TERRY & JOYCE LOSONSKY

McDonald's®

HAPPY MEAL® TOYS

IN THE U.S.A.

Schiffer Publishing Ltd

77 Lower Valley Road, Atglen, PA 19310

Published by Schiffer Publishing, Ltd.
77 Lower Valley Road
Atglen, PA 19310
Please write for a free catalog.
This book may be purchased from the publisher.
Please include $2.95 postage.
Try your bookstore first.

We are interested in hearing from authors
with book ideas on related subjects.

Every effort has been made to identify copyright holders of materials referenced in this book. Should there be omissions, the authors apologize and shall be pleased to make appropriate acknowlegements in future editions.

Printed in Hong Kong

ISBN: 0-88740-853-2

Library of Congress Cataloging-in-Publication Data

Losonsky, Terry.
McDonald's happy meal toys in the USA/Terry and Joyce Losonsky.
p. cm.
Includes index.
ISBN 0-88740-853-2 (paper)
1. McDonald's Corporation--Collectibles--Catalogs.
2. Lunchboxes--Collectors and collecting--United States--Catalogs. 3. Premiums (Retail trade)--Collectors and collecting--United States--Catalogs. I. Losonsky, Joyce. II. Title.
NK6213.L68 1995
688.7'2'093075--dc20 95-9054
CIP

THIS GUIDE IS NEITHER AUTHORIZED NOR APPROVED BY THE McDONALD'S CORPORATION.

The following trademarks and service marks TM, SM and ® are owned by McDonald's Corporation, Oak Brook, Illinois 60521:

BIG MAC, BIRDIE, BIRDIE THE EARLY BIRD, BIRTHDAYLAND, CAPTAIN CROOK, CAPTAIN (THE), CHICKEN NUGGETS, CosMc, EARLYBIRD, FRY GIRLS, FRY GUYS, FRY KIDS, GLO-TRON, GOLDENARCHES, THE GOLDENARCHES LOGO, GRIMACE, HAMBURGLAR, HAPPY MEAL, HAPPY MEALS, HAPPY PAIL, MACTONIGHT, MAYOR McCHEESE, McBOO, McBUNNY, McCAPS, McCHEESE, McDONALD'S, McDONALDLAND, McDONALD'S FT MAGAZINE LOGO, McGHOST, McGOBLIN, McJACK, McMUFFIN, McNUGGET BUDDIES, McPUNK'N, McPIZZA, McWITCH, PROFESSOR, QUARTER POUNDER, ROBOCAKES, RONALD, RONALD McDONALD, WILLIE MUNCHRIGHT.

The following trademarks and service marks TM, SM and ® are owned by the companies indicated:

101 DALMATIONS, BALOO, BAMBI, DONALD, DUCKTALES, DUMBO, BENJI, FALINE, HUEY, DUEY, LOUIS, SCROOGE, LAUNCHPAD, SNOW WHITE AND THE SEVEN DWARFS, TALESPIN, WEBBY -- WALT DISNEY COMPANY.

ACME ACRES, ANIMANIACS, BAT DUCK, BUGS, BUGS BUNNY, DAFFY DUCK, DUKES OF HAZZARD, GOGO DODO, HAMPTON, LOONEY TUNES, ROAD RUNNER, SUPER BUGS, SYLVESTER, TAS-FLASH, TINY TOON, TOONSTERS, TWEETY, WILE COYOTE, WONDER PIG -- WARNER BROS.

ARCHIES, THE NEW ARCHIES, DINO, JUGHEAD, REGGIE --PRIME DESIGNS LTD.

BARBIE, HOT WHEELS, MINI-STREEX, ATTACK PACK -- MATTEL INC.

BERENSTAIN -- S & J BERENSTAIN

BIBBLE, CORKLE, GROPPLE, THUGGER -- CURRENT INC.

BOOBER, BULLDOZER, COTTERPIN, DOOZER, FOZZIE, FRAGGLE ROCK, GOBO, BONZO, KERMIT, MOKEY, MUPPET BABIES (THE), THE GREAT MUPPET CAPER, WEMBLY, SNOOPY, CHARLIE BROWN, LUCY, LINUS, MISS PIGGY, MUPPET WORKSHOP, MUPPET, WHAT-NOT -- JIM HENSON PRODUCTIONS, INC./HENSON ASSOCIATES.

COCA-COLA, DIET COKE, SPRITE, MINUTE MAID -- COCA-COLA COMPANY, ATLANTA, GA.

COLORFORMS -- COLORFORMS

CRAYOLA -- BINNEY AND SMITH

COMMANDRONS, DRAGONOIDS, ELEPHOIDS, OCTOPOID, SCORPOID, POPPIN -- TOMY.

FIEVEL -- UNIVERSAL CITY STUDIOS.

FLINSTONES (THE) -- Copyright: UNIVERSAL CITY STUDIOS, INC AND AMBLIN ENTERTAINMENT.

FLINSTONES (THE), BARNEY, FRED, WILMA, BETTY -- Trademark: HANNA-BARBERA PRODUCTIONS INC.

FRANKENTYKE, VINNIE STOKER, CLEOFATRA, GRAVEDALE HIGH -- NBC.

GARFIELD, ODIE, POOKY -- UNITED FEATURE SYNDICATE INC.

GHOSTBUSTER, GHOSTBUSTERS, SLIMER -- COLUMBIA PICTURES INDUSTRIES INC.

GOOMBA, KOOPA, LUIGI, SUPER MARIO BROS 3, SUPER MARIO -- NINTENDO OF AMERICA INC.

HOOK, RUFIO, CAPTAIN HOOK, PETER PAN -- TRI-STAR PICTURES INC.

KIRK, KLINGONS, MCCOY, SPOCK, STAR TREK -- PARAMOUNT PICTURES

KISSYFUR -- S. L. COLBURN, MILWAUKEE, WI.

LEGO, LEGODUPLO -- LEGO GROUP

MATCHBOX -- MATCHBOX INTERNATIONAL

NASCAR -- JR MAXX, CHARLOTTE, NC.

PAAS -- SCHERING-PLOUGH

PIGGSBURG PIGS, QUACKER, HUFF, PIGHEAD, PORTLY, PUFF, REMBRANDT -- FOX CHILDREN'S NETWORK, INC.

PLAYMOBIL -- GEOBRA-BRANDSLATTER GMBH & CO.

PLAYMOBIL CHARACTERS, STOMPER, BIGFOOT -- SCHAFER MFG. CO.

RAGGEDY ANN, RAGGEDY ANDY, RAGGEDY ANN AND ANDY -- MACMILLAN INC.

SUPER MARIO BROS 3, SUPER MARIO, GOOMBA, LUIGI, KOOPA -- NINTENDO OF AMERICA INC.

THE FRIENDLY SKIES -- UNITED AIR LINES.

THE MAGIC SCHOOL BUS -- SCHOLASTIC INC., JOANNA COLE AND BRUCE DEGEN.

TOM AND JERRY - TURNER ENTERTAINMENT

Acknowledgments & Thanks

The authors would like to take this opportunity to express our sincere appreciation and gratitude to each collector who has contributed their time and knowledge. In the event of oversight, we sincerely apology for any names and familiar faces left off.

ADVISORY BOARD

Scott & Susan Chandler
Ken Clee
Ron & Eileen Corbett
Jimmy & Pat Futch
John & Eleanor Larsen
McDonald's Corporation
Bill & Pat Poe
E. J. Ritter
Rich & Laurel Seidelman

Another very special "Thank you and a hug" goes to the many wonderful collector friends who have helped us in various ways over the last twenty-one years, from offering advice to sending material or photographs. These special friends encouraged us to develop this book and our upcoming books.

Helen Farrell - McDonald's Archives
Lois Daughtery - McDonald's Archives
George Griggs - Director/Field Marketing
Kathy List - Marketing/McDonald's
Wilma Weir - Marketing/McDonald's
Ron Abler
Sam Apkarian
Dave Archer
Kathy Arne
Ron & Ethel Bacon
Linda Bailey
Richard & Crystal Banyon
Tom & Bonnie Becker
Tom Borton
Bill & Marie Boyce
Bob & Mary Ann Brown
Jeanne Bruce
Sidney & Jeanne Bruce
Vern Bryant
Gerald & Helen Buchholz
Bert & Carolyn Buckler
Eugene Cantor
Mark Carder
Carl & Rosemary Carlson
Maynard Carney
Karen Cavanaugh
Jim Challenger
Stephanie Chandler
Jim Christoffel
Ann Marie Clark
John & Brenda Clark
Judy Clark
Marilyn Clulow
Mark Coleman
David Cunningham
Clint Deale
Marvinette Dennis
Nate Downs
Robyn Duncan
Charles Duval
Gail Duzak
David Epstein
Jan Exler
Gordon & Kath Fairgrieve
Leslie Fein
Fred Fiedler
Marjorie Fontana
Mike & Deanna Fountaine
Mike & Kathy Franze
Bonnie Garnett
Cheri Garnett
Jim & Linda Gegorski
Kay Geva
Brian Gildea
Mark & Carol Gillette
Bob & Gretchen Gipson
Lance Golba
Cindy Gore
Steve Gould
Pat & Martha Gragg
Shirley Graulich
Nick Graziano
Gary & Teena Greenberg
Chuck Gustafson
David Hale
Roberta Harris
Gary & Judy Heald
Gary & Shirley Henriques
Ed Hock
Roger Hordines
Sharon Iranpour
Steven & Ann Jackson
Dave Johnson
Brian Jones
Anne King
Joyce Klassen
Pam Klemm
Curt & Janice Lafey
Robert Lanier
Jerry Ledbetter
Pat Lonergan
Kent Longmire
Chris Lucho
Darrell Lulling
Greg MacClaren
Thomas & Frankie Massey
Bill & Betty McCormick
Glen & Kathleen McElwee
Janet McGuire
Art McManis
Victor Medcalf
Don Metiva
George Miller
Julius & Margaret Mortvedt
Dick Morvan
Stanley Mull
Pat Multz
Beulah Murphy
Rene & Anne Marie Naim
Steve & Margie Nation
Steven Jr. Nation
Rebecca Nation
Rachel Nation
Tom & Terry Nelson
Jim & Cooky Oberg
Harry Oberth
Roger Olshanski
Tom & Teresa Olszeski
Joe & Dolly Pascale
Mark Patterson
Garnett Pennington
Mark & Jane Petzel
Janet Phillips
Joe & Carol Pierce
Ray Podraza
Larry & Manuella Poli
Edward & Jean Pomeroy
Jean Pomeroy
Mike Portzline
Charles & Connie Prater
Ron & Jane Prussiano
Fred Rauch
Jimmy Renella
Russell & Marie Rinehart
Alyce Roberts
Tom & Kathy Robusto
Ed Ruby
Chris & Julie Rucho
Doug & Debbie Ryan
Barbara Saitta
Essie Saunders
Ed & Sharon Scarbrock
Pat Sentell
Bob Serighino
Jim Silva
Trudy Slaven
Scott Smiles
Dan Smith
Jerry & Lorraine Soltis
Rich & JoLyn Stack
Lorie Steele
Julie Stegeman
Peggy Stockard
David Stone
Richard & Marge Taibi
Debbie Taylor
Nigel Thomas
John & Virginia Thompson
Robert & Jackie Thompson
Ray & Dorothy Tognarelli
Frances Turey
Gary & Jill Turner
Lee Turpin
Dave Tuttle
Kees & Conny Versteeg
Mitchel Versteeg
Roxana Versteeg
Taylor & Cindy Wagen
Lloyd Washburn
Fred & Elaine Waterman
Ted Waters
Toni Welsh
Gary & Karen Wenzlaff
Robert WIlkey
Meredith Williams
Don Wilson
Jim & Rosalie Wolfe
Mike & Mary Ann Wooten
Ron & Eldra Word
Frank Work
Claire Zabo
Frank Zamarripa

One reason for writing this book was to share knowledge with others who enjoy the thrill of seeking out McDonald's collectables in the family toy boxes, thrift stores, church and yard sales. McDonald's is located in at least 67 countries, distributes millions of toys every week - enough collectables for all of us.

A special thanks to the many McDonald's employees who over the years have fulfilled our request for items. We also send a special hug for their cheerful, friendly, helpful, polite manner; especially to: Chris and Betsy Shead, Janet, Fidel and Vangie, Eric, Karl, Kelly, Stacey, Heidi, Terry, Joyce and Jeff - the McDonald's crew everywhere who say with a smile, "May I take your order, please?"

We extend another very special, "thank you" for the patience and help our children and our families have given us over the years; to our children: Andrea, Natasha, Nicole and Ryan - they provided the incentive to visit McDonald's frequently; to our families: Stephen & Ann Zurko, Frank & Nancy Losonsky, Steve & Linda Zurko, Max Zurko, Phil & Alana Losonsky, Chris & Toni Losonsky and Aunt Ursula Shows - they always encouraged us.

Lastly, we would like to express the feelings of many McDonald's collectors to McDonald's Corporation, Oak Brook, Illinois. Thank you McDonald's for the McFun!

Terry and Joyce Losonsky
7506 SUMMER LEAVE LANE
COLUMBIA, MARYLAND 21046-2455
FAX: 410-381-1852

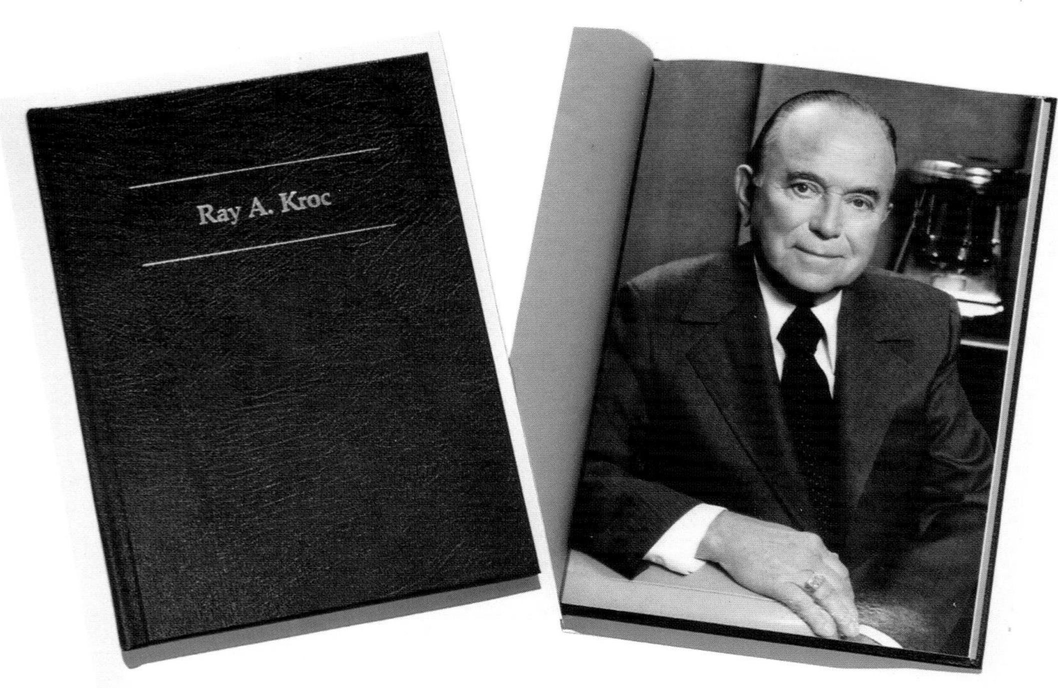

McDonald's Happy Meal Collectibles Timeline

Welcome to the world of McDonald's Happy Meal USA Collectibles. The Circus Wagon Happy Meal is considered to be the "First National Happy Meal Promotion" in the USA, June 11-July 31, 1979. Fifteen years later, Ronald McDonald Celebrates Happy Birthday Happy Meal, 1994 is promoted to commemorate "The Fifteenth Anniversary of the Happy Meal" in the USA, October 28-December 1, 1994.

Where did it all start and where is it going? The answers tell a very interesting story.

Ray Kroc is the Founder of McDonald's. Forty years have passed since Mr. Kroc opened his first McDonald's restaurant in Des Plaines, Illinois. McDonald's has grown from one to over 15,000 restaurants in over 70 countries. Incredible as it sounds, McDonald's Corporation is just beginning to settle into the American market and begin expansion worldwide.

1948 - Dick and Mac McDonald, known as the McDonald brothers opened their first limited menu, self-service McDonald's drive-in restaurant in San Bernardino, California. The operation required a lot of milk-shake machines. Ray Kroc was the salesman for milk-shake machines. Simplistically, he visited the McDonald brothers, essentially bought out their franchising operation; the rest is history. It is not quite that simple. The McDonald's story is one of many innovative twists and much marketing genius.

1952 - Dick and Mac McDonald franchised their McDonald's Speedee Service System. The building design was red and white candy striped walls with yellow neon arches going through the roof. The golden arches were born.

1955 - Ray Kroc became franchising agent for the McDonald brothers and opened his first McDonald's restaurant in Des Plaines, Illinois. April 15, 1955 is officially known as Founder's Day. The first menu was a check-off paper sheet with a limited selection of 15-cent hamburgers, $1.80 per dozen; 19-cent cheeseburgers, $2.28 per dozen; 10-cent french fries; 20-cent milk shakes-chocolate, strawberry, vanilla, 10-cent Coke or extra large Coke was 15 cents; orange or root beer sodas were 10 and 15 cents; 10-cent milk, coffee and hot chocolate. The menu was promoted by the company symbol, "Speedee", a little hamburger man. Just the concept of "Speedee" service brought speedee growth.

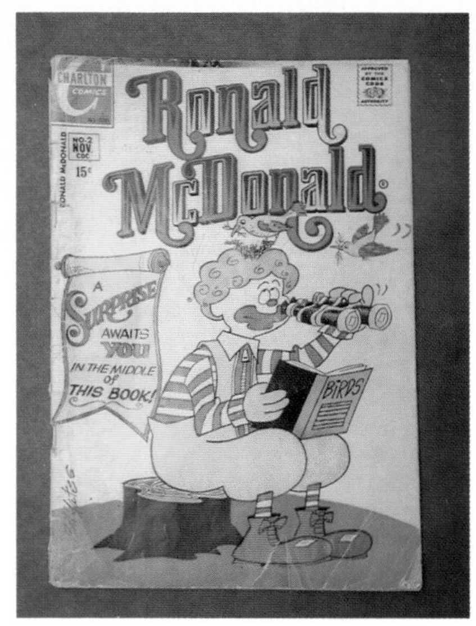

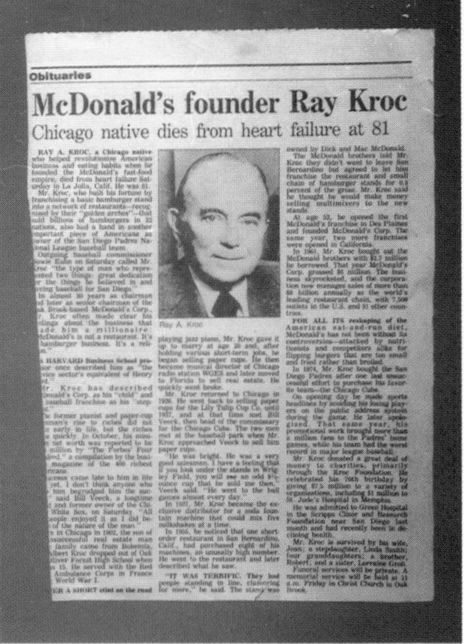
Obituaries

McDonald's founder Ray Kroc

Chicago native dies from heart failure at 81

Ray A. Kroc

Arches fall on 1st McDonald's with barely a beef about history

By Linda Sarrio and James Kane

1956 - A dozen McDonald's restaurants are added in Chicago and California. Ray Kroc considered this "slow growth." He had a dream to put a McDonald's restaurant in every neighborhood.

1959 - The 100th McDonald's restaurant is opened and celebrated in Fond Lac, Wisconsin.

1960 - The 200th McDonald's restaurant is opened in Knoxville, Tennessee and the 400 millionth hamburger was served. "Look for the Golden Arches" jingle is played on radio.

1961 - The All American Meal is launched after Ray Kroc buys out the McDonald brothers for $2.7 million. The meal includes a hamburger, fries and milk-shake. Hamburger University, a management training center is opened in Elk Grove Village, Illinois to standardize the product, place, price and promotions along with the selling agents, the employees. An early key to success was the financing operations, the land and buildings were retained by the corporation. Franchise owners bought the rights to sell the product in a controlled environment. The Golden Arches were proving to be indeed golden.

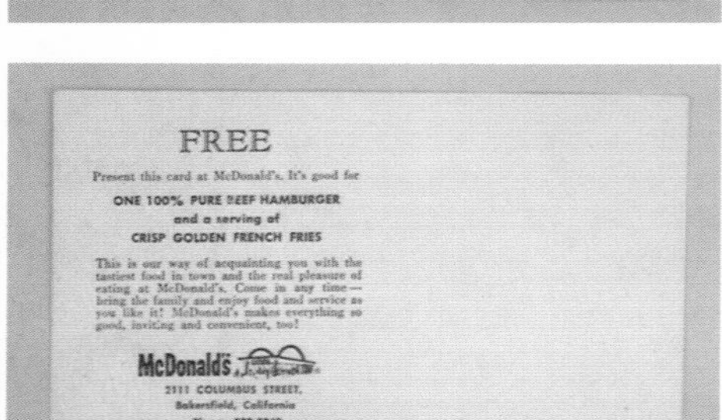

FREE

Present this card at McDonald's. It's good for

ONE 100% PURE BEEF HAMBURGER
and a serving of
CRISP GOLDEN FRENCH FRIES

This is our way of acquainting you with the tastiest food in town and the real pleasure of eating at McDonald's. Come in any time—bring the family and enjoy food and service as you like it! McDonald's makes everything so good, inviting and convenient, too!

McDonald's
2111 COLUMBUS STREET,
Bakersfield, California
Phone: 323-2242

1962 - "The Golden Arches," a modern design, replaced the Speedee logo. Advertising was placed nationally in LIFE magazine, the target market being the nation as a whole. "Go For Goodness at McDonald's" advertising slogan appeared.

1963 - Willard Scott was the "First Ronald McDonald." Ronald McDonald, Williard Scott, made his debut in Washington, D.C. at the Cherry Blossom Parade. Filet-O-Fish sandwich was added to the menu, 24-cents.

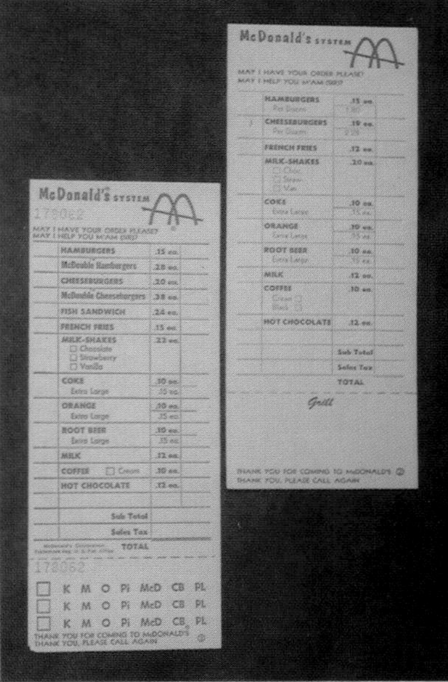

McDonald's SYSTEM

178062

MAY I HAVE YOUR ORDER PLEASE?
MAY I HELP YOU M'AM (SIR)?

HAMBURGERS	.15 ea.	
McDouble Hamburgers	.28 ea.	
CHEESEBURGERS	.20 ea.	
McDouble Cheeseburgers	.38 ea.	
FISH SANDWICH	.24 ea.	
FRENCH FRIES	.15 ea.	
MILK-SHAKES ☐ Chocolate ☐ Strawberry ☐ Vanilla	.23 ea.	
COKE / Extra Large	.10 ea. / .15 ea.	
ORANGE / Extra Large	.10 ea. / .15 ea.	
ROOT BEER / Extra Large	.10 ea. / .15 ea.	
MILK	.12 ea.	
COFFEE ☐ Cream	.10 ea.	
HOT CHOCOLATE	.12 ea.	
Sub Total		
Sales Tax		
TOTAL		

178062

☐ K M O Pi McD CB PL
☐ K M O Pi McD CB PL
☐ K M O Pi McD CB PL

THANK YOU FOR COMING TO McDONALD'S
THANK YOU, PLEASE CALL AGAIN

McDonald's SYSTEM

MAY I HAVE YOUR ORDER PLEASE?
MAY I HELP YOU M'AM (SIR)?

HAMBURGERS	.15 ea.	
CHEESEBURGERS	.19 ea.	
FRENCH FRIES	.12 ea.	
MILK-SHAKES	.20 ea.	
COKE	.10 ea.	
ORANGE	.10 ea.	
ROOT BEER	.10 ea.	
MILK	.12 ea.	
COFFEE	.10 ea.	
HOT CHOCOLATE	.12 ea.	
Sub Total		
Sales Tax		
TOTAL		

THANK YOU FOR COMING TO McDONALD'S
THANK YOU, PLEASE CALL AGAIN

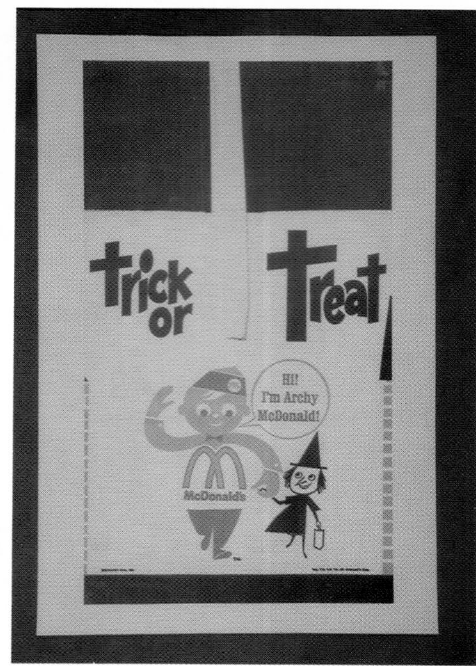

1964 - Archy McDonald logo is used on a limited number of premiums and bags.

1967 - Canada opens its first McDonald's restaurant.

1968 - Big Mac sandwich and Hot Apple Pie are added to the menu at the opening of the 1,000th restaurant in Des Plaines, Illinois. The Big Mac Attack begins. Hawaii also opens its first McDonald's.

1969 - Red and White design buildings were being replaced with a new modern design. Changing with the times promoted the QSCV concept-quality, service, cleanliness and value.

1970 - "You Deserve A Break Today-So Get Up And Get Away To McDonald's" advertising slogan proved very successful. McDonaldland concept was introduced.

1971 - Hamburglar, Grimace, Mayor McCheese, Captain Crook and The Professor join Ronald McDonald in McDonaldland.

1972 - The Quarter Pounder is added to the menu as the 2,000th store opens in Des Plaines, Illinois.

1973 - The Egg McMuffin is added to the menu and published on the cover of TIME magazine.

1974 - The First Ronald McDonald House opens in Philadelphia, Pennsylvania. McDonaldland Cookies are introduced. McDonaldland characters will change over the years; in modernizing the faces and features. Ray Kroc pays particular attention to detail; modernizes as well as McDonaldizes with the times.

1975 - The Honorary Meal of McDonaldland is introduced when the First Drive-Thru Restaurant is opened in Oklahoma City, Oklahoma. "We Do it All For You" advertising slogan is introduced. "Twoallbeefpattiesspecialsaucelettucecheesepicklesonionsonasesame seedbun" promotional jingle catches the imagination of the country. Advertising proves to be very successful for sales! The Mayor McCheese Bag promotion was specifically designed for children. Advertised as **"The Honorary Meal of McDonaldland"** the appeal to children continues with **McDonaldland Cookies** and **McDonaldland Citizenship Wall Certificates**. This special appeal to children began the process leading to the Happy Meal concept. The Captain Crook Sea Bag promotion highlighted the Filet-0-Fish sandwich. *See Honorary Meal of McDonaldland, 1975 and Sea Bag Promotion, 1975.*

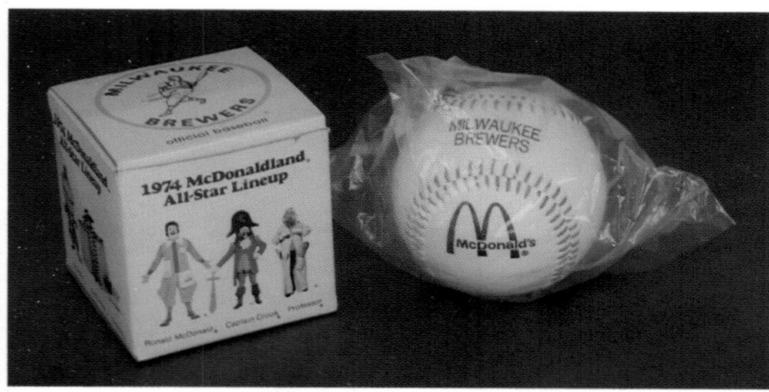

Help support Ronald McDonald House.

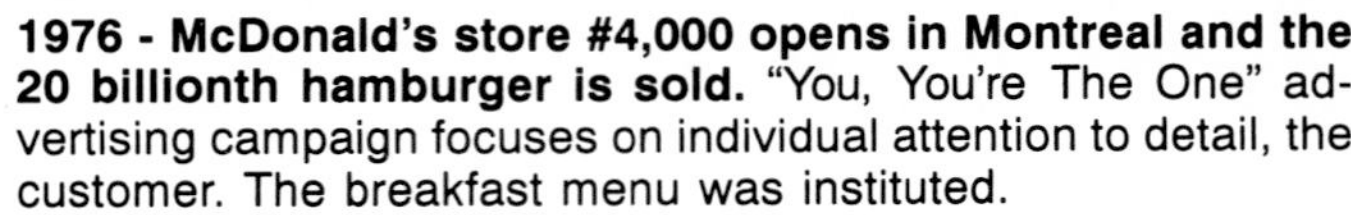

1976 - McDonald's store #4,000 opens in Montreal and the 20 billionth hamburger is sold. "You, You're The One" advertising campaign focuses on individual attention to detail, the customer. The breakfast menu was instituted.

1977 - Dick Abrams, McDonald's St. Louis Regional Advertising Manager is considered the "Father of the Happy Meal" concept. He is considered the catalyst for the evolution of the Happy Meal concept. Dick Abrams took the proposal to Chicago to support a duel test market - Fun to Go in St. Louis and Happy Meal in Kansas City. *See Fun To Go Kids Meal, 1977 and Round Top - Test I - Happy Meal, 1977.* From the Happy Plate, Happy Cup, the Happy Meal concept won out over the Fun to Go concept. The initial boxes were designed like round top metal lunch boxes.

Introducing funny-looking, great tasting McDonald's Hash Browns.

O.K., so maybe McDonald's New Hash Browns are something of an original in their hands form. But they're very old-fashioned in their scrumptious taste.

McDonald's Hash Browns are made from real slices of real potatoes. (Just like old-fashioned hash browns.)

But unlike old-fashioned hash browns, ours are deep fried, McDonald's style. To cook up crispy and golden on the outside. Tender on the inside. (Just like our world famous fries.)

And surprise! You can even eat them with your fingers. (Now just try that with your old-fashioned hash browns.)

They laughed when we said we had a fried egg and Canadian bacon you could eat with your fingers, too. Like Egg McMuffin, our Hash Browns will be a new old favorite.

At participating McDonald's.

McDonald's Kids' Day-Nov. 5, 1977

Maryland vs. Villanova 5 free children with each paying adult

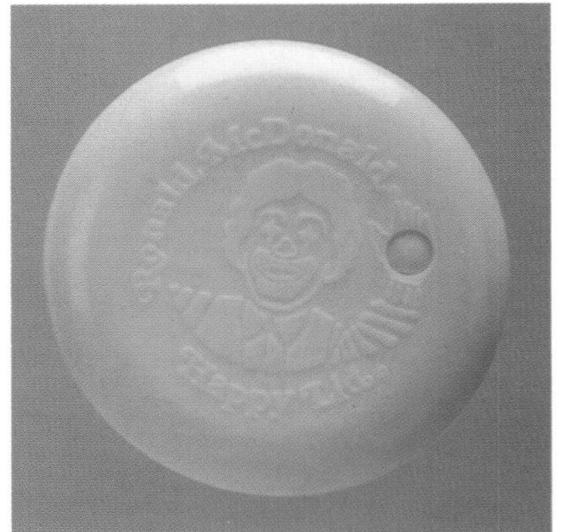

1978 - Round Top - Test II - Happy Meal, 1978 was tested in Kansas City. *See Round Top - Test II* - Happy Meal, 1978. **Round Top - Test III - Happy Meal, 1978/1979 continued in Kansas City.** *See Round Top - Test III - Happy Meal, 1978/1979.* Happy Meal tests were conducted in Albany and Buffalo, New York along with San Diego, Denver and St. Louis. The results were promising. The advertising focused on children and the "Collect all..." theme.

1979 - Circus Wagon Happy Meal was the "First National Happy Meal Promotion" and "Nobody Can Do It Like McDonald's Can" became the national advertising slogan. *See Circus Wagon Happy Meal, 1979.* The Miles Of Smiles Ronald McDonald Shows defines Ronald McDonald's theme:

Ronald McDonald's Theme

Nobody can do it like Ronald can.
Nobody else spreads laughter through the land.
He makes it fun, he's always got a joke in hand.
He's Ronald McDonald.
Nobody can do it like Ronald can.

Nobody else has a sunnier smile
Nobody else has a funnier style.
Come on along, see what he has planned.
He's Ronald McDonald.
Nobody can do it like Ronald can.

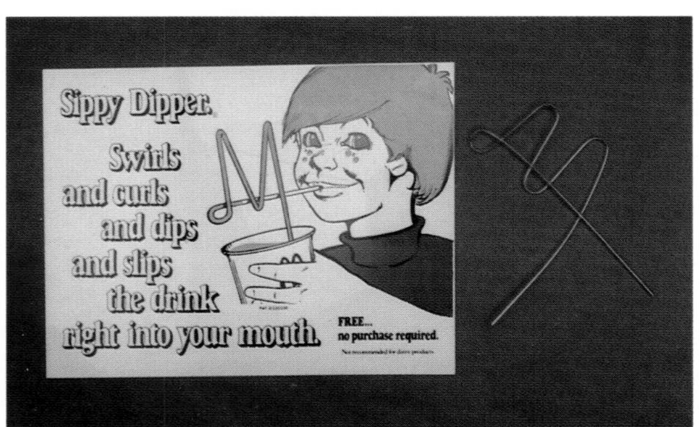

1980 - Birdie, The Early Bird joins Ronald McDonald's cast of characters in the Spring at the Breakfast Menu advertising.

1981 - The "You Deserve A Break Today" advertising campaign reached the hearts and minds of millions. The advertising slogan was a tremendous success. The emphasis was on "Collect all 6 boxes", not the premiums. *See Dinosaur Days Happy Meal, 1982/1981.*

1982 - Going Places Happy Meal, 1982 introduces a slight change in advertising focus, "A Prize in every box. Get all six." The promotion emphasized a prize and a box along with a food purchase. The premiums/prizes soon became the focus of children's attention on every visit. Because the Playmobil Happy Meal premiums contained small pieces and were potentially dangerous for small children, **McDonald's voluntarily recalled and stopped distribution of the Playmobil toys.** McDonald's began the under-3 (U-3) premium policy.

1983 - Chicken McNuggets were introduced. McDonald's restaurants are in 31 countries, 7,000th restaurant opened in Falls Church, Virginia and they served over 45 billion hamburgers.

1984 - "It's A Good Time For The Great Taste of McDonald's" slogan captured the voice of American youth who either visited McDonald's for "Food, Folks and Fun" or sought out entry level employment with their local franchisee. Either way it was a winning combination. Their youth and money was being spent at McDonald's. **The 10th Anniversary of the Ronald McDonald House was celebrated** with a national fund raiser. McDonald's commitment to Children's Charities and the Ronald McDonald Houses is to be highly commended. Over $5 million dollars was raised and 73 Ronald McDonald Houses were providing services to families in need. To always give back to the communities was a focal point of Ray Kroc's ventures. Ray Kroc epitomized excellence in American business. **Ray Kroc dies in 1984,** but his American dream lives on. **Ronald McDonald Children Charities is established in Ray Kroc's memory.**

1985 - 30th Year of Operation is celebrated. "Large Fries for Small Fries" slogan begins. McBlimp, a real blimp floats over cities and sporting events catching the advertising eye of the consumer. "The Hot Stays Hot and The Cool Stays Cool" introduces the McD. L. T. sandwich. First European Ronald McDonald House opens in Amsterdam, Holland.

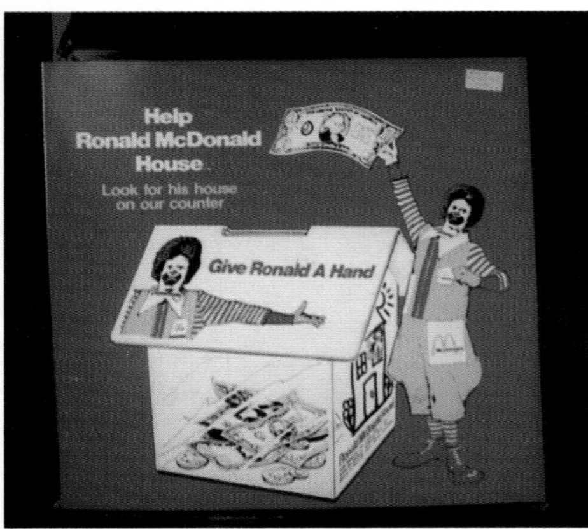

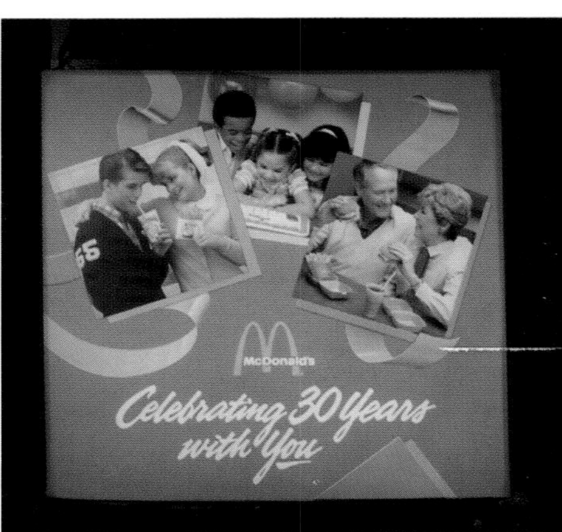

1986 - Regional Happy Meal promotions are conducted in more selected markets. The Breakfast Menu includes freshly baked buttermilk biscuits. McDonald's provides a complete food product ingredients listing to the public. Health conscious consumers respond favorably with requests for a more varied menu.

1987 - Tossed salads are added to the national menu.

1988 - 10,000th restaurant opened in Dale City, Virginia. CosMc character joins Ronald McDonald's cast of characters at McDonaldland. McKids line of clothing and products is introduced in the retail community. The retailing of McDonald's McKids merchandise expands the product line into the home.

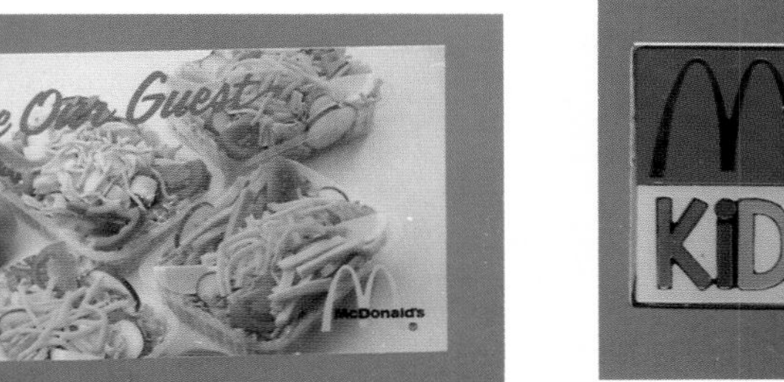

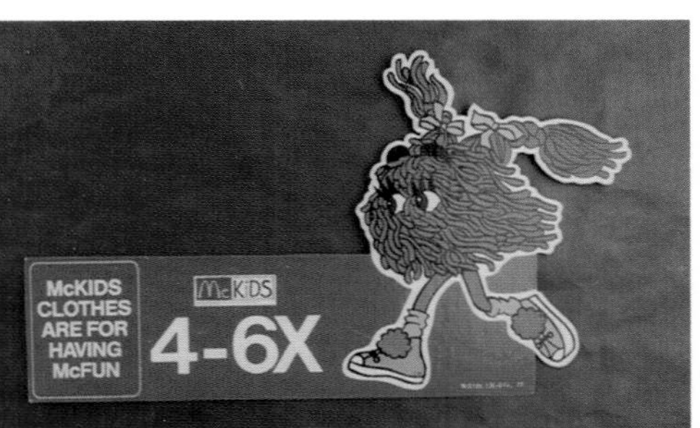

1989 - McChicken sandwich expands the menu selection.

1990 - Moscow McDonald's opens with world press. The idea that McDonald's is even in the Soviet Union awakens customers to the realization that McDonald's is a safe haven everywhere. The Golden Arches serve as a familiar and universal landmark. Recyclable packaging phases out styrofoam containers. McDonald's emphasizes the relationship between food sources and the environment. A Global Relationship is stressed. "Food, Folks and Fun" is the advertising slogan selected to promote family gatherings. McJobs, special program to hire and develop disabled persons as employees wins immediate approval. **Ray Kroc was selected by *Life* magazine as one of the Most Important Americans of the 20th Century.**

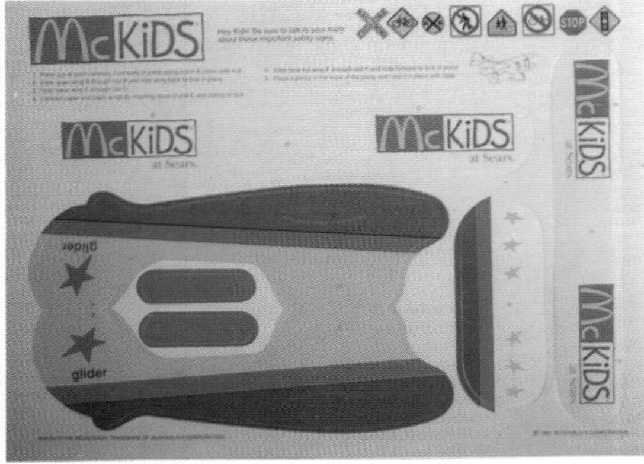

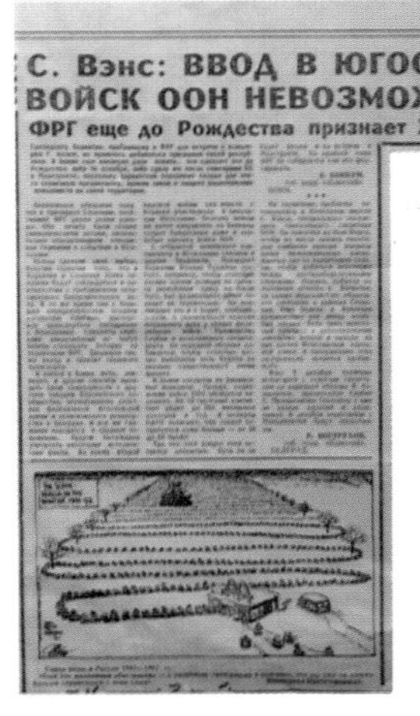
С. Вэнс: ВВОД В ЮГОСЛАВИЮ ВОЙСК ООН НЕВОЗМОЖЕН

ФРГ еще до Рождества признает Хорватию

Сцена зимы в России 1991—1992 гг.
«Еще сто миллионов «биг-маков» — и направьте телеграмму в конгресс, что мы уже не можем больше справляться с этим сами». Юниверсал Пресс-синдикат.

1991 - Smaller style Happy Meal box is introduced. Hook Happy Meal emphasizes McDonald's successful teaming with large national corporations. Indiana Jones videos are sold on a national scale. Promotions and promotional items are solidly entrenched with current movies and themes.

1992 - World's largest McDonald's opens in Beijing, China, employing over 1,000 crew members.

1993 - McWorld advertising emphasizes the global relationship between McDonald's and the Earth.

1994 - Ronald McDonald Celebrates Happy Birthday Happy Meal commemorate Fifteen Years of the Happy Meal in the USA. McDonald's serves over 26 million customers daily in over 70 countries. A new McDonald's opens every seven to ten hours worldwide and the Happy Meal leads to thousands of McDonald's collectors who have "McFun" visiting McDonald's.

1995 - McDonald's expands into smaller sales units with McStop and McSnack operations in retail stores and limited space locations. Ronald McDonald Houses continue to serve the public and Ronald McDonald Children Charities continue to focus on the needs of the needy in the communities. Forty years later, Ray Kroc's vision lives on.

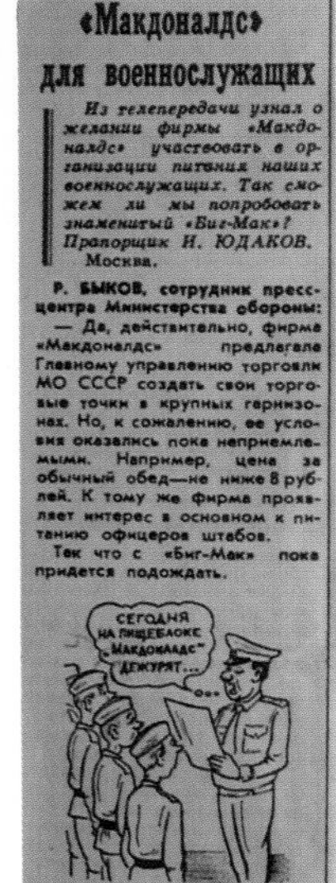

«Макдоналдс» для военнослужащих

Из телепередачи узнал о желании фирмы «Макдоналдс» участвовать в организации питания наших военнослужащих. Так сможем ли мы попробовать знаменитый «Биг-Мак»?
Прапорщик Н. ЮДАКОВ.
Москва.

Р. БЫКОВ, сотрудник пресс-центра Министерства обороны:

— Да, действительно, фирма «Макдоналдс» предлагала Главному управлению торговли МО СССР создать свои торговые точки в крупных гарнизонах. Но, к сожалению, ее условия оказались пока неприемлемыми. Например, цена за обычный обед—не ниже 8 рублей. К тому же фирма проявляет интерес в основном к питанию офицеров штабов.

Так что с «Биг-Мак» пока придется подождать.

THE GOLDEN ARCHES OF MOSCOW

15 MONTHS AFTER ITS GRAND OPENING, McDONALD'S FAST FOOD FANTASIA IS STILL WOWING IVAN

Helpful Information for Using this Book

Pricing - The price range listed is for MINT IN THE PACKAGE. Loose toys are generally 50% less. Damaged, chipped or broken toys tend to have little value with a collector. The real value of any collectible is what a buyer is willing to pay. This value may exceed the stated mint in the package (MIP) range. Likewise, since McDonald's makes millions of toys, value may be over inflated based on regional markets. Price ranges vary by regions, since some toys were distributed in specific regional markets.

Premium Names - The premiums are listed by the names on the packaging whenever possible.

Blocks - Provided for checking off mint in the package (MIP) and loose Happy Meal items.

Box Names - The boxes were named by the authors with the accompanying identifying numbering system. Whenever possible, the names came from the front panel where the words "Happy Meal" are displayed.

Number System - The numbering system reflects the **country of origin/country of distribution,** followed by the first two letters of the Happy meal or **first two letters of the Happy Meal** name or the generic representation of the Happy Meal items. The two letters are followed by the **year of distribution**; followed by a **numerical listing of the items**. The authors' intention is to reflect a different alphabetical/numerical listing for each and every item distributed.

Example: USA CI7909 = CIRCUS WAGON HAPPY MEAL, 1979

USA = Country of distribution/origin
CI = Circus Wagon Happy Meal
79 = Year of distribution
09 = Numerical listing of item

Example: USA DT8865 = DUCK TALES I HAPPY MEAL, 1988

USA = Country of distribution/origin
DT = Duck Tales I Happy Meal, 1988
88 = Year of distribution
65 = Numerical listing of an item - i.e. TRANSLITE/LG

Numerical Designator - Last two numbers of identification code; whenever possible the following last two numbers have been used.

DISPLAY: ---------------- 26	TABLE TENT: ----------- 56
HM BAG: ---------------- 30	COUNTER MAT: ------ 60
CEILING DANGLER: 41	MESSAGE C INSERT: 61
COUNTER CARD: ---- 42	HEADER CARD: ------ 62
CREW CARD: --------- 43	LUG-ON: --------------- 63
CREW POSTER: ------ 44	TRANSLITE/SM: ------ 64
REGISTER TOPPER: 45	TRANSLITE/LG: ------ 65
BUTTON: ---------------- 50	PIN: ---------------------- 95
TRAYLINER: ----------- 55	

Whenever conflict in selecting the alphabetical/numerical designator arose, the first letter of the first two names of the Happy Meal was used and/or the generic alphabetic representation of the item was used. For example, Michael Jordan/Fitness Fun Happy Meal, 1992 and/or Fitness Fun/Michael Jordan HM is noted as MJ. Likewise, some Happy Meal promotions were repeated over the years. These were consistently assigned alphabetic listings, Attack Pack becomes AP; Barbie becomes BA; Batman becomes BT; Cabbage Patch becomes CP; Funny Fry Friends becomes FF; Halloween becomes HA; Hot Wheels becomes HW; Tonka becomes TK and so on. As time progresses, it is hoped these alpha/numeric listings will become standardized. The authors apologize for all past inconsistencies in developing a system which identifies each and every item with a separate alpha/numeric label. A Cross/Numbering listing can be found in the back of this text.

McDonald's Collecting Language

HM = Happy Meal
MIP = Mint in Package
MOC = Mint on Card
MOT = Mint on Tree/plastic holder
ND = No date on item
NP = Not packaged

Clean-up week - Open time period following a Happy Meal when no specific designed toy is distributed. The stock room backlog is given out.

Counter card - advertising or customer information card or board which sits on the counter.

Counter mat - advertising mat which sits on the counter; used in early years.

Display - advertising medium which holds/displays the toys being promoted and distributed during specific time frame. These range from older bubble type to cardboard fold-up type. These are displayed in stand-up Ronald McDonald in the lobby.

Generic - item such as a box or a toy not specifically associated with a specific theme Happy Meal or promotion. The item(s) may be used in several different promotions over a period of time.

Header card - used in older Happy Meal promotions as advertising on top of the permanent display or ceiling dangler to display Happy Meal boxes or toys.

Insert card - advertising card within/along with the premium packaging.

Lug-on - sign added to the menu board.

McDonaldland - imaginary place where all Ronald McDonald's cast of characters live and play; a playland area.

National - all stores in the USA distribute the same Happy Meal at the same time; supported with national advertising.

Register Topper - advertising item placed on the top of registers.

Regional - geographical distribution was limited to specific cities or states or stores.

Self-liquidator - item intended to be sold over the counter which may or may not be included in the Happy Meal box.

Table tent - rectangle shaped advertising sign placed on the tables and counters in the lobby.

Translite - advertising transparent sign used on overhead or drive-thru menu boards to illustrate the current promotion.

U-3 - under the age of 3 premiums; specifically designed for children under the age of 3. Packaging is typically in zebra stripes around the outside of the package. The colors of the stripes vary.

1975 - 1976

HONORARY MEAL OF MCDONALDLAND, 1975
SEA BAG PROMOTION, 1975

HONORARY MEAL OF MCDONALDLAND, 1975

❑ ❑ USA HO7530 **HM BAG**, 1975, **#6 MAYOR MCCHEESE BAG W BRN/GOLD GRAPHICS** $75-100
❑ ❑ USA HO7501 **CITIZENSHIP CERTIFICATE - MAYOR PROCLAIMS "HONORARY CITIZEN/MCDLAND"** $15-20
❑ ❑ USA HO7502 **COOKIE BOX - MCDONALDLAND COOKIES,** 1975 $10-15

COMMENTS: LIMITED REGIONAL DISTRIBUTION: USA - 1975. GENERIC PREMIUMS WERE GIVEN WITH THIS HAPPY MEAL.

SEA BAG PROMOTION, 1975

❑ ❑ USA SE7530 **HM BAG,** 1975, **#6 BAG W GRAPHICS** $75-100

COMMENTS: REGIONAL DISTRIBUTION: USA - 1975. GENERIC PREMIUMS WERE GIVEN WITH THIS HAPPY MEAL.

USA HO7530

USA HO7502

1977

FUN-TO-GO KIDS MEAL, 1977
ROUND TOP - TEST I HAPPY MEAL, 1977

FUN-TO-GO KIDS MEAL, 1977

❑ ❑ USA FU7735 **KIDS MEAL BOX #1,** 1977, **20,000 FILET-O-FISH** $150-200
❑ ❑ USA FU7736 **KIDS MEAL BOX #2,** 1977, **PROFESSOR IN HIS LABORATORY** $150-200
❑ ❑ USA FU7737 **KIDS MEAL BOX #3,** 1977, **2002 HAMBURGERS/MAZE CRAZE** $150-200
❑ ❑ USA FU7738 **KIDS MEAL BOX #4,** 1977, **MCMOBILE** $150-200
❑ ❑ USA FU7739 **KIDS MEAL BOX #5,** 1977, **MCDONALD'S BREAKFAST** $150-200
❑ ❑ USA FU7740 **KIDS MEAL BOX #6,** 1977, **BIG BURGER COUNTRY** $150-200
❑ ❑ USA FU7701 **BIKE FENDER STICKER - BIG MAC,** 1977, **"OBEY ALL RULES OF THE ROAD"** $15-20
❑ ❑ USA FU7702 **BIKE FENDER STICKER - CAPTAIN CROOK,** 1977, **"DON'T TAILGATE"** $15-20
❑ ❑ USA FU7703 **BIKE FENDER STICKER - HAMBURGLAR,** 1977, **"LIGHTS ON FOR SAFETY"** $15-20

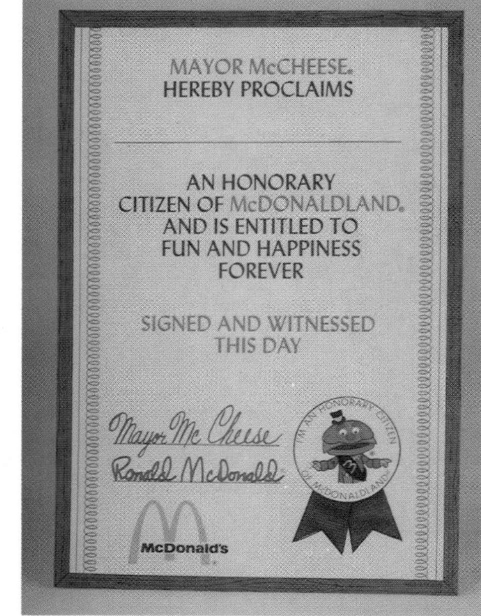

USA HO7501

USA FU7740

USA FU7701 USA FU7704 USA FU7702 USA FU7703

USA FU7706 USA FU7708

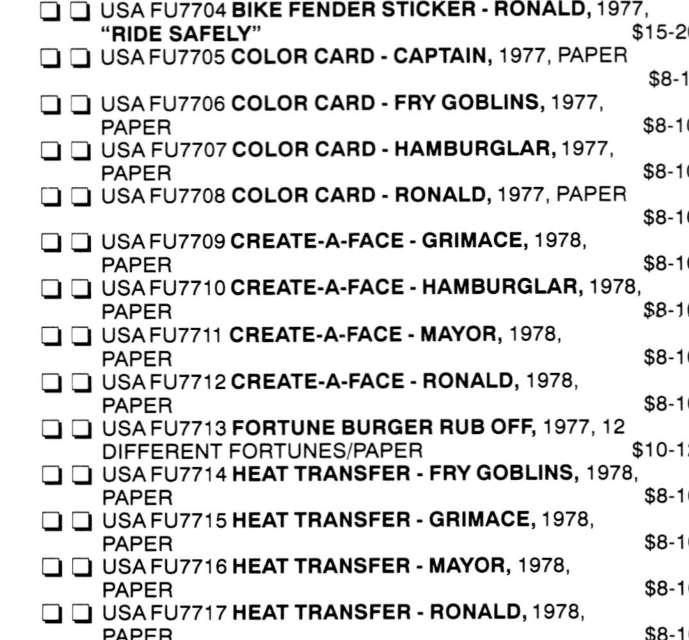

❑ ❑ USA FU7704 **BIKE FENDER STICKER - RONALD,** 1977, **"RIDE SAFELY"** $15-20

❑ ❑ USA FU7705 **COLOR CARD - CAPTAIN,** 1977, PAPER $8-10

❑ ❑ USA FU7706 **COLOR CARD - FRY GOBLINS,** 1977, PAPER $8-10

❑ ❑ USA FU7707 **COLOR CARD - HAMBURGLAR,** 1977, PAPER $8-10

❑ ❑ USA FU7708 **COLOR CARD - RONALD,** 1977, PAPER $8-10

❑ ❑ USA FU7709 **CREATE-A-FACE - GRIMACE,** 1978, PAPER $8-10

❑ ❑ USA FU7710 **CREATE-A-FACE - HAMBURGLAR,** 1978, PAPER $8-10

❑ ❑ USA FU7711 **CREATE-A-FACE - MAYOR,** 1978, PAPER $8-10

❑ ❑ USA FU7712 **CREATE-A-FACE - RONALD,** 1978, PAPER $8-10

❑ ❑ USA FU7713 **FORTUNE BURGER RUB OFF,** 1977, 12 DIFFERENT FORTUNES/PAPER $10-12

❑ ❑ USA FU7714 **HEAT TRANSFER - FRY GOBLINS,** 1978, PAPER $8-10

❑ ❑ USA FU7715 **HEAT TRANSFER - GRIMACE,** 1978, PAPER $8-10

❑ ❑ USA FU7716 **HEAT TRANSFER - MAYOR,** 1978, PAPER $8-10

❑ ❑ USA FU7717 **HEAT TRANSFER - RONALD,** 1978, PAPER $8-10

USA FU7713

USA FU7714

USA FU7710

USA FU7712

USA FU7709

USA FU7711

USA FU7715 USA FU7716

❑ ❑ USA FU7718 **STRAW/MCD - BIG MAC,** 1978, RED/BLU/GRN $20-25

❑ ❑ USA FU7719 **STRAW/MCD - GRIMACE,** 1978, RED/BLU/GRN $20-25

❑ ❑ USA FU7720 **STRAW/MCD - HAMBURGLAR,** 1978, RED/BLU/GRN/YEL $20-25

❑ ❑ USA FU7721 **STRAW/MCD - RONALD,** 1978, RED/BLU/GRN $20-25

❑ ❑ USA FU7732 **STRAW/MCD - CAPTAIN,** 1978, RED/BLU/GRN $20-25

❑ ❑ USA FU7722 **SPACE RAIDERS - BRAK,** ND, ALIEN W ROUNDED HEAD/PNK/BLU/YEL/GRN/ORG $1-2

❑ ❑ USA FU7723 **SPACE RAIDERS - DARD,** ND, ALIEN W POINTED EARS/PNK/BLU/YEL/GRN/ORG $1-2

❑ ❑ USA FU7724 **SPACE RAIDERS - HORTA,** ND, ALIEN W RAISED ARMS/PNK/BLU/YEL/GRN/ORG $1-2

❑ ❑ USA FU7725 **SPACE RAIDERS - ZAMA,** ND, ALIEN W DIVING HELMET/PNK/BLU/YEL/GRN/ORG $1-2

❑ ❑ USA FU7726 **SPACE SHIP - ALTAIR**, ND, ROCKET/NARROW PROFILE/PNK/BLU/YEL/GRN/ORG $1-2

❑ ❑ USA FU7727 **SPACE SHIP - CETI-3,** ND, ROCKET/BOOSTER NOZZLE/PNK/BLU/YEL/GRN/ORG $1-2

❑ ❑ USA FU7728 **SPACE SHIP - LYRA,** ND, FLYING SAUCER DISK/PNK/YEL/GRN/BLU/ORG $1-2

❑ ❑ USA FU7729 **SPACE SHIP - KRYGO-5,** ND, ROCKET WIDE WINGED/PNK/BLU/YEL/GRN/ORG $1-2

❑ ❑ USA FU7730 **STENCIL-A-FACE - HAMB,** 1977, PAPER $10-12

❑ ❑ USA FU7731 **STENCIL-A-FACE - RONALD,** 1977, PAPER $10-12

COMMENTS: REGIONAL TEST MARKET: USA - OCTOBER 10, 1977-OCTOBER 1978 IN THE ST. LOUIS REGION. REGION DEVELOPED THEIR OWN GENERIC PREMIUMS FOR THIS HAPPY MEAL.

USA FU7723 USA FU7725

USA FU7722 USA FU7724

USA FU7726

USA FU7728

USA FU7729

USA FU7727

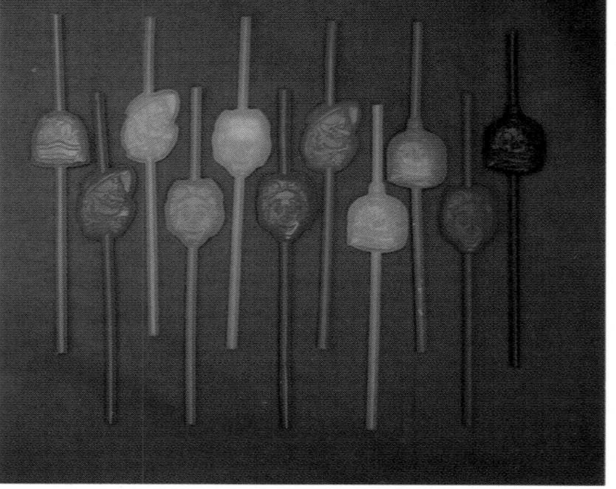

USA FU7718

USA FU7719

USA FU7720

USA FU7721

USA FU7731

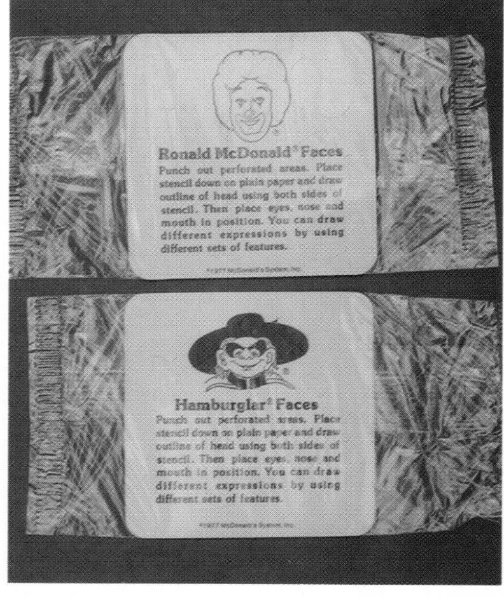

USA FU7730

USA RO7722 USA RO7721

USA RO7720

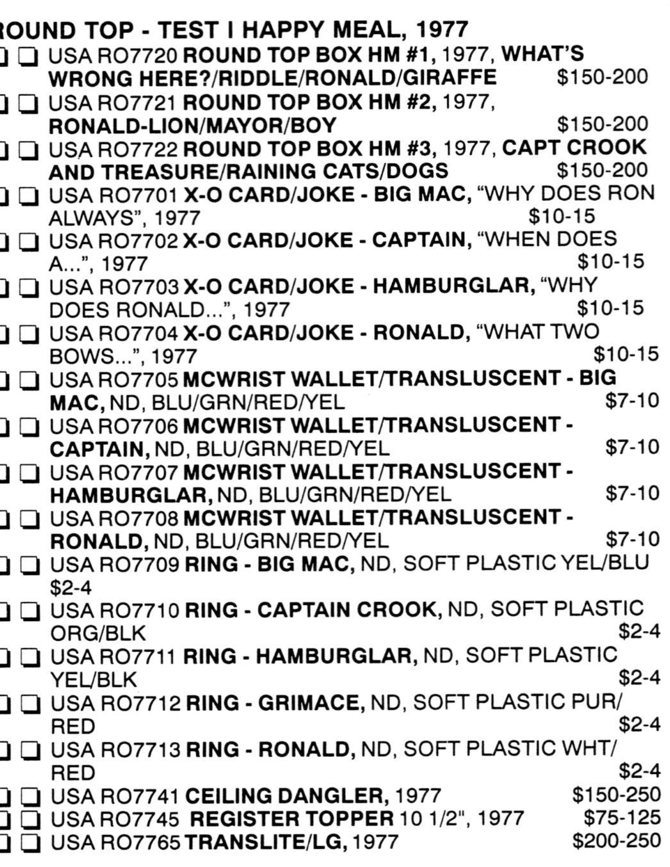

ROUND TOP - TEST I HAPPY MEAL, 1977

❑ ❑ USA RO7720 **ROUND TOP BOX HM #1,** 1977, **WHAT'S WRONG HERE?/RIDDLE/RONALD/GIRAFFE** $150-200
❑ ❑ USA RO7721 **ROUND TOP BOX HM #2,** 1977, **RONALD-LION/MAYOR/BOY** $150-200
❑ ❑ USA RO7722 **ROUND TOP BOX HM #3,** 1977, **CAPT CROOK AND TREASURE/RAINING CATS/DOGS** $150-200
❑ ❑ USA RO7701 **X-O CARD/JOKE - BIG MAC,** "WHY DOES RON ALWAYS", 1977 $10-15
❑ ❑ USA RO7702 **X-O CARD/JOKE - CAPTAIN,** "WHEN DOES A...", 1977 $10-15
❑ ❑ USA RO7703 **X-O CARD/JOKE - HAMBURGLAR,** "WHY DOES RONALD...", 1977 $10-15
❑ ❑ USA RO7704 **X-O CARD/JOKE - RONALD,** "WHAT TWO BOWS...", 1977 $10-15
❑ ❑ USA RO7705 **MCWRIST WALLET/TRANSLUSCENT - BIG MAC,** ND, BLU/GRN/RED/YEL $7-10
❑ ❑ USA RO7706 **MCWRIST WALLET/TRANSLUSCENT - CAPTAIN,** ND, BLU/GRN/RED/YEL $7-10
❑ ❑ USA RO7707 **MCWRIST WALLET/TRANSLUSCENT - HAMBURGLAR,** ND, BLU/GRN/RED/YEL $7-10
❑ ❑ USA RO7708 **MCWRIST WALLET/TRANSLUSCENT - RONALD,** ND, BLU/GRN/RED/YEL $7-10
❑ ❑ USA RO7709 **RING - BIG MAC,** ND, SOFT PLASTIC YEL/BLU $2-4
❑ ❑ USA RO7710 **RING - CAPTAIN CROOK,** ND, SOFT PLASTIC ORG/BLK $2-4
❑ ❑ USA RO7711 **RING - HAMBURGLAR,** ND, SOFT PLASTIC YEL/BLK $2-4
❑ ❑ USA RO7712 **RING - GRIMACE,** ND, SOFT PLASTIC PUR/RED $2-4
❑ ❑ USA RO7713 **RING - RONALD,** ND, SOFT PLASTIC WHT/RED $2-4
❑ ❑ USA RO7741 **CEILING DANGLER,** 1977 $150-250
❑ ❑ USA RO7745 **REGISTER TOPPER** 10 1/2", 1977 $75-125
❑ ❑ USA RO7765 **TRANSLITE/LG,** 1977 $200-250

COMMENTS: REGIONAL DISTRIBUTION: USA - NOVEMBER 4, 1977-FEBRUARY 12, 1978. THIS WAS THE VERY FIRST REGIONAL TEST OF HAPPY MEAL PROMOTION IN THE USA. THE TEST WAS CONDUCTED IN KANSAS CITY; WICHITA, KS; PHOENIX; TUCSON, AZ; AND PARTS OF NEVADA. SEVERAL REGIONS DEVELOPED THEIR OWN PREMIUMS AS WELL AS GENERIC PREMIUMS COULD HAVE BEEN USED. USA RO7705-08 MUST SAY, "PAN WESTERN RESEARCH CORP., PAT. PEND., SANTA ANA, CALIF" TO BE THE ORIGINAL MCWRIST WALLETS. OVER THE YEARS, MANY OTHER MCWRIST WALLETS HAVE BEEN PRODUCED AND DISTRIBUTED WITH A VALUE OF APPROXIMATELY $1.

USA RO7721

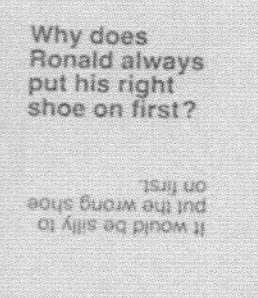

USA RO7701

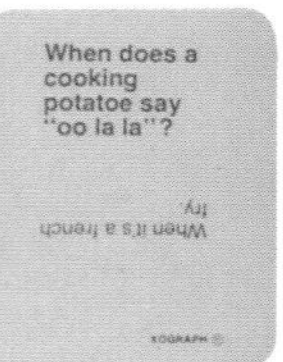

USA RO7702

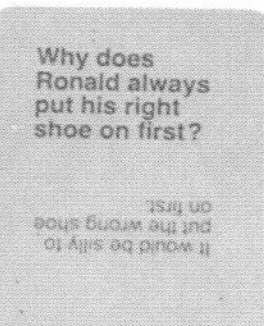

USA RO7703

USA RO7704

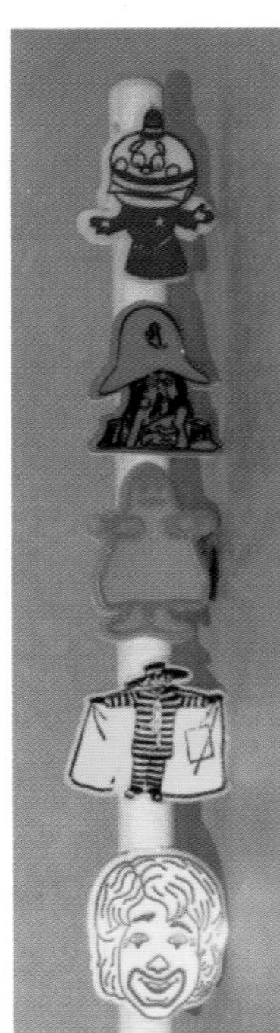

USA RO7709

USA RO7710

USA RO7712

USA RO7711

USA RO7713

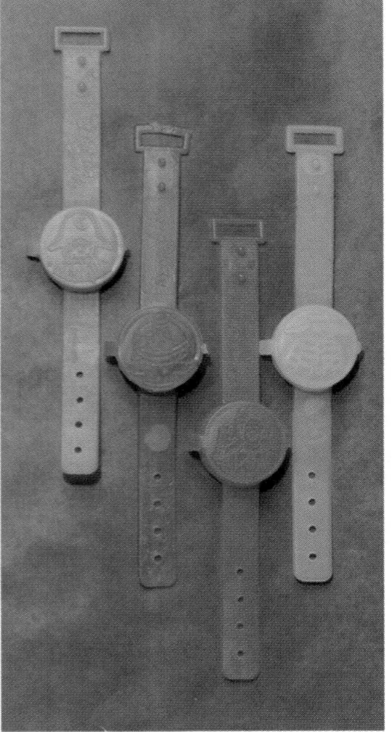

USA RO7706 USA RO7707

USA RO7705

USA RO7708

USA RO7765

USA RO7741

1978

ROUND TOP - TEST II HAPPY MEAL, 1978
ROUND TOP - TEST III HAPPY MEAL, 1978

ROUND TOP - TEST II HAPPY MEAL, 1978

- ❑ ❑ USA RO7880 **ROUND TOP HM BOX #4,** 1978, **MAKE A FACE/ MCPUZZLE** $150-200
- ❑ ❑ USA RO7881 **ROUND TOP HM BOX #5,** 1978, **BEE/ROBOT SAYS NO TO GAS PUMP** $150-200
- ❑ ❑ USA RO7882 **ROUND TOP HM BOX #6,** 1978, **WEIRD CREATURES/SPACE VIEW** $150-200
- ❑ ❑ USA RO7851 **PENCIL TOPPERS - BIG MAC,** ND, BLU/GRN/ PNK/ORG/YEL ERASER/SOFT RUBBER $5-8
- ❑ ❑ USA RO7852 **PENCIL TOPPERS - CAPTAIN,** ND, BLU/GRN/ PNK/ORG/YEL ERASER/SOFT RUBBER $5-8
- ❑ ❑ USA RO7853 **PENCIL TOPPERS - HAMBURG,** ND, BLU/GRN/ PNK/ORG/YEL ERASER/SOFT RUBBER $5-8
- ❑ ❑ USA RO7854 **PENCIL TOPPERS - RONALD,** ND, BLU/GRN/ PNK/ORG/YEL ERASER/SOFT RUBBER $5-8
- ❑ ❑ USA RO7855 **RING - UNCLE O'GRIMACY,** ND, GRN $2-3
- ❑ ❑ USA RO7856 **PRESS ON PATCH BIG MAC,** 1978, CIRCLE PATCH/WHT W BIG MAC PIC $8-10
- ❑ ❑ USA RO7857 **PRESS ON PATCH CAPTAIN,** 1978, CIRCLE PATCHWHT W CAPT PIC $8-10
- ❑ ❑ USA RO7858 **PRESS ON PATCH GRIMACE,** 1978, CIRCLE PATCH/WHT W GRIM PIC $10-12
- ❑ ❑ USA RO7859 **PRESS ON PATCH HAMBURGLAR,** 1978, CIRCLE PATCH/WHT W HAMB PIC $8-10
- ❑ ❑ USA RO7860 **PRESS ON PATCH MAYOR,** 1978, CIRCLE PATCH/ WHT W MAYOR PIC $8-10
- ❑ ❑ USA RO7861 **PRESS ON PATCH RONALD,** 1978, CIRCLE PATCH/WHT W RONALD PIC $8-10
- ❑ ❑ USA RO7862 **RONALD MAGIC PAD BOOK 1,** 1978, PAPER AD ENTERPRISES $5-8

USA RO7880

USA RO7882

USA RO7881

USA RO7856 USA RO7857

USA RO7852

USA RO7853

USA RO7854

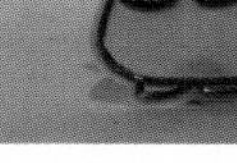

USA RO7855

USA RO7858 USA RO7859

USA RO7860 USA RO7861

USA RO7862

USA RO7864

USA RO7865

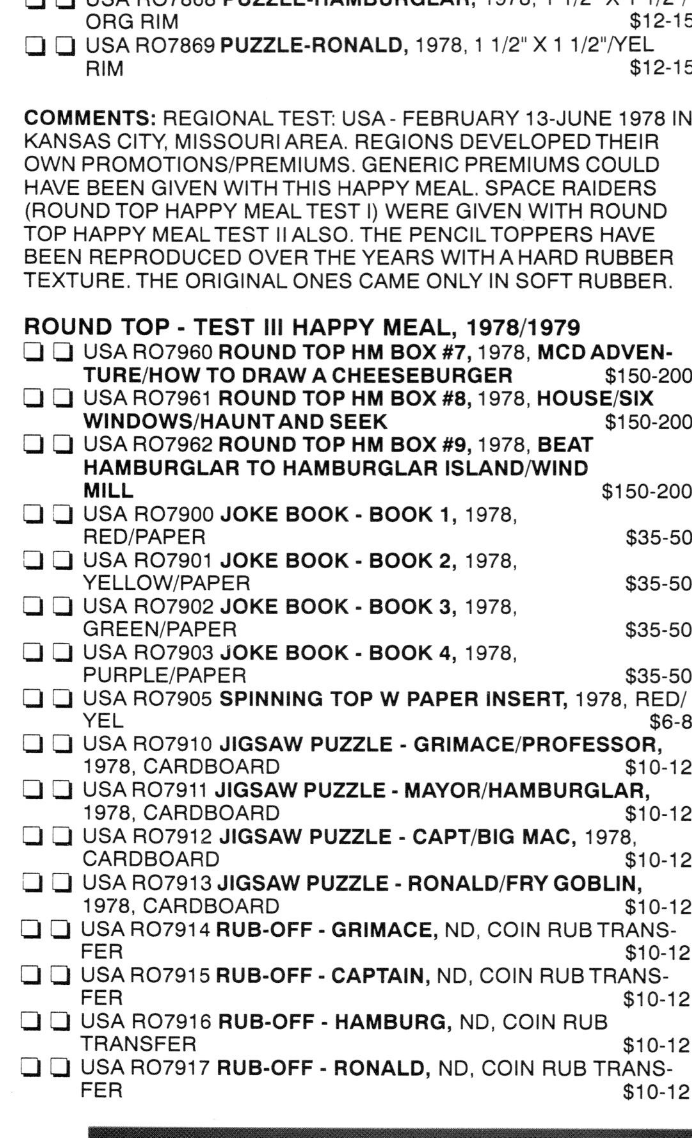

❑ ❑ USA RO7863 **RONALD MAGIC PAD BOOK 2,** 1978, PAPER/AD ENTERPRISES $5-8

❑ ❑ USA RO7864 **RONALD MAGIC PAD BOOK 3,** 1978, PAPER/AD ENTERPRISES $5-8

❑ ❑ USA RO7865 **SUNDAE SMILE RING/SAUCER** 5 3/4", 1978, BRN/RED/YEL $8-10

❑ ❑ USA RO7866 **PUZZLE-FRY KID,** 1978, 1 1/2" X 1 1/2"/GRN RIM $12-15

❑ ❑ USA RO7867 **PUZZLE-GRIMACE,** 1978, 1 1/2" X 1 1/2"/RED RIM $12-15

❑ ❑ USA RO7868 **PUZZLE-HAMBURGLAR,** 1978, 1 1/2" X 1 1/2"/ORG RIM $12-15

❑ ❑ USA RO7869 **PUZZLE-RONALD,** 1978, 1 1/2" X 1 1/2"/YEL RIM $12-15

COMMENTS: REGIONAL TEST: USA - FEBRUARY 13-JUNE 1978 IN KANSAS CITY, MISSOURI AREA. REGIONS DEVELOPED THEIR OWN PROMOTIONS/PREMIUMS. GENERIC PREMIUMS COULD HAVE BEEN GIVEN WITH THIS HAPPY MEAL. SPACE RAIDERS (ROUND TOP HAPPY MEAL TEST I) WERE GIVEN WITH ROUND TOP HAPPY MEAL TEST II ALSO. THE PENCIL TOPPERS HAVE BEEN REPRODUCED OVER THE YEARS WITH A HARD RUBBER TEXTURE. THE ORIGINAL ONES CAME ONLY IN SOFT RUBBER.

ROUND TOP - TEST III HAPPY MEAL, 1978/1979

❑ ❑ USA RO7960 **ROUND TOP HM BOX #7,** 1978, **MCD ADVENTURE/HOW TO DRAW A CHEESEBURGER** $150-200

❑ ❑ USA RO7961 **ROUND TOP HM BOX #8,** 1978, **HOUSE/SIX WINDOWS/HAUNT AND SEEK** $150-200

❑ ❑ USA RO7962 **ROUND TOP HM BOX #9,** 1978, **BEAT HAMBURGLAR TO HAMBURGLAR ISLAND/WIND MILL** $150-200

❑ ❑ USA RO7900 **JOKE BOOK - BOOK 1,** 1978, RED/PAPER $35-50

❑ ❑ USA RO7901 **JOKE BOOK - BOOK 2,** 1978, YELLOW/PAPER $35-50

❑ ❑ USA RO7902 **JOKE BOOK - BOOK 3,** 1978, GREEN/PAPER $35-50

❑ ❑ USA RO7903 **JOKE BOOK - BOOK 4,** 1978, PURPLE/PAPER $35-50

❑ ❑ USA RO7905 **SPINNING TOP W PAPER INSERT,** 1978, RED/YEL $6-8

❑ ❑ USA RO7910 **JIGSAW PUZZLE - GRIMACE/PROFESSOR,** 1978, CARDBOARD $10-12

❑ ❑ USA RO7911 **JIGSAW PUZZLE - MAYOR/HAMBURGLAR,** 1978, CARDBOARD $10-12

❑ ❑ USA RO7912 **JIGSAW PUZZLE - CAPT/BIG MAC,** 1978, CARDBOARD $10-12

❑ ❑ USA RO7913 **JIGSAW PUZZLE - RONALD/FRY GOBLIN,** 1978, CARDBOARD $10-12

❑ ❑ USA RO7914 **RUB-OFF - GRIMACE,** ND, COIN RUB TRANSFER $10-12

❑ ❑ USA RO7915 **RUB-OFF - CAPTAIN,** ND, COIN RUB TRANSFER $10-12

❑ ❑ USA RO7916 **RUB-OFF - HAMBURG,** ND, COIN RUB TRANSFER $10-12

❑ ❑ USA RO7917 **RUB-OFF - RONALD,** ND, COIN RUB TRANSFER $10-12

USA RO7868 USA RO7866 USA RO7867

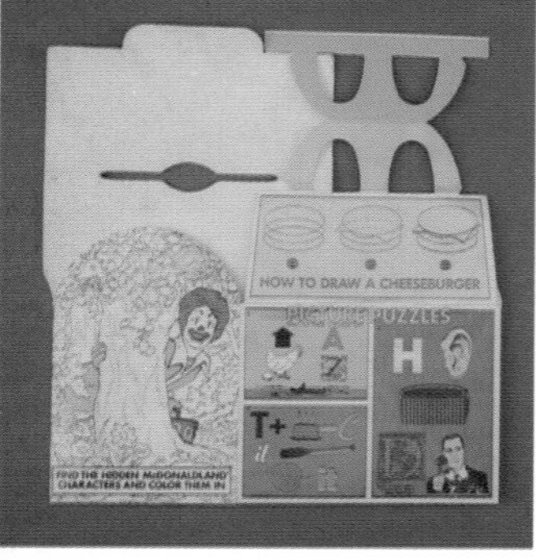

USA RO7961

USA RO7960

USA RO7962

USA RO7905

USA RO7910 USA RO7911 USA RO7912 USA RO7913

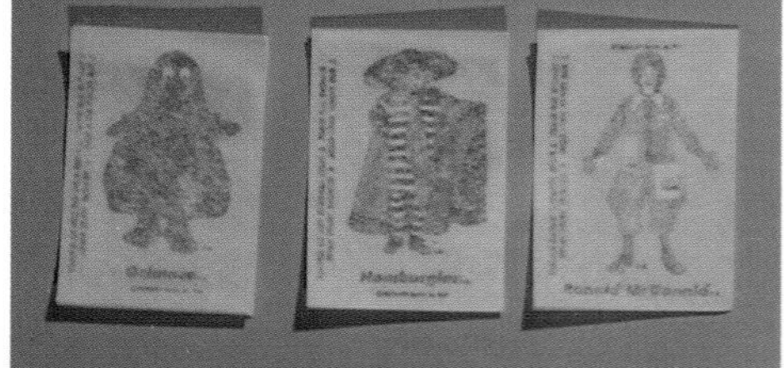

USA RO7914

USA RO7916

USA RO7917

❑ ❑ USA RO7918 **RING AROUND RONALD,** 1978, RING TOSS GAME/PAPER $8-10

❑ ❑ USA RO7919 **REFLECTOR STICKER - BIG MAC,** 1978, BLK W SIL CHARACTER $3-4

❑ ❑ USA RO7920 **REFLECTOR STICKER - CAPTAIN,** 1978, BLK W SIL CHARACTER $3-4

❑ ❑ USA RO7921 **REFLECTOR STICKER - HAMBURGLAR,** 1978, BLK W SIL CHARACTER $3-4

❑ ❑ USA RO7922 **REFLECTOR STICKER - RONALD,** 1978, BLK W SIL CHARACTER $3-4

❑ ❑ USA RO7930 **CHRISTMAS ORNAMENT - COLOR YOUR OWN GINGERBREAD HOUSE,** 1978, 5P PAPER PUNCHES $8-12

❑ ❑ USA RO7931 **CHRISTMAS ORNAMENT - COLOR YOUR OWN REINDEER,** 1978, 6P PAPER PUNCH-OUTS $8-12

❑ ❑ USA RO7932 **CHRISTMAS ORNAMENT - COLOR YOUR OWN ROCKING HORSE,** 1978, 5P PAPER PUNCH-OUTS $8-12

❑ ❑ USA RO7933 **CHRISTMAS ORNAMENT - COLOR YOUR OWN SNOWFLAKE,** 1978, 6P PAPER PUNCH-OUTS $8-12

❑ ❑ USA RO7934 **CHRISTMAS ORNAMENT - COLOR YOUR OWN SANTA,** 1978, 5P PAPER PUNCH-OUTS $8-12

❑ ❑ USA RO7935 **CHRISTMAS STOCKING - RONALD,** ND, PLASTIC/SANTA/RED/WHT $4-6

❑ ❑ USA RO7940 **COMIC BOOK - RONALD AND THE FRIES FARMERS,** 1978, PAPER $15-20

❑ ❑ USA RO7941 **COMIC BOOK - RONALD LENDS A HELPING HAND,** 1978, PAPER $15-20

❑ ❑ USA RO7942 **COMIC BOOK - THE DISAPPEARING ACT,** 1978, PAPER $15-20

❑ ❑ USA RO7965 **TRANSLITE "WE BUY JOKES" MENU BOARD,** 1978 $100-125

❑ ❑ USA RO7969 **COUNTER CARD "WE WANT JOKES",** 1978 $75-100

COMMENTS: REGIONAL TEST: USA - JUNE 11-OCTOBER 15, 1978 IN KANSAS CITY; BUFFALO, NY 7/31/78-9/19/78; PHOENIX 9/15-10/15/78 AND ST. LOUIS, MISSOURI. WITH CLEAN-UP GENERIC PREMIUMS GIVEN OUT UNTIL FEBRUARY 1979, REGIONS USED STOCK ITEMS AND DEVELOPED THEIR OWN PROMOTIONS/PREMIUMS. OTHER GENERIC PREMIUMS COULD HAVE BEEN GIVEN WITH THIS HAPPY MEAL. THIS WAS THE THIRD HM TEST IN THE USA OF THE HAPPY MEAL CONCEPT.

USA RO7918

USA RO7919 USA RO7921

USA RO7920 USA RO7922

USA RO7930 USA RO7933

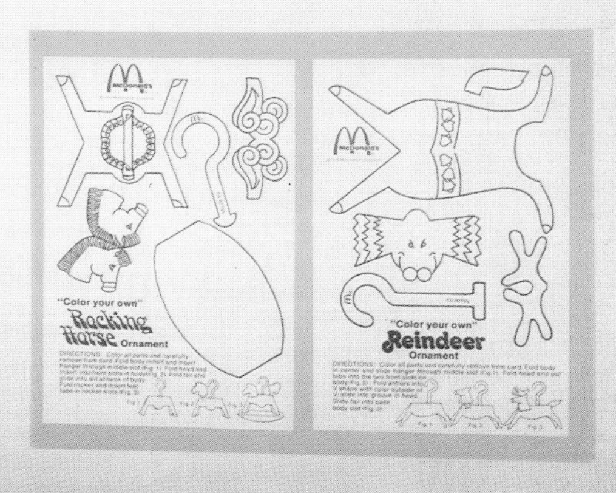

USA RO7932 USA RO7931

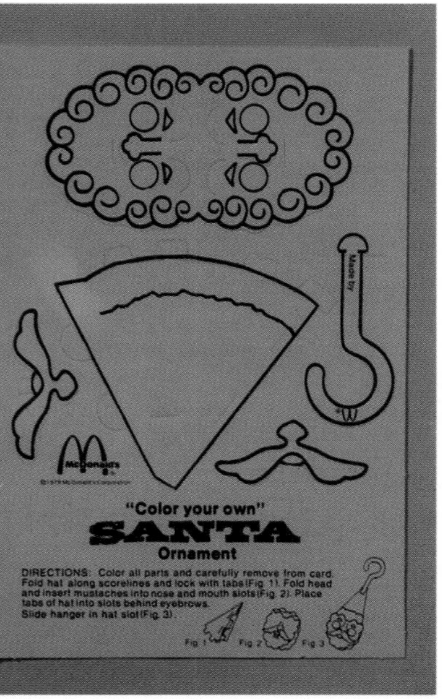

USA RO7934

USA RO7935

USA RO7942
USA RO7940
USA RO7941

USA RO7965

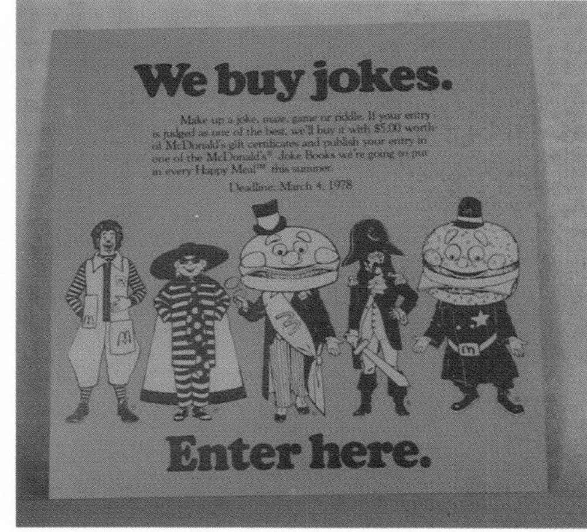

1979

HAPPY MEAL TEST - PART IV GENERIC HAPPY MEAL, 1979
CIRCUS WAGON HAPPY MEAL, 1979
SPACE THEME HAPPY MEAL, 1979
STAR TREK MEAL HAPPY MEAL, 1980/1979
USA/GENERIC PROMOTION, 1979

USA GE7930

HAPPY MEAL TEST - PART IV GENERIC HAPPY MEAL, 1979

- ❑ ❑ USA GE7930 **HM BOX,** 1979, **SMART DUCK/PAINT THE SUN** $100-125
- ❑ ❑ USA GE7931 **HM BOX,** 1979, **CHEF IN TEACUP/WHAT'S WRONG HERE** $100-125
- ❑ ❑ USA GE7932 **HM BOX,** 1979, **ANIMAL RIDDLES/PIG DRIVING AUTO/ELEPH/LION** $100-125
- ❑ ❑ USA GE7933 **HM BOX,** 1979, **LION CIRCUS/WHAT'S THIS/ RONALD/CAPT** $100-125
- ❑ ❑ USA GE7934 **HM BOX,** 1979, **SKYSCRAPERS/THERE ARE HIDDEN WORDS** $100-125
- ❑ ❑ USA GE7901 **BAJA BUGGY,** ND, CAR/SOFT PLIABLE RUBBER $1-2
- ❑ ❑ USA GE7902 **BEACH HOPPER,** ND, CAR/SOFT PLEABLE RUBBER $1-2
- ❑ ❑ USA GE7903 **COSMOBILE,** ND, CAR/SOFT PLIABLE RUBBER $1-2
- ❑ ❑ USA GE7904 **DATSUN 126X**, ND, CAR/SOFT PLIABLE RUBBER $1-2
- ❑ ❑ USA GE7905 **FANDANGO,** ND, CAR/SOFT PLIABLE RUBBER $1-2
- ❑ ❑ USA GE7906 **HAIRY HUSTLER,** ND, CAR/SOFT PLIABLE RUBBER $1-2
- ❑ ❑ USA GE7907 **HIGH TAILER,** ND, CAR/SOFT PLIABLE RUBBER $1-2
- ❑ ❑ USA GE7908 **MERCEDES 350SL,** ND, CAR/SOFT PLIABLE RUBBER $1-2
- ❑ ❑ USA GE7909 **PLANET SCOUT,** ND, CAR/SOFT PLIABLE RUBBER $1-2
- ❑ ❑ USA GE7910 **TURBO FURY,** ND, CAR/SOFT PLIABLE RUBBER $1-2

USA GE7933

USA GE7934

USA GE7901 USA GE7902 USA GE7903 USA GE7904 USA GE7905

USA GE7906 USA GE7907 USA GE7908 USA GE7909 USA GE7910

- ❑ ❑ USA GE7911 **UNCLE O'GRIMACEY INFLATABLE (UNCUT),** 1979, PLASTIC/PUPPET $5-8
- ❑ ❑ USA GE7912 **YOYO - BIG MAC,** 1979, BLU W BLU/WHT BIG MAC DECAL $10-15
- ❑ ❑ USA GE7913 **YOYO - GRIMACE,** 1979, PURP W PURP/WHT GRIM DECAL $10-15
- ❑ ❑ USA GE7914 **YOYO - HAMBURGLAR,** 1979, YEL W BLK/WHT HAMB DECAL $10-15
- ❑ ❑ USA GE7915 **YOYO - RONALD,** 1979, RED W RED/WHT RON DECAL $10-15
- ❑ ❑ USA GE7916 **LIFT-UP MYSTERY GAME,** 1978, BIG MAC TIC-TAC-TOE $5-8
- ❑ ❑ USA GE7917 **LIFT-UP MYSTERY GAME,** 1978, MAYOR WORD GUESS $5-8
- ❑ ❑ USA GE7918 **LIFT-UP MYSTERY GAME,** 1978, PROFESSOR DOT $5-8
- ❑ ❑ USA GE7919 **LIFT-UP MYSTERY GAME,** 1978, RONALD MAZE $5-8
- ❑ ❑ USA GE7920 **X-O RING - FRENCH FRY,** ND, VANISH/GR/RED/YEL/BLU $8-10
- ❑ ❑ USA GE7921 **GLIDER - RONALD,** ND, STYRO/PUNCH-OUT/RED/YEL 4 3/8" LONG $8-10
- ❑ ❑ USA GE7941 **COUNTER CARD/MINIFLEXIES,** ND, PLASTIC $20-25
- ❑ ❑ USA GE7945 **REGISTER TOPPER/MINIFLEXIES,** ND, RED CARDBOARD $20-25
- ❑ ❑ USA GE7965 **TRANSLITE/MINIFLEXIES/LG,** 1979 $45-60

COMMENTS: LIMITED REGIONAL DISTRIBUTION: USA - FEBRUARY 3-JUNE 10, 1979. THIS HAPPY MEAL WAS PART OF THE FOURTH HAPPY MEAL GENERIC TEST CONDUCTED IN ST. LOUIS, DENVER, KANSAS CITY AND BUFFALO. SOME OF THESE MARKETS DEVELOPED THEIR OWN PROMOTIONS/PREMIUMS. MCD ARCHIVES INDICATE THAT ANY OF THE ABOVE GENERIC PREMIUMS COULD HAVE BEEN GIVEN WITH THIS HAPPY MEAL. CAR NAMES ARE ON THE DOOR PANEL. NOTE: SOFT PLIABLE RUBBER PREMIUMS WERE COMMON IN 1979 AND STILL AVAILABLE IN RETAIL STORES IN THE 1990'S. BOTTOM OF THE CAR READS, "MATCHBOX IS A REG. T.M. OF LESNEY PROD. CORP. LTD ENG."

USA GE7914 USA GE7915 USA GE7912 USA GE7913

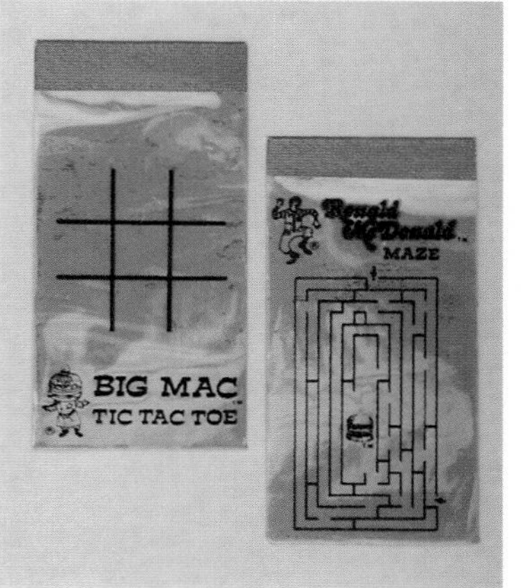

USA GE7916 USA GE7919

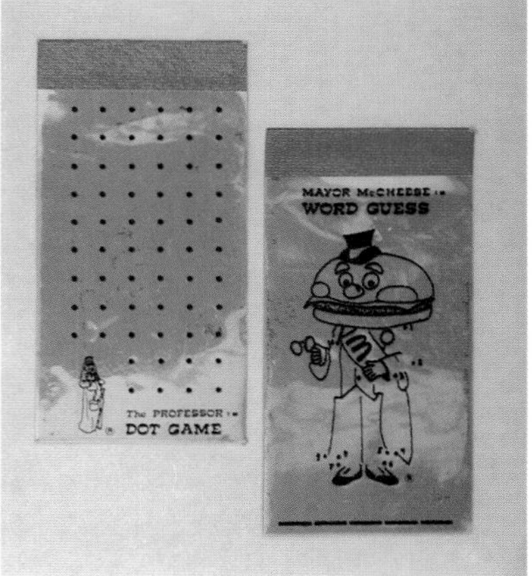

USA GE7918 USA GE7917

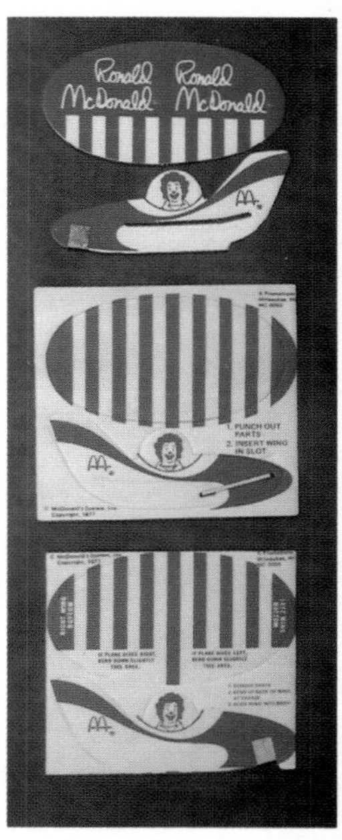

USA GE7921

USA GE7911

USA GE7945

USA GE7920

USA CI7930

CIRCUS WAGON HAPPY MEAL, 1979

- ❑ ❑ USA CI7930 **HM BOX**, 1979, **CAPT CROOK AND SEAL...SEALS NOSE 12"...** $25-40
- ❑ ❑ USA CI7931 **HM BOX**, 1979, **GRIMACE AND ELEPHANT** $25-40
- ❑ ❑ USA CI7932 **HM BOX**, 1979, **RON/HAMB/ CAPT...ROBBLE,ROBBLE...** $25-40
- ❑ ❑ USA CI7933 **HM BOX**, 1979, **RON/GOBLINS...HALF A HAMBURGER** $25-40
- ❑ ❑ USA CI7934 **HM BOX**, 1979, **RONALD/LION... WHEN DO LIONS HAVE 8 FEET?** $25-40

USA CI7933

USA CI7931

USA CI7934

USA CI7932

- ❑ ❑ USA CI7935 **HM BOX,** 1979, **RONALD/MAYOR...WHAT DO ZEBRAS...** $25-40
- ❑ ❑ USA CI7905 **ID BRACELET-BIG MAC,** 1979, YEL or RED ALPHABET STICKER SHEET $8-10
- ❑ ❑ USA CI7908 **ID BRACELET-HAMBURGLAR,** 1979, YEL or RED ALPHABET STICKER SHEET $8 -10
- ❑ ❑ USA CI7909 **ID BRACELET-RONALD,** 1979, YEL or RED ALPHABET STICKER SHEET $8-10
- ❑ ❑ USA CI7906 **DOODLER RULER-RONALD**, 1979, RED or BLU or YEL 2P $8-10
- ❑ ❑ USA CI7907 **MC PUZZLE LOCK-RONALD,** 1979, RED or BLU or YEL 5P $10-12
- ❑ ❑ USA CI7926 **FLOOR DISPLAY,** 1979 $100-150
- ❑ ❑ USA CI7941 **CEILING DANGLER,** 1979 $45-60
- ❑ ❑ USA CI7954 **CREW BADGE,** 1979, PAPER BLU/TURQ HM BOX W PINBACK $15-20
- ❑ ❑ USA CI7965 **TRANSLITE/6 BOXES/LG**, 1979 $50-75
- ❑ ❑ USA CI7966 **TRANSLITE/1 BOX/LG,** 1979 $45-65

COMMENTS: NATIONAL DISTRIBUTION: USA - JUNE 11-JULY 31, 1979. FIRST NATIONAL HAPPY MEAL PROMOTION IN THE UNITED STATES.

USA CI7906

USA CI7935

USA CI7907

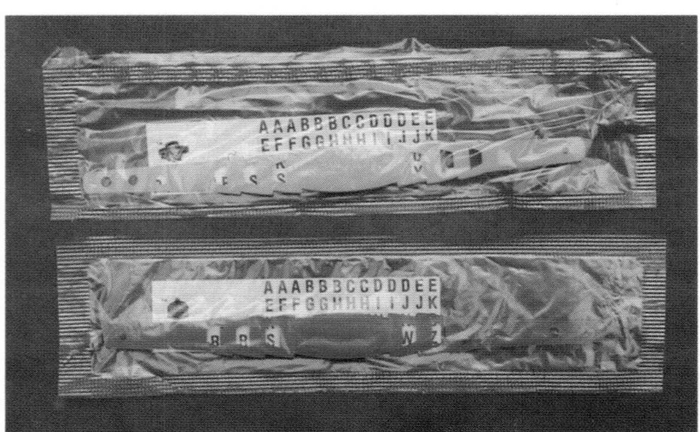

USA CI7908

USA CI7905

USA CI7954

USA CI7965

USA CI7966

SPACE THEME HAPPY MEAL, 1979

- ❑ ❑ USA SP7900 **HM BOX,** 1979, **BIG MAC/SIX MARTIANS/ FLIGHT LOG/SPACE QUIZ** $50-65
- ❑ ❑ USA SP7901 **HM BOX,** 1979, **GRIMACE/THICK SHAKE** $50-65
- ❑ ❑ USA SP7902 **HM BOX,** 1979, **SPACE CREATURES/RON FEEDING CREATURES** $50-65
- ❑ ❑ USA SP7903 **HM BOX,** 1979, **MCDONALDLAND FRIENDS IN PLANT-A-TARIUM** $50-65
- ❑ ❑ USA SP7904 **HM BOX,** 1979, **RON/STOWAWAY SPACEMEN "SIX SPACEMEN .."** $50-65

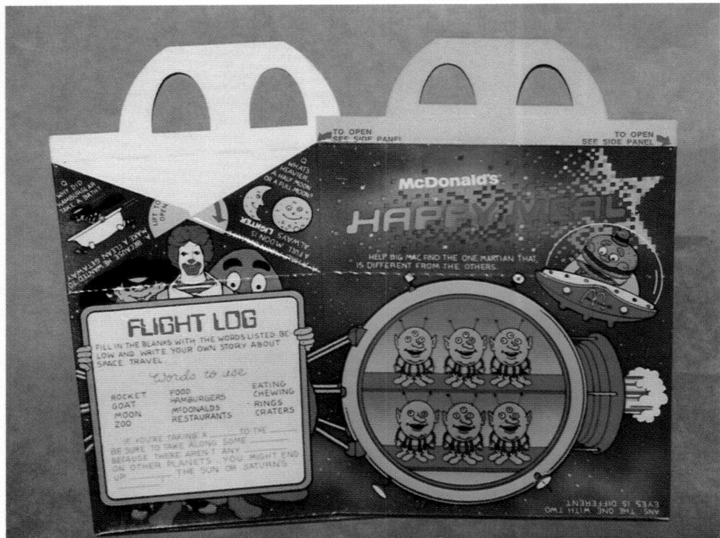

USA SP7900

USA SP7901

USA SP7902

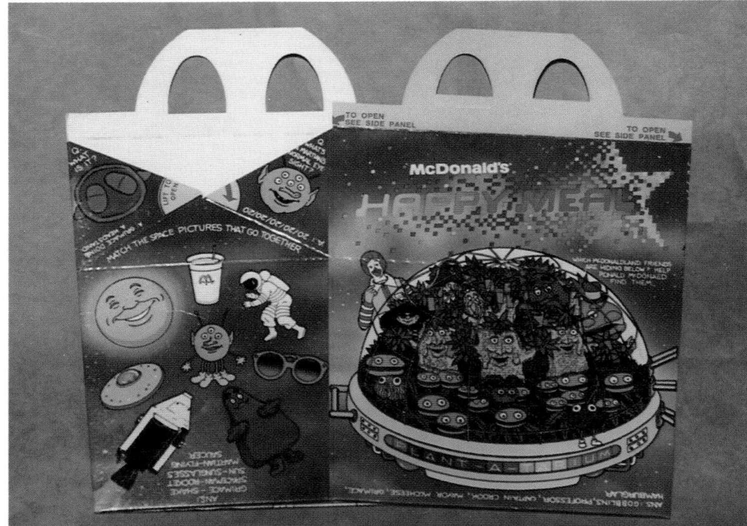

USA SP7903

USA SP7904

❑ ❑ USA SP7905 **HM BOX,** 1979, **SPACE ZOO/RONALD AND SPACE ZOO ANIMALS** $50-65
❑ ❑ USA SP7990 **GILL FACE CREATURE,** ND, ORG/PUR/YEL/BRN/GRN/BRN $1-1.50
❑ ❑ USA SP7991 **HORNED CYCLOPS,** ND, ORG/PUR/YEL/BRN/GRN/BLU $1-1.50
❑ ❑ USA SP7992 **INSECTMAN,** ND, ORG/PUR/YEL/BRN/GRN/BLU $1-1.50
❑ ❑ USA SP7993 **LIZARD MAN,** ND, ORG/PUR/YEL/BRN/GRN/BLU $1-1.50
❑ ❑ USA SP7994 **TREE TRUNK MONSTER,** ND, ORG/PUR/YEL/BRN/GRN/BLU $1-1.50
❑ ❑ USA SP7995 **VAMPIRE BAT CREATURE**, ND, ORG/PUR/YEL/BRN/GRN/BLU $1-1.50
❑ ❑ USA SP7996 **VEINED CRANIUM,** ND, ORG/PUR/YEL/BRN/GRN/BLU $1-1.50
❑ ❑ USA SP7997 **WINGED AMPHIBIAN,** ND, ORG/PUR/YEL/BRN/GRN/BLU $1-1.50
❑ ❑ USA SP7941 **CEILING DANGLER** $45-75
❑ ❑ USA SP7942 **COUNTER CARD** $35-50
❑ ❑ USA SP7965 **TRANSLITE/SPACE ALIENS,** 1979 $50-75
❑ ❑ USA SP7966 **TRANSLITE/ALIEN CREATURES,** 1979 $50-75
❑ ❑ USA SP7967 **TRANSLITE/HAPPY MEAL,** 1979 $50-75

COMMENTS: REGIONAL DISTRIBUTION: USA - JULY/DECEMBER 1979. PREMIUM MARKINGS - "DIENER IND."; SPACE RAIDERS WERE SOFT, SPACE ALIENS WERE HARD AND SOFT. REGIONS DEVELOPED THEIR OWN PROMOTIONS/PREMIUMS. OTHER GENERIC PREMIUMS COULD HAVE BEEN GIVEN WITH THE HAPPY MEAL. THESE PREMIUMS MAY HAVE BEEN GIVEN OUT IN EARLIER HAPPY MEAL OFFERINGS. USA SP7990-97 ARE STILL AVAILABLE AT RETAIL STORES IN THE 1990'S. NO MCDONALD'S MARKINGS ON PREMIUMS.

STAR TREK MEAL HAPPY MEAL, 1980/1979

❑ ❑ USA ST7920 **HM BOX,** 1979, **BRIDGE-DRAW THE ALIEN** $8-12
❑ ❑ USA ST7921 **HM BOX,** 1979, **BRIDGE-PLANET FACES** $8-12
❑ ❑ USA ST7922 **HM BOX,** 1979, **FEDERATION** $8-12
❑ ❑ USA ST7923 **HM BOX,** 1979, **KLINGONS** $8-12
❑ ❑ USA ST7924 **HM BOX,** 1979, **SPACESUIT-SPOCKS CODE** $8-12
❑ ❑ USA ST7925 **HM BOX,** 1979, **TRANSPORTER ROOM-KLINGON MATCH** $8-12

USA ST7920 USA ST7921

USA ST7922 USA ST7923

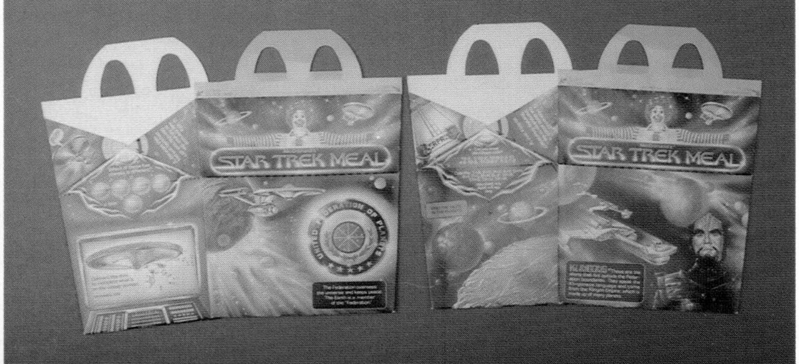

USA SP7905

USA SP7990 USA SP7992 USA SP7994 USA SP7996

USA SP7991 USA SP7993 USA SP7995 USA SP7997

USA SP7941

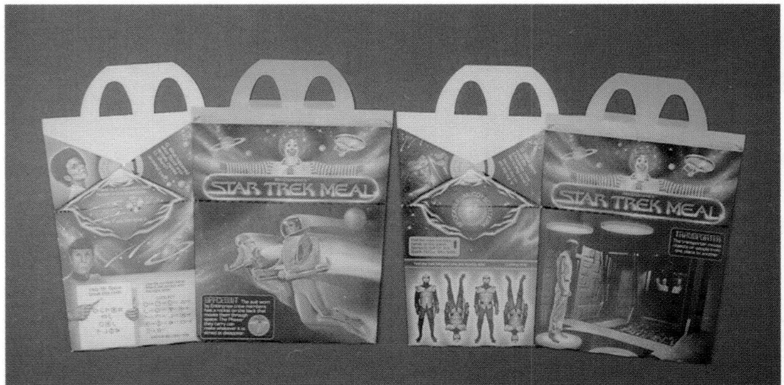

USA ST7924 USA ST7925

USA ST7905 USA ST7901 USA ST7902

- ☐ ☐ USA ST7915 **BRACELET,** 1979, NAVIGATORS CHART/ GALAXY 6 DECALS/8 3/4"/BLU $20-25
- ☐ ☐ USA ST7916 **GAME,** 1979, PAPER BOARD W REMOVABLE PIECES/5" X 10 1/4" $15-20
- ☐ ☐ USA ST7901 **VIDEO COMMUNICATOR,** 1979, GRY or BLK/ COMIC #1 - STAR TREK STARS $25-35
- ☐ ☐ USA ST7902 **VIDEO COMMUNICATOR,** 1979, GRY or BLK/ COMIC #2 - A PILL SWALLOWS THE ENTERPRISE $25-35
- ☐ ☐ USA ST7903 **VIDEO COMMUNICATOR,** 1979, GRY or BLK/ COMIC #3 - TIME & TIME & TIME AGAIN $25-35
- ☐ ☐ USA ST7904 **VIDEO COMMUNICATOR,** 1979, GRY or BLK/ COMIC #4 - VOTEC'S FREEDOM $25-35
- ☐ ☐ USA ST7905 **VIDEO COMMUNICATOR,** 1979, GRY or BLK/ COMIC #5 - STARLIGHT STARFIGHT $25-35
- ☐ ☐ USA ST7906 **RING - CAPT KIRK,** 1979, YEL or BLU or RED $25-35
- ☐ ☐ USA ST7907 **RING - U.S.S. ENTERPRISE,** 1979, YEL or BLU or RED $25-35
- ☐ ☐ USA ST7908 **RING - SPOCK,** 1979, YEL or BLU or RED $25-35
- ☐ ☐ USA ST7909 **RING - STAR TREK LOGO,** 1979, YEL or BLU or RED $25-35
- ☐ ☐ USA ST7910 **IRON-ON TRANSFER - CAPT KIRK,** 1979 $20-25
- ☐ ☐ USA ST7911 **IRON-OH TRANSFER - DR. MCCOY,** 1979 $20-25
- ☐ ☐ USA ST7912 **IRON-ON TRANSFER - LT. ILIA,** 1979 $20-25
- ☐ ☐ USA ST7913 **IRON-ON TRANSFER - MR. SPOCK,** 1979 $20-25

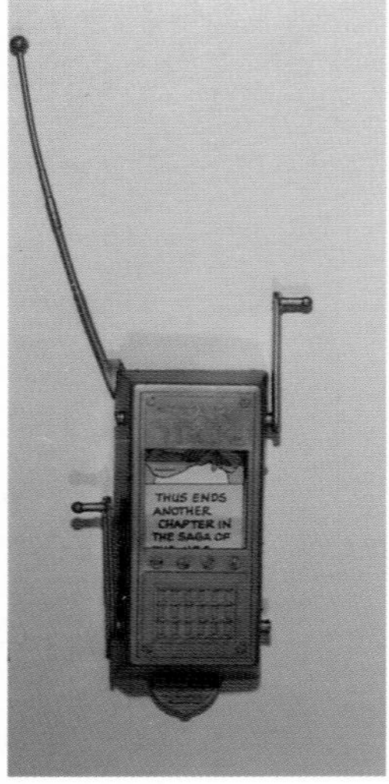

USA ST7904

USA ST7910 USA ST7911

USA ST7909 USA ST7906

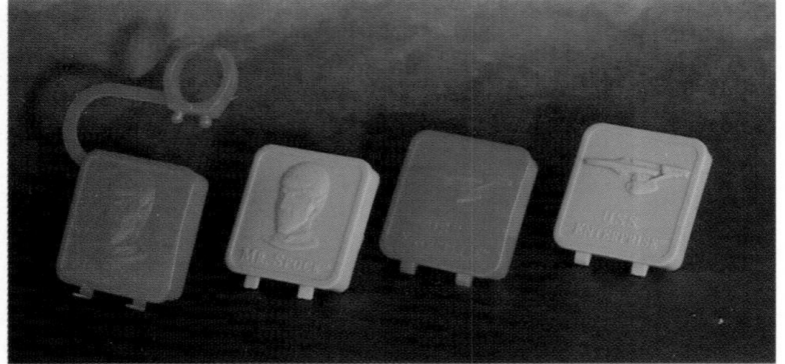

USA ST7908 USA ST7907

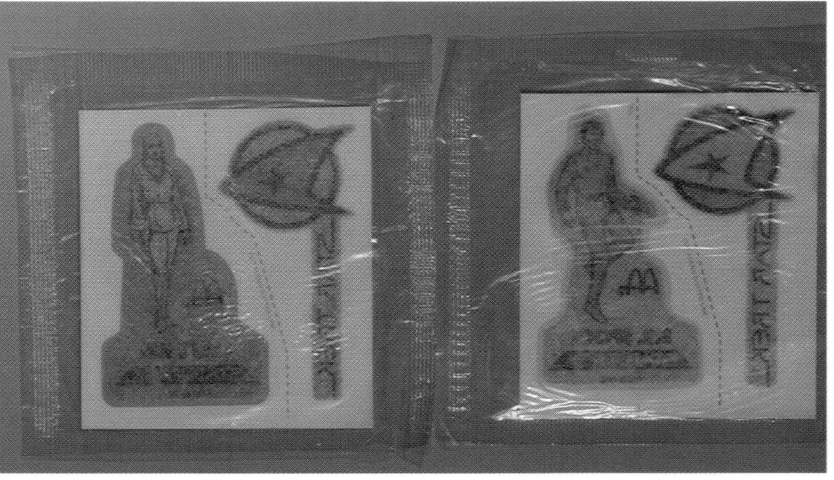

USA ST7912 USA ST7913

❑ ❑ USA ST7934 **CREW BADGE/PAPER STICK-ON** $20-25
❑ ❑ USA ST7935 **ENTRY FORM/STAR TREK THE MOTION PICTURE,** 1980, PAPER $7-10
❑ ❑ USA ST7938 **APRON/UNIFORM,** 1979, W MCD/STAR TREK LOGO $50-75
❑ ❑ USA ST7941 **CEILING DANGLER/W 5 BOXES** $200-250
❑ ❑ USA ST7942 **COUNTER CARD** $50-65

USA ST7938

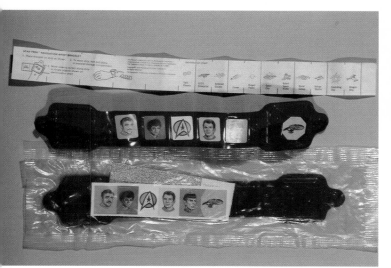

USA ST7915

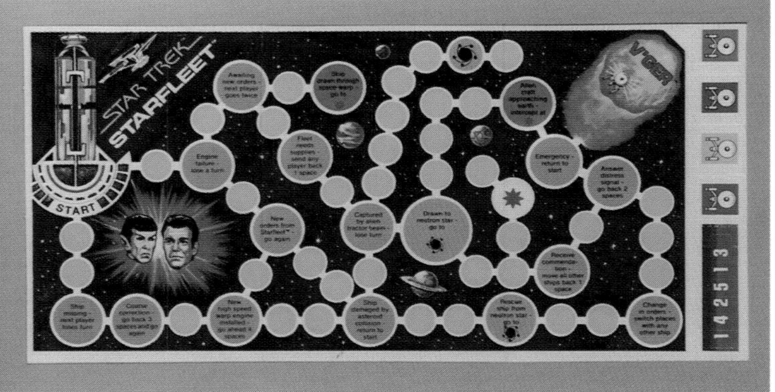

USA ST7916

USA ST7941

USA ST7934

USA ST7935

USA ST7942

USA ST7955

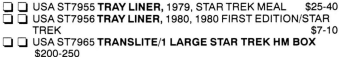

❑ ❑ USA ST7955 **TRAY LINER,** 1979, STAR TREK MEAL $25-40
❑ ❑ USA ST7956 **TRAY LINER,** 1980, 1980 FIRST EDITION/STAR TREK $7-10
❑ ❑ USA ST7965 **TRANSLITE/1 LARGE STAR TREK HM BOX** $200-250
❑ ❑ USA ST7966 **TRANSLITE/HM BOX/HAM/FRIES/SHAKE/PIN HOLES** $200-250

COMMENTS: NATIONAL DISTRIBUTION: USA - DECEMBER 26, 1979-FEBRUARY 3, 1980. THIS WAS USA'S NATIONAL HAPPY MEAL WITH PREMIUMS DESIGNED FOR THE STAR TREK THEME. COMMUNICATORS CAME WITH 1 COMIC STRIP HAVING TWO BACK-TO-BACK DIFFERENT TITLES/LISTED. SOME REGIONS DEVELOPED THEIR OWN PROMOTIONS/PREMIUMS. GENERIC PREMIUMS COULD HAVE BEEN GIVEN WITH THE HAPPY MEAL. NO UNDER 3 (U-3) PREMIUMS WERE FURNISHED. SOME STORES OFFERED ENTRY FORM TO WIN TICKETS FOR TWO FOR "STAR TREK THE MOTION PICTURE" (1980).

USA ST7956

USA/GENERIC PROMOTION, 1979

❑ ❑ USA GE7951 **RACER/MCDONALDLAND-RONALD,** 1979, RED or YEL/2P W 2 ELASTIC BANDS $12-15

COMMENT: REGIONAL DISTRIBUTION: USA - 1979 DURING CLEAN-UP WEEKS. THIS IS A SAMPLING OF GENERIC PREMIUMS GIVEN OUT DURING 1979.

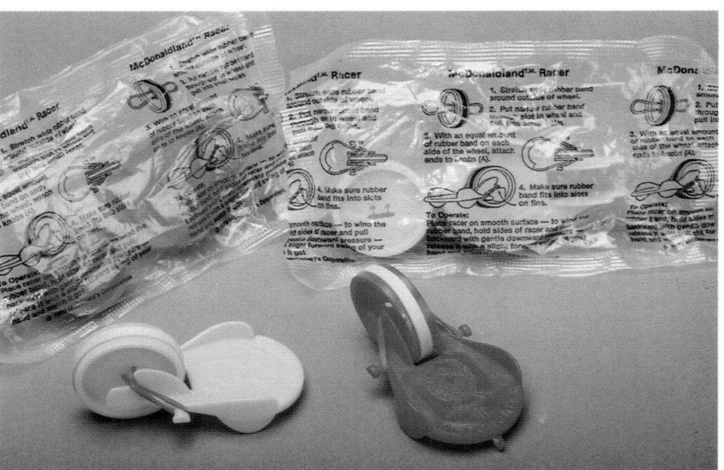

USA GE7951

USA ST7965

1980

DALLAS COWBOYS SUPER BOX HAPPY MEAL, 1980
HAPPY HOTCAKES PROMOTION, 1980
LOOK LOOK BOOKS HAPPY MEAL, 1980
SAFARI ADVENTURE MEAL HAPPY MEAL, 1980
UNDERSEA HAPPY MEAL, 1980
USA/GENERIC PROMOTION, 1980

DALLAS COWBOYS SUPER BOX HAPPY MEAL, 1980

❑ ❑ USA DA8035 **HM BOX**, 1980, **SUPER BOX I/CHUCK HOWLEY/DON PERKINS** $125-175

USA ST7966

❑ ❑ USA DA8036 **HM BOX,** 1980, **SUPER BOX II/DON MEREDITH/BOB LILLY** $125-175

❑ ❑ USA DA8037 **HM BOX,** 1980, **SUPER BOX III/ROGER STAUBACH/W. GARRISON** $125-175

COMMENTS: REGIONAL DISTRIBUTION: USA - 1980 IN DALLAS, TEXAS. TWO CUT-OUT COWBOYS COLLECTOR SERIES FOOTBALL CARDS ON EACH BOX.

HAPPY HOTCAKES PROMOTION, 1980

❑ ❑ USA HO8010 **PANCAKES WRAPPER,** 1980, **BATTER UP FOR BREAKFAST** $8-12

❑ ❑ USA HO8011 **PANCAKES WRAPPER,** 1980, **FLYIN' HIGH** $8-12

❑ ❑ USA HO8012 **PANCAKES WRAPPER,** 1980, **TOO POOPED TO PEDAL** $8-12

❑ ❑ USA HO8001 **CUP-HAPPY MILK,** 1980, RON W NET/RED BAND $4-6

❑ ❑ USA HO8002 **CUP-HAPPY MILK,** 1980, RON W BINOCULARS/BLU BAND $4-6

❑ ❑ USA HO8003 **CUP-HAPPY MILK,** 1980, RON W PILLOW/BRN BAND $4-6

❑ ❑ USA HO8004 **CUP-HAPPY MILK,** 1980, RON W BIRDIE FLYING/GRN BAND $4-6

COMMENTS: REGIONAL DISTRIBUTION: USA - 1980 IN SOUTH CAROLINA AND OHIO.

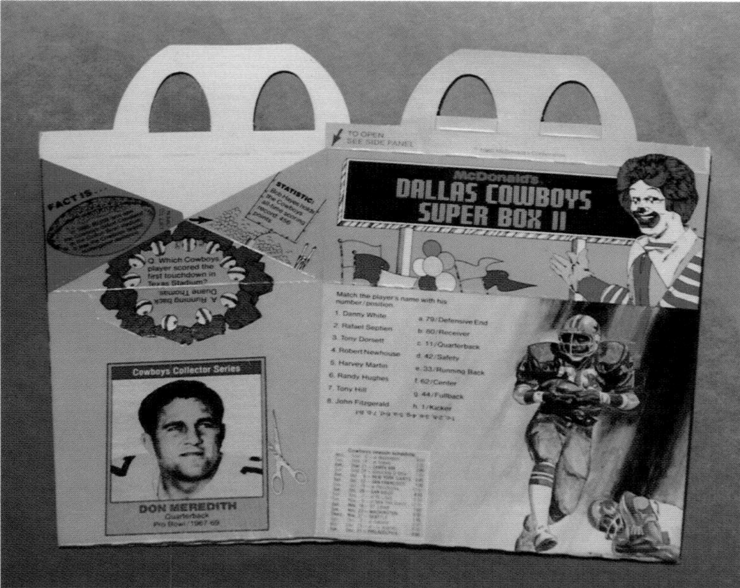

USA DA8036

USA HO8010

USA HO8012

USA HO8011

USA HO8001 USA HO8002 USA HO8003 USA HO8004

LOOK LOOK BOOKS HAPPY MEAL, 1980

❑ ❑ USA LO8000 **ANIMALS OF THE SEA,** 1980, PAPER BOOKLET $25-40
❑ ❑ USA LO8001 **ANIMALS THAT FLY,** 1980, PAPER BOOKLET $25-40
❑ ❑ USA LO8002 **CATS IN THE WILD,** 1980, PAPER BOOKLET $25-40
❑ ❑ USA LO8003 **THE BIGGEST ANIMALS,** 1980, PAPER BOOKLET $25-40
❑ ❑ USA LO8042 **COUNTER CARD/DATED APRIL 20, 1980** $25-40

COMMENTS: REGIONAL DISTRIBUTION: USA - SOUTHERN CALIFORNIA BY MARINE WORLD AND IN ST. LOUIS, MISSOURI. BOOK SIZE 5" x 4" W 12 PAGES. PACKAGED IN CELLOPHANE; BOOKS WERE PRODUCED BY WESTERN PUBLISHING WITH THE MCDONALD'S LOGO ON BACK OF BOOK.

SAFARI ADVENTURE HAPPY MEAL, 1980

❑ ❑ USA SA8015 **HM BOX,** 1980, **RONALD AND GRIMACE** $25-40
❑ ❑ USA SA8016 **HM BOX,** 1980, **RONALD AND HYENA** $25-40
❑ ❑ USA SA8017 **HM BOX,** 1980, **RONALD/MONKEY/FRY GUY** $25-40
❑ ❑ USA SA8018 **HM BOX,** 1980, **RONALD/VINES/CARROT/HIPPO** $25-40
❑ ❑ USA SA8001 **ALLIGATOR,** 1980, BLU or BRN or GRY or ORG or PNK or PUR or YEL or GRN $1-1.50
❑ ❑ USA SA8002 **APE,** 1980, BLU or BRN or GRY or ORG or PNK or PUR or YEL or GRN $1-1.50
❑ ❑ USA SA8003 **ELEPHANT,** 1980, BLU or BRN or GRY or ORG or PNK or PUR or YEL or GRN $1-1.50
❑ ❑ USA SA8004 **HIPPO,** 1980, BLU or BRN or GRY or ORG or PNK or PUR or YEL or GRN $1-1,50
❑ ❑ USA SA8005 **LION,** 1980, BLU or BRN or GRY or ORG or PNK or PUR or YEL or GRN $1-1.50
❑ ❑ USA SA8006 **MONKEY,** 1980, BLU or BRN or GRY or ORG or PNK or PUR or YEL or GRN $1-1.50
❑ ❑ USA SA8007 **RHINO,** 1980, BLU or BRN or GRY or ORG or PNK or PUR or YEL or GRN $1-1.50
❑ ❑ USA SA8008 **TIGER,** 1980, BLU or BRN or GRY or ORG or PNK or PUR or YEL or GRN $1-1.50
❑ ❑ USA SA8019 **COMB - RONALD,** 1980, RED or YEL or BLU $1-2
❑ ❑ USA SA8020 **COMB - GRIMACE,** 1080, RED or YEL or BLU $1-2
❑ ❑ USA SA8021 **SPONGE - GRIMACE,** ND, GRIMACE STANDING/PURPLE $2.50-4

USA LO8000

USA LO8001

USA LO8002

USA LO8003

USA SA8017 USA SA8016

USA SA8001 USA SA8003 USA SA8005 USA SA8007

USA SA8002 USA SA8004 USA SA8006 USA SA8008

USA SA8020

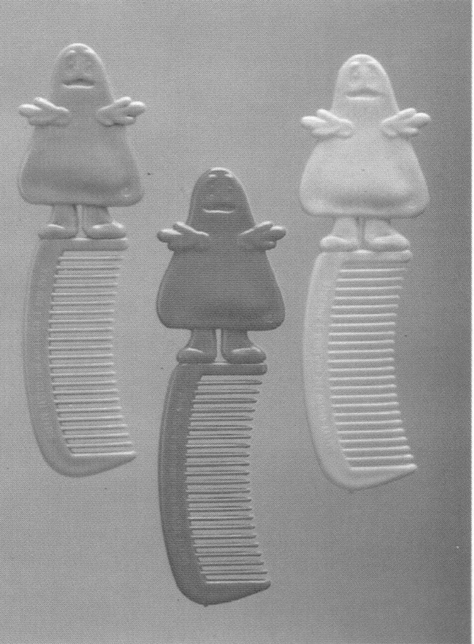

USA SA8019

USA SA8021

- ❑ ❑ USA SA8022 **SPONGE - RONALD,** ND, RONALD SITTING W ARMS/LEGS CROSSED $2.50-4
- ❑ ❑ USA SA8023 **SPONGE - HAMBURGLAR FLOATER,** ND, ORG 5 1/8" CIRCLE DISC $7-10
- ❑ ❑ USA SA8024 **COOKIE MOLD - RONALD,** 1980, RED or YEL $1-1.50
- ❑ ❑ USA SA8025 **COOKIE MOLD - GRIMACE,** 1980, RED or YEL $1-1.50
- ❑ ❑ USA SA8026 **BIG MAC - DOUBLE BALLS IN RINGS,** 1979, YEL BASE $7-10
- ❑ ❑ USA SA8027**CAPTAIN - BALL IN SLOT/3 BALLS,** 1979, YEL BASE $7-10
- ❑ ❑ USA SA8028 **HAMBURGLAR - SINGLE TOSS/2 RINGS,** 1979, YEL BASE $7-10
- ❑ ❑ USA SA8029 **MAYOR - 2 BALLS IN RING PLUS TOSS,** 1979, YEL BASE $7-10
- ❑ ❑ USA SA8030 **RONALD - DOUBLE RING TOSS/2 RINGS,** 1979, YEL BASE $7-10
- ❑ ❑ USA SA8031 **LIGHT SWITCH COVER,** 1980, RON/STICK-ON/ 4" X 2 1/2"/GLOW-IN-DARK $5-8
- ❑ ❑ USA SA8032 **RING - RONALD WHISTLE,** 1980, RED $5-7
- ❑ ❑ USA SA8033 **PENNANT - RONALD,** 1980, $15-20
- ❑ ❑ USA SA8034 **PENNANT - GRIMACE,** 1980 $15-20
- ❑ ❑ USA SA8035 **TIP 'N' TILT GAME,** 1980 $8-12
- ❑ ❑ USA SA8036 **HAMBURGLAR HOCKEY,** 1980 $4-6
- ❑ ❑ USA SA8037 **LETTERLAND STATIONARY - RONALD/ PROFESSOR,** 1980 $6-8

USA SA8030 USA SA8027

USA SA8033 USA SA8034

USA SA8022 USA SA8023

USA SA8032

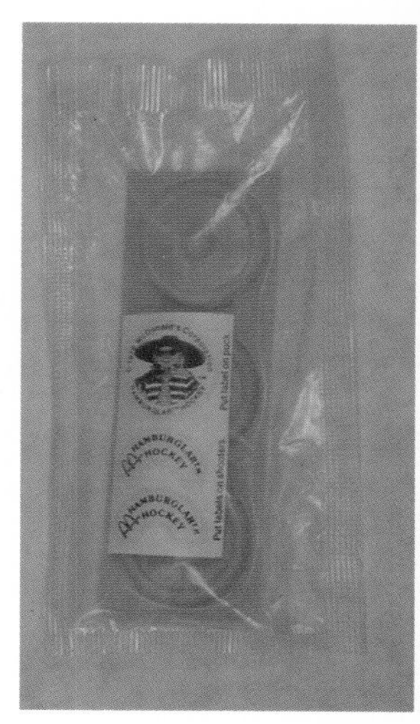

USA SA8036

USA SA8024 USA SA8025

USA SA8031

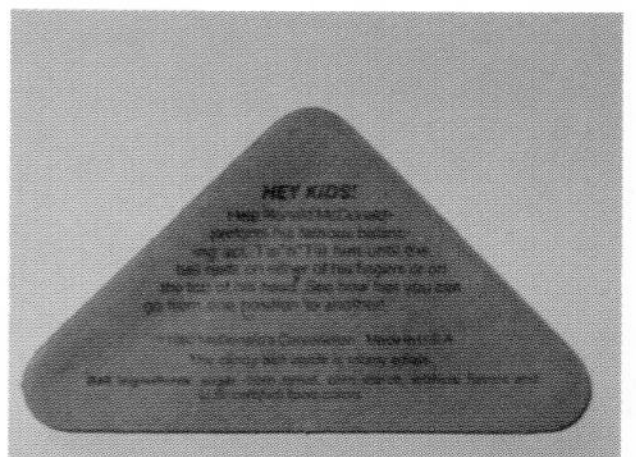

USA SA8035

USA SA8037

USA SA8026 USA SA8029 USA SA8028

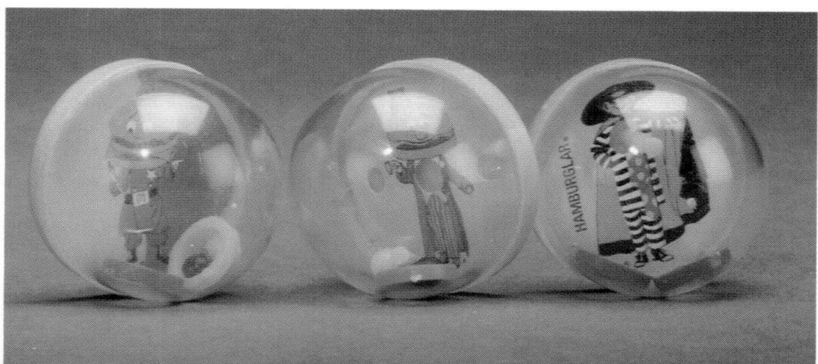

- ❑ ❑ USA SA8038 **LETTERLAND STATIONARY - CAPT/BIG MAC/ GRI/FRY GUY,** 1980 $6-8
- ❑ ❑ USA SA8039 **FISHIN' FUN GAME,** 1980, PAPER $7-10
- ❑ ❑ USA SA8040 **WHO'S IN THE ZOO? GAME,** 1980, PAPER $7-10
- ❑ ❑ USA SA8041 **CEILING DANGLER,** 1980, W/O BOXES $50-75
- ❑ ❑ USA SA8042 **COUNTER CARD,** 1980, DON'T MONKEY AROUND! $25-40
- ❑ ❑ USA SA8065 **TRANSLITE/LG,** 1980 $50-65
- ❑ ❑ USA SA8066 **TRANSLITE/LETTERLAND STATIONARY** $20-30
- ❑ ❑ USA SA8067 **TRANSLITE/FATHER'S DAY COUPONS,** 1980 $15-25

COMMENTS: NATIONAL PROMOTION: USA JUNE 2-29, 1980. FIGURINE PREMIUM MARKINGS - "DIENER IND." ALL FIGURINES WERE RUBBER. REGIONS DEVELOPED THEIR OWN PROMOTIONS/PREMIUMS DURING 1980.

USA SA8038

USA SA8066

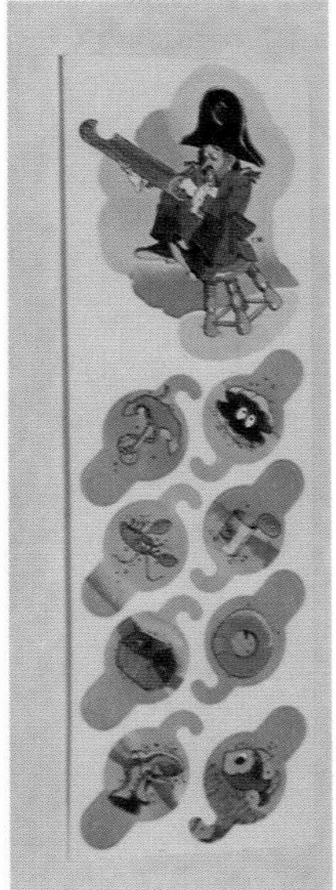

USA SA8039 USA SA8040

USA SA8067

USA SA8065

UNDERSEA HAPPY MEAL, 1980

❑ ❑ USA UN8035 **HM BOX,** 1980, **CAPTAIN CROOK/ RONALD** $35-50
❑ ❑ USA UN8036 **HM BOX,** 1980, **GRIMACE/DIVER** $35-50
❑ ❑ USA UN8037 **HM BOX,** 1980, **GRIMACE ON PORPOISE/ SQUID** $35-50
❑ ❑ USA UN8038 **HM BOX,** 1980, **SECRET MESSAGE/SEA SHELL** $35-50
❑ ❑ USA UN8039 **HM BOX,** 1980, **RONALD IN SUB-MARINE** $35-50
❑ ❑ USA UN8040 **HM BOX,** 1980, **EELS/DOG/CHICKEN** $35-50
❑ ❑ USA UN8001 **ALLIGATOR,** ND, "DIENER" MOLDED INTO FIGURINE $1-1.50
❑ ❑ USA UN8002 **DOLPHIN/PORPOISE,** ND, "DIENER" MOLDED INTO FIGURINE $1-1.50
❑ ❑ USA UN8003 **SEAL,** ND, NO COMPANY NAME $1-1.50
❑ ❑ USA UN8004 **SHARK/GREAT WHITE,** ND, NO COMPANY NAME $1-1.50
❑ ❑ USA UN8005 **SHARK/HAMMERHEAD,** ND, "HAMMERHEAD" MOLDED INTO FIGURINE $1-1.50
❑ ❑ USA UN8006 **SHARK/TIGER,** ND, "TIGER SHARK" MOLDED INTO FIGURINE $1-1.50
❑ ❑ USA UN8007 **SHARK/WHALE,** ND, "WHALESHARK" MOLDED INTO FIG $1-1.50
❑ ❑ USA UN8008 **TURTLE/SEA,** ND, "DIENER" MOLDED INTO FIGURINE $1-1.50
❑ ❑ USA UN8009 **WALRUS,** ND, "DIENER" MOLDED INTO FIG $1-1.50
❑ ❑ USA UN8010 **WHALE,** ND, "DIENER" MOLDED INTO FIG $1-1.50
❑ ❑ USA UN8041 **CEILING DANGLER W/O BOXES,** 1980 $65-90
❑ ❑ USA UN8042 **COUNTER CARD,** 1980 $25-35
❑ ❑ USA UN8065 **TRANSLITE/LG,** 1980 $50 -65

COMMENTS: NATIONAL DISTRIBUTION: USA - 1980 IN THE SPRING. ALL FIGURINES WERE SOFT RUBBER AND CAME IN ASSORTED COLORS. REGIONS COULD ACCEPT THE NATIONAL PROMOTION OR DEVELOP THEIR OWN PROMOTIONS. GENERIC PREMIUMS COULD HAVE BEEN GIVEN WITH THIS HAPPY MEAL.

USA UN8037

USA UN8038

USA SA8035

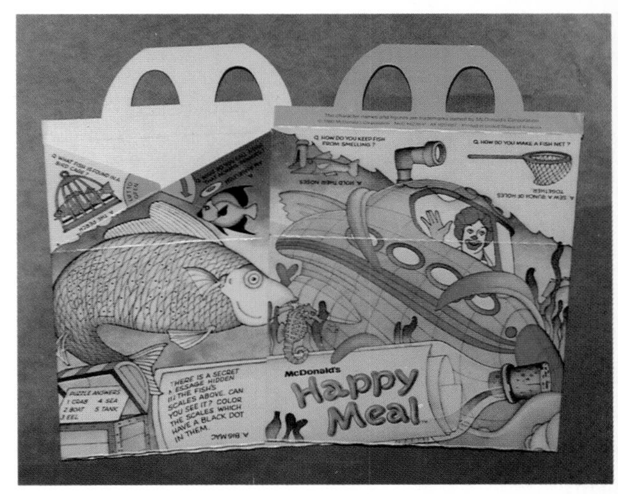

USA UN8039

USA UN8036

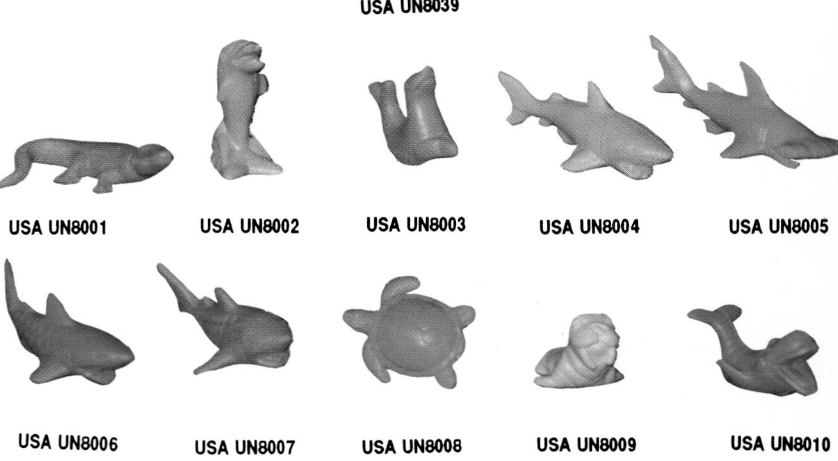
USA UN8001 USA UN8002 USA UN8003 USA UN8004 USA UN8005

USA UN8006 USA UN8007 USA UN8008 USA UN8009 USA UN8010

THE HAPPY MEAL NAME, UNDERSEA, IS NOT ON THE FRONT OF THE BOXES, BUT IS ON THE COUNTER CARD AND TRANSLITE.

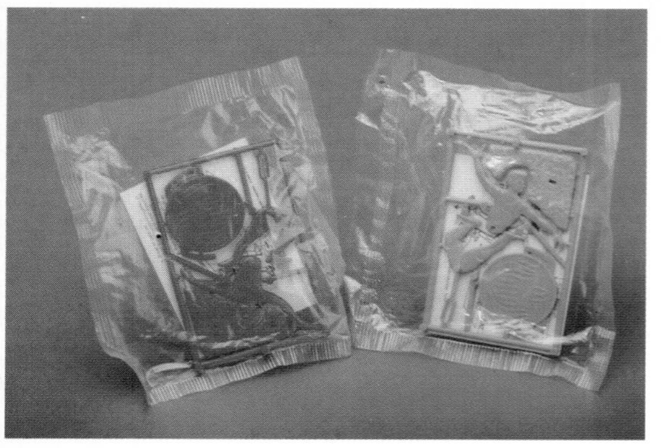
USA GE8001

USA/GENERIC PROMOTION, 1980

- ❑ ❑ USA GE8001 **GYMNASTICS/OLYMPICS - RON,** 1980, BLU or RED/4P $10-15
- ❑ ❑ USA GE8003 **JALOPY CAR-BIRDIE,** 1980, ORG or RED or YEL/5P $10-15
- ❑ ❑ USA GE8006 **JALOPY CAR-HAMB,** 1980, ORG or RED or YEL/5P $10-15
- ❑ ❑ USA GE8009 **JALOPY CAR-RONALD,** 1980, ORG or RED or YEL/5P $10-15
- ❑ ❑ USA GE8012 **ICICLY STICK,** 1980, YEL/4 1/4"/2P $3-5
- ❑ ❑ USA GE8013 **PEN - GRIMACE,** 1980, PURP W CORDED THREAD $6-8
- ❑ ❑ USA GE8014 **PEN - BIG MAC,** 1980, BRN W CORDED THREAD $6-8
- ❑ ❑ USA GE8015 **PEN - HAMB,** 1980, BLK W CORDED THREAD $6-8
- ❑ ❑ USA GE8016 **PEN - RONALD**, 1980, YEL/RED/WHT W CORDED THREAD $6-8

COMMENTS: REGIONAL DISTRIBUTION: USA - 1980. USA GE8001-02 WERE LIMITED DISTRIBUTION BECAUSE USA 1980 OLYMPICS WERE CANCELLED BY PRESIDENT CARTER.

USA GE8012 USA GE8003 USA GE8006 USA GE8009

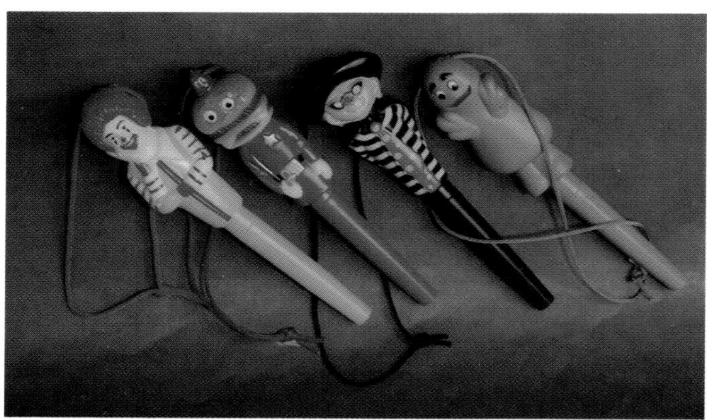
USA GE8016 USA GE8014 USA GE8015 USA GE8013

1981

3D HAPPY MEAL HAPPY MEAL, 1981
ADVENTURES OF RONALD MCDONALD HAPPY MEAL, 1981
DINOSAUR DAYS HAPPY MEAL, 1981
OLD WEST HAPPY MEAL, 1981
PLAYMOBIL I TEST MARKET HAPPY MEAL, 1981
SPACESHIP/UNIDENTIFIED HAPPY MEAL, 1981
USA/GENERIC PROMOTION, 1981

3D HAPPY MEAL HAPPY MEAL, 1981

- ❑ ❑ USA TH8155 **HM BOX,** 1981, **BUGSVILLE/HUNGRY FUNNIES** $25-40
- ❑ ❑ USA TH8156 **HM BOX,** 1981, **HIGH JINX/CLOWNISH CAPERS** $25-40

USA TH8155

USA TH8156

USA TH8156

- ❑ ❑ USA TH8157 **HM BOX,** 1981, **LOCOMOTION/LAUGHING STOCK** $25-40
- ❑ ❑ USA TH8158 **HM BOX,** 1981, **SPACE FOLLIES/GURGLE GAGS** $25-40
- ❑ ❑ USA TH8150 **3-D GLASSES,** 1981, CARDBOARD/BLU/RED CELLOPHANE/ARCHES $12-15
- ❑ ❑ USA TH8165 **TRANSLITE/LG,** 1981 $75-100

COMMENTS: REGIONAL DISTRIBUTION: USA - MAY/JUNE/NOV 1981. TEST MARKET REGIONAL PROMOTION.

ADVENTURES OF RONALD MCDONALD HAPPY MEAL, 1981

- ❑ ❑ USA AD8114 **HM BOX,** 1981, **RAINBOW/RON/GRI/HAMB** $20-25

USA TH8157

USA TH8158

USA TH8150

USA AD8114

- ❑ ❑ USA AD8115 **HM BOX,** 1981, **RODEO/RONALD BULL RIDING** $20-25
- ❑ ❑ USA AD8116 **HM BOX,** 1981, **SPEECH/MAYOR CAN'T READ SPEECH** $20-25
- ❑ ❑ USA AD8117 **HM BOX,** 1981, **EXPRESS/HAMB STEALING CHEESEBURGER** $20-25
- ❑ ❑ USA AD8118 **HM BOX,** 1981, **HIDE N' SEEK/RONALD AND FRIENDS** $20-25
- ❑ ❑ USA AD8119 **HM BOX,** 1981, **KABOOM/MAYOR FINDING LIGHT** $20-25

USA AD8115

USA AD8116

USA AD8117

USA AD8118

USA AD8119

❑ ❑ USA AD8101 **FIGURINE - BIG MAC,** 1981, 2" SOFT RUBBER $6-8
❑ ❑ USA AD8102 **FIGURINE - CAPTAIN,** 1981, 2" SOFT RUBBER $6-8
❑ ❑ USA AD8103 **FIGURINE - GRIMACE,** 1981, 2" SOFT RUBBER $6-8
❑ ❑ USA AD8104 **FIGURINE - HAMBURG,** 1981, 2" SOFT RUBBER $6-8
❑ ❑ USA AD8105 **FIGURINE - MAYOR,** 1981, 2" SOFT RUBBER $6-8
❑ ❑ USA AD8106 **FIGURINE - RONALD,** 1981, 2" SOFT RUBBER $6-8
❑ ❑ USA AD8107 **FIGURINE - BIG MAC,** 1981, 2" HARD RUBBER $7-10
❑ ❑ USA AD8108 **FIGURINE - CAPTAIN,** 1981, 2" HARD RUBBER $7-10
❑ ❑ USA AD8109 **FIGURINE - GRIMACE,** 1981, 2" HARD RUBBER $7-10
❑ ❑ USA AD8110 **FIGURINE - HAMBURGLAR,** 1981, 2" HARD RUBBER $7-10
❑ ❑ USA AD8111 **FIGURINE - MAYOR,** 1981, 2" HARD RUBBER $7-10
❑ ❑ USA AD8112 **FIGURINE - RONALD,** 1981, 2" HARD RUBBER $7-10
❑ ❑ USA AD8113 **FIGURINE - BIRDIE,** 1981, 2" HARD RUBBER $7-10
❑ ❑ USA AD8126 **DISPLAY/RON STANDING,** 1981 $150-200
❑ ❑ USA AD8165 **TRANSLITE/LG,** 1981 $50-65

COMMENTS: NATIONAL PROMOTION: USA - MAY 25-JUNE 21, 1981. DIENER THE MANUFACTURER, MADE SOFT FIGURINES IN FIVE BASIC COLORS: ORG, YEL, GRN, BLU, PNK; HARD RUBBER FIGURES CAME IN FOUR COLORS: ORG, YEL, GRN, AND BLU.

DINOSAUR DAYS HAPPY MEAL, 1982/1981

❑ ❑ USA DI8125 **HM BOX,** 1981, **(A) ANATOSAURUS (B) DIMETRODON** $20-30
❑ ❑ USA DI8126 **HM BOX,** 1981, **(A) ANKYLOSAURUS (B) CORYTHOSAURUS** $20-30

USA AD8102 USA AD8103 USA AD8104 USA AD8101
USA AD8105 USA AD8106

USA AD8108 USA AD8110 USA AD8111 USA AD8107
USA AD8109 USA AD8112 USA AD8113

USA DI8125

USA AD8165

USA DI8126

USA DI8127

USA DI8128

USA DI8129

❑ ❑ USA DI8127 **HM BOX,** 1981, **(A) BRACHIOSAURUS (B) TANYSTROPHEUS** $20-30

❑ ❑ USA DI8128 **HM BOX,** 1981, **(A) BRONTOSAURS (B) TYRANNOSAURUS REX** $20-30

❑ ❑ USA DI8129 **HM BOX,** 1981, **(A) BRONOTO (B) TYRANNO/ THREE SKELTONS** $20-30

❑ ❑ USA DI8130 **HM BOX,** 1981, **(A) WOOLY MAMMOTH (B) GIANT GROUND SLOTH** $20-30

❑ ❑ USA DI8106 **CARD #1 XOGRAPH MASTODONS,** 1981 $15-20

❑ ❑ USA DI8107 **CARD #2 XOGRAPH STEGOSAURS,** 1981 $15-20

❑ ❑ USA DI8108 **CARD #3 XOGRAPH TRICERATOPS,** 1981 $15-20

❑ ❑ USA DI8109 **CARD #4 XOGRAPH BRONTOSAURS,** 1981 $15-20

❑ ❑ USA DI8110 **CARD #5 XOGRAPH SABER-TOOTHED TIGER,** 1981 $15-20

❑ ❑ USA DI8111 **CARD #6 XOGRAPH TYRANNOSAURS REX,** 1981 $15-20

USA DI8130

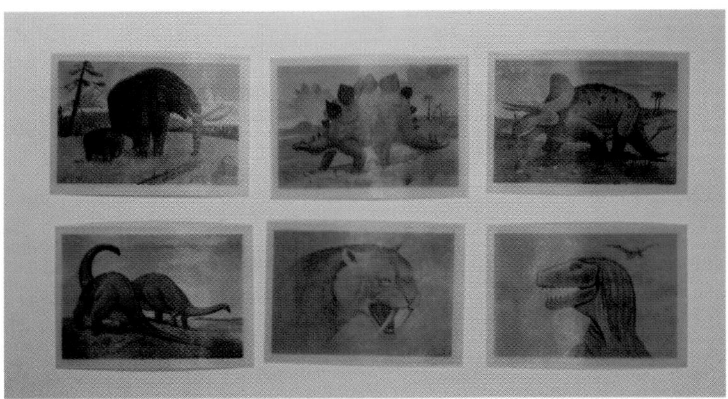

USA DI8106 USA DI8107 USA DI8108
USA DI8109 USA DI8110 USA DI8111

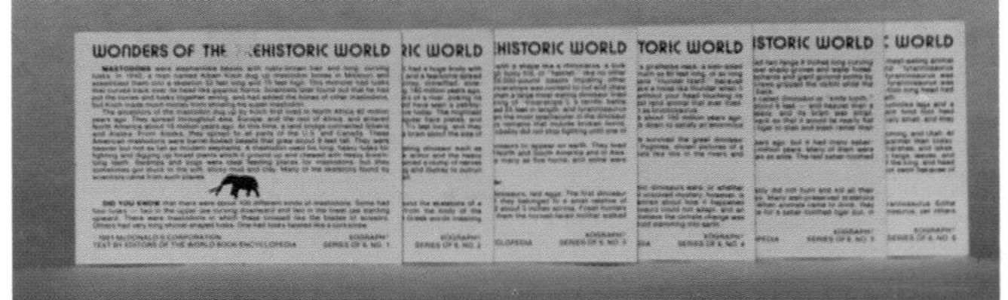

❑ ❑ USA DI8100 **DINOSAUR-ANKYLOSAURUS,** 1981, HARD RUBBER BRN or GRY or GRN or ORG or BLU $1-1.50
❑ ❑ USA DI8101 **DINOSAUR-DIMETRODON,** 1981, HARD RUBBER BRN or GRY or GRN or ORG or BLU $1-1.50
❑ ❑ USA DI8102 **DINOSAUR-PTERANODON,** 1981, HARD RUBBER BRN or GRY or GRN or ORG or BLU $1-1.50
❑ ❑ USA DI8103 **DINOSAUR-STEGOSAURUS,** 1981, HARD RUBBER BRN or GRY or GRN or ORG or BLU $1-1.50
❑ ❑ USA DI8104 **DINOSAUR-TRICERATOPS,** 1981, HARD RUBBER BRN or GRY or GRN or ORG or BLU $1-1.50
❑ ❑ USA DI8105 **DINOSAUR-TYRANNOSAURUS REX,** 1981, HARD RUBBER BRN or GRY or GRN or ORG or BLU $1-1.50
❑ ❑ USA DI8112 **SPONGE-DINOSAUR,** ND, GRN/MCD LOGO AROUND NECK $2.50-4
❑ ❑ USA DI8115 **SPONGE-BIRDIE,** ND, YEL $4-6
❑ ❑ USA DI8116 **FLYING WHEEL/FRISBEE,** 1980, "FLYER" RON/ ARMS OUTSTRETCHED/RED or YEL $2-3
❑ ❑ USA DI8117 **TIC-TAC-TOP,** ND $8-12
❑ ❑ USA DI8118 **NOSE MAZE GAME,** 1980, RONALD $4-6
❑ ❑ USA DI8119 **PATCH/POCKET,** ND, RONALD/POCKET SHAPED $4-5
❑ ❑ USA DI8120 **WHISTLE-RONALD,** ND, VERY LONG/18-21"/ YEL $4-5
❑ ❑ USA DI8121 **WHISTLE-GRIMACE,** ND, VERY LONG/18-21"/ PURP $4-5
❑ ❑ USA DI8122 **RING/GLOW,** 1980, RONALD/YEL W PAPER FRONT $8-10
❑ ❑ USA DI8123 **RING/GLOW,** 1980, GRIMACE/YEL W PAPER FRONT $8-10
❑ ❑ USA DI8136 **FORK/SPOON SET,** 1980, RONALD W HANDS UP/RED OR YELLOW $1-2
❑ ❑ USA DI8137 **FORK/SPOON SET,** 1980, GRIMACE W SHAKE/ RED OR YEL $1-2

USA DI8116

USA DI8118

USA DI8119

USA DI8100 USA DI8101 USA DI8102 USA DI8103 USA DI8104 USA DI8105

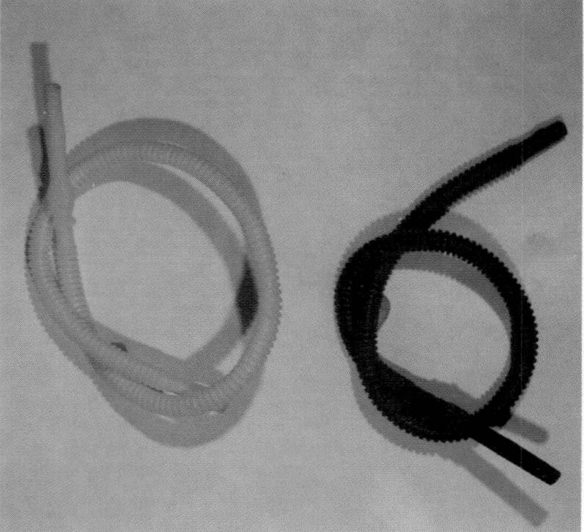
USA DI8120 USA DI8121

USA DI8122

USA DI8123

USA DI8112

USA DI8115

USA DI8136 USA DI8137

USA DI8140 USA DI8138 USA DI8139

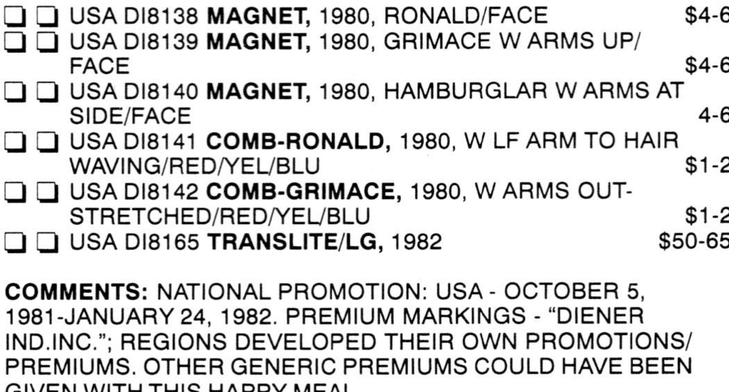

❑ ❑ USA DI8138 **MAGNET,** 1980, RONALD/FACE $4-6
❑ ❑ USA DI8139 **MAGNET,** 1980, GRIMACE W ARMS UP/FACE $4-6
❑ ❑ USA DI8140 **MAGNET,** 1980, HAMBURGLAR W ARMS AT SIDE/FACE 4-6
❑ ❑ USA DI8141 **COMB-RONALD,** 1980, W LF ARM TO HAIR WAVING/RED/YEL/BLU $1-2
❑ ❑ USA DI8142 **COMB-GRIMACE,** 1980, W ARMS OUT-STRETCHED/RED/YEL/BLU $1-2
❑ ❑ USA DI8165 **TRANSLITE/LG,** 1982 $50-65

COMMENTS: NATIONAL PROMOTION: USA - OCTOBER 5, 1981-JANUARY 24, 1982. PREMIUM MARKINGS - "DIENER IND.INC."; REGIONS DEVELOPED THEIR OWN PROMOTIONS/PREMIUMS. OTHER GENERIC PREMIUMS COULD HAVE BEEN GIVEN WITH THIS HAPPY MEAL.

USA DI8141

The most fun in a million years!
McDONALD'S
DINOSAUR DAYS
HAPPY MEAL
COLLECT ALL 6 BOXES

USA DI8165

OLD WEST HAPPY MEAL, 1981

❑ ❑ USA OL8110 **HM BOX,** 1981, **BLACKSMITH SHOP** $25-40
❑ ❑ USA OL8111 **HM BOX,** 1981, **GENERAL STORE** $25-40
❑ ❑ USA OL8112 **HM BOX,** 1981, **HOTEL** $25-40
❑ ❑ USA OL8113 **HM BOX,** 1981, **MUSIC HALL** $25-40
❑ ❑ USA OL8114 **HM BOX,** 1981, **SHERIFF'S OFFICE** $25-40
❑ ❑ USA OL8115 **HM BOX,** 1981, **TRAIN DEPOT** $25-40

USA OL8110 USA OL8111

USA OL8114

USA OL8112 USA OL8113

USA OL8115

❑ ❑ USA OL8100 **INDIAN SQUAW W HANDS CROSSED,** ND, BLU or BRN or YEL or ORG $12-15
❑ ❑ USA OL8101 **INDIAN BRAVE/FACE TO FACE,** ND, BLU or BRN or YEL or ORG $12-15
❑ ❑ USA OL8102 **COWGIRL W GUN,** ND, BLU or BRN or YEL or ORG $12-15
❑ ❑ USA OL8103 **COWBOY BEING HELD UP,** ND, BLU or BRN or YEL or ORG $12-15
❑ ❑ USA OL8104 **SHERIFF W HANDS ON SIDE,** ND, BLU or BRN or YEL or ORG $12-15
❑ ❑ USA OL8105 **WOODSMAN W KNIFE IN HAND,** ND, BLU or BRN or YEL or ORG $12-15
❑ ❑ USA OL8161 **M C INSERT/CARDBOARD,** 1981 $45-60
❑ ❑ USA OL8165 **TRANSLITE/LG,** 1981 $50-65

COMMENTS: NATIONAL OPTION: USA - SPRING 1981. PREMIUM MARKINGS - "DIENER IND." ALL FIGURINES WERE HARD RUBBER. REGIONS DEVELOPED THEIR OWN PROMOTIONS/ PREMIUMS. GENERIC PREMIUMS COULD HAVE BEEN GIVEN WITH THIS HAPPY MEAL.

PLAYMOBIL I TEST MARKET HAPPY MEAL, 1981

❑ ❑ USA PL8100 **INDIAN,** 1981, RED MAN W LT BRN HEAD-PIECE/SHIELD/SPEAR/RIFLE/5P $35-50
❑ ❑ USA PL8101 **CONSTRUCTION WORKER,** 1981, BLU MAN/ BEIGE LADDER/WHT HAT/BRN PICK/GRY SHOVEL/ 5P $35-50
❑ ❑ USA PL8102 **CAVALRY SOLDIER,** 1981, LT BLU PANTS/DK BLU HAT/SHIRT/RIFLE/FLAG W CIRCLE STARS-#1 $35-50
❑ ❑ USA PL8103 **SOLDIER'S HORSE,** 1981, LT BRN HORSE W DK BRN SADDLE/RECT OR OVAL WATER TROUGH/2P $35-50
❑ ❑ USA PL8104 **UMBRELLA GIRL,** 1981, RED MAN W BLU DRESS/WHT HAT/YEL UMB $35-50
❑ ❑ USA PL8105 **FARMER,** 1981, GRN PANTS W WHT HAT/WHT SHOVEL/RAKE/SCYTHE $35-50
❑ ❑ USA PL8106 **COW,** 1981, MEDIUM BROWN W HEAD DOWN $35-50
❑ ❑ USA PL8121 **PAMPHLET / PEOPLE/ FIGURES,** 1981 $10-15

USA OL8102 USA OL8100 USA OL8105
USA OL8103 USA OL8104 USA OL8101

USA OL8165

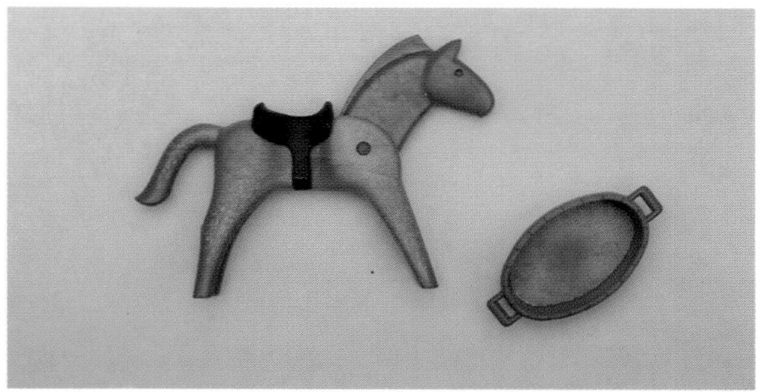

USA PL8103

USA PL8121

USA PL8122

❑ ❑ USA PL8122 **PAMHPLET /ACCESSORIES,** 1981 $10-15
❑ ❑ USA PL8155 **TRAYLINER,** 1981 $10-12

COMMENTS: REGIONAL DISTRIBUTION: USA - MAY 8-JUNE 25, 1981 IN ST. LOUIS, JEFFERSON CITY AND SPRINGFIELD, MISSOURI AS WELL AS NEBRASKA. A 5 PIECE ACCESSORY SET COULD BE ORDERED WITH THE COUPON INSERT - CANNON, CANOE/DECAL, TEPEE/DECAL, ROCKING CHAIR AND ROAD ROLLER. RECTANGLE WATERING TROUGH IS NOT ONE MOLDED PIECE, BUT THREE PIECES. NOTICE END OF TROUGH. WATERING TROUGH, MINT IN PACKAGE, IS NOT SAME AS PICTURE MINT IN PACKAGE. CANADIAN SET INCLUDED ONLY OVAL TROUGH. USA TEST MARKET SET INCLUDED BOTH/ EITHER RECTANGLE TROUGH WITH SIDE PIECES OR OVAL TROUGH.

USA SP8103 USA SP8102 USA SP8101 USA SP8100

SPACESHIP/UNIDENTIFIED HAPPY MEAL, 1981

❑ ❑ USA SP8100 **SPACESHIP #1 - 8 WINDOWS,** 1981, BLU or GRN or RED or YEL W DECALS $20-25
❑ ❑ USA SP8101 **SPACESHIP #2 - ROUND FRONT W REAR ENGINE,** 1981, BLU/GRN/RED/YEL W DECALS $20-25
❑ ❑ USA SP8102 **SPACESHIP #3 - POINTED FRONT,** 1981, BLU or GRN or RED or YEL W DECALS $20-25
❑ ❑ USA SP8103 **SPACESHIP #4 - 4 KNOBS,** 1981, BLU or GRN or RED or YEL W DECALS $20-25
❑ ❑ USA SP8104 **STICKER SHEET #1 - 8 WINDOWS** $15-20
❑ ❑ USA SP8105 **STICKER SHEET #2 - ROUND FRONT** $15-20
❑ ❑ USA SP8106 **STICKER SHEET #3 - POINTED FRONT** $15-20
❑ ❑ USA SP8107 **STICKER SHEET #4 - FOUR KNOBS** $15-20
❑ ❑ USA SP8165 **TRANSLITE/LG,** 1981 $75-100

COMMENTS: LIMITED REGIONAL DISTRIBUTION: USA - 1981 IN KANSAS CITY, KANSAS. THE UNIDENTIFIED HAPPY MEAL WAS TEST MARKETED IN THE KANSAS CITY AND ST. LOUIS AREAS. THIS SET HAD ONLY 4 LUGS HOLDING THE TOP TO THE BOTTOM. LATER, 1982 SET HAD 8 LUGS. THE SPACESHIPS CAME WITH EITHER A MOLDED "M" ON TOP OR A MOLDED "M'S" WITHIN A CIRCLE. THE TWO PIECE SPACESHIP CONTAINER HELD FOOD AND SERVED AS THE PREMIUM. THE SPACESHIP CONTAINERS HAD A DULL FINISH.

USA GE8105

USA/GENERIC PROMOTION, 1981

❑ ❑ USA GE8101 **GLOBE/AIRPLANE-BIRDIE,** 1981, BLU or WHT/PLANE/GLOBE/4P $8-12
❑ ❑ USA GE8103 **GLOBE/AIRPLANE-GRIMACE,** 1981, BLU or WHT PLANE/GLOBE/4P $8-12
❑ ❑ USA GE8105 **GLOBE/AIRPLANE-RONALD,** 1981, BLU or WHT PLANE/GLOBE/4P $8-12
❑ ❑ USA GE8107 **BLOW STRING-RON,** 1981, ORG WHISTLE/ RED STRING W INSTRUCTIONS $4-6
❑ ❑ USA GE8108 **SWING AND CATCH GAME-RONALD,** 1981, ORG or YEL RONALD/BASKETBALL HOOP/BALL/3P $7-10
❑ ❑ USA GE8109 **FOOT RULER-RONALD,** 1981, RED FOOT/ RULER/3P $2-3

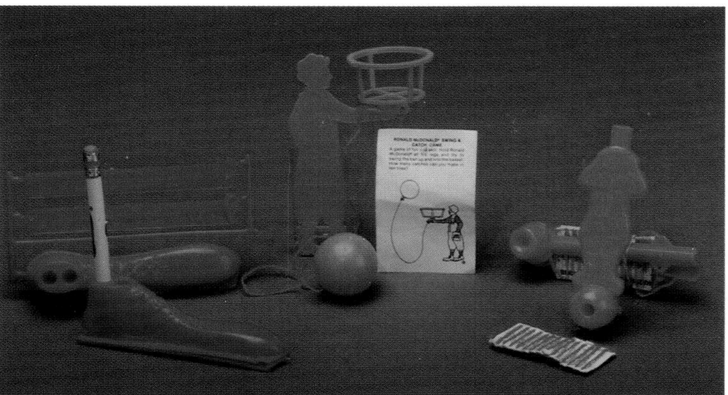

USA GE8109 USA GE8108 USA GE8107

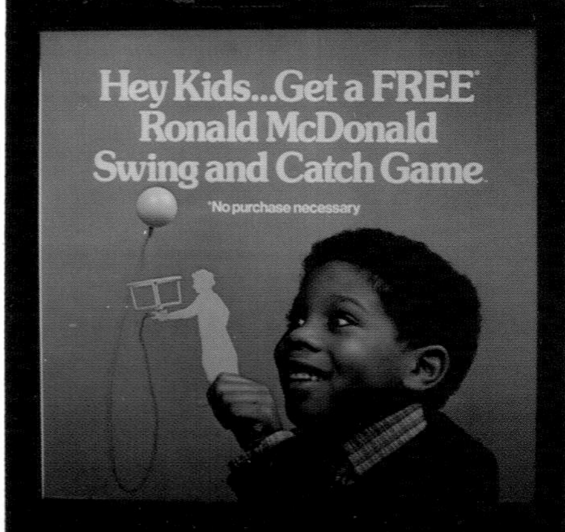

❑ ❑ USA GE8110 **MOTOR BOAT/RUBBER BAND-GRIM,** 1981, ORG or RED or YEL/RUBBER BAND/3P $8-12
❑ ❑ USA GE8113 **MOTOR BOAT/RUBBER BAND-HAMB,** 1981, ORG or RED or YEL/RUBBER BAND/3P $8-12
❑ ❑ USA GE8116 **MOTOR BOAT/RUBBER BAND-RON,** 1981, ORG or RED or YEL/RUBBER BAND/3P $8-12
❑ ❑ USA GE8119 **TIC TAC MAC,** 1981, YEL BOARD/5 GRI X/5 RON O/11P $4-6
❑ ❑ USA GE8120 **PENCIL HOLDER-BIG MAC,** 1981, RED/1P $4-6
❑ ❑ USA GE8121 **PENCIL HOLDER-CAPTAIN,** 1981, RED/1P $4-6
❑ ❑ USA GE8122 **PENCIL HOLDER-HAMBURGLAR,** 1981, RED/1P $4-6
❑ ❑ USA GE8123 **PENCIL HOLDER-RONALD,** 1981, RED/1P $4-6

COMMENTS: REGIONAL DISTRIBUTION: USA - 1981 DURING CLEAN-UP WEEKS. THIS IS A SAMPLING OF GENERIC PREMIUMS GIVEN OUT DURING 1981.

1982

DUKES OF HAZZARD HAPPY MEAL, 1982
GIGGLES AND GAMES HAPPY MEAL, 1982
GOING PLACES HAPPY MEAL, 1982
LITTLE GOLDEN BOOK HAPPY MEAL, 1982
MCDONALDLAND EXPRESS HAPPY MEAL, 1982
PLAYMOBIL II HAPPY MEAL, 1982
SKY-BUSTERS HAPPY MEAL, 1982
SPACESHIP HAPPY MEAL, 1982
WACKY HAPPY MEAL, 1982
USA/GENERIC PROMOTION, 1982

DUKES OF HAZZARD HAPPY MEAL, 1982

❑ ❑ USA DU8200 **GENERAL LEE,** 1982, ORG VACUFORM CAR $25-40
❑ ❑ USA DU8201 **BOSS HOGG CADILLAC,** 1982, WHT VACUFORM CAR $25-40
❑ ❑ USA DU8202 **SHERIFF ROSCOE CAR,** 1982, WHT VACUFORM CAR $25-40
❑ ❑ USA DU8203 **DAISEY'S JEEP,** 1982, WHT VACUFORM JEEP $25-40

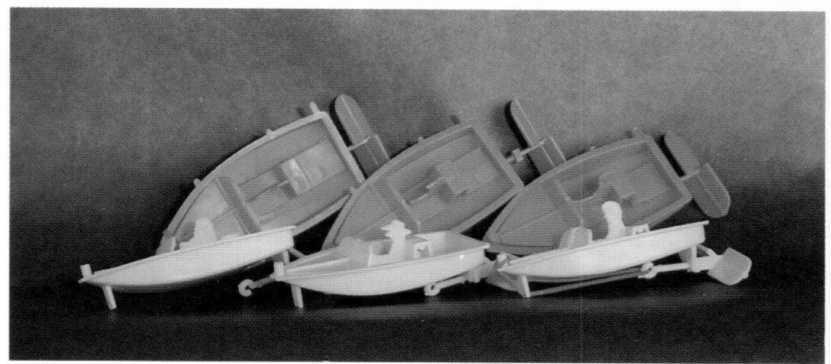

USA GE8110 USA GE8113 USA GE8116

USA GE8119

USA GE8120

USA GE8121 USA GE8122 USA GE8123

USA DU8200

USA DU8202

USA DU8201

USA DU8203

USA DU8204

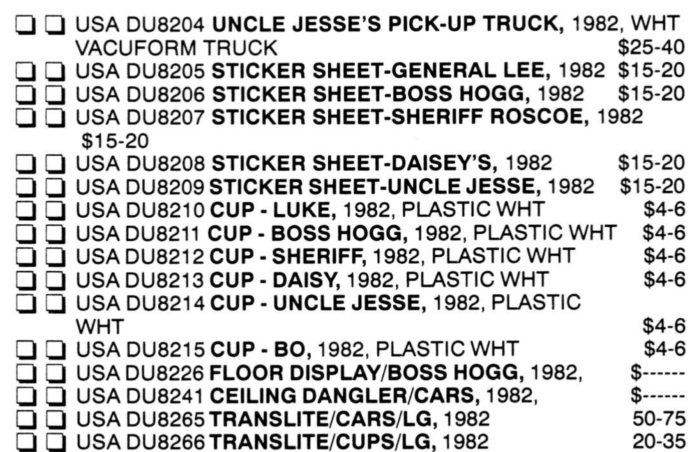

☐ ☐ USA DU8204 **UNCLE JESSE'S PICK-UP TRUCK,** 1982, WHT VACUFORM TRUCK $25-40
☐ ☐ USA DU8205 **STICKER SHEET-GENERAL LEE,** 1982 $15-20
☐ ☐ USA DU8206 **STICKER SHEET-BOSS HOGG,** 1982 $15-20
☐ ☐ USA DU8207 **STICKER SHEET-SHERIFF ROSCOE,** 1982 $15-20
☐ ☐ USA DU8208 **STICKER SHEET-DAISEY'S,** 1982 $15-20
☐ ☐ USA DU8209 **STICKER SHEET-UNCLE JESSE,** 1982 $15-20
☐ ☐ USA DU8210 **CUP - LUKE,** 1982, PLASTIC WHT $4-6
☐ ☐ USA DU8211 **CUP - BOSS HOGG,** 1982, PLASTIC WHT $4-6
☐ ☐ USA DU8212 **CUP - SHERIFF,** 1982, PLASTIC WHT $4-6
☐ ☐ USA DU8213 **CUP - DAISY,** 1982, PLASTIC WHT $4-6
☐ ☐ USA DU8214 **CUP - UNCLE JESSE,** 1982, PLASTIC WHT $4-6
☐ ☐ USA DU8215 **CUP - BO,** 1982, PLASTIC WHT $4-6
☐ ☐ USA DU8226 **FLOOR DISPLAY/BOSS HOGG,** 1982, $------
☐ ☐ USA DU8241 **CEILING DANGLER/CARS,** 1982, $------
☐ ☐ USA DU8265 **TRANSLITE/CARS/LG,** 1982 50-75
☐ ☐ USA DU8266 **TRANSLITE/CUPS/LG,** 1982 20-35

COMMENTS: LIMITED REGIONAL DISTRIBUTION: USA MAY 21-JULY 4, 1982 IN ST. LOUIS, MISSOURI. THE 16 OZ PLASTIC CUPS WERE USED AS AN ADDITIONAL PREMIUM OR FREE WITH THE PURCHASE OF A LARGE DRINK. PREMIUM WERE THE HM CONTAINERS.

USA DU8205

USA DU8211 USA DU8210
USA DU8214 USA DU8213 USA DU8212 USA DU8215

USA DU8226

USA DU8265

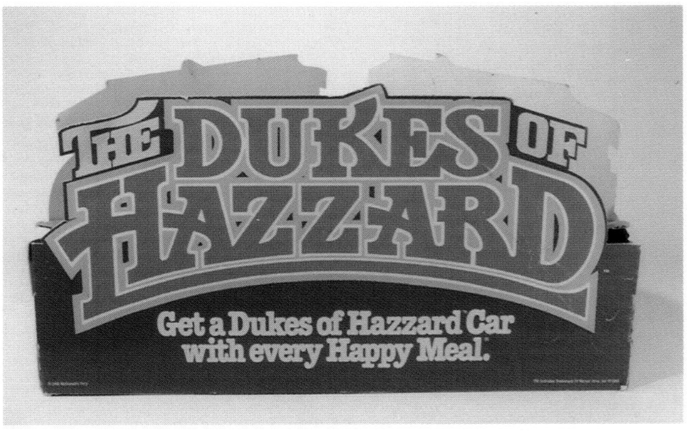

USA DU8241

GIGGLES AND GAMES HAPPY MEAL, 1982

- ❑ ❑ USA GI8200 **HM BOX,** 1982, **BUMPER CAR TAG** $25-40
- ❑ ❑ USA GI8201 **HM BOX,** 1982, **MAKE A FACE CHASE** $25-40
- ❑ ❑ USA GI8202 **HM BOX,** 1982, **MONSTER MARATHON** $25-40
- ❑ ❑ USA GI8203 **HM BOX,** 1982, **OUTER SPACE BATTLE** $25-40
- ❑ ❑ USA GI8204 **HM BOX,** 1982, **ROAD RALLY** $25-40
- ❑ ❑ USA GI8205 **HM BOX,** 1982, **SUNKEN TREASURE** $25-40
- ❑ ❑ USA GI8220 **SPONGE,** 1982, **TICKLE FEATHER/ORG** $12-15
- ❑ ❑ USA GI8221 **SLATE,** 1982, **TIC-TAC-TEETH** $2.50-4
- ❑ ❑ USA GI8222 **GOBLIN CALLER,** 1982, BLUE or RED $4-6
- ❑ ❑ USA GI8223 **GOBLIN GROOMER/COMB,** 1982, ORG or GRN $3-4
- ❑ ❑ USA GI8224 **FLYING WHEEL/FLINGER,** 1981, FRISBEE/ RONALD/YEL W RED $3-5
- ❑ ❑ USA GI8261 **M C INSERT/CARDBOARD,** 1982 $45-60
- ❑ ❑ USA GI8262 **HEADER CARD,** 1982 $25-40
- ❑ ❑ USA GI8265 **TRANSLITE/LG,** 1982 $50-65

COMMENTS: NATIONAL OPTIONAL HAPPY MEAL: USA - JUNE 28-AUGUST 29, 1982. GENERIC PREMIUMS COULD HAVE BEEN GIVEN WITH THE HAPPY MEAL. NO UNDER 3 (U-3) PREMIUMS WERE FURNISHED.

USA GI8204

USA GI8220

USA GI8200

USA GI8221

USA GI8222

USA GI8202

USA GI8223

USA GI8265

GOING PLACES HAPPY MEAL, 1982

❑ ❑ USA GO8201 **HM BOX,** 1981, **BIPLANE/RONALD** $12-15
❑ ❑ USA GO8202 **HM BOX,** 1981, **DUNE BUGGY/RONALD** $12-15
❑ ❑ USA GO8203 **HM BOX,** 1981, **ELEPHANT** $12-15
❑ ❑ USA GO8204 **HM BOX,** 1981, **FIRE ENGINE** $12-15
❑ ❑ USA GO8205 **HM BOX,** 1981, **PADDLE WHEELER** $12-15

USA GO8201

USA GO8202

USA GO8203

USA GO8204

USA GO8205

❑ ❑ USA GO8206 **HM BOX,** 1981, **STEAM ENGINE** $12-15
❑ ❑ USA GO8220 **SPONGE,** 1981, JOLLY JET $4-6
❑ ❑ USA GO8222 **MCDONALDLAND HOCKEY,** 1982, RED or BLU or YEL $4-6
❑ ❑ USA GO8223 **GOBLINS HORSESHOES,** 1982 $4-6
❑ ❑ USA GO8224 **GOBLINS BOWLING,** 1981 $4-6
❑ ❑ USA GO8225 **SCISSORS-RONALD,** 1981, YELLOW $2.50-4
❑ ❑ USA GO8261 **M C INSERT CARDBOARD,** 1981 $25-40
❑ ❑ USA GO8265 **TRANSLITE/LG,** 1981 $40-50

COMMENTS: REGIONAL DISTRIBUTION: USA - FEBRUARY 21-APRIL 28, 1982. REGIONS DEVELOPED THEIR OWN PROMOTIONS/PREMIUMS. GENERIC AND/OR REGIONAL PREMIUMS COULD HAVE BEEN GIVEN WITH THIS HAPPY MEAL. THESE HM BOXES WERE REGIONALLY DISTRIBUTED AGAIN WITH GOING PLACES/HOT WHEELS PROMOTION, 1983 ALONG WITH HOT WHEELS CARS. A GOING PLACES PLASTIC CUP WAS DISTRIBUTED IN 1983. RED/BLUE SCISSORS WERE PROTOTYPE AND NOT NATIONALLY/REGIONALLY DISTRIBUTED.

LITTLE GOLDEN BOOK HAPPY MEAL, 1982

❑ ❑ USA LI8258 **HM BOX,** 1982, **RONALD AND FRIENDS** $10-15

USA GO8223

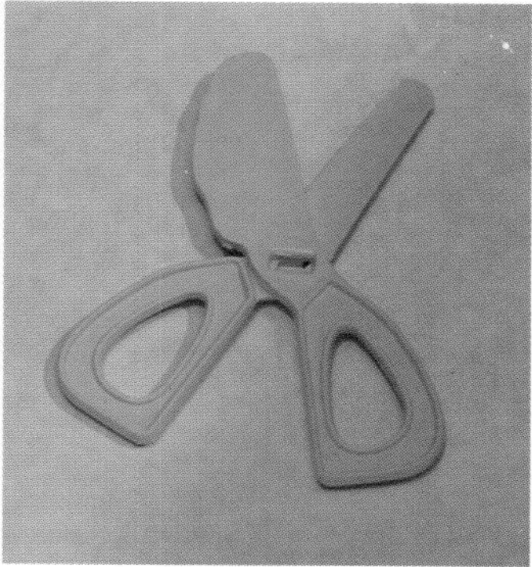

USA GO8225

USA GO8206

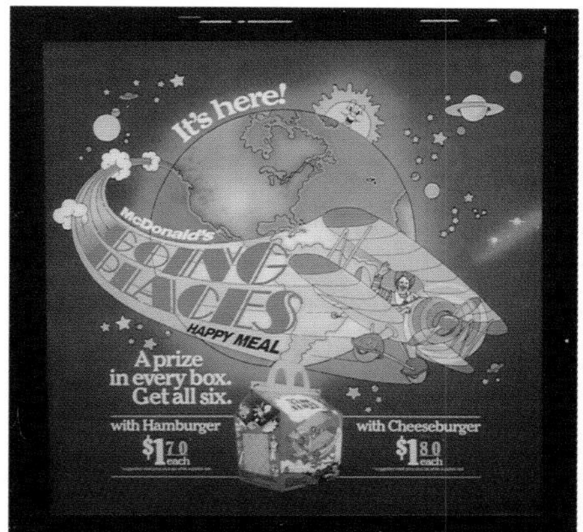

USA GO8265

USA GO8222

USA LI8258

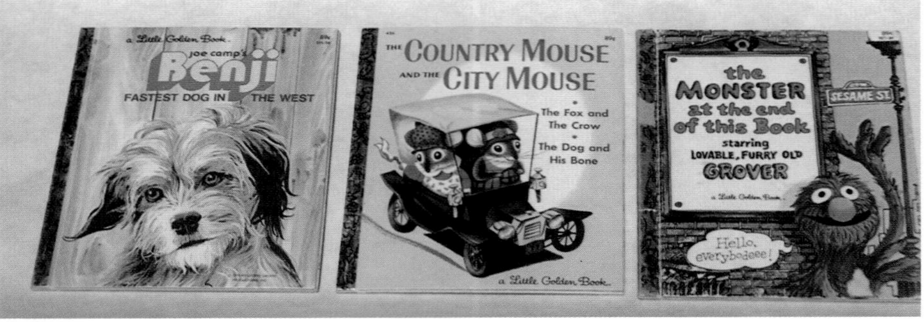

USA LI8250 USA LI8251 USA LI8252

USA LI8253 USA LI8254

- ❑ ❑ USA LI8250 **BOOK-BENJI FASTEST DOG IN THE WEST,** 1982 $4-6
- ❑ ❑ USA LI8251 **BOOK-THE COUNTRY MOUSE AND THE CITY MOUSE,** 1982 $4-6
- ❑ ❑ USA LI8252 **BOOK-THE MONSTER AT THE END OF THIS BOOK,** 1982 $4-6
- ❑ ❑ USA LI8253 **BOOK-THE POKY LITTLE PUPPY,** 1982 $4-6
- ❑ ❑ USA LI8254 **BOOK-TOM AND JERRY'S PARTY,** 1982 $4-6
- ❑ ❑ USA LI8265 **TRANSLITE/FATHER W 2 GIRLS,** 1982 $45-60
- ❑ ❑ USA LI8271 **MESSAGE CENTER/CARDBOARD,** 1982 $40-50
- ❑ ❑ USA LI8272 **COUNTER CARD/GIRL W 5 BOOKS,** 1982 $25-40
- ❑ ❑ USA LI8273 **CREW BADGE-BENJI,** 1982, PAPER/STICK ON $5-8
- ❑ ❑ USA LI8274 **CREW BADGE-COUNTRY MOUSE,** 1982, PAPER/STICK ON $5-8
- ❑ ❑ USA LI8275 **CREW BADGE-MONSTER AT THE END,** 1982, PAPER/STICK ON $5-8
- ❑ ❑ USA LI8276 **CREW BADGE-POKY LITTLE PUPPY,** 1982, PAPER/STICK ON $5-8
- ❑ ❑ USA LI8277 **CREW BADGE-TOM AND JERRY,** 1982, PAPER/STICK ON $5-8

COMMENTS: NATIONAL DISTRIBUTION: USA - JULY 16-AUGUST 23, 1982.

USA LI8265

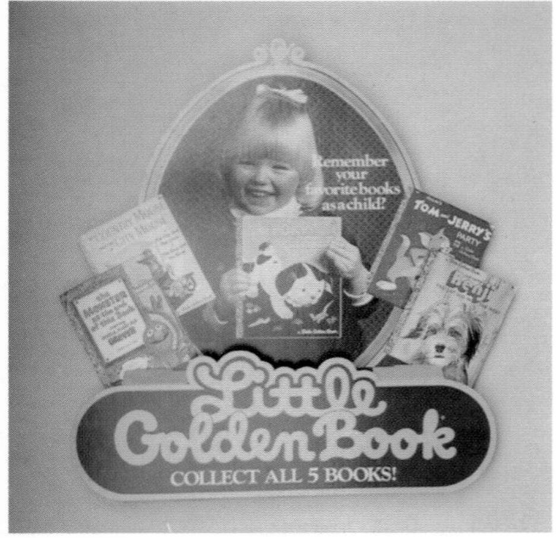

USA LI8272

USA LI8273 USA LI8271

USA LI8275 USA LI8277

MCDONALDLAND EXPRESS HAPPY MEAL, 1982

	Item	Price
❑ ❑	USA EX8200 **ENGINE,** 1982, VACUFORMED/RED or BLU	$15-20
❑ ❑	USA EX8201 **COACH,** 1982, VACUFORMED/BLU or ORG	$15-20
❑ ❑	USA EX8202 **FREIGHT CAR,** 1982, VACUFORMED/GRN or ORG	$15-20
❑ ❑	USA EX8203 **CABOOSE,** 1982, VACUFORMED/RED or GRN	$15-20
❑ ❑	USA EX8206 **STICKER SHEET-ENGINE,** 1982	$6-10
❑ ❑	USA EX8207 **STICKER SHEET-COACH,** 1982	$6-10
❑ ❑	USA EX8208 **STICKER SHEET-FREIGHT,** 1982	$6-10
❑ ❑	USA EX8209 **STICKER SHEET-CABOOSE,** 1982	$6-10
❑ ❑	USA EX8226 **DISPLAY/PREMIUMS,** 1982	$200-250
❑ ❑	USA EX8241 **CEILING DANGLER,** 1982	$75-100
❑ ❑	USA EX8250 **BUTTON,** 1982, ENGINE	$10-15
❑ ❑	USA EX8261 **M C INSERT/CARDBOARD,** 1982	$40-50
❑ ❑	USA EX8262 **HEADER CARD,** 1982	40-50
❑ ❑	USA EX8265 **TRANSLITE/LG,** 1982	$45-60

COMMENTS: NATIONAL DISTRIBUTION: USA - JUNE 11-JULY 15, 1982. VACUFORM TRAIN CARS SERVED AS THE FOOD CONTAINER AND PREMIUM.

PLAYMOBIL II HAPPY MEAL, 1982

	Item	Price
❑ ❑	USA PL8260 **HM BOX,** 1982, **BARN**	$20-25
❑ ❑	USA PL8261 **HM BOX,** 1982, **LOG CABIN**	$20-25
❑ ❑	USA PL8262 **HM BOX,** 1982, **SCHOOL HOUSE**	$20-25
❑ ❑	USA PL8263 **HM BOX,** 1982, **TRADING POST**	$20-25

USA EX8209 USA EX8208 USA EX8207 USA EX8206
USA EX8203 USA EX8202 USA EX8201 USA EX8200

USA EX8226

USA EX8250

USA EX8265

USA PL8260 USA PL8261

USA PL8262 USA PL8263

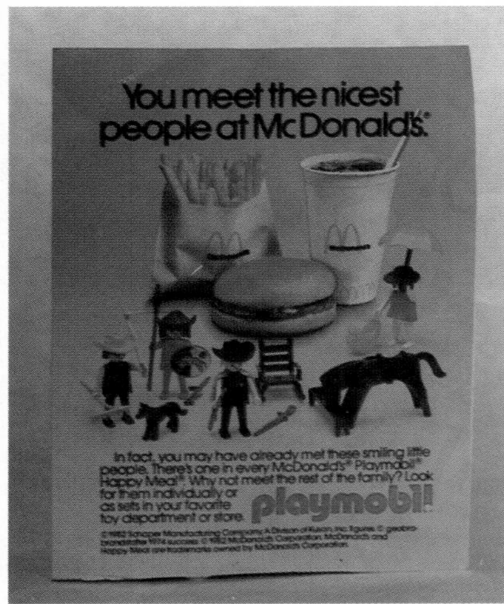

USA PL8272

❏ ❏ USA PL8250 **SET 1 SHERIFF,** 1982, W CHAIR/RIFLE/HAT/CAPE $7-10
❏ ❏ USA PL8251 **SET 2 INDIAN,** 1982, W SHIELD/STICKER/GUN/SPEAR/PEACE PIPE/HEADDRESS $7-10
❏ ❏ USA PL8252 **SET 3 HORSE,** 1982, BRN W ATTACHED SADDLE W RECT TROUGH $12-15
❏ ❏ USA PL8253 **SET 4 UMBRELLA GIRL,** 1982, W 2P UMBRELLA/YEL SUITCASE/RED DRESS/BLK HAIR $12-15
❏ ❏ USA PL8254 **SET 5 FARMER,** 1982, W GRN SHIRT/PANTS/GREY SICKLE/RAKE/YEL HAT/DOG $12-15
❏ ❏ USA PL8226 **DISPLAY/PREMIUMS,** 1982 $150-200
❏ ❏ USA PL8265 **TRANSLITE/LG,** 1982 $60-75
❏ ❏ USA PL8266 **TRANSLITE/CARDBOARD/LG,** 1982 $60-75
❏ ❏ USA PL8271 **COUNTER CARD/RECALLED NOTICE,** 1982 $20-25
❏ ❏ USA PL8272 **BUTTON,** 1982, STAR W PLAYMOBIL MEAL DEAL $10-15

COMMENTS: NATIONAL DISTRIBUTION: USA - OCTOBER 2-NOVEMBER 28, 1982. SET 1 AND 2 PREMIUMS WERE DISTRIBUTED. ALL SETS WERE RECALLED AS A RESULT OF A PRODUCT SAFETY CONCERN (SMALL PARTS). AFTER THE RECALL, MCDONALD'S BEGAN THE UNDER 3 (U-3) PREMIUM OFFERINGS. A $1.98 ACCESSORY KIT WAS OFFERED BY COUPON OFFERING IN THE PACKAGES. PLAYMOBIL PEOPLE WERE MARKED - "1974 GEOBRA". THE DOG IN USA PL8254/SET 5 CAME IN TWO VERSIONS - WITH AND WITHOUT MOUTH OPEN.

USA PL8250 USA PL8252 USA PL8253 USA PL8254
USA PL8251

SKY-BUSTERS HAPPY MEAL, 1982

❏ ❏ USA SK8201 **MIG-21,** YEL or BLU or BRN or PNK or GRN or ORG MATCHBOX (LESNEY) $1-2
❏ ❏ USA SK8202 **MIRAGE F1,** YEL or BLU or BRN or PNK or GRN or ORG MATCHBOX (LESNEY) $1-2
❏ ❏ USA SK8203 **PHANTOM F4E,** YEL or BLU or BRN or PNK or GRN or ORG MATCHBOX (LESNEY) $1-2
❏ ❏ USA SK8204 **SKY HAWK A4F,** YEL or BLU or BRN or PNK or GRN or ORG MATCHBOX (LESNEY) $1-2
❏ ❏ USA SK8205 **TORNADO,** YEL or BLU or BRN or PNK or GRN or ORG MATCHBOX (LESNEY) $1-2
❏ ❏ USA SK8206 **UNITED DC-10,** YEL or BLU or BRN or PNK or GRN or ORG MATCHBOX (LESNEY) $1-2
❏ ❏ USA SK8264 **TRANSLITE/SM,** 1982 $45-60

COMMENTS: REGIONAL DISTRIBUTION: USA - 1982. INITIALLY, HARD RUBBER PREMIUMS WERE DISTRIBUTED. LATER, SOME REGIONS MAY HAVE DISTRIBUTED SOFT RUBBER AIRPLANES. AIRPLANES ARE MARKED, "LESNEY".

USA PL8265

Dear Customer,

We have voluntarily stopped the distribution of the Playmobil toys because the Playmobil manufacturer failed to meet McDonald's specifications and governmental standards for children under the age of three.

The Playmobil toys contain pieces which, if broken, could be swallowed.

We recommend that the use of these Playmobil toys by children under the age of three be discontinued, and that these toys be returned to any McDonald's for a box of McDonald's cookies, a cone or a refund.

Thank you.

USA PL8271

USA SK8206

USA SK8205

USA SK8204

USA SK8203

USA SK8202

USA SK8201

SPACESHIP HAPPY MEAL, 1982

❑ ❑ USA SP8230 **SPACESHIP #1 - 8 WINDOWS,** 1981, BLU or GRN or RED or YEL W CIRCLE M W DECALS $15-20
❑ ❑ USA SP8231 **SPACESHIP #2 - ROUND/CIRCULAR W REAR ENGINE,** 1981, BLU or GRN or RED or YEL W DECALS $15-20
❑ ❑ USA SP8232 **SPACESHIP #3 - POINTED FRONT,** 1981, BLU or GRN or RED or YEL W DECALS $15-20
❑ ❑ USA SP8233 **SPACESHIP #4 - 4 KNOBS,** 1981, BLU or GRN or RED or YEL W DECALS $15-20
❑ ❑ USA SP8204 **STICKER SHEET #1 - 8 WINDOWS** $10-15
❑ ❑ USA SP8205 **STICKER SHEET #2 - ROUND FRONT** $10-15
❑ ❑ USA SP8206 **STICKER SHEET #3 - POINTED FRONT** $10-15
❑ ❑ USA SP8207 **STICKER SHEET #4 - FOUR KNOBS** $10-15
❑ ❑ USA SP8241 **CEILING DANGLER,** 1982 $45-60
❑ ❑ USA SP8242 **COUNTER CARD W DIFFERENT SHIPS FEATURED,** 1982 $45-60
❑ ❑ USA SP8243 **MANAGER'S GUIDE,** 1981, SHAPED LIKE SPACESHIP/RED/PAPER $20-25
❑ ❑ USA SP8244 **CREW POSTER,** 1982 $15-25
❑ ❑ USA SP8265 **TRANSLITE/LG,** 1982 $50-65

COMMENTS: NATIONAL DISTRIBUTION: USA - JANUARY 22-FEBRUARY 28, 1982. SPACESHIP HAPPY MEAL IS SOMETIMES MISTAKENLY REFERRED TO AS THE "UNIDENTIFIED" HAPPY MEAL TEST MARKETED IN THE KANSAS CITY MO. ST. LOUIS AREA IN 1981. THIS 1982 HM SET OF CONTAINERS HAD A SHINY FINISH; WITH A MOLDED "M" ON TOP OR A MOLDED "M" WITHIN A MOLDED CIRCLE. THE TOP AND BOTTOM WAS HELD TOGETHER BY 8 LUGS. THE 1981 UNIDENTIFIED SET HAD ONLY 4 LUGS. THE TWO PIECE SPACESHIP CONTAINER HELD FOOD AND SERVED AS THE PREMIUM. COLOR VARIATIONS OF THE SPACESHIPS EXIST.

USA SP8232

USA SP8204

USA SP8205

USA SP8206

USA SP8207

USA SP8230

USA SP8233

USA SP8231

USA SP8244

USA SP8265

USA SP8243

USA WA8204

WACKY HAPPY MEAL, 1982

❑ ❑ USA WA8201 **HM BOX,** 1981, **FARM** $20-25
❑ ❑ USA WA8202 **HM BOX,** 1981, **FOREST** $20-25
❑ ❑ USA WA8203 **HM BOX,** 1981, **PARTY** $20-25
❑ ❑ USA WA8204 **HM BOX,** 1981, **PARADE** $20-25
❑ ❑ USA WA8205 **HM BOX,** 1981, **PICNIC** $20-25
❑ ❑ USA WA8206 **HM BOX,** 1981, **ZOO** $20-25
❑ ❑ USA WA8210 **CUP-AIRPLANE HANGER,** ND, 8 OZ PLASTIC CUP $12-15
❑ ❑ USA WA8211 **CUP-COUNTRY CLUB,** ND, 8 OZ PLASTIC CUP $12-15
❑ ❑ USA WA8212 **CUP-FIGURE SKATING,** ND, 8 OZ PLASTIC CUP $12-15
❑ ❑ USA WA8213 **CUP-JUNGLE GYM,** ND, 8 OZ PLASTIC CUP $12-15
❑ ❑ USA WA8214 **CUP-MONKEY BUSINESS,** ND, 8 OZ PLASTIC CUP $12-15
❑ ❑ USA WA8215 **CUP-TRAFFIC JAM,** ND, 8 OZ PLASTIC CUP $12-15
❑ ❑ USA WA8262 **HEADER CARD,** 1982 $25-40
❑ ❑ USA WA8265 **TRANSLITE/LG,** 1982 $50-65

COMMENTS: LIMITED REGIONAL DISTRIBUTION: USA MARCH 1-MAY 23, 1982. BOXES WITH CUT-OUTS WERE THE PREMIUMS. THE CUPS MAY HAVE BEEN GIVEN AS AN ADDITIONAL PREMIUM IN ST. LOUIS, MISSOURI.

USA WA8206

USA/GENERIC PROMOTION, 1982

❑ ❑ USA GE8201 **BASKETBALL HOOP/SHOOTER-GRIM,** 1982, WHT HOOP/SHOOTER/BALL/6P $10-12
❑ ❑ USA GE8202 **FALLER/ZIG ZAG-BIRDIE/GRIM,** 1982, PURP/ 3P $10-12
❑ ❑ USA GE8203 **FRENCH FRY GRABBER-CAPTAIN,** 1982, BLU or ORG or PNK or RED/9P $10-12
❑ ❑ USA GE8204 **FRENCH FRY GRABBER-FRY KID,** 1982, BLU or ORG or PNK or RED/9P $10-12
❑ ❑ USA GE8205 **FRENCH FRY GRABBER-HAMBURG,** 1982, BLU or ORG or PNK or RED/9P $10-12
❑ ❑ USA GE8206 **FRENCH FRY GRABBER-RONALD,** 1982, BLU or ORG or PNK or RED/9P $10-12
❑ ❑ USA GE8207 **GYMNASTIC-RONALD,** 1982, GRN or ORG/ PARALLEL BARS/5P $7-10

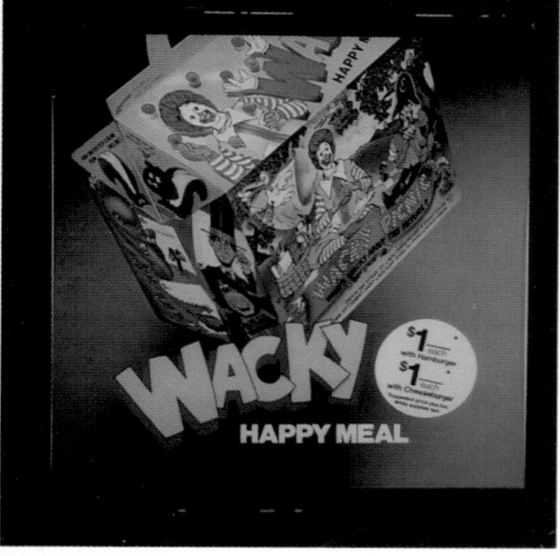

USA WA8265

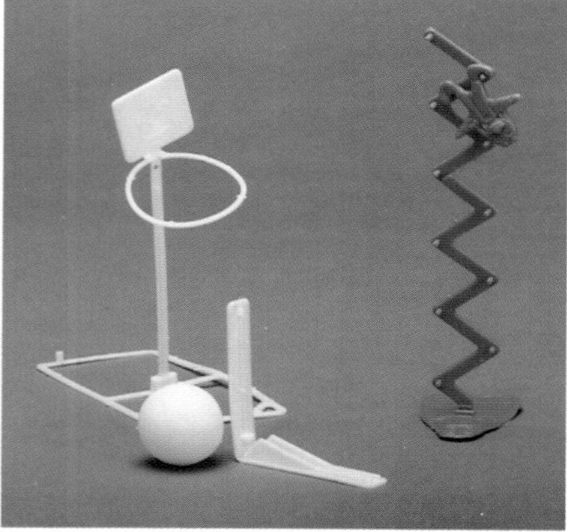

USA GE8201

USA GE8202

USA GE8205

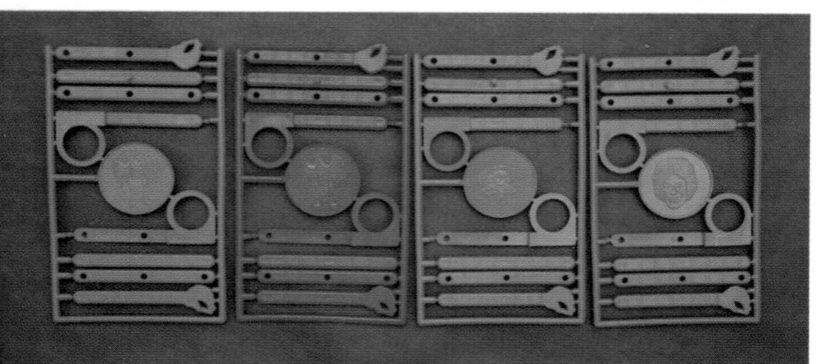

USA GE8204

USA GE8206

USA GE8207

❑ ❑ USA GE8208 **GYRO-BIRDIE,** 1982, TURQ GYRO/4P $10-12
❑ ❑ USA GE8209 **GYRO-RONALD,** 1982, TURQ GYRO/4P $10-12
❑ ❑ USA GE8210 **HANG GLIDER-HAMBURGLAR,** 1982, YEL CHAR W PNK/WHT STYRO WINGS $8-10
❑ ❑ USA GE8211 **HANG GLIDER-PROFESSOR,** 1982, YEL CHAR W PNK/WHT STYRO WINGS $8-10
❑ ❑ USA GE8212 **HANG GLIDER-RONALD,** 1982, YEL CHAR W PNK/WHT STYRO WINGS $8-10
❑ ❑ USA GE8213 **HARDWORKING BURGER BULLDOZER,** 1982, GRN or ORG $4-6
❑ ❑ USA GE8214 **HARDWORKING BURGER DUMP TRUCK,** 1982, GRN or ORG $4-6
❑ ❑ USA GE8215 **LAUNCHER-BIRDIE,** 1982, WHT/3P $5-7
❑ ❑ USA GE8216 **PEN-MAYOR,** 1982, PNK PEN/PURP CORD $8-12
❑ ❑ USA GE8217 **POP CAR-HAMB,** 1982, BLU or GRN or ORG/6P $8-12
❑ ❑ USA GE8218 **POP CAR-RON,** 1982, BLU or GRN or ORG/6P $8-12

USA GE8214 USA GE8213

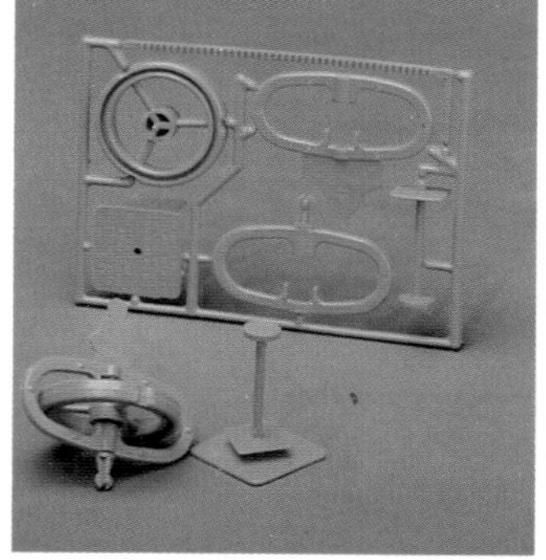
USA GE8208

USA GE8209

USA GE8215

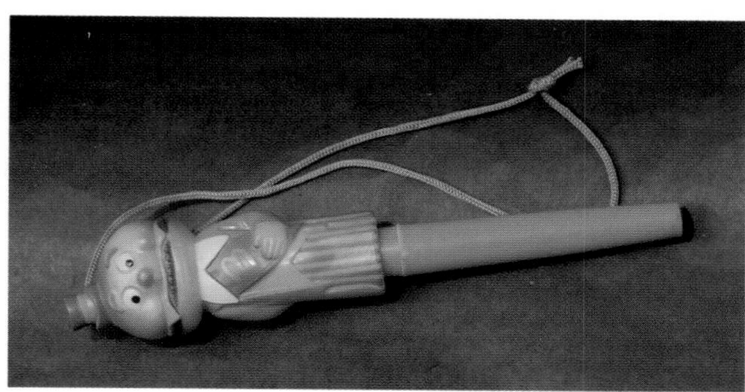
USA GE8216

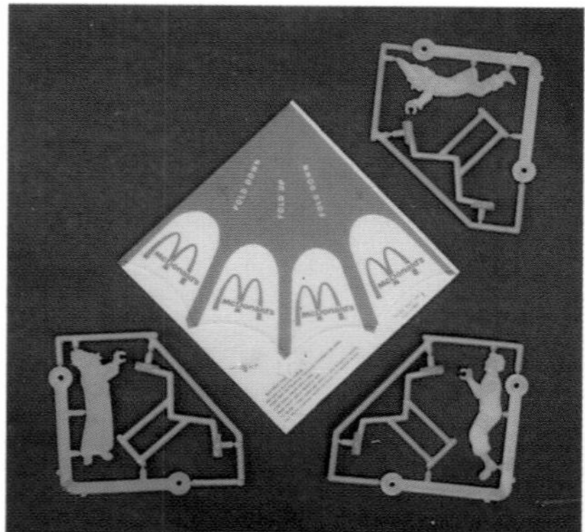
USA GE8210 USA GE8211 USA GE8212

USA GE8217

USA GE8218

USA GE8219

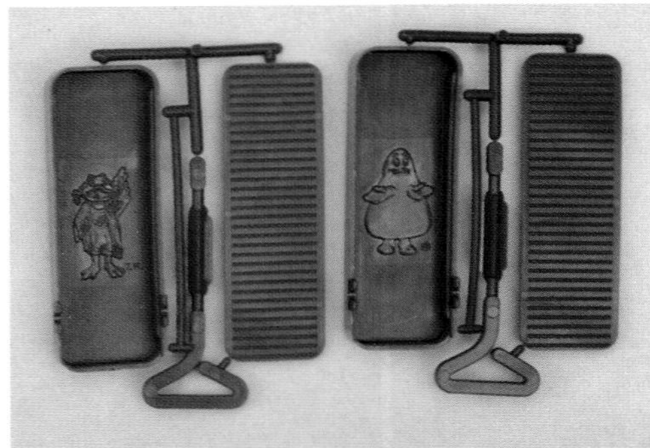

USA GE8220 USA GE8221

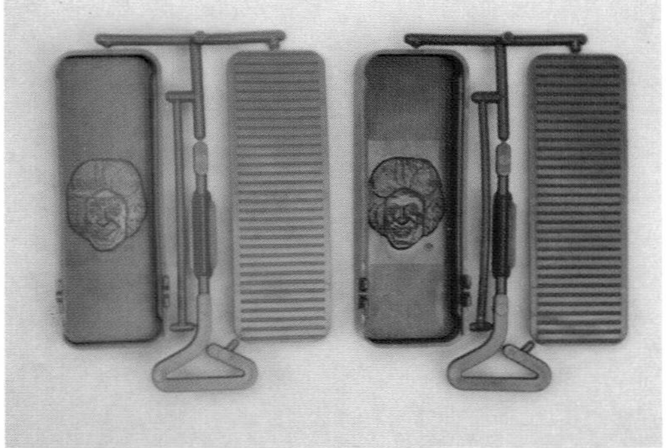

USA GE8222

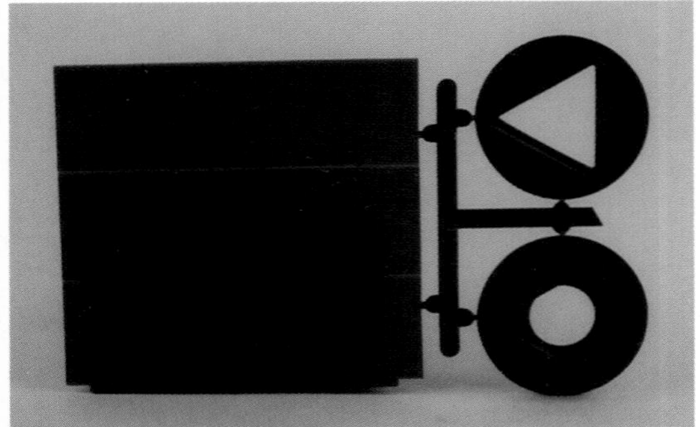

USA GE8223

☐ ☐ USA GE8219 **PUZZLE/GUESS N' GLOW,** 1982, RONALD W GHOST $4-6

☐ ☐ USA GE8220 **SARDINE CAN-BIRDIE,** 1982, BLU or YEL or PUR/3P $8-10

☐ ☐ USA GE8221 **SARDINE CAN-GRIMACE,** 1982, BLU or YEL or PUR/3P $8-10

☐ ☐ USA GE8222 **SARDINE CAN-RONALD,** 1982, BLU or YEL or PUR/3P $8-10

☐ ☐ USA GE8223 **MYSTICAL SCRAMBLER,** 1982, BLU/3P $10-15

COMMENTS: REGIONAL DISTRIBUTION: USA - 1982 DURING CLEAN-UP WEEKS. THIS IS A SAMPLING OF GENERIC PREMIUMS GIVEN AWAY DURING 1982.

1983

ASTROSNIKS I HAPPY MEAL, 1983
CIRCUS HAPPY MEAL, 1983
GOING PLACES/HOT WHEELS PROMOTION, 1983
HAPPY PAIL I HAPPY MEAL, 1983
LEGO BUILDING SETS I TEST MARKET HAPPY MEAL, 1983
MCDONALDLAND JUNCTION HAPPY MEAL, 1983
MYSTERY HAPPY MEAL, 1983
PLAY-DOH I HAPPY MEAL, 1983
SHIP SHAPE I HAPPY MEAL, 1983
WINTER WORLDS HAPPY MEAL, 1983
USA/GENERIC PROMOTION, 1983

ASTROSNIKS I HAPPY MEAL, 1983

☐ ☐ USA AS8315 **HM BOX,** 1983, **ASTROSNIK ROVER/ONE WHEEL** $50-75

USA AS8315

❑ ❑ USA AS8316 **HM BOX,** 1983, **ROUND SPACE SHIP/VOLCANO** $50-75

❑ ❑ USA AS8317 **HM BOX,** 1983, **SPACESHIP/DINOSAUR/ASTRALIA** $50-75

❑ ❑ USA AS8318 **HM BOX,** 1983, **SPACESHIP/MOON GOLF COURSE** $50-75

❑ ❑ USA AS8301 **ASTRALIA,** 1983, GIRL HOLDING CONE/W STICKER $10-15

❑ ❑ USA AS8302 **LASER,** 1983, W GUN/W STICKER $7-10

❑ ❑ USA AS8303 **ROBO-ROBOT,** 1983, GOLD/W STICKER $7-10

❑ ❑ USA AS8304 **SCOUT,** 1983, HOLDING FLAG/W STICKER $7-10

❑ ❑ USA AS8305 **SKATER,** 1983, ON ICE SKATES/W STICKER $7-10

❑ ❑ USA AS8306 **SNIKAPOTAMUS,** 1983, DINOSAUR/W STICKER $7-10

❑ ❑ USA AS8307 **SPORT,** 1983, HOLDING FOOTBALL/W STICKER $7-10

❑ ❑ USA AS8308 **THIRSTY,** 1983, HOLDING DRINK/W STICKER $7-10

❑ ❑ USA AS8355 **TRAY LINER,** 1983 $12-20

❑ ❑ USA AS8356 **TABLE TENT,** 1983 $15-25

❑ ❑ USA AS8365 **TRANSLITE/LG,** 1983 $65-90

COMMENTS: LIMITED REGIONAL DISTRIBUTION: USA - 1983. EACH FIGURE HAS A MOLDED YELLOW M; "MCDONALD'S, HONG KONG, '83 BULLY-FIGUREN" MOLDED INTO THE BOTTOM OF THE FEET. THE FIGURES CAME LOOSE; DID NOT COME WRAPPED -- "NO MINT IN PACKAGE." EACH CAME WITH A "SAFETY TESTED" STICKER ATTACHED TO THE BACK OR SIDE OF FIGURINES. STICKERS WERE EASILY REMOVED WITH HANDLING.

USA AS8305 USA AS8306 USA AS8307 USA AS8308

USA AS8355

USA AS8317

USA AS8356

USA AS8301 USA AS8302 USA AS8303 USA AS8304

CIRCUS HAPPY MEAL, 1983

❑ ❑ USA CI8315 **HM BOX,** 1983, **AMAZING ANIMAL ACTS** $25-40
❑ ❑ USA CI8316 **HM BOX,** 1983, **CIRCUS BAND** $25-40
❑ ❑ USA CI8317 **HM BOX,** 1983, **CLOWN CAR** $25-40
❑ ❑ USA CI8318 **HM BOX,** 1983, **HIGH WIRE SHOW** $25-40
❑ ❑ USA CI8319 **HM BOX,** 1983, **MONKEY CAGE** $25-40

USA CI8315

USA CI8316

USA CI8317

USA CI8318

USA CI8319

- ❑ ❑ USA CI8320 **HM BOX,** 1983, **TUMBLERS & JUGGLERS** $25-40
- ❑ ❑ USA CI8301 **FRENCH FRY FALLER,** 1982, DISK ROLLS THRU LADDER/BLU or RED or YEL $20-25
- ❑ ❑ USA CI8302 **FUN HOUSE MIRROR/RON,** 1983, W 3 VISUAL EFFECTS/BLU or RED or YEL $15-20
- ❑ ❑ USA CI8303 **FUN HOUSE MIRROR/HAMB,** 1983, W 3 VISUAL EFFECTS/BLU or RED or YEL $15-20
- ❑ ❑ USA CI8304 **GRIMACE STRONG GONG,** 1982, MALLET KNOCKS GRIMACE OFF/BLU or YEL or PURP or GRN $20-25
- ❑ ❑ USA CI8305 **RONALD ACROBAT,** 1980, RONALD HANGS FROM BAR/YEL or BLU or RED or ORG $20-25
- ❑ ❑ USA CI8306 **PUNCH OUTS MIDWAY 1,** 1983, PUPPET SHOW/ARCADE/PROF IN CAR $30-45
- ❑ ❑ USA CI8307 **PUNCH OUTS MIDWAY 2,** 1983, FUN HOUSE/ HOW STRONG/ELEPHANT/RON $30-45

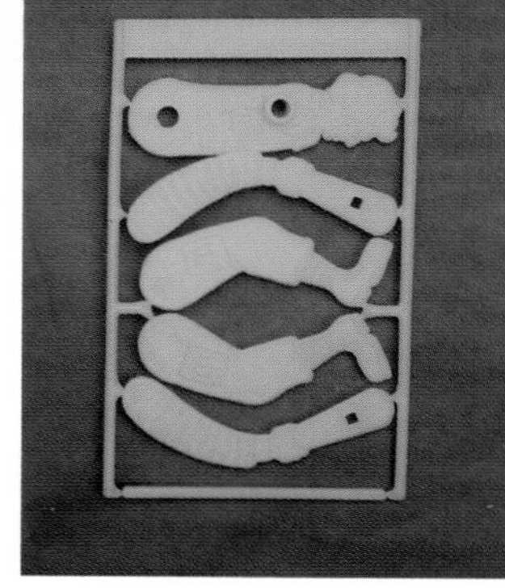

USA CI8320

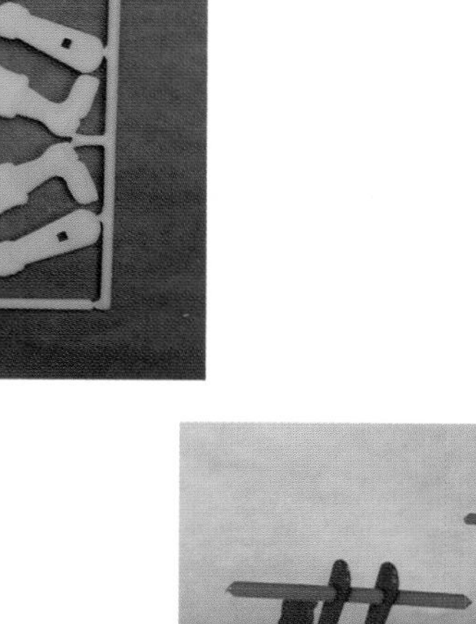

USA CI8305

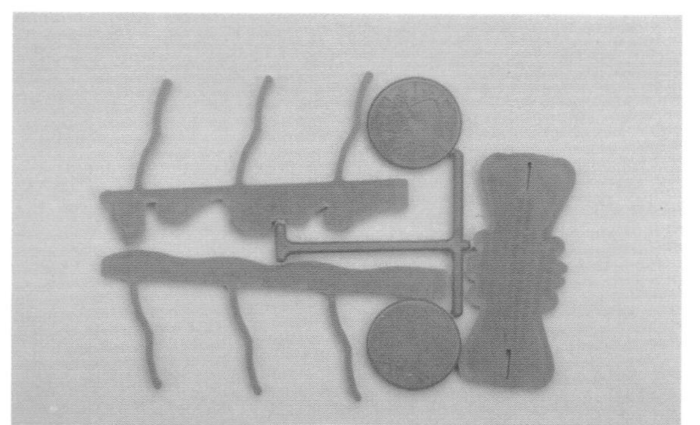

USA CI8301

USA CI8306

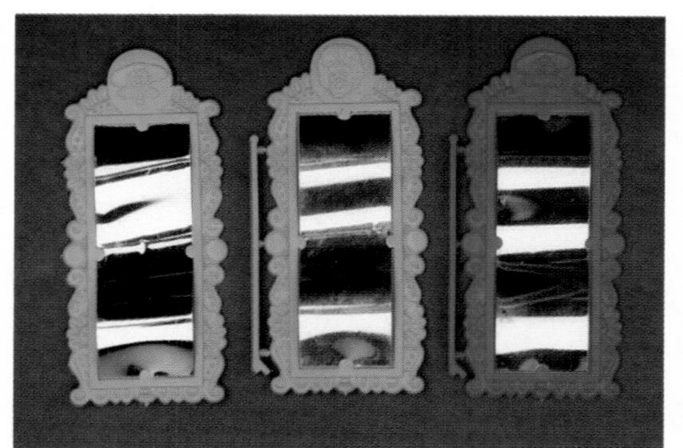

USA CI8303

USA CI8302

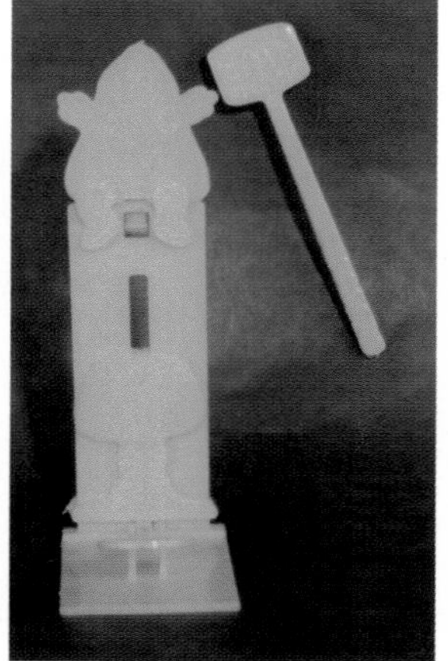

USA CI8304

USA CI8307

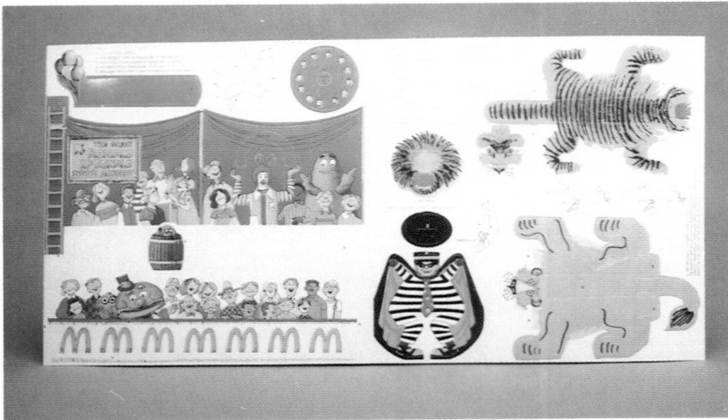

USA CI8308

USA CI8309

❑ ❑ USA CI8308 **PUNCH OUTS TENT/LEFT,** 1983, LION/TIGER/ HAMBURGLAR $30-45
❑ ❑ USA CI8309 **PUNCH OUTS TENT/RIGHT,** 1983, BIRDIE W HORSE/CIRCUS BANNER ON RIGHT $30-45
❑ ❑ USA CI8361 **M C CARDBOARD,** 1983 $40-50
❑ ❑ USA CI8362 **HEADER CARD,** 1983 $35-45
❑ ❑ USA CI8365 **TRANSLITE/LG,** 1983 $45-60

COMMENTS: NATIONAL DISTRIBUTION: USA - SEPTEMBER 30-NOVEMBER 23, 1983.

GOING PLACES/HOT WHEELS PROMOTION, 1983

❑ ❑ USA HW8330 **CORVETTE STINGRAY NO.9241** $7-10
❑ ❑ USA HW8331 **JEEP CJ-7 CAR NO.3259** $7-10
❑ ❑ USA HW8332 **3-WINDOW '34 NO.1132** $7-10
❑ ❑ USA HW8333 **56 HI-TAIL HAULER NO.9647** $7-10
❑ ❑ USA HW8334 **57 T-BIRD NO.2013** $7-10
❑ ❑ USA HW8335 **BAJA BREAKER NO.2022** $7-10
❑ ❑ USA HW8336 **CADILLAC SEVILLE NO.1698** $7-10
❑ ❑ USA HW8337 **CHEVY CITATION "X-11" NO.3362+** $7-10
❑ ❑ USA HW8338 **DATSUN 200 SX NO.3255** $7-10
❑ ❑ USA HW8339 **DIXIE CHALLENGER NO.3364** $7-10
❑ ❑ USA HW8340 **FIREBIRD FUNNY CAR NO.3250** $7-10
❑ ❑ USA HW8341 **FRONT RUNNING FAIRMONT NO.3257** $7-10
❑ ❑ USA HW8342 **LAND LORD NO.3260** $7-10
❑ ❑ USA HW8343 **MALIBU GRAND PRIX "GOODYEAR 9999" NO.9037+** $7-10
❑ ❑ USA HW8344 **MERCEDES 380/SILVER SEL NO. 3261+** $7-10
❑ ❑ USA HW8345 **MINITREK "GOOD TIME CAMPER"/WHITE NO.1697+** $7-10
❑ ❑ USA HW8346 **PORSCHE 928 NO. 5180+** $7-10
❑ ❑ USA HW8347 **RACE BAIT 308 NO.2021** $7-10
❑ ❑ USA HW8348 **SHERIFF PATROL/BLK/WHT NO.2019** $7-10
❑ ❑ USA HW8349 **SPLIT WINDOW '63 NO.1136+** $7-10
❑ ❑ USA HW8350 **TRICAR X8 NO.1130** $7-10
❑ ❑ USA HW8351 **TURISMO "10" NO.1694+** $7-10
❑ ❑ USA HW8352 **STUTZ BLACKHAWK NO.1126** $7-10
❑ ❑ USA HW8321 **CUP/GOING PLACES,** 1983, WHT PLASTIC $3-5
❑ ❑ USA HW8326 **DISPLAY/COLLECT ALL 14 CARS,** 1983 $------

USA CI8365

USA HW8326

USA HW8321

❑ ❑ USA HW8355 **TRAYLINER/COLLECT ALL 14,** 1983 $5-8
❑ ❑ USA HW8361 **HOT WHEELS HUB CAP BOX/ROUND,** 1983, GREY/HW LOGO $25-50
❑ ❑ USA HW8365 **TRANSLITE/LG,** 1983 $40-50

COMMENTS: NATIONAL OPTIONAL DISTRIBUTION: USA - 1983/89. HOT WHEELS WERE USED AS A SELF-LIQUIDATING PROMOTION WITH THE "GOING PLACES" BOXES. DIFFERENT CARS (MARKED BY +) WERE GIVEN OUT AND/OR SOLD IN DIFFERENT REGIONS. CARS COULD BE PURCHASED FOR $.59. "COLLECT ALL 14. A DIFFERENT CAR EVERY DAY". NO UNDER 3 (U-3) PREMIUMS WERE FURNISHED. THIS WAS A NATIONAL OPTION IN 1983. DATES STAMPED ON CARS DO NOT ALWAYS MATCH THE MIP PACKAGE DATE. USA GO8330-31 CARRY 1981 DATES, ALL OTHERS CARRY 1982 DATES. USA GO8352 STUTZ BLACK HAWK NO. 1126 COULD HAVE BEEN SUBSTITUTED FOR USA GO8333 HIGH TAIL HAULER NO. 9647 AND/OR USA GO8345 MINITREK GOOD TIME CAMPER NO. 1697. THIS PROMOTION WAS RUN REGIONALLY AS A SELF-LIQUIDATOR IN 1983 AND AGAIN IN 1988 AND IN TEXAS - JANUARY 27-FEBRUARY 23, 1989.

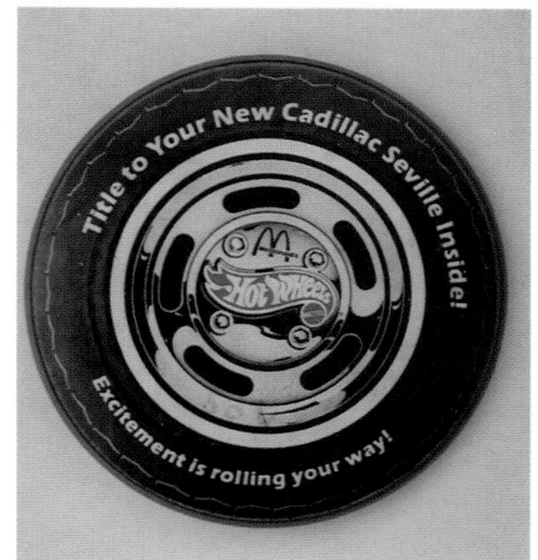

USA HW8361

USA HW8365

HAPPY PAIL I HAPPY MEAL, 1983

❑ ❑ USA HP8350 **RONALD/MAYOR UNDER UMBRELLA,** 1983, PNK PAIL/SHOVEL/LID $20-35
❑ ❑ USA HP8351 **RONALD IN AN INNER TUBE,** 1983, WHT PAIL/SHOVEL/LID $20-35
❑ ❑ USA HP8352 **AIRPLANE PULLING BANNER,** 1983, YEL PAIL/SHOVEL/LID $20-35
❑ ❑ USA HP8365 **TRANSLITE/LG,** 1983 $40-50

COMMENTS: REGIONAL DISTRIBUTION: USA - 1983 IN UPPER NEW YORK STATE AND PARTS OF NEW ENGLAND. LIDS HAD 4 HOLES IN EACH AND SHOVELS/LIDS/PAIL COLORS MATCHED.

USA HP8350 USA HP8351 USA HP8352

USA HP8365

HAPPY TEETH HAPPY MEAL, 1983

❑ ❑ USA HT8320 **TOOTHBRUSH,** 1983, REACH TOOTHBRUSH/NO LOGO $8-12
❑ ❑ USA HT8321 **TOOTHPASTE,** 1983, COLGATE/1.4 OZ/RED BOX W MCD LOGO $15-20
❑ ❑ USA HT8365 **TRANSLITE/LG,** 1983, GET A REACH YOUTH-SIZE TOOTHBRUSH W EVERY HM $------

COMMENTS: REGIONAL DISTRIBUTION: USA - 1983 IN NEW ENGLAND. HM PROMOTED INCONJUNCTION WITH DENTAL HEALTH MONTH. EXPIRATION DATE ON TOOTHPASTE - 05/84.

USA HW8355

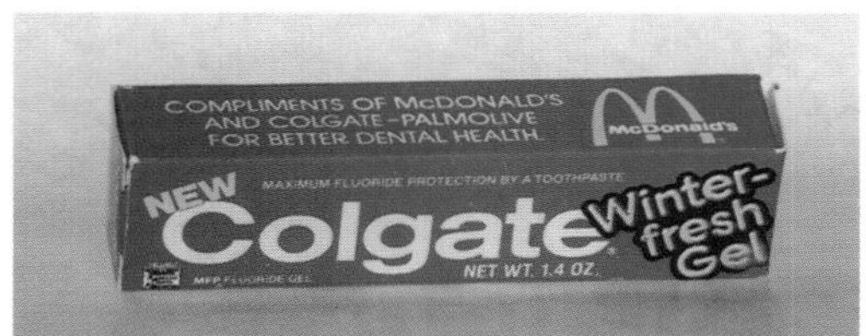

USA HT8321

USA LE8306

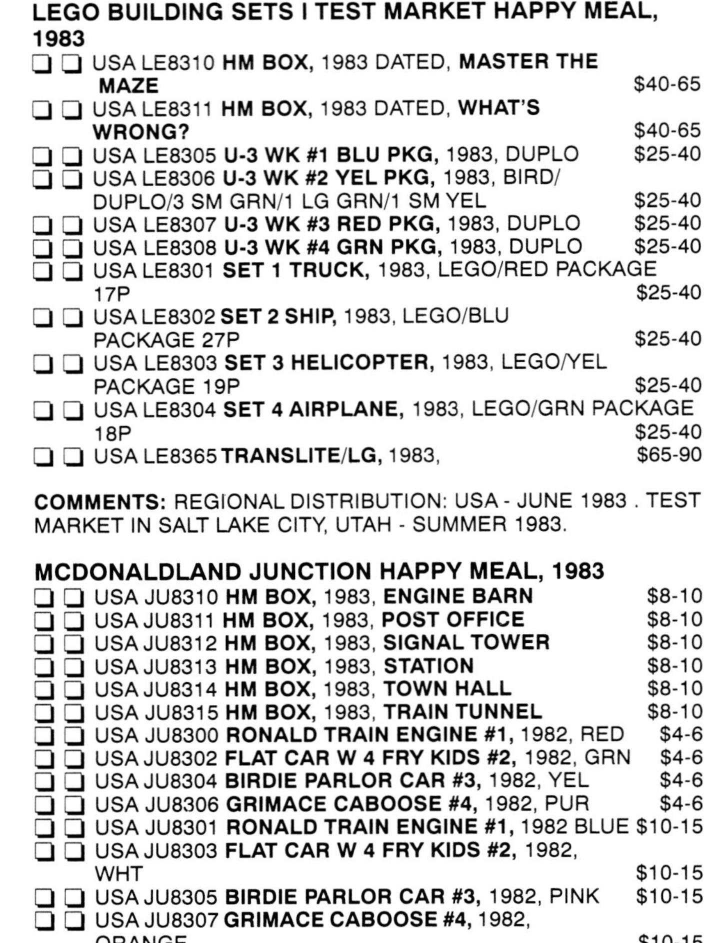

LEGO BUILDING SETS I TEST MARKET HAPPY MEAL, 1983

- ❑ ❑ USA LE8310 **HM BOX,** 1983 DATED, **MASTER THE MAZE** $40-65
- ❑ ❑ USA LE8311 **HM BOX,** 1983 DATED, **WHAT'S WRONG?** $40-65
- ❑ ❑ USA LE8305 **U-3 WK #1 BLU PKG,** 1983, DUPLO $25-40
- ❑ ❑ USA LE8306 **U-3 WK #2 YEL PKG,** 1983, BIRD/ DUPLO/3 SM GRN/1 LG GRN/1 SM YEL $25-40
- ❑ ❑ USA LE8307 **U-3 WK #3 RED PKG,** 1983, DUPLO $25-40
- ❑ ❑ USA LE8308 **U-3 WK #4 GRN PKG,** 1983, DUPLO $25-40
- ❑ ❑ USA LE8301 **SET 1 TRUCK,** 1983, LEGO/RED PACKAGE 17P $25-40
- ❑ ❑ USA LE8302 **SET 2 SHIP,** 1983, LEGO/BLU PACKAGE 27P $25-40
- ❑ ❑ USA LE8303 **SET 3 HELICOPTER,** 1983, LEGO/YEL PACKAGE 19P $25-40
- ❑ ❑ USA LE8304 **SET 4 AIRPLANE,** 1983, LEGO/GRN PACKAGE 18P $25-40
- ❑ ❑ USA LE8365 **TRANSLITE/LG,** 1983, $65-90

COMMENTS: REGIONAL DISTRIBUTION: USA - JUNE 1983 . TEST MARKET IN SALT LAKE CITY, UTAH - SUMMER 1983.

MCDONALDLAND JUNCTION HAPPY MEAL, 1983

- ❑ ❑ USA JU8310 **HM BOX,** 1983, **ENGINE BARN** $8-10
- ❑ ❑ USA JU8311 **HM BOX,** 1983, **POST OFFICE** $8-10
- ❑ ❑ USA JU8312 **HM BOX,** 1983, **SIGNAL TOWER** $8-10
- ❑ ❑ USA JU8313 **HM BOX,** 1983, **STATION** $8-10
- ❑ ❑ USA JU8314 **HM BOX,** 1983, **TOWN HALL** $8-10
- ❑ ❑ USA JU8315 **HM BOX,** 1983, **TRAIN TUNNEL** $8-10
- ❑ ❑ USA JU8300 **RONALD TRAIN ENGINE #1,** 1982, RED $4-6
- ❑ ❑ USA JU8302 **FLAT CAR W 4 FRY KIDS #2,** 1982, GRN $4-6
- ❑ ❑ USA JU8304 **BIRDIE PARLOR CAR #3,** 1982, YEL $4-6
- ❑ ❑ USA JU8306 **GRIMACE CABOOSE #4,** 1982, PUR $4-6
- ❑ ❑ USA JU8301 **RONALD TRAIN ENGINE #1,** 1982 BLUE $10-15
- ❑ ❑ USA JU8303 **FLAT CAR W 4 FRY KIDS #2,** 1982, WHT $10-15
- ❑ ❑ USA JU8305 **BIRDIE PARLOR CAR #3,** 1982, PINK $10-15
- ❑ ❑ USA JU8307 **GRIMACE CABOOSE #4,** 1982, ORANGE $10-15

USA JU8310 USA JU8311

USA JU8312 USA JU8313

USA JU8314 USA JU8315

USA JU8300 USA JU8305 USA JU8302 USA JU8303 USA JU8307

USA JU8304

USA JU8301 USA JU8306

❑ ❑ USA JU8324 **AMTRAK PAMPHLET W STICKERS,** 1983 $15-20
❑ ❑ USA JU8361 **M C INSERT/CARDBOARD,** 1983 $35-45
❑ ❑ USA JU8362 **HEADER CARD,** 1983 $20-30
❑ ❑ USA JU8363 **MENU BOARD LUG ON,** 1983 $20-30
❑ ❑ USA JU8365 **TRANSLITE/LG,** 1983 $40-50

COMMENTS: NATIONAL DISTRIBUTION: USA - JANUARY 17-MARCH 27, 1983. THE AMTRAK "ALL ABOARD" STICKER SHEET WITH PAMPHLET WAS DISTRIBUTED WITH THE HM IN THE NORTHEAST. USA JU8300/02/04/06 WERE NATIONALLY DISTRIBUTED. USA JU8301/03/05/07 WERE REGIONALLY DISTRIBUTED.

MYSTERY HAPPY MEAL, 1983

❑ ❑ USA MY8310 **HM BOX,** 1983, **DOG-GONE MYSTERY** $15-20
❑ ❑ USA MY8311 **HM BOX,** 1983, **GOLDEN KEY** $15-20
❑ ❑ USA MY8312 **HM BOX,** 1983, **MYSTERIOUS MAP** $15-20

USA JU8365

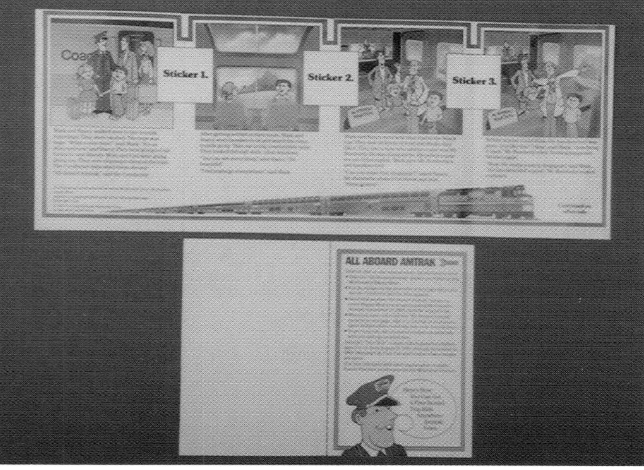

USA JU8324

USA JU8361

USA MY8310

USA MY8311

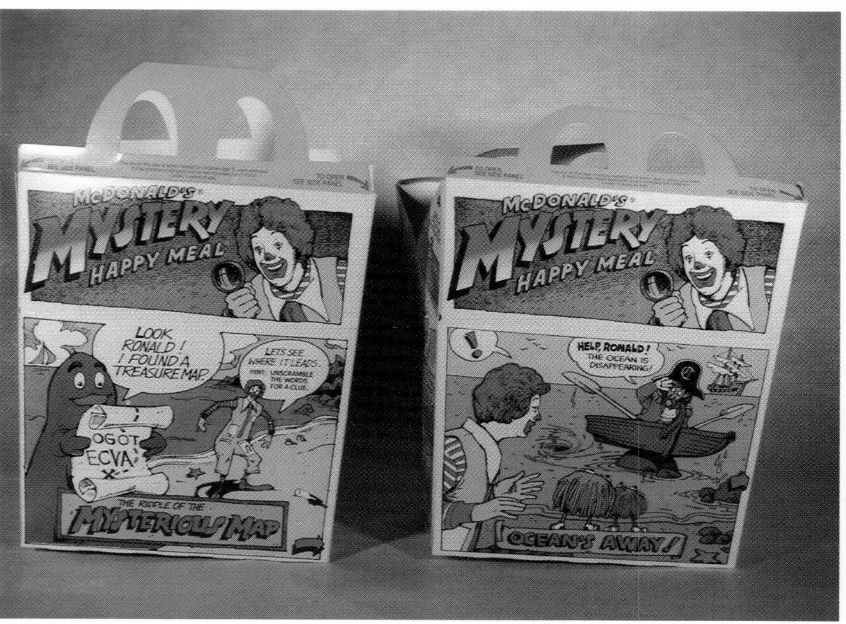

USA MY8312

USA MY8313

USA MY8314

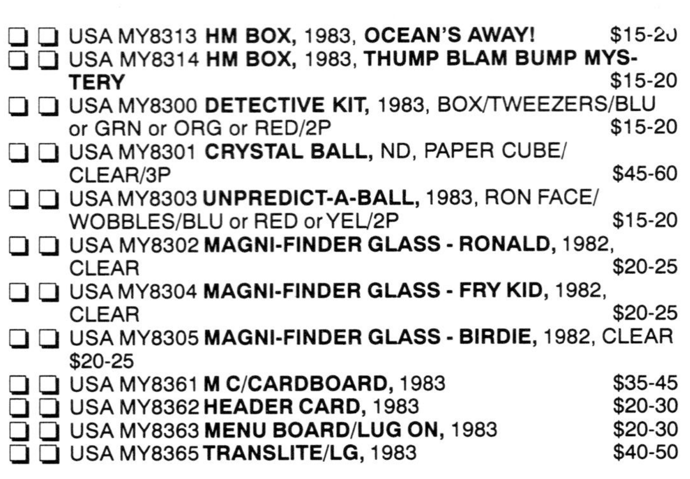

- ❑ ❑ USA MY8313 **HM BOX,** 1983, **OCEAN'S AWAY!** $15-20
- ❑ ❑ USA MY8314 **HM BOX,** 1983, **THUMP BLAM BUMP MYSTERY** $15-20
- ❑ ❑ USA MY8300 **DETECTIVE KIT,** 1983, BOX/TWEEZERS/BLU or GRN or ORG or RED/2P $15-20
- ❑ ❑ USA MY8301 **CRYSTAL BALL,** ND, PAPER CUBE/ CLEAR/3P $45-60
- ❑ ❑ USA MY8303 **UNPREDICT-A-BALL,** 1983, RON FACE/ WOBBLES/BLU or RED or YEL/2P $15-20
- ❑ ❑ USA MY8302 **MAGNI-FINDER GLASS - RONALD,** 1982, CLEAR $20-25
- ❑ ❑ USA MY8304 **MAGNI-FINDER GLASS - FRY KID,** 1982, CLEAR $20-25
- ❑ ❑ USA MY8305 **MAGNI-FINDER GLASS - BIRDIE,** 1982, CLEAR $20-25
- ❑ ❑ USA MY8361 **M C/CARDBOARD,** 1983 $35-45
- ❑ ❑ USA MY8362 **HEADER CARD,** 1983 $20-30
- ❑ ❑ USA MY8363 **MENU BOARD/LUG ON,** 1983 $20-30
- ❑ ❑ USA MY8365 **TRANSLITE/LG,** 1983 $40-50

COMMENTS: NATIONAL DISTRIBUTION: USA - MARCH 28-JUNE 5, 1983. USA MY8301 WAS RECALLED PRIOR TO NATIONAL DISTRIBUTION.

USA MY8301

USA MY8365

USA MY8300

USA PL8301 USA PL8302 USA PL8303 USA PL8304

USA MY8305 USA MY8304 USA MY8302

PLAY-DOH I HAPPY MEAL, 1983

- ❑ ❑ USA PL8301 **BLUE,** 1981, **CARDBOARD W TIN BOTTOM** $15-20
- ❑ ❑ USA PL8302 **RED,** 1981, **CARDBOARD W TIN BOTTOM** $15-20
- ❑ ❑ USA PL8303 **WHITE,** 1981, **CARDBOARD W TIN BOTTOM** $15-20
- ❑ ❑ USA PL8304 **YELLOW,** 1981, **CARDBOARD W TIN BOTTOM** $15-20
- ❑ ❑ USA PL8365 **TRANSLITE/LG,** 1983 $40-50

COMMENTS: REGIONAL DISTRIBUTION: USA - MAY 1983 IN THE BOSTON, MASS. AREA. THE 2 OUNCE CANS OF PLAY-DOH BY KENNER WERE MADE OF CARDBOARD WITH TIN BOTTOMS; NO MCDONALD'S MARKINGS. IN 1984, THE WICHITA, KS. (MARCH 23-APRIL 22) AND NEBRASKA (MARCH 2-APRIL 1) AREAS RAN THIS PLAY-DOH PROMOTION. IN 1985 PLAY-DOH WAS OFFERED AGAIN WITH 2 ADDITIONAL CANS, SEE USA PL8529-30, PLAY-DOH HAPPY MEAL, 1985.

SHIP SHAPE I HAPPY MEAL, 1983

- ❑ ❑ USA SH8301 **SPLASH DASHER-HAMBURGLAR,** 1983, WHT TOP/ORG BOTTOM $10-15
- ❑ ❑ USA SH8302 **TUBBY TUGGER-GRIMACE,** 1983, PNK TOP/BLU BOTTOM $10-15
- ❑ ❑ USA SH8303 **RUB-A-DUB SUB-CAPTAIN,** 1983, GRN TOP/GRN BOTTOM/SUBMARINE $10-15
- ❑ ❑ USA SH8304 **RIVER BOAT-RONALD,** 1983, YEL TOP/RED BOTTOM $10-15
- ❑ ❑ USA SH8305 **STICKER SHEET-SPLASH DASHER,** 1983 $4-6
- ❑ ❑ USA SH8306 **STICKER SHEET-TUBBY TUGGER,** 1983 $4-6
- ❑ ❑ USA SH8307 **STICKER SHEET-RUB-A-DUB-SUB,** 1983 $4-6
- ❑ ❑ USA SH8308 **STICKER SHEET-RIVER BOAT,** 1983 $4-6
- ❑ ❑ USA SH8326 **DISPLAY,** 1983 $150-200
- ❑ ❑ USA SH8361 **M C/CARDBOARD,** 1983 $35-45
- ❑ ❑ USA SH8365 **TRANSLITE/LG,** 1983 $40-50

COMMENTS: NATIONAL DISTRIBUTION: USA JUNE 6-JULY 18, 1983. DECALS AND CONTAINERS CARRIED 1983 DATES. THE "SPLASH DASHER" ISSUED IN 1985 HAD A LARGER DECAL.

WINTER WORLDS HAPPY MEAL, 1983

- ❑ ❑ USA WI8310 **HM BOX,** 1983, **BIRDS OF ICE AND SNOW** $5-8
- ❑ ❑ USA WI8311 **HM BOX,** 1983, **LANDS OF ICE AND SNOW** $5-8
- ❑ ❑ USA WI8312 **HM BOX,** 1983, **LANDS OF THE MIDNIGHT SUN** $5-8
- ❑ ❑ USA WI8313 **HM BOX,** 1983, **MAMMALS ON THE ICY SHORES** $5-8
- ❑ ❑ USA WI8314 **HM BOX,** 1983, **PEOPLE OF THE FROSTY FRONTIER** $5-8

USA SH8365

USA SH8326

USA SH8303 USA SH8304 USA SH8302
USA SH8301

USA WI8310 USA WI8311

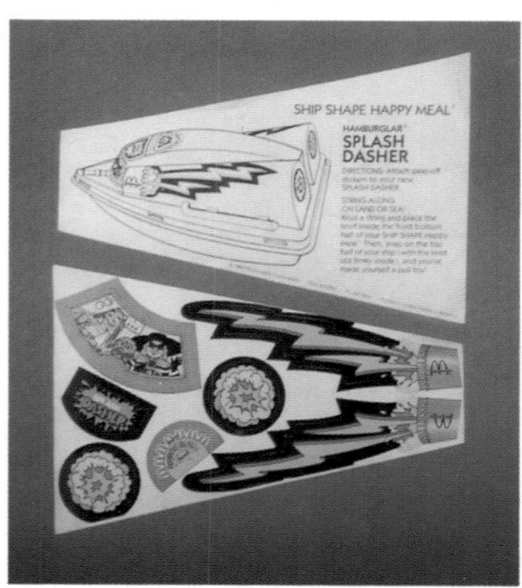

USA SH8305

USA WI8312

USA WI8313

USA WI8314

USA WI8301 USA WI8302 USA WI8303

USA WI8304 USA WI8305

USA WI8363

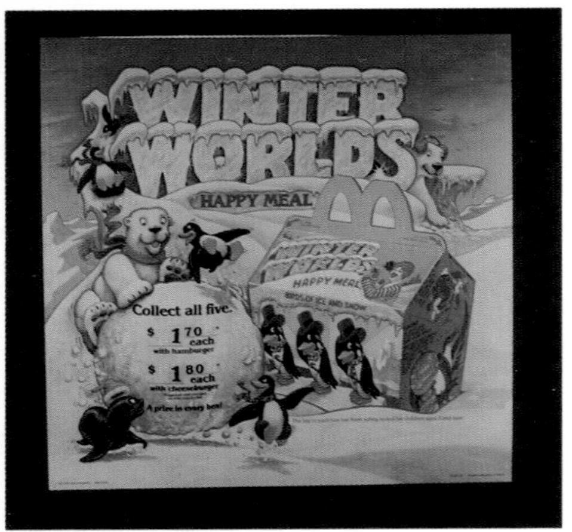

USA WI8365

USA AS8450

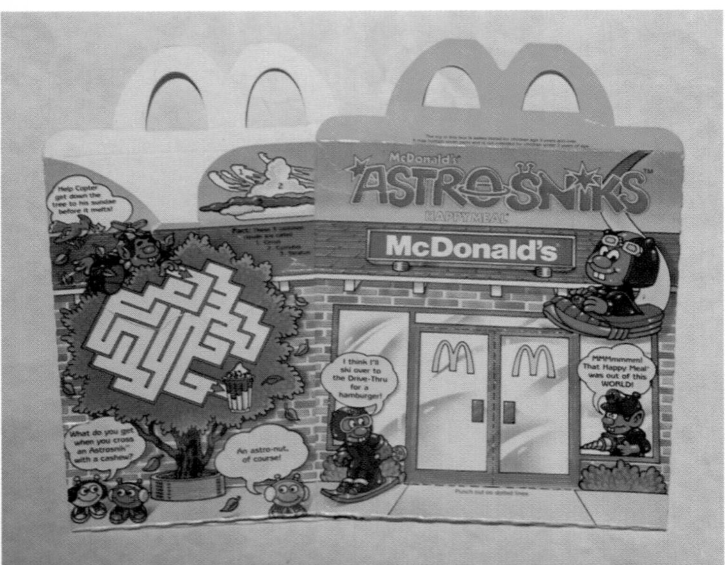

- ❑ ❑ USA WI8301 **ORNAMENT-BIRDIE,** 1983, YEL/PNK VINYL 4" W LOOPED CORD $5-8
- ❑ ❑ USA WI8302 **ORNAMENT-GRIMACE,** 1983, PUR VINYL 4" W LOOPED CORD $3-5
- ❑ ❑ USA WI8303 **ORNAMENT-HAMBURGLAR,** 1983, BLK/WHT STRIPES/VINYL 4" W LOOPED CORD $3-5
- ❑ ❑ USA WI8304 **ORNAMENT-MAYOR,** 1983, YEL/PNK/PUR VINYL 4" W LOOPED CORD $5-8
- ❑ ❑ USA WI8305 **ORNAMENT-RONALD,** 1983, RED/YEL VINYL 4" W LOOPED CORD $3-5
- ❑ ❑ USA WI8361 **M C/CARDBOARD,** 1983 $35-45
- ❑ ❑ USA WI8362 **HEADER CARD,** 1983 $20-30
- ❑ ❑ USA WI8363 **MENU BOARD/LUG ON,** 1983 $20-30
- ❑ ❑ USA WI8365 **TRANSLITE/LG,** 1983 $40-50

COMMENTS: LIMITED NATIONAL DISTRIBUTION: USA NOVEMBER 28, 1983-FEBRUARY 5, 1984. GRIMACE/RON/HAMB VINYL ORNAMENTS WERE REISSUED CHRISTMAS 1984, DATED 1984 (NOT 1983).

USA/GENERIC PROMOTION, 1983

- ❑ ❑ USA GE8301 **SPINNER BASEBALL,** 1983, GRN/5P/RON/GRI/HAMB/F KID $5-7
- ❑ ❑ USA GE8302 **FUN RULER,** 1983, INCHES/CENTIMETERS $2-3

COMMENTS: REGIONAL DISTRIBUTION: USA - 1983 DURING CLEAN-UP WEEKS. THIS IS A SAMPLING OF GENERIC PREMIUMS GIVEN AWAY DURING THIS PERIOD.

USA GE8301

USA GE8302

1984

ASTROSNIKS II HAPPY MEAL, 1984
FAST MACS I PROMOTION, 1984
GOOD SPORTS HAPPY MEAL, 1984
HAPPY HOLIDAYS HAPPY MEAL, 1984
HAPPY PAIL II OLYMPIC THEME HAPPY MEAL, 1984
LEGO BUILDING SETS II HAPPY MEAL, 1984
OLYMPIC BEACH BALL PROMOTION, 1984
OLYMPIC SPORTS I HAPPY MEAL, 1984
POPOIDS/CRAZY CREATURES I TEST MARKET HAPPY MEAL, 1984
SCHOOL DAYS HAPPY MEAL, 1984
USA/GENERIC PROMOTION, 1984

ASTROSNIKS II HAPPY MEAL, 1984

- ❑ ❑ USA AS8450 **HM BOX,** 1984, **MCDONALD'S STORE/RACER** $40-65

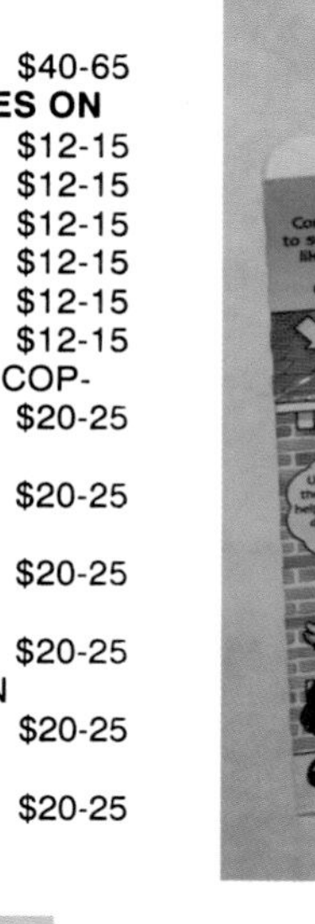

- ❑ ❑ USA AS8451 **HM BOX,** 1984, **SNIK STATION EARTH/ PERFIDO** $40-65
- ❑ ❑ USA AS8431 **COPTER,** 1984, **W HELICOPTER BLADES ON HEAD** $12-15
- ❑ ❑ USA AS8432 **RACING,** 1984, **ON SLED** $12-15
- ❑ ❑ USA AS8433 **SKI,** 1984, **W SKIS/GOGGLES** $12-15
- ❑ ❑ USA AS8434 **COMMANDER,** 1984, **W MASK** $12-15
- ❑ ❑ USA AS8435 **DRILL,** 1984, **W DRILL IN HANDS** $12-15
- ❑ ❑ USA AS8436 **PERFIDO,** 1984, **W RED CAPE** $12-15
- ❑ ❑ USA AS8437 **COPTER/WHT PRINTING,** 1984, W HELICOPTER BLADES ON HEAD $20-25
- ❑ ❑ USA AS8438 **RACING/WHT PRINTING,** 1984, ON SLED $20-25
- ❑ ❑ USA AS8439 **SKI/WHT PRINTING,** 1984, W SKIS/ GOGGLES $20-25
- ❑ ❑ USA AS8440 **COMMANDER/WHT PRINTING,** 1984, W MASK $20-25
- ❑ ❑ USA AS8441 **DRILL/WHT PRINTING,** 1984, W DRILL IN HANDS $20-25
- ❑ ❑ USA AS8442 **PERFIDO/WHT PRINTING,** 1984, W RED CAPE $20-25

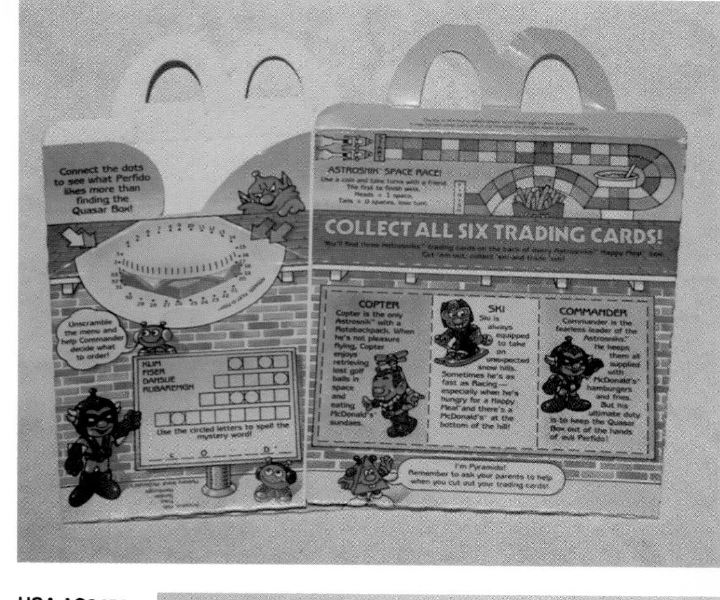

USA AS8450

USA AS8431

USA AS8432 USA AS8433 USA AS8434 USA AS8435 USA AS8436

USA AS8451

USA AS8440

USA AS8427

- ❑ ❑ USA AS8426 **FLOOR DISPLAY/4',** 1984 $100-150
- ❑ ❑ USA AS8427 **SPACEMOBILE ROCKET DISPLAY,** 1984 $50-75
- ❑ ❑ USA AS8455 **TRAY LINER,** 1984 $15-20
- ❑ ❑ USA AS8456 **TABLE TENT,** 1984 $15-20
- ❑ ❑ USA AS8465 **TRANSLITE/LG,** 1984 $75-90
- ❑ ❑ USA AS8466 **ASTROSNIKS COUPON/SAVE $4,** 1984 $5-8

COMMENTS: LIMITED REGIONAL DISTRIBUTION: USA - MARCH/APRIL AND AUGUST 10-SEPTEMBER 23, 1984 IN ST. LOUIS, MISSOURI AREA. ALL MINT FIGURES WERE ENCLOSED IN A ZIPLOCK BAG WITH A $4 OFF COUPON FOR THE SPACEMOBILE DISPLAY/SOLD IN RETAIL STORES. BAGS SAID, "THIS TOY IN THIS PACKAGE HAS BEEN SAFETY TESTED FOR CHILDREN AGE 3 YEARS AND OVER. MADE IN HONG KONG." USA AS8431-36 FIGURINES HAVE A MOLDED YELLOW LOGO M ON FIGURINE AND TRADEMARK DATA '84 BULLY-FIGUREN TM ASTROSNIK MCDONALD'S HONG KONG PRINTED ONTO BOTTOM OF FIGURINE. USA AS8437-42 WERE LIMITED REGIONAL DISTRIBUTION: USA - 1984 IN NEW ENGLAND AREAS; THE TRADEMARK DATA WAS PRINTED IN WHITE ON THE BOTTOM OF EACH FIGURINE AND THE YELLOW "M" WAS PAINTED ON.

FAST MACS I PROMOTION, 1984

- ❑ ❑ USA FA8401 **BIG MAC,** 1985, IN WHT SQUAD/POLICE CAR $8-10
- ❑ ❑ USA FA8402 **HAMBURGLAR,** 1985, IN RED SPORTS CAR/ $8-10
- ❑ ❑ USA FA8403 **MAYOR,** 1985, IN PNK SUN CRUISER/WHT ARCHES WINDSHIELD $15-20
- ❑ ❑ USA FA8404 **RONALD,** 1985, IN YEL JEEP W WHT RECTANGLE WINDSHIELD $15-20

COMMENTS: LIMITED REGIONAL DISTRIBUTION: USA - 1984. BLISTER PACK CARDS/CARS CARRY 1984 DATE. CARS WERE SOLD FOR 59 CENTS ON A BLISTER PACK. USA FA8503-04/MAYOR/RONALD WERE REDESIGNED FOR NATIONAL DISTRIBUTION IN 1985 BECOMING USA FA8506/08.

USA AS8456

Get one Astrosnik in every Happy Meal.
McDonald's
ASTROSNIKS

USA AS8466

USA FA8403 USA FA8402 USA FA8401

USA FA8404 USA FA8403

GOOD SPORTS HAPPY MEAL, 1984

❑ ❑ USA GO8415 **HM BOX,** 1984, **SKIING** $5-7
❑ ❑ USA GO8416 **HM BOX,** 1984, **SLEDDING** $5-7
❑ ❑ USA GO8417 **HM BOX,** 1984, **BASKETBALL** $5-7
❑ ❑ USA GO8418 **HM BOX,** 1984, **GYMNASTICS** $5-7
❑ ❑ USA GO8401 **STICKER/PUFFY-BIRDIE,** 1984, W SOCCER BALL $4-7
❑ ❑ USA GO8402 **STICKER/PUFFY-GRIMACE,** 1984, ON RED TOBOGGAN SLED $4-7
❑ ❑ USA GO8403 **STICKER/PUFFY-HAMBURGLAR,** 1984, W HOCKEY STICK/PUCK $4-7
❑ ❑ USA GO8404 **STICKER/PUFFY-MAYOR,** 1984, ON SKIS $4-7
❑ ❑ USA GO8405 **STICKER/PUFFY-RONALD,** 1984, ON ICE SKATES $4-7
❑ ❑ USA GO8406 **STICKER/PUFFY-SAM THE OLYMPIC EAGLE,** 1984, W BASKETBALL $4-7
❑ ❑ USA GO8461 **M C INSERT/CARDBOARD,** 1983 $25-35
❑ ❑ USA GO8462 **HEADER CARD,** 1983 $15-25
❑ ❑ USA GO8465 **TRANSLITE/LG,** 1983 $25-40

COMMENTS: NATIONAL DISTRIBUTION: USA - FEBRUARY 5-APRIL 15, 1984. SAM THE OLYMPIC EAGLE PUFFY STICKER IS DATED 1984 AND 1981/FRONT AND BACK.

USA GO8415 USA GO8416

USA GO8404 USA GO8405 USA GO8406

USA GO8417 USA GO8418

USA GO8462

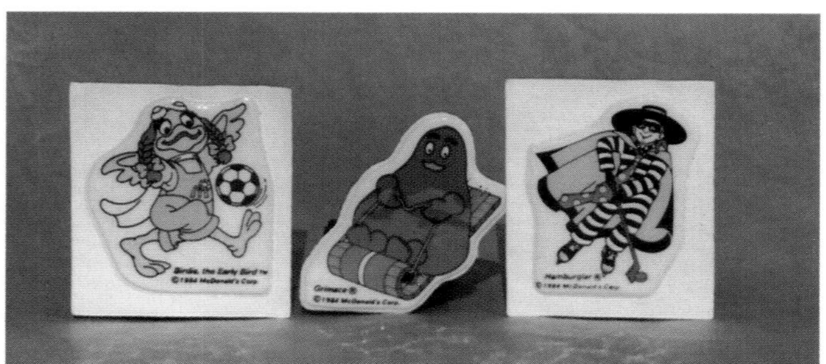

USA GO8401 USA GO8402 USA GO8403

USA GO8465

USA HH8405 USA HH8406

HAPPY HOLIDAYS HAPPY MEAL, 1984

- ☐ ☐ USA HH8405 **HM BOX,** 1984, **RED BOX/RONALD W SLEIGH** $8-12
- ☐ ☐ USA HH8406 **HM BOX,** 1984, **GRN BOX/GINGERBREAD HOUSE** $8-12
- ☐ ☐ USA HH8400 **CARD/STICKERS,** 1984, **GINGERBREAD HOUSE W STICKERS** $20 -25
- ☐ ☐ USA HH8401 **CARD/STICKERS,** 1984, **TRAIN W STICKERS** $20 -25
- ☐ ☐ USA HH8461 **M C INSERT/CARDBOARD,** 1984 $25-40
- ☐ ☐ USA HH8462 **HEADER CARD,** 1984 $20-25
- ☐ ☐ USA HH8463 **MENU BOARD LUG-ON,** 1984 $15-20
- ☐ ☐ USA HH8465 **TRANSLITE/LG,** 1984 $40-60

COMMENTS: LIMITED NATIONAL DISTRIBUTION: USA - NOVEMBER 23-DECEMBER 24, 1984.

HAPPY PAIL II OLYMPIC THEME HAPPY MEAL, 1984

- ☐ ☐ USA HP8470 **HM PAIL/ATHLETICS,** 1983, BEIGE LID/PAIL W YEL SHOVEL $5-7
- ☐ ☐ USA HP8471 **HM PAIL/CYCLING,** 1983, YEL PAIL/LID W YEL SHOVEL $5-7
- ☐ ☐ USA HP8472 **HM PAIL/OLYMPIC GAMES,** 1983, WHT PAIL/ LID W YEL SHOVEL $5-7
- ☐ ☐ USA HP8473 **HM PAIL/SWIMMING,** 1983, BLUE PAIL/LID W YEL SHOVEL $5-7
- ☐ ☐ USA HP8426 **DISPLAY/1 PAIL,** 1984 $35-50
- ☐ ☐ USA HP8461 **M C INSERT,** 1984 $25-40
- ☐ ☐ USA HP8465 **TRANSLITE/LG,** 1984 $40-50

COMMENTS: NATIONAL DISTRIBUTION: USA - MAY 18-JUNE 17, 1984. LIDS HAD 4 OPEN VENT HOLES.
YELLOW SHOVEL HAD THE WARNING "SAFETY TESTED FOR CHILDREN 3 YEARS AND OVER" MOLDED ON THEM.

USA HH8400

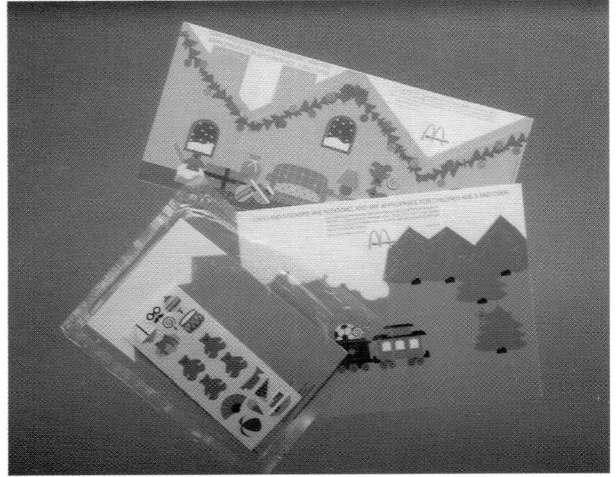

USA HH8401

USA HP8472 USA HP8473

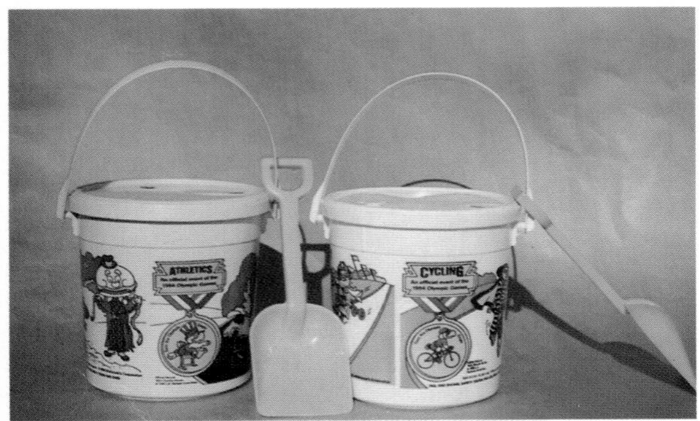

USA HP8470 USA HP8471

USA HP8426

USA HP8465

LEGO BUILDING SETS II HAPPY MEAL, 1984

❑ ❑ USA LE8435 **HM BOX,** 1984, **FIND THE FRY GUY** $5-8
❑ ❑ USA LE8436 **HM BOX,** 1984, **MASTER THE MAZE** $5-8
❑ ❑ USA LE8437 **HM BOX,** 1984, **SHIP SHAPE** $5-8
❑ ❑ USA LE8438 **HM BOX,** 1984, **WHAT'S WRONG?** $5-8
❑ ❑ USA LE8405 **U-3 BOAT W SAILOR,** 1984, DUPLO/BLU PKG "AGES 1-4"/5P $4-6
❑ ❑ USA LE8406 **U-3 BIRD W EYE,** 1984, DUPLO/RED PKG "AGES 1-4"/5P $4-6
❑ ❑ USA LE8401 **SET 1 TRUCK,** 1984, LEGO/RED PKG/17P $6-8
❑ ❑ USA LE8402 **SET 2 SHIP,** 1984, LEGO/BLU PKG/27P $6-8
❑ ❑ USA LE8403 **SET 3 HELICOPTER,** 1984, LEGO/YEL PKG/19P $6-8
❑ ❑ USA LE8404 **SET 4 AIRPLANE,** 1984, LEGO/GRN PKG/18P $6-8
❑ ❑ USA LE8426 **DISPLAY/RONALD,** 1984, LEGO W STICKER $350-500
❑ ❑ USA LE8441 **DANGLER/EACH,** 1984 $10-15
❑ ❑ USA LE8455 **TRAYLINER,** 1984 $5-8
❑ ❑ USA LE8461 **M C INSERT/CARDBOARD,** 1984 $35-50
❑ ❑ USA LE8465 **TRANSLITE/LG,** 1984 $40-60

COMMENTS: NATIONAL DISTRIBUTION: USA - OCTOBER 26-NOVEMBER 25, 1984.

USA LE8406

USA LE8435 USA LE8436

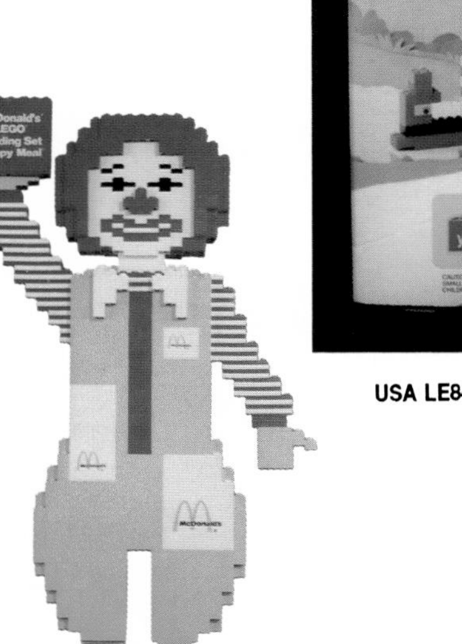
USA LE8426

USA LE8437 USA LE8438

USA LE8401 USA LE8402 USA LE8403 USA LE8404 USA LE8405 USA LE8406

USA LE8441

McDonald's Happy Meal featuring LEGO Building Sets
One set in every box... Collect all 4!
Imagine all the toys you can build!
$1 86 with Hamburger
$1 96 with Cheeseburger

USA LE8465

USA BE8400 USA BE8401 USA BE8402

USA OL8410 USA OL8411

USA OL8412 USA OL8413

USA OL8414

USA OL8463

OLYMPIC BEACH BALL PROMOTION, 1984

- ❑ ❑ USA BE8400 **BEACH BALL-BIRDIE,** 1984, IN A SAILBOAT/W OLYMPIC LOGO ON SAIL/BLUE $15-20
- ❑ ❑ USA BE8401 **BEACH BALL-GRIMACE,** 1984, IN A KAYAK/W OLYMPIC LOGO ON SAIL/GRN $15-20
- ❑ ❑ USA BE8402 **BEACH BALL-RONALD,** 1984, IN OLYMPIC EVENT/W OLYMPIC LOGO ON BANNER/RED $15-20

COMMENTS: REGIONAL DISTRIBUTION: USA - 1984. MIP CAME POLYBAGGED WITH SCOTCH TAPE CLOSURE. THIS PROMOTION COULD HAVE BEEN A REGIONAL PROMOTION AND NOT A HAPPY MEAL.

OLYMPIC SPORTS I HAPPY MEAL, 1984

- ❑ ❑ USA OL8410 **HM BOX,** 1984, **BOATS AFLOAT** $5-8
- ❑ ❑ USA OL8411 **HM BOX,** 1984, **IN THE SWIM** $5-8
- ❑ ❑ USA OL8412 **HM BOX,** 1984, **JUST FOR KICKS** $5-8
- ❑ ❑ USA OL8413 **HM BOX,** 1984, **MAKING TRACKS** $5-8
- ❑ ❑ USA OL8414 **HM BOX,** 1984, **PEDAL POWER** $5-8
- ❑ ❑ USA OL8400 **PUZZLE-GUESS WHICH GUY COMES UNDER WIRE,** 1984, FRY GUY GLOWS $20-25
- ❑ ❑ USA OL8401 **PUZZLE-GUESS WHO FINISHED SMILES AHEAD,** 1984, BIRDIE GLOWS $20-25
- ❑ ❑ USA OL8402 **PUZZLE-GUESS WHO MAKES BIGGEST SPLASH,** 1984, GRIMACE GLOWS $20-25
- ❑ ❑ USA OL8403 **PUZZLE-GUESS WHO STOLE THE WINNING GOAL,** 1984, HAMBURGLAR GLOWS $20-25
- ❑ ❑ USA OL8404 **PUZZLE-WHO DO YOU KNOW CAN HELP THEM ROW?,** 1984, RONALD GLOWS $20-25
- ❑ ❑ USA OL8461 **M C INSERT/CARDBOARD,** 1984 $35-50
- ❑ ❑ USA OL8462 **HEADER CARD,** 1984 $15-20
- ❑ ❑ USA OL8463 **MENU BOARD/LUG ON,** 1984 $20-25
- ❑ ❑ USA OL8465 **TRANSLITE/LG,** 1984 $40-65

COMMENTS: NATIONAL DISTRIBUTION: USA JUNE 18-AUGUST 20, 1984. PUZZLES WERE 4 3/4" X 3 3/4". OTHER PREMIUMS, CHARACTERS WITH PUSH HANDLES, WERE ORIGINALLY SLATED TO BE DISTRIBUTED. DUE TO PRODUCTION PROBLEMS, THESE WERE CANCELLED AND PUZZLES SUBSTITUTED.

USA OL8400 USA OL8403 USA OL8401

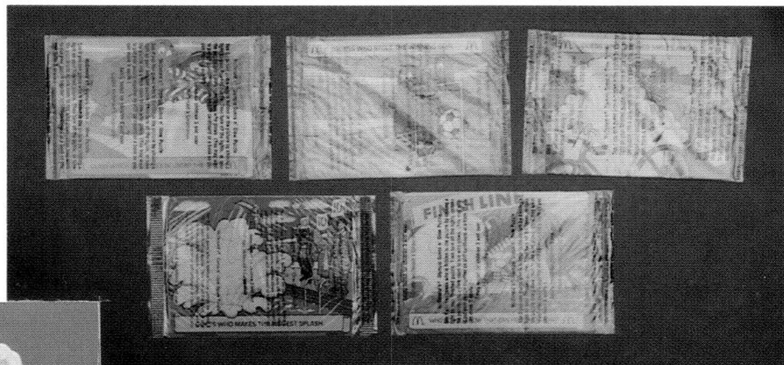

USA OL8402 USA OL8404

USA OL8462

USA OL8465

POPOIDS/CRAZY CREATURES I TEST MARKET HAPPY MEAL, 1984

❑ ❑ USA PO8410 **HM BOX,** 1984, **ELEPHOID/JUNGLE/POPOIDS SONG** $40-75
❑ ❑ USA PO8411 **HM BOX,** 1984, **OCTOPOID/UNDERSEA/ POPOIDS SONG** $40-75
❑ ❑ USA PO8400 **POPOIDS #1,** 1984, 2 BELLOWS/BLU/DK BLU/ 1 WHT BALL $40-50
❑ ❑ USA PO8401 **POPOIDS #2,** 1984, 2 BELLOWS/BLU/DK BLU/ 1 CUBE 6 HOLES $40-50
❑ ❑ USA PO8402 **POPOIDS #3,** 1984, 2 BELLOWS/BLU/DK BLU/ 1 CUBE 6 HOLES $40-50
❑ ❑ USA PO8403 **POPOIDS #4,** 1984, 2 BELLOWS/RED/YEL/ 1 PENTAHEDRON/ORG $40-50
❑ ❑ USA PO8404 **POPOIDS #5,** 1984, 2 BELLOWS/RED/YEL/ 1 COLUMN/ORG $40-50
❑ ❑ USA PO8405 **POPOIDS #6,** 1984, 3 BELLOWS/BLU/DK BLUE/YEL $40-50
❑ ❑ USA PO8456 **TABLE TENT,** 1984, $20-30

COMMENTS: REGIONAL DISTRIBUTION: USA - MARCH 30-MAY 6, 1984 IN ST. LOUIS, MISSOURI. SETS CAME IN CLEAR POLYBAG W "POPOIDS" NAME PRINTED IN RED LETTERS ACROSS THE BAG. NO MCDONALD'S MARKINGS ON THE MIP.

SCHOOL DAYS HAPPY MEAL, 1984

❑ ❑ USA SC8420 **HM BOX,** 1984, **123'S** $5-8
❑ ❑ USA SC8421 **HM BOX,** 1984, **ABC'S** $5-8
❑ ❑ USA SC8422 **HM BOX,** 1984, **HISTORY** $5-8
❑ ❑ USA SC8423 **HM BOX,** 1984, **SCIENCE** $5-8
❑ ❑ USA SC8400 **ERASER - BIRDIE,** 1984, HOLDING AN APPLE $4-6
❑ ❑ USA SC8401 **ERASER - CAPTAIN,** 1984, HOLDING A RULER AND PARROT $4-6
❑ ❑ USA SC8402 **ERASER - GRIMACE,** 1984, W PENCIL $4-6
❑ ❑ USA SC8403 **ERASER - HAMBURGLAR,** 1984, W LUNCH BAG $4-6
❑ ❑ USA SC8404 **ERASER - RONALD,** 1984, W HISTORY BOOK $4-6
❑ ❑ USA SC8405 **PENCIL - GRIMACE,** ND, WHT W PUR GRIMACE $4-6
❑ ❑ USA SC8406 **PENCIL - HAMBURGLAR,** ND, WHT ORG LOGO BLK HAMB $4-6
❑ ❑ USA SC8407 **PENCIL - RONALD,** ND, SCRIP WHT/RED LOGO $4-6
❑ ❑ USA SC8408 **PENCIL CASE - RON/BIRDIE,** 1984, THIN CLEAR VINYL $2-3
❑ ❑ USA SC8409 **PENCIL SHARPENER - GRIMACE BUST,** 1984 $5-8
❑ ❑ USA SC8410 **PENCIL SHARPENER - RONALD BUST,** 1984 $5-8
❑ ❑ USA SC8411 **RULER/NO METRIC SCALE, 1984,** RON BIRDIE(FRONT)/HAMB CAPT(BACK) $2-4

USA PO8456

USA SC8420 USA SC8421

USA SC8422 USA SC8423

USA SC8401 USA SC8403 USA SC8400
USA SC8409 USA SC8404 USA SC8402 USA SC8410

USA SC8408 USA SC8400 USA PO8404
USA SC8411
USA SC8405
USA SC8407
USA SC8406

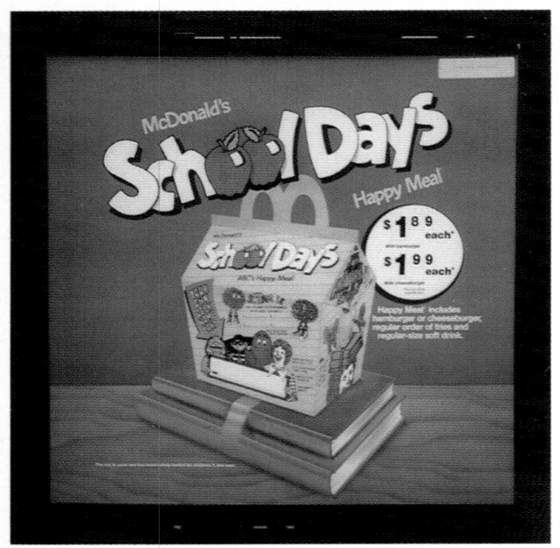

USA SC8465

- ❑ ❑ USA SC8434 **FOOD ITEM/LUG ON,** 1984 $8-12
- ❑ ❑ USA SC8461 **M C INSERT/CARDBOARD,** 1984 $35-50
- ❑ ❑ USA SC8462 **HEADER CARD,** 1984 $15-20
- ❑ ❑ USA SC8463 **MENU BOARD/LUG ON,** 1984 $15-20
- ❑ ❑ USA SC8465 **TRANSLITE/LG,** 1984 $40-60

COMMENTS: NATIONAL DISTRIBUTION: USA - AUGUST 20-OCTOBER 25, 1984. THE RULER CAN BE CONFUSED WITH '85 VERSIONS WITH METRIC SCALE INCLUDED.

USA/GENERIC PROMOTION, 1984

- ❑ ❑ USA GE8401 **SPINNER BIKE RACE-RON/HAMB,** 1984, PINK OR TURQ/4P $4-6

COMMENTS: REGIONAL DISTRIBUTION: USA - 1984 DURING CLEAN-UP WEEKS. THIS IS A SAMPLING OF GENERIC PREMIUMS GIVEN AWAY DURING THIS PERIOD.

USA GE8401

1985

ASTROSNIKS III HAPPY MEAL, 1985
BEACH BALL CHARACTERS PROMOTION, 1985
COMMANDRONS TEST MARKET HAPPY MEAL, 1985
CRAZY CREATURES W POPOIDS II HAPPY MEAL, 1985
DAY & NIGHT HAPPY MEAL, 1985
E.T. HAPPY MEAL, 1985
FAST MACS II PROMOTION, 1985
FEELING GOOD HAPPY MEAL, 1985
FLORIDA BEACH BALL/OLYMPIC BEACH BALL PROMOTION, 1985
HALLOWEEN '85 HAPPY MEAL, 1985
HOBBY BOX HAPPY MEAL, 1985
LITTLE TRAVELERS W LEGO BUILDING SETS/SUPER TRAVELERS HAPPY MEAL, 1985
MAGIC SHOW HAPPY MEAL, 1985
MUSIC HAPPY MEAL, 1985
ON THE GO I HAPPY MEAL, 1985
PICTURE PERFECT HAPPY MEAL, 1985
PLAY-DOH II HAPPY MEAL, 1985
SANTA CLAUS THE MOVIE HAPPY MEAL, 1985
SHIP SHAPE II HAPPY MEAL, 1985
STICKER CLUB HAPPY MEAL, 1985
STOMPER MINI I 4X4 PUSH-ALONG/TEST MARKET HAPPY MEAL, 1985
TOOTHBRUSH HAPPY MEAL, 1985
TRANSFORMERS / MY LITTLE PONY HAPPY MEAL, 1985
WACKY GLASSES/DRINKING STRAW PROMOTION, 1985

USA AS8571 USA AS8572 USA AS8573 USA AS8574 USA AS8575 USA AS8576 USA AS8577

USA AS8578

USA AS8595

ASTROSNIKS III HAPPY MEAL, 1985

- ❑ ❑ USA AS8571 **BANNER,** 1983, SCOUT HOLDING YEL FLAG/ "ASTRONIKS" ON FLAG $7-15
- ❑ ❑ USA AS8572 **C.B.,** 1983, GUY W HEADPHONES W RADIO/ NO "M" $7-15
- ❑ ❑ USA AS8573 **COMMANDER,** 1983, W MASK/NO YEL "M" ON BELT $7-15
- ❑ ❑ USA AS8574 **JET,** 1983, ON ROCKET/NO "M" $7-15
- ❑ ❑ USA AS8575 **JUNIOR,** 1983, HOLDING ICE CREAM CONE/ NO "M" $7-15
- ❑ ❑ USA AS8576 **LASER,** 1983, W GOLD GUN/NO "M" ON BELT $7-15
- ❑ ❑ USA AS8577 **PERFIDO,** 1983, W RED CAPE/LETTER "P" ON BACK $7-15
- ❑ ❑ USA AS8578 **PYRAMIDO,** 1983, PYRAMID SHAPE/LEFT HAND RAISED/NO "M" $7-15
- ❑ ❑ USA AS8579 **ROBO-ROBOT,** 1983, GOLD/NO "M" ON FRONT $7-15
- ❑ ❑ USA AS8580 **SNIKAPOTAMUS,** 1983, DINOSAUR/NO "M" ON SADDLE $7-15
- ❑ ❑ USA AS8581 **ASTRALIA,** 1983, GIRL/NOT HOLDING CONE/ NO "M" $7-15
- ❑ ❑ USA AS8595 **COUNTER CARD,** 1983, FEATURES 11 ASTROSNIKS/CARDBOARD $20-25

COMMENTS: LIMITED REGIONAL DISTRIBUTION: USA - NOVEMBER 1985 IN OKLAHOMA. FIGURINES DO NOT HAVE AN "M" OR "MCDONALD'S" ON THEM. MINT FIGURES CAME WRAPPED IN ZIPLOCK BAG WHICH SAID, "THIS TOY IN THIS PACKAGE HAS BEEN SAFETY TESTED FOR CHILDREN AGE 3 YEARS AND OVER. MADE IN HONG KONG." "'83 BULLY-FIGUREN '83 SCHAPER -ASTROSNIKS TM - MADE IN H.K" WAS MOLDED INTO THE BOTTOM OF FIGURINE. THESE SAME FIGURINES WERE SOLD IN RETAIL STORES.

BEACH BALL CHARACTERS PROMOTION, 1985

❑ ❑ USA BE8505 **BIRDIE,** 1985, BIRDIE IN SAILBOAT /BLUE $10-12
❑ ❑ USA BE8506 **GRIMACE,** 1985, GRIMACE W KAYAK/GRN $10-12
❑ ❑ USA BE8507 **RONALD,** 1985, RONALD WITH BEACH BALL/RED $10-12

COMMENTS: REGIONAL DISTRIBUTION: USA - 1985. THESE BEACH BALLS ARE SIMILAR TO 1984 OLYMPIC BEACH BALLS USA BE8400-02, BUT DATED 1985 WITHOUT MCD LOGO; WITHOUT OLYMPIC LOGO.

COMMANDRONS TEST MARKET HAPPY MEAL, 1985

❑ ❑ USA CO8500 **COMMANDER MAGNA,** 1985, W "AIRBORNE!" COMIC/RED/BLU/WHT TOMY/BLISTER PACK $15-20
❑ ❑ USA CO8501 **MOTRON,** 1985, W "ROBO-MANIA" COMIC/ RED/BLU/WHT TOMY/BLISTER PACK $12-15
❑ ❑ USA CO8502 **SOLARDYN,** 1985, W "THE COPY-BATS!" COMIC/RED/BLU/WHT TOMY/BLISTER PACK $12-15
❑ ❑ USA CO8503 **VELOCITOR,** 1985, W "DAWN OF THE COMMANDRONS!" COMIC/RED/BLU/WHT TOMY/BLIS PK $12-15
❑ ❑ USA CO8504 **COMMANDER MAGNA,** 1985, W "AIRBORNE!" COMIC/RED/BLU/WHT TOMY/LIGHT BLU BOX $12-15
❑ ❑ USA CO8505 **MOTRON,** 1985, W "ROBO-MANIA" COMIC/ RED/BLU/WHT TOMY/LIGHT BLUE BOX $10-12
❑ ❑ USA CO8506 **SOLARDYN,** 1985, W "THE COPY-BATS!" COMIC/RED/BLU/WHT TOMY/LIGHT BLUE BOX $10-12
❑ ❑ USA CO8507 **VELOCITOR,** 1985, W "DAW/ COMMANDRONS!" COM/RED/BLU/WHT TOMY/LIGHT BLU BOX $10-12

COMMENTS: REGIONAL DISTRIBUTION: USA - AUGUST 22-SEPTEMBER 21, 1985. BLISTER PACKS WERE PRICED AT .99 CENTS EACH WITH ANY FOOD PURCHASE. ONE SET OF COMMANDRONS CAME BLISTER PACKAGED WITH A MINI-COMIC BOOK, A SERIALIZED STORY ABOUT THAT ROBOT/ VEHICLE. NO MCDONALD'S LOGO ON THE VEHICLES. MCD LOGO IS ON EACH COMIC BOOK IN THE BLISTER PACK. A SECOND SET EXISTS PACKAGED IN A LIGHT BLUE BOX WITH A COMIC LIKE, "AIRBORNE!" WITH ROBO STRUX OFFER, EXPIRES NOV. 30, 1985. THE COMMANDRONS/LOOSE WERE SOLD IN RETAIL STORES; NOTE THE SHAPE OF THE DECALS. PRICES REFLECTS MIP/NOT LOOSE.

CRAZY CREATURES W POPOIDS II HAPPY MEAL, 1985

❑ ❑ USA CR8510 **HM BOX,** 1985, **ELEPHOIDS** $10-15
❑ ❑ USA CR8511 **HM BOX,** 1985, **DRAGONOIDS** $10-15
❑ ❑ USA CR8512 **HM BOX,** 1985, **OCTOPOID** $10-15
❑ ❑ USA CR8513 **HM BOX,** 1985, **SCORPOID** $10-15

USA CO8500 USA CO8501 USA CO8502 USA CO8503

USA CO8504

USA CR8510 USA CR8511

USA CR8512 USA CR8513

USA CR8551 USA CR8552 USA CR8550 USA CR8553

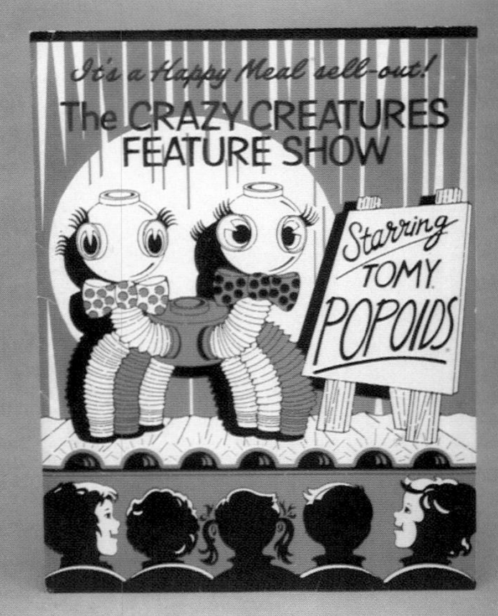

USA CR8543

USA CR8565

USA CR8555

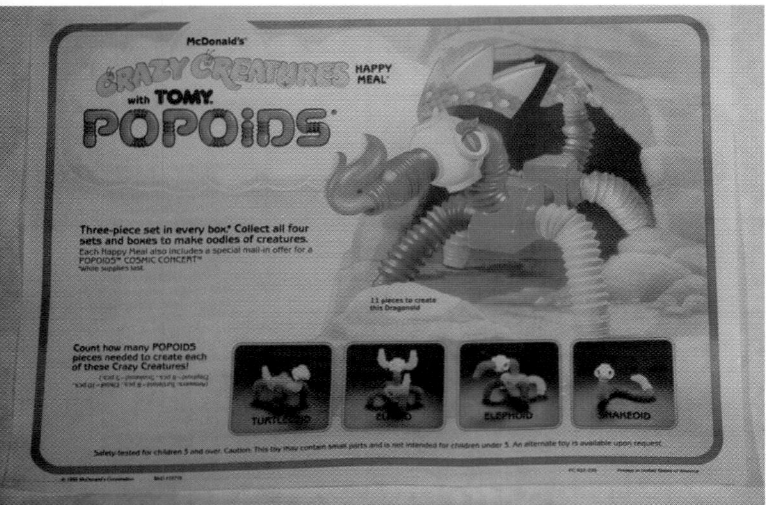

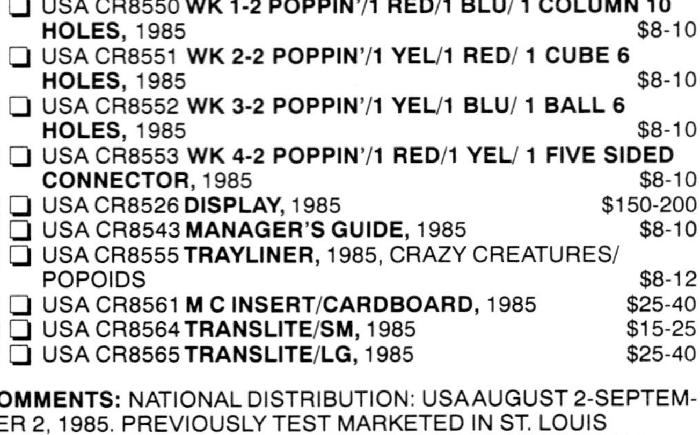

❑ ❑ USA CR8550 **WK 1-2 POPPIN'/1 RED/1 BLU/ 1 COLUMN 10 HOLES,** 1985 $8-10
❑ ❑ USA CR8551 **WK 2-2 POPPIN'/1 YEL/1 RED/ 1 CUBE 6 HOLES,** 1985 $8-10
❑ ❑ USA CR8552 **WK 3-2 POPPIN'/1 YEL/1 BLU/ 1 BALL 6 HOLES,** 1985 $8-10
❑ ❑ USA CR8553 **WK 4-2 POPPIN'/1 RED/1 YEL/ 1 FIVE SIDED CONNECTOR,** 1985 $8-10
❑ ❑ USA CR8526 **DISPLAY,** 1985 $150-200
❑ ❑ USA CR8543 **MANAGER'S GUIDE,** 1985 $8-10
❑ ❑ USA CR8555 **TRAYLINER,** 1985, CRAZY CREATURES/ POPOIDS $8-12
❑ ❑ USA CR8561 **M C INSERT/CARDBOARD,** 1985 $25-40
❑ ❑ USA CR8564 **TRANSLITE/SM,** 1985 $15-25
❑ ❑ USA CR8565 **TRANSLITE/LG,** 1985 $25-40

COMMENTS: NATIONAL DISTRIBUTION: USA AUGUST 2-SEPTEMBER 2, 1985. PREVIOUSLY TEST MARKETED IN ST. LOUIS REGION WITH 2 BOXES AND 6 PREMIUMS - MARCH/MAY 1984 - USA PO8400-05.

DAY & NIGHT HAPPY MEAL, 1985

❑ ❑ USA DA8525 **HM BOX,** 1985, **ALL STAR SUNDAY** $5-7
❑ ❑ USA DA8526 **HM BOX,** 1985, **WHO'S AFRAID OF THE DARK** $5-7

USA DA8525

USA DA8526

COMMENTS: REGIONAL DISTRIBUTION: USA - 1985 DURING CLEAN-UP WEEK HAPPY MEAL; GENERIC PREMIUMS WERE GIVEN.

E.T. HAPPY MEAL, 1985

- ❑ ❑ USA ET8510 **HM BOX,** 1985, **ET MAKES FRIENDS** $6-8
- ❑ ❑ USA ET8511 **HM BOX,** 1985, **THE GREAT ADVENTURE** $6-8
- ❑ ❑ USA ET8500 **ET BOY W BASKET/BIKE,** 1985, POSTER $10-15
- ❑ ❑ USA ET8501 **ET BOY/GIRL W SPSHIP,** 1985, POSTER/ TOUCHING FINGERS $10-15
- ❑ ❑ USA ET8502 **ET/GLOWING FINGER,** 1985, POSTER $10-15
- ❑ ❑ USA ET8503 **ET/RADIO DEVICE,** 1985, POSTER $10-15
- ❑ ❑ USA ET8523 **MENU BOARD LUG-ON,** 1985 $20-30
- ❑ ❑ USA ET8524 **WALL POSTER/E.T./GLOWING FINGER,**
- ❑ ❑ USA ET8541 **DANGLER,** 1985 $7-10
  1985 $25-40
- ❑ ❑ USA ET8561 **MESSAGE CENTER INSERT,** 1985 $15-20
- ❑ ❑ USA ET8562 **HEADER CARD/PERMANENT DISPLAY,** 1985 $7-10
- ❑ ❑ USA ET8563 **TRANSLITE/MOTION WHEEL/LG,** 1985 $35-50
- ❑ ❑ USA ET8564 **TRANSLITE/SM,** 1985 $20-35
- ❑ ❑ USA ET8565 **TRANSLITE/LG,** 1985 $25-40

COMMENTS: NATIONAL DISTRIBUTION: USA - JULY 5-AUGUST 1, 1985

USA ET8510

USA ET8511

USA ET8500

USA ET8501

USA ET8502

USA ET8503

USA ET8523

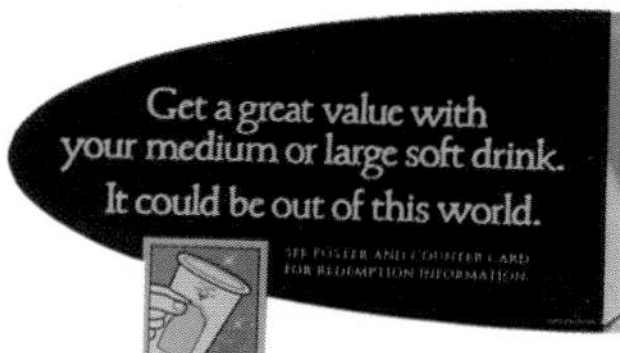

USA ET8541

USA ET8565

USA FA8508 USA FA8505 USA FA8506 USA FA8507

FAST MACS II PROMOTION, 1985

- ❑ ❑ USA FA8505 **BIG MAC,** 1985, IN WHT SQUAD/POLICE CAR $3-5
- ❑ ❑ USA FA8506 **BIRDIE,** 1985, IN PNK SUN CRUISER $3-5
- ❑ ❑ USA FA8507 **HAMBURGLAR,** 1985, IN RED SPORTS CAR $3-5
- ❑ ❑ USA FA8508 **RONALD,** 1985, IN YEL JEEP $3-5
- ❑ ❑ USA FA8515 **PROMO SIGN,** 1985, "TURN HERE FOR FAST MACS" $7-10
- ❑ ❑ USA FA8516 **PROMO SIGN,** 1985, "STOP HERE FOR FAST MACS", $7-10
- ❑ ❑ USA FA8526 **DISPLAY,** 1985 $75-100
- ❑ ❑ USA FA8565 **TRANSLITE/LG,** 1985 $25-40

COMMENTS: REGIONAL DISTRIBUTION: USA - 1985. CARS WERE SOLD FOR 59 CENTS ON A BLISTER PACK AND/OR USED AS HM PREMIUM.

FEELING GOOD HAPPY MEAL, 1985

- ❑ ❑ USA FE8515 **HM BOX,** 1985, **CHILD IN MIRROR/GUESS WHO** $5-7
- ❑ ❑ USA FE8516 **HM BOX,** 1985, **HIDDEN TOOTHBRUSHES/ FIND THE PAIRS** $5-7
- ❑ ❑ USA FE8517 **HM BOX,** 1985, **CHAR WARM UP EXERCISES/ SNOOZE BLUES** $5-7
- ❑ ❑ USA FE8518 **HM BOX,** 1985, **REVERSE MESSAGE/THE BIRDIE PATH** $5-7
- ❑ ❑ USA SH8554 **U-3 GRIMACE IN A TUB,** 1984/5, FLOATER/ YEL or GRN $2-3

USA FA8515

USA FA8516

USA FA8565

USA FA8526

USA FE8515

❑ ❑ USA SH8555 **U-3 FRY GUY ON DUCK,** 1984/5, FLOATER/ YEL or GRN $2-3
❑ ❑ USA FE8501 **TOOTHBRUSH - RONALD BUST,** 1985, WHT-RED/POLYBAGED $4-5
❑ ❑ USA FE8502 **TOOTHBRUSH - HAMB BUST,** 1985, WHT-BLK/ POLYBAGED $4-5
❑ ❑ USA FE8503 **SOAP DISH,** 1985, GRIMACE W SPREAD ARMS/PUR $4-5
❑ ❑ USA FE8504 **SPONGE - FRY GUY/SHOWER,** 1985, GRN $2-3
❑ ❑ USA FE8505 **MIRROR - BIRDIE,** 1985, YEL RECTANGLE MIRROR/POLYBAGED $3-5
❑ ❑ USA FE8506 **COMB - CAPTAIN,** 1985, RED $1-2
❑ ❑ USA FE8561 **M C INSERT/CARDBOARD,** 1985 $20-30
❑ ❑ USA FE8563 **MENU BOARD LUG-ON,** 1985 $20-30
❑ ❑ USA FE8564 **TRANSLITE/SM,** 1985 $25-40
❑ ❑ USA FE8565 **TRANSLITE/LG,** 1985 $35-50

COMMENTS: NATIONAL DISTRIBUTION: USA - DECEMBER 26, 1985-MARCH 9, 1986. OTHER CHARACTER COMBS MAY HAVE BEEN DISTRIBUTED WITH THIS HM.

USA FE8517

USA FE8516

USA FE8518

USA SH8555 USA SH8554

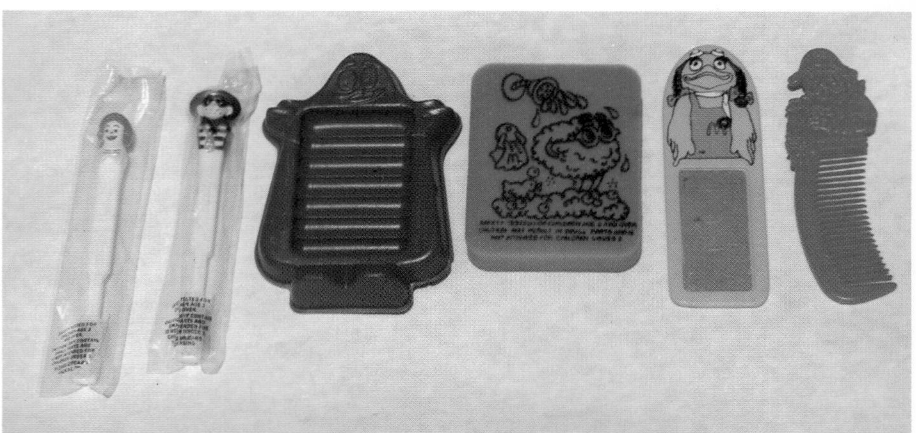

USA FE8501 USA FE8502 USA FE8503 USA FE8504 USA FE8505 USA FE8506

USA FE8565

USA FL8550 USA FL8551 USA FL8552

USA HA8500 USA HA8501 USA HA8502 USA HA8504

USA HA8565

FLORIDA BEACH BALL/OLYMPIC BEACH BALL PROMOTION, 1985

- ❑ ❑ USA FL8550 **BIRDIE,** 1985, BIRDIE IN SAILBOAT W PALM TREES/FLORIDA/BLU $10-12
- ❑ ❑ USA FL8551 **GRIMACE,** 1985, GRIMACE W KAYAK W PALM TREES/FLORIDA/GRN $10-12
- ❑ ❑ USA FL8552 **RONALD,** 1985, RONALD WITH BEACH BALL W PALM TREES/FLORIDA/RED $10-12

COMMENTS: REGIONAL DISTRIBUTION: USA - 1985 IN FLORIDA. THIS COULD HAVE BEEN A REGIONAL PROMOTION.

HALLOWEEN '85 HAPPY MEAL, 1985

- ❑ ❑ USA HA8500 **MCPUNKY,** 1985, ORG PAIL W MCPUNK'N FACE $12-15
- ❑ ❑ USA HA8501 **MCPUNK'N,** 1985, ORG PAIL $10-15
- ❑ ❑ USA HA8502 **MCGOBLIN,** 1985, ORG PAIL $10-15
- ❑ ❑ USA HA8503 **MCJACK,** 1985, ORG PAIL W MCGOBLIN FACE $15-20
- ❑ ❑ USA HA8504 **MCBOO,** 1985, ORG PAIL $10-15
- ❑ ❑ USA HA8565 **TRANSLITE/LG,** 1985 $35-50

COMMENTS: REGIONAL DISTRIBUTION: USA - OCTOBER 11-31, 1985. PAILS WERE TEST MARKETED IN NEW ENGLAND WITH 1985 DATE. LIDS HAD FOUR 1/2" OPENINGS W 12 HOLE GRID MESH.

HOBBY BOX HAPPY MEAL, 1985

- ❑ ❑ USA LU8500 **LUNCH BOX-LT GREEN,** 7 1/2 X 6 X 2 1/2" RECTANGLE W RECT HANDLE/LG M LOGO $8-12
- ❑ ❑ USA LU8501 **LUNCH BOX-YELLOW**, 7 1/2 X 6 X 2 1/2" RECTANGLE W RECT HANDLE/LG M LOGO $8-12
- ❑ ❑ USA LU8502 **LUNCH BOX-RED,** 7 1/2 X 6 X 2 1/2" RECTANGLE W RECT HANDLE/LG M LOGO $8-12
- ❑ ❑ USA LU8503 **LUNCH BOX-BLUE,** 7 1/2 X 6 X 2 1/2" RECTANGLE W RECT HANDLE/LG M LOGO $8-12
- ❑ ❑ USA LU8565 **TRANSLITE/LG,** 1985 $------

COMMENTS: REGIONAL DISTRIBUTION: USA - 1985 IN THE SOUTH. MCD LOGO ON ONE SIDE WITH "WHIRLEY INDUSTRIES, INC., WARREN, PA U.S.A." ON BACK.

USA LU8500 USA LU8501 USA LU8502 USA LU8503

USA LU8565

LITTLE TRAVELERS W LEGO BUILDING SETS/SUPER TRAVELERS HAPPY MEAL, 1985

- ❑ ❑ USA LE8515 **HM BOX,** 1985, **CAPT CROOK/FRY GUY/WHICH CAME FIRST** $40-65
- ❑ ❑ USA LE8516 **HM BOX,** 1985, **GRIMACE/VACATION/MATCH A PATCH** $40-65
- ❑ ❑ USA LE8517 **HM BOX,** 1985, **GRIMACE/SAN FRANCISCO/ANIMAL POWER** $40-65
- ❑ ❑ USA LE8518 **HM BOX,** 1985, **RON/RECORD TRIPS AROUND THE GLOBE** $40-65
- ❑ ❑ USA LE8504 **SET 1 HELICOPTER,** 1984, LEGO/PACKAGED 36P $25-35
- ❑ ❑ USA LE8505 **SET 2 AIRPLANE/PILOT,** 1984, LEGO/PACKAGED 26P $25-35
- ❑ ❑ USA LE8506 **SET 3 TANKER/BOAT,** 1984, LEGO/PACKAGED 38P $25-35
- ❑ ❑ USA LE8507 **SET 4 ROADSTER/RACE CAR,** 1984, LEGO/PACKAGED 19P $25-35
- ❑ ❑ USA LE8526 **DISPLAY W PREMIUMS,** 1985 $150-200
- ❑ ❑ USA LE8565 **TRANSLITE/LITTLE TRAVELERS/LG,** 1985 $65-90
- ❑ ❑ USA LE8566 **TRANSLITE/SUPER TRAVELERS/LG,** 1985 $50-75
- ❑ ❑ USA LE8567 **TRANSLITE/LEGO TOY DAYS/LG,** 1985 $40-50

COMMENTS: LIMITED REGIONAL DISTRIBUTION: USA - OKLAHOMA 1985. PACKAGING IS LIKE LEGO BUILDING SETS HM, EXCEPT BLUE COLOR.

MAGIC SHOW HAPPY MEAL, 1985

- ❑ ❑ USA MA8510 **HM BOX,** 1985, **GHOST WRITER/CRYING QUARTER** $8-12
- ❑ ❑ USA MA8511 **HM BOX,** 1985, **EGGS W LEGS/NICKEL TRICK** $8-12

USA LE8517

USA LE8518

USA LE8515

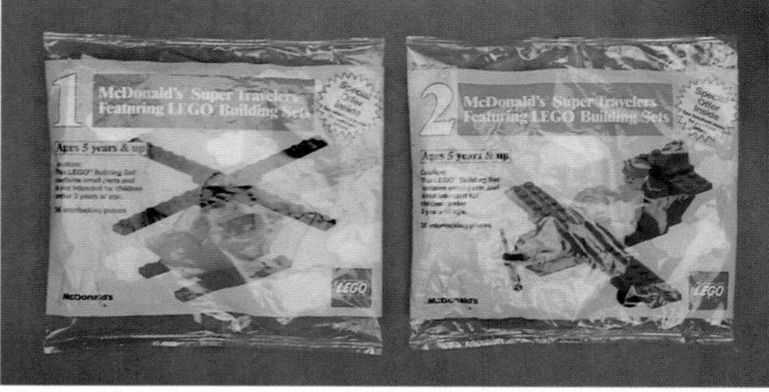

USA LE8504

USA LE8505

USA LE8516

USA LE8506

USA LE8507

USA MA8510

USA MA8511

USA MA8512 USA MA8513

USA MA8500 USA MA8502 USA MA8503 USA MA8504 USA MA8501

USA MA8565

USA MU8512

- ❑ ❑ USA MA8512 **HM BOX,** 1985, **STICKY CARD TRICK** $8-12
- ❑ ❑ USA MA8513 **HM BOX,** 1985, **TUG-O-WAR/MOVING CHECKERS** $8-12
- ❑ ❑ USA MA8500 **MAGIC TRICK - DISAPPEARING HAMBURGLAR,** 1985, 3P/EGG SHAPED/RED or BLU $6-10
- ❑ ❑ USA MA8501 **MAGIC STRING TRICK - BIRDIE,** 1985, ORG or GRN $4-7
- ❑ ❑ USA MA8502 **MAGIC TABLET,** 1985, PAPER/RON HOLDING SLATE $8-12
- ❑ ❑ USA MA8503 **MAGIC PICTURE - RONALD,** 1985, MAKE RONALD APPEAR IN COLOR $6-8
- ❑ ❑ USA MA8504 **MAGIC PICTURE - GRIMACE,** 1985, MAKE GRIMACE APPEAR IN COLOR $6-8
- ❑ ❑ USA MA8561 **M C INSERT/CARDBOARD,** 1985 $25-40
- ❑ ❑ USA MA8562 **HEADER CARD,** 1985 $20-30
- ❑ ❑ USA MA8564 **TRANSLITE/SM,** 1985 $30-45
- ❑ ❑ USA MA8565 **TRANSLITE/LG,** 1985 $45-60

COMMENTS: NATIONAL DISTRIBUTION: USA - APRIL/MAY 1985. THE U-3 TOYS WERE USA SH8554-55.

MUSIC HAPPY MEAL, 1985

- ❑ ❑ USA MU8510 **HM BOX,** 1985, **AUDIENCE CLAPPING** $40-65
- ❑ ❑ USA MU8511 **HM BOX,** 1985, **CAN YOU FIND** $40-65
- ❑ ❑ USA MU8512 **HM BOX,** 1985, **JAM SESSION** $40-65
- ❑ ❑ USA MU8513 **HM BOX,** 1985, **RONALD DIRECTING** $40-65
- ❑ ❑ USA MU8500 **IF YOU'RE HAPPY/RONALD ONE MAN BAND,** 1985, RECORD/FP/BLU PKG $5-7
- ❑ ❑ USA MU8501 **COMING ROUND THE MT/OBJ IS MUSIC,** 1985, RECORD/FP/GRN PKG $5-7
- ❑ ❑ USA MU8502 **GREAT TO BE CRAZY/MUSIC MACHINE,** 1985, RECORD/FP/PNK PKG $5-7
- ❑ ❑ USA MU8503 **HOKEY POKEY/RONALD ORCHESTRA,** 1985, RECORD/FP/YEL PKG $5-7
- ❑ ❑ USA MU8561 **M C INSERT/CARDBOARD,** 1985 $40-55
- ❑ ❑ USA MU8565 **TRANSLITE/LG,** 1985 $50-65

COMMENTS: REGIONAL DISTRIBUTION: USA - 1985 IN ST. LOUIS, MISSOURI. RECORDS ARE FISHER-PRICE 33 1/3 RPM PHONOGRAPH RECORDS.

ON THE GO I HAPPY MEAL, 1985

- ❑ ❑ USA ON8510 **HM BOX,** 1985, **BRIDGE** $5-8
- ❑ ❑ USA ON8511 **HM BOX,** 1985, **DRIVE THRU** $5-8,00

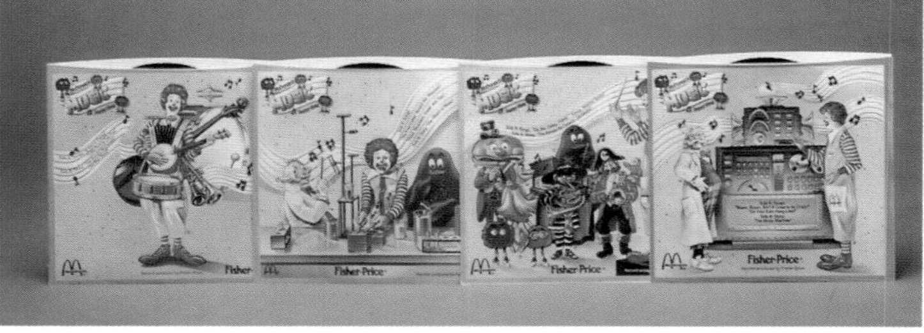

USA MU8500 USA MU8501 USA MU8503 USA MU8502

USA ON8510 USA ON8511

- ❑ ❑ USA ON8512 **HM BOX,** 1985, **GARAGE** $5-8
- ❑ ❑ USA ON8513 **HM BOX,** 1985, **TUNNEL** $5-8
- ❑ ❑ USA ON8501 **BEAD GAME/OCTAGON,** 1985, ON THE ROAD TO MCD/OCTAGON SHAPED $12-15
- ❑ ❑ USA ON8502 **MAGIC SLATE BOARD,** 1985, HAMB/LIFT PAD/ RED RACE CAR $10-12
- ❑ ❑ USA ON8503 **MAGIC SLATE BOARD,** 1985, RONALD/LIFT PAD/YELLOW CAR $10-12
- ❑ ❑ USA ON8504 **BEAD GAME/RECTANGLE,** 1985, STOP & GO/ LOOK/READ N GO/HAMB & RON AT TRAFFIC LIGHT $12-15
- ❑ ❑ USA ON8505 **TRANSFERS/GRIMACE,** 1985, DECALS $7-10
- ❑ ❑ USA ON8564 **TRANSLITE/SM,** 1985 $25-40
- ❑ ❑ USA ON8565 **TRANSLITE/LG,** 1985 $40-55

COMMENTS: REGIONAL DISTRIBUTION: USA - 1985.

PICTURE PERFECT HAPPY MEAL, 1985

- ❑ ❑ USA PI8510 **HM BOX,** 1984, **BIRDIE** $5-8
- ❑ ❑ USA PI8511 **HM BOX,** 1984, **FRY GUYS** $5-8
- ❑ ❑ USA PI8512 **HM BOX,** 1984, **GRIMACE** $5-8
- ❑ ❑ USA PI8513 **HM BOX,** 1984, **RONALD MCDONALD** $5-8
- ❑ ❑ USA PI8501 **MARKERS/COLORING - BLUE or RED/ 5 5/8"** $5-8
- ❑ ❑ USA PI8502 **MARKERS/DRAWING - ORANGE or GREEN/5"** $5-8
- ❑ ❑ USA PI8503 **CRAYONS,** 1985, 3/YEL/RED/BLU IN YEL/GRN BINNEY/SMITH/PROMO PKG $5-8
- ❑ ❑ USA PI8504 **CRAYONS,** 1985, 6/BLK/BLU/BRN/GRN/RED/ YEL/3 5/8" X 5/16" $5-8

USA ON8565

USA PI8510 USA PI8511

USA ON8512 USA ON8513

USA PI8512 USA PI8513

USA ON8501 USA ON8502 USA ON8503

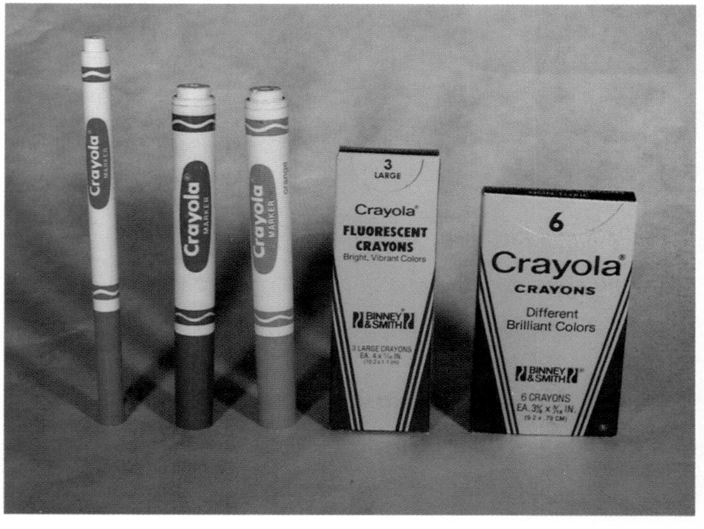

USA ON8504 USA ON8505

USA PI8501 USA PI8502 USA PI8503 USA PI8504

USA PI8565

USA PI8522

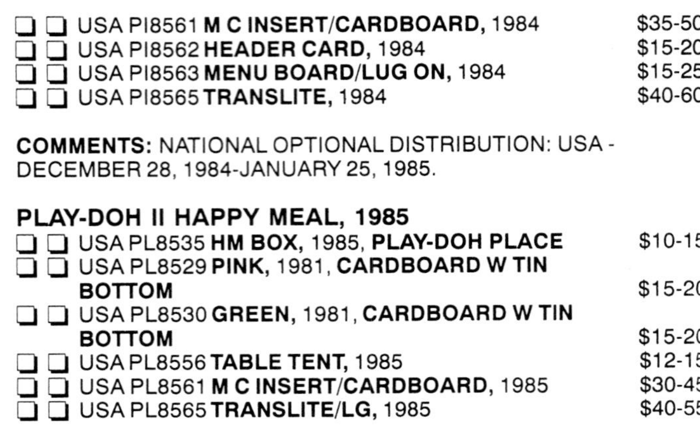

❑ ❑ USA PI8561 **M C INSERT/CARDBOARD,** 1984 $35-50
❑ ❑ USA PI8562 **HEADER CARD,** 1984 $15-20
❑ ❑ USA PI8563 **MENU BOARD/LUG ON,** 1984 $15-25
❑ ❑ USA PI8565 **TRANSLITE,** 1984 $40-60

COMMENTS: NATIONAL OPTIONAL DISTRIBUTION: USA - DECEMBER 28, 1984-JANUARY 25, 1985.

PLAY-DOH II HAPPY MEAL, 1985

❑ ❑ USA PL8535 **HM BOX,** 1985, **PLAY-DOH PLACE** $10-15
❑ ❑ USA PL8529 **PINK,** 1981, **CARDBOARD W TIN BOTTOM** $15-20
❑ ❑ USA PL8530 **GREEN,** 1981, **CARDBOARD W TIN BOTTOM** $15-20
❑ ❑ USA PL8556 **TABLE TENT,** 1985 $12-15
❑ ❑ USA PL8561 **M C INSERT/CARDBOARD,** 1985 $30-45
❑ ❑ USA PL8565 **TRANSLITE/LG,** 1985 $40-55

COMMENTS: REGIONAL DISTRIBUTION: USA - FEBRUARY 15-MARCH 29, 1985 IN KANSAS, MISSOURI, ILLINOIS, TENNESSEE, ARKANSAS, OKLAHOMA, ALABAMA, TEXAS AND INDIANA. USA PL8301-04 WERE AGAIN DISTRIBUTED WITH USA PL8529-30 FOR A TOTAL OF 6 CANS OF PLAY-DOH WITH TIN BOTTOM.

SANTA CLAUS THE MOVIE HAPPY MEAL, 1985

❑ ❑ USA SA8510 **HM BOX,** 1985, **SANTA'S COTTAGE** $5-8
❑ ❑ USA SA8511 **HM BOX,** 1985, **WORKSHOP** $5-8
❑ ❑ USA SA8500 **THE ELVES AT THE TOP OF THE WORLD,** 1985, GRN STORYBOOK $2-3
❑ ❑ USA SA8501 **THE LEGEND OF SANTA CLAUS,** 1985, RED STORYBOOK $2-3

USA PL8535

USA SA8510 USA SA8511

USA PL8529

USA PL8530

USA PL8565

USA SA8500 USA SA8501

- ❑ ❑ USA SA8502 **SLEIGHFULL OF SURPRISES,** 1985, COLORING BOOK $2-3
- ❑ ❑ USA SA8503 **WORKSHOP OF ACTIVITIES,** 1985, COLORING BOOK $2-3
- ❑ ❑ USA SA8542 **COUNTER CARD,** 1985 $15-20
- ❑ ❑ USA SA8555 **TRAY LINER,** 1985 $5-8
- ❑ ❑ USA SA8564 **TRANSLITE/SM,** 1985 $20-30
- ❑ ❑ USA SA8565 **TRANSLITE/LG,** 1985 $35-50

COMMENTS: NATIONAL DISTRIBUTION: USA - NOVEMBER 22-DECEMBER 24, 1985.

SHIP SHAPE II HAPPY MEAL, 1985

- ❑ ❑ USA SH8554 **U-3 GRIMACE IN TUB,** 1985, YEL DATED '85/ GRN DATED '84 $3-4
- ❑ ❑ USA SH8555 **U-3 FRY KID ON DUCK,** 1985, GRN DATED '85/ YEL DATED '84 $3-4
- ❑ ❑ USA SH8301 **HAMBURGLAR SPLASH DASHER,** 1983, WHT TOP/ORG BOTTOM $10-15
- ❑ ❑ USA SH8302 **GRIMACE TUBBY TUGGER,** 1983, PNK TOP/ BLU BOTTOM $10-15
- ❑ ❑ USA SH8303 **CAPT RUB-A-DUB SUB,** 1983, GRN TOP/GRN BOTTOM $10-15
- ❑ ❑ USA SH8304 **RONALD RIVER BOAT,** 1983, YEL TOP/RED BOTTOM $10-15
- ❑ ❑ USA SH8505 **STICKER SHEET - SPLASH DASHER,** 1985 $4-6
- ❑ ❑ USA SH8506 **STICKER SHEET - TUBBY TUGGER,** 1985 $4-6

USA SH8304

USA SH8555 USA SH8554

USA SA8502

USA SA8503

USA SH8303
USA SH8301 USA SH8302

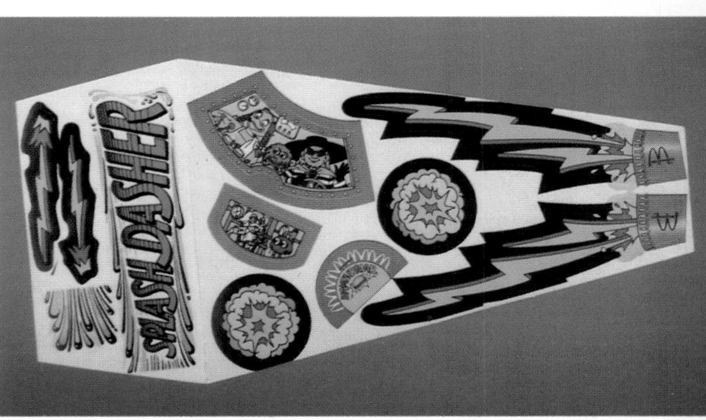

USA SH8505

USA SA8565

USA SH8506

USA SH8507

- ❑ ❑ USA SH8507 **STICKER SHEET - RUB-A-DUB-SUB,** 1985 $4-6
- ❑ ❑ USA SH8508 **STICKER SHEET - RIVER BOAT,** 1985 $4-6
- ❑ ❑ USA SH8518 **STICKER ALBUM, 1984,** HAWAII $15-20
- ❑ ❑ USA SH8526 **DISPLAY/MOTION/1 PREMIUM,** 1985 $150-200
- ❑ ❑ USA SH8561 **M C INSERT/CARDBOARD,** 1985 $20-35
- ❑ ❑ USA SH8563 **MENU BOARD/LUG-ON/3 PREMIUMS,** 1985 $45-60
- ❑ ❑ USA SH8564 **TRANSLITE/SM,** 1985 $20-35
- ❑ ❑ USA SH8565 **TRANSLITE/LG,** 1985 $25-40

COMMENTS: NATIONAL DISTRIBUTION: USA - MAY 31-JUN 30, 1985. USA SH8301-04 WERE REDISTRIBUTED IN 1985 WITH NEW DECALS. NOTE SPLASH DASHER HAD A LARGE DECAL RUNNING THE LENGTH OF THE BOAT VS THE 1983 SMALLER DECAL. ALL SHIP SHAPE '85 DECALS WERE DATED 1985.

STICKER CLUB HAPPY MEAL, 1985

- ❑ ❑ USA ST8510 **HM BOX,** 1984, **CLUB HOUSE MEETING** $6-8
- ❑ ❑ USA ST8511 **HM BOX,** 1984, **STICKER CLUB PARTY** $6-8
- ❑ ❑ USA ST8512 **HM BOX,** 1984, **STICKER CLUB PICNIC** $6-8
- ❑ ❑ USA ST8513 **HM BOX,** 1984, **TRADING DAYS** $6-8
- ❑ ❑ USA ST8501 **STICKER - PAPER,** 1985, 12 STICKERS/ MCDONALDLAND CHARACTERS $4-6
- ❑ ❑ USA ST8502 **STICKER - SCENTED/SCRATCH & SNIFF,** 1985, 5 STICKERS/HAMB/BIRDIE/RON/ FRYGUY/GRI $4-6
- ❑ ❑ USA ST8503 **STICKER - MOTION (3-D),** 1985, 4 STICKERS/ RON/PROF/HAMB/BIRDIE $4-6
- ❑ ❑ USA ST8504 **STICKER - SHINY/PRISMATIC,** 1985, 6 STICKERS/RON/GRIM/ARCHES/BIRDIE/MCCHEESE/ FRIES $4-6

USA SH8565

USA ST8510

USA ST8511

USA ST8512

USA ST8513

USA ST8501

USA ST8503

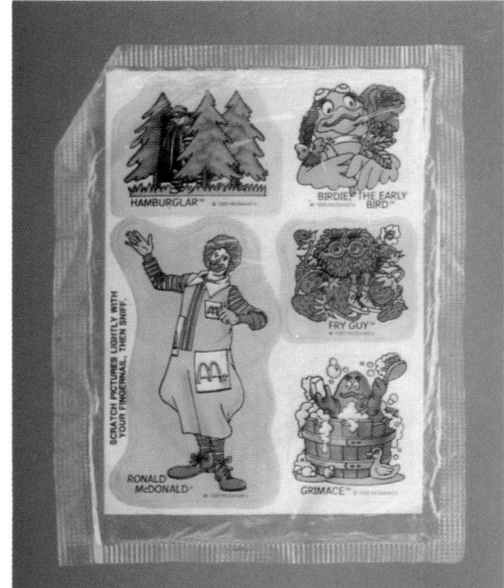

USA ST8504

USA ST8502

❑ ❑ USA ST8505 **STICKER - PUFFY,** 1985, 2 STICKERS/RON/GRIMACE $4-6
❑ ❑ USA ST8561 **M C INSERT/CARDBOARD,** 1985 $25-40
❑ ❑ USA ST8562 **HEADER CARD/PERMANENT DISPLAY,** 1985 $20-30
❑ ❑ USA ST8563 **MENU BOARD LUG-ON,** 1985 $20-30
❑ ❑ USA ST8565 **TRANSLITE/LG,** 1985 $35-50

COMMENTS: NATIONAL DISTRIBUTION: USA - MARCH 11-MAY 19, 1985.

STOMPER MINI I 4X4 PUSH-ALONG/TEST MARKET HAPPY MEAL, 1985

❑ ❑ USA PU8515 **HM BOX,** 1985, **STOMPERS W DESERT** $40-50
❑ ❑ USA PU8507 **U-3 CHEVY VAN,** 1986, YEL W PLASTIC TIRES/BLK WHEELS $4-15
❑ ❑ USA PU8508 **U-3 JEEP RENEGADE,** 1986, ORG W PLASTIC TIRES/BLK WHEELS $4-15
❑ ❑ USA PU8501 **CHEVY S-10 PICK-UP,** 1986, BLK-SIL W RUBBER TIRES/WHT WHEELS $4-15
❑ ❑ USA PU8502 **CHEVY S-10 PICK-UP,** 1986, YEL-PUR W RUBBER TIRES/WHT WHEELS $4-15
❑ ❑ USA PU8503 **CHEVY VAN,** 1986, RED-YEL W RUBBER TIRES/WHT WHEELS $4-15
❑ ❑ USA PU8504 **DODGE RAMPAGE,** 1986, WHT-BLU W RUBBER TIRES/WHT WHEELS $4-15
❑ ❑ USA PU8505 **DODGE RAMPAGE,** 1986, BLU-MAR W RUBBER TIRES/WHT WHEELS $4-15
❑ ❑ USA PU8506 **JEEP RENEGADE 78,** 1986, MAROON-WHT W RUBBER TIRES/WHT WHEELS $4-15
❑ ❑ USA PU8509 **LIMITED EDITION CHEVY/STOMPER,** 1986, WHT/GRN W ARCHES/SEND AWAY $12-15
❑ ❑ USA PU8556 **TABLE TENT,** 1986 $10-12
❑ ❑ USA PU8564 **TRANSLITE/SM,** 1986 $45-65
❑ ❑ USA PU8565 **TRANSLITE/LG,** 1986 $50-75

COMMENTS: LIMITED REGIONAL DISTRIBUTION: USA - SEPTEMBER 6-OCTOBER 17, 1985. THE CARS ARE THE SAME AS OFFERED IN THE STOMPER MINI II 4X4'S HAPPY MEAL, 1986.

TOOTHBRUSH HAPPY MEAL, 1985

❑ ❑ USA TO8501 **RONALD/FULL FIGURE,** 1984, YEL or RED or BLU/TOOTHBRUSH $40-50
❑ ❑ USA TO8565 **TRANSLITE/LG,** 1985 $75-100

COMMENTS: LIMITED REGIONAL DISTRIBUTION: USA - 1985 IN NEW ENGLAND. DISTRIBUTION WAS ONLY FOR A 2 WEEK PERIOD.

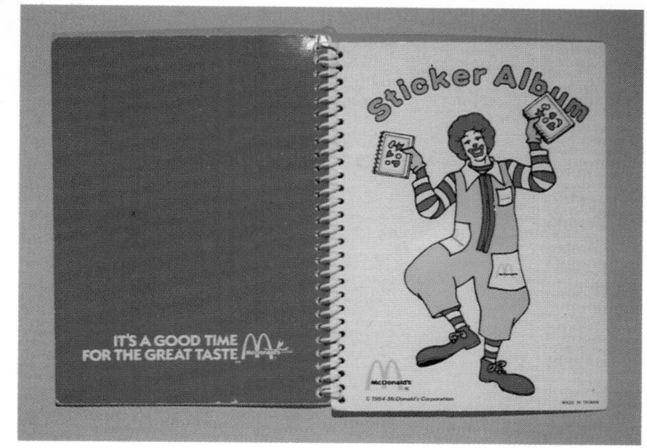

USA ST8518

USA ST8505

USA ST8565

USA PU8509

USA TO8501

USA TO8565

TRANSFORMERS / MY LITTLE PONY HAPPY MEAL, 1985

- ❑ ❑ USA TR8520 **HM BOX,** 1985, **MY LITTLE PONY/TRANSFORMERS** $65-100
- ❑ ❑ USA TR8501 **BRAWN,** 1984, ARMS OUT/GRN-BLU/RED-BLU/BLU-YEL/RED-GRN/RED-YEL/GRN-YEL $12-25
- ❑ ❑ USA TR8502 **BUMBLEBEE,** 1984, SM WINDOW/BLK-RED/WINE-BLK/YEL-BLK/BLK-BLU/BLK-GRN/VIO-BLU/TEAL-BLK $12-25
- ❑ ❑ USA TR8503 **CLIFFJUMPER,** 1984, LG WINDOW/BLK-RED/WINE-BLK/YEL-BLK/BLK-BLU/BLK-GRN/VIO-BLU/TEAL-BLK $12-25
- ❑ ❑ USA TR8504 **GEARS,** 1984, ARMS AT SIDE/GRN-BLU/RED-BLU/BLU-YEL/RED-GRN/RED-YEL/GRN-YEL $12-25
- ❑ ❑ USA TR8510 **CHARM-BLOSSOM,** 1984, PURP W FLOWER IMPRINT/HASBRO $12-20
- ❑ ❑ USA TR8511 **CHARM-BLUE BELLE,** 1984, BLU/GRY W STAR IMPRINT/HASBRO $12-20
- ❑ ❑ USA TR8512 **CHARM-BUTTERSCOTCH,** 1984, BUTTERSCOTCH W BUTTERFLY IMPRINT/HASBRO $12-20
- ❑ ❑ USA TR8513 **CHARM-COTTON CANDY,** 1984, PNK W PAW PRINT IMPRINT/HASBRO $12-20
- ❑ ❑ USA TR8514 **CHARM-MINTY,** 1984, GRN W THREE LEAF IMPRINT/HASBRO $12-20
- ❑ ❑ USA TR8515 **CHARM-SNUZZLE,** 1984, GREY W HEART IMPRINT/HASBRO $12-20
- ❑ ❑ USA TR8555 **TRAY LINER,** 1985 $7-10
- ❑ ❑ USA TR8556 **TABLE TENT,** 1985 $12-15
- ❑ ❑ USA TR8565 **TRANSLITE/LG,** 1985 $50-65

COMMENTS: LIMITED REGIONAL DISTRIBUTION: USA - 1985 IN ST. LOUIS, MISSOURI IN THE SUMMER. PREMIUM MARKINGS - "1985 HASBRO". WITH THE ADDITION OF THE TEAL-BLACK TRANSFORMERS, THE TOTAL NUMBERS ARE: 26 TRANSFORMERS/6 MY LITTLE PONY CHARMS.

USA TR8520

USA TR8501

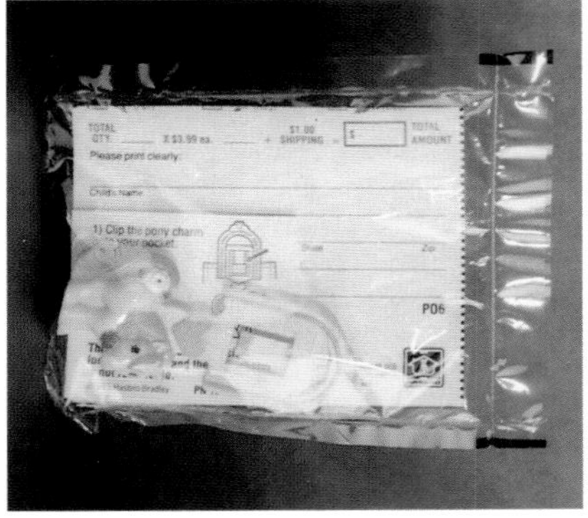
USA TR8513

USA TR8501 USA TR8502 USA TR8503 USA TR8504

USA TR8510 USA TR8511 USA TR8512 USA TR8513 USA TR8514 USA TR8515

WACKY GLASSES/DRINKING STRAW PROMOTION, 1985

- ❑ ❑ USA WA8501 **GLASSES/DRINKING STRAW-BLU,** 1985, BLU GLASSES/CLEAR TUBE $10-12
- ❑ ❑ USA WA8502 **GLASSES/DRINKING STRAW-CLEAR,** 1985, CLEAR GLASSES/CLEAR TUBE $10-12
- ❑ ❑ USA WA8503 **GLASSES/DRINKING STRAW-RED,** 1985, RED GLASSES/CLEAR TUBE $10-12
- ❑ ❑ USA WA8504 **GLASSES/DRINKING STRAW-YEL,** 1985, YEL GLASSES/CLEAR TUBE $10-12

COMMENTS: REGIONAL DISTRIBUTION: USA - 1985-88 DURING CLEAN-UP WEEKS. PAPER INSERT SAYS, "US PATENT...SANSOM INC. PHILA.,PA...MADE IN MEXICO". UNCONFIRMED DISTRIBUTION SITE/DATES.

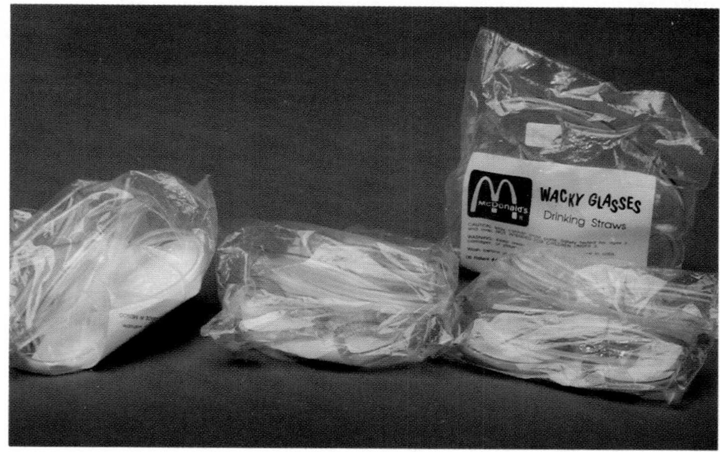

USA WA8504 USA WA8503 USA WA8502 USA WA8501

1986

AIRPORT HAPPY MEAL, 1986
AN AMERICAN TAIL HAPPY MEAL, 1986
BEACH BALL HAPPY MEAL, 1986
BEACHCOMBER HAPPY MEAL, 1986
BERENSTAIN BEARS I TEST MARKET HAPPY MEAL, 1986
COLORFORMS HAPPY MEAL, 1986
CONSTRUX ACTION BUILDING SYSTEM TEST MARKET HAPPY MEAL, 1986
CRAYOLA/CRAYON MAGIC I TEST MARKET HAPPY MEAL, 1986
GLO-TRON SPACESHIP TEST MARKET HAPPY MEAL, 1986
HALLOWEEN '86 HAPPY MEAL, 1986
HAPPY PAIL III HAPPY MEAL, 1986
HIGH FLYING KITE HAPPY MEAL, 1986
LEGO BUILDING SETS III HAPPY MEAL, 1986
METROZOO HAPPY MEAL, 1986
MUPPET BABIES I TEST MARKET HAPPY MEAL, 1986
OLD MCDONALD'S FARM/BARNYARD HAPPY MEAL, 1986
PLAY-DOH III HAPPY MEAL, 1986
STOMPER MINI II 4X4'S HAPPY MEAL, 1986
STORY OF TEXAS HAPPY MEAL, 1986
TINOSAURS HAPPY MEAL, 1986
YOUNG ASTRONAUTS I HAPPY MEAL, 1986
USA/GENERIC PROMOTION, 1986

AIRPORT HAPPY MEAL, 1986

- ❑ ❑ USA AI8675 **HM BOX,** 1986, **CONTROL TOWER** $4-5
- ❑ ❑ USA AI8676 **HM BOX,** 1986, **HANGAR** $4-5
- ❑ ❑ USA AI8677 **HM BOX,** 1986, **TERMINAL** $4-5

USA AI8675

USA AI8676

USA AI8677

USA AI8678

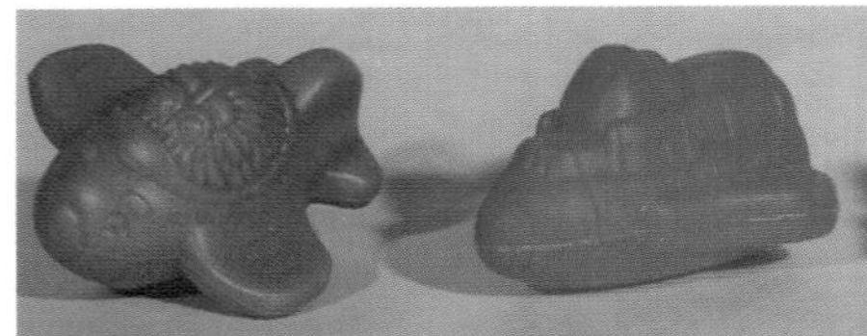

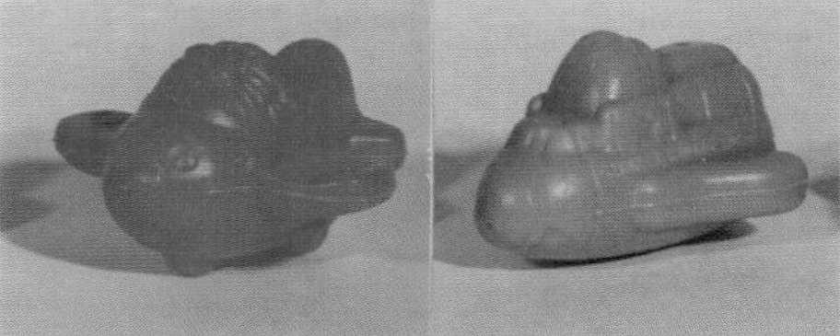

USA AI8666 USA AI8667

USA AI8651 USA AI8652 USA AI8653

USA AI8654

USA AI8655

❑ ❑ USA AI8678 **HM BOX,** 1986, **LUGGAGE CLAIM AREA** $4-5
❑ ❑ USA AI8666 **U-3 FRY GUY FRIENDLY FLYER,** 1986, BLU or RED FLOATER $2-4
❑ ❑ USA AI8667 **U-3 GRIMACE SMILING SHUTTLE,** 1986, BLU or RED FLOATER $2-4
❑ ❑ USA AI8651 **BIG MAC HELICOPTER,** 1982, GRN $4-6
❑ ❑ USA AI8652 **FRY GUY FLYER,** 1986, 3P BLU AIRPLANE $4-6
❑ ❑ USA AI8653 **RONALD SEAPLANE,** 1986, 4P RED AIRPLANE $4-6
❑ ❑ USA AI8654 **GRIMACE ACE,** 1986, 3P PUR BIPLANE $4-6
❑ ❑ USA AI8655 **BIRDIE BENT WING BRAZER,** 1986, 5P PNK BIRDIE THE EARYLY BIRD BENT WING $4-6
❑ ❑ USA AI8661 **M C INSERT/CARDBOARD,** 1986 $15-20
❑ ❑ USA AI8663 **MENU BOARD LUG-ON W 1 PREMIUM,** 1986 $10-15
❑ ❑ USA AI8664 **TRANSLITE/SM,** 1986 $15-20
❑ ❑ USA AI8665 **TRANSLITE/LG,** 1986 $15-25

COMMENTS: NATIONAL DISTRIBUTION: USA - MAR 10-MAY 18, 1986. THE RED AND BLUE BIG MAC HELICOPTERS, LIKE THE GREEN BIG MAC, WERE A 1982 GIVEAWAY AND MAY HAVE BEEN USED AGAIN WITH AIRPORT HM. ALSO DISTRIBUTED WERE THE GREEN AND RED FRY GUY FLYER. THESE WERE USED AS GENERIC FILL-IN PREMIUMS.

AN AMERICAN TAIL HAPPY MEAL, 1986

❑ ❑ USA AN8610 **HM BOX,** 1986, **MOUSE IN THE MOON** $4-5
❑ ❑ USA AN8611 **HM BOX,** 1986, **SLIPPERY SOLUTIONS** $4-5
❑ ❑ USA AN8601 **BOOK - FIEVEL'S BOAT TRIP,** 1986, PNK $2-4
❑ ❑ USA AN8602 **BOOK - FIEVEL'S FRIENDS,** 1986, YEL $2-4

USA AI8665

USA AN8610

❑ ❑ USA AN8603 **BOOK - FIEVEL AND TIGER,** 1986, PURP $2-4
❑ ❑ USA AN8604 **BOOK - TONY AND FIEVEL,** 1986, BLU/GRN $2-4
❑ ❑ USA AN8661 **M C INSERT/CARDBOARD**, 1986 $15-20
❑ ❑ USA AN8664 **TRANSLITE/SM,** 1986 $15-20
❑ ❑ USA AN8665 **TRANSLITE/LG,** 1986 $15-25

COMMENTS: NATIONAL DISTRIBUTION: USA - NOVEMBER 28-DECEMBER 24, 1986.

BEACH BALL HAPPY MEAL, 1986

❑ ❑ USA BE8607 **HM BOX,** 1986, HAVING A WONDERFUL TIME/ BY THE SEA $7-10
❑ ❑ USA BE8601 **BIRDIE,** 1986, ON BEACH W SAND CASTLE/ SAILBOAT/BLU $7-10
❑ ❑ USA BE8602 **GRIMACE,** 1986, W BEACH UMBRELLA W BIRD/FISH/SAILBOAT/YEL $7-10
❑ ❑ USA BE8603 **RONALD,** 1986, WAVING ON BEACH W PELICAN/SEAHORSE/SUN/RED $7-10
❑ ❑ USA BE8665 **TRANSLITE/LG,** 1986 $20-35

COMMENTS: REGIONAL DISTRIBUTION: USA - 1986 IN WASHINGTON, NEW YORK AND COLORADO. MIP PACKAGE CAME POLYBAGGED WITH SCOTCH TAPE ENCLOSURE.

BEACHCOMBER HAPPY MEAL, 1986

❑ ❑ USA BC8650 **PAIL - GRIMACE,** 1986, WHT PAIL $15-20
❑ ❑ USA BC8651 **PAIL - MAYOR,** 1986, WHT PAIL $15-20
❑ ❑ USA BC8652 **PAIL - RONALD,** 1986, WHT PAIL $15-20
❑ ❑ USA BC8665 **TRANSLITE/LG,** 1986 $45-60

COMMENTS: REGIONAL DISTRIBUTION: USA - SOUTH CAROLINA -1986. ALL WHITE PAILS HAD WHT LIDS W A YELLOW SHOVEL.
LIDS HAD FOUR 1/2" HOLES IN EACH.

USA AN8665

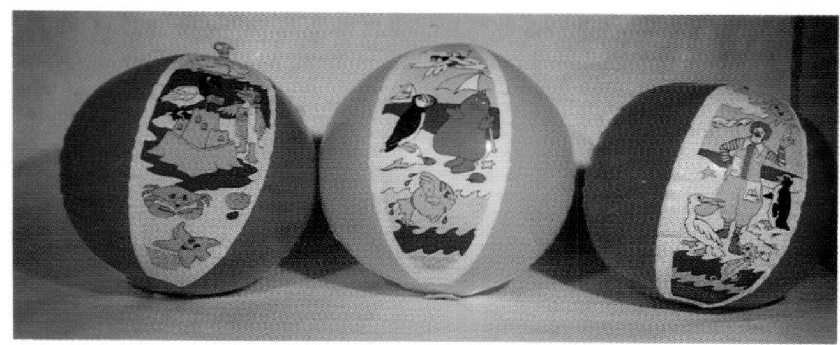

USA BE8601 USA BE8602 USA BE8603

USA BE8607

USA BE8665

USA BC8651 USA BC8652 USA BC8650

USA AN8601 USA AN8602 USA AN8603 USA AN8604

USA BE8665

USA BB8602 USA BB8603 USA BB8601 USA BB8604

BERENSTAIN BEARS I TEST MARKET HAPPY MEAL, 1986

❑ ❑ USA BB8610 **HM BOX,** 1986, **HOLLY WREATH ON FRONT DOOR/ HOLIDAY BARN DANCE** $35-50
❑ ❑ USA BB8611 **HM BOX,** 1986, **BEAR COUNTRY GENERAL STORE/HOLLY WREATH** $35-50
❑ ❑ USA BB8612 **HM BOX,** 1986, **HEAVE-HO!/WREATH ON FRONT DOOR** $35-50
❑ ❑ USA BB8613 **HM BOX,** 1986, **BEAR COUNTRY SCHOOL/ WREATHS ON WINDOWS** $35-50
❑ ❑ USA BB8603 **SET 1 SISTER,** 1986, 2P ARMS AT SIDE ON RED SLED $20-25
❑ ❑ USA BB8602 **SET 2 MAMA,** 1986, 2P FLOCKED HEAD W PANTS W YEL SHOPPING CART $20-25
❑ ❑ USA BB8601 **SET 3 PAPA,** 1986, 2P FLOCKED HEAD W BURNT ORG WHEELBARROW $20-25
❑ ❑ USA BB8604 **SET 4 BROTHER,** 1986, 2P FLOCKED HEAD ON YEL SCOOTER/GRN HANDLE BARS $20-25
❑ ❑ USA BB8664 **TRANSLITE/SM,** 1986 $40-50
❑ ❑ USA BB8665 **TRANSLITE/LG,** 1986 $45-60

COMMENTS: REGIONAL DISTRIBUTION: USA - NOVEMBER 28-DECEMBER 24, 1986 IN EVANSVILLE, INDIANA. THE NATIONAL PROMOTION FOLLOWED IN OCT-NOV 1987 WITH 4 REDESIGNED BOXES AND 2 NEW HAPPY MEAL BAGS. HANDS AND FEET WERE PAINTED, NOT NATURAL RUBBER COLOR; BEARS WERE SOFT RUBBER COMPOSITION.

COLORFORMS HAPPY MEAL, 1986

❑ ❑ USA CO8610 **HM BOX,** 1986, **BEACH PARTY** $4-5
❑ ❑ USA CO8611 **HM BOX,** 1986, **CAMP OUT** $4-5
❑ ❑ USA CO8612 **HM BOX,** 1986, **PICNIC TODAY** $4-5
❑ ❑ USA CO8613 **HM BOX,** 1986, **PLAY DAY** $4-5
❑ ❑ USA CO8606 **U-3 STICKER PLAYSET - GRIMACE/BEACH PARTY,** 1986 $5-8
❑ ❑ USA CO8607 **U-3 STICKER PLAYSET - RONALD/AT THE FARM,** 1986 $5-8

USA CO8610 USA CO8611

USA CO8613

USA CO8612

USA CO8606 USA CO8607

❑ ❑ USA CO8601 **SET 1 BEACH PARTY,** 1986, **GRIMACE** $5-8
❑ ❑ USA CO8602 **SET 2 PICNIC TODAY,** 1986, **HAMBURGLAR** $5-8
❑ ❑ USA CO8603 **SET 3 PLAY DAY,** 1986, **BIRDIE/ EARLY BIRD** $5-8
❑ ❑ USA CO8604 **SET 4 CAMP OUT,** 1986, **PROFESSOR** $5-8
❑ ❑ USA CO8605 **SET 5 FARM,** 1986, **RONALD** $5-8
❑ ❑ USA CO8661 **M C/CARDBOARD,** 1986 $15-25
❑ ❑ USA CO8664 **TRANSLITE/SM,** 1986 $15-25
❑ ❑ USA CO8665 **TRANSLITE/LG,** 1986 $20-35

COMMENTS: LIMITED REGIONAL DISTRIBUTION: USA - DECEMBER 29, 1986-FEBRUARY 1, 1987.

USA CO8665

CONSTRUX ACTION BUILDING SYSTEM TEST MARKET HAPPY MEAL, 1986

❑ ❑ USA CX8610 **HM BOX,** 1986, **COMPUTER QUICK FIX/ REPAIR STATION** $50-75
❑ ❑ USA CX8611 **HM BOX,** 1986, **MARS LANDSCAPE** $50-75
❑ ❑ USA CX8600 **SET 1 CYLINDER,** 1986, CONSTRUX PLASTIC PIECE/DECALS/WHT W GLOW PIECES $35-50
❑ ❑ USA CX8601 **SET 2 CANOPY,** 1986, CONSTRUX PLASTIC PIECE/DECALS/WHT W GLOW PIECES $35-50
❑ ❑ USA CX8602 **SET 3 WING,** 1986, CONSTRUX 12 PLASTIC PIECES/DECALS/WHT W GLOW PIECE $35-50
❑ ❑ USA CX8603 **SET 4 AXEL,** 1986, CONSTRUX PLASTIC PIECE/DECALS/WHT W GLOW PIECES $35-50

USA CO8601 USA CO8602 USA CO8603

USA CO8604 USA CO8605

USA CX8611

USA CX8602 USA CX8601 USA CX8600 USA CX8603

USA CX8600

USA CX8602

USA CX8601

USA CX8603

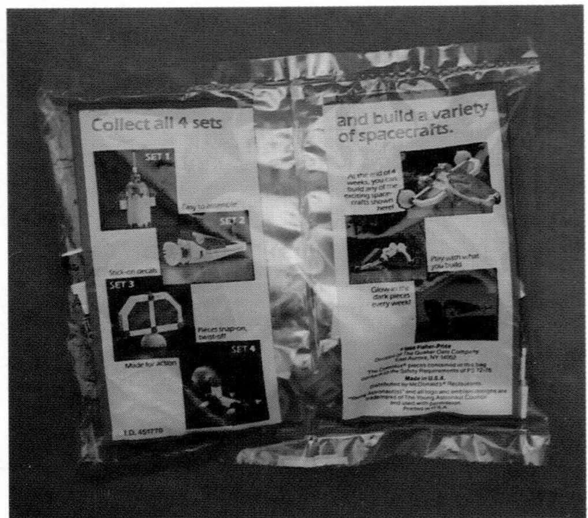

USA CX8626

USA CR8601

❑ ❑ USA CX8626 **DISPLAY,** 1986 $300-400
❑ ❑ USA CX8665 **TRANSLITE/LG,** 1986 $75-100

COMMENTS: REGIONAL DISTRIBUTION: USA - 1986. A SINGLE SPACECRAFT COULD BE BUILT BY PUTTING TOGETHER THE 4 SETS. SETS WERE DISCONTINUED AFTER THE CHALLENGER DISASTER. SET 3 CONTAINED 12 PIECES: 3 STRAIGHT WHITE/2 CURVED WHITE/4 LIGHT BLUE KNOTS/1 GLOW-N-DARK BELL/2 DARK BLUE PANELS.

CRAYOLA/CRAYON MAGIC I TEST MARKET HAPPY MEAL, 1986

❑ ❑ USA CR8610 **HM BOX,** 1986, **QUICK DRAW GRIMACE** $35-50
❑ ❑ USA CR8611 **HM BOX,** 1986, **QUICK DRAW RONALD** $35-50
❑ ❑ USA CR8601 **CIRCLE/STENCIL W 12 CUT-OUTS,** 1986, RED W 4 CRAYONS $15-20
❑ ❑ USA CR8602 **RECTANGLE/STENCIL W 22 CUT-OUTS,** 1986, RED W 4 FLOURESCENT CRAYONS $15-20
❑ ❑ USA CR8603 **TRIANGLE/STENCIL W 10 CUT-OUTS,** 1986, BLU W 1 THICK GRN CRAYOLA MARKER $15-20

USA CR8610

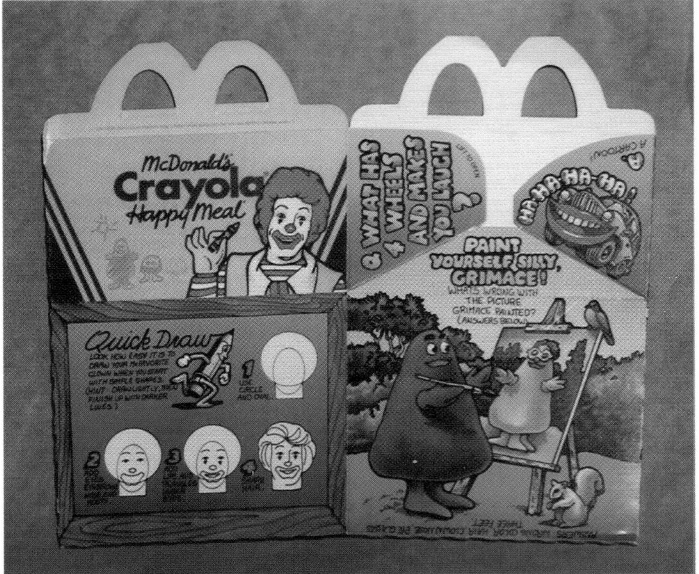

USA CR8611

❑ ❑ USA CR8604 **TRIANGLE/STENCIL W 10 CUT-OUTS,** 1986, BLU W 1 THICK ORG CRAYOLA MARKER $15-20

❑ ❑ USA CR8605 **RIGHT ANGLE/STENCIL W 9 CUT-OUTS,** 1986, BLU W 1 THIN BLUE CRAYOLA MARKER $35-40

❑ ❑ USA CR8606 **RIGHT ANGLE/STENCIL W 9 CUT-OUTS,** 1986, BLU W 1 THIN RED CRAYOLA MARKER $35-40

❑ ❑ USA CR8665 **TRANSLITE/LG,** 1986 $40-65

COMMENTS: LIMITED TEST MARKET DISTRIBUTION: USA - 1986. HM USED REDESIGNED PICTURE PERFECT HM BOXES WITH NEW TITLES.

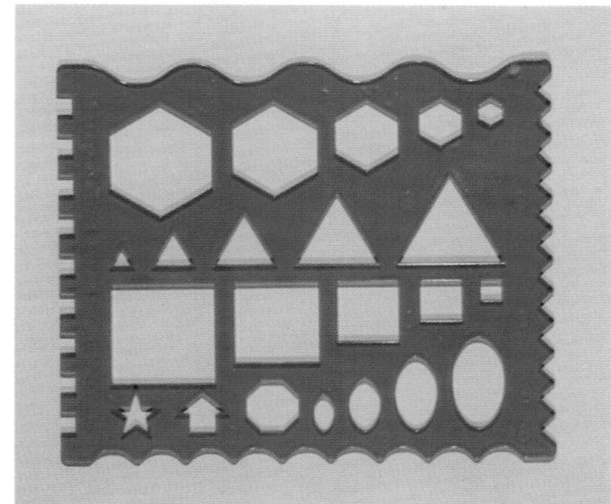

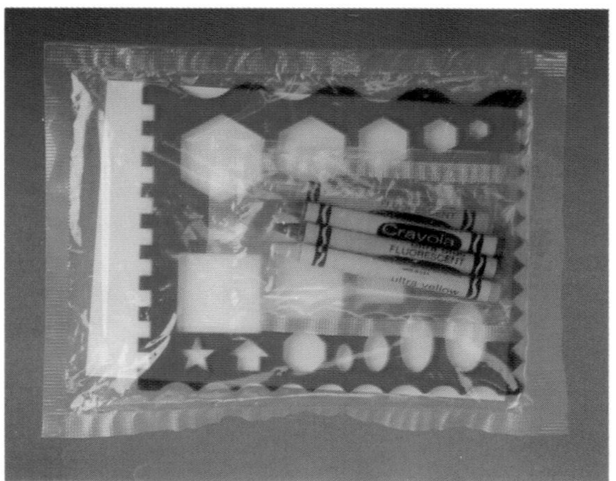

USA CR8602

USA CR8603

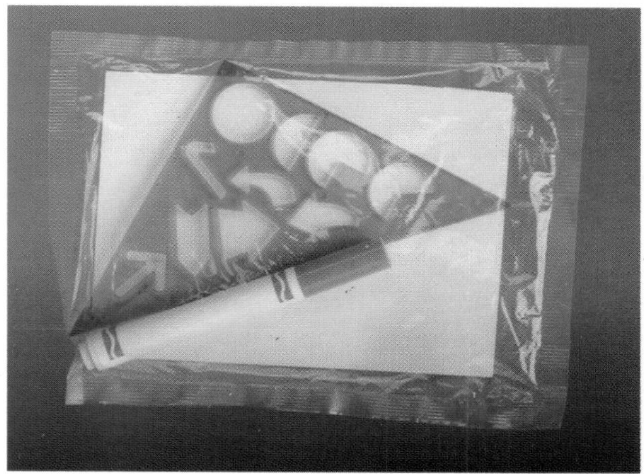

USA CR8604

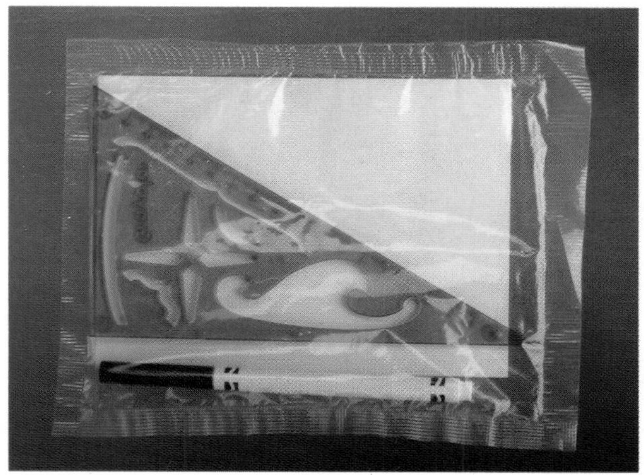

USA CR8605

USA CR8606

GLO-TRON SPACESHIP TEST MARKET HAPPY MEAL, 1986

❑ ❑ USA SP8601 **SPACESHIP 8 WINDOWS,** 1985, METALLIC GREY W GLOW STICKERS $35-50
❑ ❑ USA SP8602 **SPACESHIP W REAR ENGINE,** 1985, METALLIC BLUE W GLOW STICKERS $35-50
❑ ❑ USA SP8603 **SPACESHIP W POINTED NOSE,** 1985, METALLIC GREEN W GLOW STICKERS $35-50
❑ ❑ USA SP8604 **SPACESHIP 4 HUMPS,** 1985, METALLIC RED W GLOW STICKERS $35-50
❑ ❑ USA SP8607 **STICKER SHEET/EACH,** 1986 $20-25
❑ ❑ USA SP8665 **TRANSLITE/MENU BOARD,** 1986 $75-90

COMMENTS: REGIONAL DISTRIBUTION: USA - 1986. THE SPACESHIPS HAVE A SHINY METALLIC FLAKE FINISH. THE SPACESHIPS WERE THE VACUFORM HAPPY MEAL CONTAINERS AND THE PREMIUM. THE STICKERS ARE GLOW-IN-DARK, NOT SPACESHIPS THEMSELVES.

HALLOWEEN '86 HAPPY MEAL, 1986

❑ ❑ USA HA8601 **MCBOO,** 1986, ORGN PAIL/ORG LID $1-2
❑ ❑ USA HA8602 **MCGOBLIN,** 1986, ORG PAIL/ORG LID $1-2
❑ ❑ USA HA8603 **MCPUNK'N,** 1986, ORG PAIL/ORG LID $1-2
❑ ❑ USA HA8661 **M C INSERT/CARDBOARD,** 1986 $10-15
❑ ❑ USA HA8665 **TRANSLITE/LG,** 1986 $12-20

COMMENTS: NATIONAL DISTRIBUTION: USA - OCTOBER 13-30, 1986. LIDS HAD SIX 1/2" HOLES. HOLES WERE LARGE ENOUGH FOR FINGER ENTRAPMENT.

HAPPY PAIL III HAPPY MEAL, 1986

❑ ❑ USA HP8690 **BEACH,** 1986, BLU HANDLE/TOP/YEL SHOVEL $5-7
❑ ❑ USA HP8691 **PARADE,** 1986, ORG HANDLE/TOP/RED RAKE $5-7
❑ ❑ USA HP8692 **PICNIC,** 1986, YEL HANDLE/TOP/RED RAKE $5-7

USA SP8604 USA SP8603 USA SP8602 USA SP8601

USA SP8607

USA HA8665

USA HA8601 USA HA8602 USA HA8603

USA HP8690 USA HP8691 USA HP8692

❑ ❑ USA HP8693 **TREASURE HUNT,** 1986, RED HANDLE/TOP/ YEL SHOVEL $5-7
❑ ❑ USA HP8694 **VACATION,** 1986, GRN HANDLE/TOP/RED RAKE $5-7
❑ ❑ USA HP8626 **DISPLAY,** 1986 $35-50
❑ ❑ USA HP8641 **CEILING DANGLER,** 1986, W 5 PAILS $50-65
❑ ❑ USA HP8660 **COUNTER MAT,** 1986 $15-25
❑ ❑ USA HP8664 **TRANSLITE/SM,** 1986 $20-35
❑ ❑ USA HP8665 **TRANSLITE/LG,** 1986 $25-40

COMMENTS: NATIONAL DISTRIBUTION: USA - MAY 30-JULY 6, 1986. PAILS CAME WITH EITHER A YEL SHOVEL OR RED RAKE.

HIGH FLYING KITE HAPPY MEAL, 1986

❑ ❑ USA HI8610 **HM BOX,** 1986, **KITES** $85-125
❑ ❑ USA HI8601 **HAMBURGLAR,** 1986, BLK/WHT KITE/GRN STRING HANDLE $45-60
❑ ❑ USA HI8602 **RONALD,** 1986, BLU/WHT KITE/GRN STRING HANDLE $45-60
❑ ❑ USA HI8603 **BIRDIE,** 1986, YEL KITE/GRN STRING HANDLE $45-60

USA HP8665

USA HI8610

USA HP8693 USA HP8694

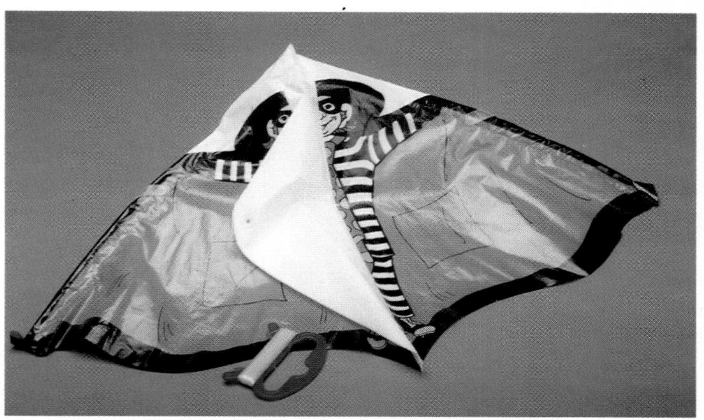
USA HI8601

USA HP8626

USA HI8602

USA HI8603

USA HI8665

❑ ❑ USA HI8664 **TRANSLITE/SM,** 1986 $50-75
❑ ❑ USA HI8665 **TRANSLITE/LG,** 1986 $85-100

COMMENTS: REGIONAL DISTRIBUTION: USA - 1987 IN PARTS OF NEW ENGLAND STATES. A BIRDIE KITE IS SHOWN ON THE PAPER INSERT AND TRANSLITE BUT HAS NOT BEEN IDENTIFIED AS READILY DISTRIBUTED.

LEGO BUILDING SETS III HAPPY MEAL, 1986

❑ ❑ USA LE8610 **HM BOX,** 1986, **CAPT CROOK/TUG BOAT/FRY GUY/WHICH CAME FIRST** $4-7
❑ ❑ USA LE8611 **HM BOX,** 1986, **GRIMACE/VACATION/MATCH THE PATCH** $4-7
❑ ❑ USA LE8612 **HM BOX,** 1986, **GRIMACE/GOLDEN GATE BRIDGE/ANIMAL POWER** $4-7
❑ ❑ USA LE8613 **HM BOX,** 1986, **RM/GLOBE/RECORD TRIPS AROUND THE WORLD** $4-7
❑ ❑ USA LE8604 **U-3 BIRD W EYE,** 1986, DUPLO/RED PKG/5P/AGES 1 1/2-4 $4-6
❑ ❑ USA LE8605 **U-3 BOAT W SAILOR,** 1986, DUPLO/BLU PKG/5P/AGES 1 1/2-4 $4-6
❑ ❑ USA LE8600 **SET A RACE CAR,** 1986, LEGO/RED PKG/16P $4-6
❑ ❑ USA LE8601 **SET B TANKER,** 1986, LEGO/BLUE PKG/27P $4-6
❑ ❑ USA LE8602 **SET C HELICOPTER,** 1986, LEGO/YELLOW PKG/19P $4-6
❑ ❑ USA LE8603 **SET D AIRPLANE,** 1986, LEGO/GREEN PKG/18P $4-6
❑ ❑ USA LE8626 **DISPLAY/PREMIUMS,** 1986 $175-250
❑ ❑ USA LE8641 **DANGLER,** 1986, 6 P CARDBOARD $35-50
❑ ❑ USA LE8661 **M C INSERT/CARBOARD,** 1986 $25-40
❑ ❑ USA LE8664 **TRANSLITE/SM,** 1986 $25-40
❑ ❑ USA LE8665 **TRANSLITE/LG,** 1986 $35-50

COMMENTS: NATIONAL DISTRIBUTION: USA - OCTOBER 31-NOVEMBER 26, 1986.

USA LE8610 USA LE8611 USA LE8613 USA LE8612

USA LE8604 USA LE8605

USA LE8641

USA LE8601 USA LE8603

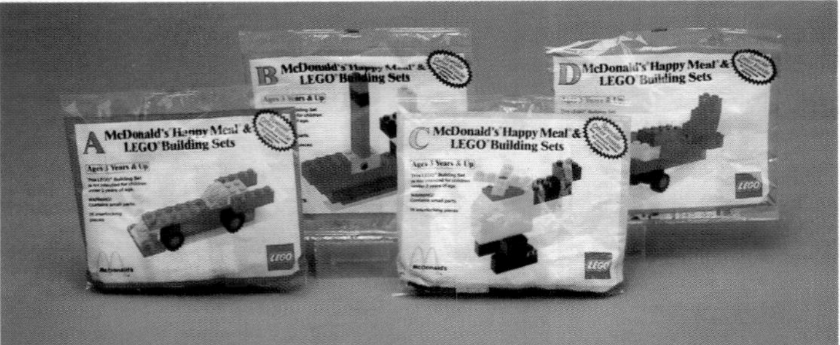

USA LE8600 USA LE8602

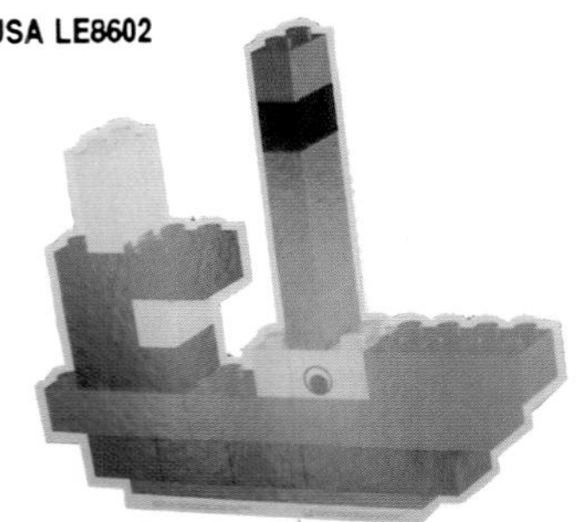

USA LE8665

USA MU8600 USA MU8601 USA MU8603

USA MU8602

USA MU8603 USA MU8601 USA MU8602 USA MU8600

USA BA8615

MUPPET BABIES I TEST MARKET HAPPY MEAL, 1986

- ❑ ❑ USA MU8600 **SET 1 GONZO,** 1986, W SUSPENDERS CROSSED IN BACK/NO SHOES/GRN BIG WHEELS $20-25
- ❑ ❑ USA MU8601 **SET 2 FOZZIE,** 1986, ON YEL HORSE $20-25
- ❑ ❑ USA MU8602 **SET 3 MISS PIGGY,** 1986, W PNK CAR/PNK RIBBON FLAT AGAINST HAIR $20-25
- ❑ ❑ USA MU8603 **SET 4 KERMIT,** 1986, ON RED SKATEBOARD $20-25

COMMENTS: LIMITED TEST MARKET: USA - AUGUST 8-SEPTEMBER 7, 1986 IN SAVANNAH, GEORGIA.

OLD MCDONALD'S FARM/BARNYARD HAPPY MEAL, 1986

- ❑ ❑ USA BA8615 **HM BOX,** 1986, **BARN** $50-75
- ❑ ❑ USA BA8616 **HM BOX,** 1986, **HOUSE** $50-75
- ❑ ❑ USA BA8601 **COW,** 1986, WHT/BRN $6-15
- ❑ ❑ USA BA8602 **HUSBAND,** 1986, WHT SHIRT/GRN PANTS W BRN HAT $6-15
- ❑ ❑ USA BA8603 **HEN,** 1986, WHT $6-15
- ❑ ❑ USA BA8604 **PIG,** 1986, BEIGE $6-15
- ❑ ❑ USA BA8605 **ROOSTER,** 1986, WHT $6-15
- ❑ ❑ USA BA8606 **SHEEP,** 1986, WHT $6-15
- ❑ ❑ USA BA8607 **WIFE,** 1986, BLU DRESS W YEL HAIR $6-20
- ❑ ❑ USA BA8665 **TRANSLITE/LG,** 1986 $65-90

USA BA8616

USA BA8603 USA BA8605

USA BA8601 USA BA8602 USA BA8604 USA BA8606

USA BA8607

COMMENTS: REGIONAL DISTRIBUTION: USA APRIL/MAY - 1986 IN ST. LOUIS, MISSOURI AND TENNESSEE. MINT FIGURINES, MADE BY PLAYMATES CO. CAME IN A CLEAR POLY BAG. ALL FIGURINES/MINT IN CLEAR PACKAGE SAY, "MADE IN HONG KONG." TRANSLITE SHOWS 5 FARM ANIMALS. HOWEVER, THE HEN MAY HAVE BEEN SUBSTITUTED FOR THE ROOSTER IN SOME NEW ENGLAND PROMOTIONS. THE HEN AND THE ROOSTER CAME MIP WITH AND WITHOUT "MADE IN HONG KONG" LOGO. SAME FIGURINES WERE SOLD IN RETAIL STORES.

PLAY-DOH III HAPPY MEAL, 1986

- ❑ ❑ USA PL8690 **HM BOX,** 1986, **CIRCUS ANIMALS** $5-8
- ❑ ❑ USA PL8691 **HM BOX,** 1986, **FARM ANIMALS** $5-8
- ❑ ❑ USA PL8692 **HM BOX,** 1986, **HOUSE PETS** $5-8
- ❑ ❑ USA PL8693 **HM BOX,** 1986, **YESTERDAY'S ANIMALS** $5 -8
- ❑ ❑ USA PL8675 **PINK/HOT PINK,** 1984, PLASTIC CONTAINER $5 -8
- ❑ ❑ USA PL8676 **BLUE,** 1984, PLASTIC CONTAINER $5-8
- ❑ ❑ USA PL8677 **PURPLE,** 1984, PLASTIC CONTAINER $5 -8
- ❑ ❑ USA PL8678 **RED,** 1984, PLASTIC CONTAINER $5 -8
- ❑ ❑ USA PL8679 **GREEN,** 1984, PLASTIC CONTAINER $5 -8
- ❑ ❑ USA PL8680 **YELLOW,** 1984, PLASTIC CONTAINER $5 -8
- ❑ ❑ USA PL8681 **ORANGE,** 1984, PLASTIC CONTAINER $5-8
- ❑ ❑ USA PL8682 **WHITE,** 1984, PLASTIC CONTAINER $5 -8
- ❑ ❑ USA PL8661 **M C INSERT/CARDBOARD,** 1986 $25-40
- ❑ ❑ USA PL8664 **TRANSLITE/SM,** 1986 $25-40
- ❑ ❑ USA PL8665 **TRANSLITE/LG,** 1986 $35-50

COMMENTS: NATIONAL DISTRIBUTION: USA - JULY 7-AUGUST 3, 1986. THE 2 OZ PLASTIC CANS HAD NO MCDONALD'S MARKINGS.

STOMPER MINI II 4X4'S HAPPY MEAL, 1986

- ❑ ❑ USA ST8600 **HM BOX,** 1986, **JALOPY JUMP** $5-8
- ❑ ❑ USA ST8601 **HM BOX,** 1986, **QUICKSAND ALLEY** $5-8
- ❑ ❑ USA ST8602 **HM BOX,** 1986, **RAMBUNCTIOUS RAMP** $5-8
- ❑ ❑ USA ST8603 **HM BOX,** 1986, **THUNDERBOLT PASS** $5-8

USA PL8675 USA PL8676 USA PL8677 USA PL8678

USA PL8679 USA PL8680 USA PL8681 USA PL8682

USA PL8665

USA PL8690 USA PL8691

USA ST8600 USA ST8601

USA PL8692 USA PL8693

USA ST8602 USA ST8603

USA ST8691 USA ST8692 USA ST8693 USA ST8694

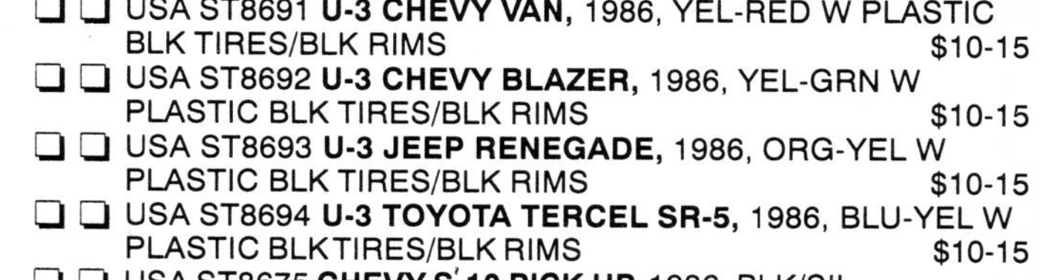

❑ ❑ USA ST8691 **U-3 CHEVY VAN,** 1986, YEL-RED W PLASTIC BLK TIRES/BLK RIMS $10-15
❑ ❑ USA ST8692 **U-3 CHEVY BLAZER,** 1986, YEL-GRN W PLASTIC BLK TIRES/BLK RIMS $10-15
❑ ❑ USA ST8693 **U-3 JEEP RENEGADE,** 1986, ORG-YEL W PLASTIC BLK TIRES/BLK RIMS $10-15
❑ ❑ USA ST8694 **U-3 TOYOTA TERCEL SR-5,** 1986, BLU-YEL W PLASTIC BLKTIRES/BLK RIMS $10-15
❑ ❑ USA ST8675 **CHEVY S-10 PICK UP,** 1986, BLK/SIL STRIPES $6-10

USA ST8677 USA ST8678 USA ST8676 USA ST8675 USA ST8679 USA ST8680

USA ST8681 USA ST8682 USA ST8683 USA ST8684 USA ST8685 USA ST8686

USA ST8687 USA ST8688 USA ST8689 USA ST8690

USA ST8626

❑ ❑ USA ST8676 **CHEVY S-10 PICK UP,** 1986, YEL/PUR STRIPES $6-10
❑ ❑ USA ST8677 **JEEP RENEGADE 78,** 1986, MAROON/WHT STRIPES $6-10
❑ ❑ USA ST8678 **JEEP RENEGADE 78,** 1986, ORG/YEL STRIPES $6-10
❑ ❑ USA ST8679 **CHEVY VAN,** 1986, RED/YEL STRIPES $6-10
❑ ❑ USA ST8680 **CHEVY VAN,** 1986, YEL/ORG STRIPES $6-10
❑ ❑ USA ST8681 **DODGE RAMPAGE PICK UP,** 1986, BLU/MAROON STRIPES $6-10
❑ ❑ USA ST8682 **DODGE RAMPAGE PICK UP,** 1986, WHT/BLU STRIPES $6-10
❑ ❑ USA ST8683 **CHEVY BLAZER 4 X 4,** 1986, YEL/GRN STRIPES $6-10
❑ ❑ USA ST8684 **CHEVY BLAZER 4 X 4,** 1986, RED/GRY STRIPES $6-10
❑ ❑ USA ST8685 **AMC EAGLE 74,** 1986, BLK/GOLD STRIPES $6-10
❑ ❑ USA ST8686 **AMC EAGLE 74,** 1986, ORG/BLU STRIPES $6-10
❑ ❑ USA ST8687 **FORD RANGER 23 PICK UP,** 1986, ORG/YEL STRIPES $6-10
❑ ❑ USA ST8688 **FORD RANGER 23 PICK UP,** 1986, RED/BLK STRIPES $6-10
❑ ❑ USA ST8689 **TOYOTA TERCEL SR-5 4 X 4,** 1986, BLU/YEL STRIPES $6-10
❑ ❑ USA ST8690 **TOYOTA TERCEL SR-5 4 X 4,** 1986, GREY/MAROON STRIPES $6-10
❑ ❑ USA ST8626 **DISPLAY W PREMIUMS,** 1986 $150-200
❑ ❑ USA ST8661 **M C INSERT/CARDBOARD,** 1986 $25-40
❑ ❑ USA ST8664 **TRANSLITE/SM,** 1986 $25-40
❑ ❑ USA ST8665 **TRANSLITE/LG,** 1986 $30-40
❑ ❑ USA ST8666 **TRANSLITE/VACUFORMED/LG,** 1986 $35-50

COMMENTS: NATIONAL DISTRIBUTION: USA - AUGUST 8-SEPTEMBER 7, 1986. ST. LOUIS TEST MARKET SEPEMBER/OCTOBER 1985 USED 4 CARS. THE U-3 PREMIUMS CAME WITH PLASTIC TIRES / BLACK HUBCAPS (RIMS). THE REGULAR PREMIUMS CAME WITH RUBBER TIRES AND WHITE HUBCAPS (RIMS).

STORY OF TEXAS HAPPY MEAL, 1986

- ❑ ❑ USA TX8610 **HM BOX,** 1986, **ALAMO/ARMADILLO** $------
- ❑ ❑ USA TX8601 **AUSTIN/BOOK - PART 1/THE BEGINNING,** 1986, 46 PAGES/KTVV-TV 36 AUSTIN $75-150
- ❑ ❑ USA TX8602 **AUSTIN/BOOK - PART 2/INDEPENDENCE,** 1986, 47 PAGES/KTVV-TV 36 AUSTIN $75-150
- ❑ ❑ USA TX8603 **AUSTIN/BOOK - PART 3/THE FRONTIER,** 1986, 46 PAGES/KTVV-TV 36 AUSTIN $75-150
- ❑ ❑ USA TX8604 **AUSTIN/BOOK - PART 4/THE 20TH CENTURY,** 46 PAGES/KTVV-TV 36 AUSTIN $75-150
- ❑ ❑ USA TX8605 **MAP,** 1986, "DISCOVER THE STORY OF TEXAS" /SIZE 22" X 24" $------
- ❑ ❑ USA TX8606 **HOUSTON/BOOK - PART 1/THE BEGINNING,** 1986, 46 PAGES/KPRC-TV 2 HOUSTON $65-130
- ❑ ❑ USA TX8607 **HOUSTON/BOOK - PART 2/INDEPENDENCE,** 1986, 47 PAGES/KPRC-TV 2 HOUSTON $65-130
- ❑ ❑ USA TX8608 **HOUSTON/BOOK - PART 3/THE FRONTIER,** 1986, 46 PAGES/KPRC-TV 2 HOUSTON $65-130
- ❑ ❑ USA TX8609 **HOUSTON/BOOK - PART 4/THE 20TH CENTURY,** 46 PAGES/KPRC-TV 2 HOUSTON $65-130
- ❑ ❑ USA TX8665 **TRANSLITE/LG,** 1986 $------

COMMENTS: REGIONAL DISTRIBUTION - 1986 IN AUSTIN AND HOUSTON, TEXAS. BOOKS PUBLISHED BY SHEARER PUBLISHING, FREDERICKSBURG, TEXAS. TWO SETS OF BOOKS WERE DISTRIBUTED -KPRC-TV-2 AND KTVV-TV-36. ANOTHER SET OF 4 BOOKS WAS SOLD BY THE PUBLISHER WITH PART 4 (ONLY) HAVING MCDONALD'S INFORMATION INSIDE THE FRONT COVER. NOT ENOUGH TRANSACTIONS TO DETERMINE PRICE ON BOX, MAP AND TRANSLITE.

USA ST8664

USA ST86

USA TX8610

USA TX8601

USA TX8605

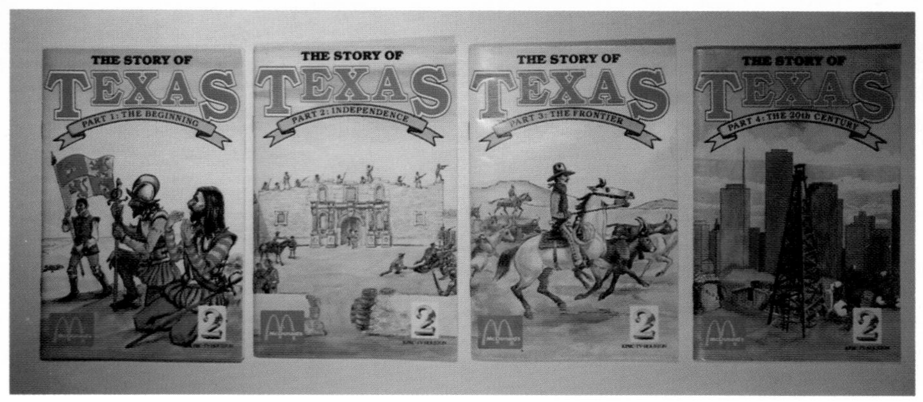

USA TX8606 USA TX8607 USA TX8608 USA TX8609

USA TX8665

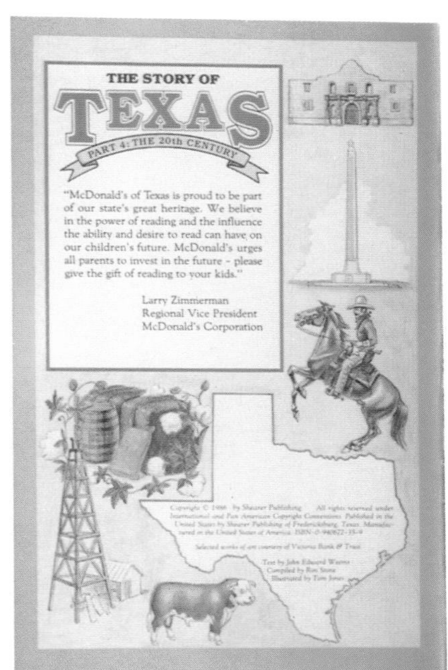

TINOSAURS HAPPY MEAL, 1986

- ❑ ❑ USA TI8615 **HM BOX,** 1986, **TINOSAURS/8 PREMIUMS** $10-15
- ❑ ❑ USA TI8601 **BONES,** 1986, GRN DINOSAUR HOLDING ORANGE STAR W M $6-12
- ❑ ❑ USA TI8602 **DINAH,** 1986, ORG DINOSAUR HOLDING PUR HEART $6-12
- ❑ ❑ USA TI8603 **FERN,** 1986, WHT GIRL TIME TRAVELER HOLDING BRN POT W M $6-12
- ❑ ❑ USA TI8604 **JAD,** 1986, PUR DRAGON W BEAD NECKLACE $6-12
- ❑ ❑ USA TI8605 **KOBBY,** 1986, PNK HORSE W GRN HAIR W WHT FEET KAVE KOLT $6-12
- ❑ ❑ USA TI8606 **LINK,** 1986, PURP ELF DOING HANDSTAND W GREEN OUTFIT $6-12
- ❑ ❑ USA TI8607 **SPELL,** 1986, BLU W GRN HANDS AND FEET SITTING GUMPIES LEADER $6-12
- ❑ ❑ USA TI8608 **TINY,** 1986, PURP DINOSAUR W M ON FOOT $6-12
- ❑ ❑ USA TI8656 **TABLE TENT,** 1986 $8-12
- ❑ ❑ USA TI8660 **COUNTER MAT,** 1986 $15-25
- ❑ ❑ USA TI8664 **TRANSLITE/SM,** 1986 $25-40
- ❑ ❑ USA TI8665 **TRANSLITE/LG,** 1986 $35-50

COMMENTS: REGIONAL DISTRIBUTION: USA - SEPTEMBER 12-OCTOBER 19, 1986 IN ST. LOUIS, MISSOURI. EACH FIGURINES HAS A YELLOW "M" AND CAME POLY-BAGGED.

USA TI8615

USA TI8601 USA TI8602 USA TI8603 USA TI8604

USA TI8605 USA TI8606 USA TI8607 USA TI8608

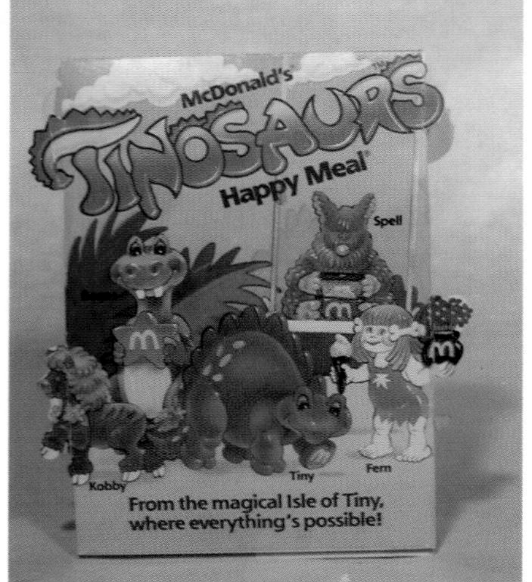

USA TI8656

YOUNG ASTRONAUTS I HAPPY MEAL, 1986

❑ ❑ USA YO8610 **HM BOX,** 1986, **MARS ADVENTURE** $6-8
❑ ❑ USA YO8611 **HM BOX,** 1986, **MOONBASE/ BLUE LETTERS "LUNAR LOOKOUT"** $6-10
❑ ❑ USA YO8612 **HM BOX,** 1986, **REPAIR STATION** $6-8
❑ ❑ USA YO8613 **HM BOX,** 1986, **SPACE STATION** $6-8
❑ ❑ USA YO8614 **HM BOX,** 1986, **MOONBASE/ PINK LETTERS "LUNAR LOOKOUT"** $6-10
❑ ❑ USA YO8601 **APOLLO COMMAND MODULE,** 1986, GRY $8-10
❑ ❑ USA YO8602 **ARGO LAND SHUTTLE,** 1986, RED $8-10
❑ ❑ USA YO8603 **CIRRUS VTOL,** 1986, BLU $8-10
❑ ❑ USA YO8604 **SPACE SHUTTLE,** 1986, WHT $8-10
❑ ❑ USA YO8661 **M C INSERT/CARDBOARD,** 1986 $20-35
❑ ❑ USA YO8664 **TRANSLITE/SM,** 1986 $20-35
❑ ❑ USA YO8665 **TRANSLITE/LG,** 1986 $25-40

USA YO8612 USA YO8613

COMMENTS: REGIONAL DISTRIBUTION: USA - SEPTEMBER 8-OCTOBER 5, 1986. THE "MOONBASE" BOX CAME IN TWO VARIATIONS/COLORS OF "LUNAR LOOKOUT."

USA YO8602 USA YO8603 USA YO8601 USA YO8604

USA YO8610 USA YO8611

USA YO8611 USA YO8614

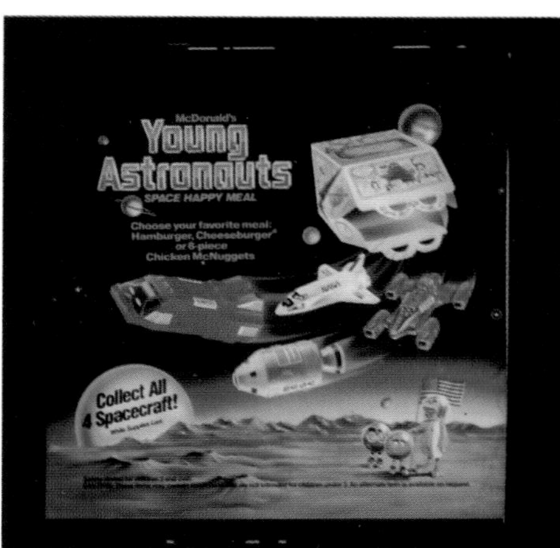

USA YO8665

USA/GENERIC PROMOTION, 1986

- ❑ ❑ USA GE8601 **MIGHTY MAC ROBOT DOZER,** 1986, DARK BLU/4P $5-7
- ❑ ❑ USA GE8602 **FOOTBALL/SUPER SPIN,** 1986, RED or GRN/4P $5-7
- ❑ ❑ USA GE8603 **HELICOPTER-BIG MAC,** 1986, BLU or RED $4-6
- ❑ ❑ USA GE8605 **HELICOPTER-HELLO! COPTER,** 1986, BLU or GRN or RED $4-6
- ❑ ❑ USA GE8608 **GRIMACE MIGHTY MAC SHUTTLE,** 1986, BLU/4P $5-7
- ❑ ❑ USA GE8609 **FINGER PUPPET-BIRDIE,** 1986, YEL $2.50-4
- ❑ ❑ USA GE8610 **FINGER PUPPET-FRY GIRL,** 1986, PURP $2.50-4
- ❑ ❑ USA GE8611 **FINGER PUPPET-GRIMACE,** 1986, PNK $2.50-4
- ❑ ❑ USA GE8612 **FINGER PUPPET-RONALD,** 1986, GRN $2.50-4
- ❑ ❑ USA GE8613 **FRY GUY FRIENDLY FLYER,** 1986, ORG FLOATER $2-4
- ❑ ❑ USA GE8614 **GRIMACE SMILING SHUTTLE,** 1986, ORG FLOATER $2-4

COMMENTS: REGIONAL DISTRIBUTION: USA - 1986 DURING CLEAN-UP WEEKS. THIS IS A SAMPLING OF GENERIC PREMIUMS GIVEN AWAY DURING 1986.

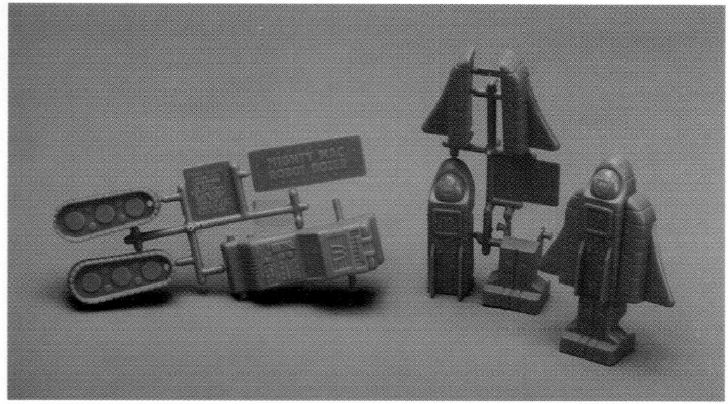

USA GE8601 USA GE8608

USA GE8602

USA GE8605

USA GE8609 USA GE8610 USA GE8611 USA GE8612

USA GE8613 USA GE8614

1987

BERENSTAIN BEARS II HAPPY MEAL, 1987
BOATS 'N FLOATS HAPPY MEAL, 1987
BIGFOOT/WITHOUT ARCHES HAPPY MEAL, 1987
BIGFOOT/WITH ARCHES HAPPY MEAL, 1987
CASTLEMAKERS/SAND CASTLE HAPPY MEAL, 1987
CHANGEABLES '87 HAPPY MEAL, 1987
CRAYOLA II HAPPY MEAL, 1987
DESIGN-O-SAURS HAPPY MEAL, 1987
DISNEY FAVORITES HAPPY MEAL, 1987
FRAGGLE ROCK/DOOZERS I TEST MARKET HM, 1987
GOOD FRIENDS HAPPY MEAL, 1987
HALLOWEEN '87 HAPPY MEAL, 1987
KISSYFUR HAPPY MEAL, 1987
LITTLE ENGINEER HAPPY MEAL, 1987
LUNCH BOX/CHARACTERS PROMOTION, 1987
MCDONALDLAND BAND HAPPY MEAL, 1987
MCDONALDLAND TV LUNCH BOX/LUNCH BUNCH HAPPY MEAL, 1987
METRO ZOO HAPPY MEAL, 1987
MUPPET BABIES II HAPPY MEAL, 1987
POTATO HEAD KIDS I HAPPY MEAL, 1987
REAL GHOSTBUSTERS I HAPPY MEAL, 1987
RUNAWAY ROBOTS HAPPY MEAL, 1987
SUPER SUMMER I TEST MARKET HAPPY MEAL, 1987
ZOO FACE I TEST MARKET HAPPY MEAL, 1987
USA/GENERIC PROMOTION, 1987

USA BB8730

BERENSTAIN BEARS II HAPPY MEAL, 1987

- ❑ ❑ USA BB8730 **HM BOX,** 1987, **BARN DANCE** $2-4
- ❑ ❑ USA BB8731 **HM BOX,** 1987, **BEAR COUNTRY GENERAL STORE** $2-4
- ❑ ❑ USA BB8732 **HM BOX,** 1987, **BEAR COUNTRY SCHOOL** $2-4
- ❑ ❑ USA BB8733 **HM BOX,** 1987, **TREE HOUSE/CLEAN AS A WHISTLE** $2-4
- ❑ ❑ USA BB8724 **U-3 MAMA,** 1987, W PAPER PUNCH OUTS/NO FLOCKING $5-8
- ❑ ❑ USA BB8725 **U-3 PAPA,** 1987, W PAPER PUNCH OUTS/NO FLOCKING $5-8
- ❑ ❑ USA BB8720 **SET 1 SISTER,** 1987, W RED WAGON/ FLOCKED $3-4
- ❑ ❑ USA BB8721 **SET 2 PAPA,** 1987, W BRN WHEELBARROW/ FLOCKED $3-4
- ❑ ❑ USA BB8722 **SET 3 BROTHER,** 1987, W GRN/YEL SCOOTER/FLOCKED $3-4
- ❑ ❑ USA BB8723 **SET 4 MAMA,** 1987, W DRESS W YEL SHOP CART/FLOCKED $3-4
- ❑ ❑ USA BB8726 **DISPLAY/PREM,** 1987 $125-175
- ❑ ❑ USA BB8750 **BUTTON/CREW,** 1987, BERENSTAIN BEARS HAPPY MEALS $5-7
- ❑ ❑ USA BB8764 **TRANSLITE/SM,** 1987 $12-15
- ❑ ❑ USA BB8765 **TRANSLITE/LG,** 1987 $15-20
- ❑ ❑ USA BB8795 **PIN,** 1987, SQUARE/GRN MCD PRESENTS BERENSTAIN BEARS $3-5

COMMENTS: NATIONAL DISTRIBUTION: USA - OCTOBER 30-NOVEMBER 29, 1987. PREMIUM MARKINGS - "S&J BERENSTAIN CHINA" OR "MCDONALDS."

USA BB8731

USA BB8721 USA BB8722 USA BB8720 USA BB8724

USA BB8723 USA BB8725

USA BB8732

USA BB8733

USA BB8726

USA BB8765

USA BB8750

USA BB8795

BIGFOOT/WITHOUT ARCHES HAPPY MEAL, 1987

❑ ❑ USA BI8725 **HM BOX,** 1987, **BIGFOOT GAME W CROSS-WORD PUZZLE** $8-12
❑ ❑ USA BI8701 **FORD BRONCO,** 1987, GRN 1 1/2" WHLS $6-8
❑ ❑ USA BI8702 **FORD PICKUP,** 1987, PURP 1 1/2" WHLS $6-8
❑ ❑ USA BI8703 **MS FORD PICKUP,** 1987, TURQ 1 1/2" WHLS $6-8
❑ ❑ USA BI8704 **SHUTTLE FORD,** 1987, RED W WHT 1 1/2" WHLS $6 -8
❑ ❑ USA BI8705 **FORD BRONCO,** 1987, ORG W 1" WHLS $6 -8
❑ ❑ USA BI8706 **FORD PICKUP,** 1987, LIGHT BLUE 1" WHLS $6-8
❑ ❑ USA BI8707 **MS FORD PICKUP,** 1987, PNK 1" WHLS $6-8
❑ ❑ USA BI8708 **SHUTTLE FORD,** 1987, BLK-SIL 1" WHLS $6-8

COMMENTS: REGIONAL DISTRIBUTION: USA - 1987 IN ST. LOUIS, MISSOURI. EACH BIGFOOT CAR CAME POLYBAGGED WITH NO MCD LOGO MARKINGS. NOTE: IN OTHER REGIONS, SEE BIGFOOT/WITH ARCHES HAPPY MEAL, 1987.

BIGFOOT/WITH ARCHES HAPPY MEAL, 1987

❑ ❑ USA BI8709 **FORD BRONCO,** 1987, GRN 1 1/2" WHLS $6-8
❑ ❑ USA BI8710 **FORD PICKUP,** 1987, PURP 1 1/2" WHLS $6-8
❑ ❑ USA BI8711 **MS FORD PICKUP,** 1987, TURQ 1 1/2" WHLS $6-8
❑ ❑ USA BI8712 **SHUTTLE FORD,** 1987, RED W WHT 1 1/2" WHLS $6-8
❑ ❑ USA BI8713 **FORD BRONCO,** 1987, ORG W 1" WHLS $6-8
❑ ❑ USA BI8714 **FORD PICKUP,** 1987, LIGHT BLU 1" WHLS $6 -8
❑ ❑ USA BI8715 **MS FORD PICKUP,** 1987, PNK W 1" WHLS $6-8
❑ ❑ USA BI8716 **SHUTTLE FORD,** 1987, BLK-SIL 1" WHLS $6-8
❑ ❑ USA BI8764 **TRANSLITE/SM,** 1987 $15-25
❑ ❑ USA BI8765 **TRANSLITE/LG,** 1987 $20-35

COMMENTS: REGIONAL DISTRIBUTION: USA - 1987 IN PARTS OF FLORIDA AND BUFFALO, NEW YORK REGIONS. EACH BIGFOOT CAR HAD MCD LOGO MARKINGS. FOR CARS WITHOUT LOGO/ARCHES, SEE BIGFOOT/WITHOUT ARCHES HAPPY MEAL, 1987.

USA BI8725

USA BI8704 USA BI8703 USA BI8702 USA BI8701

USA BI8708 USA BI8707 USA BI8706 USA BI8705

USA BI8711 USA BI8715 USA BI8710 USA BI8714

USA BI8712 USA BI8716 USA BI8709 USA BI8713

USA BI8765

BOATS' N FLOATS HAPPY MEAL, 1987

❑ ❑ USA BO8700 **HM CONTAINER - GRIMACE SKI BOAT,** 1987, PUR $6-8
❑ ❑ USA BO8701 **HM CONTAINER - FRY KIDS ON RAFT,** 1987, GRN $6-8
❑ ❑ USA BO8702 **HM CONTAINER - MCNUGGET BUDDIES LIFE BOAT,** 1987, ORG $6-8
❑ ❑ USA BO8703 **HM CONTAINER - BIRDIE ON RAFT,** 1987, YEL $6-8
❑ ❑ USA BO8704 **STICKER SHEET - SKI BOAT,** 1987 $3-5
❑ ❑ USA BO8705 **STICKER SHEET - FRY KIDS ON RAFT,** 1987 $3-5
❑ ❑ USA BO8706 **STICKER SHEET - LIFE BOAT,** 1987 $3-5
❑ ❑ USA BO8707 **STICKER SHEET - BIRDIE ON RAFT,** 1987 $3-5
❑ ❑ USA BO8764 **TRANSLITE/SM,** 1987 $12-15
❑ ❑ USA BO8765 **TRANSLITE/LG,** 1987 $15-25

COMMENTS: NATIONAL DISTRIBUTION: USA - AUGUST 7-SEPTEMBER 3, 1987. VACUFORM BOATS SERVE AS THE FOOD CONTAINER AND PREMIUM.

USA BO8701 USA BO8700 USA B08702 USA BO8703

USA BO8765

CASTLEMAKERS/SAND CASTLE HAPPY MEAL, 1987

❑ ❑ USA CA8700 **SAND MOLD - CYLINDRICAL,** 1987, YEL/8" $20-30
❑ ❑ USA CA8701 **SAND MOLD - DOMED,** 1987, BLU/8" $20-30
❑ ❑ USA CA8702 **SAND MOLD - RECTANGLE,** 1987, RED/9" $20-30
❑ ❑ USA CA8703 **SAND MOLD - SQUARE,** 1987, DK BLU/5 1/2" $20-30
❑ ❑ USA CA8764 **TRANSLITE/SM,** 1987 $40-60
❑ ❑ USA CA8765 **TRANSLITE/LG,** 1987 $50-75

COMMENTS: REGIONAL DISTRIBUTION: USA - 1987 IN MICHIGAN, ILLINOIS AND HOUSTON, TEXAS. MCD LOGO M WAS MOLDED INTO EACH TOP SECTION.

USA CA8703
USA CA8700 USA CA8701 USA CA8702

CHANGEABLES '87 HAPPY MEAL, 1987

❑ ❑ USA CH8710 **HM BOX,** 1987, **5 CHANGEABLES W/O MILK SHAKE PICTURE** $10-15
❑ ❑ USA CH8711 **HM BOX,** 1987, **6 CHANGEABLES W MILK SHAKE** $5-8

USA CH8710

USA CH8711

USA CH8711 (BACK)

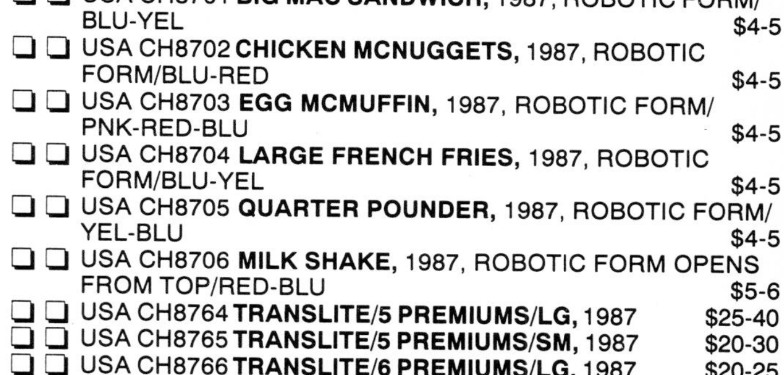

- ❑ ❑ USA CH8701 **BIG MAC SANDWICH,** 1987, ROBOTIC FORM/ BLU-YEL $4-5
- ❑ ❑ USA CH8702 **CHICKEN MCNUGGETS,** 1987, ROBOTIC FORM/BLU-RED $4-5
- ❑ ❑ USA CH8703 **EGG MCMUFFIN,** 1987, ROBOTIC FORM/ PNK-RED-BLU $4-5
- ❑ ❑ USA CH8704 **LARGE FRENCH FRIES,** 1987, ROBOTIC FORM/BLU-YEL $4-5
- ❑ ❑ USA CH8705 **QUARTER POUNDER,** 1987, ROBOTIC FORM/ YEL-BLU $4-5
- ❑ ❑ USA CH8706 **MILK SHAKE,** 1987, ROBOTIC FORM OPENS FROM TOP/RED-BLU $5-6
- ❑ ❑ USA CH8764 **TRANSLITE/5 PREMIUMS/LG,** 1987 $25-40
- ❑ ❑ USA CH8765 **TRANSLITE/5 PREMIUMS/SM,** 1987 $20-30
- ❑ ❑ USA CH8766 **TRANSLITE/6 PREMIUMS/LG,** 1987 $20-25
- ❑ ❑ USA CH8767 **TRANSLITE/6 PREMIUMS/SM,** 1987 $15-20

COMMENTS: REGIONAL DISTRIBUTION: USA - 1987. THE 1987 CHANGEABLES DO NOT HAVE PAINTED HANDS, SEE NEW FOOD CHANGEABLES FOR PAINTED CHARACTERISTICS, 1989.

USA CH8701 USA CH8702 USA CH8703 USA CH8704 USA CH8705 USA CH8706

USA CH8765

USA CH8767

CRAYOLA II HAPPY MEAL, 1987

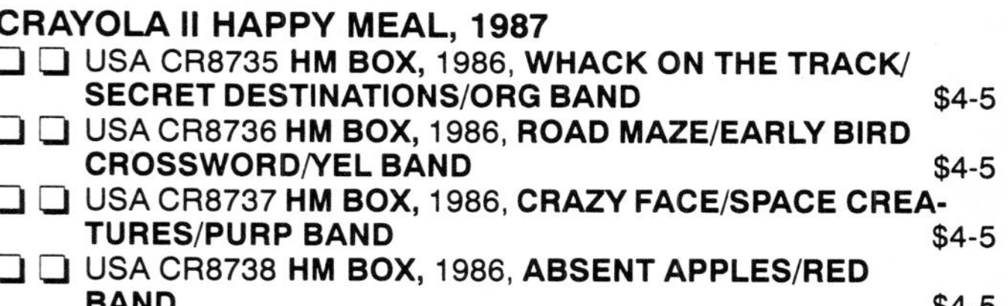

- ❑ ❑ USA CR8735 **HM BOX,** 1986, **WHACK ON THE TRACK/ SECRET DESTINATIONS/ORG BAND** $4-5
- ❑ ❑ USA CR8736 **HM BOX,** 1986, **ROAD MAZE/EARLY BIRD CROSSWORD/YEL BAND** $4-5
- ❑ ❑ USA CR8737 **HM BOX,** 1986, **CRAZY FACE/SPACE CREATURES/PURP BAND** $4-5
- ❑ ❑ USA CR8738 **HM BOX,** 1986, **ABSENT APPLES/RED BAND** $4-5

McDonald's
Crayola
Happy Meal
What's out of whack on the track?
Secret Destinations

USA CR8735

- ❑ ❑ USA CR8729 **U-3 RONALD ON FIRE ENGINE,** 1986, RED CARDBOARD W 4 CRAYONS $6-12
- ❑ ❑ USA CR8725 **SET 1 HAMBURGLAR IN STEAM ENGINE,** 1986, ORG STEN/7 FIGS W 4 REG CRAYONS $2-5
- ❑ ❑ USA CR8726 **SET 2 EARLYBIRD IN CAR,** 1986, YEL STEN W 9 FIGS THICK GRN OR ORG MARKER $2-5
- ❑ ❑ USA CR8727 **SET 3 GRIMACE IN ROCKET,** 1986, PUR STEN W 10 FIGS 4 FLUORESCENT CRAYONS $2-5
- ❑ ❑ USA CR8728 **SET 4 RONALD ON TRACTOR,** 1986, RED STEN W 7 FIGS W THIN BLU OR RED MAGIC MARKER $2-5
- ❑ ❑ USA CR8745 **HANGING BANNER,** 1987, CRAYOLA $20-25

USA CR8736

USA CR8737

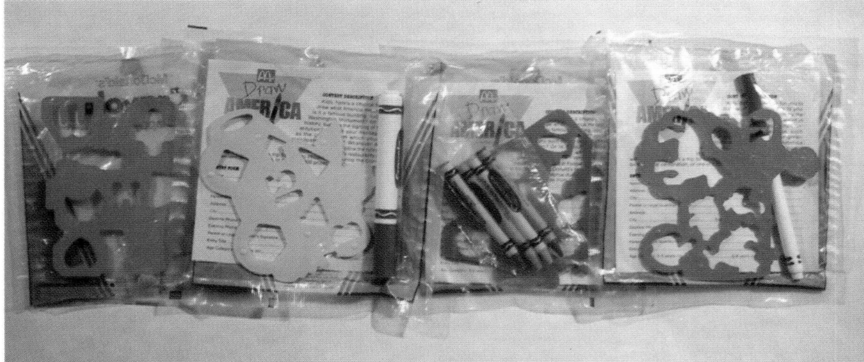

USA CR8725 USA CR8726 USA CR8727 USA CR8728

USA CR8738

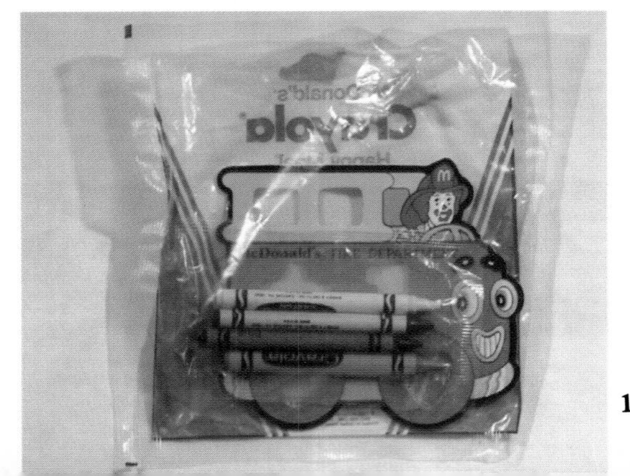

USA CR8729

USA CR8745

USA CR8750

USA CR8765

USA CR8760

USA DE8712 USA DE8711 USA DE8713

USA DE8710

❑ ❑ USA CR8750 **BUTTON,** 1986, COLLECT CRAYOLA/RECT-ANGLE $4-6
❑ ❑ USA CR8760 **COUNTER MAT,** 1986 $10-15
❑ ❑ USA CR8761 **M C INSERT/CARDBOARD,** 1986 $25-35
❑ ❑ USA CR8763 **MENU BOARD LUG-ON W 1 PREMIUM,** 1986 $25-35
❑ ❑ USA CR8764 **TRANSLITE/SM,** 1986 $20-30.00
❑ ❑ USA CR8765 **TRANSLITE/LG,** 1986 $30-45

COMMENTS: NATIONAL DISTRIBUTION: USA - MARCH 20-APRIL 26, 1987. EVANSVILLE, INDIANA CONDUCTED TEST MARKET IN THE SUMMER 1985.

DESIGN-O-SAURS HAPPY MEAL, 1987

❑ ❑ USA DE8710 **SET 1 RONALD,** 1987, ON tyRONALDsaurus rex TYRANNOSAURUS/5P RED $8-10
❑ ❑ USA DE8711 **SET 2 GRIMACE,** 1987, ON GRIMACEsaur PTERODACTYL/5P PURP $8-10
❑ ❑ USA DE8712 **SET 3 FRY GUY,** 1987, ON brontoFRY GUY BRONTOSAURUS/5P GRN $8-10
❑ ❑ USA DE8713 **SET 4 HAMBURGLAR,** 1987, ON triceraHAMBURGLAR TRICERATOPS/5P ORG $8-10

COMMENTS: LIMITED REGIONAL DISTRIBUTION: USA - JULY 2-AUGUST 6, 1987. MCDONALD'S PREMIUM ORDER FORM IDENTIFIED THE PROMOTION AS A SUSTAINING "HAPPY MEAL"/ MIX AND MATCH. PREMIUM MARKINGS -"DESIGN-O-SAURS."

DISNEY FAVORITES HAPPY MEAL, 1987

❑ ❑ USA DI8710 **HM BOX,** 1987, **CINDERELLA W GODMOTHER** $4-5
❑ ❑ USA DI8711 **HM BOX,** 1987, **CINDERELLA & PRINCE DANCING** $4-5
❑ ❑ USA DI8700 **CINDERELLA,** 1987, BOOK/PAINT WITH WATER COUPONS $3-5
❑ ❑ USA DI8701 **LADY AND THE TRAMP,** 1987, BOOK/ STICKER $3-5
❑ ❑ USA DI8702 **DUMBO,** 1987, BOOK/PRESS-OUT BOOK $3-5
❑ ❑ USA DI8703 **THE SWORD IN THE STONE,** 1987, BOOK/ ACTIVITY $3-5
❑ ❑ USA DI8763 **MENU BOARD PREM LUG-ON,** 1987 $14-20
❑ ❑ USA DI8764 **TRANSLITE/SM,** 1987 $15-25
❑ ❑ USA DI8765 **TRANSLITE/LG,** 1987 $20-35

COMMENTS: NATIONAL DISTRIBUTION: USA - NOVEMBER 30-DECEMBER 24, 1987.

USA DI8711

USA DI8701

USA DI8700

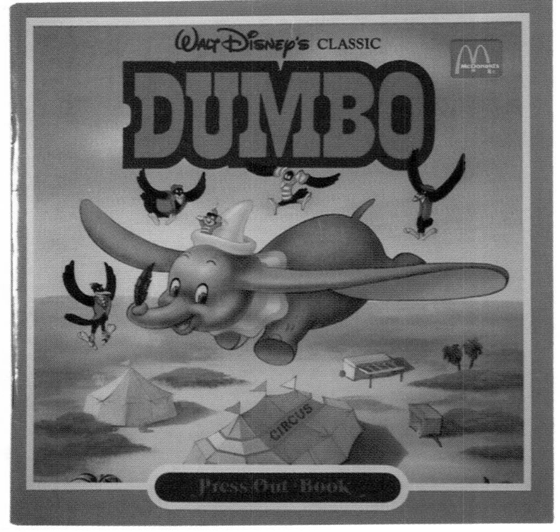

USA DI8765

USA DI8702

USA DI8703

FRAGGLE ROCK/DOOZERS I TEST MARKET HAPPY MEAL, 1987

❑ ❑ USA FR8700 **SET 1 GOBO,** 1987, IN CARROT/WHEELS OFFSET/WOBBLES/BLU PKG $30-35

❑ ❑ USA FR8701 **SET 2 BULLDOZER,** 1987, ON BULLDOZER/FRIENDS/RED PKG $30-35

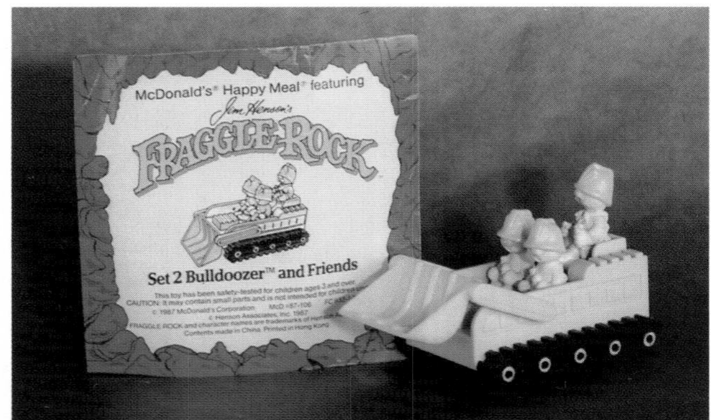

USA FR8700

USA FR8701

USA FR8702

USA FR8703

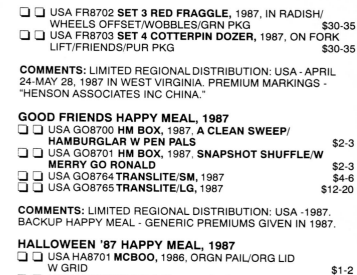

❑ ❑ USA FR8702 **SET 3 RED FRAGGLE,** 1987, IN RADISH/WHEELS OFFSET/WOBBLES/GRN PKG $30-35

❑ ❑ USA FR8703 **SET 4 COTTERPIN DOZER,** 1987, ON FORK LIFT/FRIENDS/PUR PKG $30-35

COMMENTS: LIMITED REGIONAL DISTRIBUTION: USA - APRIL 24-MAY 28, 1987 IN WEST VIRGINIA. PREMIUM MARKINGS - "HENSON ASSOCIATES INC CHINA."

GOOD FRIENDS HAPPY MEAL, 1987

❑ ❑ USA GO8700 **HM BOX,** 1987, **A CLEAN SWEEP/ HAMBURGLAR W PEN PALS** $2-3

❑ ❑ USA GO8701 **HM BOX,** 1987, **SNAPSHOT SHUFFLE/W MERRY GO RONALD** $2-3

❑ ❑ USA GO8764 **TRANSLITE/SM,** 1987 $4-6

❑ ❑ USA GO8765 **TRANSLITE/LG,** 1987 $12-20

COMMENTS: LIMITED REGIONAL DISTRIBUTION: USA -1987. BACKUP HAPPY MEAL - GENERIC PREMIUMS GIVEN IN 1987.

HALLOWEEN '87 HAPPY MEAL, 1987

❑ ❑ USA HA8701 **MCBOO,** 1986, ORGN PAIL/ORG LID W GRID $1-2

❑ ❑ USA HA8702 **MCGOBLIN,** 1986, ORG PAIL/ORG LID W GRID $1-2

❑ ❑ USA HA8703 **MCPUNK'N,** 1986, ORG PAIL/ORG LID W GRID $1-2

❑ ❑ USA HA8764 **TRANSLITE/SM,** 1987 $4-6

❑ ❑ USA HA8765 **TRANSLITE/LG,** 1987 $12-20

COMMENTS: NATIONAL DISTRIBUTION: USA - OCTOBER 16-31, 1987. USA HA8601-03 WERE GIVEN OUT WITH REDESIGNED LIDS. THE 1987 LIDS HAD GRIDS ON THE SIX 1/2" HOLES TO PREVENT FINGER ENTRAPMENT.

USA GO8700

USA GO8701

USA GO8765

USA HA8701 USA HA8702 USA HA8703

USA KI8715

USA KI8704 USA KI8706 USA KI8703 USA KI8705

USA KI8708 USA KI8707 USA KI8702 USA KI8701

USA LI8710 USA LI8711

KISSYFUR HAPPY MEAL, 1987

- ❑ ❑ USA KI8715 **HM BOX,** 1987, **GUS JUGGLING APPLES** $15-20
- ❑ ❑ USA KI8701 **BEEHONIE,** 1985, RABBIT/FLOCKED $10-15
- ❑ ❑ USA KI8702 **DUANE,** 1985, PIG/FLOCKED $10-15
- ❑ ❑ USA KI8703 **FLOYD,** 1985, MALE ALLIGATOR/GREEN/NOT FLOCKED/SMOOTH $8-15
- ❑ ❑ USA KI8704 **GUS,** 1985, FATHER BEAR/BIG BEAR/BROWN/ SMOOTH W ARMS EXTENDED UP $8-15
- ❑ ❑ USA KI8705 **JOLENE,** 1985, FEMALE ALLIGATOR/NOT FLOCKED/SMOOTH $8-15
- ❑ ❑ USA KI8706 **KISSYFUR,** 1985, BABY BEAR/LITTLE BEAR/ BROWN/SMOOTH/ARMS FOLDED $8-15
- ❑ ❑ USA KI8707 **LENNIE,** 1985, WART HOG/BROWN/ FLOCKED $10-15
- ❑ ❑ USA KI8708 **TOOT,** 1985, BEAVER/GREY/FLOCKED $10-15
- ❑ ❑ USA KI8764 **TRANSLITE/SM,** 1987 $35-50
- ❑ ❑ USA KI8765 **TRANSLITE/LG,** 1987 $40-65

COMMENTS: REGIONAL DISTRIBUTION: USA - APRIL/MAY 1987. PREMIUM MARKINGS - “1985 PHIL MENDEZ.”

LITTLE ENGINEER HAPPY MEAL, 1987

- ❑ ❑ USA LI8710 **HM BOX,** 1986, **ROUND HOUSE TRAIN GARAGE/REPAIR PAIRS** $4-6
- ❑ ❑ USA LI8711 **HM BOX,** 1986, **STATION/WAITING ROOM** $4-6
- ❑ ❑ USA LI8712 **HM BOX,** 1986, **TRESTLE/A PLACE FOR EVERYTHING** $4-6
- ❑ ❑ USA LI8713 **HM BOX,** 1986, **TUNNEL/TUNNEL PROJECT** $4-6
- ❑ ❑ USA LI8705 **U-3 FRY GUY HAPPY CAR,** 1985, TEAM MCDONALDS GRN FLOATER $2-4
- ❑ ❑ USA LI8706 **U-3 FRY GUY HAPPY CAR,** 1985, TEAM MCDONALDS YEL FLOATER $2-4
- ❑ ❑ USA LI8707 **U-3 GRIMACE HAPPY TAXI COMPANY,** 1985, GRN FLOATER $2-4
- ❑ ❑ USA LI8708 **U-3 GRIMACE HAPPY TAXI COMPANY,** 1985, YEL FLOATER $2-4
- ❑ ❑ USA LI8700 **BIRDIE'S SUNSHINE SPECIAL,** 1986, TRAIN ENGINE/YEL 3P $5-7
- ❑ ❑ USA LI8701 **FRY GIRL EXPRESS,** 1986, TRAIN ENGINE/BLU 3P W STICKERS $5-7
- ❑ ❑ USA LI8702 **FRY GUY FLYER,** 1986, TRAIN ENGINE/DAY GLO ORG 3P W STICKER $5-7
- ❑ ❑ USA LI8703 **GRIMACE PURPLE STREAK,** 1986, TRAIN ENGINE/PUR 3P W STICKERS $5-7
- ❑ ❑ USA LI8704 **RONALD'S RAILWAY,** 1986, TRAIN ENGINE/ RED 3P W STICKERS $5-7

USA LI8712 USA LI8713

USA LI8707 USA LI8708 USA LI8705 USA LI8706

❑ ❑ USA LI8763 **TRANSLITE/DRIVE-THRU STRIP INSERT,** 1986 $15-20
❑ ❑ USA LI8764 **TRANSLITE/SM,** 1986 $25-40
❑ ❑ USA LI8765 **TRANSLITE/LG,** 1986 $35-50

COMMENTS: REGIONAL DISTRIBUTION: USA - FEBRUARY 9-MARCH 15, 1987

USA LI8700 USA LI8701 USA LI8702 USA LI8703 USA LI8704

LUNCH BOX/CHARACTERS PROMOTION, 1987

❑ ❑ USA LU8700 **GRIMACE BATTING W RON/FRIENDS,** 1987, LUNCH BOX/PURP/WHT $12-15
❑ ❑ USA LU8701 **RONALD PLAYING FOOTBALL,** 1987, LUNCH BOX/BLU/WHT $12-15
❑ ❑ USA LU8702 **RONALD AND FRIENDS RAINBOW,** 1987, LUNCH BOX/YEL/WHT $12-15
❑ ❑ USA LU8703 **RONALD FLYING BUBBLE SPACESHIP,** 1987, LUNCH BOX/RED/WHT $12-15

COMMENTS: REGIONAL DISTRIBUTION: USA - 1987 IN SOUTHERN STATES.

USA LI8765

MCDONALDLAND BAND HAPPY MEAL, 1987

❑ ❑ USA MC8710 **HM BOX,** 1986, **BAND CONCERT/ONE MAN BAND** $4-6
❑ ❑ USA MC8711 **HM BOX,** 1986, **CAN YOU FIND/INSTRU RHYME TIME** $4-6
❑ ❑ USA MC8712 **HM BOX,** 1986, **JAM SESSION/SCAVENGER HUNT** $4-6
❑ ❑ USA MC8713 **HM BOX,** 1986, **PROFESSOR AND HAMBURGLAR/BAND LEADER** $4-6

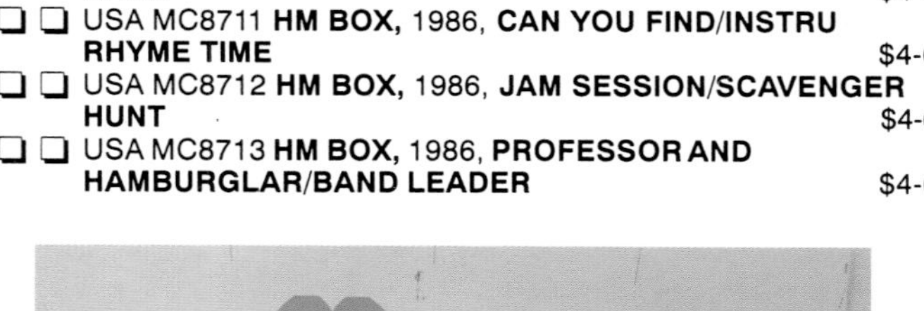

USA LU8700 USA LU8701 USA LU8702 USA LU8703

USA MC8710

USA MC8712

USA MC8711

USA MC8713

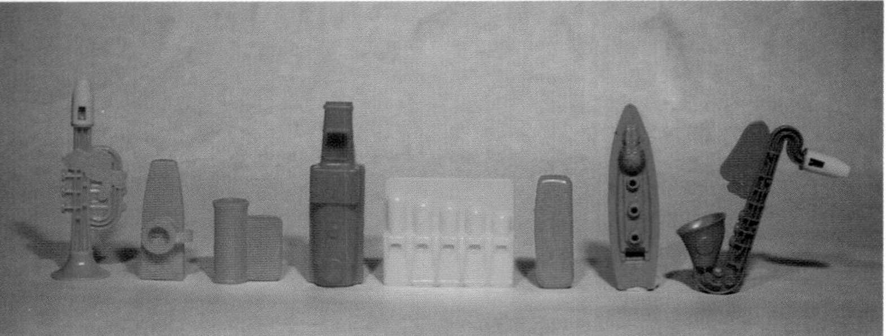

USA MC8700 USA MC8702 USA MC8704 USA MC8706
USA MC8701 USA MC8703 USA MC8705 USA MC8707

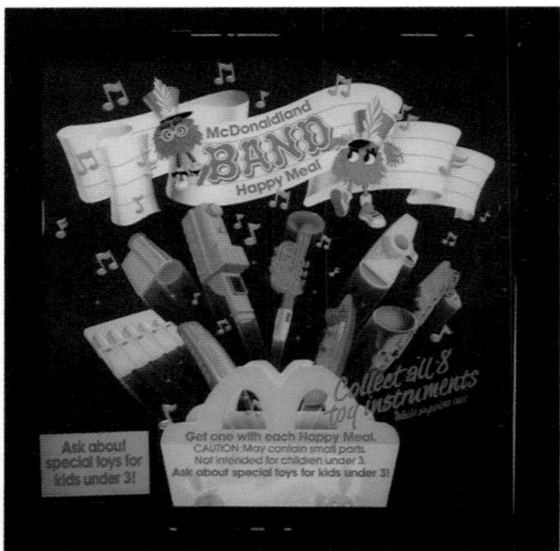

USA MC8764

USA LB8710 USA LB8713

USA LB8716 USA LB8711 USA LB8712 USA LB8719

USA LB8765

- ❑ ❑ USA MC8700 **TRUMPET,** 1986, FRY KID/GREEN $2.50-4
- ❑ ❑ USA MC8701 **KAZOO,** 1986, BIRDIE/PINK $1-1.50
- ❑ ❑ USA MC8702 **SIREN,** 1986, HAMB/ORG $1-1.50
- ❑ ❑ USA MC8703 **TRAIN ENGINE WHISTLE,** 1986, RONALD/PURP $1-1.50
- ❑ ❑ USA MC8704 **PAN PIPES,** 1986, RONALD/YEL $1.50-2
- ❑ ❑ USA MC8705 **HARMONICA,** 1986, RONALD/RED $2.50-4
- ❑ ❑ USA MC8706 **BOAT WHISTLE,** 1986, FRY KID/BLU $1-1.50
- ❑ ❑ USA MC8707 **SAXOPHONE,** 1986, GRIMACE/PURP $1-1.50
- ❑ ❑ USA MC8761 **M C INSERT/CARDBOARD,** 1986 $25-40
- ❑ ❑ USA MC8764 **TRANSLITE/SM,** 1986 $25-40
- ❑ ❑ USA MC8765 **TRANSLITE/LG,** 1986 $35-50

COMMENTS: REGIONAL DISTRIBUTION: USA - APRIL 27-JUNE 4, 1987. THE PAN PIPES AND PURPLE RONALD TRAIN WHISTLE WERE ALSO USED AS U-3 PREMIUMS. NONE WERE POLYBAGGED. DURING THE 1990'S THE PREMIUMS WERE SOLD IN RETAIL STORES ON BLISTER PACKS AND SOLD IN HALLOWEEN TREAT BAGS BY RETAIL STORES.

MCDONALDLAND TV LUNCH BOX/LUNCH BUNCH HAPPY MEAL, 1987

- ❑ ❑ USA LB8710 **LUNCH BOX - BLU,** 1987, **W TV ON BACK/** STICKERS $7-10
- ❑ ❑ USA LB8711 **LUNCH BOX - GRN,** 1987, **W TV ON BACK/** STICKERS $7-10
- ❑ ❑ USA LB8712 **LUNCH BOX - RED,** 1987, **W TV ON BACK/** STICKERS $7-10
- ❑ ❑ USA LB8713 **LUNCH BOX - YEL,** 1987, **W TV ON BACK/** STICKERS $7-10
- ❑ ❑ USA LB8716 **STICKER SHEET - BLU BOX,** 1986 $4-7
- ❑ ❑ USA LB8717 **STICKER SHEET - GRN BOX,** 1986 $4-7
- ❑ ❑ USA LB8718 **STICKER SHEET - RED BOX,** 1986 $4-7
- ❑ ❑ USA LB8719 **STICKER SHEET - YEL BOX,** 1986 $4-7
- ❑ ❑ USA LB8765 **TRANSLITE/LG,** 1987 $50-75

COMMENTS: LIMITED REGIONAL DISTRIBUTION: USA - 1987 IN NEW ENGLAND STATES. STICKER SHEETS CARRIED A 1986 DATE WITH "SAFETY TIPS FOR BACK TO SCHOOL" ON THE BACK.

METROZOO HAPPY MEAL, 1987

- ❑ ❑ USA ME8715 **HM BOX,** 1987, **ELEPHANT/TIGER "ONE OF THE WORLD'S GREAT ZOOS"** $------
- ❑ ❑ USA ME8701 **CHIMP,** BLK W TAN FACE W LEFT LEG BEHIND, 1987 $------
- ❑ ❑ USA ME8702 **ELEPHANT,** GREY W WHT TUSKS, 1987 $------
- ❑ ❑ USA ME8703 **FLAMINGO,** PINK W YEL BILL, 1987 $------
- ❑ ❑ USA ME8704 **TIGER,** WHT W RUST STRIPES, 1987 $------
- ❑ ❑ USA ME8765 **TRANSLITE/LG,** 1987 $------

COMMENTS: LIMITED REGIONAL DISTRIBUTION: USA -FEBRUARY/MARCH 1987 IN THE SOUTH FLORIDA AREA. PREMIUM MARKINGS -"BULLY ...WEST GERMANY." MIP INCLUDES FIGURINE AND LOCAL MAP WITH MIAMI ZOO LOCATION. NOT ENOUGH TRANSACTIONS TO DETERMINE PRICE.

USA ME8715

USA ME8701

USA ME8702

USA ME8703

USA ME8704

USA ME8765

MUPPET BABIES II HAPPY MEAL, 1987

- ❑ ❑ USA MU8730 **HM BOX,** 1987, **FOZZIE BEAR** $2-4
- ❑ ❑ USA MU8731 **HM BOX,** 1987, **GONZO** $2-4
- ❑ ❑ USA MU8732 **HM BOX,** 1987, **KERMIT** $2-4
- ❑ ❑ USA MU8733 **HM BOX,** 1987, **MISS PIGGY'S** $2-4
- ❑ ❑ USA MU8705 **U-3 KERMIT,** 1987, ON SKATES 1P $4-6
- ❑ ❑ USA MU8706 **U-3 MS PIGGY,** 1987, ON SKATES 1P $4-6
- ❑ ❑ USA MU8701 **SET 1 GONZO,** 1987, ON GRN BIG WHLS 2P $2-3
- ❑ ❑ USA MU8702 **SET 2 FOZZIE,** 1987, ON YEL HORSE 2P $2-3
- ❑ ❑ USA MU8703 **SET 3 MS PIGGY,** 1987, IN PNK CAR/PNK RIBBON/2P $2-3
- ❑ ❑ USA MU8704 **SET 4 KERMIT,** 1987, ON RED SKATEBOARD 2P $2-3.0O
- ❑ ❑ USA MU8726 **DISPLAY/PREMIUMS,** 1987 $125-175
- ❑ ❑ USA MU8741 **DANGLER/EACH CHARACTER,** 1987, $5-8
- ❑ ❑ USA MU8745 **REGISTER TOPPER,** 1987 $10-15
- ❑ ❑ USA MU8750 **BUTTON-GONZO,** 1987, RECTANGLE W HEART $3-5

USA MU8701 USA MU8702 USA MU8704 USA MU8706
USA MU8703 USA MU8705

USA MU8732 USA MU8733

USA MU8730 USA MU8731

USA MU8750

USA MU8751

USA MU8726

USA MU8765

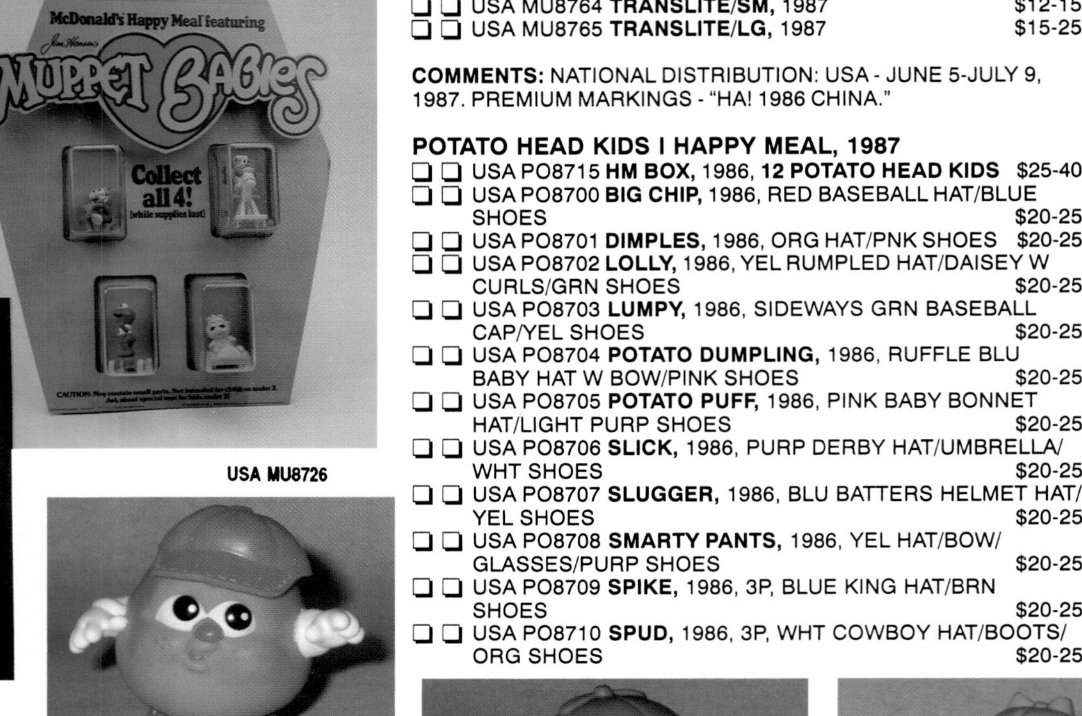

- ❑ ❑ USA MU8751 **BUTTON-MUPPET BABIES,** 1987, W HEART $3-5
- ❑ ❑ USA MU8764 **TRANSLITE/SM,** 1987 $12-15
- ❑ ❑ USA MU8765 **TRANSLITE/LG,** 1987 $15-25

COMMENTS: NATIONAL DISTRIBUTION: USA - JUNE 5-JULY 9, 1987. PREMIUM MARKINGS - "HA! 1986 CHINA."

POTATO HEAD KIDS I HAPPY MEAL, 1987

- ❑ ❑ USA PO8715 **HM BOX,** 1986, **12 POTATO HEAD KIDS** $25-40
- ❑ ❑ USA PO8700 **BIG CHIP,** 1986, RED BASEBALL HAT/BLUE SHOES $20-25
- ❑ ❑ USA PO8701 **DIMPLES,** 1986, ORG HAT/PNK SHOES $20-25
- ❑ ❑ USA PO8702 **LOLLY,** 1986, YEL RUMPLED HAT/DAISEY W CURLS/GRN SHOES $20-25
- ❑ ❑ USA PO8703 **LUMPY,** 1986, SIDEWAYS GRN BASEBALL CAP/YEL SHOES $20-25
- ❑ ❑ USA PO8704 **POTATO DUMPLING,** 1986, RUFFLE BLU BABY HAT W BOW/PINK SHOES $20-25
- ❑ ❑ USA PO8705 **POTATO PUFF,** 1986, PINK BABY BONNET HAT/LIGHT PURP SHOES $20-25
- ❑ ❑ USA PO8706 **SLICK,** 1986, PURP DERBY HAT/UMBRELLA/ WHT SHOES $20-25
- ❑ ❑ USA PO8707 **SLUGGER,** 1986, BLU BATTERS HELMET HAT/ YEL SHOES $20-25
- ❑ ❑ USA PO8708 **SMARTY PANTS,** 1986, YEL HAT/BOW/ GLASSES/PURP SHOES $20-25
- ❑ ❑ USA PO8709 **SPIKE,** 1986, 3P, BLUE KING HAT/BRN SHOES $20-25
- ❑ ❑ USA PO8710 **SPUD,** 1986, 3P, WHT COWBOY HAT/BOOTS/ ORG SHOES $20-25

USA PO8700

USA PO8701

USA PO8703

USA PO8704

USA PO8702

USA PO8705

USA PO8708

USA PO8706

USA PO8707

USA PO8715

USA PO8709

USA PO8710

USA PO8711

- ❑ ❑ USA PO8711 **TULIP,** 1986, 3P, PURP HAT/BLUE SHOES $20-25
- ❑ ❑ USA PO8741 **DANGLER,** 1986 $75-100
- ❑ ❑ USA PO8745 **REGISTER TOPPER/1 PREMIUM BLISTER PACK,** 1986 $40-50
- ❑ ❑ USA PO8765 **TRANSLITE/LG,** 1986 $75-100

COMMENTS: REGIONAL DISTRIBUTION: USA - FEBRUARY 20-MARCH 19, 1987 IN REGIONAL AREAS OF TEXAS, OKLAHOMA AND NEW MEXICO. PACKAGED IN POLYBAG WHICH SAID, "MADE IN CHINA. SAFETY TESTED FOR CHILDREN OF ALL AGES. RECOMMENDED FOR AGES 2 & U.." HASBRO SOLD THE SAME PREMIUMS AT RETAIL OUTLETS. THE COLORS OF HATS AND SHOES DO NOT ALWAYS MATCH THE COLORS ON HM BOX. COLORS LISTED ARE ACTUAL COLORS MCDONALD'S GAVE AS A PREMIUM.

REAL GHOSTBUSTERS I HAPPY MEAL, 1987

- ❑ ❑ USA RE8710 **HM BOX,** 1987, **HEADQUARTERS** $3-5
- ❑ ❑ USA RE8711 **HM BOX,** 1987, **MUSEUM** $3-5
- ❑ ❑ USA RE8712 **HM BOX,** 1987, **PUBLIC LIBRARY** $3-5
- ❑ ❑ USA RE8713 **HM BOX,** 1987, **SCHOOLHOUSE** $3-5
- ❑ ❑ USA RE8706 **U-3 RULER/NOTE PAD,** 1987, X-O-GRAPHIC/MARSHMALLOW PAD $6-10
- ❑ ❑ USA RE8701 **PENCIL CASE,** 1987, REAL GHBS CONTAINMENT CHAMBER $4 -6
- ❑ ❑ USA RE8702 **RULER,** 1987, 6" X-O-GRAPHIC GHBS $4-6
- ❑ ❑ USA RE8703 **NOTE PAD/ERASER,** 1987, MARSHMALLOW PAD/GHB ERASER $4-6
- ❑ ❑ USA RE8704 **PENCIL/PENCIL TOPPER,** 1987, W GRN SLIMER TOPPER $4-6
- ❑ ❑ USA RE8705 **PENCIL SHARPENER,** 1987, WHT GHBS $4-6
- ❑ ❑ USA RE8764 **TRANSLITE/SM,** 1987 $12-20
- ❑ ❑ USA RE8765 **TRANSLITE/LG,** 1987 $15-25

COMMENTS: LIMITED NATIONAL OPTION DISTRIBUTION: USA -SEPTEMBER 4-OCTOBER 15, 1987. ALL PREMIUMS POLYBAGGED EXCEPT FOR PENCIL CASE AND RULER.

USA RE8702

USA RE8710 USA RE8711

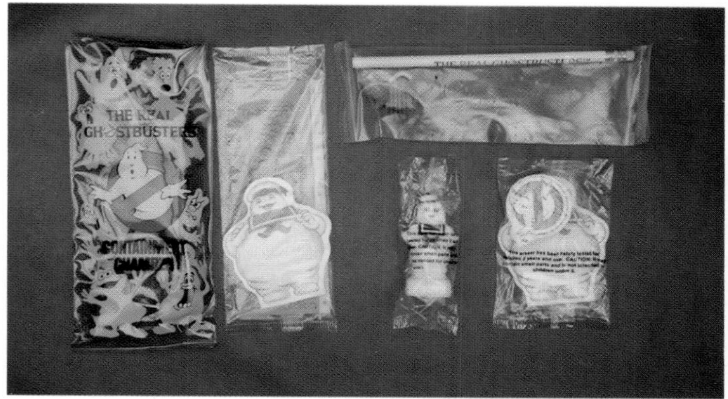
USA RE8701 USA RE8706 USA RE8704 USA RE8705 USA RE8703

USA RE8712 USA RE8713

USA RE8765

USA RU8710

USA RU8700 USA RU8701 USA RU8702 USA RU8703 USA RU8704 USA RU8705

RUNAWAY ROBOTS HAPPY MEAL, 1987

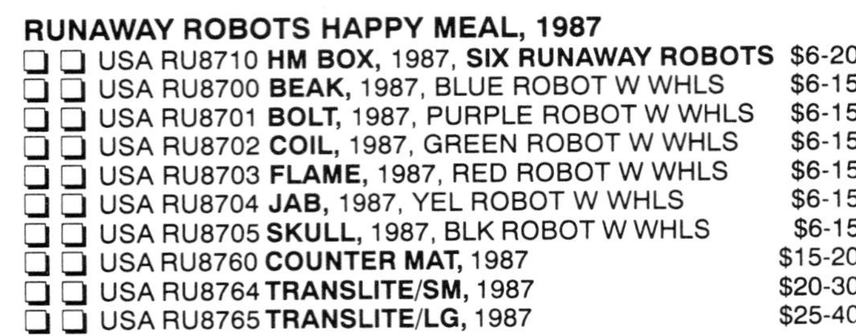

- ❑ ❑ USA RU8710 **HM BOX,** 1987, **SIX RUNAWAY ROBOTS** $6-20
- ❑ ❑ USA RU8700 **BEAK,** 1987, BLUE ROBOT W WHLS $6-15
- ❑ ❑ USA RU8701 **BOLT,** 1987, PURPLE ROBOT W WHLS $6-15
- ❑ ❑ USA RU8702 **COIL,** 1987, GREEN ROBOT W WHLS $6-15
- ❑ ❑ USA RU8703 **FLAME,** 1987, RED ROBOT W WHLS $6-15
- ❑ ❑ USA RU8704 **JAB,** 1987, YEL ROBOT W WHLS $6-15
- ❑ ❑ USA RU8705 **SKULL,** 1987, BLK ROBOT W WHLS $6-15
- ❑ ❑ USA RU8760 **COUNTER MAT,** 1987 $15-20
- ❑ ❑ USA RU8764 **TRANSLITE/SM,** 1987 $20-30
- ❑ ❑ USA RU8765 **TRANSLITE/LG,** 1987 $25-40

COMMENTS: REGIONAL DISTRIBUTION: USA - FEBRUARY 6-MARCH 22, 1987 - ST. LOUIS, MO./NE/MI/ME/MA/TN/AL. PREMIUM MARKINGS -"COLBURN CHINA."

SUPER SUMMER I TEST MARKET HAPPY MEAL, 1987

- ❑ ❑ USA SU8730 **HM BAG,** 1987, **SUPER SUMMER W NO CHARACTERS ON BAG** $10-15
- ❑ ❑ USA SU8701 **SAILBOAT,** 1987, GRIMACE/INFLATABLE/ DATED 1987/NOT 1988 $20-25
- ❑ ❑ USA SU8726 **BEACH BALL,** 1987, WHT/DATED 1987 20-25
- ❑ ❑ USA SU8731 **WATERING CAN,** ND, W MCD LOGO/ BLUE $35-45

COMMENTS: TEST DISTRIBUTION: USA - MAY 22-JUNE 25, 1987 IN FRESNO, CALIFORNIA. USA SU8701 MIP PACKAGE SAYS, "MADE IN TAIWAN" AND NOT, "CONTENTS MADE IN CHINA." BOTTOM OF HM BAG SHOWS THREE PREMIUMS.

ZOO FACE I TEST MARKET HAPPY MEAL, 1987

- ❑ ❑ USA ZO8705 **U-3 TIGER,** 1987, PAPER MASK $35-40
- ❑ ❑ USA ZO8701 **ALLIGATOR,** 1987, W PAAS MAKE-UP KIT DATED 1987/2 SMALL AIR HOLES
- ❑ ❑ USA ZO8702 **MONKEY,** 1987, W PAAS MAKE-UP KIT DATED 1987/THIN ELASTIC $20-25

USA RU8765

USA SU8731

USA SU8730

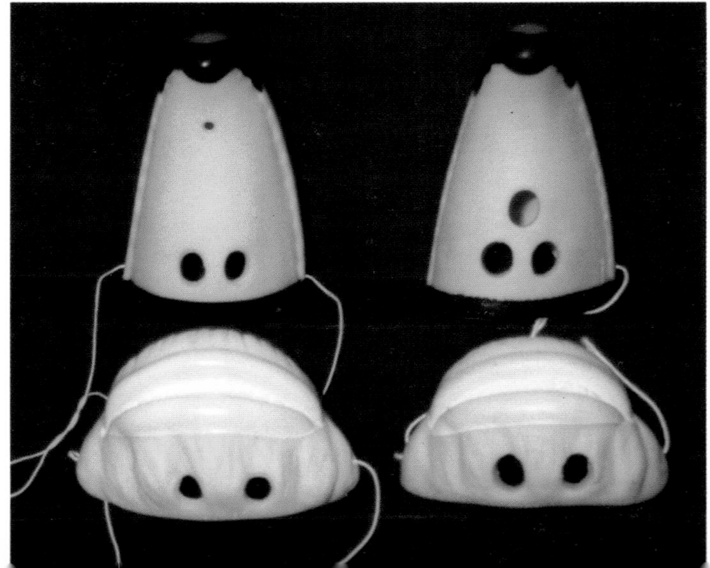
USA ZO8704

USA ZO8703

- ❑ ❑ USA ZO8703 **TIGER,** 1987, W PAAS MAKE-UP KIT DATED 1987/THIN ELASTIC $20-25
- ❑ ❑ USA ZO8704 **TOUCAN,** 1987, W PAAS MAKE-UP KIT DATED 1987/2 SMALL AIR HOLES $20-25

COMMENTS: VERY LIMITED REGIONAL TEST: USA - OCTOBER 2-31, 1987 IN EVANSVILLE, INDIANA. THE TEST MARKET PACKAGE HAS NO MCD # LISTED AND IS DATED 1987/NOT 1988.

USA/GENERIC PROMOTION, 1987

- ❑ ❑ USA GE8701 **COOKIE CUTTER/FUN MOLD-FRY KID,** 1987, GRN or RED $1-1.25
- ❑ ❑ USA GE8703 **COOKIE CUTTER/FUN MOLD-RONALD,** 1987, GRN or RED/W BALLOONS $1-1.25
- ❑ ❑ USA GE8705 **SUPER STICKER SQUARES,** 1987, 9 SCENES/ 100 STICKERS $4-6
- ❑ ❑ USA GE8706 **FRY GUY,** 1987, ON brontoFRY GUY BRONTO-SAURUS/5P YEL $8-10
- ❑ ❑ USA GE8707 **HAMBURGLAR,** 1987, ON triceraHAMBURGLAR TRICERATOPS/5P GRN or PURP $8-10

COMMENTS: REGIONAL DISTRIBUTION: USA - 1987. THESE TOYS ARE A SAMPLING OF PREMIUMS GIVEN AWAY DURING 1987.

USA ZO8701

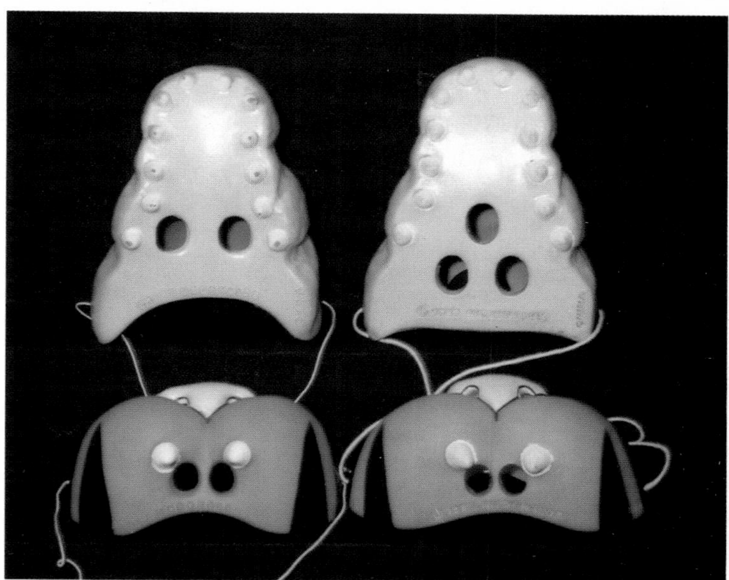

USA ZO8702

1988

BAMBI HAPPY MEAL, 1988
BIG TOP HAPPY MEAL, 1988
BLACK HISTORY HAPPY MEAL, 1988
COSMC CRAYOLA HAPPY MEAL, 1988
DUCK TALES I HAPPY MEAL, 1988
DUCK TALES II HAPPY MEAL, 1988
FLINTSTONE KIDS HAPPY MEAL, 1988
FRAGGLE ROCK II HAPPY MEAL, 1988
GARFIELD I TEST MARKET HAPPY MEAL, 1988
HALLOWEEN '88 HAPPY MEAL, 1988
HOT WHEELS HAPPY MEAL, 1988
LUGGAGE TAG PROMOTION, 1988
MAC TONIGHT TRAVEL TOYS HAPPY MEAL, 1990/1989/1988
MATCHBOX SUPER GT HAPPY MEAL, 1988
MCNUGGET BUDDIES HAPPY MEAL, 1988
MOVEABLES/MCDONALDLAND HAPPY MEAL, 1988
NEW ARCHIES HAPPY MEAL, 1988
OLIVER & COMPANY HAPPY MEAL, 1988
OLYMPIC SPORTS II CLIP-ON BUTTONS HAPPY MEAL, 1988
ON THE GO II LUNCH BOX/BAGS HAPPY MEAL, 1988
PETER RABBIT HAPPY MEAL, 1988
SAILORS HAPPY MEAL, 1988
SEA WORLD OF OHIO HAPPY MEAL, 1988
SEA WORLD OF TEXAS I HAPPY MEAL, 1988
SPORT BALL TEST MARKET HAPPY MEAL, 1990/1988
STORYBOOK MUPPET BABIES HAPPY MEAL, 1988
SUPER SUMMER II HAPPY MEAL, 1988
TURBO MACS I TEST MARKET HAPPY MEAL, 1988
ZOO FACE II/HALLOWEEN '88 HAPPY MEAL, 1988
USA/GENERIC PROMOTION, 1988
USA/MUPPET BABIES HOLIDAY PROMOTION, 1988

USA GE8701 USA GE8703

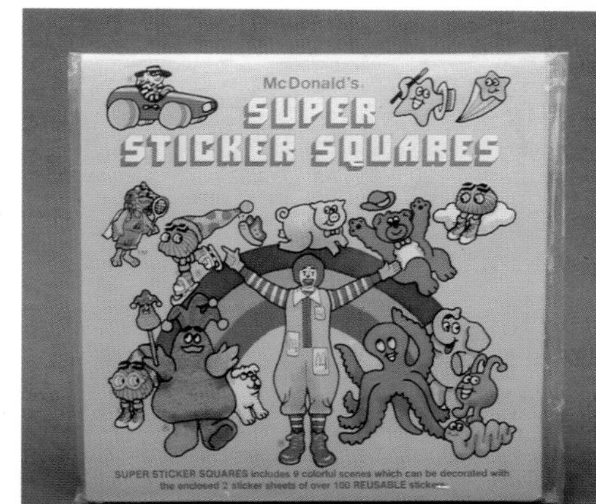

USA GE8705

BAMBI HAPPY MEAL, 1988

- ❑ ❑ USA BA8810 **HM BOX,** 1988, **FALL/SQUIRREL W THUMPER/ BAMBI** $2-4
- ❑ ❑ USA BA8811 **HM BOX,** 1988, **SPRING/BAMBI W MOTHER** $2-4
- ❑ ❑ USA BA8812 **HM BOX,** 1988, **SUMMER/BAMBI AND FALINE W OWL/FROG** $2-4
- ❑ ❑ USA BA8813 **HM BOX,** 1988, **WINTER/BAMBI AND THUMPER** $2-4
- ❑ ❑ USA BA8805 **U-3 BAMBI,** 1988, 1P W BUTTERFLY ON TAIL/ NO MOVING LEGS $4-6

USA GE8707

USA GE8706

USA BA8810 USA BA8811
USA BA8812 USA BA8813

USA BA8805 USA BA8801 USA BA8803
USA BA8806 USA BA8807 USA BA8802 USA BA8804

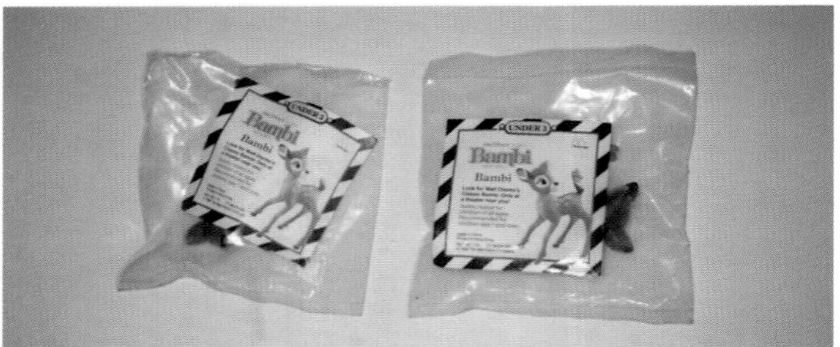

USA BA8806 USA BA8805

USA BA8826

USA BA8865

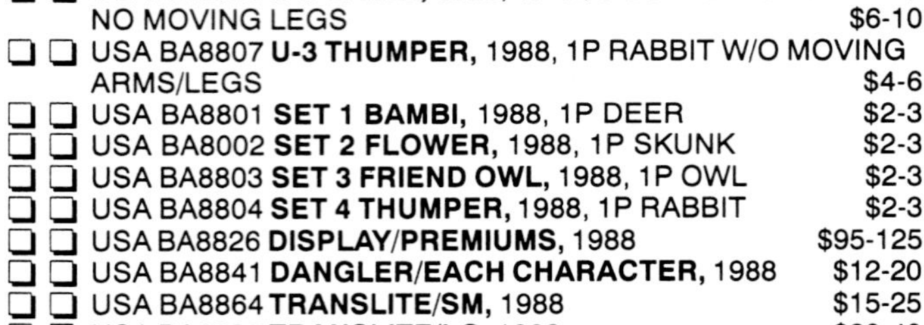

- ❑ ❑ USA BA8806 **U-3 BAMBI,** 1988, 1P W/O BUTTERFLY ON TAIL/ NO MOVING LEGS $6-10
- ❑ ❑ USA BA8807 **U-3 THUMPER,** 1988, 1P RABBIT W/O MOVING ARMS/LEGS $4-6
- ❑ ❑ USA BA8801 **SET 1 BAMBI,** 1988, 1P DEER $2-3
- ❑ ❑ USA BA8002 **SET 2 FLOWER,** 1988, 1P SKUNK $2-3
- ❑ ❑ USA BA8803 **SET 3 FRIEND OWL,** 1988, 1P OWL $2-3
- ❑ ❑ USA BA8804 **SET 4 THUMPER,** 1988, 1P RABBIT $2-3
- ❑ ❑ USA BA8826 **DISPLAY/PREMIUMS,** 1988 $95-125
- ❑ ❑ USA BA8841 **DANGLER/EACH CHARACTER,** 1988 $12-20
- ❑ ❑ USA BA8864 **TRANSLITE/SM,** 1988 $15-25
- ❑ ❑ USA BA8865 **TRANSLITE/LG,** 1988 $20-40

COMMENTS: NATIONAL DISTRIBUTION: USA - JULY 8-AUGUST 4, 1988. PREMIUM MARKINGS: "DISNEY CHINA."

BIG TOP HAPPY MEAL, 1988

- ❑ ❑ USA BI8801 **HM BOX,** 1988, **BIG TOP** $2-3

COMMENTS: REGIONAL DISTRIBUTION: USA - 1988. GIVEN AT MCD BIRTHDAY PARTIES WITH GENERIC PREMIUMS.

BLACK HISTORY HAPPY MEAL, 1988

- ❑ ❑ USA BL8805 **HM BOX,** 1988, **BLACK HISTORY** $------
- ❑ ❑ USA BL8800 **COLORING BOOK,** 1988, LITTLE MARTIN JR. COLORING BOOK VOL. 1 $------
- ❑ ❑ USA BL8801 **COLORING BOOK,** 1988, LITTLE MARTIN JR. COLORING BOOK VOL. 2 $------
- ❑ ❑ USA BL8865 **TRANSLITE/LG,** 1988 $------

USA BI8801

USA BL8805

COMMENTS: VERY LIMITED REGIONAL DISTRIBUTION: USA - 1988 IN DETROIT, MICHIGAN IN SIX STORES. THE BOOKS ARE NOT MARKED WITH MCDONALD'S LOGO. NOT ENOUGH TRANSACTIONS TO ESTABLISH A PRICE.

COSMC CRAYOLA HAPPY MEAL, 1988

- ❑ ❑ USA CO8810 **HM BOX,** 1987, **LAUNCH PAD/GRIMACE W SPACE SCRAMBLE** $3-5
- ❑ ❑ USA CO8811 **HM BOX,** 1987, **LUNAR BASE W PLANET ROUNDUP** $3-5
- ❑ ❑ USA CO8812 **HM BOX,** 1987, **PLANETS/CRATERS W TOWING TROUBLES** $3-5
- ❑ ❑ USA CO8813 **HM BOX,** 1987, **MARTIANS W FUZZY SPACE FRIENDS** $3-5
- ❑ ❑ USA CO8806 **U-3 SPACESHIP COLOR**, 1987, ACTIVITY SHEET/2 METALLIC/FLORESCENT CRAYONS $3-4
- ❑ ❑ USA CO8801 **SET 1 CRAYONS,** 1987, 4/RED/BLU/COPPER/SIL W COLORING PAGE $3-5
- ❑ ❑ USA CO8802 **SET 2 MARKER,** 1987, RED MARKER W PLANET COLORING PAGE $3-5
- ❑ ❑ USA CO8803 **SET 3 CHALK,** 1987, 4 PASTEL CHALKS W CHALK BOARD $3-5

USA CO8810 USA CO8811

USA CO8812 USA CO8813

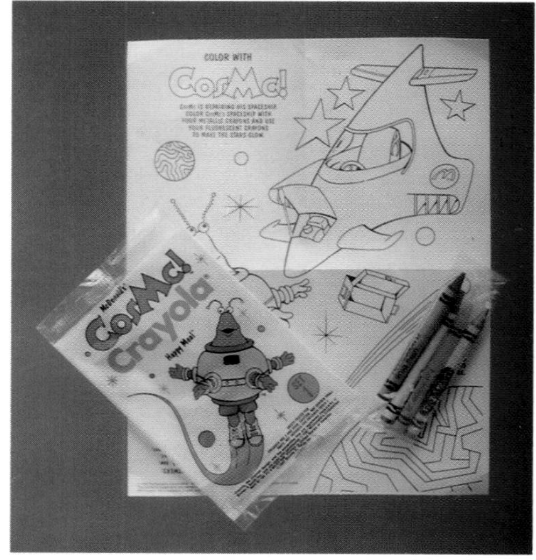

USA CO8801

USA BL8800 USA BL8801

USA CO8802

USA CO8803

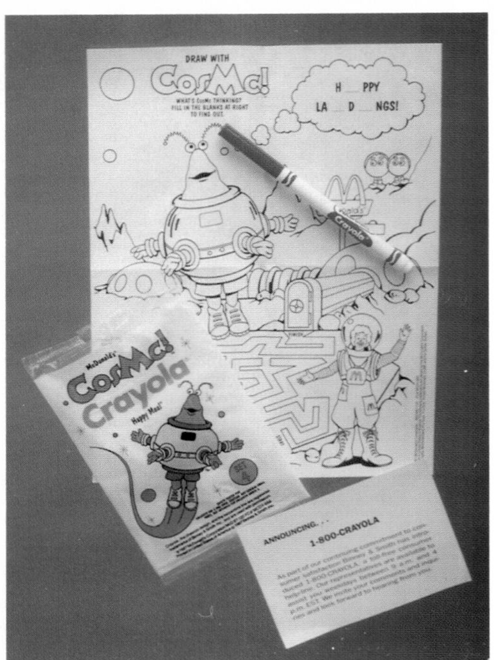

USA CO8804

- ❑ ❑ USA CO8804 **SET 4 MAGIC MARKER,** 1987, WASHABLE MARKER & COLOR PAGE $3-5
- ❑ ❑ USA CO8805 **SET 5 PAINT/NUMBER,** 1987, 3 COLOR PAINT SET/BRUSH & COLOR PAGE $3-5
- ❑ ❑ USA CO8864 **TRANSLITE/SM,** 1987 $12-20
- ❑ ❑ USA CO8865 **TRANSLITE/LG,** 1987 $15-25

COMMENTS: NATIONAL DISTRIBUTION: USA - APRIL 15-MAY 12, 1988.

DUCK TALES I HAPPY MEAL, 1988

- ❑ ❑ USA DT8810 **HM BOX,** 1987, **CITY OF GOLD** $3-5
- ❑ ❑ USA DT8811 **HM BOX,** 1987, **COOKIE OF FORTUNE** $3-5
- ❑ ❑ USA DT8812 **HM BOX,** 1987, **HULA HOOPLA** $3-5
- ❑ ❑ USA DT8813 **HM BOX,** 1987, **WESTWARD DOUGH** $3-5

USA CO8865

USA CO8805

USA DT8810 USA DT8811

USA DT8812 USA DT8813

USA CO8806

❑ ❑ USA DT8805 **U-3 MAGIC MOTION MAP,** 1987, PAPER $2-3
❑ ❑ USA DT8801 **QUACKER/WHISTLE,** 1987, ORANGE $2-3
❑ ❑ USA DT8802 **MAGNIFYING GLASS,** 1987, GRN W DECAL $2-3
❑ ❑ USA DT8803 **SPY GLASS,** 1987, YELLOW W DECAL VERTICAL or HORIZONTAL $2-3
❑ ❑ USA DT8804 **WATCH/WRIST/ENCODER,** 1987, W SECRET COMPARTMENT/BLU W DECAL $2-3
❑ ❑ USA DT8864 **TRANSLITE/SM,** 1987 $15-25
❑ ❑ USA DT8865 **TRANSLITE/LG,** 1987 $20-35

COMMENTS: NATIONAL DISTRIBUTION: USA - FEBRUARY 5-MARCH 10, 1988. U-3 WAS ONLY PREMIUM POLYBAGGED.

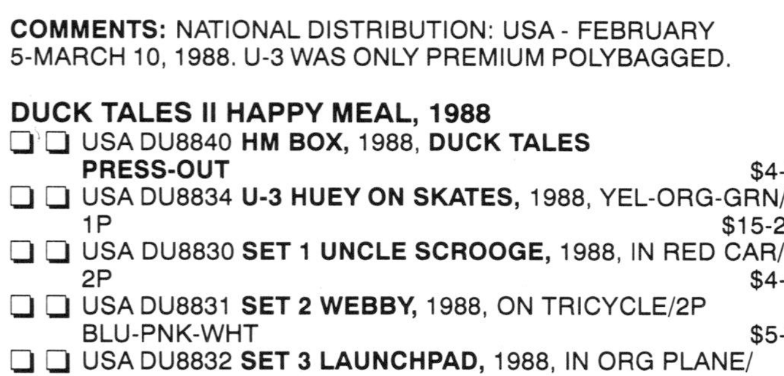

DUCK TALES II HAPPY MEAL, 1988

❑ ❑ USA DU8840 **HM BOX,** 1988, **DUCK TALES PRESS-OUT** $4-7
❑ ❑ USA DU8834 **U-3 HUEY ON SKATES,** 1988, YEL-ORG-GRN/1P $15-25
❑ ❑ USA DU8830 **SET 1 UNCLE SCROOGE,** 1988, IN RED CAR/2P $4-6
❑ ❑ USA DU8831 **SET 2 WEBBY,** 1988, ON TRICYCLE/2P BLU-PNK-WHT $5-7
❑ ❑ USA DU8832 **SET 3 LAUNCHPAD,** 1988, IN ORG PLANE/ORG-BRN-BLU $4-6
❑ ❑ USA DU8833 **SET 4 HUEY DUEY LOUIE,** 1988, ON SKI BOAT W WHEELS/YEL-GRN $4-6
❑ ❑ USA DU8835 **SET 4 HUEY DUEY LOUIE,** 1988, ON SKI BOAT W/O WHEELS/YEL-GRN $15-20
❑ ❑ USA DU8864 **TRANSLITE/SM,** 1988 $15-25
❑ ❑ USA DU8865 **TRANSLITE/LG,** 1988 $20-35

COMMENTS: REGIONAL DISTRIBUTION: USA - 1988 IN TEXAS/MICHIGAN/MARYLAND AND NEW JERSEY. PREMIUM MARKINGS "DISNEY CHINA C3" OR "MCDONALDS CHINA 1988".

USA DT8805 USA DT8801 USA DT8803 USA DT8802 USA DT8804

USA DT8865

USA DU8840

USA DU8831 USA DU8833 USA DU8832 USA DU8830 USA DU8834

USA DU8865

USA FL8810

FLINTSTONE KIDS HAPPY MEAL, 1988

❑ ❑ USA FL8810 **HM BOX,** 1987, **DRIVE IN COUNTRY** $15-25
❑ ❑ USA FL8805 **U-3 DINO,** 1987, PUR DINO/1P $15-20
❑ ❑ USA FL8801 **BARNEY,** 1987, IN BLU MASTODON CAR 2P $10-12
❑ ❑ USA FL8802 **BETTY,** 1987, IN ORG PTERYDOCTIL CAR 2P $10-12
❑ ❑ USA FL8803 **FRED,** 1987, IN GRN ALLIGATOR CAR 2P $10-12
❑ ❑ USA FL8804 **WILMA,** 1987, IN PURP DRAGON CAR 2P $10-12
❑ ❑ USA FL8864 **TRANSLITE/SM,** 1987 $25-40
❑ ❑ USA FL8865 **TRANSLITE/LG,** 1987 $40-65

COMMENTS: REGIONAL DISTRIBUTION: USA - 1988 IN NEW ENGLAND AND PARTS OF FLORIDA. PREMIUM MARKINGS - "1988 H_B PROD.INC CHINA."

FRAGGLE ROCK II HAPPY MEAL, 1988

❑ ❑ USA FR8830 **HM BOX,** 1987, **RADISH TOPS/MEET MOKEY FRAGGLE** $2-3
❑ ❑ USA FR8831 **HM BOX,** 1987, **PARTY PICKS/VOTE/MEET BOOBER FRAGGLE** $2-3
❑ ❑ USA FR8832 **HM BOX,** 1987, **RADISHES IN CAVE/MEET GOBO FRAGGLE** $2-3

USA FL8805 USA FL8801 USA FL8802 USA FL8803 USA FL8804

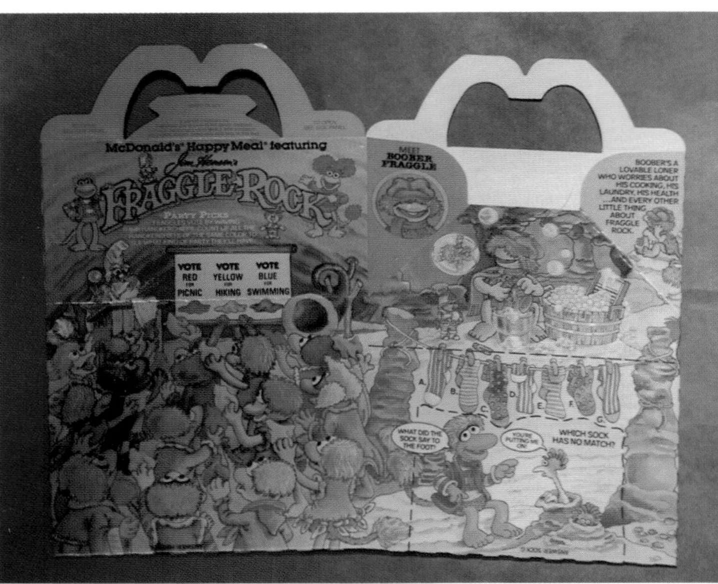

USA FR8831

USA FL8864

USA FR8832

USA FR8830

- ❑ ❑ USA FR8833 **HM BOX,** 1987, **SWIMMING HOLE BLUES/ MEET RED FRAGGLE** $2-3
- ❑ ❑ USA FR8824 **U-3 GOBO,** 1988, HOLDING LARGE CARROT $4-6
- ❑ ❑ USA FR8825 **U-3 RED,** 1988, HOLDING LARGE RADISH $4-6
- ❑ ❑ USA FR8820 **SET 1 GOBO,** 1987, IN CARROT CAR/ ORG $3-4
- ❑ ❑ USA FR8821 **SET 2 RED,** 1987, IN RADISH CAR/RED $3-4
- ❑ ❑ USA FR8822 **SET 3 MOKEY,** 1987, IN EGGPLANT CAR/ PURP $3-4
- ❑ ❑ USA FR8823 **SET 4 WEMBLY/BOOBER,** 1987, IN PICKLE CAR/GRN $3-4
- ❑ ❑ USA FR8826 **DISPLAY/W PREMIUMS,** 1988 $50-75
- ❑ ❑ USA FR8841 **DANGLER/EACH,** 1988 $12-15
- ❑ ❑ USA FR8845 **REGISTER TOPPER/EA,** 1988 $10-15
- ❑ ❑ USA FR8850 **CREW BUTTON-GOBO,** 1988 $4-6
- ❑ ❑ USA FR8851 **CREW BUTTON-RED,** 1988 $4-6
- ❑ ❑ USA FR8852 **CREW BUTTON-MONKEY,** 1988 $4-6

USA FR8826

USA FR8833

USA FR8845

USA FR8821 USA FR8820 USA FR8823 USA FR8822 USA FR8824 USA FR8825

USA FR8850 USA FR8851

USA FR8852 USA FR8853

USA FR8865

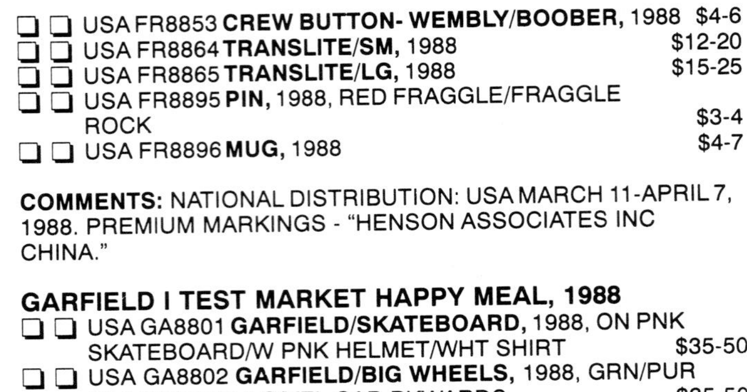

❑ ❑ USA FR8853 **CREW BUTTON- WEMBLY/BOOBER,** 1988 $4-6
❑ ❑ USA FR8864 **TRANSLITE/SM,** 1988 $12-20
❑ ❑ USA FR8865 **TRANSLITE/LG,** 1988 $15-25
❑ ❑ USA FR8895 **PIN,** 1988, RED FRAGGLE/FRAGGLE ROCK $3-4
❑ ❑ USA FR8896 **MUG,** 1988 $4-7

COMMENTS: NATIONAL DISTRIBUTION: USA MARCH 11-APRIL 7, 1988. PREMIUM MARKINGS - "HENSON ASSOCIATES INC CHINA."

GARFIELD I TEST MARKET HAPPY MEAL, 1988

❑ ❑ USA GA8801 **GARFIELD/SKATEBOARD,** 1988, ON PNK SKATEBOARD/W PNK HELMET/WHT SHIRT $35-50
❑ ❑ USA GA8802 **GARFIELD/BIG WHEELS,** 1988, GRN/PUR WHLS/BIG WHLS/YEL CAP-BKWARDS $35-50
❑ ❑ USA GA8803 **GARFIELD/SCOOTER,** 1988, ON RED SCOOTER/GRN WHLS/GRY VEST/BIG SMILE $35-50
❑ ❑ USA GA8804 **GARFIELD/CAR,** 1988, IN DARK BLU CAR/YEL TRIM/TIRES/PURP HAT/SCARF/ $35-50

COMMENTS: LIMITED REGIONAL DISTRIBUTION: USA - JULY 1988 IN ERIE, PENNSYLVANIA AND CHARLESTON, SOUTH CAROLINA. PREMIUM MARKINGS - "UNITED FEAT. SYND. CHINA H6."

HALLOWEEN '88 HAPPY MEAL, 1988

COMMENTS: NATIONAL DISTRIBUTION: USA - 1988 - SEE ZOO FACE II HAPPY MEAL, 1988.

HOT WHEELS HAPPY MEAL, 1988

❑ ❑ USA HW8820 **HM BOX,** 1988, **SPEED RAMP PUNCH OUT 12 CARS LISTED** $15-20

USA FR8896

USA FR8895

USA GA8801 USA GA8802 USA GA8803 USA GA8804

USA HW8820

❑ ❑ USA HW8800 **57 T-BIRD - TURQ,** 1988 $8-10
❑ ❑ USA HW8801 **57 T-BIRD - WHT,** 1988 $8-10
❑ ❑ USA HW8802 **80'S FIREBIRD - BLU,** 1988 $8-10
❑ ❑ USA HW8803 **80'S FIREBIRD - BLK/NO.3972** $8-10
❑ ❑ USA HW8804 **FIRE CHIEF - RED,** 1988 $8-10
❑ ❑ USA HW8805 **P-911 TURBO - BLACK/NO.3968** $8-10
❑ ❑ USA HW8806 **P-911 TURBO - WHT,** 1988 $8-10
❑ ❑ USA HW8807 **SHERIFF PATROL - BLK,** 1988 $8-10
❑ ❑ USA HW8808 **SPLIT WINDOW '63 - BLACK,** 1988 $8 -10
❑ ❑ USA HW8809 **SPLIT WINDOW '63 - SILVER,** 1988 $8-10
❑ ❑ USA HW8810 **STREET BEAST - RED,** 1988 $8-10
❑ ❑ USA HW8811 **STREET BEAST - SILVER,** 1988 $8-10
❑ ❑ USA HW8812 **CJ7 JEEP - WHT/ORG/NO.3953** $8-10
❑ ❑ USA HW8813 **CJ7 JEEP - YEL/ORG/NO.3954** $8-10
❑ ❑ USA HW8814 **CORVETTE STINGRAY - WHT/RED STRIPE/ NO.3973*** $8-10
❑ ❑ USA HW8815 **CORVETTE STINGRAY - YEL/ORG STRIPE/ NO.3974*** $8-10
❑ ❑ USA HW8816 **THUNDER STREEK -BURGAN/PURP/NO.3998*** $8-10
❑ ❑ USA HW8817 **THUNDER STREEK - BLU/YEL/NO.3999*** $8-10
❑ ❑ USA HW8818 **FIRE EATER - RED TRUCK/BLU/ NO.4000*** $8-10
❑ ❑ USA HW8819 **FIRE EATER - YEL TRUCK/BLU/ NO.4001*** $8-10
❑ ❑ USA HW8826 **DISPLAY W 12 CARS,** 1988 $250-300
❑ ❑ USA HW8864 **TRANSLITE/SM,** 1988 $15-25
❑ ❑ USA HW8865 **TRANSLITE/LG,** 1988 $20-35

COMMENTS: REGIONAL DISTRIBUTION: USA - 1988 IN TEXAS/ CONNECTICUT AND VIRGINIA. DIFFERENT CARS MAY HAVE BEEN GIVEN IN DIFFERENT REGIONS. * DENOTES CARS GIVEN OUT ON THE EAST COAST.

LUGGAGE TAG PROMOTION, 1988

❑ ❑ USA LU8801 **BIRDIE,** 1988, PNK TAG/STRAP $3-5
❑ ❑ USA LU8802 **GRIMACE,** 1988, PURP TAG/STRAP $3-5
❑ ❑ USA LU8803 **HAMBURGLAR,** 1988, BLK TAG/STRAP $3-5
❑ ❑ USA LU8804 **RONALD,** 1988, RED TAG/STRAP $3-5

COMMENTS: REGIONAL DISTRIBUTION: USA - 1988 DURING CLEAN-UP WEEKS.

USA LU8801 USA LU8802 USA LU8803 USA LU8804

MAC TONIGHT TRAVEL TOYS HAPPY MEAL, 1990/1989/ 1988

❑ ❑ USA MA8815 **HM BOX,** 1988, **ON THE ROAD/WORLD TOUR/ CREAM COLOR BOX** $3-5
❑ ❑ USA MA8830 **HM BAG,** 1989, **MAC/VEHICLES** $1-2
❑ ❑ USA MA8808 **U-3 SKATEBOARD,** 1988, MAC ON SKATE-BOARD $5-8

USA MA8815

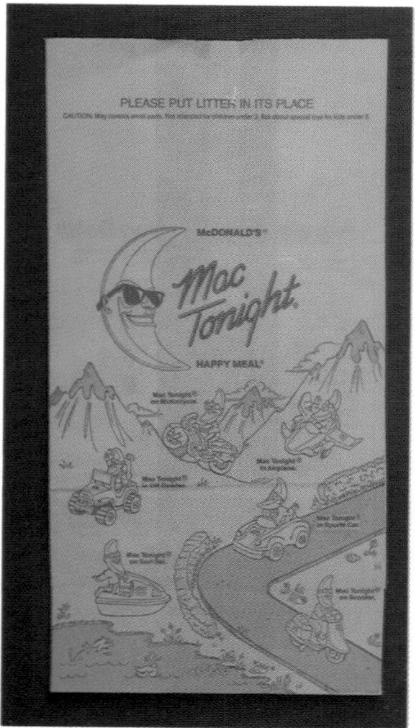

USA MA8830

USA MA8808

USA MA8800 USA MA8801 USA MA8803 USA MA8804

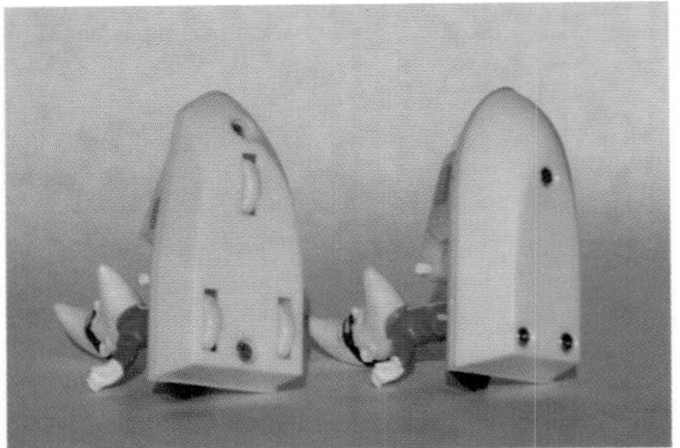

USA MA8802

USA MA8805 USA MA8807 USA MA8806

❑ ❑ USA MA8800 **SET 1 JEEP/OFF ROADER,** 1988, 4 WHEELER W MAC GRN $4-6
❑ ❑ USA MA8801 **SET 2 SPORTS CAR,** 1988, PORCHE W MAC RED $4-6
❑ ❑ USA MA8802 **SET 3 SURF SKI,** 1988, SKIBOAT W MAC **NO WHEELS**(1988) $4-6
❑ ❑ USA MA8803 **SET 3 SURF SKI,** 1988, SKIBOAT W MAC **W WHT WHEELS**(1990) $6-8
❑ ❑ USA MA8804 **SET 4 SCOOTER,** 1988, SCOOTER W MAC BLK $4-6
❑ ❑ USA MA8805 **SET 5 MOTORCYCLE,** 1988, RED W MAC TONIGHT $4-6
❑ ❑ USA MA8806 **SET 6 AIRPLANE,** 1988, BLU PLANE W MAC/ **BLU SUNGLASSES** $6-8
❑ ❑ USA MA8807 **SET 6 AIRPLANE,** 1988, BLU PLANE W MAC/ **BLK SUNGLASSES** $4-6
❑ ❑ USA MA8826 **DISPLAY/PREMIUMS,** 1988 $150-200
❑ ❑ USA MA8864 **TRANSLITE/SM,** 1988 $12-20
❑ ❑ USA MA8865 **TRANSLITE/LG,** 1988 $20-35
❑ ❑ USA MA8866 **TRANSLITE/X-O-GRAPHIC,** 1988, MAKE IT MAC TONIGHT $40-60
❑ ❑ USA MA8867 **TRANSLITE/X-O-GRAPHIC,** 1988, MAC TONIGHT $40-60

COMMENTS: REGIONAL DISTRIBUTION: USA - 1988 AND SEPTEMBER 7-OCTOBER 4, 1990 IN CALIFORNIA. HM WAS TEST MARKETED IN 1988 AND SEPTEMBER 1989. ST.LOUIS, MISSOURI TEST MARKET USED HM BAG IN EARLY 1990. CHICAGO TEST MARKET USED HM BAG IN SEPT 1990. OTHER MAC TONIGHT FIGURINES WERE SOLD IN RETAIL STORES. THESE FIGURINES MARKED WITH MCD LOGO, WERE NOT PART OF THE HAPPY MEAL PROMOTION. USA MA8816 HM BAG WAS USED IN 1989 WITH 1988 PREMIUMS. USA MA8803 SURF SKI WITH WHEELS WAS ISSUED IN 1990 IN PARTS OF NEW JERSEY.

MATCHBOX SUPER GT HAPPY MEAL, 1988

❑ ❑ USA MB8825 **HM BOX,** 1988, **SUPER GT/8 CARS** $15-20
❑ ❑ USA MB8801 **CAR ALMOND W BLACK STRIPES/BR 27/28** $8-10

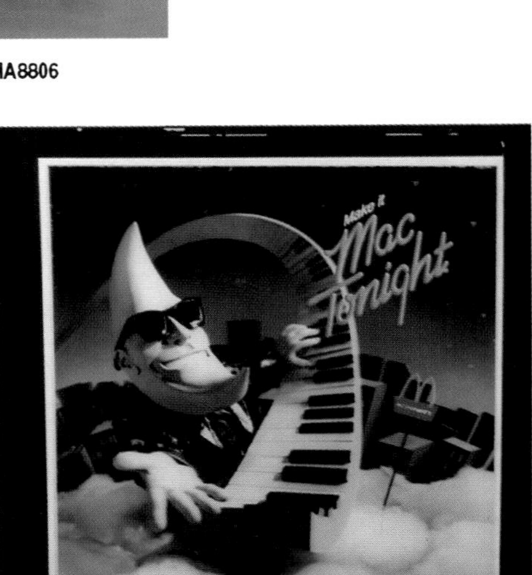

USA MA8865

USA MA8826

USA MA8866

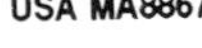

USA MA8867

USA MB8825

❑ ❑ USA MB8802 **CAR BEIGE STARFIRE W RED STRIPES/BR 23/24** $8-10
❑ ❑ USA MB8803 **CAR BLUE #8 RED FLAME GRAPHICS/BR 37/38** $8-10
❑ ❑ USA MB8804 **CAR METALLIC BLUE/YEL-GRN GRAPHICS/BR 9/10** $8-10
❑ ❑ USA MB8805 **CAR GRN #8 WHT-YEL GRAPHICS/BR 27/28** $8-10
❑ ❑ USA MB8806 **CAR ORG #6 W BLU-WHT STRIPES/BR 21/22** $8-10
❑ ❑ USA MB8807 **CAR ORANGE TURBO W WHT FLAME GRAPHICS/BR 7/8** $8-10
❑ ❑ USA MB8808 **CAR SILVER/GREY #3 BR35/36** $8-10
❑ ❑ USA MB8809 **CAR SILVER GREY W GRN/RED STRIPES/BR 5/6** $8-10
❑ ❑ USA MB8810 **CAR SILVER GREY SUPER GT W BLK/BLU STRIPE/BR 21/22** $8-10
❑ ❑ USA MB8811 **CAR WHITE #1 W RED FLAME GRAPHICS/BR 9/10** $8-10
❑ ❑ USA MB8812 **CAR WHT #18 W RED STRIPE/BR 19/20** $8-10
❑ ❑ USA MB8813 **CAR WHT #45 RACER W RED STRIPES/BR 33/34** $8-10
❑ ❑ USA MB8814 **CAR WHT W YEL-BLU GRAPHICS/BR 7/8** $8-10
❑ ❑ USA MB8815 **CAR YEL #19 W RED-BLU STRIPES/BR 31/32** $8-10
❑ ❑ USA MB8816 **CAR MUSTARD YEL W DARK BLU-ORG STRIPES/BR 29/30** $8-10
❑ ❑ USA MB8826 **COUNTER CARD W 16 PREMIUMS,** 1988 $200-250
❑ ❑ USA MB8864 **TRANSLITE/SM,** 1988 $15-25
❑ ❑ USA MB8865 **TRANSLITE/LG,** 1988 $20-30

COMMENTS: REGIONAL DISTRIBUTION: USA - 1988 IN OKLAHOMA REGION.

MCNUGGET BUDDIES HAPPY MEAL, 1988

❑ ❑ USA NU8820 **HM BOX,** 1988, **APARTMENTS** $2-4
❑ ❑ USA NU8821 **HM BOX,** 1988, **BEAUTY SHOP** $2-4
❑ ❑ USA NU8822 **HM BOX,** 1988, **GARDENS** $2-4
❑ ❑ USA NU8823 **HM BOX,** 1988, **POST OFFICE** $2-4
❑ ❑ USA NU8811 **U-3 SLUGGER,** 1988, 2P BRN W BASEBALL GLOVE $5-7
❑ ❑ USA NU8812 **U-3 DAISY,** 1988, 2P BRN/BEAR W DAISEY FLOWER ON HAT $6-10
❑ ❑ USA NU8800 **COWPOKE MCNUGGET,** 1988, 3P COWBOY HAT W SCARF $3-4
❑ ❑ USA NU8801 **FIRST CLASS,** 1988, 3P HAT W LETTER BELT $3-4
❑ ❑ USA NU8802 **SARGE MCNUGGET,** 1988, 3P HAT W CUFFS/RADIO BELT $3-4
❑ ❑ USA NU8803 **DRUMMER MCNUGGET,** 1988, 3P DRUM MAJOR HAT W DRUM BELT $3-4
❑ ❑ USA NU8804 **CORNY MCNUGGET,** 1988, 3P STRAW HAT W RED POPCORN BELT $3-4
❑ ❑ USA NU8805 **CORNY MCNUGGET,** 1988, 3P STRAW HAT W BEIGE POPCORN BELT $3-4
❑ ❑ USA NU8806 **SPARKY MCNUGGET,** 1988, 3P FIRE HAT W HATCHET/EXTINGUISH BELT $3-4
❑ ❑ USA NU8807 **BOOMERANG MCNUGGET,** 1988, 3P AUSIE HAT W BOOMERANG $3-4
❑ ❑ USA NU8808 **VOLLEY MCNUGGET,** 1988, 3P HEAD BAND E TENNIS BELT $3-4
❑ ❑ USA NU8809 **SNORKEL MCNUGGET,** 1988, 3P MASK W KNIFE/LITE BELT $3-4
❑ ❑ USA NU8810 **ROCKER MCNUGGET,** 1988, 3P ORG W HAIR & GUITAR BELT $3-4

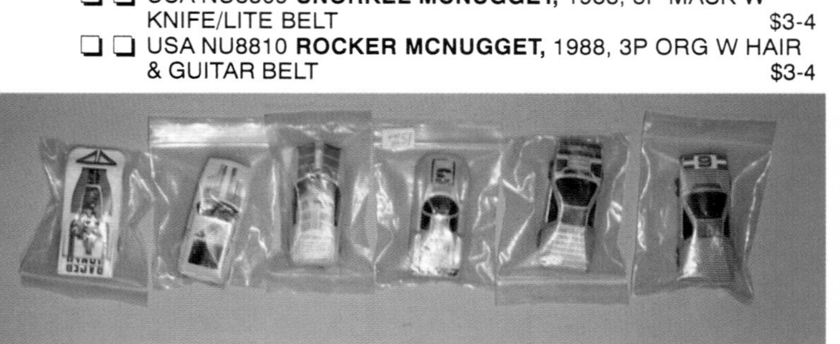

USA NU8820 USA NU8821

USA NU8822 USA NU8823

USA NU8812 USA NU8802 USA NU8804 USA NU8807 USA NU8809

USA NU8800 USA NU8801 USA NU8805 USA NU8808
USA NU8811 USA NU8803 USA NU8806 USA NU8810

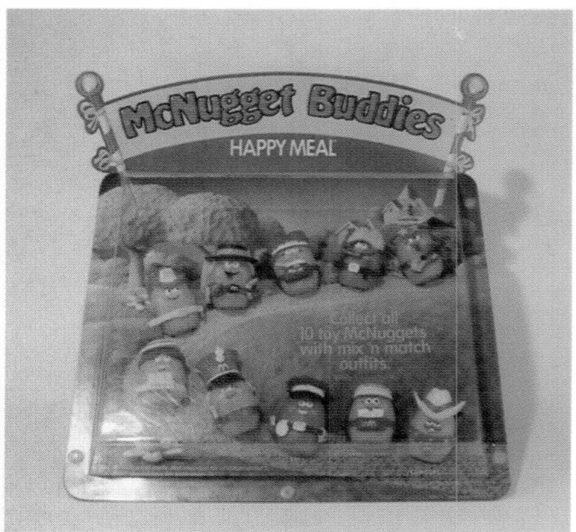

USA NU8826

- ☐ ☐ USA NU8826 **DISPLAY/PREMIUMS,** 1988 — $100-125
- ☐ ☐ USA NU8863 **MENU BOARD/LUG-ON,** 1988 — $10-15
- ☐ ☐ USA NU8864 **TRANSLITE/SM,** 1988 — $12-20
- ☐ ☐ USA NU8865 **TRANSLITE/LG,** 1988 — $15-25
- ☐ ☐ USA NU8895 **PIN,** 1988, MCNUGGET BUDDIES — $3-5

COMMENTS: NATIONAL DISTRIBUTION: USA - DECEMBER 30, 1988-JANUARY 26, 1989.

MOVEABLES/MCDONALDLAND HAPPY MEAL, 1988

- ☐ ☐ USA MO8810 **HM BOX,** 1988, **SHIP/MOVE INTO HOMES** — $8-12
- ☐ ☐ USA MO8800 **BIRDIE,** 1988, 4" HARD RUBBER — $8-10
- ☐ ☐ USA MO8801 **CAPTAIN,** 1988, 4" HARD RUBBER — $8-10
- ☐ ☐ USA MO8802 **FRY GIRL,** 1988, 2" HARD RUBBER — $8 -10
- ☐ ☐ USA MO8803 **HAMBURGLAR,** 1988, 4" HARD RUBBER — $8-10
- ☐ ☐ USA MO8804 **PROFESSOR,** 1988, 4" HARD RUBBER — $8-10
- ☐ ☐ USA MO8805 **RONALD,** 1988, 4" HARD RUBBER — $8-10
- ☐ ☐ USA MO8864 **TRANSLITE/SM,** 1988 — $12-20
- ☐ ☐ USA MO8865 **TRANSLITE/LG,** 1988 — $15-25

COMMENTS: REGIONAL DISTRIBUTION: USA - 1988 IN ST. LOUIS, MISSOURI.

NEW ARCHIES HAPPY MEAL, 1988

- ☐ ☐ USA NE8810 **HM BOX,** 1988, **ARCHIES/FUN PARK** — $20-25
- ☐ ☐ USA NE8800 **ARCHIE,** 1988, IN RED BUMPER CAR — $6-10
- ☐ ☐ USA NE8801 **BETTY,** 1988, IN BLU BUMPER CAR — $6-10
- ☐ ☐ USA NE8802 **JUGHEAD,** 1988, IN YEL BUMPER CAR — $6-10
- ☐ ☐ USA NE8803 **MOOSE,** 1988, IN PNK BUMPER CAR — $6-10
- ☐ ☐ USA NE8804 **REGGIE,** 1988, IN GRN BUMPER CAR — $6-10
- ☐ ☐ USA NE8805 **VERONICA,** 1988, IN PURP BUMPER CAR — $6-10

USA NU8865

USA NU8895

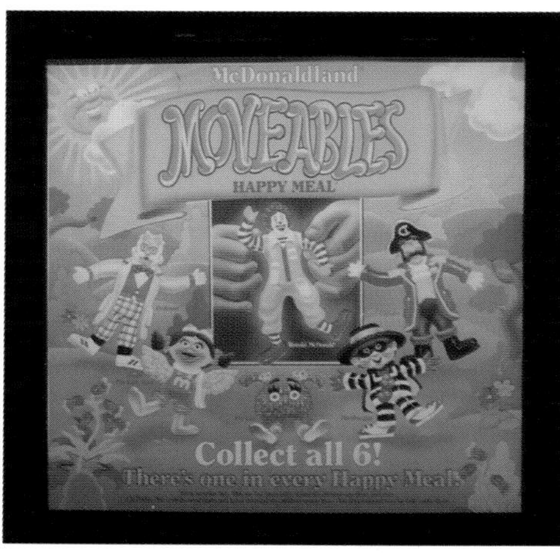

USA MO8865

USA MO8810

USA MO8800 USA MO8801 USA MO8802 USA MO8803 USA MO8804 USA MO8805

USA NE8810

USA NE8800 USA NE8801 USA NE8804 USA NE8803 USA NE8802 USA NE8805

❑ ❑ USA NE8864 **TRANSLITE/SM,** 1988 $15-30
❑ ❑ USA NE8865 **TRANSLITE/LG,** 1988 $25-40

COMMENTS: REGIONAL DISTRIBUTION: USA - SPRING-1988 IN ST. LOUIS, MISSOURI.

OLIVER & COMPANY HAPPY MEAL, 1988

❑ ❑ USA OC8810 **HM BOX,** 1988, **FUNNY BONES** $4-6
❑ ❑ USA OC8811 **HM BOX,** 1988, **NOISY NEIGHBORHOOD** $4-6
❑ ❑ USA OC8812 **HM BOX,** 1988, **SHADOW SCRAMBLE** $4-6
❑ ❑ USA OC8813 **HM BOX,** 1988, **TRICKY TRIKE** $4-6
❑ ❑ USA OC8800 **SET 1 OLIVER,** 1988, 1P KITTEN $2-3
❑ ❑ USA OC8801 **SET 2 FRANCIS,** 1988, 1P BULLDOG $2-3
❑ ❑ USA OC8802 **SET 3 GEORGETTE,** 1988, 1P FRENCH POODLE $2-3
❑ ❑ USA OC8803 **SET 4 DODGER,** 1988, 1P DOG W GOGGLES $2-3
❑ ❑ USA OC8844 **CREW POSTER,** 1988, COMPANY'S COMING! $5-8
❑ ❑ USA OC8864 **TRANSLITE/SM,** 1988 $15-25
❑ ❑ USA OC8865 **TRANSLITE/LG,** 1988 $25-40
❑ ❑ USA OC8895 **PIN,** 1988, OLIVER & COMPANY/ROUND $3-4

COMMENTS: NATIONAL DISTRIBUTION - NOVEMBER 25-DECEMBER 22, 1988. PREMIUM MARKINGS - "DISNEY CHINA P7."

USA OC8810

USA OC8811 USA OC8812 USA OC8813

USA OC8800 USA OC8801 USA OC8802 USA OC8803

USA OC8895

USA OC8865

USA OC8866

OLYMPIC SPORTS II CLIP-ON BUTTONS HAPPY MEAL, 1988

❑ ❑ USA OL8860 **HM BOX,** 1988, **HILARIOUS HURDLES** $3-5
❑ ❑ USA OL8861 **HM BOX,** 1988, **ORDER ON THE COURT** $3-5
❑ ❑ USA OL8850 **BUTTON - HAMBURGLAR,** 1988, HURDLES/1P/CLIP ON $4-6
❑ ❑ USA OL8851 **BUTTON - BIRDIE,** 1988, GYMNASTICS/1P/CLIP ON $4-6
❑ ❑ USA OL8852 **BUTTON - GRIMACE,** 1988, SOCCER/1P/CLIP ON $4-6
❑ ❑ USA OL8853 **BUTTON - FRY GIRL,** 1988, DIVING/1P/CLIP ON $4-6
❑ ❑ USA OL8854 **BUTTON - RONALD,** 1988, BICYCLING/1P/CLIP ON $4-6
❑ ❑ USA OL8855 **BUTTON - COSMC,** 1988, BASKETBALL/1P/CLIP ON $4-6
❑ ❑ USA OL8864 **TRANSLITE/SM,** 1988 $15-25
❑ ❑ USA OL8865 **TRANSLITE/LG,** 1988 $25-40

COMMENTS: LIMITED NATIONAL DISTRIBUTION - SEPTEMBER 9-29, 1988 IN ALABAMA AND GEORGIA.

USA OL8860 USA OL8861

USA OL8851 USA OL8855 USA OL8853

USA OL8852 USA OL8850 USA OL8854

USA OL8865

ON THE GO II LUNCH BOX/BAGS HAPPY MEAL, 1988

❑ ❑ USA ON8805 **U-3 LUNCH BOX,** 1988, RON IN SCHOOL/BLUE W STICKER PICTURE $7-10
❑ ❑ USA ON8801 **RED LUNCH BOX,** 1988, GRIM/RM RAISED SCENE W BULLETIN BOARD $3-5
❑ ❑ USA ON8802 **YEL LUNCH BAG,** 1988, RONALD SOFT BAG $2-3
❑ ❑ USA ON8803 **GRN LUNCH BOX,** 1988, GRIM/RM RAISED SCENE W BULLETIN BOARD $3-5
❑ ❑ USA ON8804 **BLU LUNCH BAG,** 1988, GRIMACE SOFT BAG $2-3
❑ ❑ USA ON8806 **STICKER SHEET,** 1988, FOR GRN LUNCH BOX $3-5
❑ ❑ USA ON8807 **STICKER SHEET,** 1988, FOR RED LUNCH BOX $3-5
❑ ❑ USA ON8864 **TRANSLITE/SM,** 1988 $12-20
❑ ❑ USA ON8865 **TRANSLITE/LG,** 1988 $25-40

COMMENTS: NATIONAL DISTRIBUTION: USA - AUGUST 12-SEPTEMBER 8, 1988.

USA ON8802 USA ON8804

USA ON8801 USA ON8803 USA ON8805

PETER RABBIT HAPPY MEAL, 1988

❑ ❑ USA PE8817 **HM BOX,** 1988, **MR. MCGREGOR'S GARDEN** $-------
❑ ❑ USA PE8810 **TALE OF BENJAMIN BUNNY,** 1988, BOOK/PAPER/BEATRIX POTTER $12-15

USA PE8817

USA PE8810 USA PE8811 USA PE8812 USA PE8813

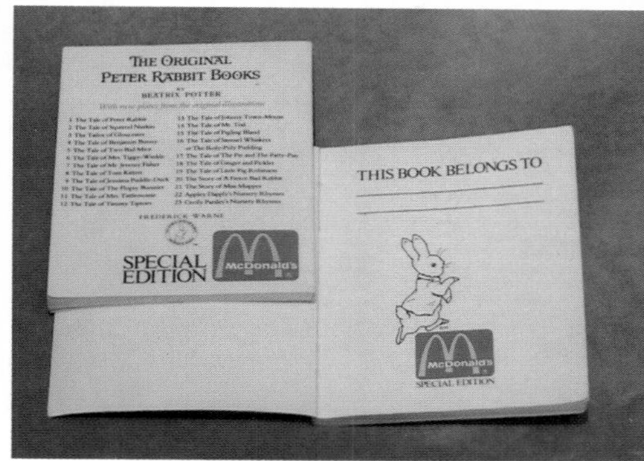

❑ ❑ USA PE8811 **TALE OF FLOPSY BUNNIES,** 1988, BOOK/PAPER/BEATRIX POTTER $12-15
❑ ❑ USA PE8812 **TALE OF PETER RABBIT,** 1988, BOOK/PAPER/BEATRIX POTTER $12-15
❑ ❑ USA PE8813 **TALE OF SQUIRREL NUTKIN,** 1988, BOOK/PAPER/BEATRIX POTTER $12-15
❑ ❑ USA PE8864 **TRANSLITE/SM,** 1988 $50-65
❑ ❑ USA PE8865 **TRANSLITE/LG,** 1988 $75-100

COMMENTS: REGIONAL DISTRIBUTION: USA - FALL 1988 IN PARTS OF NEW YORK AND PENNSYLVANIA. NOT ENOUGH TRANSACTIONS TO DETERMINE PRICE OF HM BOX.

SAILORS HAPPY MEAL, 1988

❑ ❑ USA SA8810 **HM BOX,** 1987, **FRY GUY AFLOAT** $3-5
❑ ❑ USA SA8811 **HM BOX,** 1987, **HOUSEBOAT IS WHOSE** $3-5
❑ ❑ USA SA8812 **HM BOX,** 1987, **ISLAND EYES** $3-5
❑ ❑ USA SA8813 **HM BOX,** 1987, **RONALD FISHING/CROSS-WORD** $3-5
❑ ❑ USA SA8804 **U-3 GRIMACE SPEEDBOAT,** 1987, BLU/FLOATER/1P $2-3
❑ ❑ USA SA8805 **U-3 FRY GUY ON TUBE,** 1987, BLU/FLOATER/1P $2-3
❑ ❑ USA SA8800 **GRIMACE SUBMARINE,** 1987, PUR TOP/BOTTOM/PROP/3P $3-5
❑ ❑ USA SA8801 **FRY KIDS FERRY,** 1987, GRN TOP/BOTTON/FERRY CAR/3P $4-5
❑ ❑ USA SA8802 **HAMB PIRATE SHIP,** 1987, BLU TOP/BOTTON/SAIL/3P $3-5
❑ ❑ USA SA8803 **RONALD MCD AIRBOAT,** 1987, RED BOTTON/RONALD/PROP/3P $3-5
❑ ❑ USA SA8864 **TRANSLITE/SM,** 1987 $12-20
❑ ❑ USA SA8865 **TRANSLITE/LG,** 1987 $15-25

COMMENTS: NATIONAL DISTRIBUTION: USA - JANUARY 1-28, 1988

USA SA8812 USA SA8813

USA SA8805 USA SA8804

USA SA8801 USA SA8800 USA SA8802 USA SA8803

USA SA8810

USA SA8811

USA SA8865

SEA WORLD OF OHIO HAPPY MEAL, 1988

❑ ❑ USA SE8805 **HM BOX,** 1988, **3 KIDS ON WHALE** $10-15
❑ ❑ USA SE8800 **DOLLY DOLPHIN,** 1988, BRN-WHT 3" $12-15
❑ ❑ USA SE8801 **PENNY PENGUIN,** 1988, BLK-WHT-ORG 3" $12-15
❑ ❑ USA SE8802 **SHAMU THE WHALE,** 1988, BLK-WHT 3" $12-15
❑ ❑ USA SE8864 **TRANSLITE/SM,** 1988 $20-30
❑ ❑ USA SE8865 **TRANSLITE/LG,** 1988 $25-40

COMMENTS: REGIONAL DISTRIBUTION: USA - SPRING 1988 IN CLEVELAND, OHIO. PREMIUM MARKINGS - "MADE IN CHINA, 1987, SEA WORLD, INC." ON THE BOTTOM OF FIGURINE ---NOT ON THE SIDE! FIGURINES MARKED ON THE SIDE WERE SOLD IN SEA WORLD GIFT SHOPS.

SEA WORLD OF TEXAS I HAPPY MEAL, 1988

❑ ❑ USA SW8810 **HM BOX,** 1988, **RONALD IN YEL SUB/ WITHOUT COUPON ON BOX** $10-15
❑ ❑ USA SW8800 **DOLPHIN,** 1988, GREY/WHT W BLK EYES 6" $8-12
❑ ❑ USA SW8801 **PENGUIN,** 1988, BLK-WHT W ORG PEAK/ FEET 6" $8-12
❑ ❑ USA SW8802 **WALRUS,** 1988, BROWN W WHT FACE/TUSKS 6" $8-12
❑ ❑ USA SW8803 **WHALE,** 1988, BLACK-WHT 6" $8-12
❑ ❑ USA SW8826 **COUNTER DISPLAY/PREMIUMS,** 1988 $150-200
❑ ❑ USA SW8864 **TRANSLITE/SM,** 1988 $25-40
❑ ❑ USA SW8865 **TRANSLITE/LG,** 1988 $35-50

COMMENTS: REGIONAL DISTRIBUTION: USA - SUMMER 1988 IN SAN ANTONIO, TEXAS. PREMIUM MARKINGS - DETAILED CLOTH LABEL SAYS, "SEA WORLD J3 INC KOREA."

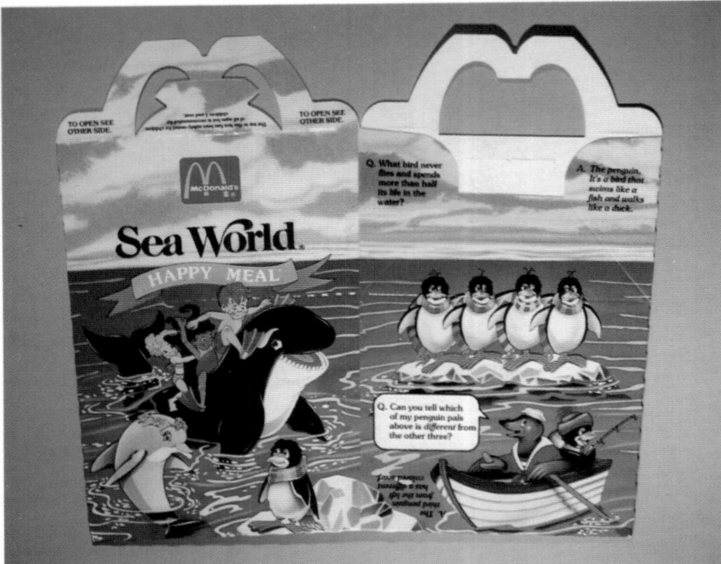

USA SE8805

USA SE8800 USA SE8801 USA SE8802

USA SW8810

USA SW8864

USA SW8803 USA SW8800 USA SW8802 USA SW8801

SPORT BALL TEST MARKET HAPPY MEAL, 1990/1988

❑ ❑ USA SP8810 **HM BOX,** 1988, **CLEAR THE COURT** $10-15
❑ ❑ USA SP8811 **HM BOX,** 1988, **MATCH POINT** $10-15
❑ ❑ USA SP8805 **U-3 BASEBALL,** 1988, 3" HARD PLASTIC/M MOLDED BOTH SIDES $20-25
❑ ❑ USA SP8801 **FOOTBALL,** 1988, YEL/RED W RED M/ RONALD MCD SIGNATURE $20-25
❑ ❑ USA SP8802 **TENNIS BALL,** 1988, SPONGE/M CUT INTO BALL $20-25
❑ ❑ USA SP8803 **BASEBALL,** 1988, HARD PLASTIC/WHT/M MOLDED INTO BALL $20-25
❑ ❑ USA SP8804 **BASKETBALL,** 1988, ORG BALL W ORG HOOP/WHT NET $30-35
❑ ❑ USA SP8826 **DISPLAY/PREMIUMS/MOTION,** 1988 $200-250
❑ ❑ USA SP8864 **TRANSLITE/SM,** 1988 $25-40
❑ ❑ USA SP8865 **TRANSLITE/LG,** 1988 $35-50

COMMENTS: REGIONAL DISTRIBUTION: USA - 1988/1990 IN SPRINGFIELD, MISSOURI.

STORYBOOK MUPPET BABIES HAPPY MEAL, 1988

❑ ❑ USA ST8860 **HM BOX,** 1988, **LIBRARY W SCARY PIT** $2-4
❑ ❑ USA ST8861 **HM BOX,** 1988, **NURSERY W TREASURE MAP** $2-4
❑ ❑ USA ST8862 **HM BOX,** 1988, **PICNIC W GOLD PAN** $2-4
❑ ❑ USA ST8850 **BOOK-JUST KERMIT AND ME,** 1988, MUPPET BABIES $1-3
❑ ❑ USA ST8851 **BOOK-THE LEGEND OF GIMME GULCH,** 1988, MUPPET BABIES $1-3
❑ ❑ USA ST8852 **BOOK-BABY PIGGY THE LIVING DOLL,** 1988, MUPPET BABIES $1-3
❑ ❑ USA ST8864 **TRANSLITE/SM,** 1988 $12-20
❑ ❑ USA ST8865 **TRANSLITE/LG,** 1988 $20-30
❑ ❑ USA ST8867 **MENU BOARD LUG-ON,** 1988 $10-12

COMMENTS: NATIONAL DISTRIBUTION: USA - OCTOBER 28-NOVEMBER 17, 1988.

SUPER SUMMER II HAPPY MEAL, 1988

❑ ❑ USA SU8835 **HM BAG,** 1987, **PICNIC PUZZLER W GRIMACE GRILLING/WHT/GRN** $1-2

USA SP8810 USA SP8811

USA SP8805 USA SP8801 USA SP8802 USA SP8803 USA SP8804

USA ST8861

USA ST8860

USA ST8862

USA ST8850

USA ST8851

USA ST8852

USA SU8835

❑ ❑ USA SU8825 **PAIL/SAND,** 1987, WHT SAND PAIL W YEL RAKE $1.50-2.50
❑ ❑ USA SU8826 **BEACH BALL,** 1987, WHT/FRY KIDS/MADE IN CHINA $1-1.50
❑ ❑ USA SU8827 **BOAT/SAIL,** 1988, INFLATABLE SAIL BOAT/GRIMACE $1-1.50
❑ ❑ USA SU8828 **SAND/FISH MOLD,** 1988, BLUE/FISH SHAPED $3-5
❑ ❑ USA SU8829 **CASTLE MOLD,** 1987, WHT CASTLE PAIL W RED SHOVEL/SAND SIFTER LID $1.50-2.50
❑ ❑ USA SU8831 **WATERING CAN,** 1988, W/O MCD LOGO/BLUE $30-40
❑ ❑ USA SU8844 **DISPLAY/FLOOR/PREMIUMS/FISH MOLD,** 1988 $65-80
❑ ❑ USA SU8864 **TRANSLITE/W FISH MOLD/SM,** 1988 $15-20
❑ ❑ USA SU8865 **TRANSLITE/W FISH MOLD/LG,** 1988 $20-25

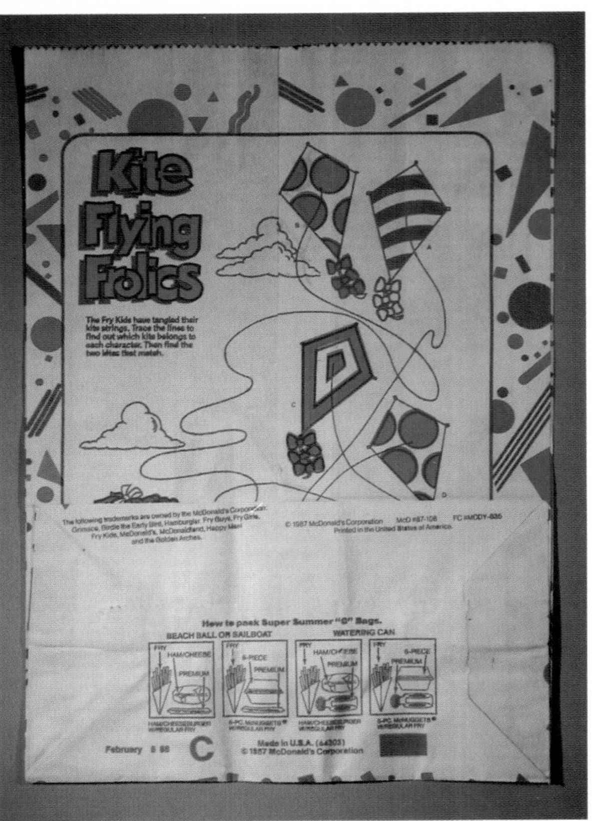

USA SU8844

USA SU8828 USA SU8826

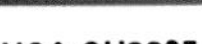
USA SU8825 USA SU8829

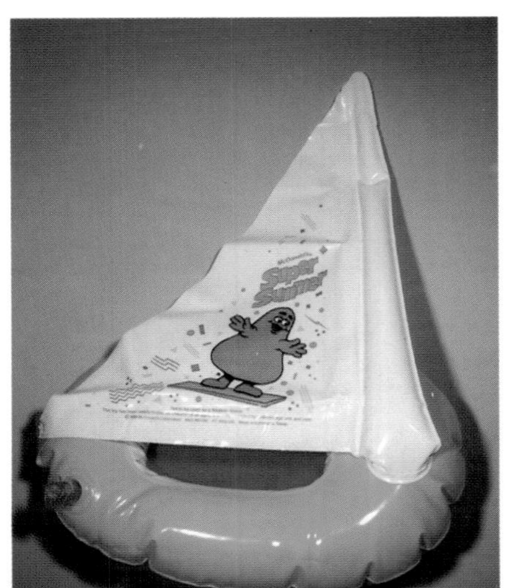

USA SU8827

USA SU8831

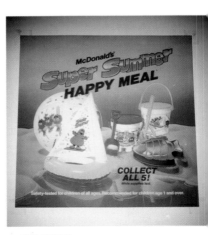

USA SU8865

❑ ❑ USA SU8866 **TRANSLITE/W WATERING CAN/SM,** 1988 $10-15
❑ ❑ USA SU8867 **TRANSLITE/W WATERING CAN/LG,** 1988 $15-20

COMMENTS: NATIONAL DISTRIBUTION: USA - MAY 20-JUNE 23, 1988. CALIFORNIA TEST MARKET: MAY-JUNE 1987. PAIL CAME WITH EITHER A RED RAKE OR YELLOW SHOVEL. IN THE NATIONAL PROMOTION THE SAND MOLD WAS SUBSTITUTED FOR THE WATERING CAN. USA SU8826 MIP SAYS, "CONTENTS MADE IN CHINA/CONTENTS PRINTED IN TAIWAN."

USA SU8867

TURBO MACS I TEST MARKET HAPPY MEAL, 1988

❑ ❑ USA TU8830 **HM BOX,** 1988, **RONALD/RED RACE CAR** $4-7
❑ ❑ USA TU8824 **U-3 RONALD,** 1988, IN RUBBER/RED CAR/YEL WHEELS/LG ARCHES $5-8
❑ ❑ USA TU8820 **BIRDIE,** 1988, PINK CAR/BRN HAIR/SMALL YEL ARCHES $4-7
❑ ❑ USA TU8821 **GRIMACE,** 1988, WHT CAR/LG YEL M ON FRONT OF CAR $4-7
❑ ❑ USA TU8822 **HAMBURGLAR,** 1988, YEL CAR/LG RED M ON FRONT OF CAR $4-7
❑ ❑ USA TU8823 **RONALD,** 1988, RED CAR/LG YEL M ON FRONT OF CAR/**TEAR DROP UNDER EYES** $4-7
❑ ❑ USA TU8826 **DISPLAY/PREMIUMS/MOTION,** 1988 $125-150
❑ ❑ USA TU8864 **TRANSLITE/SM,** 1988 $15-25
❑ ❑ USA TU8865 **TRANSLITE/LG,** 1988 $25-35

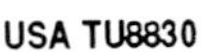

USA TU8830

COMMENTS: REGIONAL DISTRIBUTION: USA - 1988/1990 IN CALIFORNIA THROUGHOUT THE SOUTHERN BELT TO FLORIDA. USA TU8820-23 CAME POLYBAGED WITH INSERT CARD. U-3 USA TU8824 CAME POLYBAGED WITHOUT INSERT CARD AND POLYBAGGED IN A CLEAR BAG.

ZOO FACE II/HALLOWEEN '88 HAPPY MEAL, 1988

❑ ❑ USA ZO8810 **HM BOX,** 1988, **APE HOUSE** $3-5
❑ ❑ USA ZO8811 **HM BOX,** 1988, **BIRD HOUSE** $3-5
❑ ❑ USA ZO8812 **HM BOX,** 1988, **LION HOUSE** $3-5
❑ ❑ USA ZO8813 **HM BOX,** 1988, **REPTILE HOUSE** $3-5

USA TU8824 USA TU8820 USA TU8821 USA TU8822 USA TU8823

USA TU8865

USA ZO8810 USA ZO8811

USA ZO8812 USA ZO8813

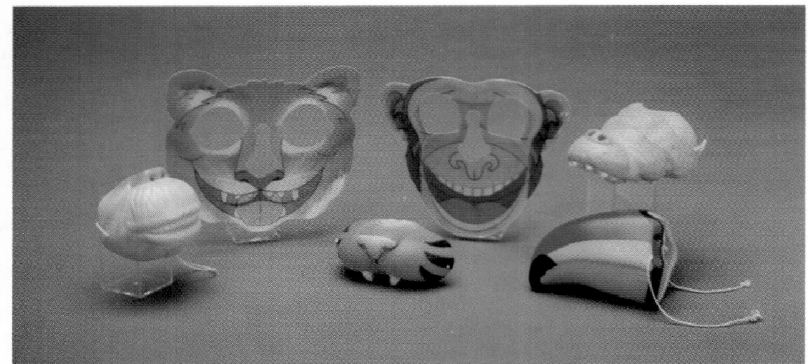

USA ZO8806 USA ZO8805 USA ZO8804
USA ZO8802 USA ZO8803 USA ZO8801

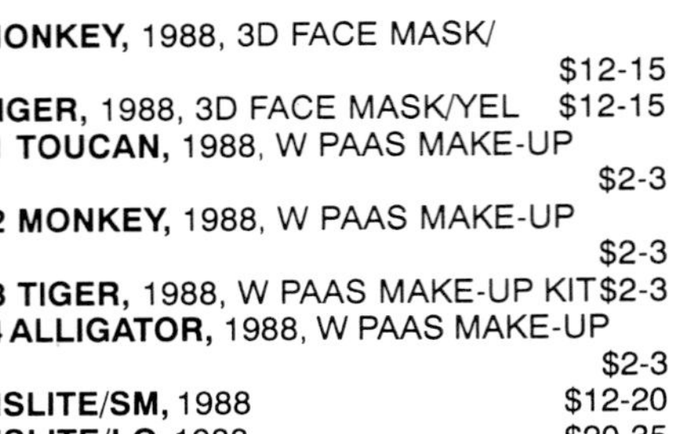

- ❑ ❑ USA ZO8805 **U-3 MONKEY,** 1988, 3D FACE MASK/ORG $12-15
- ❑ ❑ USA ZO8806 **U-3 TIGER,** 1988, 3D FACE MASK/YEL $12-15
- ❑ ❑ USA ZO8801 **SET 1 TOUCAN,** 1988, W PAAS MAKE-UP KIT $2-3
- ❑ ❑ USA ZO8802 **SET 2 MONKEY,** 1988, W PAAS MAKE-UP KIT $2-3
- ❑ ❑ USA ZO8803 **SET 3 TIGER,** 1988, W PAAS MAKE-UP KIT $2-3
- ❑ ❑ USA ZO8804 **SET 4 ALLIGATOR,** 1988, W PAAS MAKE-UP KIT $2-3
- ❑ ❑ USA ZO8864 **TRANSLITE/SM,** 1988 $12-20
- ❑ ❑ USA ZO8865 **TRANSLITE/LG,** 1988 $20-35

COMMENTS: NATIONAL DISTRIBUTION: USA - SEPTEMBER 30-OCTOBER 27, 1988. AS A RESULT OF THE TEST MARKET, HOLES WERE ENLARGED IN TOUCAN AND THE ALLIGATOR/HOLES INCREASED TO THREE. TOUCAN AND ALLIGATOR WERE RESHAPED AND HEAVIER ELASTIC STRING PROVIDED.

USA ZO8865

USA/GENERIC PROMOTION, 1988

- ❑ ❑ USA GE8810 **HM BOX,** 1988, **CONTINUITY PROGRAM** $------
- ❑ ❑ USA GE8811 **HM BOX,** 1988, **RON/BIRDIE/FRY KIDS AT THE BEACH** $7-10
- ❑ ❑ USA GE8801 **DRESS-UP MCNUGGETS,** 1988, PAPER/STICKERS/1P $1-1.25
- ❑ ❑ USA GE8802 **ZIPPER PULL-BIRDIE,** 1988, YEL/PNK W PNK LATCH $2-3
- ❑ ❑ USA GE8803 **ZIPPER PULL-GRIMACE,** 1988, PURP W PURP LATCH $2-3
- ❑ ❑ USA GE8804 **ZIPPER PULL-HAMBURGLAR,** 1988, BLK/WHT W BLK LATCH $2-3
- ❑ ❑ USA GE8805 **ZIPPER PULL-RONALD,** 1988, YEL/RED/WHT W RED LATCH $2-3
- ❑ ❑ USA GE8806 **PEN-BIRDIE,** 1988, PNK BIRDIE/PNK PEN $4-6
- ❑ ❑ USA GE8807 **PEN-FRY GIRL,** 1988, PNK/GIRL $4-6
- ❑ ❑ USA GE8808 **PEN-FRY GUY,** 1988, GRN/GUY $4-6

COMMENTS: REGIONAL DISTRIBUTION: USA - 1988. HM BOX WAS USED WHEN MCD WAS NOT SELLING SPECIFIC HM TOYS/CLEAN-UP WEEKS. BOX WAS ALSO USED IN COMMERCIALS NOT SELLING SPECIFIC HM TOYS. THESE ARE A SAMPLING OF GENERIC PREMIUMS GIVEN AWAY DURING 1988.

USA GE8810

USA GE8811

USA GE8801

USA GE8802 USA GE8804
USA GE8803 USA GE8805

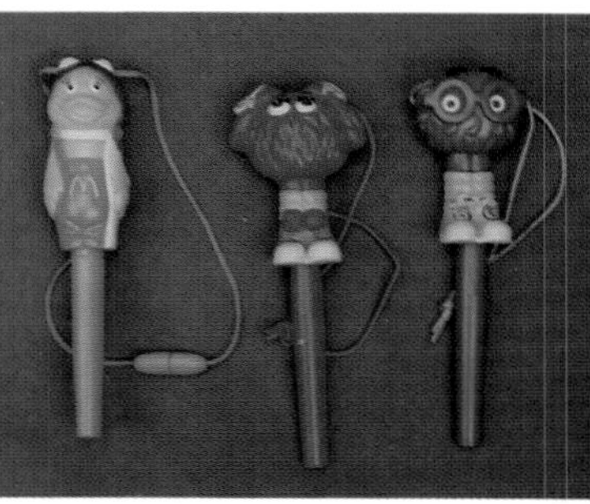

USA GE8806 USA GE8807 USA GE8808

USA/MUPPET BABIES HOLIDAY PROMOTION, 1988

❑ ❑ USA MU8801 **FOSSIE,** 1987, BRN/GOLD STUFFED DOLL $2-2.50
❑ ❑ USA MU8802 **KERMIT,** 1987, GRN/WHT/RED STUFFED DOLL $2-2.50
❑ ❑ USA MU8803 **MISS PIGGY,** 1987, RED/WHT/PNK STUFFED DOLL $2-2.50
❑ ❑ USA MU8864 **TRANSLITE/SM,** 1988 $5-8

COMMENTS: REGIONAL DISTRIBUTION: USA - 1988. DOLLS WERE SOLD FOR $1.99 DURING HOLIDAY PROMOTION.

USA MU8803 USA MU8801 USA MU8802

USA MU8864

1989

BEACH TOY I "COLLECT ALL 4"/TEST MARKET HAPPY MEAL, 1989
BEDTIME HAPPY MEAL, 1989
BURGER SIX PACK TO GO HAPPY MEAL, 1990/1989
CHIP N DALE RESCUE RANGERS HAPPY MEAL, 1989
DINOSAUR TALKING STORYBOOK HAPPY MEAL, 1989
FUN WITH FOOD HAPPY MEAL, 1989
FUNNY FRY FRIENDS I "COLLECT ALL 4"/TEST MARKET HAPPY MEAL, 1991/1989
GARFIELD II HAPPY MEAL, 1989
HALLOWEEN '89 HAPPY MEAL, 1989
LEGO MOTION IV HAPPY MEAL, 1989
LITTLE GARDENER HAPPY MEAL, 1989
MCBUNNY/EARSAN PAILS HAPPY MEAL, 1989
MICKEY'S BIRTHDAYLAND HAPPY MEAL, 1989
MIX'EM UP MONSTERS HAPPY MEAL, 1990/1989
MUPPET KIDS TEST MARKET HAPPY MEAL, 1989
NEW FOOD CHANGEABLES HAPPY MEAL, 1989
RAGGEDY ANN AND ANDY HAPPY MEAL, 1989
RAIN OR SHINE HAPPY MEAL, 1989
READ ALONG WITH RONALD HAPPY MEAL, 1989
SEA WORLD OF TEXAS II HAPPY MEAL, 1989
SUNGLASSES/MCDONALDLAND PROMOTION, 1989

BEACH TOY I "COLLECT ALL 4"/TEST MARKET HAPPY MEAL, 1989

❑ ❑ USA BT8955 **HM BAG,** 1989, **FRIENDLY REFLECTIONS** $15-20
❑ ❑ USA BT8956 **HM BAG,** 1989, **SILLY STORY** $15-20
❑ ❑ USA BT8957 **HM BAG,** 1989, **SPLASH PARTY** $15-20
❑ ❑ USA BT8958 **HM BAG,** 1989, **SUBMARINE SURPRISE** $15-20

USA BT8955

USA BT8956

USA BT8957

USA BT8958

USA BT8971 USA BT8972 USA BT8973 USA BT8970

- ❑ ❑ USA BT8971 **SET 1 FRY KID SUPER SAILOR,** 1989, RED-PUR CATAMARAN/YEL SAIL $10-12
- ❑ ❑ USA BT8972 **SET 2 GRIMACE BOUNCIN BEACH BALL,** 1989, YEL-BLU-GRN $10-12
- ❑ ❑ USA BT8973 **SET 3 RONALD FUN FLYER,** 1989, TUR-ORG RING $10-12
- ❑ ❑ USA BT8970 **SET 4 BIRDIE SEASIDE SUB,** 1988, PINK-BLU INFLATABLE $10-12
- ❑ ❑ USA BT8965 **TRANSLITE/MENU BOARD/LG,** 1989 $25-40

COMMENTS: LIMITED REGIONAL DISTRIBUTION: USA - JUNE 1989 IN GREENVILLE, SOUTH CAROLINA AND FRESNO, CALIF. "COLLECT ALL 4" WAS PRINTED ON THE MIP POLYBAGGED PACKAGE.

BEDTIME/RONALD MCDONALD HAPPY MEAL, 1989

- ❑ ❑ USA BE8910 **HM BOX,** 1988, **HIDDEN SLIPPERS** $3-4
- ❑ ❑ USA BE8911 **HM BOX,** 1988, **PILLOW FIGHT** $3-4
- ❑ ❑ USA BE8912 **HM BOX,** 1988, **SCAVENGER HUNT** $3-4
- ❑ ❑ USA BE8913 **HM BOX,** 1988, **SLUMBER PARTY** $3-4
- ❑ ❑ USA BE8901 **SET 1 TOOTHBRUSH,** 1988, YEL/RON W .85 OZ. CREST SPARKLE PASTE $5-7
- ❑ ❑ USA BE8902 **SET 2 DRINKING CUP,** 1988, RONALD ON STAR/12 OZ $2-3
- ❑ ❑ USA BE8903 **SET 3 FOAM WASH MIT,** 1988, RONALD SCRUBBING/BLU $3-5
- ❑ ❑ USA BE8904 **SET 4 NITE STAND RN,** 1988, GLOW IN THE DARK STAR/1P $1.50-2.50
- ❑ ❑ USA BE8964 **TRANSLITE/DRIVE-THRU/SM,** 1988 $12-20
- ❑ ❑ USA BE8965 **TRANSLITE/MENU BOARD/LG,** 1988 $20-35

COMMENTS: LIMITED NATIONAL DISTRIBUTION: USA - FEBRUARY 3-MARCH 2, 1989

USA BE8910 USA BE8912

USA BE8911 USA BE8913

BURGER SIX PACK TO GO HAPPY MEAL, 1990/1989

- ❑ ❑ USA BU8910 **HM BOX,** 1989, **"MCD 6 2 GO" WITHOUT ROUTE 66 SIGN** $20-25
- ❑ ❑ USA BU8911 **HM BOX,** 1990, **"SIX-PACK" W ROUTE 66 SIGN** $1-2

USA BE8901 USA BE8902 USA BE8903 USA BE8904

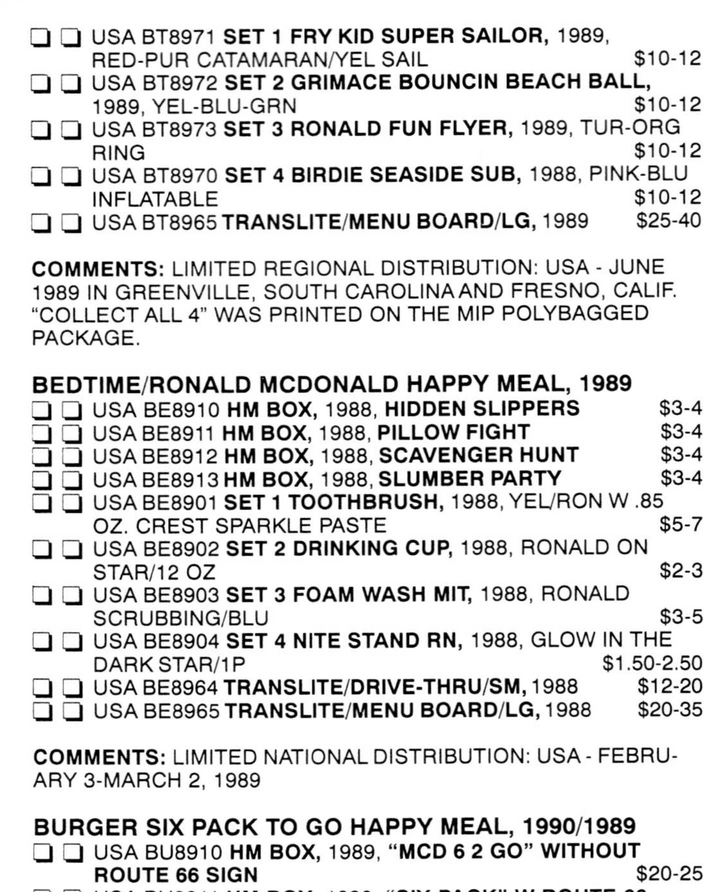

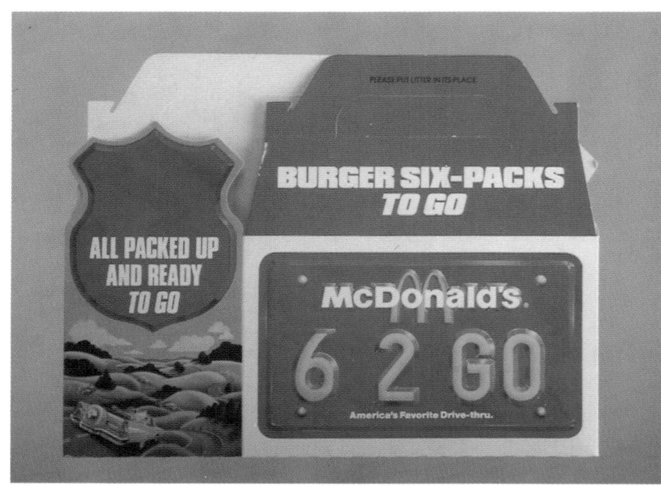

USA BU8910

USA BE8965

USA BU8911

❑ ❑ USA BU9064 **TRANSLITE/LG,** 1989, "MCD 6 2 GO" $20-25
❑ ❑ USA BU9065 **TRANSLITE/LG,** 1990, SIX-PACK $20-25

COMMENTS: LIMITED REGIONAL DISTRIBUTION: USA - 1989-94 IN CONNECTICUTT, FLORIDA AND SOUTHWEST USA-ROUTE 66. GENERIC BOX HELD SIX HAMBURGERS/CHEESEBURGERS.

USA BU9064

CHIP N DALE RESCUE RANGERS HAPPY MEAL, 1989

❑ ❑ USA CH8960 **HM BOX,** 1989, **FRAMED** $1-2
❑ ❑ USA CH8961 **HM BOX,** 1989, **ROLLIN' IN DOUGH** $1-2
❑ ❑ USA CH8962 **HM BOX,** 1989, **YOLK'S ON HIM** $1-2
❑ ❑ USA CH8963 **HM BOX,** 1989, **WHALE OF A TIME** $1-2
❑ ❑ USA CH8954 **U-3 CHIPS ROCKIN RACER,** 1989, 1P/RUBBER/RED ROCKET/CHIP $3-4
❑ ❑ USA CH8955 **U-3 GADGETS ROCKIN RIDER,** 1989, 1P/RUBBER/PNK CUP/GADGET $3-4

USA CH8960

USA CH8962

USA CH8961

USA CH8963

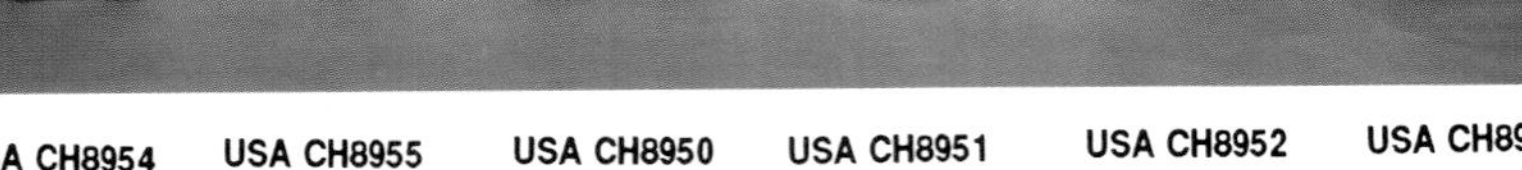
USA CH8954 USA CH8955 USA CH8950 USA CH8951 USA CH8952 USA CH8953

USA CH8926

USA CH8965

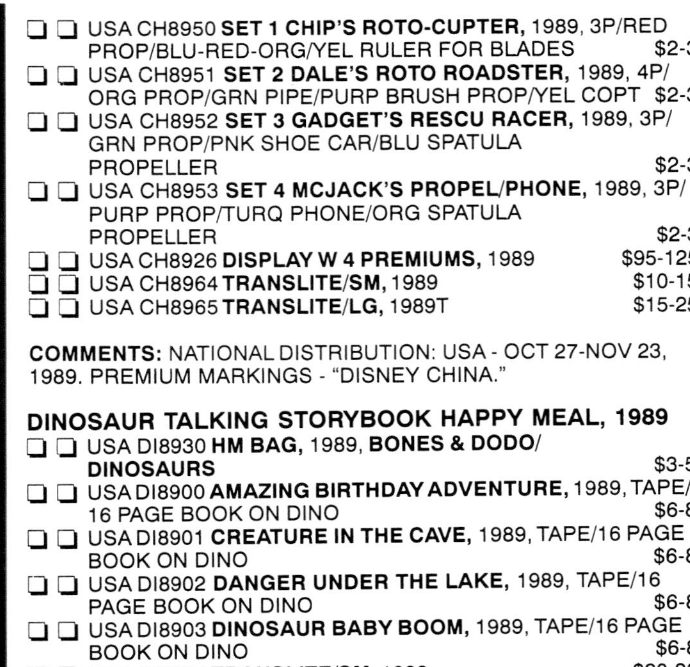
- ❑ ❑ USA CH8950 **SET 1 CHIP'S ROTO-CUPTER,** 1989, 3P/RED PROP/BLU-RED-ORG/YEL RULER FOR BLADES $2-3
- ❑ ❑ USA CH8951 **SET 2 DALE'S ROTO ROADSTER,** 1989, 4P/ORG PROP/GRN PIPE/PURP BRUSH PROP/YEL COPT $2-3
- ❑ ❑ USA CH8952 **SET 3 GADGET'S RESCU RACER,** 1989, 3P/GRN PROP/PNK SHOE CAR/BLU SPATULA PROPELLER $2-3
- ❑ ❑ USA CH8953 **SET 4 MCJACK'S PROPEL/PHONE,** 1989, 3P/PURP PROP/TURQ PHONE/ORG SPATULA PROPELLER $2-3
- ❑ ❑ USA CH8926 **DISPLAY W 4 PREMIUMS,** 1989 $95-125
- ❑ ❑ USA CH8964 **TRANSLITE/SM,** 1989 $10-15
- ❑ ❑ USA CH8965 **TRANSLITE/LG,** 1989T $15-25

COMMENTS: NATIONAL DISTRIBUTION: USA - OCT 27-NOV 23, 1989. PREMIUM MARKINGS - "DISNEY CHINA."

DINOSAUR TALKING STORYBOOK HAPPY MEAL, 1989

- ❑ ❑ USA DI8930 **HM BAG,** 1989, **BONES & DODO/DINOSAURS** $3-5
- ❑ ❑ USA DI8900 **AMAZING BIRTHDAY ADVENTURE,** 1989, TAPE/16 PAGE BOOK ON DINO $6-8
- ❑ ❑ USA DI8901 **CREATURE IN THE CAVE,** 1989, TAPE/16 PAGE BOOK ON DINO $6-8
- ❑ ❑ USA DI8902 **DANGER UNDER THE LAKE,** 1989, TAPE/16 PAGE BOOK ON DINO $6-8
- ❑ ❑ USA DI8903 **DINOSAUR BABY BOOM,** 1989, TAPE/16 PAGE BOOK ON DINO $6-8
- ❑ ❑ USA DI8964 **TRANSLITE/SM,** 1989 $20-30
- ❑ ❑ USA DI8965 **TRANSLITE/LG,** 1989 $25-40

COMMENTS: REGIONAL DISTRIBUTION: USA - SUMMER-1989 IN MICHIGANAND WISCONSIN.

USA DI8930

USA DI8965

FUN WITH FOOD HAPPY MEAL, 1989

❑ ❑ USA FU8907 **HM BOX,** 1988, **3 RING CIRCUS** A$3-4
❑ ❑ USA FU8908 **HM BOX,** 1988, **IN CONCERT** $3-4
❑ ❑ USA FU8909 **HM BOX,** 1988, **MAKING A SPLASH** $3-4
❑ ❑ USA FU8910 **HM BOX,** 1988, **MOVIE MAKING** $3-4
❑ ❑ USA FU8900 **HAMBURGER GUY,** 1989, 3P TOP/HMBG/BUN W DECAL F-PRICE $5-7
❑ ❑ USA FU8901 **FRENCH FRY GUY,** 1989, 3P BAG W FRIES W DECALS F-PRICE $5-7
❑ ❑ USA FU8902 **SOFT DRINK CUP,** 1989, 2P CUP W LID W DECALS FISHER-PRICE $5-7
❑ ❑ USA FU8903 **CHICKEN MCNUGGET GUYS,** 1989, 4P NUGGETS W CONTAINER F-PRICE $5-7
❑ ❑ USA FU8964 **TRANSLITE/SM,** 1989 $20-30
❑ ❑ USA FU8965 **TRANSLITE/LG,** 1989 $25-40

COMMENTS: LIMITED REGIONAL DISTRIBUTION: USA - SEPTEMBER 1-28, 1989.

USA FU8909

USA FU8910

USA FU8907

USA FU8900 USA FU8901 USA FU8902 USA FU8903

USA FU8908

USA FU8965

FUNNY FRY FRIENDS I "COLLECT ALL 4"/TEST MARKET HAPPY MEAL, 1991/1989

- ❑ ❑ USA FF8900 **GADZOOKS,** 1989, BLU KID W EYEGLASSES $10-12
- ❑ ❑ USA FF8901 **MATEY,** 1989, RED KID W PIRATE HAT $12-15
- ❑ ❑ USA FF8902 **TRACKER,** 1989, BLU KID W SAFARI HAT W SNAKE $10-12
- ❑ ❑ USA FF8903 **ZZZ'S,** 1989, TURQ KID W SLEEPING CAP W BEAR $10-12

COMMENTS: REGIONAL DISTRIBUTION: USA - 1989; MAY/JUNE 1991 IN CALIFORNIA, MARYLAND, PENNSYLVANIA. "COLLECT ALL 4" ON MIP INSERT CARD.

GARFIELD II HAPPY MEAL, 1989

- ❑ ❑ USA GA8910 **HM BOX,** 1989, **AHH VACATION** $2-3
- ❑ ❑ USA GA8911 **HM BOX,** 1989, **CAT WITH A MISSION** $2-3
- ❑ ❑ USA GA8912 **HM BOX,** 1989, **GARFIELD CATCHES LUNCH** $2-3
- ❑ ❑ USA GA8913 **HM BOX,** 1989, **MISCHIEF THIS MORNING** $2-3
- ❑ ❑ USA GA8914 **HM BAG,** 1989, **SAFARI GARFIELD** $10-15
- ❑ ❑ USA GA8905 **U-3 GARFIELD SKATING,** 1988, ON ROLLER SKATES $3-5
- ❑ ❑ USA GA8906 **U-3 GARFIELD W POOKY,** 1988, ON SKATE-BOARD, 1988 $3-5
- ❑ ❑ USA GA8901 **SET 1 GARFIELD ON SCOOTER,** 1988, ON YEL SCOOTER/PURP-RED WHEEL/2P $2-3
- ❑ ❑ USA GA8902 **SET 2 GARFIELD IN 4 WHEELER CAR,** 1988, ON BLU-YEL 4 WHEELER/2P $2-3
- ❑ ❑ USA GA8903 **SET 3 GARFIELD ON SKATEBOARD,** 1988, ON PNK SKATEBOARD/2P $2-3
- ❑ ❑ USA GA8904 **SET 4 GARFIELD/ODIE W SIDECAR,** 1988, ON RED MOTORCYCLE/BLU WHLS/2P $2-3
- ❑ ❑ USA GA8926 **DISPLAY/PREM,** 1989 $100-125

USA FF8900 USA FF8901 USA FF8902 USA FF8903

USA GA8912 USA GA8913

USA GA8905 USA GA8906

USA GA8901 USA GA8902 USA GA8903 USA GA8904

USA GA8910

USA GA8911

USA GA8926

❑ ❑ USA GA8941 **DANGLER/EACH,** 1989 $10-15
❑ ❑ USA GA8950 **BUTTON,** 1989, **GAR W ARCHES** $3-5
❑ ❑ USA GA8951 **PIN,** 1989, **GAR/ODIE W ARCHES** $3-5
❑ ❑ USA GA8952 **PIN,** 1989, **GAR W ARCHES** $3-5
❑ ❑ USA GA8964 **TRANSLITE/SM,** 1989 $12-15
❑ ❑ USA GA8965 **TRANSLITE/LG,** 1989 $15-25

COMMENTS: NATIONAL DISTRIBUTION: USA - JUNE 23-JULY 20, 1989. PREMIUM MARKINGS - "UNITED FEAT. SYND. CHINA H6."

HALLOWEEN '89 HAPPY MEAL, 1989

❑ ❑ USA HA8941 **PAIL-MCGHOST,** 1989, WHT W BLK FACE/WHT LID $1-1.50
❑ ❑ USA HA8942 **PAIL-MCWITCH,** 1989, GRN W GRN HAT/LID $1-1.50
❑ ❑ USA HA8964 **TRANSLITE/SM,** 1989 $4-6
❑ ❑ USA HA8965 **TRANSLITE/LG,** 1989 $8-12

COMMENTS: NATIONAL DISTRIBUTION: USA - OCTOBER 6-31, 1989. TRANSLITE SHOWS A THIRD PAIL. USA HA8725-27 PAILS WERE DISTRIBUTED AGAIN AS THIRD AND/OR FOURTH AND FIFTH PAILS. USA HA8941-42 HAD 4 GRID LIDS/NO NAME ON BACK OF PAILS.

USA GA8951

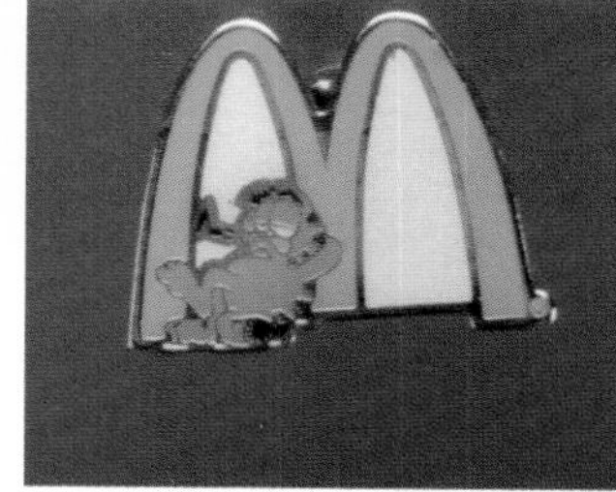

USA GA8952

USA GA8965

USA GA8941

USA HA8942 USA HA8941

USA GA8950

USA HA8965

LEGO MOTION IV HAPPY MEAL, 1989

- ❑ ❑ USA LE8915 **HM BOX,** 1989, **LAKE** $2-4
- ❑ ❑ USA LE8916 **HM BOX,** 1989, **TRAFFIC COPTER/ CLOCKS** $2-4
- ❑ ❑ USA LE8917 **HM BOX,** 1989, **ROAD RACE** $2-4
- ❑ ❑ USA LE8918 **HM BOX,** 1989, **RONALD IN HELICOPTER/ BLOCKS** $2-4
- ❑ ❑ USA LE8908 **U-3 GIDDY THE GATOR,** 1989, DUPLO/ PACKAGED 6P AGES 1 1/2-4 $2-4
- ❑ ❑ USA LE8909 **U-3 TUTTLE THE TURTLE,** 1989, DUPLO/ PACKAGED 6P AGES 1 1/2-4 $2-4
- ❑ ❑ USA LE8900 **SET 1A GYRO BIRD HELICOPTER,** 1989, LEGO/PACKAGED 19P $3-4
- ❑ ❑ USA LE8901 **SET 1B TURBO FORCE CAR,** 1989, LEGO/ PACKAGED 10P $3-4
- ❑ ❑ USA LE8902 **SET 2A SWAMP STINGER AIR BOAT,** 1989, LEGO/PACKAGED 16P $3-4
- ❑ ❑ USA LE8903 **SET 2B LIGHTNING STRIKER AIRPLANE,** 1989, LEGO/PACKAGED 14P $3-4
- ❑ ❑ USA LE8904 **SET 3A LAND LASER CAR,** 1989, LEGO/ PACKAGED 13P $3-4
- ❑ ❑ USA LE8905 **SET 3B SEA EAGLE SEAPLANE,** 1989, LEGO/ PACKAGED 15P $3-4
- ❑ ❑ USA LE8906 **SET 4A WIND WHIRLER HELICOPTER,** 1989, LEGO/PACKAGED 17P $3-4
- ❑ ❑ USA LE8907 **SET 4B SEA SKIMMER BOAT,** 1989, LEGO/ PACKAGED 17P $3-4

USA LE8915 USA LE8916

USA LE8917 USA LE8918

USA LE8909 USA LE8908

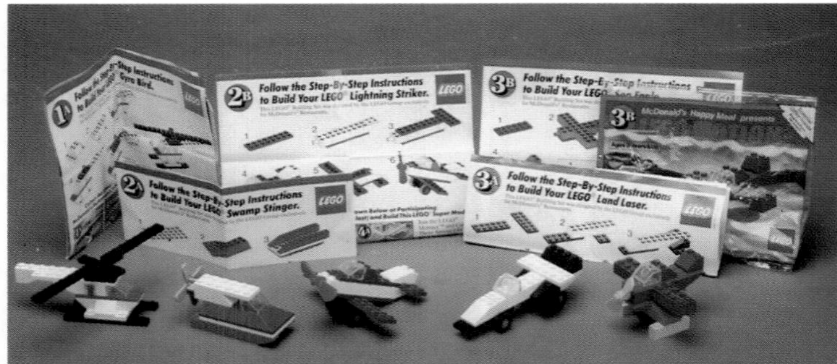

USA LE8900 USA LE8901

USA LE8902 USA LE8903

USA LE8904 USA LE8905

USA LE8906 USA LE8907

❑ ❑ USA LE8926 **DISPLAY/PREMIUMS,** 1989 $90-125
❑ ❑ USA LE8963 **MENU BOARD PREMIUM LUG-ON,** 1989 $10-12
❑ ❑ USA LE8964 **TRANSLITE/SM,** 1989 $8-12
❑ ❑ USA LE8965 **TRANSLITE/MOTION WHEEL/LG,** 1989 $25-35

COMMENTS: NATIONAL DISTRIBUTION: USA - JULY 28-AUGUST 24, 1989.

LITTLE GARDENER HAPPY MEAL, 1989

❑ ❑ USA LG8985 **HM BAG,** 1989, **BIRDIE'S BOUQUET** $1-2
❑ ❑ USA LG8986 **HM BAG,** 1989, **GARDEN GOODIES** $1-2
❑ ❑ USA LG8987 **HM BAG,** 1989, **RADISH CONTEST** $1-2
❑ ❑ USA LG8988 **HM BAG,** 1989, **WHOSE HOSE** $1-2
❑ ❑ USA LG8979 **U-3 BIRDIE'S SHOVEL,** 1988, ORG W/O ZEBRA STRIPES/NO SEEDS $4-6
❑ ❑ USA LG8975 **SET 1 BIRDIE'S SHOVEL,** 1988, ORG W BURPEE MARIGOLD SEEDS $1 -1.50
❑ ❑ USA LG8976 **SET 2 FRY KIDS PLANTER,** 1988, TURQ W PUR LID/HANDLE $1-1.50

USA LE8926

USA LE8964

USA LG8979 USA LG8975

USA LG8976 USA LG8977 USA LG8978

USA LG8985 USA LG8986

USA LG8987 USA LG8988

USA LG8965

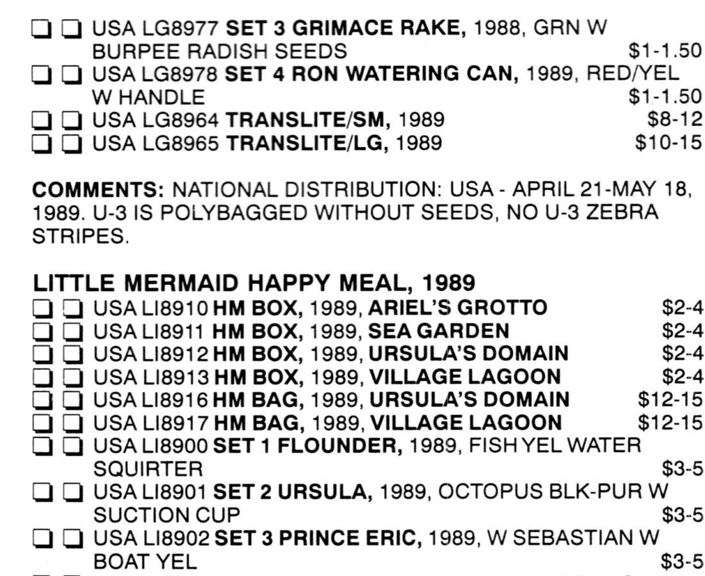

❑ ❑ USA LG8977 **SET 3 GRIMACE RAKE,** 1988, GRN W BURPEE RADISH SEEDS $1-1.50
❑ ❑ USA LG8978 **SET 4 RON WATERING CAN,** 1989, RED/YEL W HANDLE $1-1.50
❑ ❑ USA LG8964 **TRANSLITE/SM,** 1989 $8-12
❑ ❑ USA LG8965 **TRANSLITE/LG,** 1989 $10-15

COMMENTS: NATIONAL DISTRIBUTION: USA - APRIL 21-MAY 18, 1989. U-3 IS POLYBAGGED WITHOUT SEEDS, NO U-3 ZEBRA STRIPES.

LITTLE MERMAID HAPPY MEAL, 1989

❑ ❑ USA LI8910 **HM BOX,** 1989, **ARIEL'S GROTTO** $2-4
❑ ❑ USA LI8911 **HM BOX,** 1989, **SEA GARDEN** $2-4
❑ ❑ USA LI8912 **HM BOX,** 1989, **URSULA'S DOMAIN** $2-4
❑ ❑ USA LI8913 **HM BOX,** 1989, **VILLAGE LAGOON** $2-4
❑ ❑ USA LI8916 **HM BAG,** 1989, **URSULA'S DOMAIN** $12-15
❑ ❑ USA LI8917 **HM BAG,** 1989, **VILLAGE LAGOON** $12-15
❑ ❑ USA LI8900 **SET 1 FLOUNDER,** 1989, FISH YEL WATER SQUIRTER $3-5
❑ ❑ USA LI8901 **SET 2 URSULA,** 1989, OCTOPUS BLK-PUR W SUCTION CUP $3-5
❑ ❑ USA LI8902 **SET 3 PRINCE ERIC,** 1989, W SEBASTIAN W BOAT YEL $3-5
❑ ❑ USA LI8903 **SET 4 ARIEL,** 1989, MERMAID KNEELING TURQ-ORG $3-5
❑ ❑ USA LI8964 **TRANSLITE/SM,** 1989 $15-25
❑ ❑ USA LI8965 **TRANSLITE/LG,** 1989 $20-30

COMMENTS: NATIONAL DISTRIBUTION: USA - NOVEMBER 24-DECEMBER 21, 1989. TWO BAGS WERE TEST MARKETED IN SOUTH BEND IN. PREMIUM MARKINGS - "DISNEY CHINA."

USA LI8910 USA LI8911

USA LI8912 USA LI8913

USA LI8916

USA LI8900 USA LI8901 USA LI8902 USA LI8903

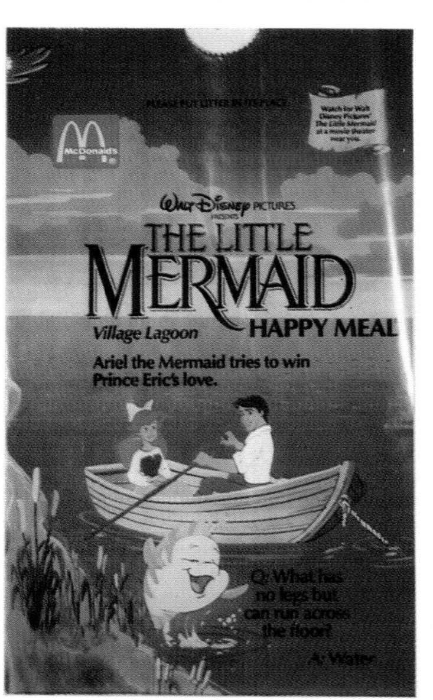

USA LI8917

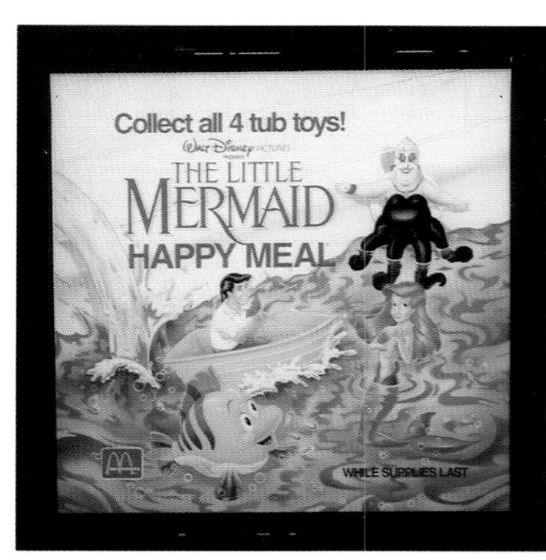

USA LI8965

MCBUNNY/EARSAN PAILS HAPPY MEAL, 1989

- ❑ ❑ USA BP8901 **FLUFFY,** 1988, PAIL/WHT-BLU W BLU LID/YEL HANDLE $5-8
- ❑ ❑ USA BP8902 **PINKY,** 1988, PAIL/WHT-YEL W YEL LID/YEL HANDLE $5-8
- ❑ ❑ USA BP8903 **WHISKERS,** 1988, PAIL/WHT-GRN GRN LID/ YEL HANDLE $5-8
- ❑ ❑ USA BP8964 **TRANSLITE/SM,** 1988 $12-15
- ❑ ❑ USA BP8965 **TRANSLITE/LG,** 1988 $15-20

COMMENTS: REGIONAL DISTRIBUTION: USA - SPRING 1989 IN ILLINOIS, CALIFORNIA, MISSOURI, ALABAMA IN THE SPRING OF 1991. NOTE: TRANSLITE SAYS, "EARS" AN OFFER.

MICKEY'S BIRTHDAYLAND HAPPY MEAL, 1989

- ❑ ❑ USA MB8915 **HM BOX,** 1988, **BARN/DAISY CAFE** $2-4
- ❑ ❑ USA MB8916 **HM BOX,** 1988, **MICKEY'S HOUSE** $2-4
- ❑ ❑ USA MB8917 **HM BOX,** 1988, **MINNIE'S DRESS SHOP** $2-4
- ❑ ❑ USA MB8918 **HM BOX,** 1988, **THEATRE** $2-4
- ❑ ❑ USA MB8919 **HM BOX,** 1988, **TRAIN STATION** $2-4
- ❑ ❑ USA MB8905 **U-3 DONALD'S JEEPSTER,** 1988, BLU W WHT WHLS/YEL STRIPES $4-6
- ❑ ❑ USA MB8911 **U-3 DONALD'S JEEPSTER,** 1988, BLU W WHT WHLS/WHT STRIPES $5-8
- ❑ ❑ USA MB8906 **U-3 DONALD'S JEEPSTER,** 1988, GRN W RED WHLS/WHT STRIPES $4-6
- ❑ ❑ USA MB8907 **U-3 GOOFY'S SEDAN,** 1988, BLU W WHT WHLS $4-6
- ❑ ❑ USA MB8908 **U-3 GOOFY'S SEDAN,** 1988, GRN W RED WHLS $4-6
- ❑ ❑ USA MB8909 **U-3 MICKEY'S ROADSTER,** 1988, RED W YEL WHLS $4-6
- ❑ ❑ USA MB8910 **U-3 MINNIE'S CONVERTIBLE,** 1988,PNK W YEL WHLS $4-6
- ❑ ❑ USA MB8900 **SET 1 DONALD'S ENGINE,** 1988, GRN $2-3
- ❑ ❑ USA MB8901 **SET 2 MINNIE CONVERTIBLE,** 1988, PINK $2-3
- ❑ ❑ USA MB8902 **SET 3 GOOFY'S JALOPY,** 1988, BLU $2-3
- ❑ ❑ USA MB8903 **SET 4 PLUTO CAR,** 1988, PURPLE $2-3
- ❑ ❑ USA MB8904 **SET 5 MICKEY ROADSTER,** 1988, RED $2-3
- ❑ ❑ USA MB8926 **DISPLAY W 2 SETS/PREMIUIMS,** 1988 $150-250

USA BP8903

USA BP8901

USA BP8965

USA MB8919

USA MB8906 USA MB8908 USA MB8910

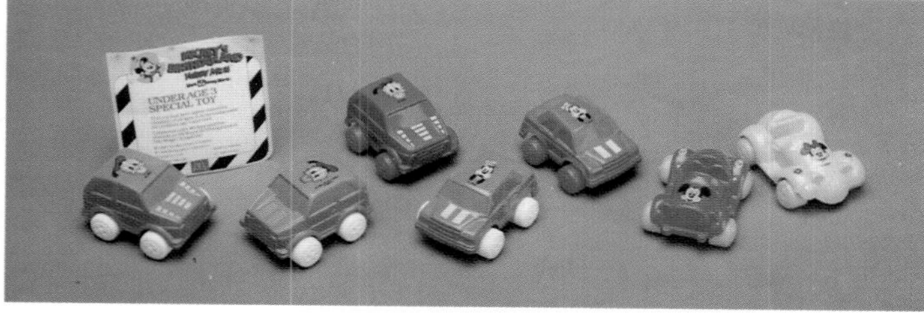

USA MB8911 USA MB8905 USA MB8907 USA MB8909

USA MB8915 USA MB8916

USA MB8900 USA MB8901 USA MB8902 USA MB8903 USA MB8904

USA MB8917 USA MB8918

USA MB8926

❑ ❑ USA MB8941 **DANGLER/EACH,** 1988 $8-12
❑ ❑ USA MB8963 **MENU BOARD LUG-ON/EACH,** 1988 $15-20
❑ ❑ USA MB8964 **TRANSLITE/SM,** 1988 $15-25
❑ ❑ USA MB8965 **TRANSLITE/LG,** 1988 $20-35

COMMENTS: NATIONAL DISTRIBUTION: USA - MARCH 17-APRIL 20, 1989. PREMIUM MARKINGS - "DISNEY CHINA."

MIX'EM UP MONSTERS HAPPY MEAL, 1990/1989

❑ ❑ USA MI8910 **HM BOX,** 1988, **MONSTERS ON MOON** $4-7
❑ ❑ USA MI8900 **BLIBBLE,** 1986, GREEN/EXTENDED EYES 3P $2-3
❑ ❑ USA MI8901 **CORKLE,** 1986, BLUE/FOLDED ARMS 3P $2-3
❑ ❑ USA MI8902 **GROPPLE,** 1986, YEL/2 HEADS 3P $2-3
❑ ❑ USA MI8903 **THUGGER,** 1986, PUR/LARGE TUSKS 3P $2-3
❑ ❑ USA MI8964 **TRANSLITE/SM,** 1988 $12-20
❑ ❑ USA MI8965 **TRANSLITE/LG,** 1988 $15-25

COMMENTS: REGIONAL DISTRIBUTION: USA - JANUARY/ SEPTEMBER 1989 AND SEPTEMBER 7-OCTOBER 4, 1990 IN NORTHERN CALIFORNIA, ST.LOUIS, MISSOURI. PREMIUM MARKINGS - "CURRENT INC CHINA F8X."

MUPPET KIDS TEST MARKET HAPPY MEAL, 1989

❑ ❑ USA MU8910 **HM BOX,** 1989, **CLUB HOUSE** $15-20
❑ ❑ USA MU8911 **HM BOX,** 1989, **SCHOOL** $15-20
❑ ❑ USA MU8900 **SET 1 KERMIT,** 1989, RED BIKE/YEL WHEEL $20-25

USA MB8965

USA MB8904

USA MU8910

USA MI8910

USA MI8902 USA MI8903 USA MI8900 USA MI8901

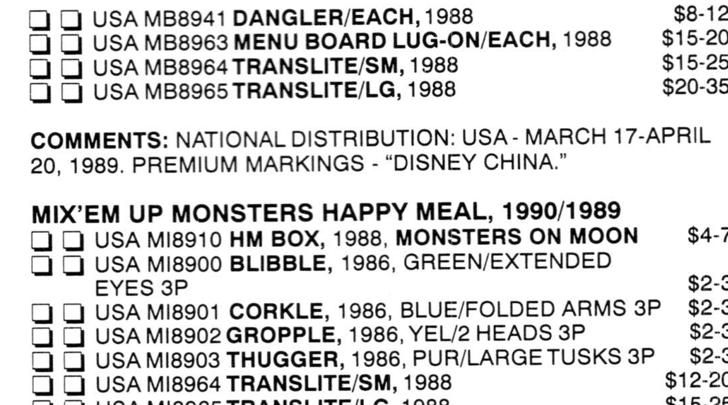

USA MI8965

USA MU8911

USA MU8900

❑ ❑ USA MU8901 **SET 2 MISS PIGGY,** 1989, PNK BIKE/GRN WHEEL/YEL $20-25

❑ ❑ USA MU8902 **SET 3 GONZO,** 1989, YEL BIKE/PNK WHEEL/RED $20-25

❑ ❑ USA MU8903 **SET 4 FOZZIE,** 1989, GRN BIKE/RED WHEEL $20-25

❑ ❑ USA MU8926 **DISPLAY/PREMIUMS,** 1989 $225-275

❑ ❑ USA MU8964 **TRANSLITE/SM,** 1989 $25-40

❑ ❑ USA MU8965 **TRANSLITE/LG,** 1989 $35-50

COMMENTS: LIMITED REGIONAL DISTRIBUTION: USA - SUMMER 1989 IN ST. LOUIS, MISSOURI TEST MARKET. DISCONTINUED AFTER HENSON DROPPED THE KIDS CONCEPT. PREMIUM MARKINGS - "HA! 1989 CHINA." OR "SIMON MKT."

NEW FOOD CHANGEABLES HAPPY MEAL, 1989

❑ ❑ USA NE8915 **HM BOX,** 1988, **LOST IN SPACE** $2-3

❑ ❑ USA NE8916 **HM BOX,** 1988, **JEEPERS/PEEPERS** $2-3

❑ ❑ USA NE8917 **HM BOX,** 1988, **TONGUE TIPPERS** $2-3

❑ ❑ USA NE8918 **HM BOX,** 1988, **WHO'S THAT** $2-3

❑ ❑ USA NE8908 **U-3 MCD PALS,** 1988, WHT CUBE W CHAR PHOTO $5-8

❑ ❑ USA NE8900 **SET 1A ROBOCAKES,** 1988, HOT CAKES/GRN HANDS $2-4

❑ ❑ USA NE8901 **SET 1B GALLACTA BURGER,** 1988, QUARTER POUNDER/PNK HANDS $2-4

❑ ❑ USA NE8902 **SET 2A FRY FORCE,** 1987, LARGE FRENCH FRIES/TURQ HANDS $2-4

❑ ❑ USA NE8903 **SET 2B KRYPTO CUP,** 1988, MILK SHAKE OPENS FROM SIDE/BLU HANDS $2-4

❑ ❑ USA NE8904 **SET 3A MACRO MAC,** 1987, BIG MAC/PNK HANDS $2-4

❑ ❑ USA NE8905 **SET 3B TURBO CONE,** 1988, ICE CREAM CONE/PNK HANDS $2-4

❑ ❑ USA NE8906 **SET 4A C2-CHEESBURGER,** 1988, CHEESEBURGER/ORG HANDS $2-4

❑ ❑ USA NE8907 **SET 4B FRY-BOT,** 1988, SMALL FRIES/PNK FEET $2-4

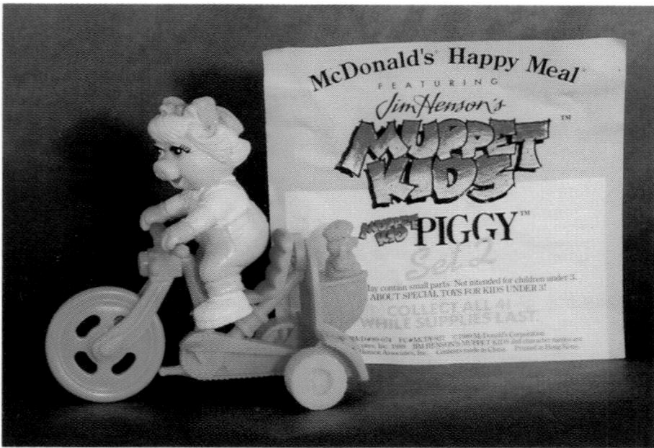

USA MU8901

USA MU8902

USA MU8903

USA NE8915 USA NE8916

USA NE8917 USA NE8918

USA NE8908 USA NE8900 USA NE8901 USA NE8902 USA NE8903

USA NE8904 USA NE8905 USA NE8906 USA NE8907

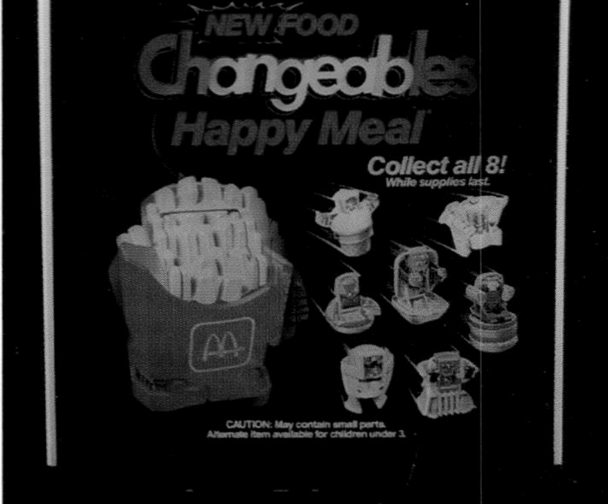

USA NE8964

USA NE8926

- ❑ ❑ USA NE8926 **DISPLAY/PREMIUMS,** 1988 $100-140
- ❑ ❑ USA NE8963 **MENU BOARD/LUG-ON,** 1988 $12-15
- ❑ ❑ USA NE8964 **TRANSLITE/SM,** 1988 $12-20
- ❑ ❑ USA NE8965 **TRANSLITE/X-O GRAPHIC/LG,** 1988 $25-40

COMMENTS: NATIONAL DISTRIBUTION: USA MAY 19-JUNE 15, 1989. VERSION 1, ISSUED IN 1987 (SEE CHANGEABLES '87) HAD 5 PREMIUMS (BIG MAC, LARGE FRENCH FRIES, EGG MCMUFFIN, CHICKEN MCNUGGETS, QUARTER POUNDER). VERSION 2 ISSUED IN 1987, ADDED A MILK SHAKE. VERSION 3, ISSUED IN 1989 (NEW FOOD CHANGEABLES), REISSUED THE LARGE FRIES AND THE BIG MAC FROM 1987 AND ADDED 6 NEW DESIGNS. THE MACRO MAC/BIG MAC HAD PINK PAINTED HANDS.

THE INVASION HAS BEGUN!
Robo-cakes
Gallacta Burger
Fry Force
Krypto Cup
Macro Mac
Turbo Cone
C2-Cheeseburger
Fry-Bot

USA NE8963

RAGGEDY ANN AND ANDY HAPPY MEAL, 1989

- ❑ ❑ USA RA8910 **HM BOX,** 1988, **SCHOOLHOUSE** $4-6
- ❑ ❑ USA RA8905 **U-3 CAMEL W WRINKLED KNEES,** 1989, 1P W/O TEETER TOTTER $8-12
- ❑ ❑ USA RA8901 **SET 1 RAGGEDY ANDY,** 1989, 3P W SLIDE $6-8
- ❑ ❑ USA RA8902 **SET 2 RAGGEDY ANN,** 1989, 5P W SWING $6-8
- ❑ ❑ USA RA8903 **SET 3 GROUCHY BEAR,** 1989, 3P W MERRY-GO-ROUND $6-8
- ❑ ❑ USA RA8904 **SET 4 CAMEL W WRINKLED KNEES,** 1989, 3P W TEETER TOTTER $6-8
- ❑ ❑ USA RA8964 **TRANSLITE/SM,** 1989 $25-40
- ❑ ❑ USA RA8965 **TRANSLITE/LG,** 1989 $35-30

USA RA8910

USA RA8905 USA RA8902 USA RA8903 USA RA8904
USA RA8901

USA RA8965

COMMENTS: REGIONAL DISTRIBUTION: USA - SEPTEMBER 1-28, 1989 IN SAN FRANCISCO, CALIFORNIA; PORTLAND, OREGON; NEVADA, HAWAII AND SOUTHERN PENNSYLVANIA. PREMIUM MARKINGS - "1988 MACMILLIAN INC CHINA OR "1989 SIMON MARKETING INC CHINA."

RAIN OR SHINE HAPPY MEAL, 1989

- ❑ ❑ USA GE8900 **HM BOX,** 1989, **BUBBLES** $1-1.50
- ❑ ❑ USA GE8901 **HM BOX,** 1989, **UMBRELLAS** $1-1.50
- ❑ ❑ USA GE8950 **BUTTON,** 1989, **BUILD YOUR OWN HM** $2-3

COMMENTS: REGIONAL DISTRIBUTION: USA - 1989 DURING CLEAN-UP WEEK. GENERIC PREMIUMS WERE USED.

READ ALONG WITH RONALD HAPPY MEAL, 1989

- ❑ ❑ USA RE8930 **HM BAG,** 1989, **MAZE/CONNECT DOT ACTIVITY** $3-5
- ❑ ❑ USA RE8900 **DINOSAUR IN MCDONALDLAND,** 1989, GRN TAPE/BOOK/2P $15-20
- ❑ ❑ USA RE8901 **GRIMACE GOES TO SCHOOL,** 1989, PURP TAPE/BOOK/2P $15-20
- ❑ ❑ USA RE8902 **THE DAY BIRDIE THE EARLY BIRD LEARNED TO FLY,** 1989, YEL TAPE/BOOK/2P $15-20
- ❑ ❑ USA RE8903 **THE MYSTERY OF THE MISSING FRENCH FRYS,** 1989, RED TAPE/BOOK/2P $15-20
- ❑ ❑ USA RE8964 **TRANSLITE/SM,** 1989 $12-20
- ❑ ❑ USA RE8965 **TRANSLITE/LG,** 1989 $15-25

COMMENTS: REGIONAL DISTRIBUTION: USA - SUMMER 1989 IN NEW ENGLAND STATES.

SEA WORLD OF TEXAS II HAPPY MEAL, 1989

- ❑ ❑ USA SE8930 **HM BOX,** 1988, **RONALD IN A YEL SUB/ W COUPON** $10-15
- ❑ ❑ USA SE8925 **SEA OTTER,** 1988, STUFFED ANIMAL/BRN/WHT/6" $8-12
- ❑ ❑ USA SW8800 **DOLPHIN,** 1988, GREY/WHT W BLK EYES 6" $8-12
- ❑ ❑ USA SW8803 **WHALE,** 1988, BLACK-WHT 6" $8-12

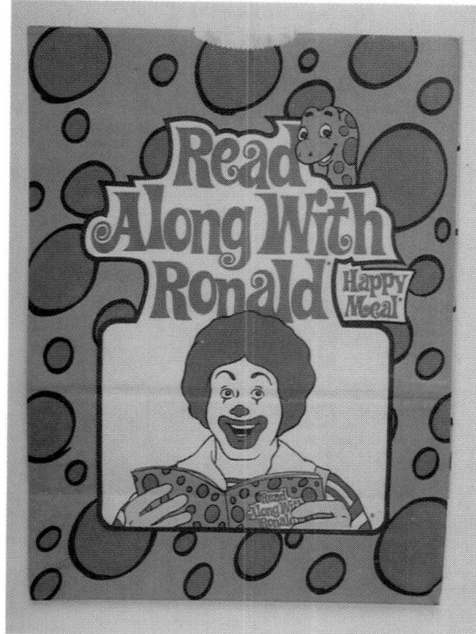

USA RE8930

USA RE8900 USA RE8901

USA GE8900 USA GE8901

USA RE8902 USA RE8903

USA GE8950

USA RE8965

USA SE8930

USA SE8926 USA SE8925 USA SE8927

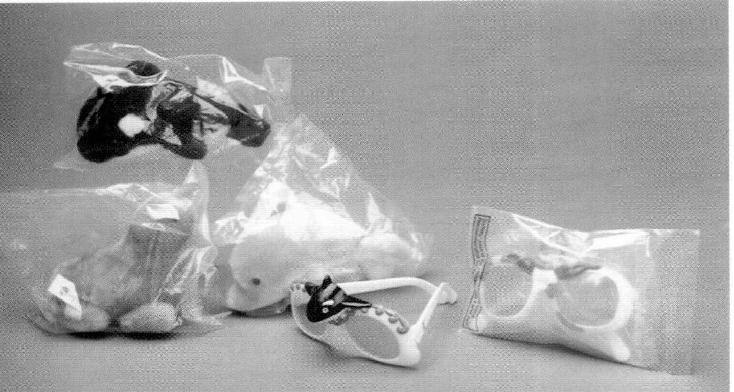

USA SU8803 USA SU8800 USA SE8926
USA SE8925 USA SE8927

USA SE8965

USA SU8901 USA SU8902 USA SU8903 USA SU8904

- ❑ ❑ USA SE8926 **PENGUIN SUNGLASSES,** 1989, BLK-WHT $15-20
- ❑ ❑ USA SE8927 **WHALE SUNGLASSES,** 1989, BLK-WHT $15-20
- ❑ ❑ USA SE8937 **DISPLAY CARD PREMIUMS,** 1989 $125-150
- ❑ ❑ USA SE8964 **TRANSLITE/SM,** 1989 $15-25
- ❑ ❑ USA SE8965 **TRANSLITE/LG,** 1989 $20-35

COMMENTS: REGIONAL DISTRIBUTION: USA - 1989 IN SAN ANTONIO, TEXAS. USA SW8800 DOLPHIN AND USA SW8803 WHALE WERE DISTRIBUTED AGAIN WITH SEA WORLD OF TEXAS II IN 1989.

SUNGLASSES/MCDONALDLAND PROMOTION, 1989

- ❑ ❑ USA SU8901 **BIRDIE THE EARLY BIRD,** 1988, WHT W BRAIDS ON TOP $3-5
- ❑ ❑ USA SU8902 **GRIMACE,** 1988, PURP W ARMS ON TOP $3-5
- ❑ ❑ USA SU8903 **HAMBURGLAR,** 1988, YEL W ARMS ON TOP $3-5
- ❑ ❑ USA SU8904 **RONALD MCDONALD,** 1988, YEL W ARMS ON TOP $3-5
- ❑ ❑ USA SU8964 **TRANSLITE/SM,** 1989 $10-15

COMMENTS: REGIONAL DISTRIBUTION: SOUTHERN USA - 1989 IN FLORIDA, GEORGIA, ALABAMA.

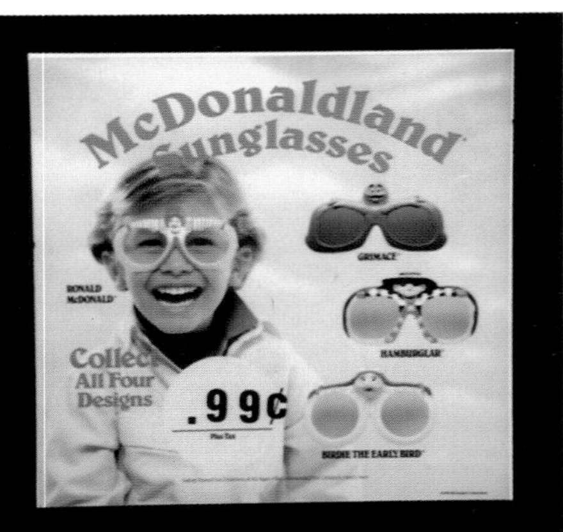

USA SU8964

1990

BARBIE / HOT WHEELS I TEST MARKET HAPPY MEAL, 1990
BEACH TOY II "COLLECT ALL 8" HAPPY MEAL, 1990
BERENSTAIN BEAR BOOKS HAPPY MEAL, 1990
CAMP MCDONALDLAND HAPPY MEAL, 1990
DINK THE LITTLE DINOSAUR HAPPY MEAL, 1990
FROM THE HEART/VALENTINE HAPPY MEAL, 1990
FRY BENDERS HAPPY MEAL, 1990
FUNNY FRY FRIENDS II "COLLECT ALL 8" HAPPY MEAL, 1990
HALLOWEEN '90 HAPPY MEAL, 1990
HATS HAPPY MEAL, 1990
I LIKE BIKES HAPPY MEAL, 1990
JUNGLE BOOK HAPPY MEAL, 1990
MCDONALDLAND CARNIVAL HAPPY MEAL, 1991/1990
MCDONALDLAND DOUGH HAPPY MEAL, 1990
MCDRIVE THRU CREW TEST MARKET HAPPY MEAL, 1990
PEANUTS HAPPY MEAL, 1990
RESCUERS DOWN UNDER HAPPY MEAL, 1990
SPORTS BALL HAPPY MEAL, 1991/1990
SUPER MARIO 3 NINTENDO HAPPY MEAL, 1990
TALE SPIN HAPPY MEAL, 1990
TOM & JERRY BAND HAPPY MEAL, 1990
TURBO MACS II HAPPY MEAL, 1990
USA/GENERIC PROMOTION, 1990

BARBIE / HOT WHEELS I TEST MARKET HAPPY MEAL, 1990

- ❑ ❑ USA BA9020 **HM BOX,** 1990, **BARBIE IN CONCERT/ GARAGE** $-----
- ❑ ❑ USA BA9021 **HM BOX,** 1990, **MOVIE STAR/ROAD RACE** $-----
- ❑ ❑ USA BA9001 **MOVIE STAR,** 1990, 1P PINK DRESS/PAPER DRESSING ROOM DIORAMA $------
- ❑ ❑ USA BA9002 **IN CONCERT,** 1990, 1P BLACK DRESS/PAPER CONCERT DIORAMA $------

USA BA9020

USA BA9002

USA BA9021

USA BA9001

USA BA9003

❑ ❑ USA BA9003 **TEA PARTY,** 1990, 1P PINK DRESS/PAPER TEA PARTY DIORAMA $------
❑ ❑ USA BA9004 **MOONLIGHT BALL,** 1990, 1P PINK GOWN/ PAPER BALLROOM DIORAMA $------
❑ ❑ USA HW9011 **SET 1 CORVETTE,** 1990, WHT W RED STRIPE $25-35
❑ ❑ USA HW9012 **SET 2 FERRARI,** 1990, RED $25-35
❑ ❑ USA HW9013 **SET 3 HOT BIRD,** 1990, SIL W PIN STRIPE $25-35
❑ ❑ USA HW9014 **SET 4 CAMARO Z-28,** 1990, TURQ W BLU STRIPE, 1990 $25-35
❑ ❑ USA BA9026 **DISPLAY/PREMIUMS,** 1990 $250-350
❑ ❑ USA BA9064 **TRANSLITE/SM,** 1990 $75-100
❑ ❑ USA BA9065 **TRANSLITE/LG,** 1990 $100-125

COMMENTS: REGIONAL DISTRIBUTION: USA TEST MARKET - JULY 1990 IN SAVANNAH, GEORGIA. PREMIUM MARKINGS - "MATTEL INC 1989 ARCO CHINA." SAME PREMIUMS WERE SOLD IN RETAIL STORES. MIP MUST INCLUDE PAPER BACKDROP.

USA BA9004

BEACH TOY II "COLLECT ALL 8" HAPPY MEAL, 1990

❑ ❑ USA BE9085 **HM BAG,** 1989, **GRIMACE W TUBE** $1-2
❑ ❑ USA BE9086 **HM BAG,** 1989, **HAMBURGLAR W BALL** $1-2

USA HW9013

USA HW9011

USA HW9014

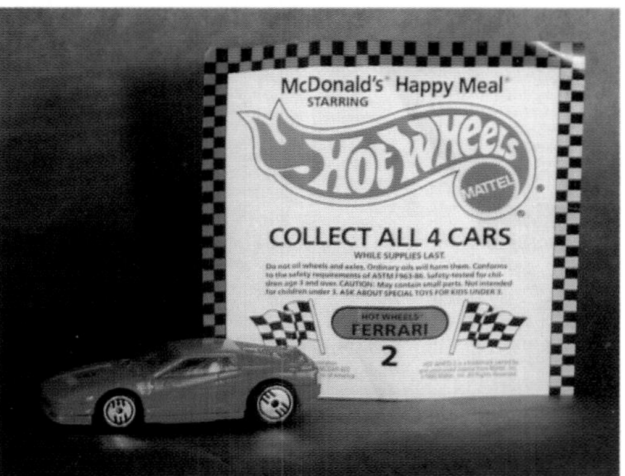

USA HW9012

USA BE9085

USA BE9086

- ❑ ❑ USA BE9087 **HM BAG**, 1989, **RONALD W STARS/SAND CASTLE** $1-2
- ❑ ❑ USA BE9088 **HM BAG**, 1989, **RONALD W TREASURE CHEST** $1-2
- ❑ ❑ USA BE9071 **SET 1 FRY KID SUPER SAILOR,** 1989, RED-PUR CATAMARAN/YEL SAIL $1-1.50
- ❑ ❑ USA BE9074 **SET 2 SAND PAIL W GRIMACE,** 1989, CLEAR PLASTIC PAIL/YEL LID-HANDLE $1-1.50
- ❑ ❑ USA BE9072 **SET 3 GRIMACE BOUNCIN BEACH BALL,** 1989, YEL-BLU-GRN $1-1.50
- ❑ ❑ USA BE9075 **SET 4 BIRDIE W SHOVEL/SAND,** 1989, RED W YEL SAND PROPELLER $1-1.50
- ❑ ❑ USA BE9073 **SET 5 RONALD FUN FLYER,** 1989, INFLATABLE TUR-ORG RING $1-1.50
- ❑ ❑ USA BE9076 **SET 6 FRY KIDS SAND CASTLE PAIL,** 1989, CLEAR PLASTIC/RED LID-HANDLE $1-1.50
- ❑ ❑ USA BE9070 **SET 7 BIRDIE SEASIDE SUBMARINE,** 1988, PINK-BLU INFLATABLE $1-1.50
- ❑ ❑ USA BE9077 **SET 8 RONALD SQUIRT GUN RAKE,** 1989, BLU-GRN $1-1.50
- ❑ ❑ USA BE9041 **CEILING DANGLER/SETS 1-4,** 1989 $20-35
- ❑ ❑ USA BE9042 **CEILING DANGLER/SETS 5-8,** 1989 $20-35
- ❑ ❑ USA BE9065 **TRANSLITE/LG,** 1989 $15-25
- ❑ ❑ USA BE9064 **TRANSLITE/SM,** 1989 $10-15

USA BE9087

USA BE9088

USA BE9071

USA BE9074

USA BE9072

USA BE9075

USA BE9073

USA BE9076

USA BE9070

USA BE9077

USA BE9065

COMMENTS: NATIONAL DISTRIBUTION: USA - JUN 1-28, 1990. "COLLECT ALL 8" PRINTED ON THE MIP PACKAGE. USA BE9070-73 = USA BT8970-73, BEACH TOY I "COLLECT ALL 4" HM, 1989, LOOSE OUT OF PACKAGE.

BERENSTAIN BEAR BOOKS HAPPY MEAL, 1990

- ❑ ❑ USA BB9040 **HM BOX,** 1989, **SHARING BRINGS GOOD THINGS** $1-2
- ❑ ❑ USA BB9041 **HM BOX,** 1989, **TEAMWORK SAVES THE DAY** $1-2
- ❑ ❑ USA BB9042 **HM BOX,** 1989, **THANK GOODNESS.. BEARS** $1-2
- ❑ ❑ USA BB9043 **HM BOX,** 1989, **WHAT TO DO DEPENDS ON YOU** $1-2
- ❑ ❑ USA BB9044 **HM BAG,** 1989, **TEAMWORK SAVES THE DAY** $15-20
- ❑ ❑ USA BB9045 **HM BAG,** 1989, **WHAT TO DO DEPENDS ON YOU** $15-20

USA BB9040

USA BB9041

USA BB9042

USA BB9043

USA BB9044

USA BB9045

❑ ❑ USA BB9025 **LIFE WITH PAPA,** 1990, STORYBOOK $2-3
❑ ❑ USA BB9026 **LIFE WITH PAPA,** 1990, ACTIVITY BOOK $2-3
❑ ❑ USA BB9027 **ATTIC TREASURE,** 1990, STORYBOOK $2-3
❑ ❑ USA BB9028 **ATTIC TREASURE,** 1990, ACTIVITY BOOK $2-3
❑ ❑ USA BB9029 **SUBSTI TEACHER,** 1990, STORYBOOK $2-3
❑ ❑ USA BB9030 **SUBSTI TEACHER,** 1990, ACTIVITY BOOK $2-3
❑ ❑ USA BB9031 **EAGER BEAVERS,** 1990, STORYBOOK $2-3
❑ ❑ USA BB9032 **EAGER BEAVERS,** 1990, ACTIVITY BOOK $2-3
❑ ❑ USA BB9064 **TRANSLITE/SM,** 1990 $8-12
❑ ❑ USA BB9065 **TRANSLITE/LG,** 1990 $10-15

COMMENTS: NATIONAL DISTRIBUTION: USA - JANUARY 26-FEBRUARY 22, 1990. TWO BAGS WERE TEST MARKETED IN SOUTH BEND, INDIANA.

CAMP MCDONALDLAND HAPPY MEAL, 1990

❑ ❑ USA CM9010 **HM BOX,** 1989, **AT THE LAKE** $1-2
❑ ❑ USA CM9011 **HM BOX,** 1989, **CAMPING OUT** $1-2
❑ ❑ USA CM9012 **HM BOX,** 1989, **NATURE WALK** $1-2
❑ ❑ USA CM9013 **HM BOX,** 1989, **PLAYTIME AT CAMP** $1-2
❑ ❑ USA CM9014 **HM BAG,** 1989, **PLAYTIME/TUG-OF-WAR** $15-20
❑ ❑ USA CM9015 **HM BAG,** 1989, **NATURE WALK** $15-20
❑ ❑ USA CM9005 **U-3 COLLAPSIBLE CUP/RONALD,** 1989, 2P RED CUP W LID $1-1.50

USA BB9025 USA BB9027 USA BB9029 USA BB9031

USA BB9026 USA BB9028 USA BB9030 USA BB9032

USA CM9010 USA CM9011

USA CM9012 USA CM9013

USA CM9014 USA CM9015

USA BB9065

USA CM9005

USA CM9000 USA CM9001 USA CM9003

USA CM9050

USA CM9002 USA CM9004

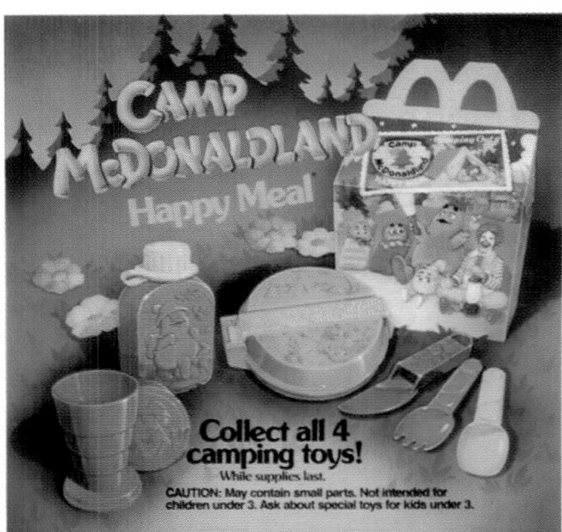

USA CM9065

- ❑ ❑ USA CM9000 **SET 1 GRIMACE CANTEEN,** 1989, 2P BLU W YEL TOP $1-1.50
- ❑ ❑ USA CM9001 **SET 2 BIRDIE CAMPER/MESS KIT,** 1989, 3P GRN W ORG HANDLE $1-1.50
- ❑ ❑ USA CM9002 **SET 3 FRY KID UTENSILS,** 1989, 3P TURQ FK/ YEL SP/PURP KN W OR W/O 5 BANDAIDS $1-1.50
- ❑ ❑ USA CM9003 **SET 4 COLLAPSIBLE CUP/RONALD,** 1989, 2P RED CUP W LID $1-1.50
- ❑ ❑ USA CM9004 **FRY KID UTENSILS,** 1989, 3P YEL FK/ BLU SP/ GRN KN W/O BANDAIDS $1.50-2.50
- ❑ ❑ USA CM9050 **BUTTON,** 1990, CAMP MCDLAND HM $3-5
- ❑ ❑ USA CM9064 **TRANSLITE/SM,** 1989 $10-15
- ❑ ❑ USA CM9065 **TRANSLITE/LG,** 1989 $15-25

COMMENTS: NATIONAL DISTRIBUTION: USA - APRIL 27-MAY 24, 1990. USA CM9003 = USA CM9005, LOOSE OUT OF PACKAGE. USA CM9004 WAS DISTRIBUTED DURING CLEAN-UP WEEKS IN 1990 AND 1991.

DINK THE LITTLE DINOSAUR HAPPY MEAL, 1990

- ❑ ❑ USA DI9010 **HM BOX,** 1990, **DINK/TOYS** $10-15
- ❑ ❑ USA DI9000 **SET 1 CRUSTY THE TURTLE,** 1989, GRN W BLU/GRN SHELL W DIORAMA $10-15
- ❑ ❑ USA DI9001 **SET 2 AMBER THE DINOSAUR,** 1989, BEIGE BODY W DIORAMA $10-15
- ❑ ❑ USA DI9002 **SET 3 SCAT THE ALLIGATOR,** 1989, GRN BODY W DIORAMA $10-15

USA DI9010

USA DI9002

❑ ❑ USA DI9003 **SET 4 SHYLER THE DINOSAUR,** 1989, GRN BODY W DIORAMA $10-15
❑ ❑ USA DI9004 **SET 5 FLAPPER THE TRIDACTYL,** 1989, BRN BODY W DIORAMA $10-15
❑ ❑ USA DI9005 **SET 6 DINK THE DINOSAUR,** 1989, GRN BODY W DIORAMA $10-15
❑ ❑ USA DI9064 **TRANSLITE/SM,** 1990 $15-25
❑ ❑ USA DI9065 **TRANSLITE/LG,** 1990 $20-30

COMMENTS: REGIONAL DISTRIBUTION: USA - AUGUST 1990 IN OKLAHOMA/TEXAS TEST MARKETS. PREMIUM MARKINGS "1989 RUBY-SPEARS INC CHINA SV." MIP MUST INCLUE DIORAMA.

FROM THE HEART/VALENTINE HAPPY MEAL, 1990

❑ ❑ USA FR9010 **HM BOX,** 1989, **PLAY MATCHMAKER** $2-3
❑ ❑ USA FR9001 **VALENTINE-FROSTING CAKE,** 1990, CHOCOLATE/SCRATCH & SNIFF $3-4
❑ ❑ USA FR9002 **VALENTINE-HOT CHOCOLATE,** 1990, CINNAMON/SCRATCH & SNIFF $3-4
❑ ❑ USA FR9064 **TRANSLITE/SM,** 1990 $15-25
❑ ❑ USA FR9065 **TRANSLITE/LG,** 1990 $20-30

COMMENTS: REGIONAL DISTRIBUTION: USA - FEBRUARY 2-FEBRUARY 14, 1990 IN SOUTHERN UNITED STATES.

FRY BENDERS HAPPY MEAL, 1990

❑ ❑ USA FB9010 **HM BOX,** 1990, **FRY BENDER CUT-OUTS/ HELP ROADIE FIND THE CLUBHOUSE** $2-3
❑ ❑ USA FB9005 **U3 TUNES,** 1989, RED SKATEBOARD W MUSIC BOX $10-15
❑ ❑ USA FB9001 **FREE STYLE,** 1989, ON ROLLER SKATES/ 2P $3-4
❑ ❑ USA FB9002 **FROGGY,** 1989, W RED SCUBA DIVER TANKS/ 2P $3-4

USA FR9010

USA DI9002 USA DI9004

USA DI9000 USA DI9001 USA DI9003 USA DI9005

USA FR9001 USA FR9002

USA FR9065

USA DI9065

USA FB9010

USA FB9001 USA FB9003 USA FB9002 USA FB9004 USA FB9005

USA FB9065

USA FF9015 USA FF9016

USA FF9017 USA FF9018

USA FF9009 USA FF9004 USA FF9005 USA FF9008

USA FF9010 USA FF9002 USA FF9006
USA FF9001 USA FF9003 USA FF9007

- ❑ ❑ USA FB9003 **GRAND SLAM,** 1989, W BASEBALL GLOVE/ 2P $3-4
- ❑ ❑ USA FB9004 **ROADIE,** 1989, THE BICYCLER/2P $3-4
- ❑ ❑ USA FB9064 **TRANSLITE/SM,** 1990 $8-12
- ❑ ❑ USA FB9065 **TRANSLITE/LG,** 1990 $10-15

COMMENTS: REGIONAL DISTRIBUTION: USA - SEPTEMBER 7-OCTOBER 4, 1990 AND MARCH-APRIL 1991. USED DURING CLEAN-UP WEEK IN MANY AREAS.

FUNNY FRY FRIENDS II "COLLECT ALL 8" HAPPY MEAL, 1990

- ❑ ❑ USA FF9015 **HM BOX,** 1989, **COOL DAY AT SCHOOL** $1-2
- ❑ ❑ USA FF9016 **HM BOX,** 1989, **CITY SIGHTS** $1-2
- ❑ ❑ USA FF9017 **HM BOX,** 1989, **SKI HOLIDAY** $1-2
- ❑ ❑ USA FF9018 **HM BOX,** 1989, **SNOWY DAY PLAY** $1-2
- ❑ ❑ USA FF9009 **U-3 LITTLE DARLING,** 1989, COW GIRL/ YEL $5-7
- ❑ ❑ USA FF9010 **U-3 LIL' CHIEF,** 1989, INDIAN CHIEF/ORG CHIEF HAT $5-7
- ❑ ❑ USA FF9001 **SET 1 HOOPS,** 1989, PURPLE KID W SWEAT B W BASKETBALL $2-3
- ❑ ❑ USA FF9002 **SET 2 ROLLIN ROCKER,** 1989, YEL GIRL W HEAD PHONES W SKATES $2-3
- ❑ ❑ USA FF9003 **SET 3 MATEY,** 1989, RED KID W PIRATE HAT $2-3
- ❑ ❑ USA FF9004 **SET 4 GADZOOKS,** 1989, BLU KID W EYE-GLASSES $2-3
- ❑ ❑ USA FF9005 **SET 5 TRACKER,** 1989, BLU KID W SAFARI HAT W SNAKE $2-3
- ❑ ❑ USA FF9006 **SET 6 ZZZ'S,** 1989, TURQ KID W SLEEPING CAP W BEAR $2-3
- ❑ ❑ USA FF9007 **SET 7 TOO TALL,** 1989, GRN KID W CLOWN HAT $2-3
- ❑ ❑ USA FF9008 **SET 8 SWEET CUDDLES,** 1989, PNK KID W BABY BONNET W BOTTLE $2-3
- ❑ ❑ USA FF9026 **DISPLAY/PREMIUMS,** 1989 $85-110
- ❑ ❑ USA FF9045 **REGISTER TOPPER/2 TYPES,** 1989, $3-5

USA FF9002

USA FF9026

USA FF9045

❑ ❑ USA FF9064 **TRANSLITE/SM,** 1989 $5-8
❑ ❑ USA FF9065 **TRANSLITE/LG,** 1989 $8-12

COMMENTS: NATIONAL DISTRIBUTION: USA - DECEMBER 22, 1989-JANUARY 18, 1990

HALLOWEEN '90 HAPPY MEAL, 1990

❑ ❑ USA HA9055 **PUMPKIN,** 1986, DAY GLO PAIL/ORG/NEON COLOR $1-2
❑ ❑ USA HA9056 **GHOST,** 1986, GLOW-IN-THE-DARK PAIL/WHT $1-2
❑ ❑ USA HA9057 **WITCH,** 1986, DAY GLO PAIL/GRN/NEON COLOR $1-2
❑ ❑ USA HA9064 **TRANSLITE/SM,** 1990 $8-12
❑ ❑ USA HA9065 **TRANSLITE/LG,** 1990 $10-15

COMMENTS: NATIONAL DISTRIBUTION: USA - OCTOBER 5-25, 1990.

HATS HAPPY MEAL, 1990

❑ ❑ USA HT9000 **BIRDIE-DERBY HAT,** 1990, GRN W FRY GUY/ RONALD ON BOTTOM MOLD $12-15
❑ ❑ USA HT9001 **FRY GUY-SAFARI HAT,** 1990, ORG W 2 FRY GUYS ON BOTTOM MOLD $12-15
❑ ❑ USA HT9002 **GRIMACE-CONSTRUCTION HAT,** 1990, YEL W HAMB/PROF ON BOTTOM MOLD $12-15
❑ ❑ USA HT9003 **RONALD-FIREMAN HAT,** 1990, RED W FRY GUY/BIRDIE ON BOTTOM MOLD $12-15
❑ ❑ USA HT9064 **TRANSLITE/SM,** 1990 $25-35
❑ ❑ USA HT9065 **TRANSLITE/LG,** 1990 $35-50

COMMENTS: REGIONAL DISTRIBUTION: USA - SEPTEMBER 7-OCTOBER 4, 1990 IN PARTS OF ALABAMA, GEORGIA, FLORIDA, AND LOUISIANA.

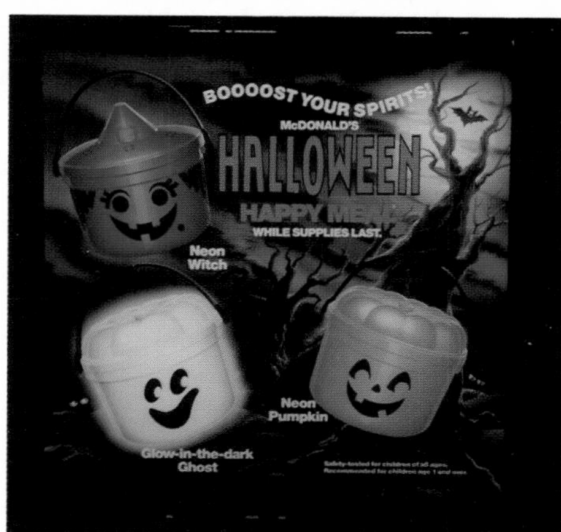

USA HA9065

USA HT9003 USA HT9002 USA HT9001 USA HT9000

USA FF9065

USA HT9065

USA HA9055 USA HA9056 USA HA9057

USA IL9002

USA IL9001 USA IL9000

I LIKE BIKES HAPPY MEAL, 1990

❑ ❑ USA IL9030 **HM BAG,** 1990, **RONALD ON A BIKE "THERE ONCE WAS A DAY"** $15-20
❑ ❑ USA IL9031 **HM BAG,** 1990, **RON/HAMB/GRI ON BIKE "WHICH RACER CAN RIDE"** $15-20
❑ ❑ USA IL9000 **SPINNER,** 1989, 1P BIRDIE ON RED PLANE/1P/ YEL SPINNER $15-25

USA IL9031 USA IL9030

- ❑ ❑ USA IL9001 **HORN,** 1989, 1P ORG/BLU FRY GUY HORN $15-25
- ❑ ❑ USA IL9002 **MIRROR,** 1990, 1P 6" REAR VIEW GRIM MIRROR $15-25
- ❑ ❑ USA IL9003 **BIKE BASKET,** 1989, 4P YEL/RON BASKET/LID/2 STRAPS $50-65
- ❑ ❑ USA IL9026 **DISPLAY/PREMIUMS,** 1990 $250-350
- ❑ ❑ USA IL9064 **TRANSLITE/SM,** 1990 $25-40
- ❑ ❑ USA IL9065 **TRANSLITE/LG,** 1990 $35-50

COMMENTS: LIMITED REGIONAL DISTRIBUTION: USA - JULY 1990 IN NORTHERN ILLINOIS AND SOUTH CAROLINA. USA "COLLECT ALL 4" DOES NOT INCLUDE A WATER BOTTLE, LIKE NATIONALLY DISTRIBUTED I LIKE BIKES HM IN EUROPE.

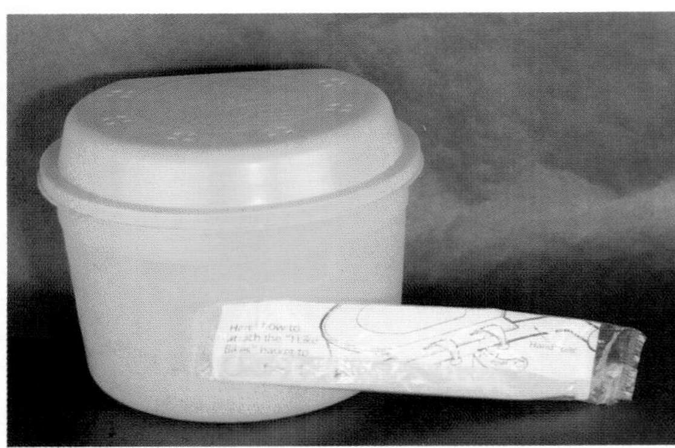

USA IL9003

JUNGLE BOOK HAPPY MEAL, 1990

- ❑ ❑ USA JU9010 **HM BOX,** 1989, **BALOO THE BEAR** $2-4
- ❑ ❑ USA JU9011 **HM BOX,** 1989, **HIDDEN ANIMAL/TIGER** $2-4
- ❑ ❑ USA JU9012 **HM BOX,** 1989, **KAA THE SNAKE** $2-4
- ❑ ❑ USA JU9013 **HM BOX,** 1989, **KING LOUIE THE ORANGUTAN** $2-4
- ❑ ❑ USA JU9004 **U-3 JUNIOR THE ELEPHANT,** 1989, GREY ELEPHANT SITTING/1P $5-7
- ❑ ❑ USA JU9005 **U-3 MOWGLI THE BOY,** 1989, BOY IN GRN CLAY POT/1P $5-7
- ❑ ❑ USA JU9000 **SET 1 BALOO,** 1989, GRY BEAR $2-3
- ❑ ❑ USA JU9001 **SET 2 KING LOUIE,** 1989, ORG ORANGUTAN $2-3
- ❑ ❑ USA JU9002 **SET 3 KAA,** 1989, GRN SNAKE $2-3
- ❑ ❑ USA JU9003 **SET 4 SHERE KHAN,** 1989, ORG TIGER $2-3
- ❑ ❑ USA JU9026 **DISPLAY W PREMIUMS,** 1989 $75-100

USA JU9010 USA JU9011

USA JU9004 USA JU9005

USA JU9000 USA JU9001 USA JU9002 USA JU9003

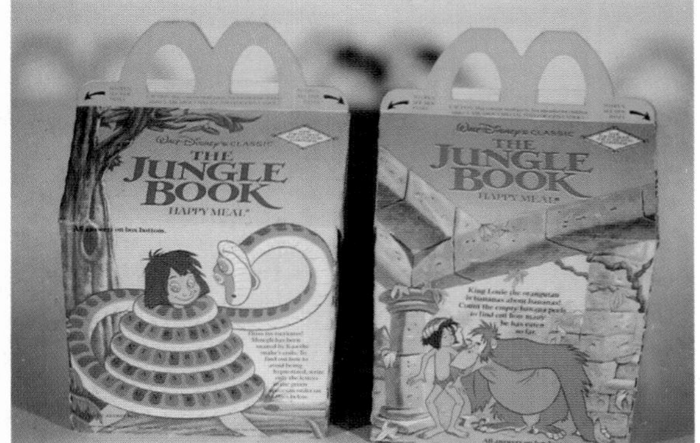

USA JU9012 USA JU9013

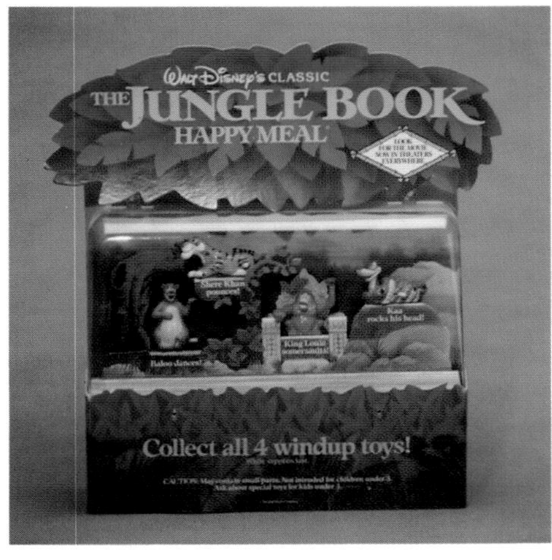

USA JU9026

- ❑ ❑ USA JU9041 **DANGLER/EACH,** 1989 $10-15
- ❑ ❑ USA JU9050 **BUTTON/CREW,** 1989 $4-7
- ❑ ❑ USA JU9051 **MUG/PLASTIC,** 1989, THE BARE NECESSITIES $2-4
- ❑ ❑ USA JU9052 **KEY CHAIN,** 1989, THE BARE NECESSITIES $2-3
- ❑ ❑ USA JU9065 **TRANSLITE/X-0 GRAPHIC/LG,** 1989 $25-35
- ❑ ❑ USA JU9064 **TRANSLITE/SM,** 1989 $8-12
- ❑ ❑ USA JU9095 **PIN,** 1989, THE BARE NECESSITIES/SQUARE SHAPED $3-4

COMMENTS: NATIONAL DISTRIBUTION: USA - JULY 6-AUGUST 2, 1990. PREMIUM MARKINGS - "DISNEY CHINA."

MCDONALDLAND CARNIVAL HAPPY MEAL, 1991/1990

- ❑ ❑ USA CA9010 **HM BOX,** 1990, **RONALD ON TRAIN** $2-3
- ❑ ❑ USA CA9004 **U-3 GRIMACE,** 1990, ON PURP ROCKER/FLOATER $7-10
- ❑ ❑ USA CA9000 **BIRDIE,** 1990, ON ORG/RED SWING/5P $3-4
- ❑ ❑ USA CA9001 **GRIMACE,** 1990, ON RED/YEL TURN-AROUND/5P $3-4
- ❑ ❑ USA CA9002 **HAMBURGLAR,** 1990, ON PURP FERRIS WHEEL/5P $3-4
- ❑ ❑ USA CA9003 **RONALD,** 1990, ON GRN TEETER TOTTER/4P $3-4
- ❑ ❑ USA CA9065 **TRANSLITE/LG,** 1990 $20-30
- ❑ ❑ USA CA9064 **TRANSLITE/SM,** 1990 $8-12

COMMENTS: REGIONAL DISTRIBUTION: USA - SEPTEMBER 7-OCTOBER 4, 1990 AND MARCH-APRIL 1991.

MCDONALDLAND DOUGH HAPPY MEAL, 1990

- ❑ ❑ USA DO9010 **HM BOX,** 1990, **HOOP TO IT** $2-4
- ❑ ❑ USA DO9011 **HM BOX,** 1990, **TIC-TAC-TOE** $2-4

USA CA9010

USA CA9000 USA CA9001 USA CA9002 USA CA9003

USA JU9050

USA CA9004

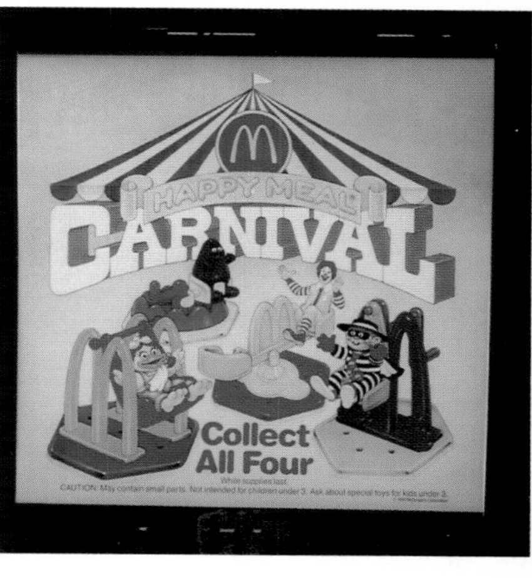

USA CA9065

USA JU9051

USA JU9064

USA JU9052

USA DO9011

USA DO9010

USA DO9000 USA DO9001 USA DO9002 USA DO9003

USA DO9004 USA DO9005 USA DO9006 USA DO9007

USA DO9065

USA MD9001 USA MD9003 USA MD9002 USA MD9000

USA PE9010 USA PE9011

- ❑ ❑ USA DO9000 **RED DOUGH/RED RONALD STAR MOLD,** 1990, RED TOP RED DOUGH $3-5
- ❑ ❑ USA DO9001 **YEL DOUGH/RED RONALD SQUARE MOLD,** 1990, YEL TOP YEL DOUGH $3-5
- ❑ ❑ USA DO9002 **GRN DOUGH/GRN FRY GIRL OCTAGON MOLD,** 1990, GRN TOP GRN DOUGH $3-5
- ❑ ❑ USA DO9003 **BLUE DOUGH/GRN FRY GUY HEXAGON MOLD,** 1990, BLU TOP BLU DOUGH $3-5
- ❑ ❑ USA DO9004 **PUR DOUGH/PURP GRIMACE SQUARE MOLD,** 1990, PUR TOP PUR DOUGH $3-5
- ❑ ❑ USA DO9005 **ORG DOUGH/PURP GRIMACE TRIANGLE MOLD,** 1990, ORG TOP ORG DOUGH $3-5
- ❑ ❑ USA DO9006 **PINK DOUGH/YEL BIRDIE HEART MOLD,** 1990, PNK TOP PNK DOUGH $3-5
- ❑ ❑ USA DO9007 **WHITE DOUGH/YEL BIRDIE CIRCLE MOLD,** 1990, WHT TOP WHT DOUGH $3-5
- ❑ ❑ USA DO9064 **TRANSLITE/SM,** 1990 $15-25
- ❑ ❑ USA DO9065 **TRANSLITE/LG,** 1990 $20-30

COMMENTS: REGIONAL DISTRIBUTION: USA - SEPTEMBER 7-OCTOBER 4, 1990 IN SOUTHERN STATES.

MCDRIVE THRU CREW TEST MARKET HAPPY MEAL, 1990

- ❑ ❑ USA MD9000 **FRIES IN POTATO SPEEDSTER,** 1990, PULL BACK FRICTION CAR $12-15
- ❑ ❑ USA MD9001 **HAMBURGLAR IN KETCHUP RACER,** 1990, PULL BACK FRICTION CAR $10-12
- ❑ ❑ USA MD9002 **MCNUGGET IN EGG ROADSTER,** 1990, PULL BACK FRICTION CAR $10-12
- ❑ ❑ USA MD9003 **SHAKE IN MILK CARTON ZOOMER,** 1990, PULL BACK FRICTION CAR $10-12

COMMENTS: REGIONAL DISTRIBUTION: USA - SEPTEMBER 7-OCTOBER 4, 1990 IN ILLINOIS AND OHIO REGIONS.

PEANUTS HAPPY MEAL, 1990

- ❑ ❑ USA PE9010 **HM BOX,** 1989, **COUNTY FAIR** $1-2
- ❑ ❑ USA PE9011 **HM BOX,** 1989, **E-I-E-I-O** $1-2
- ❑ ❑ USA PE9012 **HM BOX,** 1989, **FIELD DAY** $1-2
- ❑ ❑ USA PE9013 **HM BOX,** 1989, **HOE DOWN** $1-2
- ❑ ❑ USA PE9004 **U-3 CHARLIE B EGG BASKET,** 1989, 1P/CB W BASKET $3-4
- ❑ ❑ USA PE9005 **U-3 SNOOPY'S POTATO SACK,** 1989, 1P SNOOPY W SACK $3-4
- ❑ ❑ USA PE9000 **SET 1 SNOOPY'S HAY HAULER,** 1989, 3P/ SNOOPY/TURQ WAGON/YEL HAY $1.50-2.50
- ❑ ❑ USA PE9001 **SET 2 CB'S SEED BAG/TILLER,** 1989, 3P/ RED-BLU TILLER/YEL SACK $1.50-2.50
- ❑ ❑ USA PE9002 **SET 3 LUCY'S APPLE CART,** 1989, 3P/LUCY/ GRN WHEEELBAR/RED APPLES $1.50-2.50
- ❑ ❑ USA PE9003 **SET 4 LINUS' MILK MOVER,** 1989, 3P/LINUS/ ORG MOVER/GRY MILK CAN $1.50-2.50

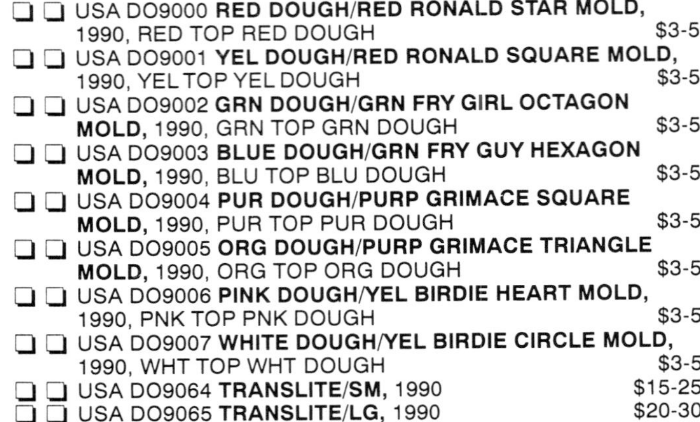

USA PE9012 USA PE9013

USA PE9005 USA PE9000 USA PE9001 USA PE9002

USA PE9004 USA PE9003

❑ ❑ USA PE9026 **DISPLAY/PREMIUMS,** 1989 $90-115
❑ ❑ USA PE9064 **TRANSLITE/SM,** 1989 $12-20
❑ ❑ USA PE9065 **TRANSLITE/LG,** 1989 $15-25

COMMENTS: NATIONAL DISTRIBUTION: USA - MARCH 30-APRIL 26, 1990. PREMIUM MARKINGS - "UNITED FEAT. SYND. CHINA."

RESCUERS DOWN UNDER HAPPY MEAL, 1990

❑ ❑ USA RE9010 **HM BOX,** 1990, **EAGLE/BERNARD/MISS BIANCA** $1-2
❑ ❑ USA RE9011 **HM BOX,** 1990, **FIREFLIES/TO LIGHT THE NIGHT** $1-2
❑ ❑ USA RE9012 **HM BOX,** 1990, **LIZARD/FRANK THE FRILL-NECKED** $1-2
❑ ❑ USA RE9013 **HM BOX,** 1990, **ROPE/MCLEACH THE VILLAIN/TOP SECRET** $1-2
❑ ❑ USA RE9004 **U-3 BERNARD,** 1990, ON A PIECE OF YEL CHEESE/RUBBER $2.50-4
❑ ❑ USA RE9000 **BERNARD & BIANCA,** 1990, GRN CAMERA/YEL LABEL $2-3
❑ ❑ USA RE9001 **JAKE,** 1990, ORANGE CAMERA/GRN LABEL $2-3
❑ ❑ USA RE9002 **CODY,** 1990, CLEAR CAMERA/BLU LABEL $2-3
❑ ❑ USA RE9003 **WILBUR,** 1990, PURP CAMERA/PNK LABEL $2-3
❑ ❑ USA RE9050 **BUTTON,** 1990, RESCUERS DOWN UNDER/RECTANGLE $3-5
❑ ❑ USA RE9064 **TRANSLITE/SM,** 1990 $8-12
❑ ❑ USA RE9065 **TRANSLITE/LG,** 1990 $10-15

COMMENTS: NATIONAL DISTRIBUTION: USA - NOVEMBER 30-DECEMBER 27, 1990.

USA RE9010 USA RE9011

USA RE9012

USA RE9013

USA PE9026

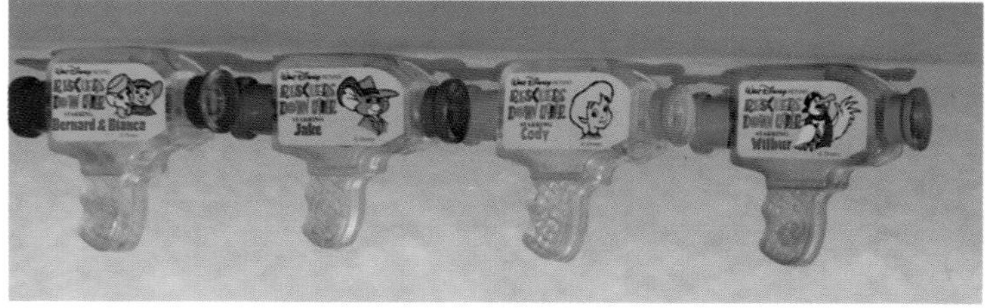

USA RE9000 USA RE9001 USA RE9002 USA RE9003

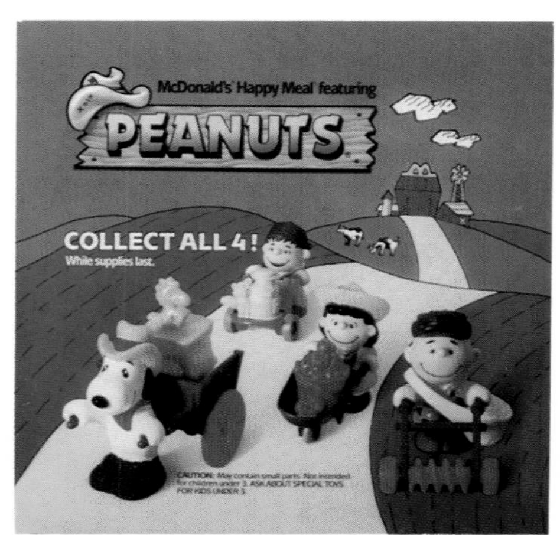

USA PE9065

USA RE9065

USA RE9004

USA RE9050

USA SP9035

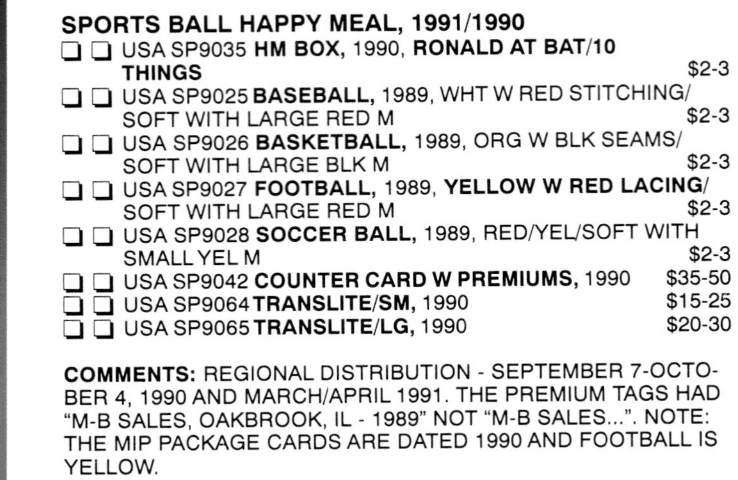

SPORTS BALL HAPPY MEAL, 1991/1990

- ❑ ❑ USA SP9035 **HM BOX,** 1990, **RONALD AT BAT/10 THINGS** $2-3
- ❑ ❑ USA SP9025 **BASEBALL,** 1989, WHT W RED STITCHING/ SOFT WITH LARGE RED M $2-3
- ❑ ❑ USA SP9026 **BASKETBALL,** 1989, ORG W BLK SEAMS/ SOFT WITH LARGE BLK M $2-3
- ❑ ❑ USA SP9027 **FOOTBALL,** 1989, **YELLOW W RED LACING/** SOFT WITH LARGE RED M $2-3
- ❑ ❑ USA SP9028 **SOCCER BALL,** 1989, RED/YEL/SOFT WITH SMALL YEL M $2-3
- ❑ ❑ USA SP9042 **COUNTER CARD W PREMIUMS,** 1990 $35-50
- ❑ ❑ USA SP9064 **TRANSLITE/SM,** 1990 $15-25
- ❑ ❑ USA SP9065 **TRANSLITE/LG,** 1990 $20-30

COMMENTS: REGIONAL DISTRIBUTION - SEPTEMBER 7-OCTOBER 4, 1990 AND MARCH/APRIL 1991. THE PREMIUM TAGS HAD "M-B SALES, OAKBROOK, IL - 1989" NOT "M-B SALES...". NOTE: THE MIP PACKAGE CARDS ARE DATED 1990 AND FOOTBALL IS YELLOW.

SUMMER SURPRISE HAPPY MEAL, 1990

- ❑ ❑ USA SS9030 **HM BAG,** 1990, **RONALD'S GOOD TIME MEAL** $1-1.25
- ❑ ❑ USA SS9031 **HM BAG,** 1990, **MCDONALD'S HM/ RONALD** $1-1.25
- ❑ ❑ USA SS9064 **TRANSLITE/SM,** 1990, A SMILE IN EVERY BOX $5-7
- ❑ ❑ USA SS9065 **TRANSLITE/LG,** 1990, A SMILE IN EVERY BOX $7-10

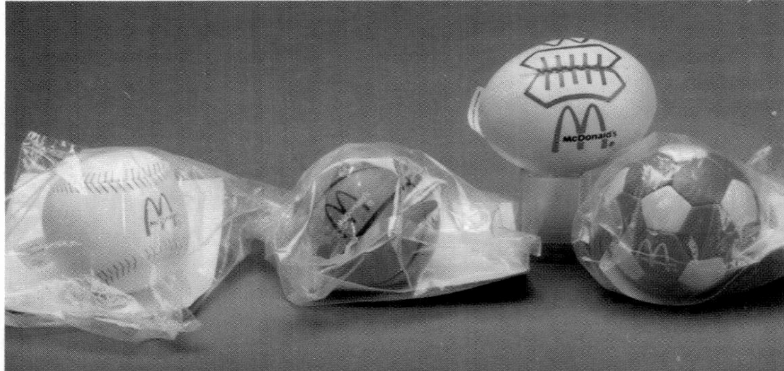

USA SP9025 USA SP9026 USA SP9027 USA SP9028

USA SS9031

USA SP9042

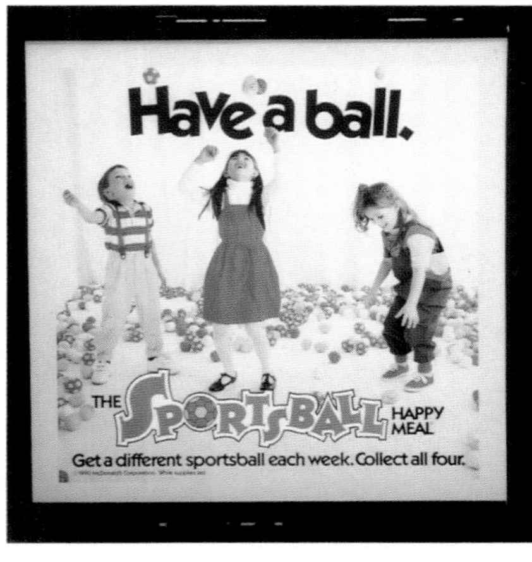

USA SP9065

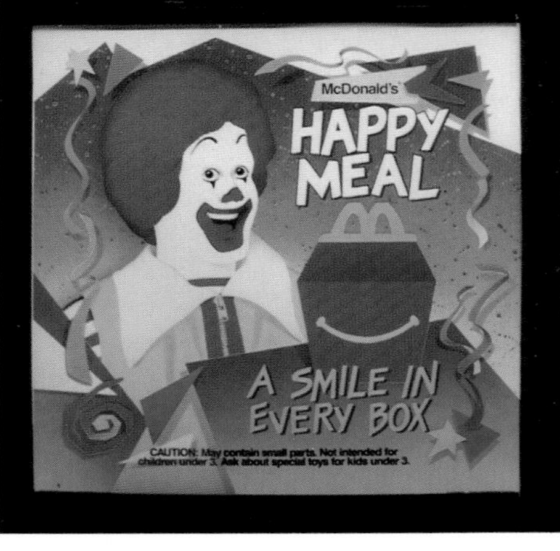

USA SS9065

❑ ❑ USA SS9050 **BUTTON,** 1990, NEON GRN/$1.99 HM $2-3
❑ ❑ USA SS9051 **BUTTON,** 1990, NEON RED/$1.99 HM $2-3

COMMENTS: REGIONAL DISTRIBUTION: USA - SUMMER 1990.

SUPER MARIO 3 NINTENDO HAPPY MEAL, 1990

❑ ❑ USA SU9010 **HM BOX,** 1990, **DESERT LAND** $1-2
❑ ❑ USA SU9011 **HM BOX,** 1990, **ISLAND WORLD** $1-2
❑ ❑ USA SU9012 **HM BOX,** 1990, **PIPE LAND** $1-2
❑ ❑ USA SU9013 **HM BOX,** 1990, **SKY LAND** $1-2
❑ ❑ USA SU9005 **U-3 SUPER MARIO,** 1990, STANDING MARIO W BLU JEANS & RED SHIRT $2.50-3.50
❑ ❑ USA SU9001 **SET 1 MARIO,** 1990, SPRING LOADED MARIO POPS UP $1.50-2
❑ ❑ USA SU9002 **SET 2 LUIGI,** 1990, LUIGI ZOOMS AROUND $1.50-2
❑ ❑ USA SU9003 **SET 3 GOOMBA,** 1990, GOOMBA FLIPS $1.50-2
❑ ❑ USA SU9004 **SET 4 KOOPA,** 1990, STANDING/HOPS $1.50-2
❑ ❑ USA SU9026 **DISPLAY/PREMIUMS,** 1990 $85-100
❑ ❑ USA SU9041 **DANGLER/EACH,** 1990 $8-12
❑ ❑ USA SU9050 **BUTTON,** 1990, NINTENDO HM $3-5
❑ ❑ USA SU9055 **TRAYLINER,** 1990 $1-2
❑ ❑ USA SU9064 **TRANSLITE/SM,** 1990 $8-12
❑ ❑ USA SU9065 **TRANSLITE/LG/X-0 GRAPHIC,** 1990 $25-40
❑ ❑ USA SU9095 **PIN,** 1990, SUPER MARIO W YEL HM BOX $3-5

COMMENTS: NATIONAL DISTRIBUTION: USA - AUGUST 3-30, 1990. PREMIUM MARKINGS - "1989 NINTENDO OF AMERICA INC. CHINA."

USA SS9051 USA SS9050

USA SU9050

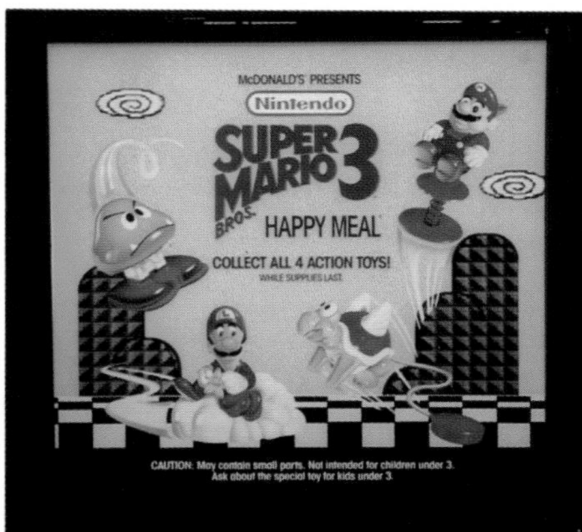

USA SU9064

USA SU9010 USA SU9011

USA SU9012

USA SU9013

USA SU9095

USA SU9026

USA SU9001 USA SU9003

USA SU9005 USA SU9002 USA SU9004

USA SU9041

USA TA9010 USA TA9011

TALE SPIN HAPPY MEAL, 1990

- ❑ ❑ USA TA9010 **HM BOX,** 1990, **HIGHER FOR HIRE** $2-3
- ❑ ❑ USA TA9011 **HM BOX,** 1990, **LOUIES** $2-3
- ❑ ❑ USA TA9012 **HM BOX,** 1990, **PIRATE ISLAND** $2-3
- ❑ ❑ USA TA9013 **HM BOX,** 1990, **SEA DUCK** $2-3
- ❑ ❑ USA TA9005 **U-3 BALOO'S SEAPLANE,** 1990, ORG SOFT PLASTIC/RUBBER $2.50-3.50
- ❑ ❑ USA TA9006 **U-3 WILDCAT'S FLYING MACHINE,** 1990, GRN SOFT PLASTIC/RUBBER $2.50-3.50
- ❑ ❑ USA TA9001 **BALOO'S SEAPLANE,** 1990, ORG-GLD DIE CAST METAL $1-1.50
- ❑ ❑ USA TA9002 **KIT'S RACING PLANE,** 1990, RED-BLU DIE CAST METAL $1-1.50
- ❑ ❑ USA TA9003 **MOLLY'S BIPLANE,** 1990, GRN-RED DIE CAST METAL $1-1.50
- ❑ ❑ USA TA9004 **WILDCAT'S FLYING MACHINE,** 1990, GRN-RED DIE CAST METAL $1-1.50
- ❑ ❑ USA TA9026 **DISPLAY/PREMIUMS,** 1990 $100-125
- ❑ ❑ USA TA9041 **CEILING DANGLER/EACH,** 1990 $8-12
- ❑ ❑ USA TA9064 **TRANSLITE/SM,** 1990 $8-12
- ❑ ❑ USA TA9065 **TRANSLITE/LG,** 1990 $10-20

COMMENTS: NATIONAL DISTRIBUTION: USA - NOVEMBER 2-29, 1990. PREMIUM MARKINGS "DISNEY KH CHINA" OR "DISNEY CH CHINA" OR DISNEY WM CHINA."

USA TA9012 USA TA9013

USA TA9026

USA TA9001

USA TA9003

USA TA9006 USA TA9005

USA TA9065

USA TA9004

USA TA9002

USA TA9041

TOM & JERRY BAND HAPPY MEAL, 1990

- ❑ ❑ USA TO9030 **HM BAG,** 1989, **LARGE WHT W FRIENDS PLAYING INSTRUMENTS** $3-5
- ❑ ❑ USA TO9031 **HM BAG,** 1990, **SMALL WHT W MORE YEL #2 BAG** $3-5
- ❑ ❑ USA TO9004 **U-3 DROOPY,** 1989, DOG W/O MICROPHONE $12-15
- ❑ ❑ USA TO9000 **SET 1 TOM W KEYBOARD,** 1989, 4P TOM/GRN KEYBOARD W 2 LEGS $7-10
- ❑ ❑ USA TO9001 **SET 2 DROOPY W MIKE,** 1989, 3P DROOPY W 2P BLK MIKE $7-10
- ❑ ❑ USA TO9002 **SET 3 JERRY W DRUMS,** 1989, 2P TOM W DRUM $7-10
- ❑ ❑ USA TO9003 **SET 4 SPIKE W BASS,** 1989, 2P SPIKE W WHT BASS $7-10
- ❑ ❑ USA TO9064 **TRANSLITE/SM,** 1989 $12-20
- ❑ ❑ USA TO9065 **TRANSLITE/LG,** 1989 $20-35

COMMENTS: NATIONAL DISTRIBUTION: USA - SEPTEMBER 2-OCTOBER 4, 1990. PREMIUM MARKINGS "1989 SIMON MARKETING CHINA"; LOS ANGELOS, CALIFORNIA TEST MARKET - JANUARY 1990. REGIONAL DISTRIBUTION: USA HAWAIIAN ISLANDS, 1990.

TURBO MACS II HAPPY MEAL, 1990

- ❑ ❑ USA TU9024 **U-3 RONALD,** 1988, RONALD/RUBBER/INSERT CARD $4-6
- ❑ ❑ USA TU9000 **BIRDIE,** 1988, PINK CAR/RED HAIR/LG YEL ARCHES $3.50-4.50
- ❑ ❑ USA TU9001 **GRIMACE,** 1988, WHT CAR/LG RED M ON FRONT OF CAR $3.50-4.50
- ❑ ❑ USA TU9002 **HAMBURGLAR,** 1988, YEL CAR/LG RED M ON FRONT OF CAR $3.50-4.50
- ❑ ❑ USA TU9003 **RONALD,** 1988, RED CAR/LG YEL M ON FRONT OF CAR/**NO TEARDROPS UNDER EYES** $3.50-4.50
- ❑ ❑ USA TU9065 **TRANSLITE/LG,** 1988, RON/NO TEARDROP $20-35

COMMENTS: LIMITED REGIONAL DISTRIBUTION: USA - SEPTEMBER 7-OCTOBER 4, 1990. IN 1990 TURBO MACS HAPPY MEAL WAS REDISTRIBUTED USING THE 1988 BOX AND 1988 CARS WITH THE LARGE ARCHES. EACH MIP CAME WITH AN INSERT CARD.

USA TO9065

USA TU9024

USA TU9000 USA TU9001 USA TU9002 USA TU9003

USA TO9030 USA TO9031

USA TO9004 USA TO9000 USA TO9001 USA TO9002 USA TO9003

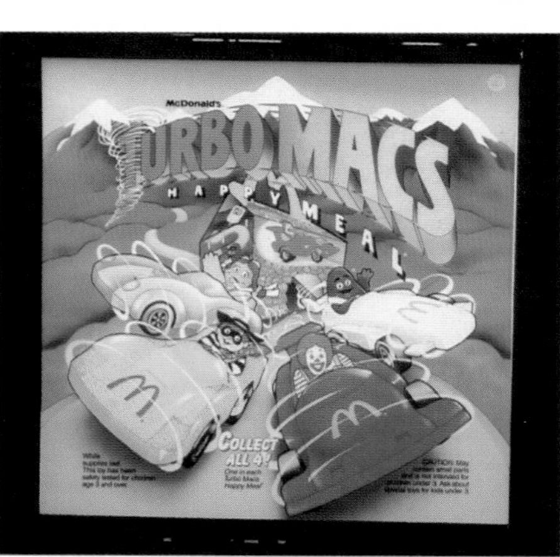

USA TU9065

USA/GENERIC PROMOTION, 1990

- ❑ ❑ USA GE9001 **HM BAG,** 1990, **KID'S COMBO MEAL** $1-1.50
- ❑ ❑ USA GE9002 **BEEF TACO HM,** 1990, HAPPY MEAL/ADV SIGN $2-4
- ❑ ❑ USA GE9065 **TRANSLITE/LG,** 1990, **KID'S COMBO MEAL** $5-8

COMMENT: REGIONAL DISTRIBUTION: USA - 1990 DURING CLEAN-UP WEEKS.

USA GE9001

USA GE9002

USA GE9065

1991

101 DALMATIONS HAPPY MEAL, 1991
ALVIN AND THE CHIPMUNKS HAPPY MEAL, 1991
BARBIE / HOT WHEELS II HAPPY MEAL, 1991
BREAKFAST HAPPY MEAL, 1991
CONNECTIBLES HAPPY MEAL, 1991
CRAZY VEHICLES HAPPY MEAL, 1991
DISCOVER THE RAIN FOREST HAPPY MEAL, 1991
FRIENDLY SKIES HAPPY MEAL, 1995/1994/1993/1992/1991
GOOD MORNING HAPPY MEAL, 1991
GRAVEDALE HIGH HAPPY MEAL, 1991
HALLOWEEN '91/MCBOO BAGS/BUCKETS HAPPY MEAL, 1991
HOOK HAPPY MEAL, 1991
MCCHARACTERS ON BIKES/MCDONALDLAND ON WHEELS HAPPY MEAL, 1991
MCDINO CHANGEABLES HAPPY MEAL, 1991
MCDONALDLAND CIRCUS PARADE HAPPY MEAL, 1993/1992/1991
MIGHTY MINI HAPPY MEAL, 1991
MUPPET BABIES III HAPPY MEAL, 1992/1991
NATURE'S HELPER HAPPY MEAL, 1991
PIGGSBURG PIGS HAPPY MEAL, 1991
PIZZA HAPPY SACK HAPPY MEAL, 1991
STENCIL/SPACE/CRAYONS GENERIC HAPPY MEAL, 1991
SPORTS BALL HAPPY MEAL, 1991
SUPER LOONEY TUNES HAPPY MEAL, 1991
TINY TOON ADVENTURES I HAPPY MEAL, 1991

101 DALMATIONS HAPPY MEAL, 1991

- ❑ ❑ USA ON9110 **HM BOX,** 1991, **BARN** $1-2
- ❑ ❑ USA ON9111 **HM BOX,** 1991, **DOG'S LEASHES** $1-2
- ❑ ❑ USA ON9112 **HM BOX,** 1991, **PIANO** $1-2
- ❑ ❑ USA ON9113 **HM BOX,** 1991, **STAIRCASE** $1-2
- ❑ ❑ USA ON9100 **SET 1 POGO THE DOG,** 1990, 1P DALMATION STANDING $1-2

USA ON9110 USA ON9111

USA ON9100 USA ON9101 USA ON9102 USA ON9103

USA ON9112 USA ON9113

❑ ❑ USA ON9101 **SET 2 LUCKY THE PUP,** 1990, 1P WHT/BLK DALMATION PUP W RED COLLAR $1-2
❑ ❑ USA ON9102 **SET 3 COLONEL/SGT.TIBBS,** 1990, 1P SHEEP DOG W CAT $1-2
❑ ❑ USA ON9103 **SET 4 CRUELA DEVILLA,** 1990, 1P YEL/BLK VILLAINESS $1-2
❑ ❑ USA ON9126 **DISPLAY W PREMIUMS,** 1991 $85-110
❑ ❑ USA ON9164 **TRANSLITE/SM,** 1991 $10-15
❑ ❑ USA ON9165 **TRANSLITE/LG,** 1991 $12-20

COMMENTS: NATIONAL DISTRIBUTION: USA - JULY 5-AUGUST 1, 1991. NOTE THE NEW SMALLER BOX SIZE. NO U-3 GIVEN.

ALVIN AND THE CHIPMUNKS HAPPY MEAL, 1991

❑ ❑ USA AL9130 **HM BAG,** 1990, **ALVIN/W TARGET COUPON** $2-4
❑ ❑ USA AL9105 **U-3 ALVIN,** 1990, 1P LEANING ON A JUKEBOX/ RUBBER $8-12
❑ ❑ USA AL9101 **ALVIN,** 1990, 2P/RED ALVIN W BLU GUITAR $8-10
❑ ❑ USA AL9102 **BRITTNEY,** 1990, 2P/PNK BRIT W GRN JUKEBOX $8-10
❑ ❑ USA AL9103 **SIMON,** 1990, 2P/YEL SIMON W PNK MOVIE CAMERA $8-10
❑ ❑ USA AL9104 **THEODORE,** 1990, 2P/TURQ/YEL THEO W RAP MACHINE $8-10
❑ ❑ USA AL9108 **TARGET COUPON,** 1990 $.50-1
❑ ❑ USA AL9127 **COUNTER CARD W PREMIUMS,** 1990 $85-100
❑ ❑ USA AL9164 **TRANSLITE/SM,** 1990 $12-20
❑ ❑ USA AL9165 **TRANSLITE/LG,** 1990 $20-25

COMMENTS: REGIONAL DISTRIBUTION: USA - MARCH 8-APRIL 12, 1991 - TEXAS. PREMIUM MARKINGS "KH CHINA 1990 M-B SALES" OR "1990 BAGDASARIAN PROD CHINA" OR "DY CHINA."

BARBIE / HOT WHEELS II HAPPY MEAL, 1991

❑ ❑ USA BA9170 **HM BOX,** 1991, **AT HOME** $1-2
❑ ❑ USA BA9171 **HM BOX,** 1991, **ON STAGE** $1-2
❑ ❑ USA BA9172 **HM BOX,** 1991, **CRUISING** $1-2
❑ ❑ USA BA9173 **HM BOX,** 1991, **RACERS** $1-2

USA AL9130

USA AL9108

USA AL9127

USA ON9126

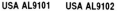

USA AL9105 USA AL9101 USA AL9102 USA AL9103 USA AL9104

USA BA9170

USA BA9171

USA ON9165

USA BA9172

USA BA9173

USA BA9141 USA BA9142 USA BA9145

USA BA9148 USA BA9149 USA BA9140 USA BA9144 USA BA9147 USA BA9143 USA BA9146

- ❑ ❑ USA BA9148 **U-3 COSTUME BALL,** 1991, 1P/PNK LONG DRESS/HOLDING PURP MASK $2-3
- ❑ ❑ USA BA9149 **U-3 WEDDING MIDGE,** 1991, 1P WHT GOWN/ PNK FLOWERS/PURP RIBBON $2-3
- ❑ ❑ USA BA9163 **U-3 TOOL SET,** 1991, 2P/PLASTIC/YEL WRENCH/RED HAMMER $2-3
- ❑ ❑ USA BA9140 **ALL AMERICAN,** 1991, #1/SHORT BLU DRESS/ REEBOK SNEAKERS $2.50-3.50
- ❑ ❑ USA BA9141 **COSTUME BALL,** 1991, #2/PNK LONG DRESS/ HOLDING PURP MASK $2.50-3.50
- ❑ ❑ USA BA9142 **LIGHTS/LACE,** 1991, #3/PNK BALLERINA DRESS/PURP STAND $2.50-3.50
- ❑ ❑ USA BA9143 **HAPPY BIRTHDAY,** 1991, #4/BLK BARBIE/PNK LONG DRESS $2 .50-3.50

USA HW9156 USA HW9158 USA HW9160 USA HW9161

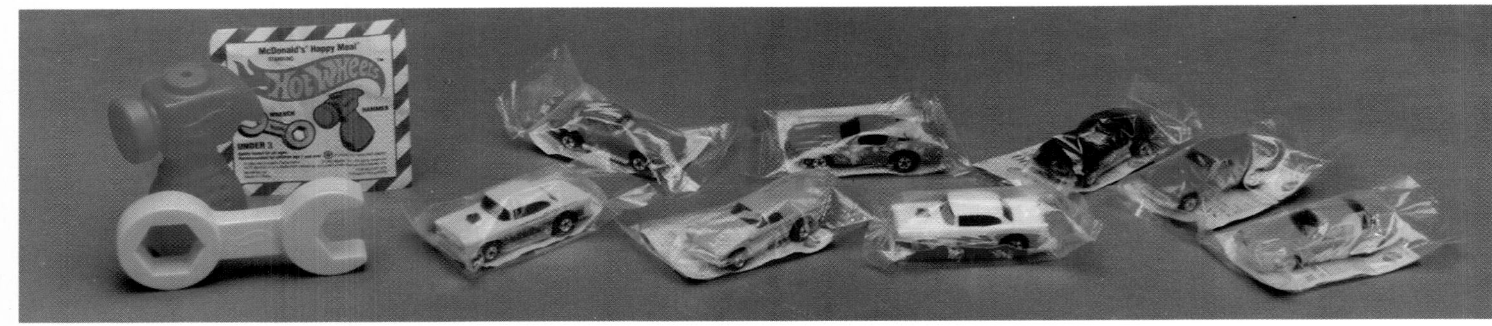

USA BA9163 USA HW9155 USA HW9157 USA HW9159 USA HW9162

USA BA9126

USA BA9150

- ❑ ❑ USA BA9144 **HAWAIIAN FUN,** 1991, #5/PNK WRAP/SEA SHELL BASE $2.50-3.50
- ❑ ❑ USA BA9145 **WEDDING DAY MIDGE,** 1991, #6/WHT GOWN/ PNK FLOWERS/PURP RIBBON $2.50-3.50
- ❑ ❑ USA BA9146 **ICE CAPADES,** 1991, #7/PURP DRESS/WHT ICE SKATES $2.50-3.50
- ❑ ❑ USA BA9147 **MY FIRST BARBIE,** 1991, #8/SPANISH BARBIE/PURP-WHT LONG DRESS $2.50-3.50
- ❑ ❑ USA HW9155 **'55 CHEVY,** 1991, #1/YEL CHEVY $2-3
- ❑ ❑ USA HW9156 **'63 CORVETTE,** 1991, #2/GRN CORVETTE $2-3
- ❑ ❑ USA HW9157 **'57 T BIRD,** 1991, #3/TURQ T BIRD $2-3
- ❑ ❑ USA HW9158 **CAMARO Z-28,** 1991, #4/PURP CAMERO $2-3
- ❑ ❑ USA HW9159 **'55 CHEVY,** 1991, #5/WHT CHEVY $2-3
- ❑ ❑ USA HW9160 **'63 CORVETTE,** 1991, #6/BLK CORVETTE $2-3
- ❑ ❑ USA HW9161 **'57 T BIRD,** 1991, #7/RED T BIRD $2-3
- ❑ ❑ USA HW9162 **CAMERO Z-28,** 1991, #8/ORG CAMERO $2-3
- ❑ ❑ USA BA9126 **DISPLAY/PREMIUMS,** 1991 $125-175
- ❑ ❑ USA BA9150 **BUTTON,** 1991, ASK ME ABOUT TODAY'S HM $4-6
- ❑ ❑ USA BA9164 **TRANSLITE/SM,** 1991 $15-25
- ❑ ❑ USA BA9165 **TRANSLITE/LG,** 1991 $20-30
- ❑ ❑ USA BA9183 **TRAY LINER,** 1991 $1-2

COMMENTS: NATIONAL DISTRIBUTION: USA - AUGUST 2-28, 1991. USA BA9141 AND USA BA9148 AS WELL AS USA BA9145 AND USA BA9149 ARE THE SAME, LOOSE OUT OF PACKAGE.

BREAKFAST HAPPY MEAL, 1991

- ❑ ❑ USA BR9101 **SQUEEZE BOTTLE,** 1991, MINUTE MAID LOGO $1.50-2.50
- ❑ ❑ USA BR8750 **BUTTON,** 1987, TRY OUR O.J. $7-10
- ❑ ❑ USA BR9164 **TRANSLITE/SM,** 1991 $4-6

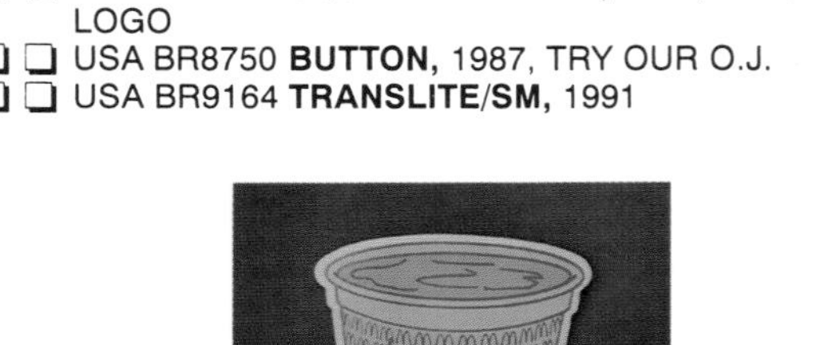

USA BA9165

USA BR9101

USA BR8750

COMMENTS: REGIONAL DISTRIBUTION: USA - 1991 IN THE SUMMER/FALL IN NORTH EASTERN UNITED STATES. BUTTON WAS ISSUED IN 1987 AND WORN AGAIN DURING 1991 PROMOTION.

CONNECTIBLES HAPPY MEAL, 1991

- ❑ ❑ USA CO9100 **BIRDIE,** 1990, 2P ON A BLU/PNK/YEL TRICYCLE $2-2.50
- ❑ ❑ USA CO9101 **GRIMACE,** 1990, 2P IN A RED WAGON $2-2.50
- ❑ ❑ USA CO9102 **HAMBURGLAR,** 1990, 2P IN A GRN/YEL AIRPLANE $2-2.50
- ❑ ❑ USA CO9103 **RONALD,** 1990, 2P IN A YEL/RED SOAPBOX RACER $2-2.50

COMMENTS: LIMITED REGIONAL DISTRIBUTION: USA - AUG 29-SEPT 5, 1991 DURING CLEAN UP WEEK. MIP INSERT CARDS ARE DATED "1991". NO SPECIFIC HM BOXES OR BAGS WERE GIVEN WITH THESE PREMIUMS.

CRAZY VEHICLES HAPPY MEAL, 1991

- ❑ ❑ USA CR9101 **BIRDIE,** 1990, IN 3P PNK/YEL/PURP AIRPLANE $2.50-3.50
- ❑ ❑ USA CR9102 **GRIMACE,** 1990, IN 3P GRN/YEL/ORG CAR $2.50-3.50
- ❑ ❑ USA CR9103 **HAMBURGLAR,** 1990, IN 3P YEL/BLU/PUR TRAIN $2.50-3.50
- ❑ ❑ USA CR9104 **RONALD,** 1990, IN 3P RED/YEL/BLU BUGGY CAR $2.50-3.50

COMMENTS: LIMITED REGIONAL DISTRIBUTION: USA DURING CLEAN-UP WEEK - AUGUST 29-SEPTEMBER 5, 1991.

DISCOVER THE RAIN FOREST HAPPY MEAL, 1991

- ❑ ❑ USA DI9130 **HM BAG,** 1991, **DISCOVER** $1-2
- ❑ ❑ USA DI9125 **SET 1 STICKER SAFARI,** 1991, 12 PAGES/14 STICKERS $1-1.50
- ❑ ❑ USA DI9126 **SET 2 PAINT IT WILD,** 1991, W PAINT BRUSH/PALLET/16 PAGES $1-1.50
- ❑ ❑ USA DI9127 **SET 3 RM IN THE JEWEL,** 1991, OF THE AMAZON KINGDOM/16 PAGES $1-1.50
- ❑ ❑ USA DI9128 **SET 4 WONDERS IN THE WILD,** 1991, 16 PAGES $1-1.50
- ❑ ❑ USA DI9164 **TRANSLITE/SM,** 1991 $6-8
- ❑ ❑ USA DI9165 **TRANSLITE/LG,** 1991 $8-12

COMMENTS: NATIONAL DISTRIBUTION: USA - SEPTEMBER 6-OCTOBER 3, 1991.

USA CR9101 USA CR9102 USA CR9103 USA CR9104

USA DI9130

USA DI9125 USA DI9126 USA DI9127 USA DI9128

USA BR9164

USA DI9165

USA CO9100 USA CO9101 USA CO9102 USA CO9103

FRIENDLY SKIES HAPPY MEAL, 1995/1994/1993/1992/1991

- ❑ ❑ USA FR9110 **HM BOX,** 1991, **TOY IN THIS BOX.../6 1/2" X 6 1/2" X 2"** $10-15
- ❑ ❑ USA FR9111 **HM BOX,** 1991, **RONALD TOY INSIDE/5 1/4" X 5 1/4" X 2"** $10-15
- ❑ ❑ USA FR9114 **HM BOX,** 1991, **GRIMACE TOY INSIDE/5 1/4" X 5 1/4" X 2"** $10-15
- ❑ ❑ USA FR9115 **HM BOX,** 1993, **WINDOWS TO THE WORLD/ SNACK PACK/5 1/4" X 5 1/4" X 2"** $4-7
- ❑ ❑ USA FR9101 **RONALD,** 1991, IN WHT 747 AIRPLANE $5-8
- ❑ ❑ USA FR9102 **GRIMACE,** 1991, IN WHT 747 UNITED AIRPLANE $7-10
- ❑ ❑ USA FR9103 **RONALD,** 1994, IN GREY/BLU 747 UNITED AIRPLANE $7-10
- ❑ ❑ USA FR9104 **GRIMACE,** 1994, IN GREY/BLU 747 UNITED AIRPLANE $7-10
- ❑ ❑ USA FR9105 **RONALD/HANGAR/PLANE,** 1994, IN GRY AIRPLANE/BLU HANGAR W RED ROOF/YEL DOOR/2P $5-8
- ❑ ❑ USA FR9112 **NAPKIN PACKET,** 1991 $2-3
- ❑ ❑ USA FR9126 **DISPLAY,** 1992, W 1 BOX $65-80
- ❑ ❑ USA FR9141 **CEILING DANGLER,** 1992, W 2 RON PREMIUMS/W 3 BOXES $65-80
- ❑ ❑ USA FR9150 **BUTTON,** 1993, UNITED FRIENDLY SKIES NOW FLYING FROM CHICAGO! $------

USA FR9111 USA FR9110

USA FR9115

USA FR9104 USA FR9103 USA FR9102 USA FR9101

USA FR9105 USA FR9416

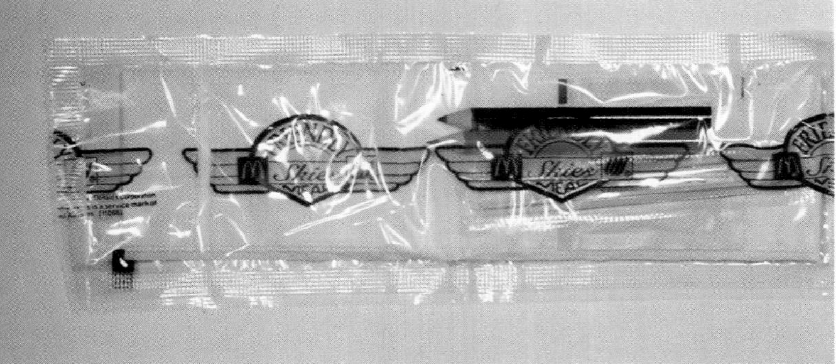

USA FR9112

USA FR9141

USA FR9150

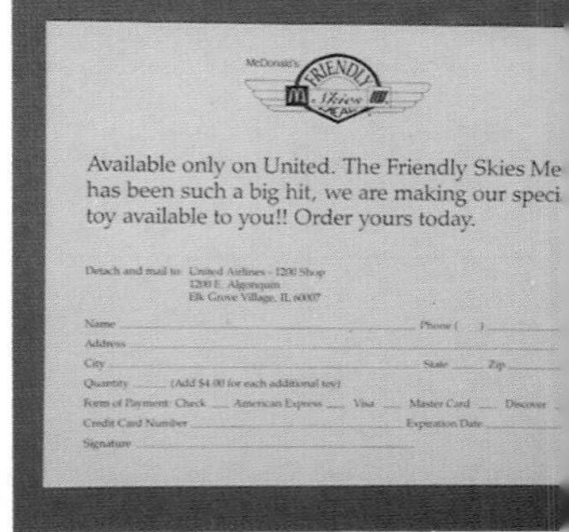

❑ ❑ USA FR9155 **TRAYLINER,** 1993, RON W CHARS $3-5
❑ ❑ USA FR9156 **TRAYLINER,** 1993, RUNWAY FUNWAY $2-3

COMMENTS: NATIONAL DISTRIBUTION: USA - OCTOBER 10-DECEMBER 1991 AND IN 1992/1993/1994/1995. THE PROMOTION WAS GIVEN ON SELECTED UNITED FLIGHTS THROUGHOUT THE USA. BOXES CAME IN TWO SIZES/4 DIFFERENT BOXES.

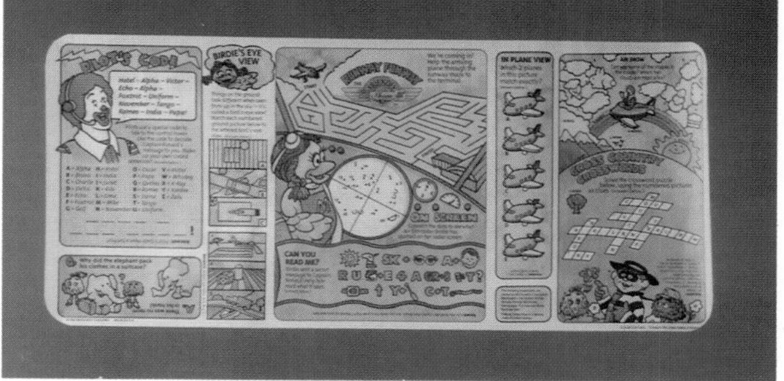

USA FR9155

GOOD MORNING HAPPY MEAL, 1991

❑ ❑ USA GO9130 **HM BAG,** 1990, **GOOD MORNING** $1-2
❑ ❑ USA GO9154 **U-3 CUP-RONALD W BUNNY,** 1990, RISING SUN BIRDS/NOT WRAPPED $1-1.50
❑ ❑ USA GO9150 **TOOTHBRUSH-RONALD,** 1989, RONALD GETTING OUT OF BED $1-1.50
❑ ❑ USA GO9151 **CLOCK-RONALD FLYING,** 1989, CLOCK HANDS PROPELLERS $1-1.50
❑ ❑ USA GO9152 **CUP-RONALD W BUNNY,** 1990, RISING SUN BIRDS/4 OZ. JUICY JUICE $1-1.50
❑ ❑ USA GO9153 **COMB,** 1990, 5 SECTION FRY KIDS COMB $1-1.50
❑ ❑ USA GO9164 **TRANSLITE/SM,** 1990 $8-12
❑ ❑ USA GO9165 **TRANSLITE/LG,** 1990 $10-15

COMMENTS: NATIONAL DISTRIBUTION: USA - JANUARY 4-31, 1991. A 2 OZ CAN OF JUICE WAS SUBSTITUTED FOR THE 4 OZ CARTON IN SOME NEW ENGLAND PROMOTIONS. USA GO9152 = USA GO9154; THEY WERE DISTRIBUTED LOOSE, WITH NO PACKAGING.

USA GO9164

USA GO9130

GRAVEDALE HIGH HAPPY MEAL, 1991

❑ ❑ USA GR9130 **HM BAG,** 1991, **CROSSWORD PUZZLE** $1.50-2
❑ ❑ USA GR9105 **U-3 CLEOFATRA,** 1991, YEL GIRL W ORG PONY TAILS - NBC LABEL $4-6
❑ ❑ USA GR9101 **SET 1 FRANKENTYKE,** 1991, GRN MONSTER W MOVABLE TONGUE $4-5
❑ ❑ USA GR9102 **SET 2 SID/INVISIBLE KID,** 1991, PUR FIGURE W MOVABLE ARMS/LEGS $4-5
❑ ❑ USA GR9103 **SET 3 VINNIE STOKER,** 1991, CASKET W ROTATING MAN $4-5
❑ ❑ USA GR9104 **SET 4 CLEOFATRA,** 1991, YEL GIRL W ORG PONY TAILS - NBC LABEL $4-5
❑ ❑ USA GR9164 **TRANSLITE/COLLECT ALL 4/SM,** 1991 $10-15
❑ ❑ USA GR9165 **TRANSLITE/COLLECT ALL 4/LG,** 1991 $12-20
❑ ❑ USA GR9166 **TRANSLITE/COLLECT ALL 3/LG,** 1991 $15-25
❑ ❑ USA GR9167 **TRANSLITE/COLLECT ALL 3/SM,** 1991 $12-20

USA GO9150 USA GO9151 USA GO9152 USA GO9153

USA GR9130

USA GR9105 USA GR9101 USA GR9102 USA GR9103 USA GR9104

USA GR9115

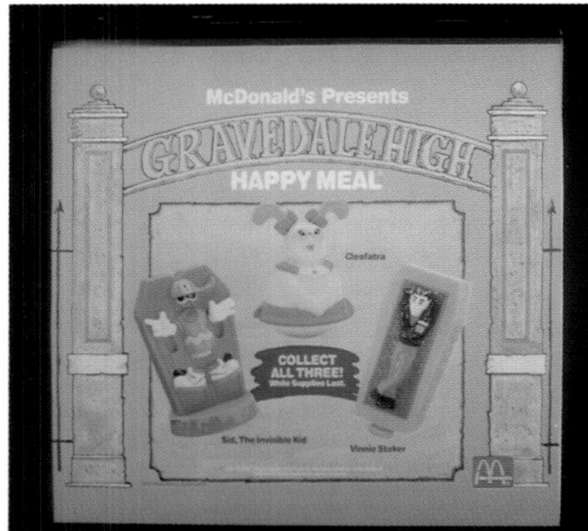

USA GR9117

COMMENTS: REGIONAL DISTRIBUTION: USA MARCH 14-APRIL 11, 1991. PREMIUM MARKINGS - "NBC CHINA." USA GR9105 U-3 = USA GR9104, LOOSE OUT OF PACKAGE. HM WAS RELEASED DURING EASTER 1991 AND DID NOT RECEIVE WIDE DISTRIBUTTION.

HALLOWEEN '91/MCBOO BAGS/BUCKETS HAPPY MEAL, 1991

- ❑ ❑ USA HA9100 **MCBOO WITCH BAG,** 1991, GRN VINYL BAG W ORG HANDLE $1-1.50
- ❑ ❑ USA HA9101 **MCBOO GHOST BAG,** 1991, PUR VINYL BAG W YEL HANDLES $1-1.50
- ❑ ❑ USA HA9102 **MCBOO MONSTER BAG,** 1991, ORG W PNK HANDLES, SKIN GLOWS $1-1.50
- ❑ ❑ USA HA9103 **MCPUNK'N,** 1986, PAIL W BLK ARCHES HANDLE W "MADE IN USA STICKER" $3-4
- ❑ ❑ USA HA9104 **GHOST,** 1986, GLOW-IN-THE-DARK PAIL/BLK AR HAN W "MADE IN USA STICKER" $3-4
- ❑ ❑ USA HA9105 **WITCH,** 1986, DAY-GLO PAIL W BLK ARCHES HANDLE W "MADE IN USA STICKER" $3-4
- ❑ ❑ USA HA9106 **MCBOO,** 1986, PAIL W BLK ARCHES HANDLE W "MADE IN USA STICKER" $3-4

USA HA9106 USA HA9107 USA HA9105 USA HA9104

USA HA9100

USA HA9102

USA HA9101

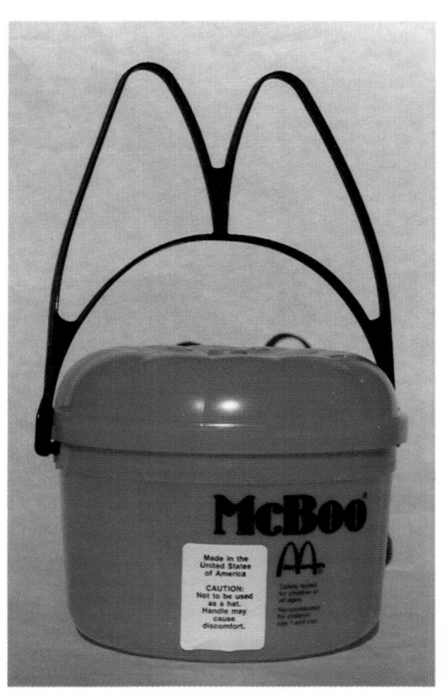

USA HA9106

- ❑ ❑ USA HA9107 **MCGOBLIN,** 1986, PAIL W BLK ARCHES HANDLE W "MADE IN USA STICKER" $3-4
- ❑ ❑ USA HA9141 **CEILING DANGLER/1 BAG,** 1991, TAKE OFF WITH A HM TODAY! $5-8
- ❑ ❑ USA HA9164 **TRANSLITE/SM,** 1991 $5-8
- ❑ ❑ USA HA9165 **TRANSLITE/LG,** 1991 $8-12

COMMENTS: NATIONAL DISTRIBUTION: USA - OCTOBER 11-OCTOBER 31, 1991. HM ALSO CALLED MCBOO BAGS/ BUCKETS HM, 1991. BAGS HAVE GLOW IN THE DARK FEATURES. IN SOME REGIONAL MARKETS, HALLOWEEN BUCKETS WERE SUBSTITUTED FOR THE NATIONAL PROMOTION.

HOOK HAPPY MEAL, 1991

- ❑ ❑ USA HO9110 **HM BOX,** 1991, **JOLLY ROGER** $1-2
- ❑ ❑ USA HO9111 **HM BOX,** 1991, **NEVER TREE** $1-2
- ❑ ❑ USA HO9112 **HM BOX,** 1991, **PIRATE TOWN** $1-2
- ❑ ❑ USA HO9113 **HM BOX,** 1991, **WENDY'S LONDON HOUSE** $1-2
- ❑ ❑ USA HO9100 **PETER PAN,** 1991, ON PURP RAFT W WHEELS/FLOATS/3P $1.50-2
- ❑ ❑ USA HO9101 **MERMAID,** 1991, BLU MERMAID WIND UP SWIMS IN WATER/1P $1.50-2
- ❑ ❑ USA HO9102 **HOOK,** 1991, CAPT HOOK IN BLU PIRATE SHIP/3P $1.50-2
- ❑ ❑ USA HO9103 **RUFIO,** 1991, BOY FLOATING ON GRN/PURP RUBBER BARRELS-SQUIRTS/1P $1.50-2
- ❑ ❑ USA HO9126 **DISPLAY/PREMIUMS,** 1991 $95-125
- ❑ ❑ USA HO9164 **TRANSLITE/SM,** 1991 $10-20
- ❑ ❑ USA HO9165 **TRANSLITE/LG,** 1991 $15-25

COMMENTS: NATIONAL DISTRIBUTION: USA - DECEMBER 13-JANUARY 9, 1992.

USA HO9110 USA HO9111

USA HO9112 USA HO9113

USA HA9141

USA HO9100 USA HO9101 USA HO9102 USA HO9103

USA HA9165

USA HO9165

USA HO9126

MCCHARACTERS ON BIKES/MCDONALDLAND ON WHEELS HAPPY MEAL, 1991

❏ ❏ USA BI9101 **BIRDIE,** 1990, ON PNK BIKE/BLU WHLS $1-2
❏ ❏ USA BI9102 **GRIMACE,** 1990, ON BLU BIKE/GRN WHLS $1-2
❏ ❏ USA BI9103 **HAMBURGLAR,** 1990, ON YEL BIKE/RED WHLS $1-2
❏ ❏ USA BI9104 **RONALD,** 1990, ON RED BIKE/YEL WHLS $1-2

COMMENTS: LIMITED REGIONAL DISTRIBUTION: USA - AUGUST 29-SEPTEMBER 6, 1991 DURING CLEAN UP WEEK. NO "MCDONALDLAND" HM BOXES OR BAGS GIVEN WITH THESE PREMIUMS. NOTE: BIKES ARE SIMILAR TO "MUPPET KIDS '89" BIKES, BUT NOT THE SAME. BIKES DATED 1989.

MCDINO CHANGEABLES HAPPY MEAL, 1991

❏ ❏ USA MC9115 **HM BAG,** 1991, **2 MCDINOS** $1-2
❏ ❏ USA MC9108 **U-3 BRONTO CHEESEBURGER,** 1990, RUBBER/BURGER W ORG DINO $2-3
❏ ❏ USA MC9109 **U-3 SMALL FRY-CERATOPS,** 1990, RUBBER/WHT FF/GRN DINO W **YEL ARCHES** $2-3
❏ ❏ USA MC9110 **U-3 SMALL FRY-CERATOPS,** 1990, RUBBER/WHT FF/GRN DINO W **RED ARCHES** $2-3
❏ ❏ USA MC9100 **HAPPY MEAL-O-DON,** 1990, 1P RED HM BOX/RED DINO $1-2
❏ ❏ USA MC9101 **QUARTER P CHEESE-O-SAUR,** 1990, 1P QP/TURQ DINO $1-2
❏ ❏ USA MC9102 **MCNUGGETS-O-SAURUS, 1990,** 1P YEL CHICK MCNUG BOX/GRN DINO $1-2
❏ ❏ USA MC9103 **HOT CAKES-O-DACTYL,** 1990, 1P WHT HOT CAKES CONT/PUR DINO $1-2
❏ ❏ USA MC9104 **BIG MAC-O-SAURUS REX,** 1990, 1P BIG MAC/ORG DINO $1-2
❏ ❏ USA MC9105 **FRY-CERATOPS,** 1990, 1P FRENCH FRIES/YEL DINO $1-2
❏ ❏ USA MC9106 **MCDINO CONE,** 1990, 1P ICE CREAM CONE/BLU DINO $1-2
❏ ❏ USA MC9107 **TRI-SHAKE-ATOPS,** 1990, 1P SHAKE/PINK DINO $1-2
❏ ❏ USA MC9126 **DISPLAY W PREMIUMS/MOTION,** 1991 $85-115

USA BI9101

USA BI9102

USA BI9103

USA BI9104

USA MC9108 USA MC9101 USA MC9103 USA MC9106

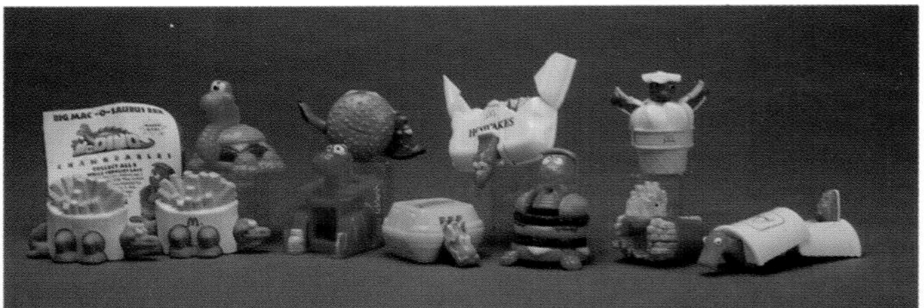
USA MC9110 USA MC9102 USA MC9105 USA MC9107
USA MC9100 USA MC9104

USA MC9115

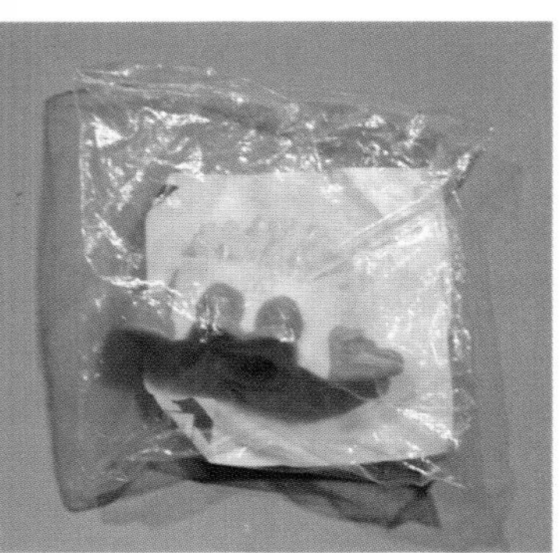
USA MC9109

USA CI9101 USA CI9102 USA CI9103 USA CI9104

USA MC9126

❑ ❑ USA MC9164 **TRANSLITE/SM,** 1991 $6-8
❑ ❑ USA MC9165 **TRANSLITE/LG,** 1991 $8-12
❑ ❑ USA MC9195 **PIN,** 1990, ORG DINO/MCDINO CHANGEABLES $3-4

COMMENTS: NATIONAL DISTRIBUTION: USA - MAY 24-JUNE 20, 1991.

MCDONALDLAND CIRCUS PARADE HAPPY MEAL, 1993/ 1992/1991

❑ ❑ USA CI9130 **HM BAG,** 1990, **CIRCUS/RONALD AS RINGMASTER** $1-1.50
❑ ❑ USA CI9101 **SET 1 RONALD,** 1989, RINGMASTER/CAR W RM $2-3
❑ ❑ USA CI9102 **SET 2 BIRDIE,** 1989, BAREBACK RIDER $2-3
❑ ❑ USA CI9103 **SET 3 FRY GUY,** 1989, ELEPHANT TRAINER $2-3
❑ ❑ USA CI9104 **SET 4 GRIMACE,** 1989, W CALLIOPE $2-3
❑ ❑ USA CI9164 **TRANSLITE/SM** 1989 $8-12
❑ ❑ USA CI9165 **TRANSLITE/LG,** 1989 $15-25
❑ ❑ USA C10166 **WINDOW DECAL,** 1989 $4-16

COMMENTS: REGIONAL DISTRIBUTION: USA - MARCH 14-APRIL 11, 1991 AND 1992/1993 DURING CLEAN-UP WEEKS.

MIGHTY MINI HAPPY MEAL, 1991

❑ ❑ USA MI9110 **HM BOX,** 1990, **DESERT SCENE W MINI CARS** $2-3
❑ ❑ USA MI9130 **HM BAG,** 1990, **MIGHTY MINI 4X4** $1-2
❑ ❑ USA MI9104 **U-3 POCKET PICKUP,** 1990, BLU W BLK TIRES/ RUBBER $3-5
❑ ❑ USA MI9100 **SET 1 DUNE BUSTER VW,** 1990, PNK W LONG TWIST CRANK $2-3
❑ ❑ USA MI9101 **SET 2 LI'L CLASSIC T BIRD,** 1990, YEL W LONG TWIST CRANK $2-3
❑ ❑ USA MI9102 **SET 3 CARGO CLIMBER VAN,** 1990, ORG W LONG TWIST CRANK $2-3
❑ ❑ USA MI9103 **SET 4 POCKET PICKUP,** 1990, RED W LONG TWIST CRANK $2-3
❑ ❑ USA MI9164 **TRANSLITE/SM,** 1990 $15-25
❑ ❑ USA MI9165 **TRANSLITE/LG,** 1990 $20-30

COMMENTS: REGIONAL DISTRIBUTION: USA - MARCH 14-APRIL 11, 1991. DISTRIBUTED IN CALIFORNIA, WASHINGTON, PENNSYLVANIIA AND PARTS OF NEW ENGLAND.

USA CI9130

USA CI9165

USA CI9102 USA CI9103 USA CI9104 USA CI9101

USA MC9165

USA MI9110

USA MI9111

USA MC9164

USA MC9195

USA MI9104 USA MI9100 USA MI9101 USA MI9102 USA MI9103

MUPPET BABIES III HAPPY MEAL, 1992/1991

❑ ❑ USA MU9130 **HM BAG,** 1990, **RACE TO THE FINISH** $3-4
❑ ❑ USA MU9100 **FOSSIE,** 1990, ON RED WAGON 2P $1-2
❑ ❑ USA MU9101 **GONZO,** 1990, IN GRN AIRPLANE 2P $1-2
❑ ❑ USA MU9102 **KERMIT,** 1990, ON YEL RACER 2P $1-2
❑ ❑ USA MU9103 **MISS PIGGY,** 1990, ON BLUE TRICYCLE 2P $1-2
❑ ❑ USA MU9164 **TRANSLITE/SM,** 1990 $12-25
❑ ❑ USA MU9165 **TRANSLITE/LG,** 1990 $20-30

COMMENTS: REGIONAL DISTRIBUTION: USA - MARCH 8-APRIL 12, 1991 AND 1992 DURING CLEAN-UP WEEKS. PREMIUM MARKINGS "HA! 1990 CHINA." NO U-3. ALL SETS RECOMMENDED FOR CHILDREN AGE 1 AND OVER.

USA MU9130

USA MU9165

USA MU9100 USA MU9101 USA MU9102 USA MU9103

NATURE'S HELPERS HAPPY MEAL, 1991

❑ ❑ USA NA9130 **HM BAG,** 1990, **SUN/GARDEN/WHAT THINGS** $1-1.50
❑ ❑ USA NA9105 **U-3 GARDEN RAKE,** 1990, YEL W MOLDED M AND WORM PIC/NO SEEDS 1P $1-1.50
❑ ❑ USA NA9100 **DOUBLE DIGGER,** 1990, GRN/W CUCUMBER SEEDS & "WHY TREES/VEGIES?" FLYER 2P $1-1.25
❑ ❑ USA NA9101 **BIRD FEEDER,** 1990, W "WHY BIRDS?" FLYER GRN/WHT/ORG 3P $1-1.50
❑ ❑ USA NA9102 **WATER CAN,** 1990, W "WHY FLOWERS?" FLYER/BLU W YEL TOP 1P $1-1.25
❑ ❑ USA NA9103 **TERRARIUM,** 1990, W COLEUS SEEDS/ "HOW..WORLD.."FLYER/GRN BASE/DOME 2P $1-1.50
❑ ❑ USA NA9104 **RAKE,** 1990, YEL W MARIGOLD SEEDS 1P $1-1.25
❑ ❑ USA NA9164 **TRANSLITE/SM,** 1990 $8-12
❑ ❑ USA NA9165 **TRANSLITE/LG,** 1990 $10-15

COMMENTS: NATIONAL DISTRIBUTION: USA - APRIL 12-MAY 16, 1991.

USA NA9130

USA NA9165

PIGGSBURG PIGS HAPPY MEAL, 1991

❑ ❑ USA PG9130 **HM BAG,** 1990, **PIGGSBURG PIGS** $1-1.50

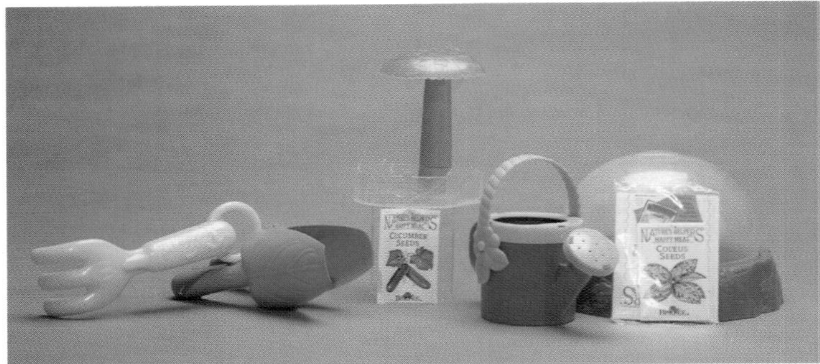

USA NA9105 USA NA9100 USA NA9101 USA NA9102 USA NA9103

USA PG9130

❑ ❑ USA PG9100 **SET 1 PORTLY/PIG HEAD,** 1990, ON BRN CYCLE W GRN SIDE CAR $3-4
❑ ❑ USA PG9101 **SET 2 PIGGY/QUACKERS,** 1990, ON BRN CRATE RACER $3-4
❑ ❑ USA PG9102 **SET 3 REMBRANDT,** 1990, IN RED BARNYARD HOT ROD $3-4
❑ ❑ USA PG9103 **SET 4 HUFF/PUFF,** 1990, ON YEL/BRN CATA-PULT 2P $3-4
❑ ❑ USA PG9164 **TRANSLITE/SM,** 1990 $15-25
❑ ❑ USA PG9165 **TRANSLITE/LG,** 1990 $20-30

COMMENTS: REGIONAL DISTRIBUTION: USA - MARCH 14-APRIL 11, 1991 IN FLORIDA. NO U-3. ALL SETS FOR AGE 1 AND OVER. PREMIUM MARKINGS - "1990 FOX CH'S NET INC CHINA."

PIZZA HAPPY SACK HAPPY MEAL, 1991

❑ ❑ USA PI9130 **HM BAG,** 1989, **"WELCOME TO MY PIZZA PARTY" MCD#90-043** $12-15
❑ ❑ USA PI9101 **HAMBURGLAR FIGURINE,** ND, 2 1/2" HAMBURGLAR STANDING/RUBBER $10-15

COMMENTS: REGIONAL DISTRIBUTION: USA - 1990 AND MAY 1991 IN CONNECTICUTT AND PARTS OF NEW ENGLAND. GENERIC TOYS COULD HAVE BEEN GIVEN. THE TEST MARKET WAS SUPPOSE TO INCLUDED A 2 1/2" RUBBER HAMBURGLAR FIGURINE.

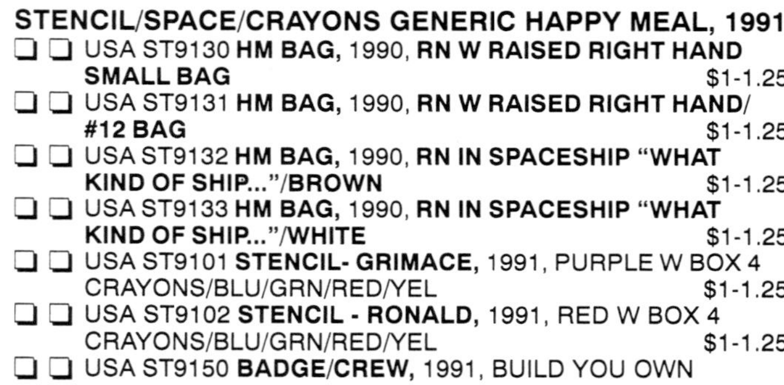

STENCIL/SPACE/CRAYONS GENERIC HAPPY MEAL, 1991

❑ ❑ USA ST9130 **HM BAG,** 1990, **RN W RAISED RIGHT HAND SMALL BAG** $1-1.25
❑ ❑ USA ST9131 **HM BAG,** 1990, **RN W RAISED RIGHT HAND/ #12 BAG** $1-1.25
❑ ❑ USA ST9132 **HM BAG,** 1990, **RN IN SPACESHIP "WHAT KIND OF SHIP..."/BROWN** $1-1.25
❑ ❑ USA ST9133 **HM BAG,** 1990, **RN IN SPACESHIP "WHAT KIND OF SHIP..."/WHITE** $1-1.25
❑ ❑ USA ST9101 **STENCIL- GRIMACE,** 1991, PURPLE W BOX 4 CRAYONS/BLU/GRN/RED/YEL $1-1.25
❑ ❑ USA ST9102 **STENCIL - RONALD,** 1991, RED W BOX 4 CRAYONS/BLU/GRN/RED/YEL $1-1.25
❑ ❑ USA ST9150 **BADGE/CREW,** 1991, BUILD YOU OWN HM $4-6

COMMENTS: REGIONAL DISTRIBUTION: USA - 1991. CLEAN-UP WEEK HAPPY MEAL - GENERIC STENCILS GIVEN.

USA PI9130

USA PI9101

USA ST9130 USA ST9131

USA PG9100 USA PG9101 USA PG9102 USA PG9103

USA PG9165

USA ST9102 USA ST9101

USA ST9150

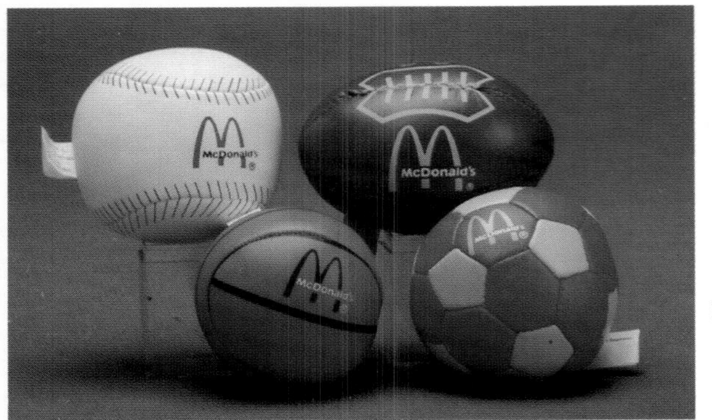

USA SP9157

USA SP9158

USA SP9155 USA SP9156

SPORTS BALL HAPPY MEAL, 1991

- ❑ ❑ USA SP9155 **BASEBALL,** 1989, WHT W RED STITCHING/ SOFT W LARGE RED M $2-3
- ❑ ❑ USA SP9156 **BASKETBALL,** 1989, ORG W BLK SEAMS/ SOFT W LARGE BLK M $2-3
- ❑ ❑ USA SP9157 **FOOTBALL,** 1989, BROWN W YEL LACING/ SOFT W LARGE YEL M $2-3
- ❑ ❑ USA SP9158 **SOCCER BALL,** 1989, RED/YEL/SOFT W SMALL YEL M $2-3

COMMENTS: REGIONAL DISTRIBUTION: USA - AUGUST/ SEPTEMBER 1991. SOME TEST AREAS INCLUDED KANSAS CITY, INDIANA / NEW ENGLAND AREAS. NOTE: THE SAME TEST MARKET PREMIUMS WERE REGIONALLY ISSUED DURING CLEAN-UP WEEK SEPTEMBER 1991. THE PREMIUM "TAGS" HAD "M-B SALES ALL NEW MATERIAL AND NOT "OAK BROOK, IL". NOTE: THE DIFFERENT COLORS OF THE FOOTBALL-BROWN (1991) VERSUS YELLOW.

USA SU9126

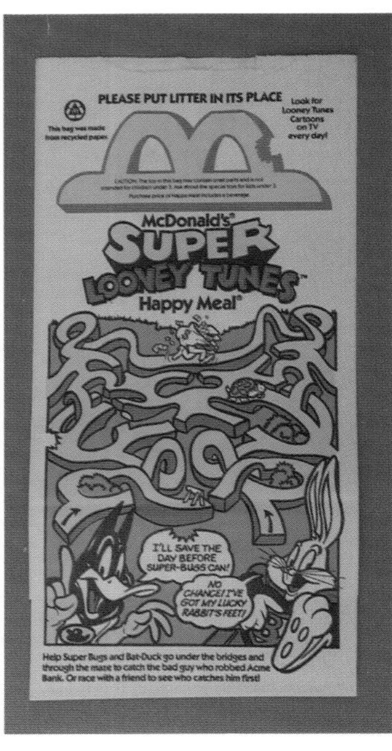

USA SU9130

SUPER LOONEY TUNES HAPPY MEAL, 1991

- ❑ ❑ USA SU9130 **HM BAG,** 1991, **MAZE** $1-1.25
- ❑ ❑ USA SU9105 **U-3 BAT DUCK,** 1991, ROCKING IN HIS BATMOBILE $2.50-3.50
- ❑ ❑ USA SU9101 **BUGS BUNNY/SUPERBUGS,** 1991, W RED/BLU BATMAN COSTUME $1-2
- ❑ ❑ USA SU9102 **TASMANIAN DEVIL/TAZ-FLASH,** 1991, W RED DEVIL SUIT $1-2
- ❑ ❑ USA SU9103 **PETUNIA PIG/WONDER PIG,** 1991, W RED/ WHT/BLU WONDER WOMAN SUIT $1-2
- ❑ ❑ USA SU9104 **DAFFY DUCK/BAT DUCK,** 1991, W BLU/GREY BATMAN SUIT $1-2
- ❑ ❑ USA SU9126 **DISPLAY/PREMIUMS,** 1991 $85-100
- ❑ ❑ USA SU9164 **TRANSLITE/SM,** 1991 $6-8
- ❑ ❑ USA SU9165 **TRANSLITE/LG,** 1991 $8-12
- ❑ ❑ USA SU9195 **PIN,** 1991, BUGS/SUPER LOONEY TUNES $3-5

COMMENTS: NATIONAL DISTRIBUTION: USA - NOVEMBER 8-DECEMBER 5, 1991.

TINY TOON ADVENTURES I HAPPY MEAL, 1991

- ❑ ❑ USA TI9110 **HM BOX,** 1990, **ACME ACRES GENERAL STORE** $1-2
- ❑ ❑ USA TI9111 **HM BOX,** 1990, **FOREST** $1-2

USA SU9105 USA SU9101 USA SU9102 USA SU9103 USA SU9104

USA TI9110 USA TI9111

USA SU9165

USA TI9112 USA TI9113

❑ ❑ USA TI9112 **HM BOX,** 1990, **LOONIVERSITY** $1-2
❑ ❑ USA TI9113 **HM BOX,** 1990, **WACKY LAND** $1-2
❑ ❑ USA TI9105 **U-3 GOGO DODO,** 1990, IN WHT BATH TUB/ SOFT RUBBER $2.50-3.50
❑ ❑ USA TI9106 **U-3 PLUCKY DUCK,** 1990, IN RED BOAT/SOFT RUBBER $2.50-3.50
❑ ❑ USA TI9101 **BABS BUNNY,** 1990, IN PHONE/PLUCKY DUCK IN SPEED BOAT $1.50-2.50
❑ ❑ USA TI9102 **BUSTER BUNNY,** 1990, IN CARROT/ELMIRA IN WAGON $1.50-2.50
❑ ❑ USA TI9103 **MONTANA MAX,** 1990, IN GRN CAR/GOGO DODO IN BATH TUB $1.50-2.50
❑ ❑ USA TI9104 **HAMPTON PIG,** 1990, IN HERO SANDWICH/ DIZZY DEVIL IN AMP $1.50-2.50
❑ ❑ USA TI9126 **DISPLAY/PREMIUMS,** 1990 $75-100
❑ ❑ USA TI9164 **TRANSLITE/SM,** 1990 $8-12
❑ ❑ USA TI9165 **TRANSLITE/X-0 GRAPHIC/LG,** 1990 $25-40

COMMENTS: NATIONAL DISTRIBUTION: USA - FEBRUARY 8-MARCH 7, 1991. PREMIUM MARKINGS "1990 WARNER BROS."

1992

BACK TO THE FUTURE HAPPY MEAL, 1992
BARBIE / HOT WHEELS MINI-STREEX III HAPPY MEAL, 1992
BATMAN HAPPY MEAL, 1992
BEHIND THE SCENES HAPPY MEAL, 1992
CABBAGE PATCH KIDS/TONKA HAPPY MEAL, 1992
CRAYON SKETCH HAPPY MEAL, 1992
CRAYON SQUEEZE BOTTLE HAPPY MEAL, 1992
FITNESS FUN/MICHAEL JORDAN HAPPY MEAL, 1992
HALLOWEEN '92 HAPPY MEAL, 1992
MYSTERY OF THE LOST ARCHES HAPPY MEAL, 1992
NATURE'S WATCH HAPPY MEAL, 1992
POTATO HEAD KIDS II HAPPY MEAL, 1992
REAL GHOSTBUSTERS II HAPPY MEAL, 1992
TINY TOON ADVENTURES II HAPPY MEAL, 1992
WATER GAMES HAPPY MEAL, 1992
WILD FRIENDS HAPPY MEAL, 1992
YO, YOGI! HAPPY MEAL, 1992
YOUNG ASTRONAUTS II HAPPY MEAL, 1992

BACK TO THE FUTURE HAPPY MEAL, 1992

❑ ❑ USA BK9210 **HM BOX,** 1991, **DRIVE THROUGH DINOCITY** $1-2
❑ ❑ USA BK9211 **HM BOX,** 1991, **HILL VALLEY HOTEL** $1-2
❑ ❑ USA BK9212 **HM BOX,** 1991, **MAKE A DRAWBRIDGE** $1-2
❑ ❑ USA BK9213 **HM BOX,** 1991, **MAKE A ROMAN TEMPLE** $1-2

USA TI9105 USA TI9106

USA TI9126

USA TI9165

USA TI9101 USA TI9102 USA TI9103 USA TI9104

USA BK9210 USA BK9211

USA BK9212 USA BK9213

USA BK9204

USA BK9201 USA BK9202 USA BK9203

USA BK9226

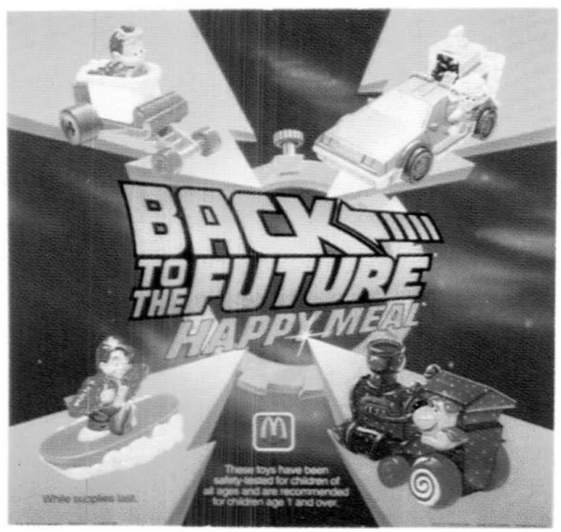

USA BK9264

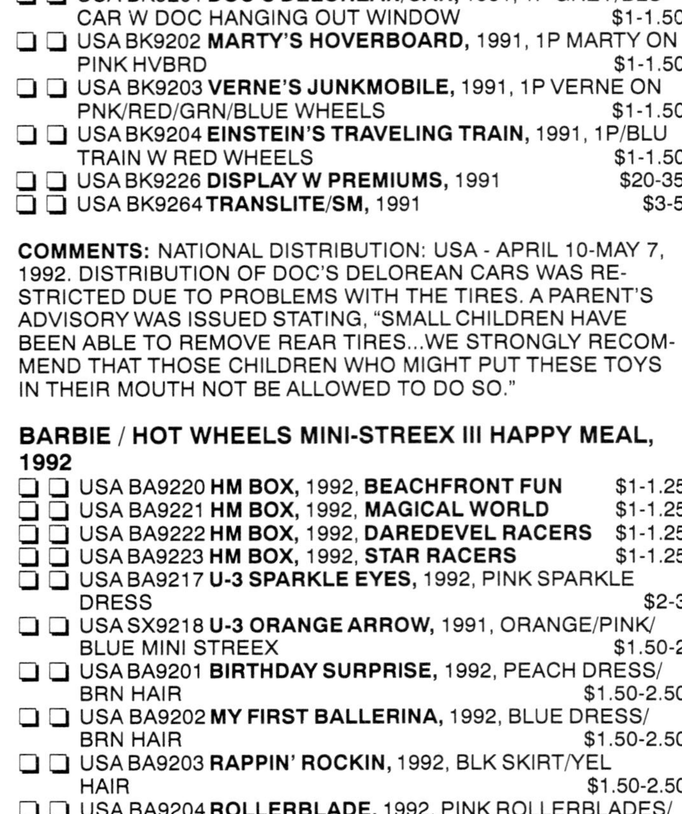

- ❏ ❏ USA BK9201 **DOC'S DELOREAN/CAR,** 1991, 1P GREY/BLU CAR W DOC HANGING OUT WINDOW $1-1.50
- ❏ ❏ USA BK9202 **MARTY'S HOVERBOARD,** 1991, 1P MARTY ON PINK HVBRD $1-1.50
- ❏ ❏ USA BK9203 **VERNE'S JUNKMOBILE,** 1991, 1P VERNE ON PNK/RED/GRN/BLUE WHEELS $1-1.50
- ❏ ❏ USA BK9204 **EINSTEIN'S TRAVELING TRAIN,** 1991, 1P/BLU TRAIN W RED WHEELS $1-1.50
- ❏ ❏ USA BK9226 **DISPLAY W PREMIUMS,** 1991 $20-35
- ❏ ❏ USA BK9264 **TRANSLITE/SM,** 1991 $3-5

COMMENTS: NATIONAL DISTRIBUTION: USA - APRIL 10-MAY 7, 1992. DISTRIBUTION OF DOC'S DELOREAN CARS WAS RESTRICTED DUE TO PROBLEMS WITH THE TIRES. A PARENT'S ADVISORY WAS ISSUED STATING, "SMALL CHILDREN HAVE BEEN ABLE TO REMOVE REAR TIRES...WE STRONGLY RECOMMEND THAT THOSE CHILDREN WHO MIGHT PUT THESE TOYS IN THEIR MOUTH NOT BE ALLOWED TO DO SO."

BARBIE / HOT WHEELS MINI-STREEX III HAPPY MEAL, 1992

- ❏ ❏ USA BA9220 **HM BOX,** 1992, **BEACHFRONT FUN** $1-1.25
- ❏ ❏ USA BA9221 **HM BOX,** 1992, **MAGICAL WORLD** $1-1.25
- ❏ ❏ USA BA9222 **HM BOX,** 1992, **DAREDEVEL RACERS** $1-1.25
- ❏ ❏ USA BA9223 **HM BOX,** 1992, **STAR RACERS** $1-1.25
- ❏ ❏ USA BA9217 **U-3 SPARKLE EYES,** 1992, PINK SPARKLE DRESS $2-3
- ❏ ❏ USA SX9218 **U-3 ORANGE ARROW,** 1991, ORANGE/PINK/BLUE MINI STREEX $1.50-2
- ❏ ❏ USA BA9201 **BIRTHDAY SURPRISE,** 1992, PEACH DRESS/BRN HAIR $1.50-2.50
- ❏ ❏ USA BA9202 **MY FIRST BALLERINA,** 1992, BLUE DRESS/BRN HAIR $1.50-2.50
- ❏ ❏ USA BA9203 **RAPPIN' ROCKIN,** 1992, BLK SKIRT/YEL HAIR $1.50-2.50
- ❏ ❏ USA BA9204 **ROLLERBLADE,** 1992, PINK ROLLERBLADES/YEL HAIR $1.50-2.50

USA BA9220 USA BA9221

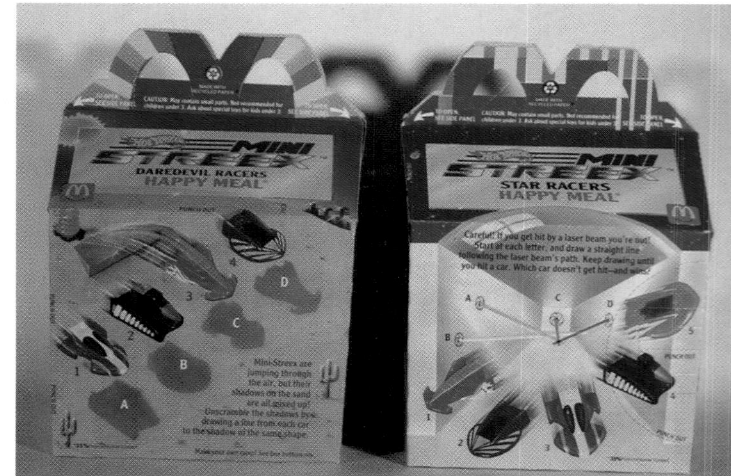

USA BA9222 USA BA9223

- ❑ ❑ USA BA9205 **ROSE BRIDE,** 1992, WHITE BRIDE DRESS $1.50-2.50
- ❑ ❑ USA BA9206 **SNAP'N PLAY,** 1992, 2P TURQ SKIRT/ PINK-PURP DRESS $1.50-2.50
- ❑ ❑ USA BA9207 **SPARKLE EYES,** 1992, PINK SPARKLE DRESS $1.50-2.50
- ❑ ❑ USA BA9208 **SUN SENSATION,** 1992, GOLD SWIM SUIT/ TURQ WRAP $1.50-2.50
- ❑ ❑ USA SX9209 **BLACK ARROW,** 1991, 2P BLK/PUR/GRN W PNK LAUNCHER $1-1.50
- ❑ ❑ USA SX9210 **BLADE BURNER,** 1991, 2P YEL/BLU/PNK W LIGHT BLU LAUNCHER $1-1.50
- ❑ ❑ USA SX9211 **FLAME-OUT,** 1991, 2P BLU/RED/YEL W RED LAUNCHER $1-1.50
- ❑ ❑ USA SX9212 **HOT SHOCK,** 1991, 2P RED/PURP/YEL W YEL LAUNCHER $1-1.50
- ❑ ❑ USA SX9213 **NIGHT SHADOW,** 1991, 2P BLK/BLU/GRN/YEL/ PNK W PURP/PINKISH LAUNCHER $1-1.50
- ❑ ❑ USA SX9214 **QUICK-FLASH,** 1991, 2P LAUNCHER/PURP/ BLU/GRN W PURP LAUNCHER $1-1.50
- ❑ ❑ USA SX9215 **RACER-TRACER,** 1991, 2P GRN/PNK/BLU W GRN LAUNCHER $1-1.50
- ❑ ❑ USA SX9216 **TURBO FLYER,** 1991, 2P BLU/YEL/PNK W DARK BLUE LAUNCHER $1-1.50
- ❑ ❑ USA BA9226 **DISPLAY/PREMIUMS,** 1991 $50-75
- ❑ ❑ USA BA9264 **TRANSLITE/SM,** 1992 $5-8

COMMENTS: NATIONAL DISTRIBUTION: USA - AUGUST 7-SEPTEMBER 3, 1992. NOTE: USA BA9207 SPARKLE EYES BARBIE = USA BA9217, EXCEPT FOR THE PACKAGING.

BATMAN HAPPY MEAL, 1992

- ❑ ❑ USA BT9230 **HM BAG,** 1991, **BATMAN IS HERO** $1-1.50
- ❑ ❑ USA BT9201 **BATMAN/BATMISSLE,** 1991, BLK CAR WITH BATMAN INSIDE/1P $1.50-2
- ❑ ❑ USA BT9202 **BATMOBILE,** 1991, BLK BATMISSILE/ BATMOBILE/2P $1.50-2
- ❑ ❑ USA BT9203 **CATWOMAN CAT COUPE,** 1991, PURPLE CAT W BATWOMAN/TAIL MOVES/1P $1.50-2
- ❑ ❑ USA BT9204 **PENGUIN ROTO-ROADSTER,** 1991, YEL CAR W UMB RED/WHT FRONT/1P $1.50-2

USA SX9218

USA BA9264

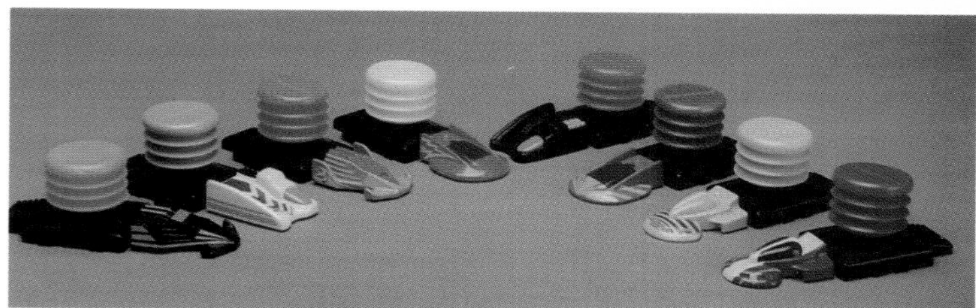
USA SX9209 USA SX9212 USA SX9213 USA SX9216
USA SX9211 USA SX9214
USA SX9210 USA SX9215

USA BA9226

USA BA9205 USA BA9206 USA BA9207 USA BA9208

USA BA9217 USA BA9201 USA BA9202 USA BA9203 USA BA9204

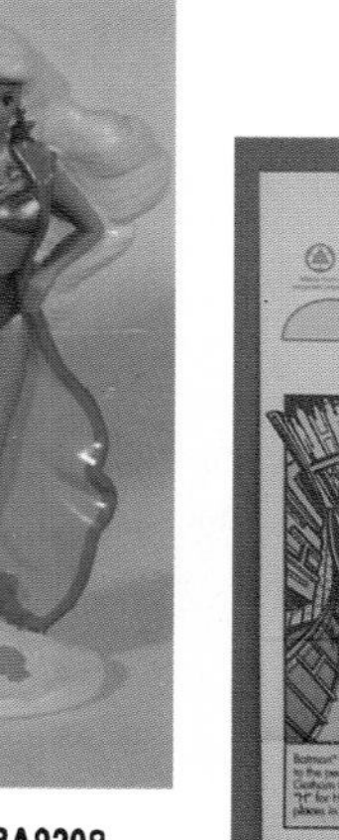

USA BT9230

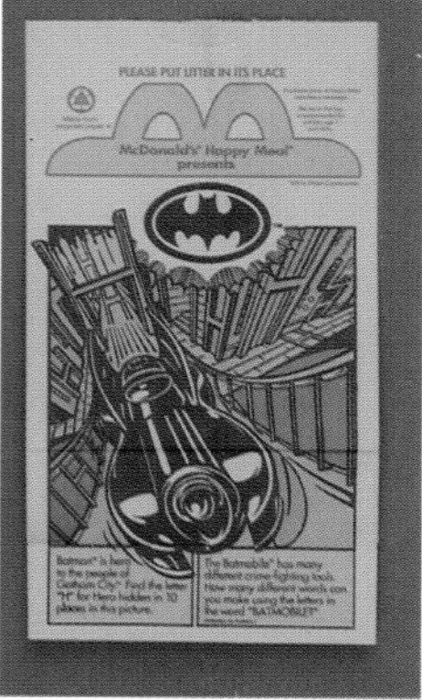

USA BT9203

USA BT9201 USA BT9202 USA BT9204

USA BT9264

USA BT9295

USA BT9296

- ❑ ❑ USA BT9226 **DISPLAY/PREMIUMS,** 1992 $45-60
- ❑ ❑ USA BT9264 **TRANSLITE/SM,** 1992 $8-12
- ❑ ❑ USA BT9295 **PIN,** 1992, SQUARE/BLK/WHT BATMAN RETURNS MCD $4-5
- ❑ ❑ USA BT9296 **PIN,** 1992, BATMAN'S FACE/MCDONALD'S $4-5

COMMENTS: NATIONAL DISTRIBUTION: USA - JUNE 12-JULY 9, 1992. A BATMAN RETURNS BROWN BAG PRECEEDED THE PROMOTION. PROMOTION INCLUDED 10 BATMAN RELATED PLASTIC CUPS FOR DRINKS, PLUS 2 EXTRA CUPS - SPECIAL ORDERED.

BEHIND THE SCENES HAPPY MEAL, 1992

- ❑ ❑ USA BE9230 **HM BAG,** 1992, **TAKE A PEEK/SCREEN PLAY** $1-1.25
- ❑ ❑ USA BE9201 **ANIMATION WHEEL,** 1992, BLK/BLU W 4 CARTOON STRIPS/BOOKLET/2P $1-1.50
- ❑ ❑ USA BE9202 **BALANCE BUILDERS,** 1992, ORG/BLU/YEL/GRN/RED STACKING FIGURES/5P $1-1.50
- ❑ ❑ USA BE9203 **RUB/DRAW TEMPLATES,** 1992, 6 TEMPLATES/1 TURQ HOLDER/7P $1-1.50
- ❑ ❑ USA BE9204 **RAINBOW VIEWER,** 1992, TURQ/PURP RECT COLOR WHEEL/1P $1-1.50
- ❑ ❑ USA BE9226 **DISPLAY W PREMIUMS,** 1992 $20-35
- ❑ ❑ USA BE9264 **TRANSLITE/SM,** 1992 $4-7

COMMENTS: NATIONAL DISTRIBUTION: USA - SEPTEMBER 11-OCTOBER 7, 1992.

CABBAGE PATCH KIDS/TONKA HAPPY MEAL, 1992

- ❑ ❑ USA CP9230 **HM BAG,** 1992, **UNSCRAMBLE THE LETTERS** $1-1.25
- ❑ ❑ USA CP9211 **U-3 ANNE LOUISE,** 1992, BABY SITTING/PURP BEAR/RUBBER $2-3
- ❑ ❑ USA TK9212 **U-3 DUMP TRUCK,** 1992, YEL/BLU/BLK WHEELS $1.50-2
- ❑ ❑ USA CP9201 **ALL DRESSED UP,** 1992, RED PARTY DRESS/HOLDING GIFT $1.50-2.50
- ❑ ❑ USA CP9202 **ALI MARIE,** 1992, TINY DANCER/PURP BODY SUIT/GOLD STAR $1.50-2.50
- ❑ ❑ USA CP9203 **FUN ON ICE,** 1992, GRN/RED/WHT MUFF W WHT SKATES $1.50-2.50
- ❑ ❑ USA CP9204 **HOLIDAY DREAMER,** 1992, PNK/BLU PJS W GRN STOCKING/BEAR $1.50-2.50
- ❑ ❑ USA CP9205 **HOLIDAY PAGEANT,** 1992, WHT ANGEL/GOLD LONG HAIR $1.50-2.50

USA BE9230

USA BE9264

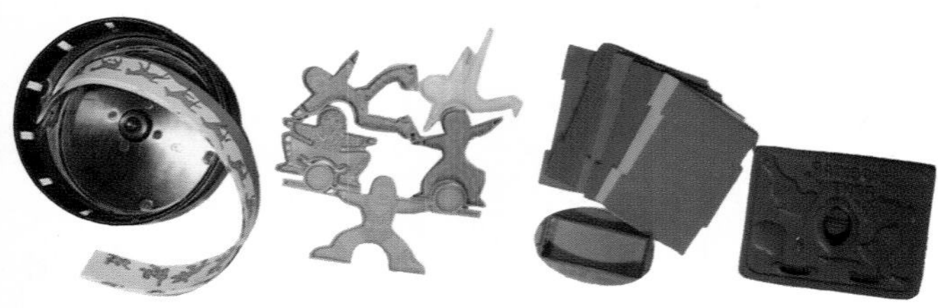
USA BE9201 USA BE9202 USA BE9203 USA BE9204

USA CP9230

USA CP9211 USA CP9201 USA CP9202 USA CP9203 USA CP9204 USA CP9

USA TK9212 USA TK9206 USA TK9207 USA TK9208 USA TK9209 USA TK9210

USA CP9226

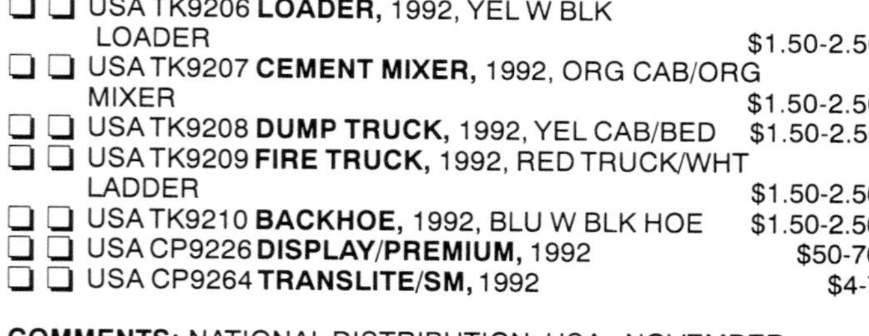

❑ ❑ USA TK9206 **LOADER,** 1992, YEL W BLK LOADER $1.50-2.50
❑ ❑ USA TK9207 **CEMENT MIXER,** 1992, ORG CAB/ORG MIXER $1.50-2.50
❑ ❑ USA TK9208 **DUMP TRUCK,** 1992, YEL CAB/BED $1.50-2.50
❑ ❑ USA TK9209 **FIRE TRUCK,** 1992, RED TRUCK/WHT LADDER $1.50-2.50
❑ ❑ USA TK9210 **BACKHOE,** 1992, BLU W BLK HOE $1.50-2.50
❑ ❑ USA CP9226 **DISPLAY/PREMIUM,** 1992 $50-70
❑ ❑ USA CP9264 **TRANSLITE/SM,** 1992 $4-7

COMMENTS: NATIONAL DISTRIBUTION: USA - NOVEMBER 27-DECEMBER 31, 1992.

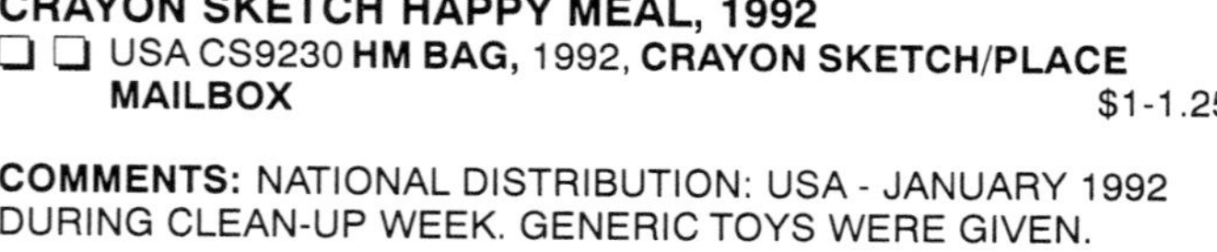

CRAYON SKETCH HAPPY MEAL, 1992

❑ ❑ USA CS9230 **HM BAG,** 1992, **CRAYON SKETCH/PLACE MAILBOX** $1-1.25

COMMENTS: NATIONAL DISTRIBUTION: USA - JANUARY 1992 DURING CLEAN-UP WEEK. GENERIC TOYS WERE GIVEN.

USA CP9264

USA CS9230

CRAYON SQUEEZE BOTTLE HAPPY MEAL, 1992

❑ ❑ USA CR9230 **HM BAG,** 1991, **KAY BEE AMERICA'S STORE/ FINISH W $5 OFF COUPON** $1-1.50
❑ ❑ USA CR9201 **BLU SQUEEZE BOTTLE,** 1992, 4P/BLU CUP/ LID/CLEAR STRAW/3 CRAYONS/YEL BOX $4.50-6
❑ ❑ USA CR9202 **GRN SQUEEZE BOTTLE,** 1992, 4P/GRN CUP/ LID/CLEAR STRAW/3 CRAYONS/YEL BOX $4.50-6
❑ ❑ USA CR9203 **RED SQUEEZE BOTTLE,** 1992, 4P/RED CUP/ LID/CLEAR STRAW/3 CRAYONS/YEL BOX $4.50-6
❑ ❑ USA CR9204 **YEL SQUEEZE BOTTLE,** 1992, 4P/YEL CUP/ LID/CLEAR STRAW/3 CRAYONS/YEL BOX $4.50-6
❑ ❑ USA CR9264 **TRANSLITE/SM,** 1992 $8-12
❑ ❑ USA CR9265 **TRANSLITE/LG,** 1992 $10-15

COMMENTS: REGIONAL DISTRIBUTION: USA - JANUARY 31-MARCH 5, 1992 IN ALBANY, NEW YORK AND CONNECTICUT. EACH HM CAME WITH A $5 OFF YELLOW COUPON FROM KAY BEE TOY STORE. CUPS ARE CRAYON SHAPED.

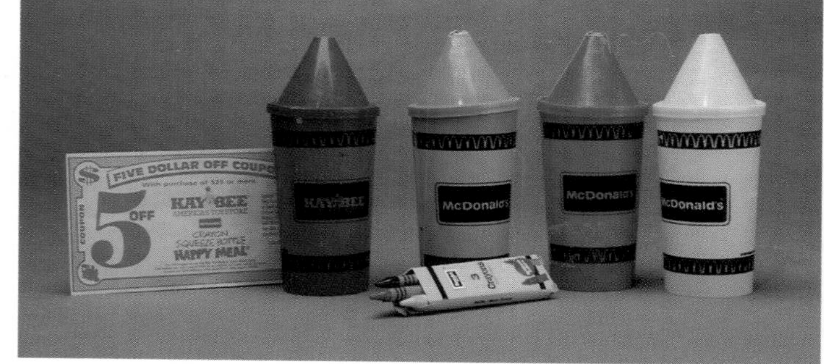

USA CR9201 USA CR9202 USA CR9203 USA CR9204

USA CR9230

USA CR9265

USA MJ9230

FITNESS FUN/MICHAEL JORDAN HAPPY MEAL, 1992

- ❑ ❑ USA MJ9230 **HM BAG,** 1991, **MJ FITNESS FUN** $1-1.25
- ❑ ❑ USA MJ9201 **BASEBALL,** 1991, 1P WHT W MJ LOGO $1-1.25
- ❑ ❑ USA MJ9202 **BASKETBALL,** ND, 1P ORG W MJ LOGO $1-1.25
- ❑ ❑ USA MJ9203 **FLYING DISC,** 1991, 1P TURQ W MJ LOGO $1-1.25
- ❑ ❑ USA MJ9204 **FOOTBALL,** 1991, 1P RED/YEL/TURQ/GRN W MJ LOGO $1-1.25
- ❑ ❑ USA MJ9205 **JUMP ROPE,** ND, 1P GRN W PURP HANDLE $1-1.25
- ❑ ❑ USA MJ9206 **SOCCER BALL,** 1991, 1P INFLATABLE BLK/ WHT SOCCER BALL $1-1.25
- ❑ ❑ USA MJ9207 **STOP WATCH,** 1991,1P BLK/GRN STOP WATCH W MJ $1-1.25
- ❑ ❑ USA MJ9208 **SQUEEZE BOTTLE,** 1991, 3P/BLUE BOTTLE/ PURP LID/ORG STRAW $1-1.25
- ❑ ❑ USA MJ9226 **DISPLAY/PREMIUMS,** 1992 $15-25
- ❑ ❑ USA MJ9264 **TRANSLITE/SM,** 1991 $5-8

COMMENTS: NATIONAL DISTRIBUTION: USA - JULY 10-AUGUST 6, 1992. EACH HM PREMIUM CAME WITH A MINI ACTIVITY BOOKLET WITH MICHAEL JORDAN'S PHOTO.

HALLOWEEN '92 HAPPY MEAL, 1992

- ❑ ❑ USA HA9201 **GHOST,** 1986, 3P WHT W COOKIE CUTTER LID/ BLK HANDLE $1-1.25
- ❑ ❑ USA HA9202 **PUMPKIN,** 1986, 3P ORG COOKIE CUTTER LID/ BLK HANDLE $1-1.25
- ❑ ❑ USA HA9203 **WITCH,** 1986, 3P GRN COOKIE CUTTER INSERT W BLK HANDLE $1-1.25

USA MJ9201 USA MJ9202 USA MJ9203 USA MJ9204

USA MJ9205 USA MJ9206 USA MJ9207 USA MJ9208

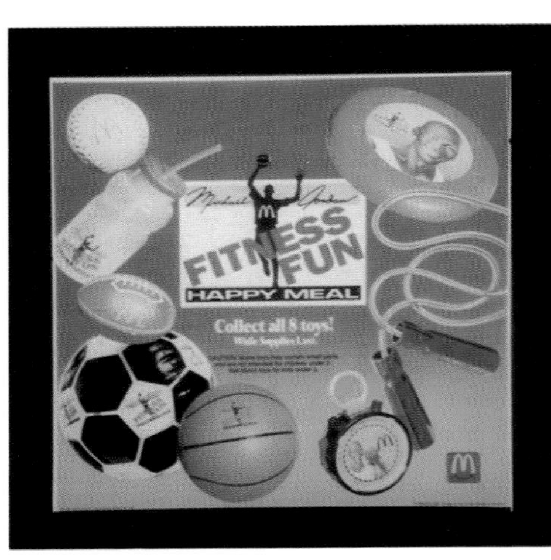

USA MJ9264

USA MJ9226

USA HA9201 USA HA9202 USA HA9203

❑ ❑ USA HA9226 **DISPLAY/PAPER/PURPLE BOX,** 1992 $2-3
❑ ❑ USA HA9264 **TRANSLITE/SM,** 1992 $4-7

COMMENTS: NATIONAL DISTRIBUTION: USA - OCTOBER 9-29, 1992.

USA HA9226

USA HA9264

MYSTERY OF THE LOST ARCHES HAPPY MEAL, 1992

❑ ❑ USA MY9230 **HM BAG,** 1991, **RONALD/PYRAMIDS** $1-1.25
❑ ❑ USA MY9205 **U-3 MAGIC LENS CAMERA,** 1991, 1P W WHT "SEARCH TEAM" DECAL $3-4
❑ ❑ USA MY9201 **MAGIC LENS CAMERA,** 1991, 1P W SILVER "SEARCH TEAM" DECAL $1-1.25
❑ ❑ USA MY9202 **MICRO-CASSETTE/MAGNIFIER,** 1991, 1P GRN W SLIDE OUT MAGNIFIER $1-1.25
❑ ❑ USA MY9203 **PHONE/PERISCOPE,** 1991, 1P ORG PHONE $1-1.25
❑ ❑ USA MY9204 **FLASHLIGHT/TELESCOPE,** 1991, 1P **RED/BLUE** $1-1.25
❑ ❑ USA MY9206 **FLASHLIGHT/TELESCOPE,** 1991, 1P **RED/YELLOW** $1-1.25
❑ ❑ USA MY9255 **TRAYLINER,** 1991 $1-1.25
❑ ❑ USA MY9264 **TRANSLITE/SM,** 1991 $6-8
❑ ❑ USA MY9265 **TRANSLITE/LG,** 1991 $8-12

COMMENTS: NATIONAL DISTRIBUTION: USA - JANUARY 3-FEBRUARY 2, 1992. THE U-3 AND MAGIC LENS CAMERA WERE RECALLED DURING THE NATIONAL PROMOTION DUE TO FINGER ENTRAPMENT. MAJORITY OF PREMIUMS WERE GIVEN OUT PRIOR TO RECALL.

USA MY9201 USA MY9205

USA MY9203 USA MY9202 USA MY9206 USA MY9204

NATURE'S WATCH HAPPY MEAL, 1992

❑ ❑ USA NA9230 **HM BAG,** 1991, **BARK LIKE A TREE!/RON IS ON A NATURE HUNT** $1-1.25
❑ ❑ USA NA9205 **U-3 DOUBLE SHOVEL-RAKE,** 1991, 2P RED SHOVEL/PURP RAKE $1-1.50
❑ ❑ USA NA9201 **BIRD FEEDER,** 1991, 3P ORG LID/CLEAR CONT/YEL BOT $1-1.25
❑ ❑ USA NA9202 **DOUBLE SHOVEL-RAKE,** 1991, 2P RED SHOVEL/PURP RAKE $1-1.25
❑ ❑ USA NA9203 **GREENHOUSE,** 1991, 2P CLEAR DOME TOP/GRN BOT W PKG MARIGOLD SEEDS $1-1.25
❑ ❑ USA NA9204 **SPRINKLER,** 1991, GRN SPRINKLER CAN W YEL NOZZLE $1-1.25
❑ ❑ USA NA9295 **PIN,** 1992, RECTANGLE/TURQ MCDONALD'S NATURE'S WATCH $3-4

USA MY9230

USA MY9265

USA NA9201 USA NA9202 USA NA9203 USA NA9204

USA NA9230

- ❏ ❏ USA NA9226 **DISPLAY/PREMIUMS,** 1992 $15-25
- ❏ ❏ USA NA9264 **TRANSLITE/SM,** 1991 $4-7

COMMENTS: NATIONAL DISTRIBUTION: MAY 8-JUNE 4, 1992. HM BAG CAME WITH ATTACHED "TOYS R US" COUPONS. BIRD FEEDERS USA NA9203 CAME PACKAGED WITH AND WITHOUT 2 CURAD HAPPY STRIP BANDADES. USA NA9202 = USA NA9205, LOOSE OUT OF PACKAGE.

POTATO HEAD KIDS II HAPPY MEAL, 1992

- ❏ ❏ USA PO9230 **HM BAG,** 1991, **EIGHT POTATO HEAD KIDS** $1-1.50
- ❏ ❏ USA PO9201 **DIMPLES,** 1986, 3P PH WITH BLU/YEL HAT W PURP SHOES $2.50-3.50
- ❏ ❏ USA PO9202 **SPIKE,** 1986, 3P SLINGSHOT PH WITH GRN HAT W YEL SHOES $2.50-3.50
- ❏ ❏ USA PO9203 **POTATO DUMPLING,** 1986, 3P PH WITH BLU HAT W PNK SHOES $2.50-3.50
- ❏ ❏ USA PO9204 **SLUGGER,** 1986, 3P BASEBALL GLOVE PH W PH SKINS BLU HAT W YEL SHOES $2.50-3.50
- ❏ ❏ USA PO9205 **SLICK,** 1986, 3P HOLDING UMBRELLA PH W PINKISH DERBY HAT W WHT SHOES $2.50-3.50
- ❏ ❏ USA PO9206 **TULIP,** 1986, 3P PH W PNK HAT W BLU SHOES $2.50-3.50
- ❏ ❏ USA PO9207 **POTATO PUFF,** 1986, 3P PH WITH PNK HAT W PURP SHOES $2.50-3.50
- ❏ ❏ USA PO9208 **SPUD,** 1986, 3P LRG YEL EYEBROW PH W WHT COWBOY HAT W RED COWBOY SHOES $2.50-3.50
- ❏ ❏ USA PO9245 **REGISTER TOPPER/HOLDS 2 PH/EACH,** 1992 $12-15
- ❏ ❏ USA PO9264 **TRANSLITE/SM,** 1992 $8-12
- ❏ ❏ USA PO9265 **TRANSLITE/LG,** 1992 $12-15

COMMENTS: REGIONAL DISTRIBUTION: USA - JANUARY 31-MARCH 5, 1992 IN OKLAHOMA, TEXAS, NORTHERN FLORIDA, DELAWARE/NJ/CT.

USA NA9226

USA NA9264

USA PO9230

USA PO9201 USA PO9202 USA PO9203 USA PO9204

USA PO9205 USA PO9206 USA PO9207 USA PO9208

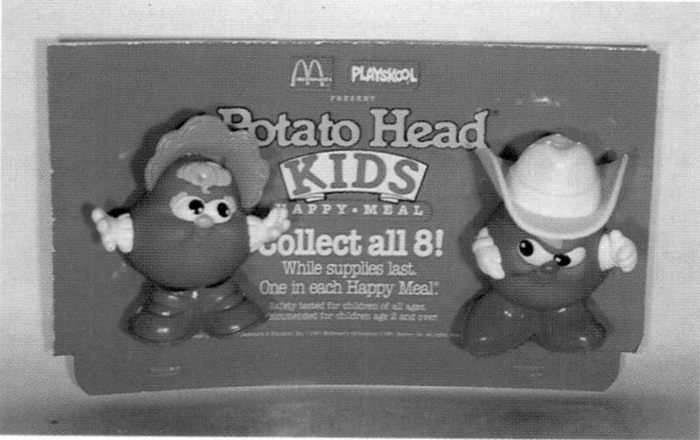

USA PO9265

USA PO9245

USA RE9230

REAL GHOSTBUSTERS II HAPPY MEAL, 1992

- ❑ ❑ USA RE9230 **HM BAG,** 1991, **REAL GB HM/BE AN AMAZING GB TOO** $1-1.25
- ❑ ❑ USA RE9258 **U-3 SQUIRTING SLIMER SQUEEZER,** 1984, 1P GRN HEAD SLIMER $3-4
- ❑ ❑ USA RE9250 **ECTO SIREN,** 1984, 1P BIKE SIREN/WHT ECTO CAR W ECTO-1 STICK SHEET $3-4
- ❑ ❑ USA RE9253 **EGON SPINNER,** 1984, 3P GRN BIKE ATTACHMENT/BLUE SPINNER/YEL MAN $3-4
- ❑ ❑ USA RE9254 **WATER BOTTLE (P.K.E.),** 1984, 2P YEL BOTTLE/BLU W GB STICKER SHEET $10-12
- ❑ ❑ USA RE9257 **SLIMER HORN,** 1984, 1P GRN SLIMER ATTACHED TO BLUE HORN ON BIKE $3-4
- ❑ ❑ USA RE9264 **TRANSLITE/SM,** 1992 $8-12
- ❑ ❑ USA RE9265 **TRANSLITE/LG,** 1992 $12-20

COMMENTS: REGIONAL DISTRIBUTION: USA - JANUARY 31-MARCH 5, 1992 IN KANSAS CITY, KANSAS. THE WATER BOTTLE WAS RECALLED PRIOR TO DISTRIBUTION DUE TO QUALITY CONTROL.

USA RE9258 USA RE9250 USA RE9253 USA RE9254 USA RE9257

TINY TOON ADVENTURES II HAPPY MEAL, 1992

- ❑ ❑ USA TI9210 **HM BOX,** 1992, **ARCTIC** $1-1.25
- ❑ ❑ USA TI9211 **HM BOX,** 1992, **CAFE/WACKYLAND** $1-1.25
- ❑ ❑ USA TI9212 **HM BOX,** 1992, **FOREST/REDWOOD** $1-1.25
- ❑ ❑ USA TI9213 **HM BOX,** 1992, **JUNGLE** $1-1.25
- ❑ ❑ USA TI9209 **U-3 SWEETIE,** 1992, 1P PINK BUNNY ON PAVEMENT ROLLER $2-2.50
- ❑ ❑ USA TI9201 **BABS BUNNY,** 1992, 1P PINK BUNNY W TINY TOONS RECORD PLAYER IN BUBBLE $1.50-2.50
- ❑ ❑ USA TI9202 **BUSTER BUNNY,** 1992, 1P BLU BUNNY IN RED BUMPER CAR/BASKETBALL BUBBLE $1.50-2.50
- ❑ ❑ USA TI9203 **DIZZY DEVIL,** 1992, 1P PUR DIZZY DEVIL IN ORG BUBBLE CAR $1.50-2.50
- ❑ ❑ USA TI9204 **ELMYRA,** 1992, 1P GIRL W YEL HAT IN GRN CAR W BUNNY IN BUBBLE $1.50-2.50
- ❑ ❑ USA TI9205 **GOGO DODO,** 1992, 1P GRN GOGO DODO ON YEL 3 WHEEL ROLLER $1.50-2.50
- ❑ ❑ USA TI9206 **MONTANA MAX,** 1992, 1P MAX IN GRN CASH REGISTER CAR $1.50-2.50
- ❑ ❑ USA TI9207 **PLUCKY DUCK,** 1992, 1P PLUCKY IN BLU STEAM ROLLER CAR $1.50-2.50
- ❑ ❑ USA TI9208 **SWEETIE,** 1992, 1P PINK BUNNY ON PAVEMENT ROLLER $1.50-2.50
- ❑ ❑ USA TI9226 **DISPLAY/PREMIUMS,** 1992 $40-65
- ❑ ❑ USA TI9264 **TRANSLITE/SM,** 1992 $5-8

USA TI9210 USA TI9213

USA TI9212 USA TI9211

USA TI9202 USA TI9204 USA TI9207

USA TI9201 USA TI9203 USA TI9205 USA TI9206 USA TI9208

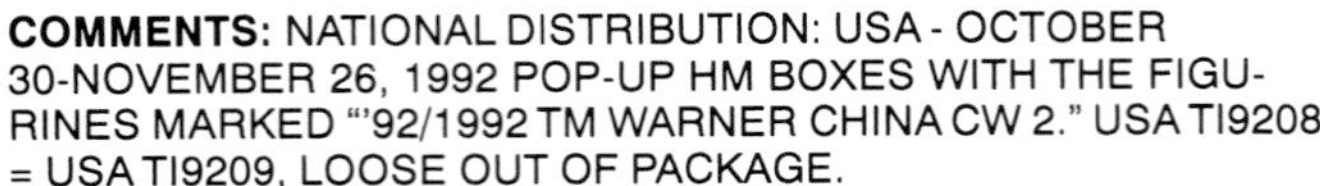

COMMENTS: NATIONAL DISTRIBUTION: USA - OCTOBER 30-NOVEMBER 26, 1992 POP-UP HM BOXES WITH THE FIGURINES MARKED "'92/1992 TM WARNER CHINA CW 2." USA TI9208 = USA TI9209, LOOSE OUT OF PACKAGE.

WATER GAMES HAPPY MEAL, 1992

- ❑ ❑ USA WA9230 **HM BAG,** 1991, **RONALD/DOT-TO-DOT/HOW CAN RON FIND ALL HIS FRIENDS** $1-1.50
- ❑ ❑ USA WA9205 **U-3 GRIMACE/SQUIRTING CAMERA,** 1991, 1P RUBBER PURP/YEL GRI $10-15
- ❑ ❑ USA WA9201 **RONALD CATCHING FRENCH FRIES,** 1991, 1P YELLOW RECTANGLE $3-4
- ❑ ❑ USA WA9202 **GRIMACE JUGGLINE SHAKES,** 1991, 1P GRN RECTANGLE $3-4
- ❑ ❑ USA WA9203 **HAMBURGLAR STACKING BURGERS,** 1991, 1P ORANGE RECTANGLE $3-4
- ❑ ❑ USA WA9204 **BIRDIE SORTING EGGS,** 1991, 1P PINK RECTANGLE 2" X 3 1/2" $3-4
- ❑ ❑ USA WA9206 **DISCLAIMER CARD,** 1991 $1-1.25
- ❑ ❑ USA WA9264 **TRANSLITE/SM,** 1991 $12-20
- ❑ ❑ USA WA9265 **TRANSLITE/LG,** 1991 $15-25

COMMENTS: REGIONAL DISTRIBUTION: USA - JANUARY 31-MARCH 5, 1992 IN MARYLAND, HAWAII, ILLINOIS AND WASHINGTON STATE. THE U-3 GRIMACE WITH SQUIRTING CAMERA WAS RECALLED PRIOR TO FULL DISTRIBUTION DUE TO QUALITY CONTROL PROBLEMS. THE MCDONALDLAND WATER GAMES CAME WITH A YELLOW "PARENTS! PLEASE READ FIRST!" CARD NOTING "AFTER FILL-UP, AND WITH NORMAL PLAY, SOME WATER EXPOSURE IS EXPECTED."

USA TI9226

USA TI9264

USA WA9230

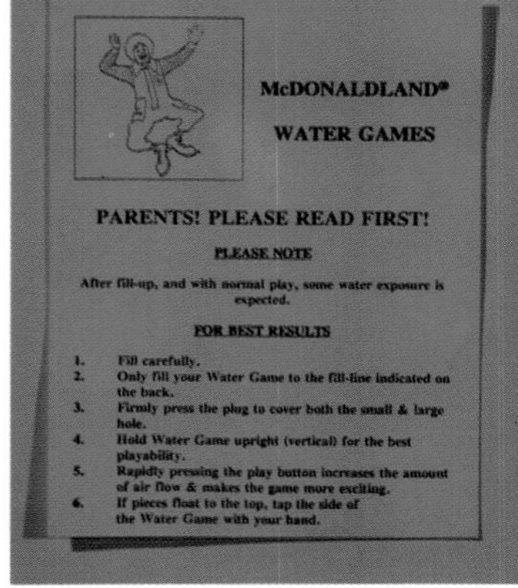

McDONALDLAND®

WATER GAMES

PARENTS! PLEASE READ FIRST!

PLEASE NOTE

After fill-up, and with normal play, some water exposure is expected.

FOR BEST RESULTS

1. Fill carefully.
2. Only fill your Water Game to the fill-line indicated on the back.
3. Firmly press the plug to cover both the small & large hole.
4. Hold Water Game upright (vertical) for the best playability.
5. Rapidly pressing the play button increases the amount of air flow & makes the game more exciting.
6. If pieces float to the top, tap the side of the Water Game with your hand.

USA WA9206

USA WA9205 USA WA9201 USA WA9202 USA WA9203 USA WA9204

USA WA9265

WILD FRIENDS HAPPY MEAL, 1992

❑ ❑ USA WI9230 **HM BAG,** 1991, **4 WILD FRIENDS/GORILLA/ ELEPHANT/CROCK/PANDA** $1-1.50
❑ ❑ USA WI9205 **U-3 GIANT PANDA,** ND, 1P BLK/WHT SOFT RUBBER PANDA W GRN BAMBO $4-5
❑ ❑ USA WI9201 **ELEPHANT,** 1992, GRN BOOK/MOVING GREY ELEPH $3-4
❑ ❑ USA WI9202 **CROCODILE,** 1992, PNK BOOK/W GRN CROC $3-4
❑ ❑ USA WI9203 **GORILLA,** 1992, YEL BOOK/W MOVING GREY GORILLA $3-4
❑ ❑ USA WI9204 **GIANT PANDA,** 1992, BLU BOOK/W BLK/WHT PANDA $3-4
❑ ❑ USA WI9241 **DANGLER/DISPLAY,** 1992 $15-20
❑ ❑ USA WI9264 **TRANSLITE/SM,** 1992 $12-20
❑ ❑ USA WI9265 **TRANSLITE/LG,** 1992 $15-25

COMMENTS: REGIONAL DISTRIBUTION: USA - JANUARY 31-MARCH 5, 1992 IN SOUTHERN CALIFORNIA AND INDIANA. THE ATTACHED MINI BOOKS ARE MARKED WITH MCDONALD'S LOGO.

YO, YOGI! HAPPY MEAL, 1992

❑ ❑ USA YO9230 **HM BAG,** 1991, **YOGI/JELLYSTONE PARK** $1-1.50
❑ ❑ USA YO9201 **YO, YOGI,** 1991, **LAF 1** ORG SQUAD WAVE JUMPER $3-4
❑ ❑ USA YO9202 **CINDY BEAR,** 1991, **LAF 2** GRN SQUAD SCOOTER $3-4
❑ ❑ USA YO9203 **HUCKLEBERRY HOUND,** 1991, **LAF 3** YEL RACE CAR $3-4
❑ ❑ USA YO9204 **BOO BOO BEAR,** 1991, **LAF 4** SQUAD SKATE BOARD $3-4
❑ ❑ USA YO9264 **TRANSLITE/SM,** 1992 $12-20
❑ ❑ USA YO9265 **TRANSLITE/LG,** 1992 $15-25

COMMENTS: REGIONAL DISTRIBUTION: USA - JANUARY 31-MARCH 5, 1992 IN CALIFORNIA, NORTHERN FLORIDA, NORTHERN GEORGIA AND PARTS OF ALABAMA.

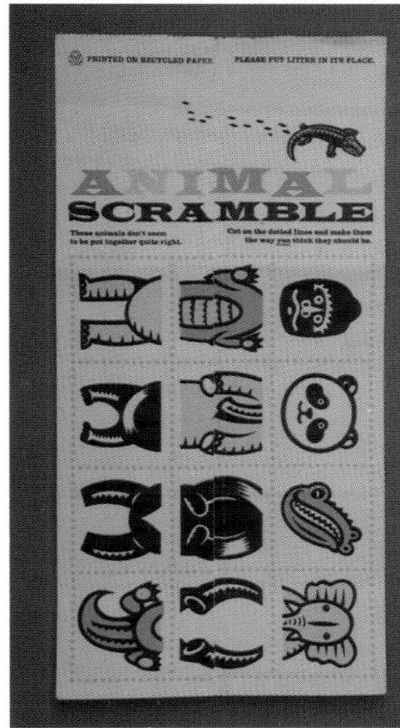

USA WI9230

USA WI9265

USA WI9205 USA WI9201 USA WI9202 USA WI9203 USA WI9204

USA WI9241

USA YO9230

USA YO9265

USA YO9201 USA YO9203 USA YO9202 USA YO9204

USA AS9230

USA AS9205

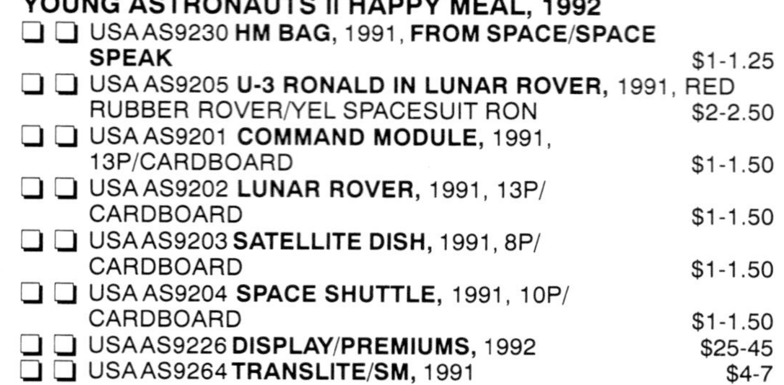

YOUNG ASTRONAUTS II HAPPY MEAL, 1992

- ❑ ❑ USA AS9230 **HM BAG,** 1991, **FROM SPACE/SPACE SPEAK** $1-1.25
- ❑ ❑ USA AS9205 **U-3 RONALD IN LUNAR ROVER,** 1991, RED RUBBER ROVER/YEL SPACESUIT RON $2-2.50
- ❑ ❑ USA AS9201 **COMMAND MODULE,** 1991, 13P/CARDBOARD $1-1.50
- ❑ ❑ USA AS9202 **LUNAR ROVER,** 1991, 13P/ CARDBOARD $1-1.50
- ❑ ❑ USA AS9203 **SATELLITE DISH,** 1991, 8P/ CARDBOARD $1-1.50
- ❑ ❑ USA AS9204 **SPACE SHUTTLE,** 1991, 10P/ CARDBOARD $1-1.50
- ❑ ❑ USA AS9226 **DISPLAY/PREMIUMS,** 1992 $25-45
- ❑ ❑ USA AS9264 **TRANSLITE/SM,** 1991 $4-7

COMMENTS: NATIONAL DISTRIBUTION: USA - MARCH 6-APRIL 2, 1992. SETS CONSIST OF HEAVY PRINTED CARDBOARD PIECES WITH A BLACK RUBBER CONNECTOR.

USA AS9201

USA AS9202

USA AS9226

USA AS9203

USA AS9204

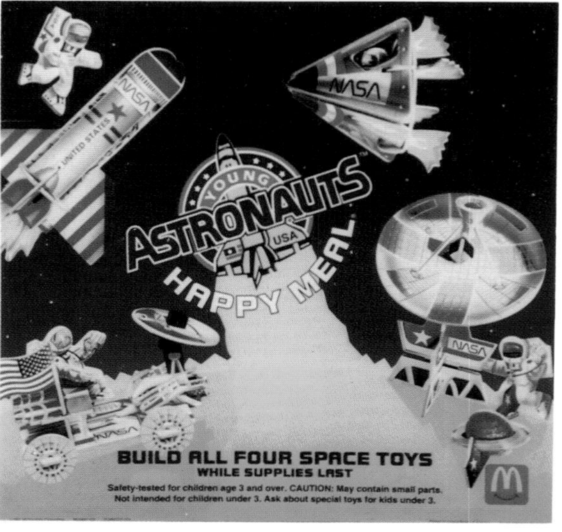

USA AS9264

1993

BARBIE / HOT WHEELS IV HAPPY MEAL, 1993
BATMAN, THE ANIMATED SERIES HAPPY MEAL, 1993
DINO-MOTION DINOSAURS HAPPY MEAL, 1993
FIELD TRIP HAPPY MEAL, 1993
FOOD FUNDAMENTALS HAPPY MEAL, 1993
HALLOWEEN '93 MCNUGGET BUDDIES HAPPY MEAL, 1993
LINKABLES HAPPY MEAL, 1993
LOONEY TUNES QUACK UP CAR CHASE HAPPY MEAL, 1993
M SQUAD HAPPY MEAL, 1993
NICKELODEON GAME GADGETS HAPPY MEAL, 1993
OUT FOR FUN HAPPY MEAL, 1993
SNOW WHITE AND THE SEVEN DWARFS HAPPY MEAL, 1993
TOTALLY TOY HOLIDAY HAPPY MEAL, 1993

BARBIE / HOT WHEELS IV HAPPY MEAL, 1993

- ❑ ❑ USA BA9330 **HM BAG,** 1993, **BARBIE/HOT WHEELS** $1-1.25
- ❑ ❑ USA BA9317 **U-3 TOOL SET,** 1991, 2P/PLASTIC/BLU WRENCH/YEL HAMMER $1.50-2
- ❑ ❑ USA BA9301 **BIRTHDAY PARTY,** 1993, BLK BARBIE/BIRTHDAY CAKE $1.50-2.50
- ❑ ❑ USA BA9302 **HOLLYWOOD HAIR,** 1993, GOLD SHORT DRESS/BLU STAR BASE $1.50-2.50
- ❑ ❑ USA BA9303 **MY FIRST BALLERINA,** 1993, PURP BALLERINA DRESS/BRN LONG SYN HAIR $1.50-2.50
- ❑ ❑ USA BA9304 **PAINT 'N DAZZLE,** 1993, PNK SHORT SKIRT/"B" STAGE/LONG BLONDE SYN HAIR $1.50-2.50
- ❑ ❑ USA BA9305 **ROMANTIC BRIDE,** 1993, WHT LONG GOWN W PEACH BOUQUET/LONG BLOND HAIR $1.50-2.50
- ❑ ❑ USA BA9306 **SECRET HEART,** 1993, WHT/ROSE LONG GOWN/HOLDING RED HEART/LONG BLOND HAIR $1.50-2.50
- ❑ ❑ USA BA9307 **TWINKLE LIGHTS,** 1993, PINK/WHT GOWN/ WHT PURSE/LONG BLONDE SYN HAIR $1.50-2.50
- ❑ ❑ USA BA9308 **WESTERN STAMPIN',** 1993, BLU/SILVER OUTFIT/COW GIRL HAT $1.50-2.50
- ❑ ❑ USA HW9309 **MCD FUNNY CAR,** 1993, RED/WHT/ "MCDONALD'S" ON SIDE $1-1.50
- ❑ ❑ USA HW9310 **QUAKER STATE RACER #62,** 1993, GRN QUAKER STATE #62 $1-1.50
- ❑ ❑ USA HW9311 **MCD THUNDERBIRD #27,** 1993, RED THUNDERBIRD #27 W "M" LOGO ON HOOD $1-1.50
- ❑ ❑ USA HW9312 **HOT WHEELS FUNNY CAR,** 1993, WHT/RED/ YEL "HOT WHEELS" ON SIDE FUNNY CAR $1-1.50
- ❑ ❑ USA HW9313 **MCD DRAGSTER,** 1993, RED DRAGSTER W "MCD" LOGO ON SIDE/HOOD $1-1.50
- ❑ ❑ USA HW9314 **HOT WHEELS CAMARO #1,** 1993, BLU CAMARO W "HOT WHEELS 1" ON SIDE $1-1.50
- ❑ ❑ USA HW9315 **DURACELL RACER #88,** 1993, YEL W "DURACELL" ON SIDE AND HOOD $1-1.50
- ❑ ❑ USA HW9316 **HOT WHEELS DRAGSTER,** 1993, BLK/YEL DRAGSTER W "HOT WHEELS" ON SIDE $1-1.50
- ❑ ❑ USA BA9326 **DISPLAY W PREMIUMS,** 1993 $50-75
- ❑ ❑ USA BA9364 **TRANSLITE/SM,** 1993 $4-7

COMMENTS: NATIONAL DISTRIBUTION: USA - AUGUST 6-SEPTEMBER 2, 1993. USA BA9205 "ROSE BRIDE BARBIE" FROM 1992 PROMOTION (NO U-3 MARKINGS ON THE MIP PACKAGE) WAS SUBSTITUTED FOR THE U-3 GIRL PREMIUM. THE U-3 BOY PREMIUM WAS THE HOT WHEELS WRENCH AND HAMMER SET (U-3 ZEBRA-STRIPED BAG).

USA BA9330

USA BA9326

USA BA9301 USA BA9302 USA BA9303 USA BA9304

USA BA9305 USA BA9306 USA BA9307 USA BA9308

USA BA9317

USA HW9311 USA HW9314
USA HW9310 USA HW9313 USA HW9315
USA HW9309 USA HW9312 USA HW9316

USA BA9364

USA BT9310 USA BT9311

USA BT9302 USA BT9304

USA BT9309 USA BT9301 USA BT9303 USA BT9307 USA BT9308 USA BT9306 USA BT9305

USA BT9326

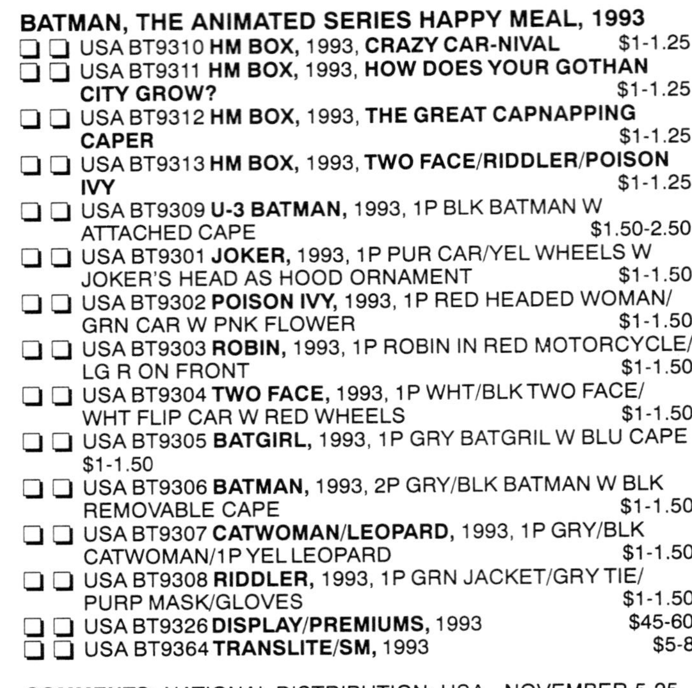

BATMAN, THE ANIMATED SERIES HAPPY MEAL, 1993

- ❑ ❑ USA BT9310 **HM BOX,** 1993, **CRAZY CAR-NIVAL** $1-1.25
- ❑ ❑ USA BT9311 **HM BOX,** 1993, **HOW DOES YOUR GOTHAN CITY GROW?** $1-1.25
- ❑ ❑ USA BT9312 **HM BOX,** 1993, **THE GREAT CAPNAPPING CAPER** $1-1.25
- ❑ ❑ USA BT9313 **HM BOX,** 1993, **TWO FACE/RIDDLER/POISON IVY** $1-1.25
- ❑ ❑ USA BT9309 **U-3 BATMAN,** 1993, 1P BLK BATMAN W ATTACHED CAPE $1.50-2.50
- ❑ ❑ USA BT9301 **JOKER,** 1993, 1P PUR CAR/YEL WHEELS W JOKER'S HEAD AS HOOD ORNAMENT $1-1.50
- ❑ ❑ USA BT9302 **POISON IVY,** 1993, 1P RED HEADED WOMAN/ GRN CAR W PNK FLOWER $1-1.50
- ❑ ❑ USA BT9303 **ROBIN,** 1993, 1P ROBIN IN RED MOTORCYCLE/ LG R ON FRONT $1-1.50
- ❑ ❑ USA BT9304 **TWO FACE,** 1993, 1P WHT/BLK TWO FACE/ WHT FLIP CAR W RED WHEELS $1-1.50
- ❑ ❑ USA BT9305 **BATGIRL,** 1993, 1P GRY BATGRIL W BLU CAPE $1-1.50
- ❑ ❑ USA BT9306 **BATMAN,** 1993, 2P GRY/BLK BATMAN W BLK REMOVABLE CAPE $1-1.50
- ❑ ❑ USA BT9307 **CATWOMAN/LEOPARD,** 1993, 1P GRY/BLK CATWOMAN/1P YEL LEOPARD $1-1.50
- ❑ ❑ USA BT9308 **RIDDLER,** 1993, 1P GRN JACKET/GRY TIE/ PURP MASK/GLOVES $1-1.50
- ❑ ❑ USA BT9326 **DISPLAY/PREMIUMS,** 1993 $45-60
- ❑ ❑ USA BT9364 **TRANSLITE/SM,** 1993 $5-8

COMMENTS: NATIONAL DISTRIBUTION: USA - NOVEMBER 5-25, 1993. THE CARS ARE MARKED "1993 DC CHINA." NOTE: NO MCDONALD'S MARKINGS.

DINO-MOTION DINOSAURS HAPPY MEAL, 1993

- ❑ ❑ USA DI9310 **HM BOX,** 1992, **A TREE-MENDOUS LUNCH** $1-1.25

USA BT9364

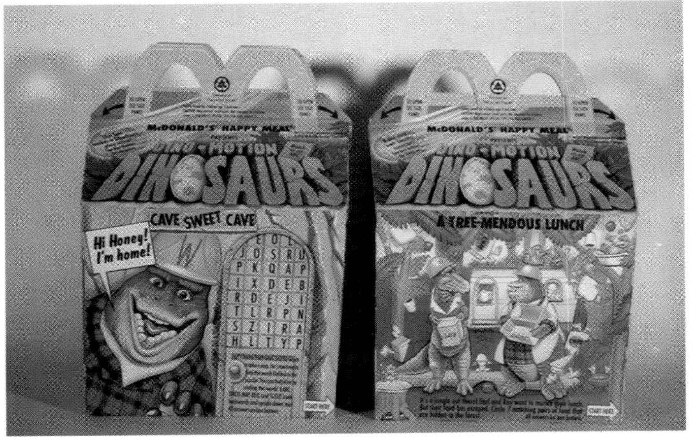

USA DI9310

❑ ❑ USA DI9311 **HM BOX,** 1992, **BABY FOOD** $1-1.25
❑ ❑ USA DI9312 **HM BOX,** 1992, **BOB-LABREA HIGH SCHOOL** $1-1.25
❑ ❑ USA DI9313 **HM BOX,** 1992, **CAVE SWEET CAVE** $1-1.25
❑ ❑ USA DI9307 **U-3 BABY SINCLAIR,** 1992, 1P RUBBER YEL BABY IN EGGSHELL $1.50-2
❑ ❑ USA DI9301 **BABY SINCLAIR,** 1992, 1P YEL BABY DINO HOLDING POT $1-1.50
❑ ❑ USA DI9302 **CHARLENE SINCLAIR,** 1992, 1P GRN MOTHER W PHONE $1-1.50
❑ ❑ USA DI9303 **EARL SINCLAIR,** 1992, 1P BLU/GRN POP W LUNCH BOX $1-1.50
❑ ❑ USA DI9304 **FRAN SINCLAIR,** 1992, 2P PNK/GRN HOLDING SPOON $1-1.50
❑ ❑ USA DI9305 **GRANDMA ETHYL,** 1992, 1P PNK/PUR IN CHAIR $1-1.50
❑ ❑ USA DI9306 **ROBBIE SINCLAIR,** 1992, 1P RED/GRN W GUITAR $1-1.50
❑ ❑ USA DI9326 **DISPLAY/PREMIUMS,** 1992 $45-60
❑ ❑ USA DI9364 **TRANSLITE/SM,** 1992 $4-7

COMMENTS: NATIONAL DISTRIBUTION: USA - FEBRUARY 5-MARCH 4, 1993.

FIELD TRIP HAPPY MEAL, 1993

❑ ❑ USA FI9330 **HM BAG,** 1993, **WHAT DO LEAVES SAY...** $1-1.25
❑ ❑ USA FI9301 **NATURE VIEWER,** 1993, 2P MAGNIFIER BOTTLE $1-1.25
❑ ❑ USA FI9302 **LEAF PRINTER,** 1993, 2P RED CRAYON W YEL LEAF HOLDER $1-1.25
❑ ❑ USA FI9303 **KALEIDOSCOPE,** 1993, 2P $1-1.25
❑ ❑ USA FI9304 **VINYL BAG,** 1993, EXPLORER BAG WHT/GRN PLASTIC $1-1.25
❑ ❑ USA FI9326 **DISPLAY/PREMIUMS,** 1993 $15-25
❑ ❑ USA FI9364 **TRANSLITE/SM,** 1993 $3-5

USA DI9311

USA DI9312

USA DI9307

USA DI9364

USA DI9301 USA DI9302 USA DI9303

USA DI9326

USA DI9304 USA DI9305 USA DI9306

USA FI9330

USA FI9326

USA FI9301 USA FI9302 USA FI9303 USA FI9304

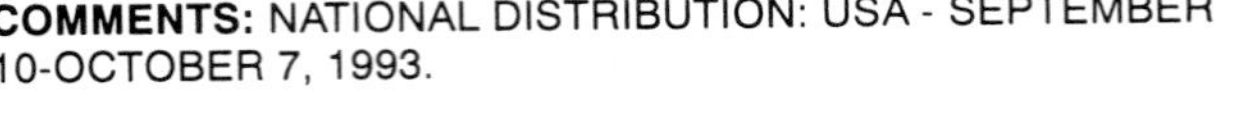

COMMENTS: NATIONAL DISTRIBUTION: USA - SEPTEMBER 10-OCTOBER 7, 1993.

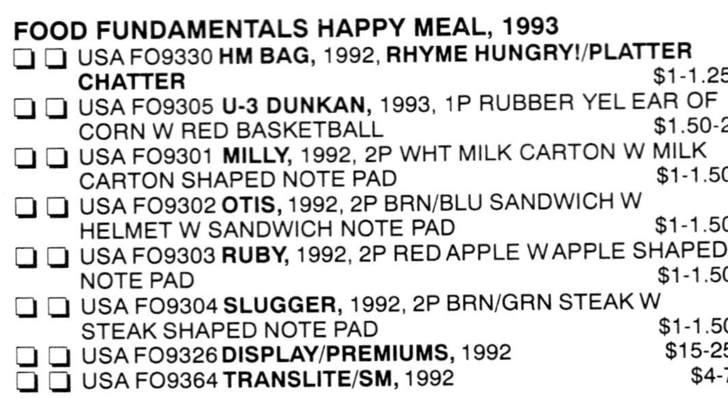

FOOD FUNDAMENTALS HAPPY MEAL, 1993

- ❑ ❑ USA FO9330 **HM BAG,** 1992, **RHYME HUNGRY!/PLATTER CHATTER** $1-1.25
- ❑ ❑ USA FO9305 **U-3 DUNKAN,** 1993, 1P RUBBER YEL EAR OF CORN W RED BASKETBALL $1.50-2
- ❑ ❑ USA FO9301 **MILLY,** 1992, 2P WHT MILK CARTON W MILK CARTON SHAPED NOTE PAD $1-1.50
- ❑ ❑ USA FO9302 **OTIS,** 1992, 2P BRN/BLU SANDWICH W HELMET W SANDWICH NOTE PAD $1-1.50
- ❑ ❑ USA FO9303 **RUBY,** 1992, 2P RED APPLE W APPLE SHAPED NOTE PAD $1-1.50
- ❑ ❑ USA FO9304 **SLUGGER,** 1992, 2P BRN/GRN STEAK W STEAK SHAPED NOTE PAD $1-1.50
- ❑ ❑ USA FO9326 **DISPLAY/PREMIUMS,** 1992 $15-25
- ❑ ❑ USA FO9364 **TRANSLITE/SM,** 1992 $4-7

COMMENTS: NATIONAL DISTRIBUTION: USA - MARCH 5-APRIL 8, 1993.

HALLOWEEN '93 MCNUGGET BUDDIES HAPPY MEAL, 1993

- ❑ ❑ USA HA9310 **HM BOX,** 1993, **BOBBIN FOR ...WHAT?/ PUMPKIN** $1-1.25
- ❑ ❑ USA HA9311 **HM BOX,** 1993, **MUMMIE MCNUGGET/SKELETON** $1-1.25
- ❑ ❑ USA HA9312 **HM BOX,** 1993, **VAMPIRE HOTEL/BAT** $1-1.25
- ❑ ❑ USA HA9307 **U-3 MCBOO MCNUGGET,** 1992, 2P WHT GHOST $2-2.50
- ❑ ❑ USA HA9301 **MCBOO MCNUGGET,** 1992, 2P WHT GHOST $2-2.50
- ❑ ❑ USA HA9302 **MONSTER MCNUGGET,** 1992, 3P GRN HAT/ PUR PANTS/GRN HANDS $2-2.50
- ❑ ❑ USA HA9303 **MUMMY MCNUGGET,** 1992, 3P WHT HAT/ SPIDER/WHT PANTS $2-2.50

USA FI9364

USA FO9330

USA FO9326

USA FO9364

USA HA9307

USA FO9305 USA FO9301 USA FO9302 USA FO9303 USA FO9304

USA HA9310 USA HA9311 USA HA9312

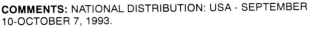

- ❑ ❑ USA HA9304 **MCNUGGLA,** 1992, 3P BLK HAT/BAT/BLK CAPE $2-2.50
- ❑ ❑ USA HA9305 **PUMPKIN MCNUGGET,** 1992, 3P ORG PUMP HAT/PUMP BASE $2-2.50
- ❑ ❑ USA HA9306 **WITCHIE MCNUGGET,** 1992, 3P BLK WITCH HAT/PUR CAPE/BROOM $2-2.50
- ❑ ❑ USA HA9313 **NICKELODEON MAGAZINE,** 1993 $.50-1
- ❑ ❑ USA HA9326 **DISPLAY/PREMIUMS,** 1993 $65-90
- ❑ ❑ USA HA9364 **TRANSLITE/SM,** 1993 $3-5

COMMENTS: NATIONAL DISTRIBUTION: USA - OCTOBER 8-29, 1993. THE NICKELODEON HALLOWEEN MAGAZINE WAS DISTRIBUTED WITH THE HAPPY MEAL. USA HA9301 = HA9307, LOOSE OUT OF PACKAGE.

LINKABLES HAPPY MEAL, 1993

- ❑ ❑ USA LI9301 **BIRDIE,** 1990, ON TRICYCLE/2P BLU/PNK/YEL $3-4
- ❑ ❑ USA LI9302 **GRIMACE,** 1990. IN A WAGON/2P RED WAGON $3-4
- ❑ ❑ USA LI9303 **HAMBURGLAR,** 1990, IN AN AIRPLANE/2P GRN/YEL $3-4
- ❑ ❑ USA LI9304 **RONALD,** 1990, IN A SOAP-BOX RACER/2P YEL/RED $3-4

COMMENTS: LIMITED REGIONAL DISTRITUTION: USA -AUGUST/SEPTEMBER 1993 DURING CLEAN-UP WEEK IN VERMONT AND PARTS OF NEW ENGLAND. RELEASED IN 1993 WITH PACKAGE DATED 1990. NO SPECIFIC HM BOXES WERE GIVEN WITH THESE PREMIUMS.

LOONEY TUNES QUACK UP CAR CHASE HAPPY MEAL, 1993

- ❑ ❑ USA LO9310 **HM BOX,** 1992, **KOOKY COLOR WORLD /PURP** $1-1.25
- ❑ ❑ USA LO9311 **HM BOX,** 1992, **MIXED-UP WORLD/BLU** $1-1.25

USA LI9301 USA LI9302 USA LI9303 USA LI9304

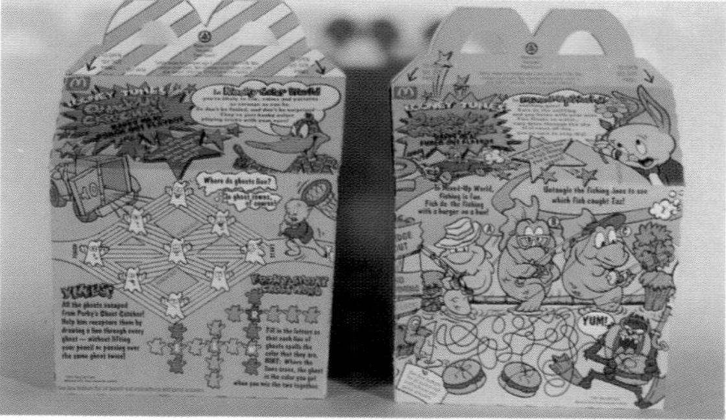

USA LO9310

USA LO9311

USA HA9304 USA HA9306 USA HA9301

USA HA9302 USA HA9305 USA HA9303

USA HA9326

USA HA9364

USA LO9312 USA LO9313

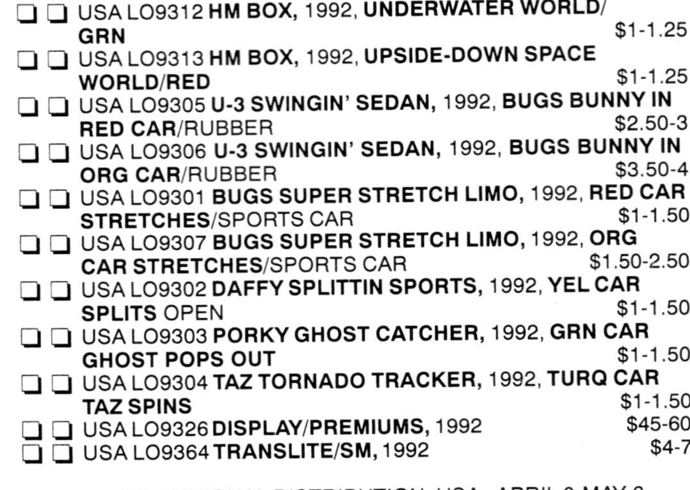

- ❑ ❑ USA LO9312 **HM BOX,** 1992, **UNDERWATER WORLD/ GRN** $1-1.25
- ❑ ❑ USA LO9313 **HM BOX,** 1992, **UPSIDE-DOWN SPACE WORLD/RED** $1-1.25
- ❑ ❑ USA LO9305 **U-3 SWINGIN' SEDAN,** 1992, **BUGS BUNNY IN RED CAR**/RUBBER $2.50-3
- ❑ ❑ USA LO9306 **U-3 SWINGIN' SEDAN,** 1992, **BUGS BUNNY IN ORG CAR**/RUBBER $3.50-4
- ❑ ❑ USA LO9301 **BUGS SUPER STRETCH LIMO,** 1992, **RED CAR STRETCHES**/SPORTS CAR $1-1.50
- ❑ ❑ USA LO9307 **BUGS SUPER STRETCH LIMO,** 1992, **ORG CAR STRETCHES**/SPORTS CAR $1.50-2.50
- ❑ ❑ USA LO9302 **DAFFY SPLITTIN SPORTS,** 1992, **YEL CAR SPLITS** OPEN $1-1.50
- ❑ ❑ USA LO9303 **PORKY GHOST CATCHER,** 1992, **GRN CAR GHOST POPS OUT** $1-1.50
- ❑ ❑ USA LO9304 **TAZ TORNADO TRACKER,** 1992, **TURQ CAR TAZ SPINS** $1-1.50
- ❑ ❑ USA LO9326 **DISPLAY/PREMIUMS,** 1992 $45-60
- ❑ ❑ USA LO9364 **TRANSLITE/SM,** 1992 $4-7

COMMENTS: NATIONAL DISTRIBUTION: USA - APRIL 9-MAY 6, 1993. THE ORANGE U-3 AND ORG STRETCH LIMO WERE DISTRIBUTED IN THE SOUTHEAST.

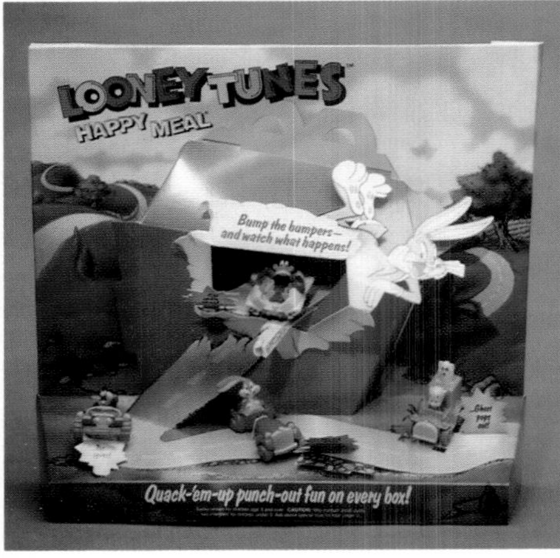

USA LO9326

USA LO9305 USA LO9306 USA LO9301 USA LO9307 USA LO9302 USA LO9303 USA LO9304

M SQUAD HAPPY MEAL, 1993

- ❑ ❑ USA MS9330 **HM BAG,** 1992, **TOP SECRET** $1-1.25
- ❑ ❑ USA MS9305 **U-3 SPY-TRACKER WATCH,** 1992, WATCH BECOMES A COMPASS/1P $1-1.50
- ❑ ❑ USA MS9301 **SPY-CODER,** 1992, WALKIE-TALKIE W BLU/ RED CRAYON W DECODER/3P $1-1.50
- ❑ ❑ USA MS9302 **SPY-NOCULARS,** 1992, RED/BLU VIDEO CAM THAT TURNS INTO BINOCULARS/1P $1-1.50
- ❑ ❑ USA MS9303 **SPY-STAMPER PAD,** 1992, STAMPER W INK PAD TURNS INTO A CALCULATOR/2P $1 -1.50
- ❑ ❑ USA MS9304 **SPY-TRACKER WATCH,** 1992, WATCH BECOMES A COMPASS/OPENS/1P $1-1.50
- ❑ ❑ USA MS9326 **DISPLAY W PREMIUMS,** 1992 $15-25
- ❑ ❑ USA MS9364 **TRANSLITE/SM,** 1992 $4-7

COMMENTS: NATIONAL DISTRIBUTION: USA - JANUARY 8-FEBRUARY 4, 1993.

USA LO9364

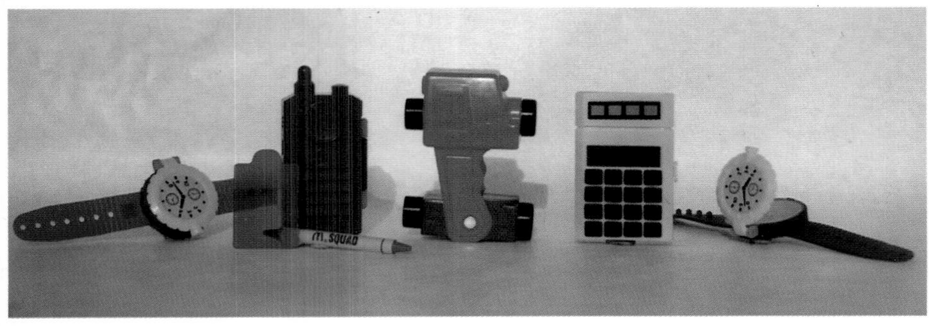

USA MS9305 USA MS9301 USA MS9302 USA MS9303 USA MS9304

USA MS9330

NICKELODEON GAME GADGETS HAPPY MEAL, 1993

- ❑ ❑ USA NI9330 **HM BAG,** 1991, **NICKELODEON GAME GADGETS** $1-1.25
- ❑ ❑ USA NI9305 **U-3 BLIMP,** 1992, 1P RED BLIMP/RUBBER $1.50-2
- ❑ ❑ USA NI9301 **APPLAUSE PAWS,** 1992, 1P YEL CLAPPING HANDS/BLU BASE $1-1.25
- ❑ ❑ USA NI9302 **BLIMP GAME,** 1992, 1P GRN BLIMP W WHISTLES/SPINS $1-1.25
- ❑ ❑ USA NI9303 **GOTCHA GUSHER,** 1992, 1P FLY SPRAY CAN SQUIRTER $1-1.25
- ❑ ❑ USA NI9304 **LOUD-MOUTH MIKE,** 1992, 1P PNK/GRN MICROPHONE $1-1.25
- ❑ ❑ USA NI9326 **DISPLAY/PREMIUMS,** 1992 $30-45
- ❑ ❑ USA NI9364 **TRANSLITE/SM,** 1992 $4-7

COMMENTS: NATIONAL DISTRIBUTION: USA - JUNE 11-JULY 8, 1993.

USA MS9326

USA NI9330

USA NI9305

USA MS9364

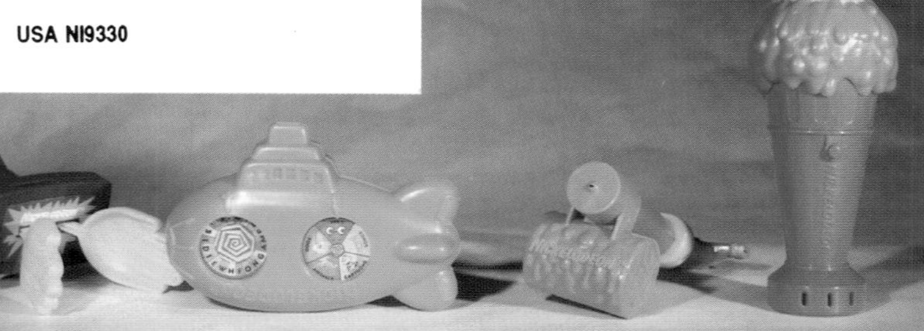
USA NI9301 USA NI9302 USA NI9303 USA NI9304

USA NI9364

USA NI9326

USA OU9330

OUT FOR FUN HAPPY MEAL, 1993

- ❑ ❑ USA OU9330 **HM BAG,** 1992, **OUT FOR FUN** $1-1.25
- ❑ ❑ USA OU9301 **BALLOON BALL,** 1992, RONALD/BLU BEACH BALL/BLOW UP BALL INSIDE $1-1.25
- ❑ ❑ USA OU9302 **BUBBLE SHOE WAND,** 1992 2P RED/YEL $1-1.50
- ❑ ❑ USA OU9303 **SAND PAIL,** 1992, RON/FRIENDS ON BEACH/ YEL HANDLE $1-1.25
- ❑ ❑ USA OU9304 **SUNGLASSES,** 1992, 1P BLU/GRN $1-1.25
- ❑ ❑ USA OU9326 **DISPLAY/PREMIUMS,** 1992 $15-25
- ❑ ❑ USA OU9364 **TRANSLITE/SM,** 1992 $4-7

COMMENTS: NATIONAL DISTRIBUTION: USA - MAY 7-JUNE 10, 1993. SAND PAIL- USA OU9303, WAS ALSO THE U-3 PREMIUM (NO PACKAGING). USA OU9304 WERE WIDELY DISTRIBUTED DURING CLEAN-UP WEEK - 1993.

USA OU9364

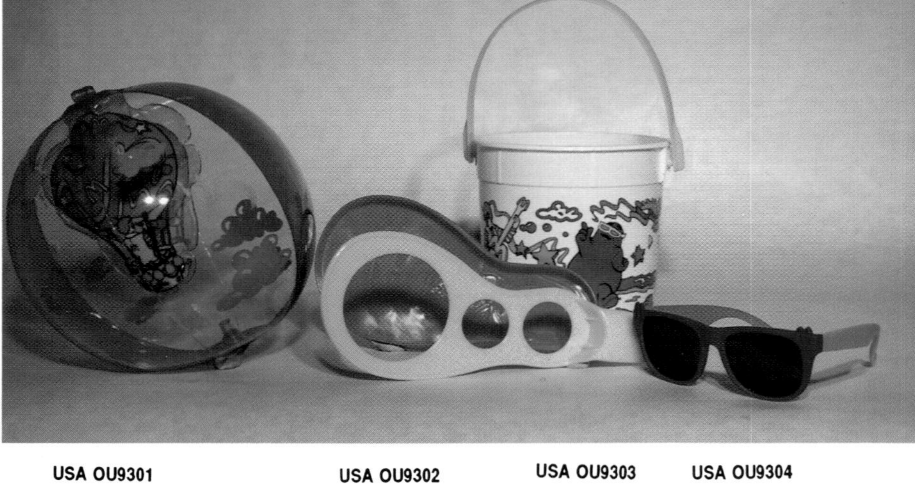

USA OU9301 USA OU9302 USA OU9303 USA OU9304

USA SN9321 USA SN9322

USA SN9323 USA SN9320

SNOW WHITE AND THE SEVEN DWARFS HAPPY MEAL, 1993

- ❑ ❑ USA SN9320 **HM BOX,** 1992, **SEVEN DRAWFS IN THE DIAMOND MINE** $1-1.50
- ❑ ❑ USA SN9321 **HM BOX,** 1992, **SEVEN DRAWFS AT COTTAGE** $1-1.50
- ❑ ❑ USA SN9322 **HM BOX,** 1992, **SNOW WHITE W BASHFUL AT CASTLE** $1-1.50
- ❑ ❑ USA SN9323 **HM BOX,** 1992, **SNOW WHITE W PRINCE W DRAWFS** $1-1.50
- ❑ ❑ USA SN9309 **U-3 DOPEY/SNEEZY SPIN,** 1992, IN BLU COAT ON A PUR RUG $2.50-3.50
- ❑ ❑ USA SN9301 **BASHFUL,** 1992, PEEKS FROM BEHIND HIS DIAMONDS $2.50-3.50
- ❑ ❑ USA SN9302 **DOC,** 1992, W DIAMOND CART. DIAMOND SPINS WHEN CART ROLLS $2.50-3.50
- ❑ ❑ USA SN9303 **DOPEY/SNEEZY SPIN,** 1992, IN BLU COAT ON A PUR RUG $2.50-3.50
- ❑ ❑ USA SN9304 **HAPPY AND GRUMPY,** 1992, ON RAILROAD PUSH CAR $3-5

USA SN9309 USA SN9301 USA SN9302 USA SN9303 USA SN9304

- ❑ ❑ USA SN9305 **PRINCE W HORSE,** 1992, W RED CAPE W WHT HORSE **W/O GRN BASE** $2.50-3.50
- ❑ ❑ USA SN9310 **PRINCE W HORSE,** 1992, W RED CAPE W WHT HORSE **W GRN BASE** $4-6
- ❑ ❑ USA SN9306 **QUEEN-WITCH,** 1992, W 2P BLK DRESS/FLIPS TO FORM WITCH/QUEEN $2.50-3.50
- ❑ ❑ USA SN9307 **SLEEPY,** 1992, 1P, WHT BEARD W PUR SWEATER EYES OPEN AND CLOSE $2.50-3.50
- ❑ ❑ USA SN9308 **SNOW WHITE/WISHING WELL,** 1992, YEL SKIRT W GRN WISHING WELL $2.50-3.50
- ❑ ❑ USA SN9326 **DISPLAY/PREMIUMS,** 1992 $85-115
- ❑ ❑ USA SN9364 **TRANSLITE/SM,** 1992 $15-20

COMMENTS: NATIONAL DISTRIBUTION: USA - JULY 9-AUGUST 5, 1993. THE PRINCE CAME IN TWO VERSIONS - WITH AND WITHOUT THE GREEN BASE MIP. USA SN9303 = USA SN9309, LOOSE OUT OF PACKAGE.

USA SN9326

USA SN9305 USA SN9310 USA SN9306 USA SN9307 USA SN9308

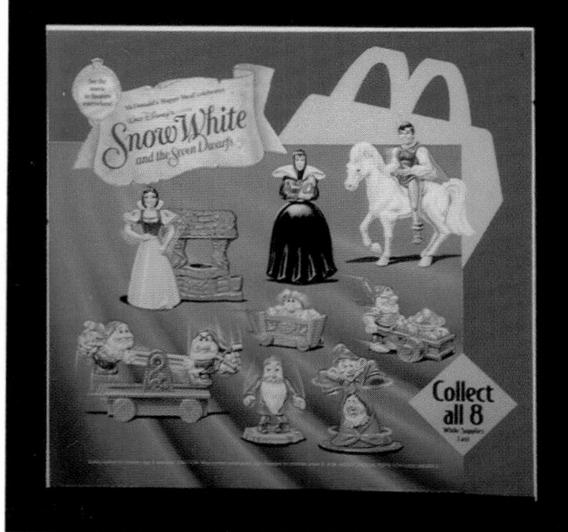

USA SN9364

TOTALLY TOY HOLIDAY HAPPY MEAL, 1993

- ❑ ❑ USA TO9330 **HM BAG,** 1993, **KIDS! LET'S WRAP!** $1-1.25
- ❑ ❑ USA TO9313 **U-3 KEY FORCE CAR,** 1993, 1P RED CAR W GREY KEY ON ROOF $2-2.50
- ❑ ❑ USA TO9314 **U-3 MAGIC NURSERY DOLL/BOY,** 1993, 1P BLU PJS/CANDY CANE CLOTH BODY/PLAST FACE $3.50-5
- ❑ ❑ USA TO9315 **U-3 MAGIC NURSURY DOLL/GIRL,** 1993, 1P PNK PJS/HOLLY CLOTH BODY W HARD PLAST FACE $2.50-3
- ❑ ❑ USA TO9301 **HOLIDAY BARBIE - SNOW DOME,** 1993, GRN DOME/RED RED DRESSED BARBIE/1P/RECALLED $75-100
- ❑ ❑ USA TO9302 **LIL MISS CANDI STRIPES,** 1993, 2P WHT DOLL/GRN TUTU/SNAP ON RED/WHT DRESS $1-1.50
- ❑ ❑ USA TO9303 **MAGIC NURSERY DOLL/BOY,** 1993, 1P BLU PJS/HOLLY CLOTH BODY DOLL/PLASTIC FACE $1-1.50
- ❑ ❑ USA TO9304 **MAGIC NURSERY DOLL/GIRL,** 1993, 1P PNK PJS/CANDY CANE CLOTH BODY/PLAST FACE $1-1.50
- ❑ ❑ USA TO9305 **POLLY POCKET,** 1993, GREEN/RED HINGED CASE W YEL FIG $1-1.50
- ❑ ❑ USA TO9306 **SALLY SECRETS (BLACK),** 1993, 1P BLK DOLL/BRN HAIR/PUNCH OUTS SHAPES/STICKERS $2-2.50
- ❑ ❑ USA TO9307 **SALLY SECRETS (WHITE),** 1993, 1P WHT DOLL/BLD HAIR/PUNCH OUT SHAPES/STICKERS $1-1.50
- ❑ ❑ USA TO9308 **ATTACK PACK VEHICLE,** 1993, HW BLU SHARK/CAR/HOOK TRUCK/LG BLK WHLS $1-1.50
- ❑ ❑ USA TO9309 **KEY FORCE CAR,** 1993, HW RED CAR W GREY KEY ON ROOF $1-1.50

USA TO9301

USA TO9330

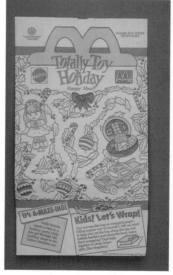

USA TO9301 USA TO9302 USA TO9303 USA TO9304 USA TO9305

USA TO9306 USA TO9307 USA TO9308 USA TO9309

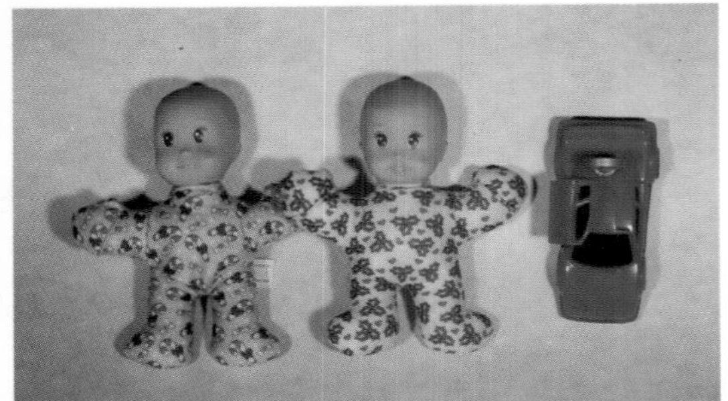

USA TO9314 USA TO9315 USA TO9313

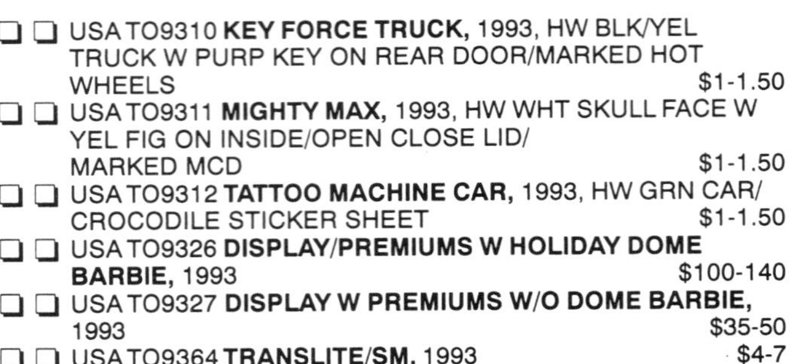

❑ ❑ USA TO9310 **KEY FORCE TRUCK,** 1993, HW BLK/YEL TRUCK W PURP KEY ON REAR DOOR/MARKED HOT WHEELS $1-1.50

❑ ❑ USA TO9311 **MIGHTY MAX,** 1993, HW WHT SKULL FACE W YEL FIG ON INSIDE/OPEN CLOSE LID/ MARKED MCD $1-1.50

❑ ❑ USA TO9312 **TATTOO MACHINE CAR,** 1993, HW GRN CAR/ CROCODILE STICKER SHEET $1-1.50

❑ ❑ USA TO9326 **DISPLAY/PREMIUMS W HOLIDAY DOME BARBIE,** 1993 $100-140

❑ ❑ USA TO9327 **DISPLAY W PREMIUMS W/O DOME BARBIE,** 1993 $35-50

❑ ❑ USA TO9364 **TRANSLITE/SM,** 1993 $4-7

COMMENTS: NATIONAL DISTRIBUTION: USA - DECEMBER 10, 1993-JANUARY 6, 1994. HOLIDAY BARBIE DOME WAS RECALLED DUE TO LEAKAGE. HOLIDAY BARBIE GREEN DOME WAS PRESENT ON THE DISPLAYS IN THE STORES, PRIOR TO RECALL. USA TO9312-16 ARE HOT WHEELS (HW) CARS.

USA TO9310 USA TO9311 USA TO9312

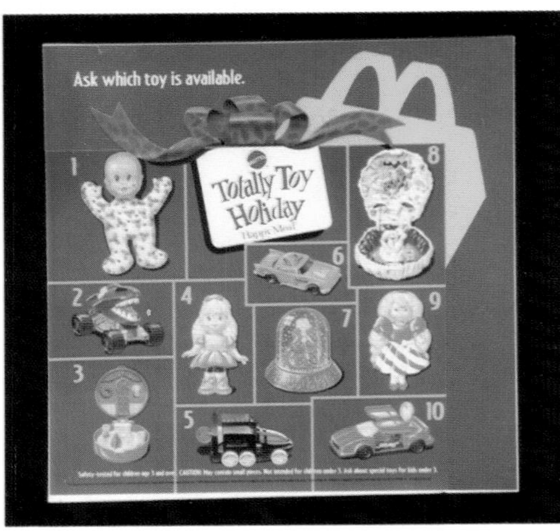

USA TO9364

USA TO9326

1994

ANIMANIACS HAPPY MEAL, 1994
BARBIE / HOT WHEELS V HAPPY MEAL, 1994
BOBBY'S WORLD HAPPY MEAL, 1994
CABBAGE PATCH KIDS/TONKA HAPPY MEAL, 1994
EARTH DAYS HAPPY MEAL, 1994
FLINTSTONES HAPPY MEAL, 1994
HALLOWEEN '94 HAPPY MEAL, 1994
MAGIC SCHOOL BUS HAPPY MEAL, 1994
MAKIN' MOVIES HAPPY MEAL, 1994
MICKEY & FRIENDS/EPCOT CENTER '94 ADVENTURE HAPPY MEAL, 1994
RONALD CELEBRATES HAPPY BIRTHDAY HAPPY MEAL, 1994
SONIC 3 THE HEDGEHOG HAPPY MEAL, 1994
USA/GENERIC PROMOTION, 1994

USA AN9413 USA AN9410

ANIMANIACS HAPPY MEAL, 1994

❑ ❑ USA AN9410 **HM BOX,** 1993, **DOT/EZ WITH R MOUTHS** $1-1.25

❑ ❑ USA AN9411 **HM BOX,** 1993, **GOOD SKATE GOOD FEATHERS** $1-1.25

❑ ❑ USA AN9412 **HM BOX,** 1993, **TRIO BICYCLE** $1-1.25

❑ ❑ USA AN9413 **HM BOX,** 1993, **PINY** $1-1.25

❑ ❑ USA AN9409 **U-3 BICYCLE BUILT FOR TRIO,** 1993, 1P PURP BIKE W 3 RED WHLS/3 CHARS RIDING $1.50-2

❑ ❑ USA AN9401 **BICYCLE BUILT FOR TRIO,** 1993, 1P PURP BIKE W 3 RED WHLS/3 CHARS RIDING $1-1.50

❑ ❑ USA AN9402 **DOT'S ICE CREAM MACHINE,** 1993, 1P ICE CREAM TRUCK W 3 PNK WHEELS/DOT RIDING $1-1.50

USA AN9412 USA AN9411

USA AN9401 USA AN9402 USA AN9403 USA AN9404

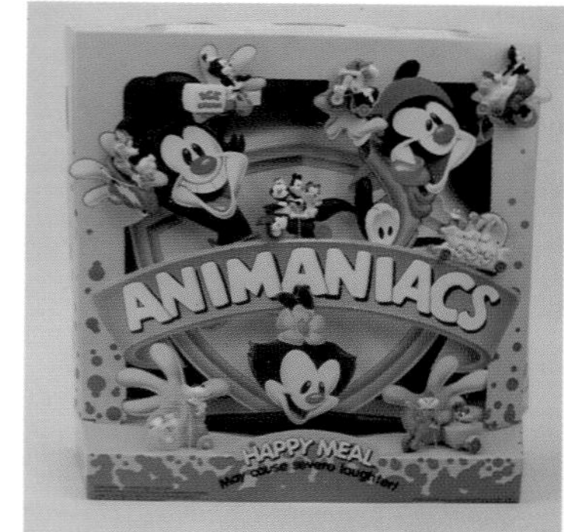

USA AN9426

USA AN9405 USA AN9406 USA AN9407 USA AN9408

❑ ❑ USA AN9403 **GOODSKATE GOODFEATHERS,** 1993, 1P YEL SKATEBOARD/BLU WHELS/3 BIRDLIKE CHARS RIDING $1-1.50
❑ ❑ USA AN9404 **MINDY/BUTTONS' WILD RIDE,** 1993, 1P TURQ AUTO/BOY AND ANIMAL RIDING $1-1.50
❑ ❑ USA AN9405 **PINKY AND THE BRAIN MOBILE,** 1993, 1P ORG TRICYCLE W CHAR RIDING IN FRONT WHEEL $1-1.50
❑ ❑ USA AN9406 **SLAPPY/SKIPPY'S CHOPPER,** 1993, 1P PNK/GRN CYCLE W SIDE CAR/2 CHARS RIDING $1-1.50
❑ ❑ USA AN9407 **UPSIDE-DOWN WAKKO,** 1993, 1P GRN TRICYCLE/PUR WHEELS W CHAR RIDING UP SIDE DOWN $1-1.50
❑ ❑ USA AN9408 **YAKKO RIDIN' RALPH,** 1993, 1P CHAR RIDING RALPH AS A TRICYCLE $1-1.50
❑ ❑ USA AN9426 **DISPLAY W PREMIUMS,** 1993 $20-25
❑ ❑ USA AN9464 **TRANSLITE/SM,** 1993 $4-7

USA AN9464

COMMENTS: NATIONAL DISTRIBUTION: USA - MAY 6-JUNE 2, 1994. PREMIUM MARKINGS "1993 WARNER BROS". THE U-3 IS THE SAME AS USA AN9401, LOOSE OUT OF PACKAGE.

BARBIE / HOT WHEELS HAPPY MEAL, 1994

❑ ❑ USA BA9430 **HM BAG,** 1994, **BARBIE AND FRIENDS/WORLD OF HOT WHEELS** $1-1.25
❑ ❑ USA BA9417 **U-3 BARBIE BALL,** 1994, LILAC BALL W BARBIE PICTURE $1-1.50

USA BA9419

USA BA9401 USA BA9404 USA BA9420 USA BA9407

USA BA9417 USA BA9402 USA BA9405 USA BA9421

USA BA9403 USA BA9406 USA BA9408

USA BA9430

USA HW9418 USA HW9409 USA HW9410 USA HW9411 USA HW9412

USA BA9426

USA HW9413 USA HW9414 USA HW9415 USA HW9416

USA BA9464

USA BO9410 USA BO9413

- ❑ ❑ USA HW9418 **U-3 FAST FORWARD,** 1991, GRN/PURPLE MINI-STREEX W WHEELS $1-1.50
- ❑ ❑ USA BA9401 **#1 BICYCLIN BARBIE,** 1994, GRN/PNK BARBIE ON PNK BIKE $1-1.50
- ❑ ❑ USA BA9402 **#2 JEWEL/GLITTER SHANI,** 1994, BLACK BARBIE W ORG DRESS $1-1.50
- ❑ ❑ USA BA9403 **#3 CAMP BARBIE,** 1994, PNK JACKET/BLONDE HAIR/BLU SHORTS/GRN BASE $1-1.50
- ❑ ❑ USA BA9404 **#4 CAMP TERESA,** 1994, BLU SHIRT/YEL SUNGLASSES/BRN HAIR/YEL PANTS $1-1.50
- ❑ ❑ USA BA9419 **#4 CAMP TERESA,** 1994, BLU SHIRT/BLU SUNGLASSES/BLU FISHING PATCH ON YEL PANTS $2.50-4
- ❑ ❑ USA BA9405 **#5 LOCKET SURPRISE BARBIE,** 1994, WHT BARBIE/PNK PARTY DRESS/BLONDE HAIR/PNK HEELS $1-1.50
- ❑ ❑ USA BA9420 **#5 LOCKET SURPRISE BARBIE,** 1994, BLK BARBIE/PNK PARTY DRESS/BLONDE HAIR/PNK HEELS $3-5
- ❑ ❑ USA BA9406 **#6 LOCKET SURPRISE KEN,** 1994, WHT KEN W GOLD JACKET/TURQ SLACKS $1-1.50
- ❑ ❑ USA BA9421 **#6 LOCKET SURPRISE KEN,** 1994, BLK KEN W GOLD JACKET/TURQ SLACKS $3-5
- ❑ ❑ USA BA9407 **#7 JEWEL/GLITTER BRIDE,** 1994, WHT LONG DRESS/BLONDE HAIR/PNK FLOWERS $1-1.50
- ❑ ❑ USA BA9408 **#8 BRIDESMAID SKIPPER,** 1994, LILAC DRESS/BLONDE HAIR $1-1.50
- ❑ ❑ USA HW9409 **#9 BOLD EAGLE,** 1994, YEL/SILVER HOT ROD $1-1.50
- ❑ ❑ USA HW9410 **#10 BLACK,** 1994, BLACK HOT ROD $1-1.50
- ❑ ❑ USA HW9411 **#11 FLAME RIDER,** 1994, BLK/RED HOT ROD W MCD LOGO $1-1.50
- ❑ ❑ USA HW9412 **#12 GAS HOG,** 1994, RED CONVERTIBLE $1-1.50
- ❑ ❑ USA HW9413 **#13 TURBINE 4-2,** 1994, BLU TURBINE/JET CAR $1-1.50
- ❑ ❑ USA HW9414 **#14 2-COOL,** 1994, PURP/SIL SPORTS CAR $1-1.50
- ❑ ❑ USA HW9415 **#15 STREET SHOCKER,** 1994, GRN SPORTS CAR $1-1.50
- ❑ ❑ USA HW9416 **#16 X21J CRUISER,** 1994, BLU/SIL FORMULA 1 CAR $1-1.50
- ❑ ❑ USA BA9426 **DISPLAY/PREMIUMS,** 1994 $50-75
- ❑ ❑ USA BA9464 **TRANSLITE/SM,** 1994 $4-6

COMMENTS: NATIONAL DISTRIBUTION: USA - AUGUST 5-SEPTEMBER 8, 1994

BOBBY'S WORLD HAPPY MEAL, 1994

- ❑ ❑ USA BO9410 **HM BOX,** 1993, **CHEAP SKATES/BOBBY SKATING** $1-1.25
- ❑ ❑ USA BO9411 **HM BOX,** 1993, **DRAG/BOBBY IN WAGON** $1-1.25
- ❑ ❑ USA BO9412 **HM BOX,** 1993, **PLAN(ET)/BOBBY ON BIG WHEELS** $1-1.25
- ❑ ❑ USA BO9413 **HM BOX,** 1993, **WAVE/BOBBY IN POOL** $1-1.25
- ❑ ❑ USA BO9405 **U-3 BOBBY/INNER TUBE,** 1993, 1P BOBBY IN INNERTUBET $1.50-2
- ❑ ❑ USA BO9401 **3-WHEELER/SPACESHIP,** 1993, YEL 3-WHEELER/RED SPACESHIP/3P $1-1.50
- ❑ ❑ USA BO9402 **INNERTUBE/SUBMARINE,** 1993, GRN INNERTUBE/ORG SUBMARINE/3P $1-1.50
- ❑ ❑ USA BO9403 **SKATES/ROLLER COASTER,** 1993, BLU SKATES/GRN ROLLER COASTER/3P $1.OO - 1.50
- ❑ ❑ USA BO9404 **WAGON/RACE CAR,** 1993, RED WAGON/BLU RACE CAR/3P $1-1.50
- ❑ ❑ USA BO9426 **DISPLAY W PREMIUMS,** 1993 $15-25
- ❑ ❑ USA BO9464 **TRANSLITE/SM,** 1993 $3-5

COMMENTS: NATIONAL DISTRIBUTION: USA - MARCH 4-31, 1994.

USA BO9411 USA BO9412

USA BO9401 USA BO9402 USA BO9403 USA BO9404

USA BO9405

CABBAGE PATCH KIDS/TONKA HAPPY MEAL, 1994

- ❑ ❑ USA CP9430 **HM BAG,** 1994, **CABBAGE PATCH KIDS/ TONKA** $1-1.25
- ❑ ❑ USA CP9409 **U-3 SARAJANE,** 1994, CPK DOLL/ RUBBER $1.50-2
- ❑ ❑ USA TK9410 **U-3 DUMP TRUCK,** 1994, YEL/BLU RUBBER $1.50-2
- ❑ ❑ USA CP9401 **WK 1 MIMI KRISTINA,** 1994, ANGEL/GOLD HORN $1-1.50
- ❑ ❑ USA CP9402 **WK 2 KIMBERLY KATHERINE,** 1994, SANTA'S HELPER/WHT APRON $1-1.50
- ❑ ❑ USA CP9403 **WK 3 ABIGAIL LYNN,** 1994, TOY SOLDIER/BLU TOP HAT/CANDY CANE/BLK DOLL $1-1.50
- ❑ ❑ USA CP9404 **WK 4 MICHELLE ELYSE,** 1994, SNOW FAIRY/ WHT DRESS/SNOWFLAKE/WHT DOLL $1-1.50

USA BO9426

USA CP9430

USA CP9401 USA CP9402 USA CP9403 USA CP9404

USA BO9464

USA TK9410 USA CP9409

USA TK9405 USA TK9406 USA TK9407 USA TK9408

❑ ❑ USA TK9405 **WK 1 LOADER,** 1994, 1P ORG W BLK LIFT $1-1.50
❑ ❑ USA TK9406 **WK 2 CRANE,** 1994, 1P GRN W BLK HOOK $1-1.50
❑ ❑ USA TK9407 **WK 3 GRADER,** 1994, 1P YEL W YEL BLADE $1-1.50
❑ ❑ USA TK9408 **WK 4 BULLDOZER,** 1994, 1P YEL W BLK BLADE $1-1.50
❑ ❑ USA CP9426 **DISPLAY W PREMIUMS,** 1994 $40-60
❑ ❑ USA CP9464 **TRANSLITE/SM,** 1994 $4-7

COMMENTS: NATIONAL DISTRIBUTION: USA - DECEMBER 2-29, 1994.

EARTH DAYS HAPPY MEAL, 1994

❑ ❑ USA EA9430 **HM BAG,** 1993, **EARTH DAYS** $1-1.25
❑ ❑ USA EA9405 **U-3 TOOL CARRIER,** 1993, BLU W RED SHOVEL W YEL STRAP $1.25-1.50
❑ ❑ USA EA9401 **BINOCULARS,** 1993, 1P HINGE OPEN EARTH SHAPED/GRN $1-1.25
❑ ❑ USA EA9402 **BIRDFEEDER,** 1993, BIRD HOUSE SHAPED BIRDFEEDER $1-1.25
❑ ❑ USA EA9403 **TERRARIUM/GLOBE,** 1993, CLEAR CYCLINDER TOP W BOTTOM $1-1.25
❑ ❑ USA EA9404 **TOOL CARRIER,** 1993, BLU W RED SHOVEL W YEL STRAP/3P $1-1.25

USA EA9405

USA CP9426

USA EA9430

USA EA9426

USA CP9464

USA EA9401 USA EA9402 USA EA9403 USA EA9404

❑ ❑ USA EA9426 **DISPLAY/PREMIUMS,** 1993 $10-20
❑ ❑ USA EA9464 **TRANSLITE/SM,** 1993 $3-5

COMMENTS: NATIONAL DISTRIBUTION: USA - APRIL 8-MAY 5, 1994.

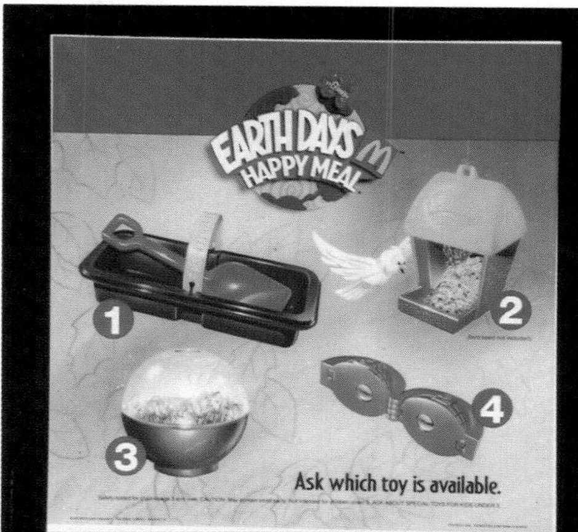

USA EA9464

FLINTSTONES HAPPY MEAL, 1994

❑ ❑ USA FL9430 **HM BAG,** 1993, **ROC DONALD'S DRIVE-THRU/ LOOK OUT!** $1-1.25
❑ ❑ USA FL9406 **U-3 ROCKING DINO,** 1993, 1P PURP RUBBER DINO DINOSAUR $2-2.50
❑ ❑ USA FL9401 **BARNEY/FOSSIL FILL-UP,** 1993, 2P/GREY BLDG/DOOR/BARNEY IN CAR/STICKER SHEET $1.50-2
❑ ❑ USA FL9402 **BETTY/BAMM BAMM/ROC D,** 1993, 2P/YEL BLDG/DOOR/BETTY IN BRN-LOG CAR/STICKER $1.50-2
❑ ❑ USA FL9403 **FRED/BEDR BOWL-O-RAMA,** 1993, 2P/GRN BLDG/DOOR/FRED IN RED CAR/STICKER $1.50-2
❑ ❑ USA FL9404 **PEBBLES/DINO/TOYS-S-A,** 1993, 2P/RED BLDG/DOOR/PEEBBLES IN BLU CYCLE/STICKER $1.50-2
❑ ❑ USA FL9405 **WILMA/FLINSTONE HOUSE,** 1993, 2P/PEACH BLDG/DOOR/WILMA IN GRY CAR/STICKER $1.50-2
❑ ❑ USA FL9426 **DISPLAY W PREMIUMS,** 1993 $20-35
❑ ❑ USA FL9450 **BUTTON,** 1993, I LOVE ROC DONALD'S $2-3
❑ ❑ USA FL9464 **TRANSLITE/SM,** 1993 $3-5
❑ ❑ USA FL9495 **PIN,** 1994, THE FLINTSTONES/ROC DONALD'S SUMMER '94 $3-4
❑ ❑ USA FL9496 **PIN,** 1994, GRAND POOBAH MEALS $2.50-3

COMMENTS: NATIONAL DISTRIBUTION: USA - JUNE 3-JULY 7, 1994.

USA FL9406 USA FL9405 USA FL9404

USA FL9402 USA FL9407 USA FL9403

USA FL9450

USA FL9430

USA FL9495

USA FL9426

USA FL9496

USA FL9464

HALLOWEEN '94 HAPPY MEAL, 1994

- ❑ ❑ USA HA9401 **GHOST,** 1986, 3P WHT GHOST W COOKIE CUTTER INSERT W BLK HANDLE $1-1.50
- ❑ ❑ USA HA9402 **PUMPKIN,** 1986, 3P ORG PUMPKIN W COOKIE CUTTER INSERT W BLK HANDLE $1-1.50
- ❑ ❑ USA HA9403 **WITCH,** 1986 3P PURP WITCH W COOKIE CUTTER INSERT W BLK HANDLE $1-1.50
- ❑ ❑ USA HA9426 **DISPLAY,** 1994 $10-20
- ❑ ❑ USA HA9464 **TRANSLITE/SM,** 1994 $3-5

COMMENTS: NATIONAL DISTRIBUTION OCTOBER 7-OCTOBER 27, 1994.

MAGIC SCHOOL BUS HAPPY MEAL, 1994

- ❑ ❑ USA MA9430 **HM BAG,** 1994, **THE MAGIC SCHOOL BUS/ WAHOO!** $1-1.25
- ❑ ❑ USA MA9405 **U-3 UNDERSEA ADVENTURE GAME,** 1994, GRN BEAD GAME WITHOUT TAB/1P $1-1.50
- ❑ ❑ USA MA9401 **COLLECTOR CARD KIT,** 1994, YEL SCHOOL BUS/10 CARDS/STICKER SHEET $1-1.25
- ❑ ❑ USA MA9402 **GEO FOSSIL FINDER,** 1994, FOSSIL TRACER W PENCIL/4P $1-1.25
- ❑ ❑ USA MA9403 **SPACE TRACER,** 1994, BLU TRACING PROTRACTOR/PLANETS/1P $1-1.25
- ❑ ❑ USA MA9404 **UNDERSEA ADVENTURE GAME,** 1994, GRN BEAD GAME W YEL TAB/1P $1-1.25
- ❑ ❑ USA MA9426 **DISPLAY,** 1994 $10-20
- ❑ ❑ USA MA9464 **TRANSLITE/SM,** 1994 $4-6

COMMENTS: NATIONAL DISTRIBUTION: USA - SEPTEMBER 9-OCTOBER 6, 1994

USA HA9402 USA HA9401 USA HA9403

USA HA9426

USA HA9464

USA MA9430

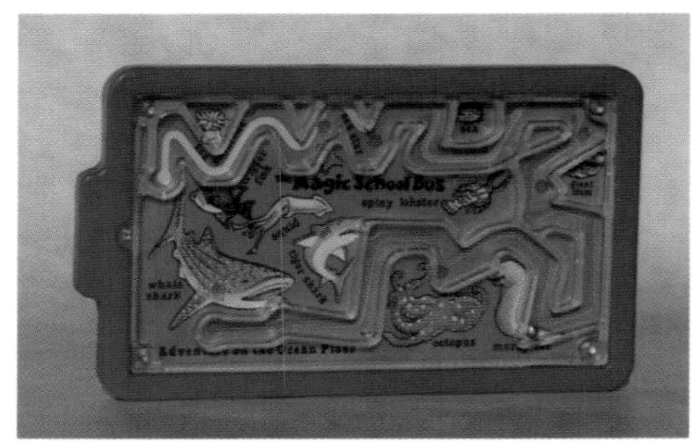

USA MA9405

USA MA9404

USA MA9402 USA MA9403 USA MA9401

USA MA9464

USA MA9426

USA MM9401 USA MM9402 USA MM9403 USA MM9404

MAKIN' MOVIES HAPPY MEAL, 1994

❑ ❑ USA MM9410 **HM BOX,** 1993, **MAKING PRINTS** $1-1.25
❑ ❑ USA MM9411 **HM BOX,** 1993, **POPCORN** $1-1.25
❑ ❑ USA MM9412 **HM BOX,** 1993, **SCOREBOARD** $1-1.25
❑ ❑ USA MM9413 **HM BOX,** 1993, **TICKETS** $1-1.25
❑ ❑ USA MM9405 **U-3 SOUND MACHINE,** 1993, 1P PURP/TURQ/BLK $1-1.50
❑ ❑ USA MM9401 **CLAPBOARD,** 1993, BLK CHALK BOARD W CHALK/2P $1-1.25
❑ ❑ USA MM9402 **MEGAPHONE/DIRECTOR'S,** 1993, 1P RED/YEL MEGAPHONE $1-1.25
❑ ❑ USA MM9403 **MOVIE CAMERA,** 1993, 1P BLU/YEL/BLK/RED MOVIE CAMERA $1-1.25
❑ ❑ USA MM9404 **SOUND EFFECTS MACHINE,** 1993, 1P PURP/TURQ/BLK SOUND MACHINE $1-1.25
❑ ❑ USA MM9426 **DISPLAY W PREMIUMS,** 1993 $15-25
❑ ❑ USA MM9464 **TRANSLITE/SM,** 1993 $3-5

COMMENTS: NATIONAL DISTRIBUTION: USA - JANUARY 7-FEBRUARY 3, 1994.

USA MM9426

USA MM9410 USA MM9411

USA MM9412 USA MM9413

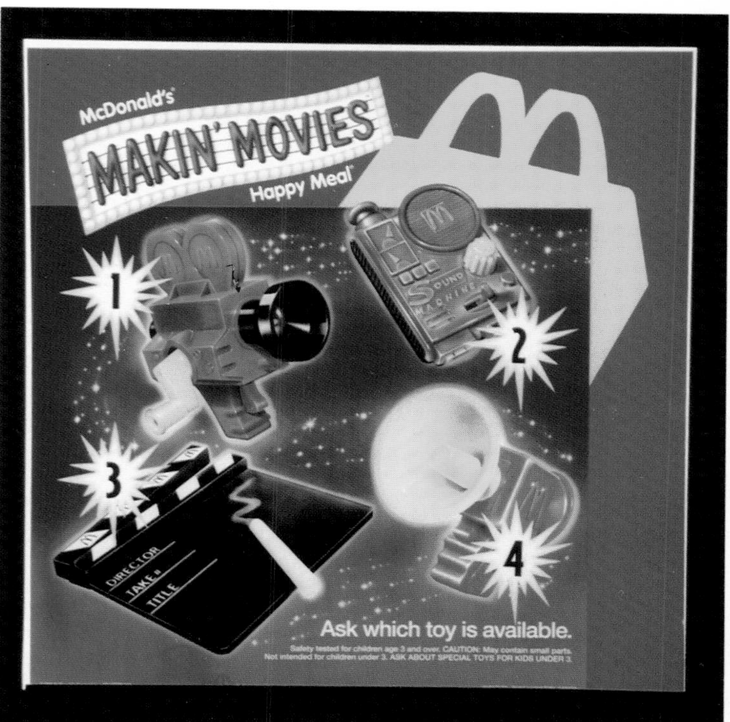

USA MM9464

USA MI9426

MICKEY & FRIENDS/EPCOT CENTER '94 ADVENTURE HAPPY MEAL, 1994

- ❑ ❑ USA MI9410 **HM BOX,** 1994, **CHIP IN CHINA/DALE IN MOROCCO** $1-1.25
- ❑ ❑ USA MI9411 **HM BOX,** 1994, **DAISY IN GERMANY/DONNALD IN MEXICO** $1-1.25
- ❑ ❑ USA MI9412 **HM BOX,** 1994, **MICKEY IN USA/MINNIE IN JAPAN** $1-1.25
- ❑ ❑ USA MI9413 **HM BOX,** 1994, **PLUTO IN FRANCE/GOOFY IN NORWAY** $1-1.25
- ❑ ❑ USA MI9409 **U-3 MICKEY IN U.S.A.,** 1994, 1P MICKEY MOUSE WITH ARMS EXTENDED $1.50-2

USA MI9410 USA MI9411 USA MI9412 USA MI9413

USA MI9464

- ❑ ❑ USA MI9401 **CHIP IN CHINA,** 1994, 1P CHIP W CHINESE HAT $1-1.50
- ❑ ❑ USA MI9402 **DAISY IN GERMANY,** 1994, 1P DAISY DUCK $1-1.50
- ❑ ❑ USA MI9403 **DALE IN MOROCCO,** 1994, 1P DALE $1-1.50
- ❑ ❑ USA MI9404 **DONALD IN MEXICO,** 1994, 1P DONALD DUCK $1-1.50
- ❑ ❑ USA MI9405 **GOOFY IN NORWAY,** 1994, 1P GOOFY $1-1.50
- ❑ ❑ USA MI9406 **MICKEY MOUSE,** 1994, 1P MICKEY WITH ARMS EXTENDED $1-1.50
- ❑ ❑ USA MI9407 **MINNIE IN JAPAN,** 1994, 1P MINNIE $1-1.50
- ❑ ❑ USA MI9408 **PLUTO IN FRANCE,** 1994, 1P PLUTO $1-1.50
- ❑ ❑ USA MI9426 **DISPLAY/PREMIUMS,** 1994 $50-65
- ❑ ❑ USA MI9464 **TRANSLITE/SM,** 1994 $5-10

COMMENTS: NATIONAL DISTRIBUTION: USA - JULY 8-AUGUST 4, 1994.

USA MI9407 USA MI9402 USA MI9403 USA MI9404

USA MI9405 USA MI9406 USA MI9407 USA MI9408

RONALD CELEBRATES HAPPY BIRTHDAY HAPPY MEAL, 1994

- ❑ ❑ USA FI9420 **HM BOX,** 1994, **CANDIES/FIND ALL** $1-1.25
- ❑ ❑ USA FI9421 **HM BOX,** 1994, **PARTY/RONALD INVITED** $1-1.25
- ❑ ❑ USA FI9422 **HM BOX,** 1994, **PORTRAIT/BERENSTAIN BEARS** $1-1.25

USA FI9420 USA FI9421

❑ ❑ USA FI9423 **HM BOX,** 1994, **PARADE/BIRTHDAY PARTY** $1-1.25

❑ ❑ USA FI9416 **U-3 RONALD MCDONALD,** 1994, IN RED HM BOX $2.50-3

❑ ❑ USA FI9401 **WK 1 RONALD MCDONALD,** 1994, IN RED HM BOX WAVING/1P $2-2.50

❑ ❑ USA FI9402 **WK 1 BARBIE,** 1994, PNK BALLERINA/PURP STAND $2-2.50

❑ ❑ USA FI9403 **WK 1 HOT WHEELS,** 1994, BLU HW CAR IN ORG TRACK $2-2.50

❑ ❑ USA FI9404 **WK 2 E.T.,** 1994, W PURP HAT ON BLU STAGE $2-2.50

❑ ❑ USA FI9405 **WK 2 SONIC THE HEDGEHOG,** 1994, ON PNK TV $2-2.50

❑ ❑ USA FI9406 **WK 2 BERENSTAIN BEARS,** 1994, ON YEL SEESAW $2-2.50

❑ ❑ USA FI9407 **WK 3 CABBAGE PATCH KIDS,** 1994, ON BLU ROCKING HORSE $2-2.50

❑ ❑ USA FI9408 **WK 3 TONKA,** 1994, YEL TRUCK CARRYING RED PACKAGE $2-2.50

❑ ❑ USA FI9409 **WK 3 101 DALMATIANS,** 1994, DOGS ON BLK/WHT BOX $2-2.50

❑ ❑ USA FI9410 **WK 4 PEANUTS,** 1994, IN GRN CALLIOPE $2-2.50

❑ ❑ USA FI9411 **WK 4 MUPPET BABIES,** 1994, MISS PIGGY/KERMIT W WHT TIE ON BLU BASE $2-2.50

❑ ❑ USA FI9412 **WK 4 LITTLE MERMAID,** 1994, W FLOUNDER ON BLU BASE $2-2.50

❑ ❑ USA FI9413 **WK 5 TINY TOONS,** 1994, W PNK CAKE/WHT CANDLE $2-2.50

❑ ❑ USA FI9414 **WK 5 LOONEY TUNES,** 1994, BUGS/SYLVESTER W HORN/SYMBOLS $2-2.50

❑ ❑ USA FI9415 **WK 5 HAPPY MEAL GUYS,** 1994, HAMB/FRIES/SKAKE $2-2.50

❑ ❑ USA FI9417 **WK 4 MUPPET BABIES,** 1994, MISS PIGGY/KERMIT W BLU TIE ON BLU BASE $3.50-5

❑ ❑ USA FI9425 **TOY SAFETY NOTICE,** 1994 $2-3

❑ ❑ USA FI9426 **DISPLAY/PREMIUMS,** 1994 $65-100

❑ ❑ USA FI9464 **TRANSLITE/SM,** 1994 $5-8

COMMENTS: NATIONAL DISTRIBUTION: USA - OCTOBER 28-DECEMBER 1, 1994. FIFTEENTH ANNIVERSARY/BIRTHDAY OF USA HAPPY MEAL. USA FI9402 BARBIE WAS RECALLED FOR SAFETY CONCERNS; RECALL WAS AT THE END OF DISTRIBUTION CYCLE. USA FI9411 WAS DISTRIBUTED BOTH WAYS, WITH WHITE TIE AND WITH BLUE PAINTED TIE.

USA FI9423

USA FI9422

USA FI9417 USA FI9411

USA FI9409 USA FI9412 USA FI9411 USA FI9410 USA FI9413 USA FI9414 USA FI9415

USA FI9401 USA FI9402 USA FI9403 USA FI9406 USA FI9405 USA FI9404 USA FI9408 USA FI9407

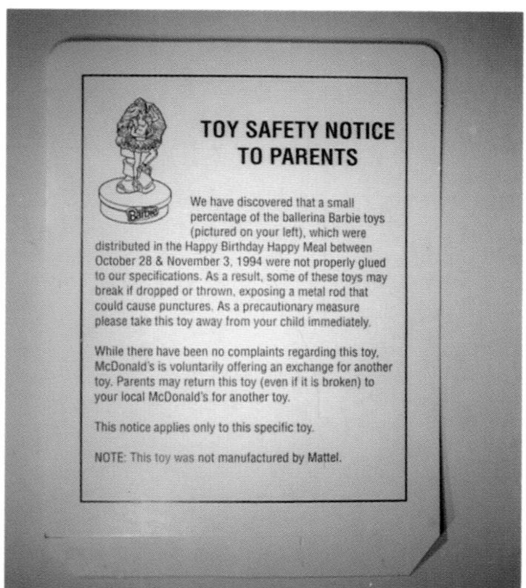

TOY SAFETY NOTICE TO PARENTS

We have discovered that a small percentage of the ballerina Barbie toys (pictured on your left), which were distributed in the Happy Birthday Happy Meal between October 28 & November 3, 1994 were not properly glued to our specifications. As a result, some of these toys may break if dropped or thrown, exposing a metal rod that could cause punctures. As a precautionary measure please take this toy away from your child immediately.

While there have been no complaints regarding this toy, McDonald's is voluntarily offering an exchange for another toy. Parents may return this toy (even if it is broken) to your local McDonald's for another toy.

This notice applies only to this specific toy.

NOTE: This toy was not manufactured by Mattel.

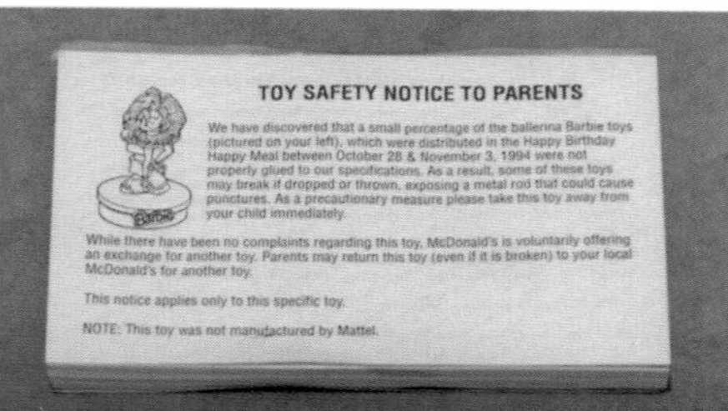

TOY SAFETY NOTICE TO PARENTS

We have discovered that a small percentage of the ballerina Barbie toys (pictured on your left), which were distributed in the Happy Birthday Happy Meal between October 28 & November 3, 1994 were not properly glued to our specifications. As a result, some of these toys may break if dropped or thrown, exposing a metal rod that could cause punctures. As a precautionary measure please take this toy away from your child immediately.

While there have been no complaints regarding this toy, McDonald's is voluntarily offering an exchange for another toy. Parents may return this toy (even if it is broken) to your local McDonald's for another toy.

This notice applies only to this specific toy.

NOTE: This toy was not manufactured by Mattel.

USA FI9425

USA FI9426

USA FI9464

USA SO9430

USA SO9405

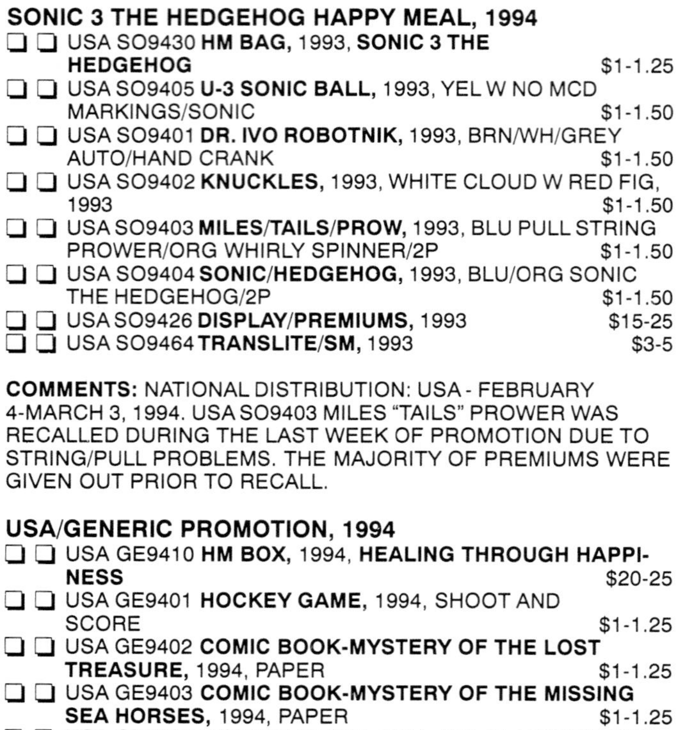

SONIC 3 THE HEDGEHOG HAPPY MEAL, 1994

- ❑ ❑ USA SO9430 **HM BAG,** 1993, **SONIC 3 THE HEDGEHOG** $1-1.25
- ❑ ❑ USA SO9405 **U-3 SONIC BALL,** 1993, YEL W NO MCD MARKINGS/SONIC $1-1.50
- ❑ ❑ USA SO9401 **DR. IVO ROBOTNIK,** 1993, BRN/WH/GREY AUTO/HAND CRANK $1-1.50
- ❑ ❑ USA SO9402 **KNUCKLES,** 1993, WHITE CLOUD W RED FIG, 1993 $1-1.50
- ❑ ❑ USA SO9403 **MILES/TAILS/PROW,** 1993, BLU PULL STRING PROWER/ORG WHIRLY SPINNER/2P $1-1.50
- ❑ ❑ USA SO9404 **SONIC/HEDGEHOG,** 1993, BLU/ORG SONIC THE HEDGEHOG/2P $1-1.50
- ❑ ❑ USA SO9426 **DISPLAY/PREMIUMS,** 1993 $15-25
- ❑ ❑ USA SO9464 **TRANSLITE/SM,** 1993 $3-5

COMMENTS: NATIONAL DISTRIBUTION: USA - FEBRUARY 4-MARCH 3, 1994. USA SO9403 MILES "TAILS" PROWER WAS RECALLED DURING THE LAST WEEK OF PROMOTION DUE TO STRING/PULL PROBLEMS. THE MAJORITY OF PREMIUMS WERE GIVEN OUT PRIOR TO RECALL.

USA/GENERIC PROMOTION, 1994

- ❑ ❑ USA GE9410 **HM BOX,** 1994, **HEALING THROUGH HAPPINESS** $20-25
- ❑ ❑ USA GE9401 **HOCKEY GAME,** 1994, SHOOT AND SCORE $1-1.25
- ❑ ❑ USA GE9402 **COMIC BOOK-MYSTERY OF THE LOST TREASURE,** 1994, PAPER $1-1.25
- ❑ ❑ USA GE9403 **COMIC BOOK-MYSTERY OF THE MISSING SEA HORSES,** 1994, PAPER $1-1.25
- ❑ ❑ USA GE9404 **LICENSE PLATE,** 1994, YEL PLASTIC W RED STICKERS $1-1.25
- ❑ ❑ USA GE9405 **PAINT KIT,** 1994, 4 1/4" X 5 1/4"/4 PGS $1.25-1.50

USA SO9401 USA SO9402 USA SO9403 USA SO9404

USA SO9464

USA SO9426

USA GE9410

❑ ❑ USA GE9406 **STICKERS-RON/GRIM,** 1994, SCRATCH 'N SNIFF $1-1.25
❑ ❑ USA GE9407 **STICKERS-BIRDIE/HAMB,** 1994, SCRATCH 'N SNIFF $1-1.25
❑ ❑ USA GE9408 **TATTOO FUN,** 1994 $1-1.25
❑ ❑ USA GE9409 **ACTIVITY BOOK-TIME OUT FOR FUN,** 1994, 5 1/2" X 8 1/2"/8 PGS $1.25-1.50
❑❑ USA GE9411 **GREETING CARD-FRIENDS LIKE YOU,** 1994, PAPER $1-1.25
❑ ❑ USA GE9412 **GREETING CARD-YOU'RE TOTALLY COOL,** 1994, PAPER $1-1.25

COMMENTS: REGIONAL DISTRIBUTION: USA - 1994 DURING FUN TREAT PERIODS. USA GE9410 HM BOX WAS DISTRIBUTED ONLY AT THE MCDONALD'S COLLECTORS CLUB CONVENTION IN CHICAGO, ILLINOIS DURING APRIL 1994. THESE ARE A SAMPLING OF THE GENERIC PREMIUMS GIVEN OUT.

USA GE9401

USA GE9402 USA GE9403

1995

AMAZING WILDLIFE HAPPY MEAL, 1995
MUPPET WORKSHOP HAPPY MEAL, 1995
POLLY POCKET / ATTACK PACK HAPPY MEAL, 1995
SPACE RESCUE HAPPY MEAL, 1995
USA/GENERIC PROMOTION, 1995

AMAZING WILDLIFE HAPPY MEAL, 1995

❑ ❑ USA AM9510 **HM BOX,** 1994, **AFRICA** $1-1.25
❑ ❑ USA AM9511 **HM BOX,** 1994, **ARCTIC** $1-1.25
❑ ❑ USA AM9512 **HM BOX,** 1994, **GALAPAGOS ISL.** $1-1.25
❑ ❑ USA AM9513 **HM BOX,** 1994, **GIR FOREST** $1-1.25
❑ ❑ USA AM9501 **ASIATIC LION,** 1994, BEIGE/TAN STUFFED LION $1-1.25
❑ ❑ USA AM9502 **CHIMPANZEE,** 1994, BRN/TAN STUFFED CHIMPANZEE $1-1.25
❑ ❑ USA AM9503 **AFRICAN ELEPHANT,** 1994, GRY STUFFED ELEPHANT $1-1.25
❑ ❑ USA AM9504 **KOALA,** 1994, TAN/WHT STUFFED BEAR $1-1.25
❑ ❑ USA AM9505 **DROMEDARY CAMEL,** 1994, BRN STUFFED CAMEL $1-1.25
❑ ❑ USA AM9506 **GALAPAGOS TORTOISE,** 1994, GRN STUFFED TORTOISE $1-1.25
❑ ❑ USA AM9507 **POLAR BEAR,** 1994, WHT STUFFED BEAR $1-1.25
❑ ❑ USA AM9508 **SIBERIAN TIGER,** 1994, GOLD/BLK/WHT STUFFED TIGER $1-1.25
❑ ❑ USA AM9526 **DISPLAY,** 1994, W 8 PREMIUMS $10-15
❑ ❑ USA AM9543 **CREW REFERENCE SHEET,** 1995, BLK/WHT PIC/TOYS $1-1.50
❑ ❑ USA AM9544 **CREW POSTER,** 1995 $1.50-3
❑ ❑ USA AM9564 **TRANSLITE,** 1994 $3-5

COMMENTS: NATIONAL DISTRIBUTION: USA - APRIL 1-28, 1995. THE ADVERTISING TIE-IN PARTNER WAS THE NATIONAL WILDLIFE FEDERATION. PROMOTION INCLUDED PROMO AD FOR RANGER RICK MAGAZINE.

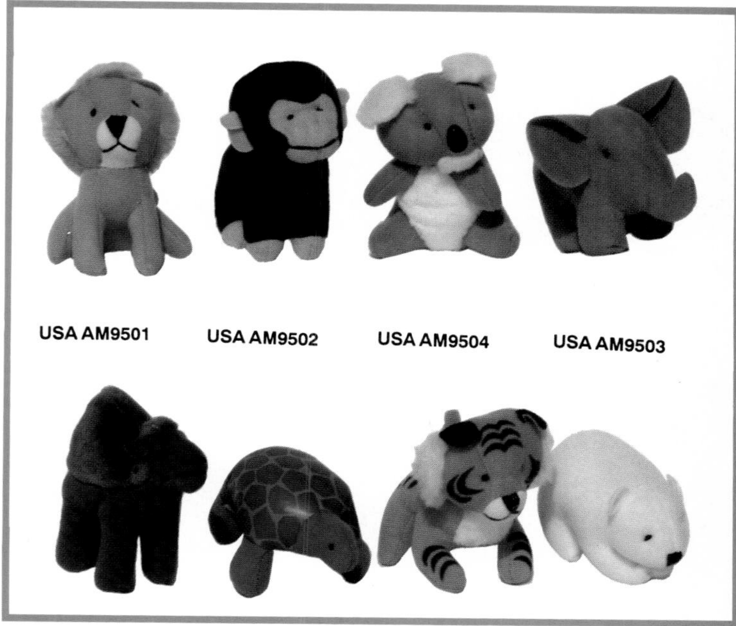

USA AM9501 USA AM9502 USA AM9504 USA AM9503

USA AM9505 USA AM9506 USA AM9508 USA AM9507

MUPPET WORKSHOP HAPPY MEAL, 1995

❑ ❑ USA MU9510 **HM BOX,** 1994, BIRD PUPPET $1-1.25
❑ ❑ USA MU9511 **HM BOX,** 1994, DOG PUPPET $1-1.25

USA MU9510 USA MU9512

USA MU9511 USA MU9513

ASIATIC LION
CHIMPANZEE
KOALA
AFRICAN ELEPHANT
AMAZING WILDLIFE
HAPPY MEAL
DROMEDARY CAMEL
GALAPAGOS TORTOISE
POLAR BEAR
April 1–28, 1995

USA AM9501 USA AM9502 USA AM9504 USA AM9503 USA AM9505 USA AM9506 USA AM9508 USA AM9507

USA MU9501 USA MU9502 USA MU9503 USA MU9504

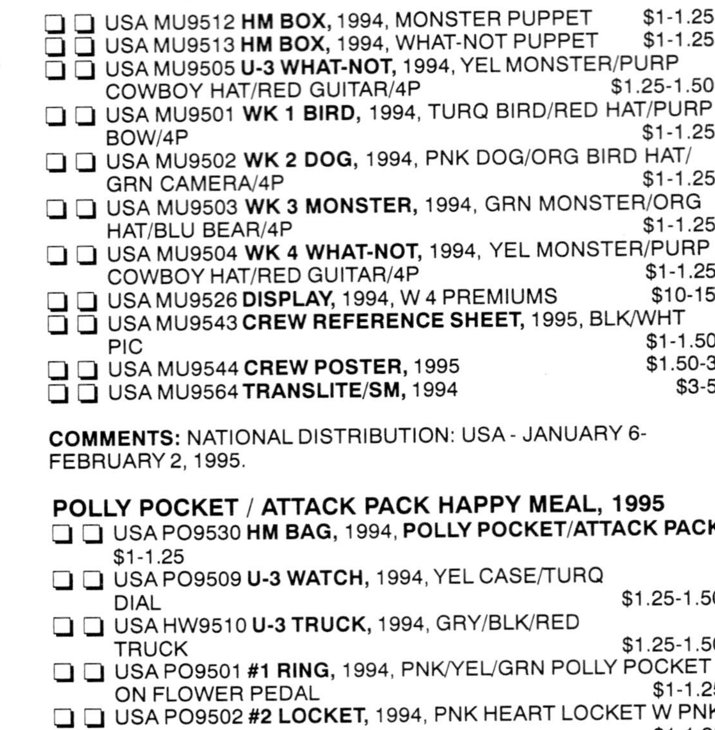

❑ ❑ USA MU9512 **HM BOX,** 1994, MONSTER PUPPET $1-1.25
❑ ❑ USA MU9513 **HM BOX,** 1994, WHAT-NOT PUPPET $1-1.25
❑ ❑ USA MU9505 **U-3 WHAT-NOT,** 1994, YEL MONSTER/PURP COWBOY HAT/RED GUITAR/4P $1.25-1.50
❑ ❑ USA MU9501 **WK 1 BIRD,** 1994, TURQ BIRD/RED HAT/PURP BOW/4P $1-1.25
❑ ❑ USA MU9502 **WK 2 DOG,** 1994, PNK DOG/ORG BIRD HAT/ GRN CAMERA/4P $1-1.25
❑ ❑ USA MU9503 **WK 3 MONSTER,** 1994, GRN MONSTER/ORG HAT/BLU BEAR/4P $1-1.25
❑ ❑ USA MU9504 **WK 4 WHAT-NOT,** 1994, YEL MONSTER/PURP COWBOY HAT/RED GUITAR/4P $1-1.25
❑ ❑ USA MU9526 **DISPLAY,** 1994, W 4 PREMIUMS $10-15
❑ ❑ USA MU9543 **CREW REFERENCE SHEET,** 1995, BLK/WHT PIC $1-1.50
❑ ❑ USA MU9544 **CREW POSTER,** 1995 $1.50-3
❑ ❑ USA MU9564 **TRANSLITE/SM,** 1994 $3-5

COMMENTS: NATIONAL DISTRIBUTION: USA - JANUARY 6-FEBRUARY 2, 1995.

POLLY POCKET / ATTACK PACK HAPPY MEAL, 1995

❑ ❑ USA PO9530 **HM BAG,** 1994, **POLLY POCKET/ATTACK PACK** $1-1.25
❑ ❑ USA PO9509 **U-3 WATCH,** 1994, YEL CASE/TURQ DIAL $1.25-1.50
❑ ❑ USA HW9510 **U-3 TRUCK,** 1994, GRY/BLK/RED TRUCK $1.25-1.50
❑ ❑ USA PO9501 **#1 RING,** 1994, PNK/YEL/GRN POLLY POCKET ON FLOWER PEDAL $1-1.25
❑ ❑ USA PO9502 **#2 LOCKET,** 1994, PNK HEART LOCKET W PNK CORD/OPENS $1-1.25

USA MU9526

USA MU9564

USA PO9530

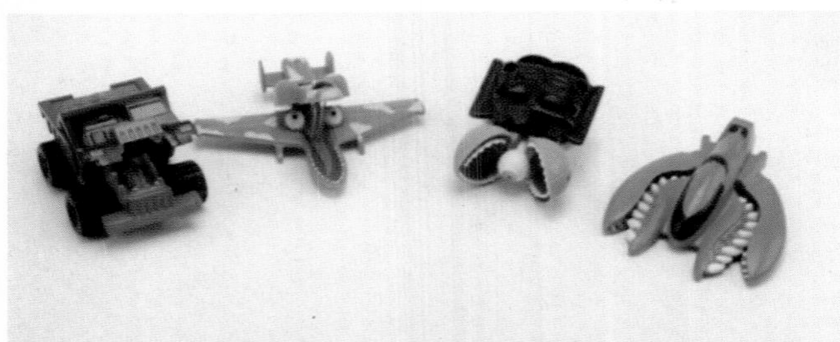

USA HW510 USA HW9505 USA HW9506 USA HW9507

USA PO9526

USA PO9501 USA PO9502 USA PO9503 USA PO9504

- ❑ ❑ USA PO9503 **#3 WATCH,** 1994, YEL CASE/TURQ DIAL/ CLIP-ON $1-1.25
- ❑ ❑ USA PO9504 **#4 BRACELET,** 1994, PNK/TURQ BUTTERFLY/ YEL STRAP/OPENS $1-1.25
- ❑ ❑ USA HW9505 **TRUCK,** 1994, PURP/BRN/BLK TRUCK $1-1.25
- ❑ ❑ USA HW9506 **BATTLE BIRD,** 1994, GRN/WHT AIRPLANE $1-1.25
- ❑ ❑ USA HW9507 **LUNAR INVADER,** 1994, YEL/BLK/GRY LUNAR MODULE $1-1.25
- ❑ ❑ USA HW9508 **SEA CREATURE,** 1994, TURQ/RED/WHT SEA CREATURE $1-1.25
- ❑ ❑ USA PO9526 **DISPLAY,** 1994, W 4 PREMIUMS $10-15
- ❑ ❑ USA PO9543 **CREW REFERENCE SHEET,** 1995, BLK/WHT PIC $1-1.50
- ❑ ❑ USA PO9544 **CREW POSTER,** 1995 $1.50-3
- ❑ ❑ USA PO9564 **TRANSLITE/SM,** 1994 $3-5

COMMENTS: NATIONAL DISTRIBUTION: USA - FEBRUARY 3-MARCH 2, 1995. USA PO9509/HW9510 = USA PO9503/HW9505, LOOSE OUT OF PACKAGE.

USA PO9543

USA PO9564

SPACE RESCUE HAPPY MEAL, 1995

- ❑ ❑ USA SP9530 **HM BAG**, 1995, **SPACE RESCUE** $1-1.25
- ❑ ❑ USA SP9505 **U-3 ASTRO VIEWER**, 1994, WHT LABEL $1-1.25
- ❑ ❑ USA SP95O1 **ASTRO VIEWER**, 1994, PINK LABLE $1-1.50
- ❑ ❑ USA SP9502 **TELE COMMUNICATOR**, 1994, ORG/GRN $1-1.25
- ❑ ❑ USA SP9503 **SPACE SLATE**, 1994, BLU/PURP/ORG W PURP PEN/2P $1-1.25
- ❑ ❑ USA SP9504 **LUNAR GRABBER**, 1994, BLU/GRN/ORG $1-1.25
- ❑ ❑ USA SP9526 **DISPLAY**, 1995, W 4 PREMIUMS $10-15
- ❑ ❑ USA SP9543 **CREW REFERENCE SHEET**, 1995, BLK/WHT/ PIC $1-1.50
- ❑ ❑ USA SP9544 **CREW POSTER**, 1995
- ❑ ❑ USA SP9564 **TRANSLITE/SM** $3-5

USA SP9526

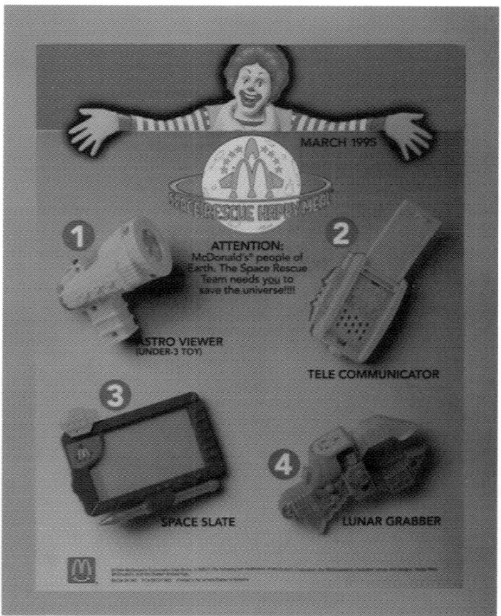

USA SP9543

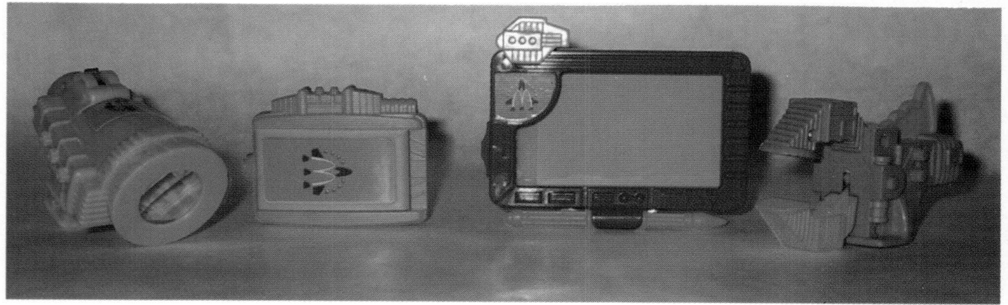

USA SP9501 USA SP9502 USA SP9503 USA SP9504

USA/GENERIC PROMOTION, 1995

❑ ❑ USA GE9501 **CALENDAR/READY, SET, GO!**, 1995, PAPER W STICKERS $1-1.25

❑ ❑ USA GE9502 **FUN TIMES**, 1995, ISSUE 1-1995 $1-1.25

COMMENTS: REGIONAL DISTRIBUTION: USA - 1995.

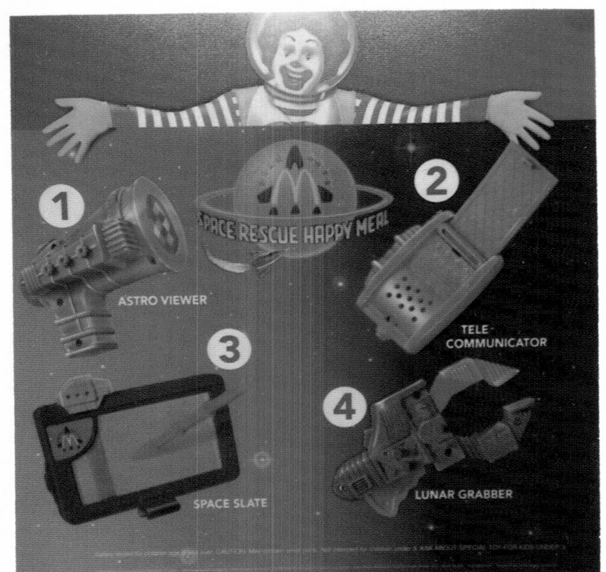

SPACE RESCUE HAPPY MEAL
1
ASTRO VIEWER
2
TELE-COMMUNICATOR
3
SPACE SLATE
4
LUNAR GRABBER

USA SP9564

USA GE9502

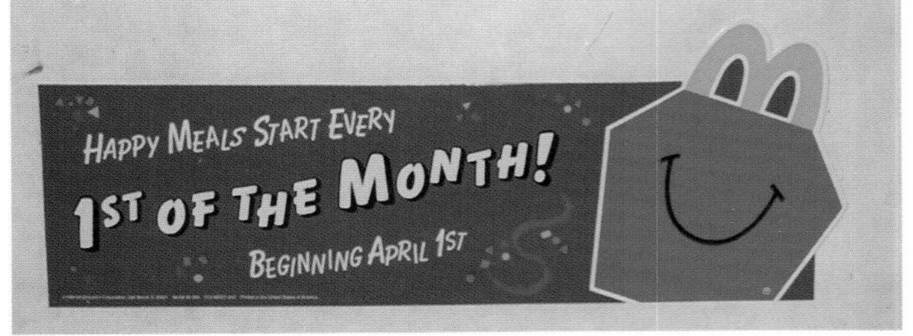

USA GE9501

CROSS REFERENCE GUIDE

The following list gives the identification numbers for this book in alphabetical order, followed by the numbers for the same items in M. Williams' book.

LOSONSKY#=WILLIAMS#
(1995) = (1992)

USA AD8101 = AD8001
USA AD8102 = AD8002
USA AD8103 = AD8003
USA AD8104 = AD8004
USA AD8105 = AD8005
USA AD8106 = AD8006
USA AD8107 = AD8007
USA AD8108 = AD8008
USA AD8109 = AD8009
USA AD8110 = AD8010
USA AD8111 = AD8011
USA AD8112 = AD8012
USA AD8113 = AD8013
USA AD8114 = AD8014
USA AD8115 = AD8015
USA AD8116 = AD8016
USA AD8117 = AD8011
USA AD8118 = AD8012
USA AD8119 = AD8013
USA AD8126 =
USA AD8165 = AD8025

USA AI8651 = AI6061
USA AI8652 = AI6062
USA AI8653 = AI6063
USA AI8654 = AI6064
USA AI8655 = AI6065
USA AI8661 = AI6087
USA AI8663 = AI6088
USA AI8664 = AI6086
USA AI8665 = AI6085
USA AI8666 = AI6066
USA AI8667 = AI6067
USA AI8675 = AI6075
USA AI8676 = AI6076
USA AI8677 = AI6077
USA AI8678 = AI6078

USA AL9101 = AL4001
USA AL9102 = AL4002
USA AL9103 = AL4003
USA AL9104 = AL4004
USA AL9105 = AL4005
USA AL9108 = AL4008
USA AL9127 = AL4027
USA AL9130 = AL4011
USA AL9164 = AL4026
USA AL9165 = AL4025

USA AM9501 =
USA AM9502 =
USA AM9503 =
USA AM9504 =
USA AM9505 =
USA AM9506 =
USA AM9507 =
USA AM9508 =
USA AM9510 =
USA AM9511 =
USA AM9512 =
USA AM9513 =
USA AM9526 =
USA AM9543 =
USA AM9544 =
USA AM9564 =

USA AN8601 = AN5001
USA AN8602 = AN5002
USA AN8603 = AN5003
USA AN8604 = AN5004
USA AN8610 = AN5010
USA AN8611 = AN5011
USA AN8661 = AN5022
USA AN8664 = AN5021
USA AN8665 = AN5020

USA AN9401 =
USA AN9402 =
USA AN9403 =
USA AN9404 =
USA AN9405 =
USA AN9406 =
USA AN9407 =
USA AN9408 =
USA AN9409 =
USA AN9410 =
USA AN9411 =
USA AN9412 =
USA AN9413 =
USA AN9426 =
USA AN9464 =

USA AP9505 =
USA AP9506 =
USA AP9507 =
USA AP9508 =
USA AP9510 =

USA AS8301 = AS7701
USA AS8302 = AS7702
USA AS8303 = AS7703
USA AS8304 = AS7704
USA AS8305 = AS7705
USA AS8306 = AS7706
USA AS8307 = AS7707
USA AS8308 = AS7708
USA AS8315 = AS7715
USA AS8316 = AS7716
USA AS8317 = AS7717
USA AS8318 = AS7718
USA AS8355 = AS7721
USA AS8356 = AS7722
USA AS8365 = AS7720

USA AS8426 = AS7761
USA AS8427 =
USA AS8431 = AS7731
USA AS8432 = AS7732
USA AS8433 = AS7733
USA AS8434 = AS7734
USA AS8435 = AS7735
USA AS8436 = AS7736
USA AS8437 = AS7737
USA AS8438 = AS7738
USA AS8439 = AS7739
USA AS8440 = AS7740
USA AS8441 = AS7741
USA AS8442 = AS7742
USA AS8450 = AS7750
USA AS8451 = AS7751
USA AS8455 = AS7763
USA AS8456 = AS7762
USA AS8465 = AS7760
USA AS8466 =

USA AS8571 = AS7771
USA AS8572 = AS7772
USA AS8573 = AS7773
USA AS8574 = AS7774
USA AS8575 = AS7775
USA AS8576 = AS7776
USA AS8577 = AS7777
USA AS8578 = AS7778
USA AS8579 = AS7779
USA AS8580 = AS7780
USA AS8581 = AS7781
USA AS8595 = AS7795

USA AS9201 =
USA AS9202 =
USA AS9203 =
USA AS9204 =
USA AS9205 =
USA AS9226 =
USA AS9230 =
USA AS9264 =

USA BA8601 = BA5501
USA BA8602 = BA5502
USA BA8603 = BA5503
USA BA8604 = BA5504
USA BA8605 = BA5505
USA BA8606 = BA5506
USA BA8607 = BA5507
USA BA8615 = BA5515
USA BA8616 = BA5516
USA BA8665 = BA5520

USA BA8801 = BA2001
USA BA8802 = BA2002
USA BA8803 = BA2003
USA BA8804 = BA2004
USA BA8805 = BA2005
USA BA8806 = BA2006
USA BA8807 = BA2007
USA BA8810 = BA2010
USA BA8811 = BA2011
USA BA8812 = BA2012
USA BA8813 = BA2013
USA BA8826 = BA2022
USA BA8841 = BA2023
USA BA8864 = BA2021
USA BA8865 = BA2020

USA BA9001 = BA4001
USA BA9002 = BA4002
USA BA9003 = BA4003
USA BA9004 = BA4004
USA BA9020 = BA4020
USA BA9021 = BA4021
USA BA9026 = BA4032
USA BA9064 = BA4031
USA BA9065 = BA4030

USA BA9126 = BA4082
USA BA9140 = BA4040
USA BA9141 = BA4041

USA BA9142 = BA4042
USA BA9143 = BA4043
USA BA9144 = BA4044
USA BA9145 = BA4045
USA BA9146 = BA4046
USA BA9147 = BA4047
USA BA9148 = BA4048
USA BA9149 = BA4049
USA BA9150 = BA4084
USA BA9163 = BA4063
USA BA9164 = BA4081
USA BA9165 = BA4080
USA BA9170 = BA4070
USA BA9171 = BA4071
USA BA9172 = BA4072
USA BA9173 = BA4073
USA BA9183 = BA4083

USA BA9201 =
USA BA9202 =
USA BA9203 =
USA BA9204 =
USA BA9205 =
USA BA9206 =
USA BA9207 =
USA BA9208 =
USA BA9217 =
USA BA9220 =
USA BA9221 =
USA BA9222 =
USA BA9223 =
USA BA9226 =
USA BA9264 =

USA BA9301 =
USA BA9302 =
USA BA9303 =
USA BA9304 =
USA BA9305 =
USA BA9306 =
USA BA9307 =
USA BA9317 =
USA BA9318 =
USA BA9326 =
USA BA9330 =
USA BA9364 =

USA BA9401 =
USA BA9402 =
USA BA9403 =
USA BA9404 =
USA BA9405 =
USA BA9406 =
USA BA9407 =
USA BA9408 =
USA BA9417 =
USA BA9419 =
USA BA9420 =
USA BA9421 =
USA BA9426 =
USA BA9430 =
USA BA9464 =

USA BB8601 = BE7301
USA BB8602 = BE7302
USA BB8603 = BE7303
USA BB8604 = BE7304
USA BB8610 = BE7310
USA BB8611 = BE7311
USA BB8612 = BE7312
USA BB8613 = BE7313
USA BB8664 = BE7321
USA BB8665 = BE7320

USA BB8720 = BE7520
USA BB8721 = BE7521
USA BB8722 = BE7522
USA BB8723 = BE7523
USA BB8724 = BE7524
USA BB8725 = BE7525
USA BB8726 = BE7542
USA BB8730 = BE7530
USA BB8731 = BE7531
USA BB8732 = BE7532
USA BB8733 = BE7633
USA BB8750 = BE7543
USA BB8764 = BE7541
USA BB8765 = BE7540
USA BB8795 =

USA BB9025 = BE7625
USA BB9026 = BE7626
USA BB9027 = BE7627
USA BB9028 = BE7628
USA BB9029 = BE7629
USA BB9030 = BE7630
USA BB9031 = BE7631
USA BB9032 = BE7632
USA BB9040 = BE7640
USA BB9041 = BE7641
USA BB9042 = BE7642
USA BB9043 = BE7643
USA BB9044 = BE7644
USA BB9045 = BE7645
USA BB9064 = BE7651
USA BB9065 = BE7650

USA BC8650 = BE1550
USA BC8651 = BE1551
USA BC8652 = BE1552
USA BC8665 = BE1556

USA BE8400 = BE0400
USA BE8401 = BE0401
USA BE8402 = BE0402

USA BE8505 = BE0505
USA BE8506 = BE0506
USA BE8507 = BE0507

USA BE8601 = BE0601
USA BE8602 = BE0602
USA BE8603 = BE0603
USA BE8607 = BE0607
USA BE8665 = BE0615

USA BE8901 = BE4001
USA BE8902 = BE4002
USA BE8903 = BE4003
USA BE8904 = BE4004
USA BE8910 = BE4010
USA BE8911 = BE4011
USA BE8912 = BE4012
USA BE8913 = BE4013
USA BE8964 = BE4021
USA BE8965 = BE4020

USA BE9041 = BE1193
USA BE9042 = BE1194
USA BE9064 = BE1192
USA BE9065 = BE1191
USA BE9070 = BE1170
USA BE9071 = BE1171
USA BE9072 = BE1172
USA BE9073 = BE1173
USA BE9074 = BE1174
USA BE9075 = BE1175
USA BE9076 = BE1176
USA BE9077 = BE1177
USA BE9085 = BE1185
USA BE9086 = BE1186
USA BE9087 = BE1187
USA BE9088 = BE1188

USA BE9201 =
USA BE9202 =
USA BE9203 =
USA BE9204 =
USA BE9226 =
USA BE9230 =
USA BE9264 =

USA BI8701 = BI3001
USA BI8702 = BI3002
USA BI8703 = BI3003
USA BI8704 = BI3004
USA BI8705 = BI3005
USA BI8706 = BI3006
USA BI8707 = BI3007
USA BI8708 = BI3008

USA BI8709 = BI3009
USA BI8710 = BI3010
USA BI8711 = BI3011
USA BI8712 = BI3012
USA BI8713 = BI3013
USA BI8714 = BI3014
USA BI8715 = BI3015
USA BI8716 = BI3016
USA BI8725 = BI3025
USA BI8764 = BI3031
USA BI8765 = BI3030

USA BI8801 = BI3401

USA BI9101 = MC2001
USA BI9102 = MC2002
USA BI9103 = MC2003
USA BI9104 = MC2004

USA BK9201 =
USA BK9202 =
USA BK9203 =
USA BK9204 =
USA BK9210 =
USA BK9211 =
USA BK9212 =
USA BK9213 =
USA BK9226 =
USA BK9264 =

USA BL8800 = BL1300
USA BL8801 = BL1301
USA BL8805 = BL1305
USA BL8865 =

USA BO8700 = BO1500
USA BO8701 = BO1501
USA BO8702 = BO1502
USA BO8703 = BO1503
USA BO8704 =
USA BO8705 =
USA BO8706 = BO1506
USA BO8707 =
USA BO8764 = BO1511
USA BO8765 = BO1510

USA BO9401 =
USA BO9402 =
USA BO9403 =
USA BO9404 =
USA BO9405 =
USA BO9410 =
USA BO9411 =
USA BO9412 =
USA BO9413 =
USA BO9426 =
USA BO9464 =

USA BP8901 = MC1101
USA BP8902 = MC1102
USA BP8903 = MC1103
USA BP8964 = MC1106
USA BP8965 = MC1105

USA BR9101 =
USA BR9150 =
USA BR9164 =

USA BT8955 = BE1155
USA BT8956 = BE1156
USA BT8957 = BE1157
USA BT8958 = BE1157
USA BT8960 = BE1160
USA BT8970 = BE1150
USA BT8971 = BD1151
USA BT8972 = BE1152
USA BT8973 = BE1153

USA BT9201 =
USA BT9202 =
USA BT9203 =
USA BT9205 =
USA BT9226 =
USA BT9230 =
USA BT9264 =
USA BT9295 =
USA BT9296 =

USA BT9301 =
USA BT9302 =
USA BT9303 =
USA BT9304 =
USA BT9305 =
USA BT9306 =
USA BT9307 =
USA BT9308 =
USA BT9309 =
USA BT9310 =
USA BT9311 =
USA BT9312 =
USA BT9313 =
USA BT9326 =
USA BT9364 =

USA BU8910 =
USA BU8911 =
USA BU9064 =
USA BU9065 =

USA CA8700 = CA7500
USA CA8701 = CA7501
USA CA8702 = CA7502
USA CA8703 = CA7503
USA CA8764 = CA7516
USA CA8765 = CA7515

USA CA9000 = CA6300
USA CA9001 = CA6301
USA CA9002 = CA6302
USA CA9003 = CA6303
USA CA9004 = CA6304
USA CA9010 = CA6310
USA CA9064 = CA6315
USA CA9065 = CA6316

USA CH8701 = CH1001
USA CH8702 = CH1002
USA CH8703 = CH1003
USA CH8704 = CH1004
USA CH8705 = CH1005
USA CH8706 = CH1006
USA CH8710 = CH1010
USA CH8711 = CH1011
USA CH8764 = CH1021
USA CH8765 = CH1020
USA CH8766 = CH1023
USA CH8767 = CH1022

USA CH8926 = CH4072
USA CH8950 = CH4050
USA CH8951 = CH4051
USA CH8952 = CH4052
USA CH8953 = CH4053
USA CH8954 = CH4054
USA CH8955 = CH4055
USA CH8960 = CH4060
USA CH8961 = CH4061
USA CH8962 = CH4062
USA CH8963 = CH4063
USA CH8964 = CH4071
USA CH8965 = CH4070

USA CI7905 = CI6805
USA CI7906 = CI6806
USA CI7907 = CI6807
USA CI7908 = CI6805
USA CI7909 = CI6805
USA CI7926 = CI6853
USA CI7930 = CI6830
USA CI7931 = CI6831
USA CI7932 = CI6832
USA CI7933 = CI6833
USA CI7934 = CI6834
USA CI7935 = CI6835
USA CI7941 = CI6852
USA CI7954 = CI6854
USA CI7965 = CI6850
USA CI7966 = CI6851

USA CI8301 = CI6001
USA CI8302 = CI6002
USA CI8303 = CI6003
USA CI8304 = CI6004
USA CI8305 = CI6005
USA CI8306 = CI6006
USA CI8307 = CI6007
USA CI8308 = CI6008
USA CI8309 = CI6009
USA CI8315 = CI6015
USA CI8316 = CI6016
USA CI8317 = CI6017
USA CI8318 = CI6018
USA CI8319 = CI6019
USA CI8320 = CI6020
USA CI8326 = CI6026
USA CI8327 = CI6027
USA CI8365 = CI6025

USA CI9101 = CI6701
USA CI9102 = CI6702
USA CI9103 = CI6703
USA CI9104 = CI6704
USA CI9130 = CI6710
USA CI9164 = CI6716
USA CI9165 = CI6715
USA CI9166 = CI6717

USA CM9000 = CA3100
USA CM9001 = CA3101
USA CM9002 = CA3102
USA CM9003 = CA3103
USA CM9004 = CA3104
USA CM9005 = CA3105
USA CM9010 = CA3110
USA CM9011 = CA3111
USA CM9012 = CA3112
USA CM9013 = CA3113
USA CM9014 = CA3114
USA CM9015 = CA3115
USA CM9050 =
USA CM9064 = CA3121
USA CM9065 = CA3120

USA CO8500 = CO2000
USA CO8501 = CO2001
USA CO8502 = CO2002
USA CO8503 = CO2003
USA CO8504 =
USA CO8505 =
USA CO8506 =
USA CO8507 =

USA CO8601 = CO1501
USA CO8602 = CO1502
USA CO8603 = CO1503
USA CO8604 = CO1504
USA CO8605 = CO1505
USA CO8606 = CO1506
USA CO8607 = CO1507
USA CO8610 = CO1510
USA CO8611 = CO1511
USA CO8612 = CO1512
USA CO8613 = CO1513
USA CO8661 = CO1522
USA CO8664 = CO1521
USA CO8665 = CO1520

USA CO8801 = CO5501
USA CO8802 = CO5502
USA CO8803 = CO5503
USA CO8804 = CO5504
USA CO8805 = CO5505
USA CO8806 = CO5506
USA CO8810 = CO5510
USA CO8811 = CO5511
USA CO8812 = CO5512
USA CO8813 = CO5513
USA CO8864 = CO5521
USA CO8865 = CO5520

USA CO9100 = CO3200
USA CO9101 = CO3201
USA CO9102 = CO3202
USA CO9103 = CO3203

USA CP9201 =
USA CP9202 =
USA CP9203 =
USA CP9204 =
USA CP9205 =
USA CP9211 =
USA CP9226 =
USA CP9230 =
USA CP9264 =

USA CP9401 =
USA CP9402 =
USA CP9403 =
USA CP9404 =
USA CP9409 =
USA CP9426 =
USA CP9430 =
USA CP9464 =

USA CR8510 = CR1960
USA CR8511 = CR1961
USA CR8512 = CR1962
USA CR8513 = CR1963
USA CR8526 = CR1968
USA CR8543 =
USA CR8550 = CR1950
USA CR8551 = CR1951
USA CR8552 = CR1952
USA CR8553 = CR1953
USA CR8555 =
USA CR8561 = CR1966
USA CR8564 = CR1967
USA CR8565 = CR1965

USA CR8601 = CR1701
USA CR8602 = CR1702
USA CR8603 = CR1703
USA CR8604 = CR1704
USA CR8605 =
USA CR8606 =
USA CR8610 = CR1710
USA CR8611 = CR1711
USA CR8665 = CR1715

USA CR8725 = CR1725
USA CR8726 = CR1726
USA CR8727 = CR1727
USA CR8728 = CR1728
USA CR8729 = CR1729
USA CR8735 = CR1735
USA CR8736 = CR1736
USA CR8737 = CR1737
USA CR8738 = CR1738
USA CR8745 =
USA CR8750 =
USA CR8760 = CR1744
USA CR8761 = CR1742
USA CR8763 = CR1743
USA CR8764 = CR1741
USA CR8765 = CR1740

USA CR9101 = CR2001
USA CR9102 = CR2002
USA CR9103 = CR2003
USA CR9104 = CR2004

USA CR9201 = CR1801
USA CR9202 = CR1802
USA CR9203 = CR1803
USA CR9204 = CR1804
USA CR9230 = CR1810
USA CR9264 = CR1816
USA CR9265 = CR1815

USA CS9230 = CR1790

USA CX8600 = CO3500
USA CX8601 = CO3501
USA CX8602 = CO3502
USA CX8603 = CO3503
USA CX8610 = CO3510
USA CX8611 = CO3511
USA CX8626 = CO3516
USA CX8665 = CO3515

USA DA8035 = DA4035
USA DA8036 = DA4036
USA DA8037 = DA4037

USA DA8525 = DA8525
USA DA8526 = DA8526

USA DE8710 = DE6010

USA DE8711 = DE6011
USA DE8712 = DE6012
USA DE8713 = DE6013
USA DI8100 = DI1200
USA DI8101 = DI1201
USA DI8102 = DI1202
USA DI8103 = DI1203
USA DI8104 = DI1204
USA DI8105 = DI1205
USA DI8106 = DI1206
USA DI8107 = DI1207
USA DI8108 = DI1208
USA DI8109 = DI1209
USA DI8110 = DI1210
USA DI8111 = DI1211
USA DI8112 = DI1212
USA DI8115 =
USA DI8116 =
USA DI8117 =
USA DI8118 =
USA DI8119 =
USA DI8120 =
USA DI8121 =
USA DI8122 =
USA DI8123 =
USA DI8125 = DI1225
USA DI8126 = DI1226
USA DI8127 = DI1227
USA DI8128 = DI1228
USA DI8129 = DI1229
USA DI8130 = DI1230
USA DI8136 =
USA DI8137 =
USA DI8138 =
USA DI8139 =
USA DI8140 =
USA DI8141 =
USA DI8142 =
USA DI8165 = DI1235

USA DI8700 = DI3300
USA DI8701 = DI3301
USA DI8702 = DI3302
USA DI8703 = DI3303
USA DI8710 = DI3310
USA DI8711 = DI3311
USA DI8763 = DI3322
USA DI8764 = DI3321
USA DI8765 = DI3320

USA DI8900 = DI1300
USA DI8901 = DI1301
USA DI8902 = DI1302
USA DI8903 = DI1303
USA DI8930 = DI1310
USA DI8964 = DI1316
USA DI8965 = DI1315

USA DI9000 = DI1100
USA DI9001 = DI1101
USA DI9002 = DI1102
USA DI9003 = DI1103
USA DI9004 = DI1104
USA DI9005 = DI1105
USA DI9010 = DI1110

USA DI9064 = DI1116
USA DI9065 = DI1115

USA DI9125 = DI3025
USA DI9126 = DI3026
USA DI9127 = DI3027
USA DI9128 = DI3028
USA DI9130 = DI3030
USA DI9164 = DI3036
USA DI9165 = DI3035

USA DI9301 =
USA DI9302 =
USA DI9303 =
USA DI9304 =
USA DI9305 =
USA DI9306 =
USA DI9307 =
USA DI9310 =
USA DI9311 =
USA DI9312 =
USA DI9313 =
USA DI9326 =
USA DI9364 =

USA DO9000 = MC4500
USA DO9001 = MC4501
USA DO9002 = MC4502
USA DO9003 = MC4503
USA DO9004 = MC4504
USA DO9005 = MC4505
USA DO9006 = MC4506
USA DO9007 = MC4507
USA DO9010 = MC4510
USA DO9011 = MC4511
USA DO9064 = MC4516
USA DO9065 = MC4515

USA DT8801 = DU1001
USA DT8802 = DU1002
USA DT8803 = DU1003
USA DT8804 = DU1004
USA DT8805 = DU1005
USA DT8810 = DU1010
USA DT8811 = DU1011
USA DT8812 = DU1012
USA DT8813 = DU1013
USA DT8864 = DU1021
USA DT8865 = DU1020

USA DU8200 = DU1200
USA DU8201 = DU1201
USA DU8202 = DU1202
USA DU8203 = DU1203
USA DU8204 = DU1204
USA DU8205 =
USA DU8206 =
USA DU8207 = DU1207
USA DU8208 =
USA DU8209 =
USA DU8210 = DU1210
USA DU8211 = DU1211
USA DU8212 = DU1212
USA DU8213 = DU1213
USA DU8214 = DU1214

USA DU8215 = DU1215
USA DU8226 = DU1228
USA DU8241 = DU1227
USA DU8265 = DU1225
USA DU8266 = DU1226

USA DU8830 = DU1030
USA DU8831 = DU1031
USA DU8832 = DU1032
USA DU8833 = DU1033
USA DU8834 = DU1034
USA DU8835 =
USA DU8840 = DU1040
USA DU8864 = DU1046
USA DU8865 = DU1045

USA EA9401 =
USA EA9402 =
USA EA9403 =
USA EA9404 =
USA EA9405 =
USA EA9426 =
USA EA9430 =
USA EA9464 =

USA ET8500 = ET7000
USA ET8501 = ET7001
USA ET8502 = ET7002
USA ET8503 = ET7003
USA ET8510 = ET7010
USA ET8511 = ET7011
USA ET8523 = ET7023
USA ET8524 = ET7024
USA ET8541 =
USA ET8561 = ET7025
USA ET8562 = ET7026
USA ET8563 = ET7020
USA ET8564 = ET7022
USA ET8565 = ET7021

USA EX8200 = MC4800
USA EX8201 = MC4801
USA EX8202 = MC4802
USA EX8203 = MC4803
USA EX8206 = MC4806
USA EX8207 =
USA EX8208 =
USA EX8209 =
USA EX8226 = MC4812
USA EX8241 = MC4813
USA EX8250 =
USA EX8261 = MC4811
USA EX8262 = MC4814
USA EX8265 = MC4810

USA FA8401 =
USA FA8402 =
USA FA8403 =
USA FA8404 =

USA FA8505 =
USA FA8506 =
USA FA8507 =
USA FA8508 =
USA FA8515 =

USA FA8516 =
USA FA8526 =
USA FA8565 =

USA FB9001 = FR2001
USA FB9002 = FR2002
USA FB9003 = FR2003
USA FB9004 = FR2004
USA FB9005 = FR2005
USA FB9010 = FR2010
USA FB9064 = FR2016
USA FB9065 = FR2015

USA FE8501 = FE1001
USA FE8502 = FE1002
USA FE8503 = FE1003
USA FE8504 = FE1004
USA FE8505 = FE1005
USA FE8506 = FE1006
USA FE8515 = FE1015
USA FE8516 = FE1016
USA FE8517 = FE1017
USA FE8518 = FE1018
USA FE8561 = FE1027
USA FE8563 = FE1-28
USA FE8564 = FE1026
USA FE8565 = FE1025

USA FF8900 = FU5200
USA FF8901 = FU5201
USA FF8902 = FU5202
USA FF8903 = FU5203

USA FF9001 = FU5210
USA FF9002 = FR5211
USA FF9003 = FU5212
USA FF9004 = FU5213
USA FF9005 = FU5214
USA FF9006 = FU5215
USA FF9007 = FU5216
USA FF9008 = FU5217
USA FF9009 = FU5218
USA FF9010 = FU5219
USA FF9015 = FU5225
USA FF9016 = FU5226
USA FF9017 = FU5227
USA FF9018 = FU5228
USA FF9026 = FU5237
USA FF9045 =
USA FF9064 = FU5236
USA FF9065 = FU5235

USA FI9301 =
USA FI9302 =
USA FI9303 =
USA FI9304 =
USA FI9326 =
USA FI9330 =
USA FI9364 =

USA FI9401 =
USA FI9402 =
USA FI9403 =
USA FI9404 =
USA FI9405 =

USA FI9406 =
USA FI9407 =
USA FI9408 =
USA FI9409 =
USA FI9410 =
USA FI9411 =
USA FI9412 =
USA FI9413 =
USA FI9414 =
USA FI9415 =
USA FI9416 =
USA FI9417 =
USA FI9420 =
USA FI9421 =
USA FI9422 =
USA FI9423 =
USA FI9425 =
USA FI9426 =
USA FI9464 =

USA FL8550 = BE0550
USA FL8551 = BE0551
USA FL8552 = BE0552

USA FL8801 = FL4001
USA FL8802 = FL4002
USA FL8803 = FL4003
USA FL8804 = FL4004
USA FL8805 = FL4005
USA FL8810 = FL4010
USA FL8864 =
USA FL8865 = FL4015

USA FL9401 =
USA FL9402 =
USA FL9403 =
USA FL9404 =
USA FL9405 =
USA FL9406 =
USA FL9426 =
USA FL9430 =
USA FL9450 =
USA FL9464 =
USA FL9495 =
USA FL9496 =

USA FO9301 =
USA FO9302 =
USA FO9303 =
USA FO9304 =
USA FO9305 =
USA FO9326 =
USA FO9330 =
USA FO9364 =

USA FR8700 = FR1100
USA FR8701 = FR1101
USA FR8702 = FR1102
USA FR8703 = FR1103

USA FR8820 = FR1120
USA FR8821 = FR1121
USA FR8822 = FR1122
USA FR8823 = FR1123
USA FR8824 = FR1124
USA FR8825 = FR1125
USA FR8826 = FR1143
USA FR8830 = FR1130
USA FR8831 = FR1131
USA FR8832 = FR1132
USA FR8833 = FR1133
USA FR8841 = FR1142
USA FR8845 = FR1144
USA FR8850 = FR1145
USA FR8851 =
USA FR8852 =
USA FR8853 =
USA FR8864 = FR1141
USA FR8865 = FR1140
USA FR8895 =
USA FR8896 =

USA FR9001 = FR1501
USA FR9002 = FR1502
USA FR9010 = FR1510
USA FR9064 = FR1516
USA FR9065 = FR1515

USA FR9101 = FR1301
USA FR9102 = FR1302
USA FR9103 =
USA FR9104 =
USA FR9105 =
USA FR9110 = FR1310
USA FR9111 = FR1311
USA FR9112 = FR1312
USA FR9114 =
USA FR9115 =
USA FR9126 =
USA FR9141 =
USA FR9150 =
USA FR9155 =
USA FR9156 =
USA FU7701 = FU7001
USA FU7702 = FU7002
USA FU7703 = FU7003
USA FU7704 = FU7004
USA FU7705 = FU7005
USA FU7706 = FU7006
USA FU7707 = FU7007
USA FU7708 = FU7008
USA FU7709 = FU7009
USA FU7710 = FU7010
USA FU7711 = FU7011
USA FU7712 = FU7012
USA FU7713 = FU7013
USA FU7714 = FU7014
USA FU7715 = FU7015
USA FU7716 = FU7016
USA FU7717 = FU7017
USA FU7718 = FU7018
USA FU7719 = FU7019
USA FU7720 = FU7020
USA FU7721 = FU7021
USA FU7722 = FU7022
USA FU7723 = FU7023
USA FU7724 = FU7024
USA FU7725 = FU7025
USA FU7726 = FU7026
USA FU7727 = FU7027
USA FU7728 = FU7028
USA FU7729 = FU7029
USA FU7730 = FU7030
USA FU7731 = FU7031
USA FU7732 =
USA FU7735 = FU7035
USA FU7736 = FU7036
USA FU7737 = FU7037
USA FU7738 = FU7038
USA FU7739 = FU7039
USA FU7740 = FU7040

USA FU8900 = FU5000
USA FU8901 = FU5001
USA FU8902 = FU5002
USA FU8903 = FU5003
USA FU8907 = FU5007
USA FU8908 = FU5008
USA FU8909 = FU5009
USA FU8910 = FU5010
USA FU8964 = FU5016
USA FU8965 = FU5015

USA GA8801 = GA5501
USA GA8802 = GA5502
USA GA8803 = GA5503
USA GA8804 = GA5504

USA GA8901 = GA6001
USA GA8902 = GA6002
USA GA8903 = GA6003
USA GA8904 = GA6004
USA GA8905 = GA6005
USA GA8906 = GA6006
USA GA8910 = GA6010
USA GA8911 = GA6011
USA GA8912 = GA6012
USA GA8913 = GA6013
USA GA8914 = GA6014
USA GA8926 = GA6022
USA GA8941 = GA6023
USA GA8950 =
USA GA8951 =
USA GA8952 =
USA GA8964 = GA6021
USA GA8965 = GA6020

USA GE7901 = GE4101
USA GE7902 = GE4102
USA GE7903 = GE4103
USA GE7904 = GE4104
USA GE7905 = GE4105
USA GE7906 = GE4106
USA GE7907 = GE4107
USA GE7908 = GE4108
USA GE7909 = GE4109
USA GE7910 = GE4110
USA GE7911 = GE4111
USA GE7912 = GE4112
USA GE7913 = GE4113
USA GE7914 = GE4114
USA GE7915 = GE4115
USA GE7916 = GE4116
USA GE7917 = GE4117
USA GE7918 = GE4118
USA GE7919 = GE4119
USA GE7920 = GE4120
USA GE7921 = GE4121
USA GE7930 = GE4130
USA GE7931 = GE4131
USA GE7932 = GE4132
USA GE7933 = GE4133
USA GE7934 = GE4134
USA GE7941 = GE4141
USA GE7945 = GE4142
USA GE7965 = GE4140

USA GE7951 =

USA GE8001 =
USA GE8003 =
USA GE8006 =
USA GE8009 =
USA GE8012 =
USA GE8013 =
USA GE8014 =
USA GE8015 =
USA GE8016 =
USA GE8101 =
USA GE8103 =
USA GE8105 =
USA GE8107 =
USA GE8108 =
USA GE8109 =
USA GE8110 =
USA GE8113 =
USA GE8116 =
USA GE8119 =
USA GE8120 =
USA GE8121 =
USA GE8122 =
USA GE8123 =

USA GE8201 =
USA GE8202 =
USA GE8203 =
USA GE8204 =
USA GE8205 =
USA GE8206 =
USA GE8207 =
USA GE8208 =
USA GE8209 =
USA GE8210 =
USA GE8211 =
USA GE8212 =
USA GE8213 =
USA GE8214 =
USA GE8215 =
USA GE8216 =
USA GE8217 =
USA GE8218 =
USA GE8219 =
USA GE8220 =
USA GE8221 =
USA GE8222 =
USA GE8223 =

USA GE8301 =
USA GE8302 =

USA GE8401 =

USA GE8601 =
USA GE8602 =
USA GE8603 =
USA GE8605 =
USA GE8608 =
USA GE8609 =
USA GE8610 =
USA GE8611 =
USA GE8612 =
USA GE8613 =
USA GE8614 =

USA GE8701 =
USA GE8703 =
USA GE8705 =
USA GE8706 =
USA GE8707 =

USA GE8801 =
USA GE8802 =
USA GE8803 =
USA GE8804 =
USA GE8805 =
USA GE8806 =
USA GE8807 =
USA GE8808 =
USA GE8810 =
USA GE8811 =

USA GE8900 = RA4000
USA GE8901 = RA4001
USA GE8950 =

USA GE9001 =
USA GE9002 =
USA GE9003 =

USA GE9401 =
USA GE9402 =
USA GE9403 =
USA GE9404 =
USA GE9405 =
USA GE9406 =
USA GE9407 =
USA GE9409 =
USA GE9410 =
USA GE9411 =
USA GE9412 =

USA GE9501 =
USA GE9502 =

USA GI8200 = GI4500
USA GI8201 = GI4501
USA GI8202 = GI4502
USA GI8203 = GI4503
USA GI8204 = GI4504
USA GI8205 = GI4505
USA GI8220 =
USA GI8221 =
USA GI8222 =
USA GI8223 =
USA GI8224 =

USA GI8261 = GI4511
USA GI8262 = GI4512
USA GI8265 = GI4510

USA GO8201 = GO3001
USA GO8202 = GO3002
USA GO8203 = GO3003
USA GO8204 = GO3004
USA GO8205 = GO3005
USA GO8206 = GO3006
USA GO8220 =
USA GO8222 =
USA GO8223 =
USA GO8224 =
USA GO8225 =
USA GO8261 = GO3011
USA GO8265 = GO3010
USA GO8401 = GO5701
USA GO8402 = GO5702
USA GO8403 = GO5703
USA GO8404 = GO5704
USA GO8405 = GO5705
USA GO8406 = GO5706
USA GO8415 = GO5715
USA GO8416 = GO5716
USA GO8417 = GO5717
USA GO8418 = GO5718
USA GO8461 = GO5726
USA GO8462 = GO5727
USA GO8465 = GO5725

USA GO8700 = GO5300
USA GO8701 = GO5301
USA GO8764 = GO5306
USA GO8765 = GO5305

USA GO9130 = GO5460
USA GO9150 = GO5450
USA GO9151 = GO5451
USA GO9152 = GO5452
USA GO9153 = GO5453
USA GO9154 =
USA GO9164 = GO5466
USA GO9165 = GO5465

USA GR9101 = GR1101
USA GR9102 = GR1102
USA GR9103 = GR1103
USA GR9104 = GR1104
USA GR9105 = GR1105
USA GR9130 = GR1110
USA GR9164 = GR1116
USA GR9165 = GR1115
USA GR9166 =
USA GR9167 =

USA HA8500 = HA1500
USA HA8501 = HA1501
USA HA8502 = HA1502
USA HA8503 = HA1503
USA HA8504 = HA1504
USA HA8565 = HA1510

USA HA8601 = HA1515
USA HA8602 = HA1516

USA HA8603 = HA1517
USA HA8661 = HA1521
USA HA8665 = HA1520

USA HA8701 = HA1525
USA HA8702 = HA1526
USA HA8703 = HA1527
USA HA8764 = HA1531
USA HA8765 = HA1530

USA HA8941 = HA1541
USA HA8942 = HA1542
USA HA8964 = HA1546
USA HA8965 = HA1545

USA HA9055 = HA1555
USA HA9056 = HA1556
USA HA9057 = HA1557
USA HA9064 = HA1566
USA HA9065 = HA1565

USA HA9100 = MC1000
USA HA9101 = MC1001
USA HA9102 = MC1002
USA HA9103 = MC1003
USA HA9104 = MC1004
USA HA9105 = MC1005
USA HA9106 =
USA HA9107 =
USA HA9141 = MC1012
USA HA9164 = MC1011
USA HA9165 = MC1010

USA HA9201 =
USA HA9202 =
USA HA9203 =
USA HA9226 =
USA HA9264 =

USA HA9301 =
USA HA9302 =
USA HA9303 =
USA HA9304 =
USA HA9305 =
USA HA9306 =
USA HA9307 =
USA HA9310 =
USA HA9311 =
USA HA9312 =
USA HA9313 =
USA HA9326 =
USA HA9364 =

USA HA9401 =
USA HA9402 =
USA HA9403 =
USA HA9426 =
USA HA9464 =

USA HH8400 = HA5000
USA HH8401 = HA5001
USA HH8405 = HA5005
USA HH8406 = HA5006
USA HH8461 = HA5011
USA HH8462 = HA5012

USA HH8463 = HA5013
USA HH8465 = HA5010

USA HI8601 =
USA HI8602 = HI4501
USA HI8610 = HI4502
USA HI8664 = HI4516
USA HI8665 = HI4515

USA HO7501 =
USA HO7502 =
USA HO7530 =

USA HO8001 =
USA HO8002 =
USA HO8003 =
USA HO8004 =
USA HO8010 =
USA HO8011 =
USA HO8012 =

USA HO9100 = HO4500
USA HO9101 = HO4501
USA HO9102 = HO4502
USA HO9103 = HO4503
USA HO9110 = HO4510
USA HO9111 = HO4511
USA HO9112 = HO4512
USA HO9113 = HO4513
USA HO9126 = HO4522
USA HO9164 = HO4521
USA HO9165 = HO4520

USA HP8350 = HA5650
USA HP8351 = HA5651
USA HP8352 = HA5652
USA HP8365 = HA5655

USA HP8426 = HA5682
USA HP8461 = HA5681
USA HP8465 = HA5680
USA HP8470 = HA5670
USA HP8471 = HA5671
USA HP8472 = HA5672
USA HP8473 = HA5673

USA HP8626 = HA5698
USA HP8641 = HA5600
USA HP8660 = HA5699
USA HP8664 = HA5697
USA HP8665 = HA5696
USA HP8690 = HA5690
USA HP8691 = HA5691
USA HP8692 = HA5692
USA HP8693 = HA5693
USA HP8694 = HA5694

USA HT8320 = HA5720
USA HT8321 =
USA HT8365 = HA5730

USA HT9000 = HA8000
USA HT9001 = HA8001
USA HT9002 = HA8002
USA HT9003 = HA8003

USA HT9064 = HA8011
USA HT9065 = HA8010
USA HW8321 =
USA HW8326 =
USA HW8330 =
USA HW8331 =
USA HW8332 =
USA HW8333 =
USA HW8334 =
USA HW8335 =
USA HW8336 =
USA HW8337 =
USA HW8338 =
USA HW8339 =
USA HW8340 =
USA HW8341 =
USA HW8342 =
USA HW8343 =
USA HW8344 =
USA HW8345 =
USA HW8346 =
USA HW8347 =
USA HW8348 =
USA HW8349 =
USA HW8350 =
USA HW8351 =
USA HW8352 =
USA HW8355 =
USA HW8361 =
USA HW8365 =

USA HW8800 = HO7000
USA HW8801 = HO7001
USA HW8802 = HO7002
USA HW8803 = HO7003
USA HW8804 = HO7004
USA HW8805 = HO7005
USA HW8806 = HO7006
USA HW8807 = HO7007
USA HW8808 = HO7008
USA HW8809 = HO7009
USA HW8810 = HO7010
USA HW8811 = HO7011
USA HW8812 =
USA HW8813 =
USA HW8814 =
USA HW8815 =
USA HW8816 =
USA HW8817 =
USA HW8818 =
USA HW8819 =
USA HW8820 = HO7020
USA HW8826 = HO7027
USA HW8864 = HO7026
USA HW8865 = HO7025

USA HW9011 = BA4011
USA HW9012 = BA4012
USA HW9013 = BA4013
USA HW9014 = BA4014

USA HW9155 = BA4055
USA HW9156 = BA4056
USA HW9157 = BA4057
USA HW9158 = BA4058

USA HW9159 = BA4059
USA HW9160 = BA4060
USA HW9161 = BA4061
USA HW9162 = BA4062

USA HW9309 =
USA HW9310 =
USA HW9311 =
USA HW9312 =
USA HW9313 =
USA HW9314 =
USA HW9315 =
USA HW9316 =

USA HW9409 =
USA HW9410 =
USA HW9411 =
USA HW9412 =
USA HW9413 =
USA HW9414 =
USA HW9415 =
USA HW9416 =

USA HW9505 =
USAHW9506 =
USAHW9507 =
USAHW9508 =
USAHW9510 =

USA IL9000 = IL3000
USA IL9001 = IL3001
USA IL9002 = IL3002
USA IL9003 = IL3003
USA IL9026 = IL3017
USA IL9030 = IL3010
USA IL9031 = IL3011
USA IL9064 = IL3016
USA IL9065 = IL3015

USA JU8300 = MC5400
USA JU8301 = MC5401
USA JU8302 = MC5402
USA JU8303 = MC5403
USA JU8304 = MC5404
USA JU8305 = MC5405
USA JU8306 = MC5406
USA JU8307 = MC5407
USA JU8310 = MC5410
USA JU8311 = MC5411
USA JU8312 = MC5412
USA JU8313 = MC5413
USA JU8314 = MC5414
USA JU8315 = MC5415
USA JU8324 =
USA JU8361 = MC5421
USA JU8362 = MC5422
USA JU8363 = MC5423
USA JU8365 = MC5420

USA JU9000 = JU8500
USA JU9001 = JU8501
USA JU9002 = JU8502
USA JU9003 = JU8503
USA JU9004 = JU8504
USA JU9005 = JU8505

USA JU9010 = JU8510
USA JU9011 = JU8511
USA JU9012 = JU8512
USA JU9013 = JU8513
USA JU9026 = JU8522
USA JU9041 = JU8523
USA JU9050 = JU8524
USA JU9051 =
USA JU9052 =
USA JU9064 = JU8521
USA JU9065 = JU8520
USA JU9095 =

USA KI8701 = KI5001
USA KI8702 = KI5002
USA KI8703 = KI5003
USA KI8704 = KI5004
USA KI8705 = KI5005
USA KI8706 = KI5006
USA KI8707 = KI5007
USA KI8708 = KI5008
USA KI8715 = KI5015
USA KI8764 = KI5021
USA KI8765 = KI5020

USA LB8710 = LU5810
USA LB8711 = LU5811
USA LB8712 = LU5812
USA LB8713 = LU5813
USA LB8716 = LU5816
USA LB8717 =
USA LB8718 =
USA LB8719 =
USA LB8765 = LU5820

USA LE8301 = LE2001
USA LE8302 = LE2002
USA LE8303 = LE2003
USA LE8304 = LE2004
USA LE8305 = LE2005
USA LE8306 = LE2006
USA LE8307 = LE2007
USA LE8308 = LE2008
USA LE8310 = LE2010
USA LE8311 = LE2011
USA LE8365 = LE2015

USA LE8401 = LE2025
USA LE8402 = LE2026
USA LE8403 = LE2027
USA LE8404 = LE2028
USA LE8405 = LE2029
USA LE8406 = LE2030
USA LE8426 = LE2042
USA LE8435 = LE2035
USA LE8436 = LE2036
USA LE8437 = LE2037
USA LE8438 = LE2038
USA LE8441 = LE2043
USA LE8455 = LE2044
USA LE8461 = LE2041
USA LE8465 = LE2040

USA LE8504 = LE2504
USA LE8505 = LE2505

USA LE8506 = LE2506
USA LE8507 = LE2507
USA LE8515 = LE2515
USA LE8516 = LE2516
USA LE8517 = LE2517
USA LE8518 = LE2518
USA LE8526 = LE2523
USA LE8565 = LE2520
USA LE8566 = LE2521
USA LE8567 = LE2522

USA LE8600 = LE2200
USA LE8601 = LE2201
USA LE8602 = LE2202
USA LE8603 = LE2203
USA LE8604 = LE2204
USA LE8605 = LE2205
USA LE8610 = LE2210
USA LE8611 = LE2211
USA LE8612 = LE2212
USA LE8613 = LE2213
USA LE8626 = LE2223
USA LE8641 =
USA LE8661 = LE2222
USA LE8664 = LE2221
USA LE8665 = LE2220

USA LE8900 = LE2700
USA LE8901 = LE2701
USA LE8902 = LE2702
USA LE8903 = LE2703
USA LE8904 = LE2704
USA LE8905 = LE2705
USA LE8906 = LE2706
USA LE8907 = LE2707
USA LE8908 = LE2708
USA LE8909 = LE2709
USA LE8915 = LE2715
USA LE8916 = LE2716
USA LE8917 = LE2717
USA LE8918 = LE2718
USA LE8926 = LE2727
USA LE8963 = LE2728
USA LE8964 = LE2726
USA LE8965 = LE2725

USA LG8964 = LI3496
USA LG8965 = LI3495
USA LG8975 = LI3475
USA LG8976 = LI3576
USA LG8977 = LI3477
USA LG8978 = LI3478
USA LG8979 = LI3479
USA LG8985 = LI3485
USA LG8986 = LI3486
USA LG8987 = LI3487
USA LG8988 = LI3488

USA LI8250 = LI3550
USA LI8251 = LI3551
USA LI8252 = LI3552
USA LI8253 = LI3553
USA LI8254 = LI3554
USA LI8258 = LI3558
USA LI8265 = LI3560

USA LI8271 = LI3561
USA LI8272 = LI3562
USA LI8273 = LI3563
USA LI8274 = LI3564
USA LI8275 = LI3565
USA LI8276 = LI3566
USA LI8277 = LI3567

USA LI8700 = LI3400
USA LI8701 = LI3401
USA LI8702 = LI3402
USA LI8703 = LI3403
USA LI8704 = LI3404
USA LI8705 = LI3405
USA LI8706 =
USA LI8707 = LI3406
USA LI8708 =
USA LI8710 = LI3410
USA LI8711 = LI3411
USA LI8712 = LI3412
USA LI8713 = LI3413
USA LI8763 = LI3420
USA LI8764 = LI3419
USA LI8765 = LI3418

USA LI8900 = LI3900
USA LI8901 = LI3901
USA LI8902 = LI3902
USA LI8903 = LI3903
USA LI8910 = LI3910
USA LI8911 = LI3911
USA LI8912 = LI3912
USA LI8913 = LI3913
USA LI8916 = LI3916
USA LI8917 = LI3917
USA LI8964 = LI3921
USA LI8965 = LI3920

USA LI9301 =
USA LI9302 =
USA LI9303 =
USA LI9304 =

USA LO8000 = LO5600
USA LO8001 = LO5601
USA LO8002 = LO5602
USA LO8003 = LO5603
USA LO8042 = LO5610

USA LO9301 =
USA LO9302 =
USA LO9303 =
USA LO9304 =
USA LO9305 =
USA LO9306 =
USA LO9307 =
USA LO9310 =
USA LO9311 =
USA LO9312 =
USA LO9313 =
USA LO9326 =
USA LO9364 =

USA LU8500 = LU5200
USA LU8501 = LU5201
USA LU8502 = LU5202
USA LU8503 = LU5203
USA LU8565 =

USA LU8700 = LU5800
USA LU8701 = LU5801
USA LU8702 = LU5802
USA LU8703 = LU5803

USA LU8801 =
USA LU8802 =
USA LU8803 =
USA LU8804 =

USA MA8500 = MA3500
USA MA8501 = MA3501
USA MA8502 = MA3502
USA MA8503 = MA3503
USA MA8504 =
USA MA8510 = MA3510
USA MA8511 = MA3511
USA MA8512 = MA3512
USA MA8513 = MA3513
USA MA8561 = MA3522
USA MA8562 = MA3523
USA MA8564 = MA3521
USA MA8565 = MA3520

USA MA8800 = MA0800
USA MA8801 = MA0801
USA MA8802 = MA0802
USA MA8803 = MA0803
USA MA8804 = MA0804
USA MA8805 = MA0805
USA MA8806 = MA0806
USA MA8807 = MA0807
USA MA8808 = MA0808
USA MA8815 = MA0815
USA MA8826 = MA0827
USA MA8830 = MA0816
USA MA8864 = MA0826
USA MA8865 = MA0825
USA MA8866 =
USA MA8867 =

USA MA9401 =
USA MA9402 =
USA MA9403 =
USA MA9404 =
USA MA9405 =
USA MA9426 =
USA MA9430 =
USA MA9464 =

USA MB8801 = MA7501
USA MB8802 = MA7502
USA MB8803 = MA7503
USA MB8804 = MA7504
USA MB8805 = MA7505
USA MB8806 = MA7506
USA MB8807 = MA7507
USA MB8808 = MA7508
USA MB8809 = MA7509
USA MB8810 = MA7510
USA MB8811 = MA7511
USA MB8812 = MA7512
USA MB8813 = MA7513
USA MB8814 = MA7514
USA MB8815 = MA7515
USA MB8816 = MA7516
USA MB8825 = MA7525
USA MB8826 = MA7532
USA MB8864 = MA7531
USA MB8865 = MA7530

USA MB8900 = MI1100
USA MB8901 = MI1101
USA MB8902 = MI1102
USA MB8903 = MI1103
USA MB8904 = MI1104
USA MB8905 = MI1105
USA MB8906 =
USA MB8907 = MI1106
USA MB8908 =
USA MB8909 = MI1107
USA MB8910 = MI1108
USA MB8911 =
USA MB8915 = MI1115
USA MB8916 = MI1116
USA MB8917 = MI1117
USA MB8918 = MI1118
USA MB8919 = MI1119
USA MB8926 = MI1127
USA MB8941 =
USA MB8963 = MI1128
USA MB8964 = MI1126
USA MB8965 = MI1125

USA MC8700 = MC4000
USA MC8701 = MC4001
USA MC8702 = MC4002
USA MC8703 = MC4003
USA MC8704 = MC4004
USA MC8705 = MC4005
USA MC8706 = MC4006
USA MC8707 = MC4007
USA MC8710 = MC4010
USA MC8711 = MC4011
USA MC8712 = MC4012
USA MC8713 = MC4013
USA MC8761 = MC4022
USA MC8764 = MC4021
USA MC8765 = MC4020

USA MC9100 = MC3000
USA MC9101 = MC3001
USA MC9102 = MC3002
USA MC9103 = MC3003
USA MC9104 = MC3004
USA MC9105 = MC3005
USA MC9106 = MC3006
USA MC9107 = MC3007
USA MC9108 = MC3008
USA MC9109 = MC3009
USA MC9110 =
USA MC9115 = MC3015
USA MC9126 = MC3022
USA MC9164 = MC3021
USA MC9165 = MC3020
USA MC9195 =
USA MD9000 = MC5900
USA MD9001 = MC5901
USA MD9002 = MC5902
USA MD9003 = MC5903

USA ME8701 = ME8001
USA ME8702 = ME8002
USA ME8703 = ME8003
USA ME8704 = ME8004
USA ME8715 = ME8015
USA ME8765 = ME8020

USA MI8900 = MI9000
USA MI8901 = MI9001
USA MI8902 = MI9002
USA MI8903 = MI9003
USA MI8910 = MI9010
USA MI8964 =
USA MI8965 =

USA MI9100 = MI5000
USA MI9101 = MI5001
USA MI9102 = MI5002
USA MI9103 = MI5003
USA MI9104 = MI5004
USA MI9110 = MI5010
USA MI9130 = MI5011
USA MI9164 = MI5016
USA MI9165 = MI5015

USA MI9401 =
USA MI9402 =
USA MI9403 =
USA MI9404 =
USA MI9405 =
USA MI9406 =
USA MI9407 =
USA MI9408 =
USA MI9409 =
USA MI9410 =
USA MI9411 =
USA MI9412 =
USA MI9413 =
USA MI9426 =
USA MI9464 =

USA MJ9201 =
USA MJ9202 =
USA MJ9203 =
USA MJ9204 =
USA MJ9205 =
USA MJ9206 =
USA MJ9207 =
USA MJ9208 =
USA MJ9226 =
USA MJ9230 =
USA MJ9264 =

USA MM9401 =
USA MM9402 =
USA MM9403 =
USA MM9404 =
USA MM9405 =
USA MM9410 =
USA MM9411 =

USA MM9412 =
USA MM9413 =
USA MM9426 =
USA MM9464 =

USA MO8800 = MO8900
USA MO8801 = MO8901
USA MO8802 = MO8902
USA MO8803 = MO8903
USA MO8804 = MO8904
USA MO8805 = MO8905
USA MO8810 = MO8910
USA MO8864 = MO8916
USA MO8865 = MO8915

USA MS9301 =
USA MS9302 =
USA MS9303 =
USA MS9304 =
USA MS9305 =
USA MS9326 =
USA MS9330 =
USA MS9364 =

USA MU8500 = MU7500
USA MU8501 = MU7501
USA MU8502 = MU7502
USA MU8503 = MU7503
USA MU8510 = MU7510
USA MU8511 = MU7511
USA MU8512 = MU7512
USA MU8513 = MU7513
USA MU8561 = MU7521
USA MU8565 = MU7520

USA MU8600 = MU6000
USA MU8601 = MU6001
USA MU8602 = MU6002
USA MU8603 = MU6003

USA MU8701 = MU6021
USA MU8702 = MU6022
USA MU8703 = MU6023
USA MU8704 = MU6024
USA MU8705 = MU6025
USA MU8706 = MU6026
USA MU8726 = MU6042
USA MU8730 = MU6030
USA MU8731 = MU6031
USA MU8732 = MU6032
USA MU8733 = MU6033
USA MU8741 =
USA MU8745 = MU6043
USA MU8750 =
USA MU8751 =
USA MU8764 = MU6041
USA MU8765 = MU6040

USA MU8801 =
USA MU8802 =
USA MU8803 =
USA MU8864 =

USA MU8900 = MU6800
USA MU8901 = MU6801

USA MU8902 = MU6802
USA MU8903 = MU6803
USA MU8910 = MU6810
USA MU8911 = MU6811
USA MU8926 = MU6817
USA MU8964 = MU6816
USA MU8965 = MU6815

USA MU9100 = MU6500
USA MU9101 = MU6501
USA MU9102 = MU6502
USA MU9103 = MU6503
USA MU9130 = MU6510
USA MU9164 = MU6516
USA MU9165 = MU6515
USA MU9501 =
USA MU9502 =
USA MU9503 =
USA MU9504 =
USA MU9505 =
USA MU9510 =
USA MU9511 =
USA MU9512 =
USA MU9513 =
USA MU9526 =
USA MU9543 =
USA MU9544 =
USA MU9564 =

USA MY8300 = MY8000
USA MY8301 = MY8001
USA MY8302 = MY8002
USA MY8303 = MY8003
USA MY8304 =
USA MY8305 =
USA MY8310 = MY8010
USA MY8311 = MY8011
USA MY8312 = MY8012
USA MY8313 = MY8013
USA MY8314 = MY8014
USA MY8361 = MY8021
USA MY8362 = MY8022
USA MY8363 = MY8023
USA MY8365 = MY8020

USA MY9201 = MY8501
USA MY9202 = MY8502
USA MY9203 = MY8503
USA MY9204 = MY8504
USA MY9205 = MY8505
USA MY9206 =
USA MY9230 = MY8510
USA MY9255 = MY8517
USA MY9264 = MY8516
USA MY9265 = MY8515

USA NA9100 = NA8000
USA NA9101 = NA8001
USA NA9102 = NA8002
USA NA9103 = NA8003
USA NA9104 = NA8004
USA NA9105 = NA8005
USA NA9130 = NA8010
USA NA9164 = NA8016
USA NA9165 = NA8015

USA NA9201 =
USA NA9202 =
USA NA9203 =
USA NA9204 =
USA NA9205 =
USA NA9226 =
USA NA9230 =
USA NA9264 =
USA NA9295 =

USA NE8800 = NE8000
USA NE8801 = NE8001
USA NE8802 = NE8002
USA NE8803 = NE8003
USA NE8804 = NE8004
USA NE8805 = NE8005
USA NE8810 = NE8010
USA NE8864 = NE8016
USA NE8865 = NE8015

USA NE8900 = NE8400
USA NE8901 = NE8401
USA NE8902 = NE8402
USA NE8903 = NE8403
USA NE8904 = NE8404
USA NE8905 = NE8405
USA NE8906 = NE8406
USA NE8907 = NE8407
USA NE8908 = NE8408
USA NE8915 = NE8415
USA NE8916 = NE8416
USA NE8917 = NE8417
USA NE8918 = NE8418
USA NE8926 = NE8427
USA NE8963 = NE8428
USA NE8964 = NE8426
USA NE8965 = NE8425

USA NI9301 =
USA NI9302 =
USA NI9303 =
USA NI9304 =
USA NI9305 =
USA NI9326 =
USA NI9330 =
USA NI9364 =

USA NU8800 = MC7000
USA NU8801 = MC7001
USA NU8802 = MC7002
USA NU8803 = MC7003
USA NU8804 = MC7004
USA NU8805 = MC7005
USA NU8806 = MC7006
USA NU8807 = MC7007
USA NU8808 = MC7008
USA NU8809 = MC7009
USA NU8810 = MC7010
USA NU8811 = MC7011
USA NU8812 = MC7012
USA NU8820 = MC7020
USA NU8821 = MC7021
USA NU8822 = MC7022
USA NU8823 = MC7023
USA NU8826 = MC7032

USA NU8863 = MC7033
USA NU8864 = MC7031
USA NU8865 = MC7030
USA NU8895 =

USA OC8800 = OL4400
USA OC8801 = OL4401
USA OC8802 = OL4402
USA OC8803 = OL4403
USA OC8810 = OL4410
USA OC8811 = OL4411
USA OC8812 = OL4412
USA OC8813 = OL4413
USA OC8844 =
USA OC8864 = OL4421
USA OC8865 = OL4420
USA OC8895 =

USA OL8100 = OL4100
USA OL8101 = OL4101
USA OL8102 = OL4102
USA OL8103 = OL4103
USA OL8104 = OL4104
USA OL8105 = OL4105
USA OL8110 = OL4110
USA OL8111 = OL4111
USA OL8112 = OL4112
USA OL8113 = OL4113
USA OL8114 = OL4114
USA OL8115 = OL4115
USA OL8161 = OL4121
USA OL8165 = OL4120

USA OL8400 = OL4800
USA OL8401 = OL4801
USA OL8402 = OL4802
USA OL8403 = OL4803
USA OL8404 = OL4804
USA OL8410 = OL4810
USA OL8411 = OL4811
USA OL8412 = OL4812
USA OL8413 = OL4813
USA OL8414 = OL4814
USA OL8461 = OL4823
USA OL8462 = OL4822
USA OL8463 = OL4821
USA OL8465 = OL4820

USA OL8850 = OL4850
USA OL8851 = OL4851
USA OL8852 = OL4852
USA OL8853 = OL4853
USA OL8854 = OL4854
USA OL8855 = OL4855
USA OL8860 = OL4860
USA OL8861 = OL4861
USA OL8864 = OL4866
USA OL8865 = OL4865

USA ON8501 = ON5501
USA ON8502 = ON5502
USA ON8503 = ON5503
USA ON8504 = ON5504
USA ON8505 = ON5505
USA ON8510 = ON5510

USA ON8511 = ON5511
USA ON8512 = ON5512
USA ON8513 = ON5513
USA ON8564 = ON5521
USA ON8565 = ON5520

USA ON8801 = ON5601
USA ON8802 = ON5602
USA ON8803 = ON5603
USA ON8804 = ON5604
USA ON8805 = ON5605
USA ON8806 = ON5608
USA ON8807 =
USA ON8864 = ON5616
USA ON8865 = ON5615

USA ON9100 = ON5700
USA ON9101 = ON5701
USA ON9102 = ON5702
USA ON9103 = ON5703
USA ON9110 = ON5710
USA ON9111 = ON5711
USA ON9112 = ON5712
USA ON9113 = ON5713
USA ON9126 = ON5723
USA ON9164 = ON5722
USA ON9165 = ON5721

USA OU9301 =
USA OU9302 =
USA OU9303 =
USA OU9304 =
USA OU9330 =
USA OU9364 =

USA PE8810 = PE8010
USA PE8811 = PE8011
USA PE8812 = PE8012
USA PE8813 = PE8013
USA PE8817 = PE8017
USA PE8864 = PE8021
USA PE8865 = PE8020

USA PE9000 = PE1100
USA PE9001 = PE1101
USA PE9002 = PE1102
USA PE9003 = PE1103
USA PE9004 = PE1104
USA PE9005 = PE1105
USA PE9010 = PE1110
USA PE9011 = PE1111
USA PE9012 = PE1112
USA PE9013 = PE1113
USA PE9026 = PE1122
USA PE9064 = PE1121
USA PE9065 = PE1120

USA PG9100 = PI3500
USA PG9101 = PI3501
USA PG9102 = PI3502
USA PG9103 = PI3503
USA PG9130 = PI3510
USA PG9164 = PI3516
USA PG9165 = PI3515
USA PI8501 = PI1501
USA PI8502 = PI1502
USA PI8503 = PI1503
USA PI8504 = PI1504
USA PI8510 = PI1510
USA PI8511 = PI1511
USA PI8512 = PI1512
USA PI8513 = PI1513
USA PI8561 = PI1521
USA PI8562 = PI1522
USA PI8563 = PI1523
USA PI8565 = PI1520

USA PI9101 =
USA PI9130 = PI1901

USA PL8100 = PL7900
USA PL8101 = PL7901
USA PL8102 = PL7902
USA PL8103 = PL7903
USA PL8104 = PL7904
USA PL8105 = PL7905
USA PL8106 = PL7906
USA PL8121 =
USA PL8122 =
USA PL8155 = PL7920

USA PL8226 =
USA PL8250 = PL7950
USA PL8251 = PL7951
USA PL8252 = PL7952
USA PL8253 = PL7953
USA PL8254 = PL7954
USA PL8260 = PL7960
USA PL8261 = PL7961
USA PL8262 = PL7962
USA PL8263 = PL7963
USA PL8265 =
USA PL8266 = PL7970
USA PL8271 = PL7971
USA PL8272 = PL7972

USA PL8301 = PL6001
USA PL8302 = PL6002
USA PL8303 = PL6003
USA PL8304 = PL6004
USA PL8365 = PL6015

USA PL8529 = PL7029
USA PL8530 = PL7030
USA PL8535 = PL7035
USA PL8556 = PL7041
USA PL8561 = PL7042
USA PL8565 = PL7040

USA PL8661 = PL7097
USA PL8664 = PL7096
USA PL8665 = PL7095
USA PL8675 = PL7075
USA PL8676 = PL7076
USA PL8677 = PL7077
USA PL8678 = PL7078
USA PL8679 = PL7079
USA PL8680 = PL7080
USA PL8681 = PL7081
USA PL8682 = PL7082
USA PL8690 = PL7090
USA PL8691 = PL7091
USA PL8692 = PL7092
USA PL8693 = PL7093

USA PO8400 = PO7500
USA PO8401 = PO7501
USA PO8402 = PO7502
USA PO8403 = PO7503
USA PO8404 = PO7504
USA PO8405 = PO7505
USA PO8410 = PO7510
USA PO8411 = PO7511
USA PO8456 = PO7516

USA PO8700 = PO8000
USA PO8701 = PO8001
USA PO8702 = PO8002
USA PO8703 = PO8003
USA PO8704 = PO8004
USA PO8705 = PO8005
USA PO8706 = PO8006
USA PO8707 = PO8007
USA PO8708 = PO8008
USA PO8709 = PO8009
USA PO8710 = PO8010
USA PO8711 = PO8011
USA PO8715 = PO8015
USA PO8741 = PO8021
USA PO8745 = PO8022
USA PO8765 = PO8020

USA PO9201 = PO9001
USA PO9202 = PO9002
USA PO9203 = PO9003
USA PO9204 = PO9004
USA PO9205 = PO9005
USA PO9206 = PO9006
USA PO9207 = PO9007
USA PO9208 = PO9008
USA PO9230 = PO9015
USA PO9245 = PO9022
USA PO9264 = PO9021
USA PO9265 = PO9020

USA PO9501 =
USA PO9502 =
USA PO9503 =
USA PO9504 =
USA PO9509 =
USA PO9526 =
USA PO9530 =
USA PO9543 =
USA PO9544 =
USA PO9564 =

USA PU8501 = ST5501
USA PU8502 = ST5502
USA PU8503 = ST5503
USA PU8504 = ST5504
USA PU8505 = ST5505
USA PU8506 = ST5506
USA PU8507 = ST5507
USA PU8508 = ST5508
USA PU8509 = ST5509
USA PU8515 = ST5515
USA PU8556 = ST5522
USA PU8564 = ST5521

USA RA8901 = RA3001
USA RA8902 = RA3002
USA RA8903 = RA3003
USA RA8904 = RA3004
USA RA8905 = RA3005
USA RA8910 = RA3010
USA RA8964 = RA3021
USA RA8965 = RA3020

USA RE8701 = RE1101
USA RE8702 = RE1102
USA RE8703 = RE1103
USA RE8704 = RE1104
USA RE8705 = RE1105
USA RE8706 = RE1106
USA RE8710 = RE1110
USA RE8711 = RE1111
USA RE8712 = RE1112
USA RE8713 = RE1113
USA RE8764 = RE1121
USA RE8765 = RE1120

USA RE8900 = RE0500
USA RE8901 = RE0501
USA RE8902 = RE0502
USA RE8903 = RE0503
USA RE8930 = RE0510
USA RE8964 = RE0516
USA RE8965 = RE0515

USA RE9000 = RE6100
USA RE9001 = RE6101
USA RE9002 = RE6102
USA RE9003 = RE6103
USA RE9004 = RE6104
USA RE9010 = RE6110
USA RE9011 = RE6111
USA RE9012 = RE6112
USA RE9013 = RE6113
USA RE9050 =
USA RE9064 = RE6121
USA RE9065 = RE6120

USA RE9230 = RE1163
USA RE9250 = RE1150
USA RE9253 = RE1153
USA RE9254 = RE1154
USA RE9257 = RE1157
USA RE9258 = RE1158
USA RE9264 = RE1166
USA RE9265 = RE1165

USA RO7701 = RO7001
USA RO7702 = RO7002
USA RO7703 = RO7003
USA RO7704 = RO7004
USA RO7705 = RO7005
USA RO7706 = RO7006
USA RO7707 = RO7007
USA RO7708 = RO7008
USA RO7709 = RO7009

USA RO7710 = RO7010
USA RO7711 = RO7011
USA RO7712 = RO7012
USA RO7713 = RO7013
USA RO7720 = RO7020
USA RO7721 = RO7021
USA RO7722 = RO7022
USA RO7741 = RO7030
USA RO7745 = RO7029
USA RO7765 = RO7028

USA RO7851 = RO7051
USA RO7852 = RO7052
USA RO7853 = RO7053
USA RO7854 = RO7054
USA RO7855 = RO7055
USA RO7856 = RO7056
USA RO7857 = RO7057
USA RO7858 = RO7058
USA RO7859 = RO7059
USA RO7860 = RO7060
USA RO7861 = RO7061
USA RO7862 = RO7062
USA RO7863 = RO7063
USA RO7864 = RO7064
USA RO7865 = RO7065
USA RO7866 =
USA RO7867 =
USA RO7868 =
USA RO7869 =
USA RO7880 = RO7080
USA RO7881 = RO7081
USA RO7882 = RO7082

USA RO7900 = RO7100
USA RO7901 = RO7101
USA RO7902 = RO7102
USA RO7903 = RO7103
USA RO7905 = RO7105
USA RO7910 = RO7110
USA RO7911 = RO7111
USA RO7912 = RO7112
USA RO7913 = RO7113
USA RO7914 = RO7114
USA RO7915 = RO7115
USA RO7916 = RO7116
USA RO7917 = RO7117
USA RO7918 = RO7118
USA RO7919 = RO7119
USA RO7920 = RO7120
USA RO7921 = RO7121
USA RO7922 = RO7122
USA RO7930 = RO7130
USA RO7931 = RO7131
USA RO7932 = RO7132
USA RO7933 = RO7133
USA RO7934 = RO7134
USA RO7935 = RO7135
USA RO7940 = RO7140
USA RO7941 = RO7141
USA RO7942 = RO7142
USA RO7960 = RO7160
USA RO7961 = RO7161
USA RO7962 = RO7162
USA RO7965 = RO7168

USA RO7969 = RO7169

USA RU8700 = RU5000
USA RU8701 = RU5001
USA RU8702 = RU5002
USA RU8703 = RU5003
USA RU8704 = RU5004
USA RU8705 = RU5005
USA RU8710 = RU5010
USA RU8760 = RU5017
USA RU8764 = RU5016
USA RU8765 = RU5015

USA SA8001 = SA1001
USA SA8002 = SA1002
USA SA8003 = SA1003
USA SA8004 = SA1004
USA SA8005 = SA1005
USA SA8006 = SA1006
USA SA8007 = SA1007
USA SA8008 = SA1008
USA SA8015 = SA1015
USA SA8016 = SA1016
USA SA8017 = SA1017
USA SA8018 = SA1018
USA SA8019 =
USA SA8020 =
USA SA8021 =
USA SA8022 =
USA SA8023 =
USA SA8024 =
USA SA8025 =
USA SA8026 =
USA SA8027 =
USA SA8028 =
USA SA8029 =
USA SA8030 =
USA SA8031 =
USA SA8032 =
USA SA8033 =
USA SA8034 =
USA SA8035 =
USA SA8036 =
USA SA8037 =
USA SA8038 =
USA SA8039 =
USA SA8040 =
USA SA8041 = SA1021
USA SA8042 = SA1022
USA SA8065 = SA1020
USA SA8066 =
USA SA8067 =

USA SA8500 = SA5600
USA SA8501 = SA5601
USA SA8502 = SA5602
USA SA8503 = SA5603
USA SA8510 = SA5610
USA SA8511 = SA5611
USA SA8542 = SA5617
USA SA8555 = SA5618
USA SA8564 = SA5616
USA SA8565 = SA5615
USA SA8800 = SA2700
USA SA8801 = SA2701

USA SA8802 = SA2702
USA SA8803 = SA2703
USA SA8804 = SA2704
USA SA8805 = SA2705
USA SA8810 = SA2710
USA SA8811 = SA2711
USA SA8812 = SA2712
USA SA8813 = SA2713
USA SA8864 = SA2721
USA SA8865 = SA2720

USA SC8400 = SC3400
USA SC8401 = SC3401
USA SC8402 = SC3402
USA SC8403 = SC3403
USA SC8404 = SC3404
USA SC8405 = SC3405
USA SC8406 = SC3406
USA SC8407 = SC3407
USA SC8408 = SC3408
USA SC8409 = SC3409
USA SC8410 = SC3410
USA SC8411 = SC3411
USA SC8420 = SC3420
USA SC8421 = SC3421
USA SC8422 = SC3422
USA SC8423 = SC3423
USA SC8434 = SC3434
USA SC8461 = SC3431
USA SC8462 = SC3432
USA SC8463 = SC3433
USA SC8465 = SC3430

USA SE7530 =

USA SE8800 = SE0200
USA SE8801 = SE0201
USA SE8802 = SE0202
USA SE8805 = SE0205
USA SE8864 = SE0211
USA SE8865 = SE0210

USA SE8925 = SE0825
USA SE8926 = SE0826
USA SE8927 = SE0827
USA SE8930 = SE0830
USA SE8937 = SE0837
USA SE8964 = SE0836
USA SE8965 = SE0835

USA SH8301 = SH5001
USA SH8302 = SH5002
USA SH8303 = SH5003
USA SH8304 = SH5004
USA SH8305 = SH5007
USA SH8306 =
USA SH8307 =
USA SH8308 =
USA SH8326 = SH5017
USA SH8361 = SH5016
USA SH8365 = SH5015

USA SH8505 = SH5052
USA SH8506 =
USA SH8507 =

USA SH8508 =
USA SH8518 =
USA SH8526 = SH5063
USA SH8554 = SH5054
USA SH8555 = SH5055
USA SH8561 = SH5062
USA SH8563 = SH5064
USA SH8564 = SH5061
USA SH8565 = SH5060

USA SK8201 = SK8001
USA SK8202 = SKK802
USA SK8203 = SK8003
USA SK8204 = SK8004
USA SK8205 = SK8005
USA SK8206 = SK8006
USA SK8264 = SK8O15

USA SN9301 =
USA SN9302 =
USA SN9303 =
USA SN9304 =
USA SN9305 =
USA SN9306 =
USA SN9307 =
USA SN9308 =
USA SN9309 =
USA SN9310 =
USA SN9320 =
USA SN9321 =
USA SN9322 =
USA SN9323 =
USA SN9326 =
USA SN9365 =

USA SO9401 =
USA SO9402 =
USA SO9403 =
USA SO9404 =
USA SO9405 =
USA SO9426 =
USA SO9430 =
USA SO9464 =

USA SP7900 = SP0100
USA SP7901 = SP0101
USA SP7902 = SP0102
USA SP7903 = SP0103
USA SP7904 = SP0104
USA SP7905 = SP0105
USA SP7941 = SP0114
USA SP7942 = SP0113
USA SP7965 = SP0110
USA SP7966 = SP0111
USA SP7967 = SP0112
USA SP7990 = SP0090
USA SP7991 = SP0091
USA SP7992 = SP0092
USA SP7993 = SP0093
USA SP7994 = SP0094
USA SP7995 = SP0095
USA SP7996 = SP0096
USA SP7997 = SP0097
USA SP8100 = SP0200
USA SP8101 = SP0201

USA SP8102 = SP0202
USA SP8103 = SP0203
USA SP8104 =
USA SP8105 =
USA SP8106 = SP0206
USA SP8107 =
USA SP8165 = SP0210

USA SP8204 = SP0236
USA SP8205 =
USA SP8206 =
USA SP8207 =
USA SP8230 = SP0230
USA SP8231 = SP0231
USA SP8232 = SP0232
USA SP8233 = SP0233
USA SP8241 = SP0241
USA SP8242 = SP0242
USA SP8243 =
USA SP8244 =
USA SP8265 = SP0240

USA SP8601 = SP0301
USA SP8602 = SP0302
USA SP8603 = SP0303
USA SP8604 = SP0304
USA SP8607 = SP0307
USA SP8665 = SP0315

USA SP8801 = SP7001
USA SP8802 = SP7002
USA SP8803 = SP7003
USA SP8804 = SP7004
USA SP8805 = SP7005
USA SP8810 = SP7010
USA SP8811 = SP7011
USA SP8826 = SP7017
USA SP8864 = SP7016
USA SP8865 = SP7015

USA SP9025 = SP7025
USA SP9026 = SP7026
USA SP9027 = SP7027
USA SP9028 = SP7028
USA SP9035 = SP7035
USA SP9042 = SP7042
USA SP9064 = SP7041
USA SP9065 = SP7040

USA SP9155 = SP7055
USA SP9156 = SP7056
USA SP9157 = SP7057
USA SP9158 = SP7058

USA SP9501 =
USA SP9502 =
USA SP9503 =
USA SP9504 =
USA SP9505 =
USA SP9526 =
USA SP9530 =
USA SP9543 =
USA SP9544 =
USA SP9564 =

USA SS9030 = SU5101
USA SS9031 = SU5102
USA SS9050 =
USA SS9051 =
USA SS9064 = SU5106
USA SS9065 = SU5105

USA ST7901 = ST2001
USA ST7902 = ST2002
USA ST7903 = ST2003
USA ST7904 = ST2004
USA ST7905 = ST2005
USA ST7906 = ST2006
USA ST7907 = ST2007
USA ST7908 = ST2008
USA ST7909 = ST2009
USA ST7910 = ST2010
USA ST7911 = ST2011
USA ST7912 = ST2012
USA ST7913 = ST2013
USA ST7915 = ST2015
USA ST7916 = ST2016
USA ST7920 = ST2020
USA ST7921 = ST2021
USA ST7922 = ST2022
USA ST7923 = ST2023
USA ST7924 = ST2024
USA ST7925 = ST2025
USA ST7934 = ST2034
USA ST7935 =
USA ST7938 =
USA ST7941 = ST2032
USA ST7942 = ST2033
USA ST7955 =
USA ST7956 =
USA ST7965 = ST2030
USA ST7966 = ST2031
USA ST8501 = ST4001
USA ST8502 = ST4002
USA ST8503 = ST4003
USA ST8504 = ST4004
USA ST8505 = ST4005
USA ST8510 = ST4010
USA ST8511 = ST4011
USA ST8512 = ST4012
USA ST8513 = ST4013
USA ST8561 = ST4021
USA ST8562 = ST4022
USA ST8563 = ST4023
USA ST8565 = ST4020

USA ST8600 = ST5600
USA ST8601 = ST5601
USA ST8602 = ST5602
USA ST8603 = ST5603
USA ST8626 = ST5613
USA ST8661 = ST5612
USA ST8664 = ST5611
USA ST8665 =
USA ST8666 = ST5610
USA ST8675 = ST5575
USA ST8676 = ST5576
USA ST8677 = ST5577
USA ST8678 = ST5578

USA ST8679 = ST5579
USA ST8680 = ST5580
USA ST8681 = ST5581
USA ST8682 = ST5582
USA ST8683 = ST5583
USA ST8684 = ST5584
USA ST8685 = ST5585
USA ST8686 = ST5586
USA ST8687 = ST5587
USA ST8688 = ST5588
USA ST8689 = ST5589
USA ST8690 = ST5590
USA ST8691 = ST5591
USA ST8692 = ST5592
USA ST8693 = ST5593
USA ST8694 = ST5594

USA ST8850 = ST5850
USA ST8851 = ST5851
USA ST8852 = ST5852
USA ST8860 = ST5860
USA ST8861 = ST5861
USA ST8862 = ST5862
USA ST8864 = ST5866
USA ST8865 = ST5865
USA ST8867 = ST5867

USA ST9101 = ST3101
USA ST9102 = ST3102
USA ST9130 =
USA ST9131 =
USA ST9132 =
USA ST9133 =
USA ST9150 =

USA SU8701 = SU7501
USA SU8726 =
USA SU8730 = SU7510
USA SU8731 =

USA SU8825 = SU7525
USA SU8826 = SU7526
USA SU8827 = SU7527
USA SU8828 = SU7528
USA SU8829 = SU7529
USA SU8831 = SU7530
USA SU8835 = SU7535
USA SU8844 = SU7544
USA SU8864 = SU7541
USA SU8865 = SU7540
USA SU8866 = SU7543
USA SU8867 = SU7542

USA SU8901 =
USA SU8902 =
USA SU8903 =
USA SU8904 =
USA SU8964 =

USA SU9001 = SU7101
USA SU9002 = SU7102
USA SU9003 = SU7103
USA SU9004 = SU7104
USA SU9005 = SU7105
USA SU9010 = SU7110

USA SU9011 = SU7111
USA SU9012 = SU7112
USA SU9013 = SU7113
USA SU9026 = SU7120
USA SU9041 = SU7121
USA SU9050 =
USA SU9055 = SU7122
USA SU9064 = SU7119
USA SU9065 = SU7118
USA SU9095 =

USA SU9101 = SU7025
USA SU9102 = SU7026
USA SU9103 = SU7027
USA SU9104 = SU7028
USA SU9105 = SU7029
USA SU9126 = SU7037
USA SU9130 = SU7030
USA SU9164 = SU7036
USA SU9165 = SU7035
USA SU9195 =

USA SW8800 = SE0800
USA SW8801 = SE0801
USA SW8802 = SE0802
USA SW8803 = SE0803
USA SW8810 = SE0810
USA SW8826 = SE0817
USA SW8864 = SE0816
USA SW8865 = SE0815

USA SX9209 =
USA SX9210 =
USA SX9211 =
USA SX9212 =
USA SX9213 =
USA SX9214 =
USA SX9215 =
USA SX9216 =
USA SX9218 =
USA SX9418 =

USA TA9001 = TA6501
USA TA9002 = TA6502
USA TA9003 = TA6503
USA TA9004 = TA6504
USA TA9005 = TA6505
USA TA9006 = TA6506
USA TA9010 = TA6510
USA TA9011 = TA6511
USA TA9012 = TA6512
USA TA9013 = TA6513
USA TA9026 = TA6522
USA TA9041 = TA6523
USA TA9064 = TA6521
USA TA9065 = TA6520

USA TH8150 = TH5550
USA TH8155 = TH5555
USA TH8156 = TH5556
USA TH8157 = TH5557
USA TH8158 = TH5558
USA TH8165 = TH5565

USA TI8601 = TI5501

USA TI8602 = TI5502
USA TI8603 = TI5503
USA TI8604 = TI5504
USA TI8605 = TI5505
USA TI8606 = TI5506
USA TI8607 = TI5507
USA TI8608 = TI5508
USA TI8615 = TI5515
USA TI8656 = TI5523
USA TI8660 = TI5522
USA TI8664 = TI5521
USA TI8665 = TI5520

USA TI9101 = TI5801
USA TI9102 = TI5802
USA TI9103 = TI5803
USA TI9104 = TI5804
USA TI9105 = TI5805
USA TI9106 = TI5806
USA TI9110 = TI5810
USA TI9111 = TI5811
USA TI9112 = TI5812
USA TI9113 = TI5813
USA TI9126 = TI5822
USA TI9164 = TI5821
USA TI9165 = TI5820

USA TI9201 =
USA TI9202 =
USA TI9203 =
USA TI9204 =
USA TI9205 =
USA TI9206 =
USA TI9207 =
USA TI9208 =
USA TI9209 =
USA TI9210 =
USA TI9211 =
USA TI9211 =
USA TI9212 =
USA TI9213 =
USA TI9226 =
USA TI9264 =

USA TK9206 =
USA TK9207 =
USA TK9208 =
USA TK9209 =
USA TK9210 =
USA TK9212 =

USA TK9405 =
USA TK9406 =
USA TK9407 =
USA TK9408 =
USA TK9410 =

USA TO8501 = TO5601
USA TO8565 = TO5608

USA TO9000 = TO5500
USA TO9001 = TO5501
USA TO9002 = TO5502
USA TO9003 = TO5503

USA TO9004 = TO5504
USA TO9030 = TO5508
USA TO9031 = TO5509
USA TO9064 = TO5516
USA TO9065 = TO5515

USA TO9301 =
USA TO9302 =
USA TO9303 =
USA TO9304 =
USA TO9305 =
USA TO9306 =
USA TO9307 =
USA TO9308 =
USA TO9309 =
USA TO9310 =
USA TO9311 =
USA TO9312 =
USA TO9313 =
USA TO9314 =
USA TO9315 =
USA TO9326 =
USA TO9327 =
USA TO9330 =
USA TO9364 =

USA TR8501 = TR0601
USA TR8502 = TR0602
USA TR8503 = TR0603
USA TR8504 = TR0604
USA TR8510 = TR0610
USA TR8511 = TR0611
USA TR8512 = TR0612
USA TR8513 = TR0613
USA TR8514 = TR0614
USA TR8515 = TR0615
USA TR8520 = TR0620
USA TR8555 = TR0627
USA TR8556 = TR0626
USA TR8565 = TR0625

USA TU8820 = TU7120
USA TU8821 = TU7121
USA TU8822 = TU7122
USA TU8823 = TU7123
USA TU8824 = TU7124
USA TU8826 = TU7137
USA TU8830 = TU7130
USA TU8864 = TU7136
USA TU8865 = TU7135

USA TU9000 = TU7200
USA TU9001 = TU7201
USA TU9002 = TU7202
USA TU9003 = TU7203
USA TU9024 = TU7204
USA TU9065 =

USA TX8601 = ST5801
USA TX8602 = ST5802
USA TX8603 = ST5803
USA TX8604 = ST5804
USA TX8605 = ST5805
USA TX8606 =

USA TX8607 =
USA TX8608 =
USA TX8609 =
USA TX8610 = ST5808
USA TX8665 = ST5815

USA UN8001 = UN3101
USA UN8002 = UN3102
USA UN8003 = UN3103
USA UN8004 = UN3104
USA UN8005 = UN3105
USA UN8006 = UN3106
USA UN8007 = UN3107
USA UN8008 = UN3108
USA UN8009 = UN3109
USA UN8010 = UN3110
USA UN8035 = UN3135
USA UN8036 = UN3136
USA UN8037 = UN3137
USA UN8038 = UN3138
USA UN8039 = UN3139
USA UN8040 = UN3140
USA UN8041 = UN3147
USA UN8042 = UN3146
USA UN8065 = UN3145

USA WA8201 = WA0501
USA WA8202 = WA0502
USA WA8203 = WA0503
USA WA8205 = WA0504
USA WA8206 = WA0506
USA WA8210 = WA0510
USA WA8211 = WA0511
USA WA8212 = WA0512
USA WA8213 = WA0513
USA WA8214 = WA0514
USA WA8215 = WA0515
USA WA8262 = WA0521
USA WA8265 = WA0520

USA WA8501 =
USA WA8502 =
USA WA8503 =
USA WA8504 =

USA WA9201 = WA8001
USA WA9202 = WA8002
USA WA9203 = WA8003
USA WA9204 = WA8004
USA WA9205 = WA8005
USA WA9206 =
USA WA9230 = WA8010
USA WA9264 = WA8016
USA WA9265 = WA8015

USA WI8301 = WI6101
USA WI8302 = WI6102
USA WI8303 = WI6103
USA WI8304 = WI6104
USA WI8305 = WI6105
USA WI8310 = WI6110
USA WI8311 = WI6111
USA WI8312 = WI6112
USA WI8313 = WI6113

USA WI8314 = WI6114
USA WI8361 = WI6119
USA WI8362 = WI6120
USA WI8363 = WI6121
USA WI8365 = WI6118

USA WI9201 = WI4501
USA WI9202 = WI4502
USA WI9203 = WI4503
USA WI9204 = WI4504
USA WI9205 = WI4505
USA WI9230 = WI4510
USA WI9241 =
USA WI9264 = WI4516
USA WI9265 = WI4515

USA YO8601 = YO7101
USA YO8602 = YO7102
USA YO8603 = YO7103
USA YO8604 = YO7104
USA YO8610 = YO7110
USA YO8611 = YO7111
USA YO8612 = YO7112
USA YO8613 = YO7113
USA YO8614 =
USA YO8661 = YO7120
USA YO8664 = YO7119
USA YO8665 = YO7118

USA YO9201 = YO4501
USA YO9202 = YO4503
USA YO9203 = YO4502
USA YO9204 = YO4504
USA YO9230 = YO4510
USA YO9264 = YO4516
USA YO9265 = YO4515

USA ZO8701 = ZO5501
USA ZO8702 = ZO5502
USA ZO8703 = ZO5503
USA ZO8704 = ZO5504
USA ZO8705 = ZO5505

USA ZO8801 = ZO5601
USA ZO8802 = ZO5602
USA ZO8803 = ZO5603
USA ZO8804 = ZO5604
USA ZO8805 = ZO5605
USA ZO8806 = ZO5606
USA ZO8810 = ZO5610
USA ZO8811 = ZO5611
USA ZO8812 = ZO5612
USA ZO8813 = ZO5613
USA ZO8864 = ZO5621
USA ZO8865 = ZO5620

INDEX